BISMARCK

ALSO BY EDWARD CRANKSHAW

Joseph Conrad: Aspects of the Art of the Novel
Vienna: The Image of a Culture in Decline
Britain and Russia
Russia and the Russians
Russia by Daylight
The Forsaken Idea: A Study of Viscount Milner
Gestapo: Instrument of Tyranny
Russia Without Stalin
Khrushchev's Russia
The New Cold War: Moscow v. Pekin
The Fall of the House of Habsburg
Khrushchev: A Biography
Maria Theresa
The Habsburgs
Tolstoy: The Making of a Novelist
The Shadow of the Winter Palace

NOVELS

Nina Lessing
What Glory?
The Creedy Case

BISMARCK

EDWARD
CRANKSHAW

M

ISBN: 0 333 18364 9

First published in Great Britain 1981 by
MACMILLAN LONDON LIMITED
London and Basingstoke
Associated companies in Auckland Dallas
Delhi Dublin Hong Kong Johannesburg Lagos
Manzini Melbourne Nairobi New York Singapore
Tokyo Washington and Zaria

Printed in the United States of America

Page 451 constitutes an extension of the copyright page.

PREFACE

Although this study covers all the years of its subject's life, it is not a cradle-to-the-grave biography. It sets out to explore the nature of a man whose genius was fully developed long before he came to dominate the European scene. So I have treated the years of preparation and the great positive achievements of Bismarck's middle years in far greater detail than the last phase, when all the world regarded him with awe. This makes sense to me, and I hope it will make sense to the reader. When all is said, it is very rare to find a public figure past sixty whose life and work suddenly take on a new dimension. One thinks of Winston Churchill in this connection; but then he did not become prime minister until he was well into his sixties. Bismarck, on the other hand, became minister-president of Prussia when he was forty-seven, and in less than ten years he had exhibited the full range of his powers for good and evil and raised his own monument. What happened after that belongs more to the history of modern Europe than to the story of Bismarck, which in fact became very repetitive indeed.

Perhaps I should add that this book was completed and in the publisher's hands before the appearance in September 1980 of Professor Lothar Gall's magisterial biography. A good deal more than twice as long as the present volume, it is a major landmark in Bismarck studies. Had it appeared a year or two earlier the writing of my own book would have been made easier.

E.C.

December 1980

CONTENTS

CONTENTS

PART THREE
TO WHAT END?

LIST OF ILLUSTRATIONS

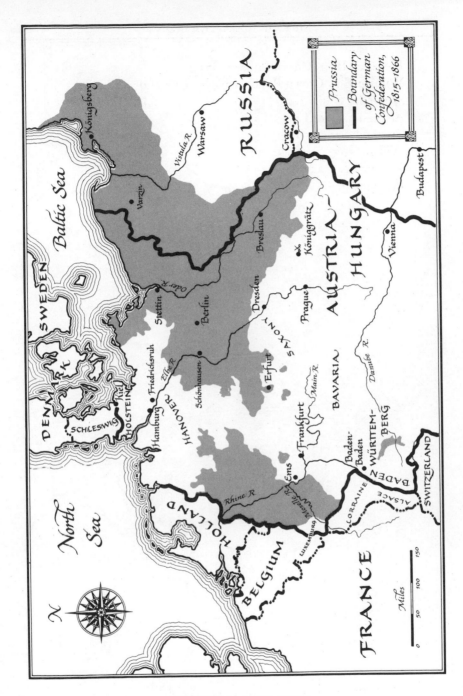

PRUSSIA AND THE
GERMAN CONFEDERATION 1866

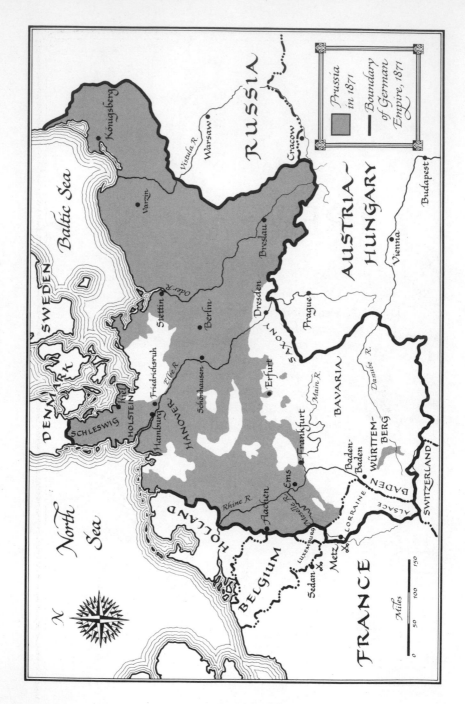

PRUSSIA AND THE
GERMAN EMPIRE 1871

PART ONE

PREPARATION

... a ruler of the great Germanic type, lion-like
in temperament as in the glance of his powerful eyes;
dangerous to enemies and allies, demoniacally defiant
in his strength, crushing, pitiless ...
—ERICH MARCKS, 1902

Unfortunately there is only one great man in each
century and Bismarck is the one in ours.
—PROSPER MÉRIMÉE, 1864

... that faithless, lawless man named Bismarck.
—LORD CLARENDON, 1864

CHAPTER I

THE PRUSSIAN INHERITANCE

Otto von Bismarck-Schönhausen was born in 1815 on All Fool's Day. His contemporaries might usefully have taken more account of this conjunction; but no doubt they were deceived by his very solid ancestry, on his father's side at least. Even when it was clear that he was the joker in the pack, they went on thinking of him as a Prussian and a Junker above all. Certainly he did a great deal to encourage this misunderstanding, frequently asserting his faith in the austere Prussian virtues and raising Prussian power and glory to unimagined heights. Few noticed that he was using Prussia to raise himself, and such was his hypnotic persuasiveness that fewer still found it odd when this most disobedient and disloyal of monarchists exalted the traditional Prussian qualities of honour, obedience, loyalty, courage. Courage he possessed absolutely. But he used the throne as his footstool and ridiculed his king to foreign diplomats and others. Even when in 1866 he contrived a revolutionary civil war in the name of that king, who had stubbornly resisted it, few seriously questioned his credentials as a conservative. The matter of honour is more complex: it is probable that this was a concept he did not understand, except in the duellist's sense.

Certainly he came to confuse cynicism with honesty, while his marvellous freedom from cant was so consciously exploited that it generated its own sort of cant. He developed rather slowly into the supreme political virtuoso of his age, but perhaps his most remarkable gift was his skill in convincing others of his own infallibility. To his brilliance was added, when he chose to bring it forward, much charm. And with his coarse, brutal, and bullying ways went in his early days great delicacy of feeling: some of his

3

letters to his wife, before and after marriage, are among the best ever written—high-spirited, sparkling, enchanting, good. His courage, limitless, was of a special kind, the varieties of which have been insufficiently explored: I mean the courage which enables its possessor to stand alone against the world and which appears to depend upon an unquestioning conviction of personal rectitude. There are many colours and shades of this sort of courage, which has been the mark of saints and holy martyrs as well as some of the most unpleasant men who have ever lived.

But although Bismarck exhibited to a greater or lesser degree those insufferable characteristics which are common to all self-consciously 'great' men who set themselves up above their fellows, in him there were strong disarming features. For example, to important matters he could more often than not bring a sense of proportion unusual in a genius. He was a past-master in the arts of the possible. His megalomania lacked the uncomprehending purity which distinguished the megalomania of, again for example, those deluded and deluding scourges of modern times Napoleon Bonaparte, Lenin, Hitler. He protested too much and argued too much. On another level, he ate too much and paraded too much. One has only to speculate on the compulsions which drove this nerve-ravaged prince of diplomacy and civilian subtlety to make himself ill with over-eating and get himself up so preposterously in spiked helmet and cavalry jack-boots, his gigantic figure a caricature of nineteenth-century militarism, to understand at once that here was a very complex man who never, with all his dazzling renown, managed to satisfy himself. His courage was not the courage of the boring 'great leader,' unspeculatively advancing to destruction in the conviction of his own infallibility. He never believed that he knew the answer to everything; it was, rather, that when he made up his mind to a thing, the fact that he had done so made him right. What he prided himself upon above all was the instinct that enabled him, he believed, to sense the movement of history so that he could profit by a process of which others were oblivious. Or he would say that he listened for God's footfall, and seize the hem of His garment as it brushed by invisibly. He created and propagated his own legend, of course; but it takes two to make a legend, and the people of Prussia, then of all Germany, far from questioning this most remarkable fantasy, after initial scepticism rushed to embrace it and make it their own.

The year of Bismarck's birth, 1815, was also the year in which the survival and enlargement of Prussia as a power was finally confirmed. She was lucky to exist at all. Less than a decade before, after Napoleon's shattering victories at Jena and Friedland, it had looked like the end for the rather barren state so dourly and laboriously built up for the greater glory of Hohenzollern. The Bismarck ancestral home, just across the River Elbe at Schönhausen in Mark Brandenburg, was itself occupied by French troops, and Bismarck's parents had to run for it. In the shadow of Napoleon at the very peak of his career, the current Hohenzollern, Frederick William III, colourless, indeterminate, and rather mean, lost the will to fight, and the proud achievement of the Great Elector and Frederick the Great seemed to pass into oblivion. But two men of extraordinary talents and vision, a civilian and a soldier, achieved a miracle. In a very short time, and with little help from the crown, they succeeded in transforming a demoralized society and a beaten army until both were fit to fight again, and this time with a national consciousness never known before. The irony was that neither of these men was a Prussian by birth nor ancestry. The civilian, Baron Heinrich vom und zum Stein, belonged to a family of imperial knights from Nassau, while the soldier, Gerhard von Scharnhorst, was a Hanoverian. Other moving spirits behind the resurgence of Prussia also came from outside—most notably Prince Karl von Hardenberg, another Hanoverian, who conducted his adopted country's foreign policy with coolness and skill in a period of confusion.

The remarkable thing about Prussia's fighting revival was that she owed nothing to the monarch by whose family that state had been created and for whom it existed, very little to the luminaries of the traditional army, and everything to the national spirit nourished by Stein and to the determination of a people's army created by Scharnhorst and the reforming war minister General Hermann von Boyen, and supplied by them with an unparalleled array of brilliant staff officers—from the comparative veteran Gneisenau, who was Blücher's chief-of-staff at Waterloo, to the much younger Clausewitz, who was to achieve world fame through his teaching only after his relatively early death. The spirit behind the new army, which proved itself at Leipzig in 1813 and then at Waterloo nearly two years later, was the spirit which had pushed through Stein's domestic reforms, most notably the abolition of serfdom; and it was a spirit actively opposed by the traditional masters of Prussia, the Junker landowners, who had presided over their country's humiliation and were soon most to benefit from its recovery. But the spirit conquered, and, after Waterloo, the people expected great things.

They expected in vain. Stein, weary with struggling and receiving no gratitude from the dynasty he had saved, slipped away into private life. Scharnhorst was already dead, mortally wounded at Lützen in 1813. Frederick William was free with promises of a constitution, but he managed to drift along with those promises unfulfilled for twenty-five uninspired years, during which, in exchange for security and a quiet life, he was content for Prussia to be treated in the international arena as an appendage of Russia.

Just over thirty years after Waterloo and the Congress of Vienna, the young Bismarck embarked upon his political career with a scornful attack on the Liberal assertion that the people of Prussia had earned their right to constitutional government by their sacrifices in the 'War of Liberation' against Napoleon. The Liberal spokesman was wrong, he proclaimed, to say that the people had rallied to the crown because the king had promised them a constitution. In fact Bismarck in his maiden parliamentary speech contrived to twist the words of his opponent with that angry and yet glacial effrontery which a half-hypnotized, half-intimidated people was to learn to know so well.[1] * The promise, nevertheless, had been made by Frederick William, not once but many times, and its fulfilment would have crowned the work of Stein and Hardenberg. But after Waterloo the social and political (but not industrial) development of Prussia regressed—until in 1848, the year of revolutions, the people took things into their own hands and came very close to overthrowing the dynasty. It was in the spirit of counter-revolution that Bismarck emerged from the Pomeranian backwoods to open up for Prussia a new direction which would have been a cause of grief to his great predecessor, Stein, who had died in 1831 and was almost a forgotten man.

The Prussia of 1815, the creation of the Congress of Vienna, was an altogether grander and richer property than the Prussia smitten by Napoleon at Jena. When the representatives of the powers assembled in Vienna to unscramble Napoleonic Europe and inaugurate a new era of perpetual peace, one of their main tasks was to re-create some sort of a viable conglomerate of German states to take the place of the old Holy Roman Empire, presided over for long by a Habsburg emperor and abolished by Napoleon nine years earlier. There was no question of restoring the three hundred and more kingdoms, electorates, principalities, duchies, free cities, bishoprics, which had made up the old empire, all bound by lip-service to the emperor in Vienna. What was required was some sort of a federation which would include at least one strong and useful power to fill

---

* The superscript figures refer to the Notes on Sources that begin on p. 415.

the central European void as a buffer between Russia and France. The reigning Habsburg monarch, Francis II, was now pleased to style himself emperor of Austria, and the greater part of his empire was populated not by Germans but by Slavs of various degrees, and by Magyars, Italians, and others. Even so, he was still regarded as being in some way paramount in Germany, not least by the king of Prussia, so that when powers brought into being the German Confederation, or *Bund*, consisting of representatives of all the German states, it was natural for Austria to preside over this institution.

The states had been reduced by mediation and amalgamation from more than three hundred to thirty-eight in number including five kingdoms: Prussia, Bavaria, Saxony, Hanover, and Württemberg. Among the free cities remaining was Frankfurt-on-Main, designated as the seat of the Diet, purported voice of the newly created *Bund*. Of all those states Prussia had made by far the most important territorial gains, acquiring the Rhineland and Westphalia as well as the northern half of Saxony. She lost only a part of her share of Poland. The already sprawling territories of the Hohenzollern crown now stretched from France and Holland in the west to Russia and Russian-dominated Poland (the tiny rump of Poland established at the Congress of Vienna) in the east. Victory had thus brought this austere, agrarian, Protestant, still feudally minded state (with its overwhelmingly strong military tradition) not only a solid block of Roman Catholic subjects and the most densely populated area of Germany but also the mineral wealth and industrial potential of the Ruhr, the extent and richness of which was then appreciated by nobody. Among the newly acquired subjects of the Prussian crown were a steel-worker of Essen, Friedrich Krupp, and the parents-to-be of Karl Marx and Friedrich Engels, the one to be born at Trier in 1818, the other at Barmen in 1820—three and five years respectively after Bismarck.

But the heart and soul of the old Prussia lay far away from the Rhine. It lay to the east between the rivers Elbe and Oder, in Brandenburg and Pomerania—and still farther, in those uncertain borderlands where Slav and Teuton had clashed savagely (and intermarried) in past centuries and where now Russia and Prussia divided between themselves, more or less amicably, those parts of the violated body of a once independent Poland which had not fallen to the lot of Austria. This was the Junker country. The Bismarcks themselves were Junkers, members of that peculiarly Prussian nobility which set more store by lineage and antiquity than material wealth or show, knew little of the outer world (including the rest of

7

Germany), asked nothing of it and gave nothing beyond allegiance to their king in return for the exclusive right to officer his army. They belonged very much to the eastern marches, able to nurse and develop their feudal habit in remote withdrawal from the western lands because they were not grand enough to excite the jealousy of their monarch or the envious hatred of their peasantry. There were no great manufactories. Their lands as a whole were hungry, though abounding in timber and game. As a rule they worked their own estates, which might include distilleries, saw-mills, etc., rarely conducting themselves as absentee landlords. Those who did not live on their ancestral lands were soldiers, members of a highly professional caste, or courtiers, diplomats, civil servants. They tended to be upright, uncorrupt, and spartan, sometimes deeply pious, but also narrow, rigid, hectoring. They were apt to confuse arrogance with pride.

This was the class to which the Bismarck family belonged, inextricably involved in the fortunes of a dynasty which kept the dullest court in Europe. Otto was to remark in his off-hand manner that the Bismarcks were older than the Hohenzollerns—'a Swabian family no better than my own.'[2] Certainly Bismarcks had been in Prussia longer than the Hohenzollerns. Their line went back into the mists of Pomeranian antiquity, whereas the Hohenzollerns came from the neighbourhood of Stuttgart, far away to the south. (There was still a Catholic branch of the Hohenzollern family in Württemberg, which is to play a fleeting but critical part in our story.) The first Hohenzollern ruler in Prussia had been appointed in 1415 by the emperor Sigismund to the margravate of Brandenburg to hold the north-eastern marches of the empire. Thereafter the Bismarcks were content to serve the new dynasty without any marked devotion for generation after generation, even after a mid-sixteenth-century Hohenzollern had so coveted their ancestral estate, Burgstall, in Pomerania, that he virtually turned them out of it when they refused to sell, giving them Schönhausen in Brandenburg in exchange. While Prussia was being painfully transformed into a European power, Bismarcks fought in all her wars, some attaining high rank, some dying in battle. Three of Otto's uncles fought as a matter of course against Napoleon at Jena. Only his father, the youngest of four brothers, did not.

This Prussia of the Junkers owed its position as a power to the military virtues and administrative efficiency. After the devastation of the Thirty Years War the Great Elector, Frederick William (1640–88), had created for this hungry land a firm economic base and a respectable army, rendering it outstanding among the German states. It was reasonable enough for the emperor Leopold I in 1701 to elevate the electorate into a kingdom. The Habsburg emperor in Vienna could not foresee that precisely forty years later the young king Frederick II (the Great, as he came to be called) would fall upon his granddaughter, the twenty-four-year-old Maria Theresa, tearing from her in the War of the Austrian Succession the cherished province of Silesia and somehow managing to hold on to it through all the disasters of the Seven Years War that followed.

All societies have their contradictions, but the contradictions built into the state of Prussia, even before the post-Napoleonic era, had a strange, violent quality. They were expressed in the character of Frederick—with differing emphases, in later Hohenzollerns too. They were expressed in the character of Bismarck.

Frederick the Great's father, Frederick William I (1688–1740), was rough, overbearing, soldierly in the barrack-square manner, and harsh to the point of mania. He sacrificed his state to the building up of a superb army which he could never bring himself to use, watching over it as his dearest possession and protecting it from all possible injury. Frederick—despised and vindictively punished by his father, a suppressed homosexual, composer, accomplished flutist, patron of Voltaire—developed into a military genius and a ruler skilled in diplomatic chicanery. He condemned himself to a life of incessant fighting and was never out of his jack-boots. And this after he had fled the battlefield in his first encounter with the Austrians at Mollwitz in 1741 ('His only friend was his horse!' observed Voltaire), waking up next day to discover that the generals he had abandoned in the field had turned defeat into victory. He was never to lose his nerve again, but this element of near hysteria shadowed many of his actions, in which he drove himself and his people to the limit, sometimes beyond it. The most striking paradox of this man, who was a bundle of paradoxes, was his despising of all Germans, including his own Prussians: while fighting all his life for the aggrandizement of Prussia he looked to France for inspiration. Bismarck also despised most Germans, above all German politicians, but he did not look to France—or, indeed, anywhere at all. He was self-sufficient to an extreme degree.

'I am a Junker and I mean to take full advantage of that fact,'[3] Bismarck declared flatly enough in the year of revolutions, 1848. This was an exact statement of the situation. He was indeed by birth a Junker, but his main concern in early days was to extract the greatest possible advantage from his membership of a class in which he took no devoted interest. His father was a decent but not a shining examplar of that class: although his tastes were the conventional tastes of the country squire, he failed in his not very exacting task of managing the family estates in a countryside which, in spite of Stein's reforms, was still in spirit manorial and serf-owning. Whether the son was ashamed of the father's unmartial mediocrity we do not know. He said he loved him for his easygoing indulgence. Certainly he made no attempt to make up for it when the time came for him to do his own military service: he postponed his call-up as long as he could, and when it could be put off no longer felt no shame in pleading unfitness. But the medical board paid no attention to this: they had before them a giant of a young man who had fought innumerable student duels and was obviously malingering, not because he feared the perils of a soldier's life but because he rejected discipline.

Indeed, he rejected subordination of any kind, and in this he was as far removed from the Junker career officer as from the clerks of the Berlin bureaucracy whom he would despise and detest all his days.

The powerful leaven in the Junker blood was introduced by his mother, who was far removed in background from her husband—so far that the betrothal must have seemed to many the mistake the marrige turned out to be. For Wilhelmine Mencken was the daughter of Ludwig Mencken, one of the most gifted and distinguished civil servants of his day, who had been the trusted adviser of Frederick the Great and his successors, Frederick William II and Frederick William III, and although under a cloud for a time because of his Jacobin opinions, had been virtually minister of the interior, running the domestic economy on behalf of his royal master.

Like Stein, who thought highly of him, like Scharnhorst, Hardenberg, and so many of the most loyal and talented servants of the Hohenzollerns, Mencken was not a Prussian at all. He was a Saxon from Leipzig and came from a family of university professors. His daughter, Wilhelmine, had some of the makings of a blue-stocking, but she was also ambitious in the worldly sense, handsome and, in her son's words 'a lover of display.'[4] Ludwig Mencken died in 1801, when she was only nine, and after that, in recognition of her father's services, she was taken under the wing of Queen Louise herself and brought up as a court familiar and as a playmate for the royal children. Perhaps it was to break out of this position of dependence that, at sixteen, she decided to marry the Junker squire, dull and not very well-off, more than twice her age, but kind, and a nobleman all the same. Before very long she knew she had made a mistake and would have to find what fulfilment she could in her children. In this, too, she failed.

CHAPTER II

MISLEADING DIRECTIONS

Bismarck's childhood and youth gave no indication of the way he was to go. As a boy he was intelligent, rebellious, intensely emotional, bursting with undirected vitality—and lazy. This sort of mixture, unappealing to most schoolmasters and parents, has distinguished many great men in their youth, but it is not, alas, enough in itself to guarantee greatness. Out of the ordinary its possessor will almost certainly be, but he could as well develop into an out of the ordinary lay-about or an enterprising burglar. There is nothing to promise the future statesman, artist, prophet. Even the celebrated Franz Krüger portrait of Bismarck the uncannily precocious schoolboy, with its fascinating mixture of self-satisfaction and wariness, slyness and determination, conscious charm, wilfulness, incipient arrogance, and, of all things, smugness—even this study does not suggest an attacking temperament; rather, extreme self-containment and a disturbingly sceptical intelligence.

From his mother the boy received no warmth of love; he was little more than an extension of her own ambition. Her criteria were scholastic achievement and an alert and cheerful compliance to her wishes. Later on, he was to speak of his early alienation from his parents, above all from his mother's coldly material outlook.[1] Since for most of the time at school the boy was bored with his work, doing only enough to ensure himself a quiet life, and she was doomed never to see him at his best: she thought he was a philistine and a rowdy philistine at that. And she was dead long before he found his direction and began to dazzle Europe in a manner beyond her wildest hopes—if by a means which, as an enlightened liberal, she must have reprehended, at least in the early days.

11

He was twelve years old when the Krüger portrait was painted, and in his last term at the Plamann Institute in Berlin. His mother had sent him away to school with his elder brother Bernard when he was six, and he never forgave her for tearing him away from the delight of fields, woods, rivers, and condemning him to city streets. Nearly sixty years later he would still show bitterness. Lucius von Ballhausen reports a dinner-table complaint in 1878: 'For my cultivated mother child-rearing was too inconvenient and she freed herself of it very early, at least in her feelings.'[2]

It was not the Schönhausen countryside. When the infant Otto was twelve months old his parents had moved out of the fairly imposing manor-house with its musicians' gallery, its library, and other appurtenances of the hereditary landowner. They migrated to Kniephof, far to the north-east, in Pomerania, one of three contiguous small estates brought into the family by Bismarck's paternal grandmother. Schönhausen was left for the time being in the hands of a bailiff, or factor. The Kniephof land, not far from Stettin and only thirty miles from the Baltic coast, was less grateful to farm and the house was insignificant compared with Schönhausen. But the countryside was remote, attractively broken, and full of game: for a small boy it was enchantment; for Wilhelmine, already discontented with her husband, purgatory. Berlin was very far away, much farther away than it had been from Schönhausen. There was nobody for her to talk to; nobody to understand the latest intellectual fashions, which absorbed her: her children would grow up to be barbarians. But she lived for the day when one or other of the boys would 'penetrate far deeper into the world of ideas than has been possible for me, a mere woman.'[3] If she could get them away to school in Berlin it would mean not only a brighter future for them, the chance to transcend their Junker background and be a credit to cultivated Mencken forebears, but also that she herself would have a proper excuse for visiting Berlin.

Thus the conventional pattern for the education of the son of a Prussian nobleman was set aside. The normal course would have been to employ a private tutor to prepare the boy for the cavalry cadet school (whether or not he proposed to make a career in the army), allowing every spare moment away from books to be spent in the open air, shooting, fishing, riding. Instead the child was bundled off to be taught in alien surroundings, largely among the children of an alien class, in a city school which, in theory at least, was an early and famous embodiment of the far-fetched notion that the proper development of the intellect is contingent upon the rigorous cultivation of the body—a doctrine which the mature Bismarck with his gross appetite and razor-sharp mind was to refute with every breath he drew.

After leaving the Plamann Institute at twelve, he had five more years of school in Berlin, three at the Friedrich Wilhelm Gymnasium, two more at the ancient and highly thought of Grauen Kloster. Soon Wilhelmine got her way and established a household in Berlin. She would probably have spent all her time there but for the unexpected and belated birth of a daughter, Malwine: until Malwine herself was old enough to go to school in Berlin she was looked after by her mother in summertime at Kniephof. So the boys sometimes lived in the Berlin apartment with their parents, and were sometimes boarded out with one of the schoolmasters. It did not matter. Bismarck detested Berlin and never forgave it for swallowing up eleven years of his life: at the very summit of his glory he refused to make a proper home there, treating the chancellor's official residence as a sort of lodging-house and demonstratively spending all the time he could, even in moments of crisis (especially, perhaps, at moments of crisis), on one or other of the great, remote estates presented to him by a grateful nation.

But his hatred of city life does not seem to have extended to his schools as such. There, he did reasonably well, particularly at the Grauen Kloster, which he liked. He made at least two good friends from his own part of the world. One of these, Oskar von Arnim, was to become his brother-in-law, and the other, Moritz von Blanckenburg, was indirectly to serve as a decisive influence on his development. It was Blanckenburg who, much later, recalled that although Bismarck appeared to do no work at school he nevertheless contrived to know all that needed to be known. He never came near to catching fire, however. French he learnt to speak and write well, although it was then still a highly unpopular language (perhaps just because it was this?); but he never fell under the spell of French literature, and the classics meant little more to him than exercises to be mastered. Goethe and Schiller he enjoyed, at any rate in part, and Shakespeare and Byron even more. Mathematics did not speak to him at all. Science meant nothing. He appeared to have no particular views on his own future. Of his general attitude towards life he was to write sixty years later in the opening words of his memoirs: 'I left school at Easter, 1832, a normal product of our State education system, a Pantheist and, if not quite a republican, at least convinced that the republic was the most rational form of government.'

He had, he went on, imbibed something of the spirit of German nationalism from the Plamann Institute, but not enough to overcome his inborn

13

Prussian-monarchist instincts. His inclinations were on the side of authority. Brutus, he said, he regarded as a criminal, William Tell as a rebel and a murderer.[4] He did not say by what means a republic was to be established without rebellion.

Time and again throughout his career Bismarck was to insist on his natural republicanism—usually at moments of emotional stress, or more than usual exasperation with the ways of his royal master, or when tired out. The most notable instance occurred at a dinner-table conversation on 28 September 1870 at Ferrières, the spectacular Rothschild mansion outside Paris which had been commandeered as King William's GHQ. Sedan had fallen, the emperor Napoleon III had surrendered and gone into exile, the triumphant German army was completing the envelopment of Paris: Bismarck's greatest and most critical gamble had come off. Within a few months in the Hall of Mirrors at Versailles he was to present his Prussian master with the new imperial crown of a united Germany. The king, so soon to be emperor, was nothing without the servant; but the servant remained a servant. In his own words:

'If I were no longer a Christian I would not serve the king another hour.

'If I did not put my trust in God I should certainly place none in my earthly masters. . . . A resolute faith in life after death—for that reason I am a royalist, otherwise I am by nature a republican.'[5]

Bismarck's latent republicanism and his idiosyncratic Christianity are brought forward here, because both are of extreme importance in any attempt to understand the man. For just as his Christianity amounted really to a special relationship with the Almighty, whom he appropriated to his own purposes, so his republicanism was essentially no more than a declaration of the special rights of Otto von Bismarck, which could be overridden only by divine sanction operating through a hereditary monarch. It was almost as though Bismarck invented his God so that he could serve his king without loss of face.

It has been suggested that Bismarck's Christianity resembled Oliver Cromwell's. Nothing could be further from the truth. Certainly both men professed their faith in the Christian God; each made war to gain his ends. But Cromwell was possessed by the conviction that he was the hammer of God, His instrument on earth, whereas Bismarck, pursuing his own purposes, found in God an indispensable ally. This partnership, however, took a long time to develop. And for fourteen years after leaving school our hero was, it is not too much to say, all over the place: wild, erratic, uncontrollable by himself or anybody else, driven by an almost desperate vitality which, carving no new channel for itself, vanished into the sands. It was not until he was thirty-one that, almost in a thunder-clap, he steadied down, found his level and his direction, and thereafter, for many years to come, followed it with all that galvanic, convulsive vitality harnessed to a single end—with what results! Until then he was a genius in embryo. He was Bismarck struggling to be Bismarck; but he did not know who Bismarck was. He was seized with destructive energy because there could be no constructive activity for him except in an intolerably subordinate position.

In 1832 he went to Göttingen in Hanover, the most sought after and liberal of all German universities, founded in 1734 by George II of England. He made a mess of it. He was to study law in preparation for the Prussian diplomatic service. But he idled and drank far too much, demonstrating his rebellion to excess, womanizing, dressing with a flamboyant eccentricity which exaggerated his great height and emphasized his pallor, and fighting a great many student duels—at least twenty-five, we are told. After an initial flirtation with his contemporaries in the noisily patriotic *Burschenschaften* with their German nationalist and radical ideas he soon decided that a Prussian Junker had no business in that company and joined the exclusive and aristocratic Hanovera Corps, the equivalent of the celebrated Borussia Corps at Heidelberg.

It was characteristic, nevertheless, that while ostentatiously idling and missing lectures, cutting himself off, that is to say, from the ideas of some of the most famous teachers of the age, Bismarck still contrived to do enough work to pass his critical examinations. Not all of it at Göttingen, however: he ran himself so heavily into debt that for his last academic year he transferred himself to Berlin, where he could attend the university and save money by living at home. But he still avoided lectures, spent a great deal of time in circles close to the court, exploited his despised mother's connections, and relied on a crammer to get him through his finals.

Two aspects of his university days made an impact on his whole life. He read a great deal more than he admitted, widely and intelligently, and he made two friends who for the rest of his days were to act as a kind of lifeline linking him with a decent and disinterested humanity in which he did not really believe. These were the American, John Lothrop Motley, future ambassador for his country and historian of the Dutch Republic, and Count Alexander von Keyserling, an aristocrat marked by an intellectual and cultural distinction unusual in the Prussia of his day.

As things turned out that year in Berlin, during which the very tall, very

15

pale, rather strangely defensive yet patronizing youth developed his acquaintanceship with members of the royal family, was to pay rich dividends. How was it that fifteen years later, in the revolutionary confusion of 1848, this particular scion of a Junker family, one among thousands, and only recently emerged from the backwoods, was able with apparently no effort at all to march straight into the royal apartments at Potsdam and start laying down the law to his monarch and intriguing with his family? The answer is that he had come to be treated almost as one of that family; and this he owed to his mother, whom he never thanked.

The benefit of her connections began to come in almost at once. The young Bismarck's first job in the service of his country was a posting to the administration at Aachen (Aix-la-Chapelle). This could have been instructive; Aachen, for centuries a free city, Charlemagne's city, where for seven hundred years the German kings were crowned, was Catholic and far removed in spirit from Prussian Lutheranism. For twenty years, under Napoleon, it had been a part of France and in 1815 was not at all happy about being handed over to Prussia. Now, in 1836, its affairs were still regulated by the Napoleonic Code (as they were to continue until 1905). Bismarck exhibited not a flicker of curiosity about this extremely interesting situation. Aachen was still a spa, as it had been since Roman days and, although no longer fashionable, was a staging-post for foreigners, above all the English, on their way to other more famous and showy resorts. The young Bismarck was enraptured by his first contact with foreigners, and aristocratic foreigners at that—above all with the unfamiliar charms of well-born English girls. In a rather fatuous letter home he boasted of his new acquaintanceship with English high society.[6] He played with the idea of being in love with a niece of the duchess of Cleveland—until he fell really in love with another charmer, Isabella Lorraine-Smith, the daughter of a fox-hunting parson from the Shires.

The wooing of Miss Lorraine-Smith produced the first display of that formidable force and singleness of purpose, the searing concentration, the recklessness, too, which were to distinguish Bismarck's grand operations on the international stage in years to come. It was July 1837. He had had just over a year in his new post. Now the Lorraine-Smiths were due to move on to Wiesbaden and farther south. Bismarck demanded a fortnight's leave to accompany them. At Wiesbaden he tried to emulate the manners of an English milord or a Russian prince incognito, spending extravagantly (far more than he could afford) on midnight champagne suppers. When the time came for Isabella to move, leaving Wiesbaden for Switzerland, he already considered himself engaged to her. With perfect disregard of his duties or his career prospects, and without a word to his superior in Aachen, he travelled on with her family to Switzerland, afraid to let the girl out of his sight. For a time it seemed he had been accepted and there was serious talk of marriage. It was not until the end of September that Bismarck remembered his more immediate obligations and wrote to his master, Count Adolf von Arnim-Boitzenburg, coolly apologizing for his long absence but explaining that in the circumstances he could not be expected to return just yet. Arnim replied by suspending him from his post. In November the young man was back in Kniephof with his tail between his legs, no job, and the affair with Isabella at an end.[7]

It was now that Wilhelmine's connections proved their value. She, as did her husband, not unnaturally regarded the whole episode with disapproval and considerable dismay. Like the parents of other headstrong children whose genius has been less immediately apparent than their capacity for idling (the young Karl Marx, to take a more or less contemporary example) they were filled with apprehension for the future. But the Mencken influence was equal to the occasion, and the central bureaucracy found work at Potsdam for the prodigal while he recovered his balance and decided what to do next.

What he decided to do in the spring of 1838 was to get through his twelve months of military service which, as a government official, he had been able to postpone. As a recruit in a Guards Jaeger regiment at Greifswald he pretended to be bored almost to distraction by every minute of the day—although, almost secretly, he was taking a course in agricultural economy. But once again Wilhelmine came to the rescue, this time involuntarily. She fell seriously ill and after only six months' service her son was able to go home for long stretches of compassionate leave. On New Year's Day 1839, she died, a disappointed woman who had lived for the time when she would launch at least one of her sons on a dazzling career in the great world, but had ended the wife of a hard-up and ineffectual squire deep in Pomerania, which she hated. Her death meant that Bismarck could become a farmer too. Papa Bismarck was packed off to Schönhausen, which more or less ran itself, while the two brothers set to work to make a going concern of the Kniephof lands. In October 1839 Bismarck submitted his formal resignation from the state service and subsided to all appearances into rustic obscurity. He was twenty-four.

* * *

What went on in his mind at this crisis of decision? Had he abandoned all ambition to shine in the public service? Had he decided, once and for all as far as he knew, to desert the city for the life of a country squire? Or was he drawing back to collect himself? If so, for what?

The first thing to say, and Erich Marcks has said it, is that there was nothing particularly individual or far-fetched about his choice.[8] It had been the natural choice of innumerable Bismarck ancestors: it grew from the tradition into which he had been born. His love of the countryside, of the soil, above all of trees, was inbred. So, it could be said, was his rejection of authority: the Junkers were far from being as grand or as rich or as powerful as the high nobility of England or France, but they were stubborn in the defence of their independence and their privileges, and although they officered the king's army and to an increasing degree staffed his ministries their devotion to the Hohenzollern was a comparatively recent growth. Furthermore, even now it was by no means absolute and was shot through, as we shall see, with a strain of what may be called selective disloyalty not commonly found among the champions of autocratic systems, but destined in Prussia to persist as a constant feature deep into the twentieth century.

In a word, by turning his back on the state service the twenty-four-year-old Bismarck was coming home. Some years later he was to write to his fiancée a little ruefully about the tedious aspects of estate management and country life; but in those early days he contemplated his chosen occupation through rose-coloured spectacles—or as he himself put it: 'as through the heavenly blue mists of mountain distances!'[9]

Of course, there was a conflict. Was there anything unusual about that? A genius is not obliged to have a one-track mind, even though most geniuses do. That conflict is clearly shown in a long letter he wrote to his cousin the Countess Caroline Bismarck-Bohlen, who had begged him not to turn his back on the public service and bury himself in Pomerania. The best-known passage in that letter is his comparison of the Prussian official to an orchestral player who, 'whether he plays first violin or triangle,' has no part in deciding what is to be played, or how, and has to do what he is told whether he thinks it good or not. 'But I wish to make music that seems good to me, or none at all.'

There is, however, a great deal more in the letter than that simple declaration of nonsubmission. He seems to be seizing an opportunity to sort out his own thoughts. He argues under three heads, the three determinants, as he sees it, of anyone's career. Duty and service to others? By all means. But what happens when the public servant is required by his superiors to acquiesce in, or actively pursue, policies in which he does not believe, or which he believes to be totally wrong? Even in his own small experience of the public service he has heard, he continues, 'highly placed officials' privately saying that 'this or that regulation is injurious, oppressive, unjust, and yet not daring to make even a most respectful protest but, on the contrary, were themselves obliged, against their conviction, to further them with all their might.' He, Bismarck, knew very well that he might quite frequently find himself opposing policies he was supposed to uphold. How, therefore, as a matter of conscience, serve?

Ambition? Yes, indeed, 'it is clear that more people are moved by the wish to command, to be admired, to win fame' than by the desire to serve. 'I must confess that I am not free from this passion, and many kinds of distinction—that of a soldier in war, of a statesman under a free constitution, like Peel, O'Connell, Mirabeau, etc., of a participant in some vigorous political movement—would attract me as the flame does the moth.' But what were the chances of such a career? What he could not stand, even though he renounced the glittering prizes with reluctance, was the conventional climb to the top: 'the well-worn road which leads through examinations, connections, the study of acts and papers, seniority, the favour of superiors.'

That left the problem of making a living. The life of the farmer showed a clear advantage, since to make the sort of living he considered proper for a public servant ('so that, in no matter what situation, I can present myself with fitting brilliance, and at the same time be in a position to surrender any advantage afforded by my office if and when my official duties are in conflict with my convictions or my taste') a large private fortune was required.

And so, he concludes: 'I am finally resolved not to surrender my convictions, my independence, my whole vital force and activity, so long as there are thousands, many distinguished individuals among them, to whose taste these prizes are sufficiently precious to make them only too pleased to fill the place which I leave vacant. . . .'[10]

What is most remarkable about this effusion is that eight years after it was written Bismarck himself was moved to dig it out (or, rather, an 'extract' he had had made to show his father, who died in 1845: the only version that exists) to send to his young fiancée for her to read as a contribution 'to the history of your future life-companion.'[11] If Bismarck at thirty-two, on the eve of marriage and, whether he knew it or not, about to

launch himself upon a great career, thought this letter sufficiently important to show to Johanna von Puttkamer, I think we should keep it at the
back of our minds as we watch that career unfolding.

Anything less on the surface like the pompous, priggish, self-justifying
young man of twenty-three exhibited in that letter than the Otto von Bismarck who now settled down to rescue the Kniephof estates with his
brother, it would be hard to imagine. 'The wild Bismarck,' he was called,
and all those favourite anecdotes—the seduction and rape of the village
maidens, the reckless moonlight gallops over neighbours' crops, letting a
fox loose in a lady's drawing-room, waking up a friend by firing a pistol
through his bedroom window—seem designed to bear out the legend of an
irresponsible young man driven almost desperate by boredom and frustration because he had missed his way. I think the perspective is here at
fault.[12] Many of these tales are true enough as far as they go, and the
young squire was evidently driven by the same furious and uncontainable
energies that ruled his university days. But just as he had not allowed his
noisy violence at Göttingen and his idleness in Berlin to wreck his examination prospects, so now, almost under cover, as it were, of his imitation of
a reckless, hard-drinking, hard-living landowner—surely more a matter of
letting off an intolerable head of steam in a rather theatrical manner than
the desperate activity of a lost soul—he turned himself into a competent
farmer and landowner while casting about for a wider theatre of operations, if he still did not know what it was.

Even before his return to Kniephof, he had been actively preparing
himself for estate management, making time to attend courses in book-
keeping and soil chemistry in his off-duty hours as a soldier at Greifswald.
Once established at Kniephof with his brother he proceeded to turn the
neglected estate into a going concern. He was not one of the great agricultural innovators: he had neither the passion nor the capital. But he made
Kniephof pay and treated his peasants well, and when in the end he sold
out to his brother, holding him to a very unbrotherly bargain indeed, the
value of the estate had been increased by at least one-third, and this in
spite of a run of bad years. At the same time he read deeply and devour-
ingly. By the summer of 1841, he was feeling settled enough to marry,
something he had not thought of, so far as is known, since the furious in-
fatuation that had sent him chasing Miss Lorraine-Smith over half of
Europe four years earlier. This time the chosen one was Ottoline von
Puttkamer, the daughter of a rich Junker neighbour. But the courtship

came to grief against the resistance of Ottoline's mother: young Bismarck was relatively poor and he had a bad reputation; it would not do. Young Bismarck was affronted, angry, and depressed. It seems likely that he was affected by the humiliation far more than by the loss of the prospective bride. He did not take snubs lying down. But how fight back against a woman? On his father's urging in the following year he sailed from Hamburg to Edinburgh *en route to a holiday in England, which had always attracted him—first Shakespeare and Byron, then the fair-haired beauties from the Shires, now Fielding and Sterne, whom he had been reading with enjoyment: his English was good. He visited York Minster and the cotton-mills of Manchester, and he wrote to his father, among other things, adeq*uate professional comments on English husbandry and grain production.[13] He finished up by going south to London and Portsmouth, returning home via Paris after three months away. He liked England and was to go on liking it as a country, even when he was bringing his formidable hatred to bear on all those, real or imaginary, who sought to spread British influence in Germany, from Queen Victoria downwards. His understanding of English politicians, however, was throughout his career to be faulty in the extreme.

It was October 1842. He was twenty-seven and still restless. On his way home he ran into an old school friend and Junker neighbour, Oskar von Arnim, red-haired, rich, and cheerfully bumbling. Arnim was on his way back from a grand tour of the Far East. He was full of stories to touch the imagination of his friend, and for a moment Bismarck played with the idea of travelling to the Middle East; then he had the even more splendid idea of entering the service of England in the Indian army. The impulse was soon dead. 'I asked myself,' he remarked much later, 'what harm the Indians had done to me.'[14]

In fact he was at last on the edge of finding himself, a process bound up with romantic love and the discovery of God. A number of forces were to come together, each of them working in its special way to shake him out of limbo and bear him into the main current of life.

Thus, for example, in the autumn of 1843 his sixteen-year-old sister, Malwine, of whom he had seen very little, finished her Berlin education and returned to the motherless home at Schönhausen. Bismarck papa decided that it would be a good thing for her to stay some time at Kniephof with her brother. Brother and much younger sister hit it off and became devoted to one other, each bringing out the other's cheerful, boisterous jokiness. He was to become, perhaps, closer to Malwine than to any other human being. It was a sad and forlorn moment for Bismarck when within a year she had become engaged to, and married, the red-haired and very rich young Oskar von Arnim. It was all the sadder for him because less than a month earlier he had had to face the bitterness of seeing the girl who had all the makings of the greatest love of his life married to another old friend. Her name was Marie von Thadden, and she was to be a decisive influence on his career, as much through her early death as through her life.

It would be impossible to imagine a family further removed from the conventional picture of the Prussian than the Thaddens of Trieglaf in Pomerania. This proves nothing, however, but the inadequacy of the conventional picture of the Prussian. The Thaddens belonged to an old Junker family with large estates and the usual military tradition. But they were something else as well. With their extreme conservatism they were also deeply religious in the evangelical style, the centre of a remarkable circle of Lutheran fundamentalists—pietists whose faith ruled their own lives without in the least requiring them to view censoriously their more worldly neighbours. The circle itself, indeed, attracted within its periphery a number of distinguished men of affairs occupying high positions in the government and at court.

Bismarck was introduced into this circle by his old school friend Moritz von Blanckenburg, who was engaged to Marie von Thadden. Blanckenburg, who was later to establish himself as a Conservative leader in the Prussian parliament, saw in Bismarck a contemporary of outstanding gifts being driven to sterility, if not despair, by his alienation from God: he made it his business to effect his friend's conversion, and he went at it hammer and tongs. Admirable fellow as he was, he had the tact of an elephant and a total absence of humour. More than once relations between the two friends were strained because Bismarck took exception to being told that he was lost and miserable and desperate for lack of faith. He was comfortable as he was, he retorted in effect; surely a man might show a certain curiosity about a religion that had moved so many millions for so long without committing himself one way or the other?[15] All the same, he obviously did feel a lack, and he returned for more. Very soon he found himself sitting at the feet of Blanckenburg's twenty-year-old fiancée, who was also determined to save him for God. And that was a different matter.

No adequate description of Marie von Thadden exists, but everyone who ever met her and recorded his impressions was ravished by her robust beauty, her intelligence, her vitality, and her charm. She was as profoundly believing as her father, as her solemn young fiancé, but she was also gay. She could take her faith for granted and allow full play to her high spirits and irrepressible interest in the theatre, music, painting—all artefacts of man, but man had been made by God. For Bismarck the meeting was too late. He was susceptible by nature, and Marie von Thadden hit him between the eyes at a moment when he was more than ready for marriage. It is evident that on her side, and from the safe but rather dull haven of Moritz's affection, Marie allowed herself the luxury of falling at least a little in love with her fiancé's friend. He himself was rather more than usually unsettled. God he still could not find, even for the sake of Marie's eyes, but in May 1844 he did take the extraordinary step of re-entering the civil service to make a new start—only to resign in less than a month, declaring that he was temperamentally incapable of working under anybody. He then took a solitary holiday on the Baltic coast and grew a beard. There is no record at all of his feelings at this time, but soon he had steadied down sufficiently to join in the lively social life on the Blanckenburg estate at Kardemin, where many members of the old Trieglaf circle now congregated. Above all he seems to have enjoyed taking part in various intellectual pastimes, such as readings from Shakespeare organized by Marie. And in the high summer of 1846 he felt sure enough of himself to go on holiday with Marie and her husband and a number of other friends into the Harz mountains far to the south, all waterfalls and gorges and misty crags. He was to look back on this holiday as the most delightful time he had ever enjoyed, and he certainly pulled his weight, injecting the heady element of pagan champagne suppers into the romantic Christian celebration of the rugged beauties of nature.

It would be safe to say, I think, that this communal idyll marked in effect his farewell to doubt. They had the gayest time imaginable and nothing went wrong. He and Marie (she, married two years by now) were electrically and profoundly conscious of each other, but all was under control: honour was well-guarded and God was standing in the wings. Otto von Bismarck, at thirty-one, had survived the upsets of his father's death in 1845 and his sister's marriage a year earlier. He had reconciled himself to the loss of Marie. And something else was happening of critical importance to his future career. Through the Thaddens he had met two brothers, Generals Leopold and Ludwig von Gerlach, both almost mystical in their conservatism, both members of the Trieglaf circle, both close to the king and his heir apparent, his brother the Prince of Prussia, key members of the court circle. In Moritz von Blanckenburg's uncle he met another, younger soldier, brusque, but highly intelligent and well-read, Major Albrecht von Roon, who was to become minister for war, the next king's most trusted confidant, and Bismarck's own most powerful sponsor.

The immediate point is that for more than a year before the holiday in the Harz mountains Bismarck had been in the habit of making the journey to Magdeburg, where Ludwig von Gerlach as head of the provincial judiciary held court, in order to discuss affairs of state with someone whose view he could sympathize with and respect. The respect was soon mutual. What was happening, and it must have been happening consciously, was that Bismarck was quietly laying the foundations for a political career, even though with half his mind he might disclaim this. For how could he make a political career, or any other, if he found it impossible to subordinate himself to any living soul?

Within two months of the Harz idyll all had changed. Marie, struck down by an obscure epidemic that swept Pomerania and killed her mother and a younger brother, was soon fighting in vain for her life. As she lay dying Bismarck, for the first time since his school-days, found himself on his knees and praying. As he put it, the news of Marie's illness 'tore the first ardent prayer from my heart, without pondering as to its reasonableness.'[16] Thus, with her illness and death Marie accomplished what all the magic of her living presence had failed to do. In the shock of desolation Bismarck could no longer accept and live with the meaninglessness of life without God. He capitulated. But he was still Otto von Bismarck, and what his surrender meant in fact was that from now on he took the Almighty into full partnership. He himself could write of Marie's death to his prospective father-in-law: 'God did not hear my prayer on that occasion but neither did he reject it, for I have never again lost the capacity to plead with Him, and I feel within me, if not peace, at least confidence and courage such as I never knew before.'[17] That was one side of the coin. The other was that the future statesman from now on could rely upon divine authority for all his actions.

The future father-in-law was Heinrich von Puttkamer, himself in deep sympathy with the Trieglaf circle, although he lived on his estate at Reinfeld in 'farther, farther Pomerania,' to use Marie's phrase. Bismarck had met his daughter, Johanna, at the Blanckenburg wedding: she was one of Marie's dearest friends (and a distant relative of the Ottoline von Puttkamer whose hand Bismarck had sought in vain some years before). He knew that Marie had hoped and prayed that he would marry Johanna, and he was to tell his father-in-law that he had been on the edge of proposing to her ever since the Harz holiday that summer. Perhaps he had been, but it took the shock of Marie's death in October to push him to a decision, and it was not until December that he came out with it. Johanna was ready to accept him, but first he must be accepted by her father, who would require to be convinced of the reality of his conversion. It was thus that in the closing days of 1846 Bismarck sat down to write a remarkable letter which was his first essay in diplomacy, and, apart from a spirited article in defence of fox-hunting in the English manner (on horseback, that is, behind a pack of hounds, as opposed to the Continental pattern of a shoot with beaters) his first set-piece of advocacy. And already in that letter, with its brilliantly effective and understated self-dramatization, its apparently total candour, its admission of faults and failures only partly offset by the nobility of the underlying motives, its exploitation of that sort of humility whereby the repentant sinner contrives in the most innocent way imaginable to upstage the virtuous—in this letter we find ourselves faced with the question-mark which will recur again and again for the next fifty years: how much of what Bismarck tells us are we to believe? How much did he himself believe?

It is a commonplace that Bismarck the statesman spoke more frankly and openly than any other statesman in history. But frankness and openness may be weapons of deception. And although Bismarck valued the truth, his approach to it was idiosyncratic in the extreme. The truth for him was not an elusive light to be pursued down an endless road of endless questioning; it was a weapon—a weapon to be swiftly seized and employed as part of the armoury of attack, which also included the lie.

'I know,' he opened himself to Herr von Puttkamer, 'that even irrespective of all obstacles in space and time which can increase your difficulty in forming an opinion of me, through my own efforts I can never be in a position to give you such guarantees for the future as would, from your point of view, justify entrusting me with a pledge so precious, unless you supplement by trust in God that which trust in human beings cannot supply.'

This breath-taking effrontery—a young man seeking to demonstrate his belief in God, in this way turning the tables on a true believer—not only displays Bismarck's marvellous instinct for attack disguised as defence but also raises the question: was he himself aware of the extent of that effrontery? Or was he so wholly self-absorbed that he could not see it for what it was?

And so he goes on, describing with stoic self-restraint his unhappy childhood, his unfortunate upbringing, his loss of faith, his floundering among the philosophers—Spinoza, Hegel, then Strauss, Feuerbach, and Bruno Bauer—leading him 'ever deeper into the blind alley of doubt.' Then the slow awakening through Moritz von Blanckenburg and the Thaddens, and how in the Trieglaf circle he found 'people who made me ashamed that, with the scanty light of my understanding, I had undertaken to investigate things accepted with childlike faith as true and holy by such superior spirits.' And, he went on, 'I saw that the members of this circle were, in their outward life, in almost every way models of what I wished to be.' But still faith could not be compelled: 'Through the advice of others, and through my own impulse, I was brought to read the Scriptures more consistently, sometimes checking my own judgement with all possible severity. That which already stirred within me came to life when the news of the fatal illness of our late friend in Kardemin tore the first ardent prayer from my heart. . . .'

He now prostrates himself and continues with the aplomb of a practised diplomat, which he was not: 'I refrain from any assurances of my feelings and purposes with reference to your daughter, for the step I am taking speaks of them more loudly and eloquently than words. So, too, no promises for the future would be of use to you, since you know better than I, the untrustworthiness of the human heart and the only pledge I can offer for the welfare of your daughter lies in my prayer for the Lord's blessing.'[18]

Within days he received a reply which, without promising, allowed him to hope. He wanted to rush off to Reinfeld at once, but was held back by his newly assumed responsibilities as superintendent of the Elbe dykes. So he wrote instead: 'You ask me, most honoured Herr von Puttkamer, whether "my foothold is *secure*." I can reply only by giving an affirmative answer to your next question—that I am firmly and manfully resolved to seek to live in peace with every man, and seek also that holiness without which no man shall see the Lord. That my foothold is as secure as I could wish, I dare not assert; I regard myself rather as a cripple who will stumble, but whom the Grace of the Lord will uphold.'[19] One would have thought that this was a little too much even for a simple pietist to swallow, but evidently it was not.

And after all he was able to make a dash through snow to Reinfeld (it took him three days' arduous travel) and there prevailed. The betrothal was announced in February 1847. In July he was married.

* * *

For Marie von Thadden, Johanna had been the perfect foil. She was not in the least beautiful and her uninteresting features were distinguished by a very short upper lip and a long, inquisitive nose. But she had plenty of fine black hair and her eyes (blue-black, her fiancé called them) had a sparkle. She was not in the least original or self-willed, but Marie had been beautiful and original and self-willed enough for two; and Johanna, modest enough on the surface, had a sharp eye for human weakness and that rather acid humour that so often goes with people who sit back deceivingly in the shade while others act. Much later in life, she came to be disliked and feared for her gossiping and malicious tongue.[20] In 1846, however, she had been submissive, on the face of it rather prim and mouselike, content to be outshone by her radiant friend. And yet even then it was clear that she knew what she wanted and how to get it and was capable of independent initiative. In August 1846, for example, on the way back to Pomerania from the holiday in the Harz mountains with the Blanckenburgs and Bismarck, she wanted to give her friends a private concert in Berlin. She hired a music-room on the premises of a well-known pianoforte maker (Kisting), persuaded a new friend, Robert von Keudell, an accomplished pianist, to play for them (she herself was an enthusiastic but untrained and lazy pianist). It was Keudell's first meeting with the man whose confidential aide he would later become, and he was impressed by Bismarck's 'open and friendly look. . . . He was very youthful-seeming, but he had the presence of a man already perfectly mature.' When, at Johanna's request, Keudell played the Beethoven opus 57 F-minor sonata no. 23 (the *Appassionata*), which was to be for ever, and characteristically, Bismarck's favourite composition, he saw tears in the young Junker's eyes as he came to the end of the last movement.[21]

Bismarck was a romantic at heart, an anarchist too, still touched by the *Sturm and Drang* of an earlier age, but for most of the time the heart heavily and rigidly disciplined by the head. There is no sterner champion of order than the man who has glimpsed chaos in his own depths, as Goethe so well knew. Goethe feared even to recognize the elemental forces within himself. Bismarck feared only the destructive passions of the mob: his own violence he could unleash and canalize.

Certainly his early love for Johanna was a page straight out of a romance. It was as though he had said to himself that he would never now aspire to a passionate relationship. Very well, he would be the knightly protector, the cherisher, his lady's shield against the passions of the world;

and in return he would count on her absolute devotion. To his brother he could write that she was a woman of rare spirit and rare nobility of character—*facile à vivre* into the bargain, more so than any girl I have ever known.' and again, when announcing his 'conversion' (with strong reservations not apparent in the account given to his prospective father-in-law), 'besides, I like piety in a woman, and abhor all feminine cleverness.'[22] But he was tenderness itself, solicitude and enchantment too, in his letters to Johanna. It is interesting to see how this tenderness sometimes breaks out into manic romanticism. The spirit that drove him to wake up a friend by shooting through his bedroom window was still very much alive. There are moments when he is in a mood to seize his bride and ride off with her on a white horse. He writes with intoxicated enjoyment about the whirling snowflakes of a raging blizzard; of a great storm at night. He rejoices to feel part of the storm. He quotes at length from *Childe Harold* (although he does not identify the source) the description of a great storm in the Swiss Alps:

> 'And this is the night;—most glorious night!
> Thou wert not sent for slumber! Let me be
> A sharer in thy fierce and fair delight—
> A portion of the tempest and of thee!'

And then, more extravagantly, he continues: 'On a night like this I feel uncommonly moved myself to become a sharer of delight, a portion of the tempest and of night, and, mounted on a runaway horse, to hurl myself over the cliff into the foam and fury of the Rhine, or something similar.' And he mocks himself: 'A pleasure of that kind, unfortunately, one can only enjoy but once in this life.'[23]

This sort of explosion of furiously seething energy, at a time when he was without question happier than at any time in his life so far, makes the violence of 'the wild Bismarck' of a few years earlier seem less the outcome of desperation than of sheer overflowing vitality. The man was energy incarnate, but the electricity had nowhere to flow, so it sparked and leapt gaps. It was the sort of energy which seizes a man and makes him spoil for a fight for no reason at all but to release the voltage. Its continuing presence is the explanation of so many of the more disconcerting actions of the statesman to be.

He had a slight outlet now. He had been appointed Superintendent of Dykes, or dyke-reeve, responsible for protecting the low-lying lands along the Elbe from flooding. It was an honorary appointment, going always to a landowner in the district, but no less important for that. The great test came each year with the breaking of the winter ice. His main concern was to be ready for the breaching of the embankments by the loose ice-blocks, grinding, shattering, rearing up against and over each other, spilling over the confining banks and breaking down the dykes. Because of this he was kept away from Johanna more than he liked in the first months of their engagement, but he wrote to her often and at length. 'As the thaw approaches,' he writes, 'when you are snugly ensconced on the sofa in the evening . . . you may think how the tattered little banner of your knight and servant flutters in the nocturnal storm and rain on the brink of riotous floods, he on a brown horse that pricks its ears and snorts in its terror at the thunderous roar of the gigantic ice-floes as they crash against each other. . . . Have you never seen the ice-drive of a great river? It is one of Nature's most imposing spectacles.'[24]

And again in a quieter, brooding mood (he has been up all night): 'It is now, at 7 a.m., minus 2 degrees centigrade, but feels warmer to me. For the last hour the snow has been falling lightly and quite vertically without the slightest breath of wind; mist lies over all the land; and, as here in this room there is no sound but the ticking of the big clock, so there is no sound outside but the slight clink of the gliding ice on the river and the monotonous calling of the wild geese, which bring me the welcome news that the thaw is here to stay. Even the people on the dyke are quiet today. They let themselves be snowed on like posts, and all look sleepy—for which I can hardly blame them, as they had the worst night-watch, from twelve to six. Four times in twenty-four hours they are relieved, but I never.'[25]

He writes to her about the flowers at Schönhausen, imagining the camellia blooms that will soon appear. But he does not really like them. He could easily become passionate for flowers, he says, but ever since childhood he has not cared for those scentless ones, the pride of most gardeners—dahlias, paeonies [sic], tulips, camellias.[26]

He can laugh with her too. Writing with considerable scepticism about the prospects of a mutual acquaintance who was rushing into a second marriage, he cites his version of the familiar anecdote (when was it invented?): 'Do you know the story of the French tiler who falls from the roof and as he passes the second-floor window, cries out: "*Ça va bien, pourvu que ça dure!*"?'[27]

He shows immense but muted pride in his ancestry, and gives her a picture of Schönhausen with its family portraits—'from knights in clanking mail to cavaliers of the Thirty Years War with their long hair and pointed beards; then the wearers of gigantic periwigs, strutting on their *talons rouges*, then the pig-tailed trooper who fell in one of Frederick's battles—down to the degenerate offspring who now lies at the feet of a black-haired girl.'[28]

But although he addressed the black-haired girl with tenderness and the most delicate respect he was quite prepared to command her. Writing of the sense of gratification that possessed him when he contemplated the length of service which marked the retainers, high and low, at Schönhausen, he explains that he has extreme reluctance ever to dismiss a man who has once been in his service, and he hopes she will feel the same about the women.[29]

He knows just what to say when Johanna is overcome with a sense of the tragedy of life and is inclined to blame herself: she is simply growing up. And after contrasting the cheerful innocence of childhood with the mature understanding of suffering he goes on prophetically: 'To be exalted to the level of cheerfulness (in the higher sense) and contentment gives the conception of majesty, of the divine, which the human being can only feebly reflect in exceptional, favoured moments and aspects. The thing that in an earthly sense is impressive and affecting, that can ordinarily be represented by human means, is always related to the fallen angel, who is beautiful, but without peace; great in his plans and endeavours, but without success; proud and sad.' And he continues: 'If your mind has grown more receptive of the poetry of autumn, of frost on a night in May, and all human experience of this kind, it simply goes to show that you are no longer a twelve-year-old. The storm that rages in the tops of the old trees, bending and breaking them, passes over the heads of children, children in body and mind, as it does over the little trees in the forest; on becoming larger they grow up in the region of storms, and their roots must become stronger if they are not to fail.'

' "words, words, words," you will say! . . .'[30]

He also had much to say about religion. For some time before the death of Marie he had been reading night and morning from two devotional books introduced to him by her: *Watchwords and Precepts* and *Daily Refreshment for Christians*. Now, an acknowledged convert, he read steadily and thoughtfully in the Bible, above all the New Testament, most particularly the Pauline Epistles. He was not happy about the tendency of, as he put it, Pietists to become Quietists. He saw this happening to Johanna and was determined to prevent it. Now he would take her to task for declaring that she cared for nobody in the world, quoting the Scriptures and the general experience of life to prove her wrong. Now he is arguing with detailed chapter and verse against the divorce of faith from worldly activity, against monasticism, against exclusive withdrawal of every kind. In one letter he drives home his message with well over a dozen separate scriptural references— 'Yet how is it that most of you have so little confidence in your own faith, and wrap it carefully in the cotton-wool of isolation, lest it take cold from any draught from the world; while others reproach you for being too holy to mingle with publicans, etc. If everyone who thinks he has found the truth behaved like this—and many serious, upright, humble seekers do believe they find the truth elsewhere or in another form—what a Pennsylvanian solitary-confinement prison would God's beautiful earth become, divided up into thousands and thousands of exclusive coteries by insuperable partitions. . . .' And he concludes: 'There are many who are honestly striving and who attach more importance to passages like James ii.14 than to Mark xvi.16, and for the latter passage offer expositions, believing them to be correct, which do not literally agree with yours.'[31]

It was not necessary for him to do more than cite the references to Johanna, who would have looked them up, first Mark: '*He that believeth and is baptized shall be saved; but he that believeth not shall be damned*'; then James: '*What doth it profit, my brethren, though a man say he hath faith, and have not works? Can faith save him?*'

Within three months of writing that letter, and before ever he was married, Bismarck had embarked upon a lifetime of works, of furious activity supported (he was to insist again and again) by an unconquerable faith, sometimes straining the Christian concept of works rather further, one hazards, than would have pleased St. James.

Faith unconquerable? We have his word for it. Yet in that very letter to Johanna he sends her as a postscript two more quotations. The first 'By Moore, I think; perhaps Byron':

> '*Sad dreams, as when the spirit of our youth*
> *Returns in sleep, sparkling with all the truth*
> *And innocence once ours, and leads us back*
> *In mournful mockery over the shining track*
> *Of our young life, and points out every ray*
> *Of hope and peace we've lost upon the way!*'

The second, Macbeth's soliloquy: 'Tomorrow and tomorrow and tomorrow . . .' down to '. . . a tale told by an idiot, full of sound and fury, signifying nothing.'

A formidable personality was building up. It was soon to be unleashed.

CHAPTER III

A SMALL BEGINNING

In 1847 King Frederick William IV had been on the throne of Prussia seven years. During all this time he had inhabited a dream world of his own imagining, but at last reality was on the point of breaking in. He was a good and kind man, widely read, knowledgeable, deeply cultivated, unreliable. Outwardly he was impressive, with a noble forehead, the hairline receding fast, square of jaw, and with a powerful chin that diverted the eye from the rather weak mouth. His eyes were bright, open, and expressive. Inwardly, however, he was cloudily romantic, vacillating, and confused. In his dealing with his advisers obstinacy and evasiveness alternated, doing duty for decisiveness. He was a dreamer, his heart dwelling in a medieval never-never land. He believed with unquestioning conviction in the divine right of kings: indeed, he believed that kings themselves shared the very quality of divinity and thus were not merely raised above their subjects but were different in kind and inevitably superior in intellect and understanding to any ministerial adviser. To his close friend, the diplomat Baron Christian von Bunsen, he solemnly declared: 'There are things that only a king can know.' All the same, as absolute monarch of Prussia, he was ready (indeed eager) to recognize as his liege lord the Habsburg emperor in Vienna, even though the Holy Roman Empire, of which Prussia had once been part, was vanished for ever.

Sadly for him, he altogether lacked the strength and ability to sustain this lofty role. His sister, the almost equally cultivated and far more sensible Princess Charlotte, would have made a better ruler. But she was married to Nicholas I of Russia, who, as the undisputed champion of reaction, did his best from a distance to keep his unsatisfactory brother-in-law up to

33

the mark and expected him at least to pull his weight in the struggle of autocracy against the evil spirit of the age, *le génie du mal*—i.e., liberalism of whatsoever colour. The tsar's expectations were not realized. In 1848 Frederick William disgraced himself by capitulating to the demands of the revolutionary nationalists in Berlin. He soon recanted, but the damage was done, and Nicholas in St. Petersburg regarded him as a traitor to his class: 'Through your caprice Prussia has come to renounce the traditions which have been her strength, her glory, her prosperity for centuries past . . . the old Prussia has *ceased to be.*'[1]

This was the man into whom the young Bismarck in that very year at the outset of his own political career tried to put some stiffening. Ten years later it had to be officially admitted that the king's mind had gone and his younger brother, Prince William of Prussia, was appointed regent. With his respect for scholarship and the arts, Frederick William should have been born into quieter times—preferably, indeed, not to the throne at all but to a comfortable inheritance which would have enabled him to blossom as an aristocratic dilettante and a valued patron of scholars, artists, and philosophers.

Instead, he was born into a very difficult time indeed. He had come to the throne in 1840 at the age of forty-five expecting tranquillity and oblivious of the great head of steam that had been building up among the European peoples and was soon to explode and shatter the post-Napoleonic arrangements ordered for so long by Metternich. His father, the characterless Frederick William III, had been very much a part of those arrangements. At the Congress of Vienna he had played a minor role, happy to secure the territorial gains which gave greater weight to Prussia than she had ever yet enjoyed, and thereafter acting in an obedient and colourless manner as the third partner in the Holy Alliance, regarded by two successive Russian tsars, Alexander I and Nicholas I, for all practical purposes as the faithful seconder of Russian aspirations. His greatly enlarged kingdom, which was also enriched beyond his understanding by the skills of the Rhineland bourgeoisie as well as vast mineral deposits, had radically developed its economy from 1819 onwards first under the shield of the Prussian-inspired and -organized Customs Union, the Zollverein, then further stimulated by the swift development of railways afteer 1835; but this economic development, and the consequent changes in the social balance, were not reflected in the fossilized political institutions of the Prussian state. In the eyes of the king and his advisers Prussia still consisted of the nobility (*Ritterschaft*) and the peasantry, plus a small and nondescript and, in their eyes, contemptible class of town-dwelling burghers.

34

Frederick William III had been conscious of divisive voices leading what purported to be a popular demand for representative government, for a written constitution. But this clamour had easily been stilled. On five separate occasions he had promised a constitution, first under the shock of defeat by Napoleon, then again and again as it became plain to the more intelligent and articulate of his subjects that untramelled monarchical rule could never hope to weld into an organic unity the old and the new parts of Prussia. The only real hope that anything might be done lay in Stein's old partner, Prince Karl von Hardenberg. Hardenberg died in 1822, and thereafter through another two decades of political (but not industrial) stagnation nothing happened. The only concession Frederick William had made was to decree in 1820 that the government must never raise a loan without the consent of an elected representative assembly.

It was this concession which, in 1847, at last brought Frederick William IV, bewildered and outraged, face to face with reality. He wanted to raise some money, but the representative assembly to authorize a loan did not exist.

In the spring of 1847 the king was faced with an urgent need for a new railway to link Berlin with Königsberg in East Prussia. For ten years past there had been a fever of railway construction all over Europe, and in Germany the pace was even fiercer than elsewhere. In most of the German kingdoms and principalities the new lines were run by the state from the beginning; but in Prussia, as in England, the building of the various lines and the provision of rolling stock and all the necessary services were left to private enterprise—with the state, however, taking powers to buy large blocks of shares, ultimately to assume full control. This procedure was satisfactory in those areas and between those centres where quick profits might be expected; but the king and his government had to think in military as well as economic terms, and by the winter of 1846 it was clear that the most urgently needed strategic line linking Berlin with the extremities of East Prussia would have to be constructed by the state, even if this meant calling a representative assembly to authorize the floating of a loan.

What kind of assembly? Obviously, declared the Liberals, a properly elected parliament reposing on a fairly broad suffrage, such as already existed in a number of smaller German states. The king thought otherwise. He saw himself presiding in a grand but paternal manner over a quasi-feudal body, a States General of delegates from the three estates of the realm. The delegates would be representatives of the existing eight provincial diets. They would meet with due ceremony, loyally accede to his demands, do homage to the crown, and disperse to their homes—until more money was required.

It did not turn out like that at all. The estates were summoned as the king desired. They formed what was called the United Diet, delegates being nominated by the existing provincial assemblies. Frederick William opened the proceedings in April 1847, wholly ignorant of the prevailing mood or of the fact that he was presiding over a climacteric in his country's history, quite enjoying the occasion, which he thought of as a civilian parade, a demonstration of loyalty. But here, in fact, was the birth of an organized and formal opposition to king and government. It was not a straightforward opposition between Liberals and Conservatives: all but a very small minority of that innocuous-seeming assembly were united in rejection of the monarch's attitude.

What happened was that a combination of intelligent and practical men of affairs, important in their own home provinces, tired of being treated like children by a king lacking any understanding of contemporary reality, some of them (from the Rhineland especially) inhabiting a world an age away from the Prussia of the Elbe flats and far beyond, which had scarcely changed in half a millennium, were determined to use the Diet not to discuss the railway bill but to push their claims to a share in responsible government, for a written constitution, for the creation of a permanent representative assembly. In his opening address Frederick William had declared, almost as a self-evident truth, that the idea of a constitution was absurd—and worse than absurd: 'I shall never allow a piece of paper to come between myself and my people,' he assured his fascinated hearers, who were as much 'the people' as anyone else in the land.

The leader of the opposition was very far from being a liberal. He was Baron Georg von Vincke, a red-haired, short-tempered, somewhat overbearing representative of an ancient and distinguished Westphalian family, who, with his supporters, had no difficulty in overwhelming the king's party. For this consisted of a handful of ultra-royalists and army officers of the old school, men for the most part of perfect integrity and a religious belief in the divinity of a king whose attitudinizings and vacillations nevertheless sometimes drove them to distraction. Two of the most distinguished of these were Bismarck's new friends, the Gerlach brothers. They were not good in debate, and it seemed there was nobody on the side of monarchical legitimacy able to stand up to the avalanche of criticism from men condemned too long to impotence and silence.

The position of the crown was made worse by a remarkable concession on the part of the king: he flatly rejected the idea of a constitution and a properly representative assembly, but he conceded, of all things, a free press, doing away with the censorship, that indispensable weapon of absolutism. Thus it was that every word of criticism uttered in the Diet was immediately published far and wide. Throughout Prussia ordinary citizens for the first time became aware of the depth and intensity of the dissatisfaction of the vast majority with the way things were being done. The whole country, it is not too much to say, was on the move; and even though it was known that the king could suspend the Diet at will and need never convene it again, it was clear that the return to the old ways was out of the question. The battle from now on had to be fought in public, and it was going to take a very able, strong, and combative man indeed to stand up as an effective champion of the *status quo*.

The man, however, was there, and his name was Bismarck. Very few of the delegates had even heard of him when he got up to make his maiden speech on Monday, 17 May 1847, but within minutes he had outraged the assembly and made a reputation for himself as the most extreme reactionary of a reactionary class. It was a reputation that misled his contemporaries and confused them for many years to come.

How had Bismarck got to Berlin? And what was he doing in that gallery?

Just nine days earlier he had written to Johanna an ebullient, apologetic, triumphant letter. It started: 'DEAREST, ONE AND ONLY; BELOVED JUANITA! *BETTER HALF OF MYSELF!* [these last words in English]' And it went on to confide the startling news that the squire of Schönhausen had suddenly been transformed into a politician, a delegate to the United Diet, no less, for Magdeburg in Prussian Saxony. He had been chosen above the heads of senior and technically better-qualified candidates to replace the formally appointed delegate, who had fallen ill. He could not, he explained, conceivably refuse without giving offence to the Magdeburg Estates, which had honoured him with their confidence in his ability.[2]

A legend, intermittently fostered by Bismarck himself (we shall find that almost all the stories about Bismarck, true or false, were at one time or another put about by him), insisted that this eruption into politics was unforeseen and undesired, that he was content at Schönhausen, preparing to settle down as a country squire with his bride, but that the summons came, and had to be obeyed. Why, he had not even approved of the convocation of the Landtag, or Diet.

This last observation was true, but this did not mean that he was not anxious to find a place in it once it had been convened. Indeed, the very day after delivering his maiden speech he was confessing to Johanna that it had been his 'ardent desire to be a member of the Landtag.' The only fly in the ointment, he went on, was that it meant being away from her and Reinfeld. But already he had made things plain enough, when in his first letter announcing the news of his appointment he had explained (boasted, indeed) that he had been chosen because the senior candidate was incompetent to serve and because the Magdeburg Estates 'had a quite unusual degree of confidence in me.' They had, he continued, actually moved heaven and earth to get him into the Landtag sooner.[3]

Unless Johanna was an idiot, which she was not, she must have understood at least from the first weeks of their betrothal that her future lord and master was by no means intent on a life of rustic seclusion. Already, as we have seen, he was putting himself out to make a place for himself in local government, above all by winning the confidence of the Gerlach brothers. The superintendency of the dykes had been the first fruit of this; the seat on the provincial diet of Magdeburg had followed because Ludwig von Gerlach was president of the provincial judiciary. On quite a different plane, very soon after his engagement to Johanna, he was urging her not to be too modest in her dress but to go in for brighter colours ('Why are you so sad, black in dress and heart, my angel?'), to work harder and more systematically at her music, above all to learn French: 'I do beg you to pay some attention to French,' he wrote . . . 'not for my own sake, for we shall understand each other in our mother tongue; but in the larger world there will often be times when you will find it unpleasant, even mortifying if you are unfamiliar with French.'[4] What world? we may ask. Why should the wife of a Pomeranian squire need French?

That was on 7 February 1847, and he was obviously thinking a great deal about the larger world and the place his wife would have to assume in it. There are enough hints of his temper in those early letters to make it clear that the negative rejection of subordination was giving way to the positive instinct to command—if only because, impatient of the hesitations, the incompetence of others, he was coming to think that nothing was well done unless he did it himself. Thus, for example, over the matter of the Elbe dykes he wrote one day to describe for Johanna the organization (*his* organization!) of watchers, horsemen, messengers to bring swift news of a breach at any time of day or night and to reinforce each other. 'It is true that fiancé and dyke-reeve are almost incompatible; but were I not the latter, I have not the slightest idea who would be. The revenues of the office are small, and the duties somewhat laborious; the gentlemen of the neighbourhood, however, are deeply concerned, and yet without public spirit. And even if anyone were found willing to undertake it for the sake of the title, which is, strange to say, much coveted in these parts, there is not one among them who (may God forgive me) would not be either unfit for the business or faint-hearted. A fine opinion, you will think, I have of myself, that I alone am not lacking in this; but I assert with all my native modesty that I have all these faults in less degree than the others in this part of the country—which is, in fact, not saying much.'[5]

He might have said the same thing of the national politicians—indeed, in private he did so many times—more crisply and without the ironic apology, when he held Germany in his hands at the height of his career.

This is another glimpse of that impatience with incompetence in a very early letter to Johanna, this time about the shortcomings of his brother, Bernhard, as an agricultural partner: he has run over from Schönhausen to see how Kniephof is getting on, and he describes how Bernhard greeted him, 'according to his habit, by dumping a woolsack full of tiresome news about Kniephof at my feet: disorderly inspectors, masses of dead sheep, chronically drunk distillers, thoroughbred colts foundered (naturally the best of them) potatoes gone rotten—poured in a rolling torrent from his all too readily opened mouth upon my somewhat travel-worn self. I have to exclaim in horror and lamentation to please my brother; for my indifferent manner on receiving news of misfortune upsets him, and if I don't express surprise he has ever new and still worse news in store.'[6]

So he might have written of his sovereign William I twenty years later.

One of the characteristics of a certain kind of Prussian, to generalize extremely, is a propensity for shouting. The reverse of the coin is a willingness to be shouted at. That is to say, the average Prussian official when shouted at is apt to crumple before the naked display of evident authority. But why does true authority find it necessary to shout? There is a thesis to be written about the origins and functions of shouting, as displayed also on the barrack square in Britain and America. This kind of sergeant-major yelling went on all over Prussia, later all over Germany, and was quite taken for granted. But the greatest sergeant-major of them all, Otto von Bismarck, did not shout, and this simple fact may have had something to do with the unease with which he was commonly regarded. He was a tall man, well over six feet; the great bulk was yet to come. The framework was there, the shoulders broad and powerful; but he was then narrow-waisted and long-legged. His hands and feet were small, his hands particularly delicate, and the bones of his head were small and compact, so that once his beard was shaved off he had the air of a thoroughbred, an appearance enhanced by the flaring nostrils, the tucked-in chin, and very large, wide-set eyes, with an odd slant which suggested that, like a nervous horse, he could see too much, and yet not enough for comfort, of what was going on behind him. When this long and striking figure unfolded itself, standing high above the assembly, the words which fell from his lips came out not in a powerful bass but, rather, in a thin, high tenor—a light baritone, Robert von Keudell called it; a pipe said others. The words were vitriolic, or coldly cutting, or bitterly sarcastic, or dismissive—but never shouted. His hearers would have felt more at home if he had shouted. They could have shouted him down. But about this contemptuous, pallid young man from the back-blocks there was a quiet, cold savagery, very hard to counter.

It was not so much what he said as the way he said it. What he said, in effect, was that he took exception to Liberal claims that the people of Prussia in 1813 had been moved to rise against Napoleon not by the determination to free the country from a foreign tyrant but by their opposition to a domestic tyranny, agreeing to fight only if their king would promise them a constitution. This, he observed, did little honour to the name of Prussia and he did not thank those who had spread the notion. At this point his voice was drowned in uproar, and he acted out the celebrated scene, which he himself recalled with noteworthy self-satisfaction in his memoirs nearly fifty years later; he simply stood there, not attempting to make himself heard above the racket, and picked up a newspaper which happened to be lying handy and glanced through it pretending to read until the uproar subsided.[7]

The cause of the uproar was not only that the young newcomer had twisted the words of previous speakers but also the insolent manner in which he contemptuously dismissed his seniors. For the immediate object of Bismarck's attack was a deeply respected deputy from East Prussia who was a veteran of the campaigns against Napoleon and had fought in Russia as well as in Germany and France. Neither he nor anybody else had said that the people had fought in return for the promise of a constitution; only that they had fought better because that promise had brought king and country closer to each other than before. The young Bismarck could thus, even in his maiden speech, twist his opponent's words as to the manner born; and he seemed to take a positive delight in taunting his elders and slighting their service to the state. Add to this iconoclasm the fact that he brought to the defence of reaction the classic behaviour of the young rebel, and the resultant mixture is unusual indeed. It was part of the mixture that was to confound first Germany and then Europe, for decades to come: the entrenched defender of the *status quo*, the apparent reactionary, who brought to his campaigns the armament of the revolutionary and the temperament of a Jacobin.

In those early days, of course, he was himself confused: there was no deliberate attempt then to use his Junker traditions and prejudices as a cover for his scheming: he had no schemes. He might despise most of his Junker neighbours, but the growing bourgeoisie he scarcely recognized, at best he saw them as a parasitic growth on the state. It suited him to be called the Vincke-baiter. It gave him publicity, and he genuinely abhorred a man of noble blood who, as he saw it, betrayed his class by seeking to put fetters on the monarch. But there were aspects of confusion in his other attitudes. He amazed his hearers by speaking up for the punitive game-laws (laws of a kind that Maria Theresa in Austria had done away with just a century earlier), which was perfectly in character; but in the next breath he found himself on the same side as his detested Liberals in demanding at least that the Diet should be convened at regular intervals, not simply dismissed at the monarch's will—perhaps never to sit again. The reason for this was that if the Diet vanished into limbo after this one session, the promising political career of Otto von Bismarck might vanish with it.

This whole episode of the first United Diet lasted little more than two months. At the end of June the railway was voted out: there would be no loan unless the king kept his father's promise and conceded a constitution. Frederick William, refusing to capitulate, simply dissolved the Diet, giving no indication that he would ever convoke it again. He did this, moreover, without a word of thanks or even recognition to his most loyal and articulate supporter. Bismarck himself recorded in his later years how at one court function after another his monarch quite pointedly contrived to avoid even speaking to his champion. He was puzzled and hurt, but the king's instinct was correct. Frederick William was angry with his subjects for demanding a share in government which no self-respecting sovereign could concede; but the fact remained, they were his children, who, given time and patience, might be brought to understand the error of their ways. It was no part of the King's desire to see his peoples divided, one faction consigning another to the outer darkness. The caustic and fire-eating Bismarck was a loyal and devoted servant, no doubt; but how could he, Frederick William, stand benevolently above his people if he smiled on the man who was importing elements of bitterness and hatred into a family argument?

More interesting is the question how this violent fire-eater came to be seriously considered for a ministerial appointment less than eighteen months after his political debut, and still only thirty-three? The answer is by sheer manifest ability and weight of character.

The king was aware of both, even when he demonstratively avoided his new champion. Bismarck had shown himself already head and shoulders above anyone else in that assembly. After initially offending them he had gathered round him all the Conservatives who saw him as a natural leader—as he wrote to Johanna, he had gained an influence over delegates of 'the so-called court-party and other Ultra-Conservatives from several provinces, which I employ in restraining them as far as possible from bolting and awkward shying, *which I can do in the most unsuspected fashion when once I have plainly expressed my inclination.*'[8] (my italics)

Bismarck at thirty-two, convinced now of his own powers of leadership, and Johanna, nine years younger, from whom he needed neither stimulation nor understanding but only devotion, were married from the bride's home on 28 July, just a month after the end of that first session of the United Diet. The groom had filled that month with activity, arranging for the letting and development of his Kniephof property, fixing up details of the wedding, seeing that Schönhausen was ready for Johanna, above all making certain dispositions calculated to carry him deeper into politics. Chief among these was the planning with the Gerlach brothers of a Conservative newspaper designed to exploit the new press freedom which had so far most benefited the opposition. But even at this moment when he might have been expected to concentrate on securing the foundations of a career in politics, Bismarck showed that detachment, that economy of effort, that inborn ability to decide when it was necessary to push hard, when not, which was to be his trademark. The Gerlachs wanted him to take Johanna to Bavaria or Switzerland for the honeymoon, where he could easily be reached for further discussion. Bismarck would have nothing to do with this. He had promised Johanna a July wedding, and he kept that promise. He was, moreover, determined to give her the time of her life by way of a honeymoon: politics could wait. So at this critical moment of his career he was incommunicado.

This will be worth remembering when, much later, we have to consider those long absences from Berlin when he was virtual dictator, buried deep in the country for weeks and sometimes months on end, sometimes offering ill-health as an excuse, sometimes not. Many reasons have been offered for this behaviour except the obvious one: that from time to time he was flooded with a complex and overpowering need: at one and the same time to get away from people and to assert himself absolutely, demonstrating that he knew he would be found indispensable whether he was physically present or not.

Now Johanna was given a miniature grand tour of the Habsburg Empire on the eve of the storm which would start shaking that empire apart: to Vienna via Prague, thence up the Danube by steamer to Linz; from Linz overland again to Salzburg and the Tirol, with a little gentle mountaineering; then over the Alps via the Brenner Pass to Merano with its terraced promenades, its terraced vineyards, its marvellous backdrop of the High Adige, its southern aspect open to the Italian skies (their first glimpse of the warm south); then on, at last, to Venice.

Johanna was enchanted with it all, but her husband obtained his satisfaction, which was deep, from her enjoyment. Back in Schönhausen he wrote to his sister, Malwine: 'For me the time seems to be past when one can be impressed by new sights, so that my chief delight has been in Johanna's pleasure.'[9] Of course he dramatized himself, the disillusioned hero looking at life from the other side of good and evil. But he was almost certainly partly speaking the sad truth, the truth of a man who has put away childish things and is already so blinkered that all the richness of Italy encountered for the first time is no more than a novelty, a toy. Already, and now for ever more, his immense vitality was to be concentrated on the exploitation of a known quantity, the exercise of power over his fellow-men. Only his skill could grow.

The nine weeks' honeymoon did one thing for him besides giving him the pleasure of entertaining his bride. At the theatre in Venice he encountered his sovereign, himself on holiday on what was then Austrian soil. Here there was no ostentatious avoidance. Frederick William greeted his young champion and his bride with manifest pleasure, invited them to dine, and indicated clearly enough that he was pleased to have the young man on his side, regardless of earlier appearances to the contrary.

That was in September. The Bismarcks returned to Schönhausen for the winter, soon to find themselves in an atmosphere of threatening crisis. Before the coming of spring king and administration had been all but swept away.

CHAPTER IV

CHAMPION OF REACTION

By the middle of March 1848 it must have seemed that the whole of Europe would be riven apart in violence. In February the Parisians had risen against Louis Philippe and driven him into limbo. Austria was in tumult, Metternich had fled the country, and almost at once the kindly, half-witted Emperor Ferdinand had to be whisked away from the Hofburg in Vienna to the safety of the grim old fortress at Olmütz in Moravia. And even while the Viennese were driving out Metternich, the Habsburgs' subject peoples—Italians, Magyars, Czechs—all rose in revolt. State after state in Germany joined in the tumult. Foreign visitors to the waters and the gaming-rooms of Baden-Baden, the idyllic Black Forest spa beloved above all by Russians, were appalled by the flare of violent feeling that had been building up below the surface for a year. Even in England, faced with a recrudescence of the Chartist movement, the government feared the worst. An army of special constables was enrolled in London, and when the great demonstration fizzled out with the presentation on 10 April of Feargus O'Connor's monster petition demanding parliamentary and electoral reform, Palmerston could write from the Foreign Office that it had been a glorious day, 'the Waterloo of peace and order.'[1]

Palmerston also wrote: 'There is a general fight going on all over the Continent between governors and governed, between law and disorder, between those who have and those who want to have, between honest men and rogues.'[2] It was not so simple as that, though in fact it was truer of Chartist England (apart from the equating of honesty with property) than of anywhere else. For what was happening all over the Continent was the breakup of the system devised by Metternich and imposed by the Con-

45

gress of Vienna in 1815. This post-Napoleonic order had been steadily undermined by the development of industry and railways, which had greatly expanded the new middle classes, at the same time upsetting the balance between town and country, pauperizing many who were already poor and destroying the livelihood of innumerable artisans and craftsmen. Of course the downtrodden and the oppressed seized their chance to riot. But throughout the Germanies and Austria the real drive behind the revolutions came from the new middle classes: it was they who turned against absolutist rule, demanded a voice in government, and at the same time discovered in nationalism, in the concept of the nation of which they formed an indisputable part, a cause to set against the principle of aristocratic privilege that so evidently transcended all considerations of nationhood.

1848 was indeed the year of the Communist Manifesto: 'A spectre is haunting Europe—the spectre of Communism,' this stirring document began; and it ended, 'Let the ruling classes tremble at a communist revolution,' and, borrowing from Marat, 'The proletarians have nothing to lose but their chains. They have a world to win.' But very few people had heard of Karl Marx or read his manifesto, which was not to come into its own until much later. And when demonstrators came out into the streets, first in Paris, then in city after city throughout western and central Europe, Marxist internationalism and the solidarity of the working-class were far from their minds.

Paradoxically, the one appeal to internationalism that made itself heard anywhere in Europe during those tumultuous months came from the students of Vienna university, who were the first in Austria to raise the flag of revolt, led by a young Liberal doctor, Adolf Fischhof, who demanded in rational and at the same time deeply moving tones all the now familiar freedoms and, above all, the free coming together in equality and fruitful accord of the several nationalities comprehended in the great empire. But the voice of Fischhof, when Metternich fled, was soon shouted down, first by hungry workers pouring out of their tenements and demanding bread, then by German nationalists who demanded an Austria for the Germans as noisily as Czechs, Magyars, Italians under Habsburg rule called for their own independence.

All were soon put down: The Italians by Count Joseph Radetzky, the Bohemians and the Viennese by the legendary Field-Marshal Windischgraetz. In Paris the counter-revolution did not succeed until the new Republic had let loose General Louis Cavaignac to drown in their own blood the Socialist workers who wanted more. In North Italy the Piedmontese had to be defeated at Novara; in Prague the ancient city was formally bombarded; in Vienna the minister for war was strung up on a lamp-post and imperial troops carried out a full-dress siege with heavy and sustained bombardment; in Hungary a Russian army was dispatched by Nicholas I to rescue his fellow-monarch, the young Francis Joseph, and to aid him in crushing a nation in arms under the rebel Lajos Kossuth, who fought on into 1849. In that year, too, there were renewed outbreaks of revolutionary violence in Saxony and Baden. In Dresden the professional Russian anarchist Michael Bakunin joined hands with Richard Wagner in proclaiming a revolution which threatened the composer's sovereign and patron, King John of Saxony. In Baden the insurrection was finally put down by units of the Prussian army.

Amidst all this violence and confusion Prussia itself was let off lightly. It did not look like that at the time. The French Revolution was still close enough to the men of 1848 to seem alive, almost as an inevitably continuing process in the manner of a smouldering subterranean fire. When all was said, there had been more than a lick of flame in 1830. And there had been bread-riots intermittently—the last in Berlin in 1847. There was very bitter discontent among the starving weavers of Silesia, among the coal-miners of the Rhineland, the factory workers and dispossessed peasantry of Baden and elsewhere. Even the demands of the Prussian Liberals in that short-lived United Diet of 1847 had verged on a direct threat to the crown.

The news of the flight of the French king to England and the fall of Guizot, his prime minister, set off a wave of unrest in Germany, at first among students at Bonn, Heidelberg, and elsewhere. But, although there was clamour for the ending of absolutism and the granting of a constitution, this made far less impression on Frederick William than the agitation for a united Germany, symbolized by the black, red, and gold tricolour of national liberation (black for foreign oppression, red for the blood of battle, gold for the sunlight of victory and freedom . . .). In this Frederick William found a mystical appeal after his own heart.

Thus even before the news of Metternich's fall reached Berlin (that was on 16 March, three days after the event) it was clear that serious trouble must be expected and prepared for in advance. The generals, broadly speaking, wanted the king out of Berlin, leaving the army a free hand to get on with what they considered its proper job, crushing any revolt and securing the safety of the realm. Frederick William vacillated and showed himself at his worst, driving his entourage nearly to distraction. He was as determined as ever not to surrender a fraction of his own sovereignty, but he was prepared to recall the United Diet. At the same time his imagination had been caught by the blaze of nationalist emotion and in some dreamy and unclear way he saw himself leading Prussia into a united Germany. Indeed, his personal envoy had already gone to Vienna to discuss with Metternich himself ways and means of reforming the German Confederation, the Bund, when the blow fell.

The fall of Metternich stimulated Frederick William to feverish action. On 17 March he decreed the convening of the United Diet for 4 April, to prepare for a constitution. At the same time he proposed a radically reformed Confederation. Although the streets were full of demonstrating crowds, he still insisted on staying in Berlin and not slipping away to Potsdam as his generals begged him to do. But while declaring that his place was with his 'dear Berliners' he quite omitted to instruct the military to clear the city of the troops they had been piling in during the past weeks. And the army had for so long been detested as a symbol of absolutism and repression that it required no more than the least show of force to infuriate the crowds. This is what happened on the fine Saturday afternoon of March 18 when a vast concourse was demonstrating in front of the royal palace. There was a collision. Shots were fired, whether by accident or in panic it is impossible to tell. The crowd grew ugly. There was more shooting. There were corpses on the palace square and the damage was done. The demonstrators forced back from the square spread the news of what had happened, and with surprising speed street barricades were rigged up throughout the city so that the troops, who had no training in street fighting, could do nothing useful short of a full-scale and damaging assault with artillery.

Once again the generals begged the king to leave Berlin while he could. Once again he refused. For a whole day he seems to have been virtually incommunicado, crushed by the enormity of the events of that Saturday afternoon. But he still insisted that he, not his generals, was in command. And even while the military were finding, much to their surprise, that clearing the city without shelling it to ruin was not an easy job, came the first serious call to the king to end the fighting. It came from Vincke, the hot-headed conservative moderate from Westphalia, the only man who had been able to stand up to the insolent taunts of the young Bismarck in that short-lived session of the United Diet. He argued urgently that quite apart from the horror of further bloodshed, the troops, unprepared and untrained, were already shaken and on the edge of total demoralization: soon they would have to be withdrawn in any case. Frederick William was shocked, and he was still more shocked some hours later when General Prittwitz, the man whose orders had brought about the fatal clash and who had been foremost in urging the king's departure and a free hand for the military, announced that he could not hold on for more than forty-eight hours at the most: after that it would be a matter of withdrawing his troops, regrouping outside, and blockading the city to starve it into surrender.

This was the situation that brought about the capitulation which was to turn Frederick William for a time into a 'king of shadows' and earn him the bitter and costly contempt of his brother-in-law Nicholas I of Russia. There is no need here to dwell in detail on the events of that night of 18 March, on the composition of the royal address to 'My dear Berliners' which made about every possible mistake, but which, after creating endless confusion, was misinterpreted by Prittwitz to mean that he should clear the city of all troops more radically and quickly than poor Frederick William had dreamed of, leaving the monarch exposed and with no choice at all but to bow to the demands of the crowd, who next day completely surrounded the palace. 'Come down and salute the dead!' they yelled at him. And Frederick William obediently descended from the palace balcony and stood bare-headed before the corpses of the slain, laid out for his inspection. That same day he formally transferred responsibility for law and order to a civilian militia. The final act of abnegation came two days later. A king without an army, he marched at the head of an extraordinary procession from the royal palace to the university. Wearing on his sleeve the black-red-gold armband, he made two separate speeches proclaiming his faith in a united Germany and Prussia's place in it: 'From now on Prussia merges with Germany!'

This was the day that Bismarck descended flamboyantly on Potsdam. He had been staying with friends not far from Schönhausen when the news of the Berlin troubles reached him. He had known about the rioting. He had known that, although the Prussian countryside was quiet, there was tension and unrest even in quite small towns. He must have known something about the starving weavers in Silesia and the discontent among the miners and the steel workers of the Rhineland, the dispossessed peasantry and the factory workers in Baden. But these appeared as local matters to be dealt with firmly. The turbulence in France and throughout the

Habsburg Empire were, however, by him entirely unforeseen: the future grand master of diplomacy and foreign affairs had not yet raised his eyes beyond the horizon of his own land.

His immediate reaction to the news that the king was a prisoner of the mob was at the same time parochial and hysterical. He had rushed home to Schönhausen to defend his own. All was quiet, but the next day deputations from the neighbouring market-towns toured the villages, demanding the running up of the black-red-gold flag on the church towers. Bismarck, outraged, organized a collecting point for all the firearms in the village and put his own into the pool. Shot-guns were then served out to specially trusted peasants with orders to chase the intruders out of the district, while Bismarck and Johanna made a circuit of neighbouring villages to rouse them. He was then nearing his thirty-third birthday, and he was in such a state of nervous excitement that when one of his neighbours suggested that this kind of violent reaction was asking for trouble, he turned on him and threatened to shoot him down if he tried to hold the peasants back.[3]

This was the overture to an astonishing display of unguarded hysteria that was to last several days and offer an invaluable insight into the character behind the mask, a key to much that is otherwise baffling about the 'iron chancellor's' actions in later years—baffling because his contemporaries never looked at his rare moments of self-revelation but saw only the contrived image. They never saw behind this to the qualities of the artist, who controls with icy cerebration the movement of his emotions at white heat. Bismarck was an artist above all.

But in 1848 he was still a beginner, unpractised, and in far from perfect control of the passions that drove him. Self-dramatization for the moment had the upper hand. And the curious thing is that although his behaviour was so odd and his acting so flamboyant, this was not one of the episodes he chose to suppress when he came to write his memoirs forty years later. He seems to have seen nothing untoward about the self-dramatization and hysteria, telling with evident self-approbation the story of how, once he had put Schönhausen into a state of defence, he pocketed a revolver and four rounds of ammunition (why four?) and hurried off to Potsdam, determined single-handed to save the king from the mob and himself.[4]

He seems to have soared into a world of total fantasy. He alone, he believed, could persuade his sovereign to give the army its head and allow it to reoccupy Berlin and drive out the revolutionaries, cost what it might. To the soldiers, specifically to his old acquaintance of the Trieglaf days, Roon, he offered to raise a levy from among the peasants and march them to the capital to rescue the king. And he seems not to have felt snubbed, only let down, when the military replied that they could do without his amateur private army, but he could make himself useful by going back to Schönhausen and organizing a reliable source of supply in the shape of bread and fodder for the regular troops and their horses.

This would not do at all. More than ever it was clear to him that he and he alone could save the king, still isolated in Berlin. So he set off for Berlin by train, sketchily and ineffectively disguised (he shaved his beard off and put on a broad-brimmed hat with a black-red-gold cockade), presented himself at the palace, was refused admittance. Still undaunted, he returned to Potsdam. If the king could not save himself, then Prussia must be saved for the crown in spite of him. The best thing would be for the king's younger brother and heir apparent, William, Prince of Prussia, to persuade him to abdicate and himself take over the succession. William was very much a martinet and an army man: he was just what was needed. But William, alas, the future king, the future German emperor, a soldier bred in the bone, was unpopular outside the army and knew it: he had already made himself small, taking refuge on an island in the middle of the River Havel, on which Potsdam stands, as a first stage on his flight to England, leaving behind him his wife, Augusta.

Very well! There was a second brother, Charles, notoriously hot-tempered, impulsive, irresponsible, with a liking for intrigue. And it was Charles whose interest Bismarck at last managed to enlist and who came up with the idea that since the king was unable to act, and since the Prince of Prussia was in hiding and in any case would never agree to lead the army against his brother to whom, as a soldier, he had sworn the loyal oath, the prince's sixteen-year-old son, Frederick, should be made regent. All that was required now was to win the support of the boy's mother, Augusta of Saxe-Weimar, who had stayed on in Potsdam while her husband slipped prudently away. But Augusta was a no-nonsense woman. She was the daughter of Charles Augustus, grand duke of Saxe-Weimar, the enlightened ruler who had persuaded Goethe to enter his service as minister of state. Her mother had become Goethe's close friend, respected and admired by him above all other women for her lively intelligence and as a patroness of the arts. Augusta lacked her mother's mind, but she had a good deal of her character and spirit. She was, moreover, a granddaughter of Catherine the Great of Russia and niece of two tsars, the brothers Alexander I and Nicholas I.

Bismarck's approach to this extremely assured and collected woman was ludicrous. She already disliked what she knew of him, and her brother-in-law Charles, who now thrust him at her, she detested. There is no accurate record of what took place at the interview (which Augusta chose to hold in the servants' quarters in the Town Palace at Potsdam), but when Bismarck emerged from it he had made a powerful enemy for life, having convinced his future queen and empress that he was trying to manipulate the royal house for his own obscure purposes and was nothing but an intriguing and disloyal careerist, as well as reactionary to the point of caricature. She would have nothing to do with any scheme concocted or approved by Prince Charles. The very idea of turning against her brother-in-law the king was treason. The notion that she might persuade her own husband to renounce the throne was no better. It was characteristic of Bismarck that when he came to publish his memoirs, he turned the story upside down (Augusta was then dead and could not contradict him[5]): in his own account it was Augusta herself who proposed that her brother-in-law should abdicate and her husband renounce the throne in favour of her son. It is a commentary on the position of women in nineteenth-century Germany that Bismarck was able to rise and survive as he did when William became king and Augusta queen.

It has been suggested that Bismarck's plan was reasonable because something like it was actually conceived and executed in Vienna. But there the emperor Ferdinand was a dear old man, half an imbecile and an epileptic, while his daughter-in-law Sophie of Bavaria, a woman of the strongest character, boundless ambition, and passionate dynastic sense, knew that her own husband was not up to the job of saving the empire. Instead, she had under her hand a nineteen-year-old son, Francis Joseph, a presentable youth of evident ability, whom she could guide, and a group of exceptionally strong and gifted men to subdue the revolutionaries, put the new emperor on the throne, and keep him there.

Frederick William, however, had not run from Berlin, as Ferdinand had been persuaded to run from Vienna. He was very much the king, and he was now proposing to give his people a constitution of sorts. The only power that could stop him was the army, its commanders already sulking after being ordered not to shoot down any more civilians. But Frederick William was not afraid of his army. Ten days after the start of the whole affair, 25 March, he felt sure enough of himself to leave Berlin and go to Potsdam, where he called together the officers of the Berlin and Potsdam garrisons to thank them formally for their loyalty and obedience. It was of this occasion that Bismarck told in his memoirs how when the king went on to express his confidence also in the loyalty of the people of Berlin the officers all but mutinied: 'there arose such a murmuring and such a rattling of sabres in their scabbards as no king of Prussia had ever heard before in the midst of his officers, nor, I trust, will ever hear again.'[6] The army came to heel, all the same.

Bismarck was an eyewitness of that scene in the Marble Hall of the Town Palace. He had been back to Schönhausen to tell his peasants not, after all, to march; and now he was depressed almost beyond endurance. It looked like the beginning of the end of the monarchy. It also looked like the end of his own career before it had really started. There was at last to be an elected constituent assembly, but nothing was more plain than that the furiously reactionary Otto von Bismarck had shot his bolt and would never be elected to the new parliament. He had nothing to lose by lifting up his voice in an impassioned protest against the present conduct of affairs.

He found his opportunity when, a week later, the United Diet (of which he was still a member) was convened to prepare the way for the elections. One item on the agenda was the moving of a formal vote of thanks to the sovereign for his generous concessions to the popular will. This was too much for Bismarck, who uncoiled his great height to deliver his protest. He began by proclaiming his acceptance of the situation as it was and his promise of what little help he might be able to give to the only power that could ensure stability and order. Having said that, he went on to register his dissent from the tone of the loyal address. What he could not stomach was the glad acceptance of humiliation: 'The past is buried,' he declared, 'and I regret far more than most of you that it is beyond all human power to restore it to life, now that the crown itself has cast earth upon its coffin.'[7]

He had said what he wanted to say, and after a few more words, overcome with emotion, and on the verge of tears, he broke off in the middle of a sentence and stepped down. To judge from his letter to Johanna the next day his tears were tears of rage rather than grief. He had spoken for one reason and one reason only, he explained: to show that he was not to be counted among 'those venal bureaucrats who turn their coats with contemptible shamelessness according to the wind.'[8] In the light of his proclaimed convictions and his record many must have thought that this was the young Junker's swan-song as a politician. They did not think it for long.

* * *

Nicholas in St. Petersburg had given up Prussia too soon when he poured scorn and fury on the head of his unfortunate brother-in-law for betraying the monarchical ideal. Frederick William's thought-processes were always obscure, never more so than when yielding to the popular explosion of March 1848, but his heart was in the right monarchical place: he might permit the inauguration of an elected parliament, but he would never allow it to usurp effective power.

This determination did not preclude a good deal of wavering, but within a matter of weeks the Liberal ministers who started off so full of hope found themselves opposed and obstructed at every turn outside the assembly by a compact Conservative group which gathered round the king to strengthen his will and define his purpose. In the light of later German history it is important to stress that this group (the Camarilla, or *Ministère Occulte*, as its members called it) was overwhelmingly military in composition. It was dominated by four extreme conservatives—the Gerlach brothers, Leopold and Ludwig, and Generals Edwin von Manteuffel, and Ludwig von Rauch—who set themselves up to thwart the will of the civilian assembly, chiefly lawyers, professors, businessmen, and so on, representatives of the new middle class. The Camarilla had their own newspaper, the *Neue Preussische Zeitung*, also known as the '*Kreuzzeitung*' because of the iron cross blazoned on its front page (this was the paper long planned by the Gerlach brothers, who had enlisted Bismarck's interest a year earlier), and they had the initial support of the heir apparent, William, Prince of Prussia—who firmly refused to countenance any move against the king, his brother, but could be counted on to stiffen his resistance to Liberal demands.

These demands came not only from the Prussian assembly, which aspired in vain to win for itself something of the authority and power of the English parliament, but even more from the revolutionary, 'All-German' parliament which had been meeting in St. Paul's Church in Frankfurt since the fall of Metternich and the consequent collapse of the old Confederation. For Frankfurt appealed to both the radically minded and the German nationalists of Prussia, who dreamt of a larger and sometimes dangerously dynamic patriotism embracing their German-speaking brothers everywhere.

In October 1848 the Frankfurt Diet demanded that each German state should place its army under a central command appointed by itself. This was a direct attempt on the Hohenzollern palladium, and as such outraged every Prussian Conservative and also shocked a great many parliamentary

54

Liberals who had little or no love for the army but were loyal monarchists all the same. A major crisis seemed to be developing just six months after the March upheaval; but the crisis never came. What happened was that the Conservative forces in Austria launched a counter-stroke, executed with ruthless determination by a trinity of able generals organized and driven by the civilian aristocrat Prince Felix zu Schwarzenberg. Towards the end of October, Prince Alfred zu Windischgraetz, commander-in-chief of the imperial forces still loyal to the Austrian crown, energetically bombarded Prague into submission and then turned his guns on Vienna itself, where, at the cost of much bloodshed and bitterness, the revolution was finally crushed. This was the penultimate step in a particularly atrocious civil war in which Slav was set against Magyar, German against Slav.

The last straw for Frederick William in Potsdam was the demand by radicals in the Prussian assembly that Prussian troops be sent to the aid of the Viennese revolutionaries. Since the great mass of the deputies were also deeply shocked by this demand, which reflected the growing power of the revolutionary masses, as opposed to the radical middle classes, the time had evidently come for Prussia to stage her own counter-revolution. And it was now that Frederick William showed his essential decency. Resisting strong pressure from his generals of the Camarilla to bring in troops to break up the assembly by force, he preferred to adjourn it quietly in a routine manner, with the promise of reconvening it three weeks later, preferably away from Berlin when tempers had cooled. This much accomplished (it was 9 November), well-disciplined troops under General Friedrich von Wrangel moved quietly into the centre of the city, taking over from the people's militia without violence or bloodshed, and held the ring while the king formed a new 'Ministry of Loyal Servants' presided over by his morganatically born cousin, Count Brandenburg, as the prelude to the promulgation, on 5 December, of a new constitution. This preserved the principle of divine right for the monarchy but conceded to the parliamentarians a great deal more than the Camarilla liked. There were to be two assemblies, an Upper House (Herrenhaus) of delegates appointed by provincial governments, and a Lower House (Landtag), its deputies chosen by the members of an elaborately organized electoral college. From the point of view of those who aspired to parliamentary government the trouble was that the king conceded not one fraction of his divine right: he could veto any legislation that did not appeal to him and he could suspend the activities of both houses and govern by emergency decree.

* * *

During all this time Bismarck had been hyperactive. He was not put down by the snubs he had suffered in Potsdam and Berlin. And for a man who was now clearly bent on a political career he was, to say the least, singularly unaccommodating, scarcely able to conceal his contempt for Frederick William's weakness, and sometimes exhibiting a downright offensiveness that only a monarch of extreme magnanimity could have tolerated. It is the curiously erratic, not to say reckless, behaviour of this newcomer that strikes one—apparently uncontrollable rages alternating unpredictably with interludes of frigid detachment. Thus, within a few weeks of stumbling out of the chamber, choking with emotion, after publicly accusing his king of betraying his heritage, we find him loftily assuring an influential journalist friend that all is well with Prussia: 'We have been saved by the specifically Prussian virtues. The old Prussian concepts of honour, loyalty, obedience, and courage inspire the army. . . . Prussians we are and Prussians we remain.'[9]

As the challenge of the Radicals intensified, we find him careering about the countryside as a kind of informal liaison officer between the various monarchist centres, seeking to inspire a military *coup*. He was among those most disappointed when the assembly was suspended and Berlin bloodlessly reoccupied by the military. He regarded the Constitution as a betrayal of principle. This did not, however, prevent him from standing for election to the new Landtag, and actually canvassing in person for the votes of tradesmen. He won his seat quite comfortably and was not in the least embarrassed by the fact that he owed it to a Jew, when only recently he had vehemently opposed a movement to emancipate the Jews.

That was in February 1849. Three months earlier Ludwig von Gerlach had suddenly realized that his young protégé, whom he had thought of as 'the very active and intelligent adjutant at our Camarilla headquarters,'[10] was a serious candidate for office. Very well, responsibility might sober him! At any rate, he suggested him for a post in the new Conservative government of Count Brandenburg, but Frederick William said 'No!'—the disconcerting newcomer was to be used 'only when the bayonet rules without restraint.'[11]

Was this to be wondered at? The young Bismarck had first come to his notice barely eighteen months before with that violently provocative speech to the United Diet in which he poured scorn on worthy veterans of the Napoleonic wars old enough to be his grandfather. Since then the king must have heard again and again his sister-in-law Augusta's version of the young man's extraordinary plan to embroil her in a plot against him. Since then, again, the same young man had publicly accused his sovereign of casting earth upon the coffin of Prussia's great past. In spite of all this, Frederick William could still put himself out to win the loyalty of this impetuous and difficult subject. In June he invited him to dine at Sans Souci and disarmed him with a patient and profoundly sincere account of all he had gone through during those terrible March days when he had to decide whether or not to use his army to destroy his people. Queen Elisabeth also tried to make this tiresome but formidable young hot-head understand something of the responsibilities and agonies of high office: for nights on end, she told him, the king had been unable to sleep. 'A king *must* sleep,' retorted Bismarck.[12]

But the new harmony did not last. A few weeks later, enraged by the threats of one of the Liberal ministry's attempts to curtail the privileges of hereditary landowners, this champion of loyalty and obedience drew up a preposterous letter to the king, sending it round for his fellow-Junkers to sign, which not only objected violently to any action involving 'the confiscation of private property' but threatened the king himself with eternal disgrace: 'the great mass of the Prussian people,' the letter declared, 'will hold Your Majesty responsible before God and Eternity!'[13] To show that they were serious and to defend their own interest, the Junkers organized a sort of counter-parliament, in which Bismarck sat.

Bismarck had more than two years to go before he was given a responsible appointment, and during those years, although still prone to intemperate outbursts, his judgement became more balanced, his perceptions more subtle, his emotions more controlled. During that time, also, his domestic life was firmly and finally subordinated to his public career. Johanna's first child, a girl, christened Marie, was born during the row over the Junker parliament (August 1848); her second, Herbert, sixteen months later (December 1849). But the delighted father saw little of his children, or of their mother herself. He was increasingly active as the organizer (to use his own phrase) of court and cabinet intrigues—a role that kept him on the move. He wrote often to Johanna when she was not with him, delightfully and in terms of extreme affection, as he continued to do in later life whenever they were away from one another. But certainly he grew away from her, in the sense that he was moving ever more deeply into politics, while politics interested her hardly at all. He must have foreseen this at the time of his marriage. Everything we know about him indicates that he was one of those men who would not know what to do with a highly intelligent wife, actively interested in all the details of his work. Furthermore, he was a German, and Germany then and for many years thereafter was the land where women were kept in their place. His own enjoyment of social life was soon to die away, but for the time being it was stimulated by the growing recognition that he was a politician to be reckoned with, still more by the presence in Berlin of his beloved sister, Malwine, and her husband. Malwine was now a striking figure; her husband, the red-haired von Arnim, was very rich indeed; both were popular at court. It was with Malwine, not Johanna, on his arm that Bismarck now started to appear at smart functions.

He was also working hard, sitting on any parliamentary committee that would have him, winding himself into tortuous political intrigues, delivering an occasional speech which showed his real quality; but still in no way influential. The main focus of governmental interest now lay in Prussia's relations with the other German states and Austria. Austria, guided by Schwarzenberg and with the new young emperor Francis Joseph at its head, was pulling herself together after the uncertainties and humiliations of the past year. In March 1849 Lombardy was reconquered brilliantly at Novara by the eighty-three-year-old veteran of the Napoleonic wars Field-Marshal Joseph Radetzky, but the Hungarian rebel army, which included many officers from the imperial army, was a tougher nut to crack, and it took the powerful Russian intervention to secure victory for the Habsburg crown. Until this was done Austria was in no condition to concentrate on the restoration of the *status quo* in Germany.

At first it looked as though she would be helped in this by Prussia. The so-called Frankfurt Parliament included some extremely able and enlightened men, bending their minds to the creation of a constitution for a united Germany, to the appointment of federal ministers, to reformist enactments of all kinds. They forgot only one thing—that governments, benevolent as well as tyrannical, are based on power. And Frankfurt had no power.

The most furious discussion centred on the question of a Greater versus a Lesser Germany (Grossdeutschland versus Kleindeutschland). Greater Germany could include all those parts of the Austrian Empire inhabited by people of German blood—and exclude, therefore, Italians, Magyars, Slavs. The extreme and most irresponsible nationalists were giving nationalism a bad name by also calling for the inclusion in a Greater Germany of all those lands where some sort of German was spoken—e.g., Switzerland, the Baltic provinces of Russia, Alsace, and even Holland. But since no Austrian statesman or monarch would conceivably agree to this sort of conjuring trick (and, indeed, Schwarzenberg's vision, supported by the economic arguments of his brilliant commerce minister, Baron Karl von Bruck, was of a great 'Empire of Seventy Millions'—all the Germanies, plus the various nationalities of the Habsburg Empire, under Austrian dominion), Frankfurt had to make do with the hope of a Lesser Germany; and it was to Prussia, as the strongest state after Austria, that it must look for its power. Thus it was that the democratic Frankfurt Parliament solemnly offered the imperial crown and the title King of the Germans to Frederick William, who refused it with disdain. It was the crown of the gutter, he said in effect. It was not Frankfurt's crown to offer. He could only accept a crown that was offered by all the German princes, who alone had the right to dispose of it.

This decision Bismarck himself applauded. He made his own contribution to the debate. German unity was the proper desire of all who spoke German, he declared, but Frankfurt would only destroy Prussia, 'that house of state raised over the centuries by glory and patriotic ardour and bathed in the blood of our ancestors.' The Frankfurt crown might shine alluringly, he went on, 'but the gold which gives reality to its lustre must first be obtained by casting the crown of Prussia into the melting pot.'[14]

In fact Frederick William could never have assumed the imperial crown: Austria would not have allowed it. Nobody in Prussia had yet realized how complete the Austrian recovery was turning out to be. Nobody had realized that Felix Schwarzenberg was a statesman of great brilliance and extreme ruthlessness. This head of a most ancient, rich, and noble family, with a Byronic past behind him, was a natural aristocrat who had nothing but contempt for most of his fellow-aristocrats, despising them for their stupidity, ignorance, and feebleness of purpose. His character is well indicated by the apocryphal remark attributed to him when he accepted the assistance against the Hungarian rebels offered so eagerly by Nicholas of Russia; his opponents had been urging the danger involved in putting Austria under any obligation to Russia: 'Austria,' Schwarzenberg is supposed to have retorted, 'will astonish the world by the magnitude of her ingratitude.' And so, to Nicholas's grave chagrin, she very soon did.

Schwarzenberg also astonished the world by his ruthlessness. When the Hungarian rebellion was at last put down and Kossuth fled in 1849, the question arose: what to do with the rebel generals, some of them very senior officers in the service of the emperor against whom they had fought.

If only to save blood in future and, more immediately, to avoid tarnishing the image of the new young emperor, the argument for leniency was strong. But Schwarzenberg had his own ideas: 'Mercy by all means,' he observed, 'mercy is a very good thing. But first let us have a little hanging.' He allowed the gifted but unbalanced and sadistical General Julius von Haynau to go on the rampage. He confirmed the execution of Count Bathyany, one of the most noble and respected of the Hungarian magnates, arousing the indignation of the world. On the other hand, he showed great skill in using men of liberal or radical inclination (including some who had fought on the 'wrong' side of the barricades in Vienna) to share in government: and he turned the ramshackle old empire, shaken into fragments by the new spirit of nationalism, into a centralized bureaucratic state. He did all this in three years, between 1849 and 1852, when, at the age of fifty-two he died.

By dying he robbed Europe of a fascinating spectacle: the struggle that might have been between this arrogant and handsome Austrian prince, ruling in the name of his inexperienced but very determined and tight-lipped young emperor, and the Prussian Junker, Bismarck, who in some ways was so uncannily like him, in others very different.

Thus, for example, we find Bismarck in Berlin writing to his mother-in-law after Bathyany's execution (Frau von Puttkamer was taking the line followed by almost everybody outside Austria and all but a very few inside, that it was unforgivable to execute the old man):

'You have so much sympathy with the relatives of Bathyany, but have you none for the thousands upon thousands of *innocent* persons whose wives have been widowed and whose children have been orphaned through the insane ambition or presumption of these rebels. . . ? Can the execution of one man provide a sufficiency of earthly justice as retribution for the burnt cities, the devastated provinces, the murdered populations whose blood cries from the earth to the emperor of Austria, whom God has entrusted with the sword of authority?'[15]

How interesting to reflect that just fifteen years after this rhetorical outburst Bismarck, now minister-president of Prussia, would be actively conspiring with the survivors among those same Hungarian rebels against that same emperor of Austria.

Still, in 1849, not understanding that Schwarzenberg was about to turn Austria into a more formidable power than ever before, if only briefly, and with Prussia once more under control, King Frederick William decided to take advantage of the general confusion into which all the Germanies had been plunged in order to strengthen Prussia's position. He worked through a strange, anachronistic creature, General Joseph von Radowitz—a Roman Catholic of Hungarian origin, who now for some eighteen months acted as the chief minister of a Protestant house in conflict with a Catholic house which claimed the Hungarian crown. Radowitz managed to stitch together a union of minor German princes and hoped also to bring Hanover and Saxony into a new confederation to be dominated by Prussia. A grand assembly was called to discuss the matter formally at Erfurt, not far from Weimar, in March 1850, the so-called Erfurt Parliament, seen as the northern nucleus of a new German Union to take the place of Metternich's old Austrian-dominated Confederation, which had become a dead letter with the inauguration of the Frankfurt Parliament.

But Radowitz was reckoning without Schwarzenberg, who was now preparing to re-establish Austrian supremacy in Germany. This remarkable man launched his campaign just two months after the opening of the Erfurt Parliament by calling together in Frankfurt a number of lesser German states and proclaiming to the world that Metternich's Confederation lived again, thus throwing down a direct challenge to Prussia. He now only needed an excuse to confront Prussia directly, and the chance arose six months later, in September, when the harshly reactionary Elector of Hesse-Kassel, in trouble with his subjects, appealed to Austria for support instead of to Prussia, as he should have done. Prussia was on the verge of declaring war. Hesse-Kassel was one of those states which separated two parts of Prussia, and to have Austrian troops astride the main road between Berlin and Cologne was not to be borne. Both sides mobilized, but in fact war would have been suicide for Prussia; Austria would have brought Bavaria into the fight with her, jealous of Hohenzollern pretensions, and almost certainly other states as well. The day was really saved for Prussia in her own despite by Nicholas I in St. Petersburg, who took it upon himself to arbitrate between his fellow-monarchs, fellow-heirs to the half-forgotten Holy Alliance, and came down heavily in favour of Austria. The Austrians had a perfect right to reconstitute the German Confederation, Nicholas declared, therefore Prussia had no business in Hesse-Kassel. Paradoxically, it was this bitterly resented 'betrayal' which saved Prussia from eclipse. Schwarzenberg was spoiling for a fight that Austria would have won. Instead, the dynasts got together. Schwarzenberg was told by his new young emperor to hold back, while Frederick William threw Radowitz overboard and sent his replacement, Otto von Manteuffel, to Olmütz to negotiate with the Austrians. There was no negotiation. Schwarzenberg appeared in person and with his cold, cutting, unforgiving arrogance demanded total capitulation. Poor Manteuffel had to agree to take Prussia's troops out of Hesse, to demobilize her army, and to enter the revived Confederation under Austrian leadership, as though nothing at all had changed.

Thus, by the Punctation of Olmütz, Austria, so recently in ruins, re-established her supremacy in Germany for all to see. It had only sixteen years to run, and it was Bismarck who was to break it, once and for ever, in 1866. But in 1850, after a brief moment when he dreamt of a dashing and romantic little war, it was he who stood out as the most articulate defender of Olmütz. From the beginning of the campaign for a northern union he had treated the notion with derision. In his first major speech to the new Prussian Landtag he had gone further, coming very close to accusing the king of betraying the memory of his ancestor Frederick the Great. Either the king should have allied Prussia with Austria to fight revolution wherever it showed its head, he argued, or he should have taken advantage of the general disarray and quite simply occupied all Germany down to the River Main, forcibly incorporating the whole in a Greater Prussia.[16]

But his disaffection had not prevented him from taking his seat in the parliament in Erfurt in March 1850, and it was here that at last, seeking to undermine the Liberal view from the inside, he began to show a serious concern for the idea of Prussia—as distinct from the Junkers of Branden-burg and Pomerania—as distinct from the dynasty itself. His moment thus came when most of his fellow-parliamentarians were shocked into si-lence by the humiliation of Olmütz. And in standing up to deliver the most important speech he had so far made to applaud the climb-down of the king he had so often charged with weakness, he made his bow as a potential statesman, capable of prudence, apparent moderation, far-sightedness, breadth of view—and above morality.

War for Hesse, he said in effect, was insupportable because it would have been essentially a frivolous war. 'The only healthy foundation for a large state—and this is what distinguishes it from a small state—is state egoism rather than romanticism, and it is unworthy of a great state to fight for something which does not affect its own interest. Gentlemen, show me an objective worth a war and I will go along with you. It is easy enough for a statesman to ride the popular wave from the comfort of his own fireside, making thunderous speeches from the rostrum, letting the public sound the trumpets of war, and leaving it to the musketeer, bleeding out his life's blood in the snowy wastes, to settle whether policies end in glory or in fail-ure. Nothing is simpler—but woe to any statesman who, at such a time, fails to find a cause of war which will stand up to scrutiny once the fighting is over.'[17]

Here he begins to unfold the blueprint of his thinking. Here is the first cool, unequivocal statement of Bismarckian *Realpolitik*, untrammelled by emotion or moral inhibition. Here also is the blind spot which will prevent him throughout his career from understanding that the real, long-term interests of a state may be in direct conflict with more immediate interests. Here, not least, is the imagination and the courage of a politician capable of visualizing the effects of his policies in terms of shattered bodies on the battlefield and the suffering of wives and mothers. In 1850 the man who was, in his own time, to savage first Denmark, then Austria, then France, in the supposed interests of Prussia offered a pre-view of his quality by welcoming as a victory of common-sense what others regarded as a shameful defeat. Bismarck understood that Nicholas of Russia had in fact saved Prussia from destruction. The other man who understood this was Prince Schwarzenberg in Vienna. Schwarzenberg enjoyed his triumph at Olmütz, but he would have enjoyed a military victory still more: 'War would perhaps have been better,' he observed, 'and would have brought peace for fifty years—perhaps! . . . What an embarrassment, alas, is conscience!'[18]

Russia still loomed hugely in the wings. Austria found it hard to bear the knowledge that she owed so much to Nicholas. Prussia found it hard to forgive the tsar for supporting Austria against her.

CHAPTER V

'I AM PRUSSIAN...'

The year 1850 had been critical. By the end of it Bismarck's reputation with the king stood higher than ever before, but he could still see no way ahead, and he was seriously worried about money. Already he had been forced to let some of the best land at Schönhausen to pay for his parliamentary adventures, and now, with no prospect of a ministerial post, he was even thinking of taking up employment outside Prussia. The duke of Anhalt was in need of a minister to run his tiny but extremely productive territory, fertile in soil and rich in minerals, traversed by the middle Elbe above Magdeburg; and he was tempted ('The Duke is an imbecile, the Minister is Duke!' he wrote to Johanna).[1] But in April came salvation, unexpectedly and out of the blue. Prussia had to find a new representative for the reconstituted Federal Diet, the Bundestag, now starting work in Frankfurt. The extremely delicate task confronting him would be to heal the breach with Austria while at the same time making it clear to Vienna and all the world that Prussia expected to be treated as an equal: Austria and Prussia were powers; that is to say, the kingdoms of Bavaria, Hanover, Saxony, and Württemberg were not.

Bismarck, with his furious directness and insolent manner towards all who crossed him, was not the first man to spring to mind as a candidate for such a post. What recommended him was his increasingly evident ability, his courage, his refusal to be over-awed, above all the fact that he had been among the few who had favoured the Austrian solution at Olmütz and therefore could be expected to get on good terms with the Austrians. He was too talented a man not to be used; Frankfurt was a long way away from Berlin and it might be just the place for this difficult but valuable defender of the Prussian crown to develop self-discipline and a sense of responsibility. After some agonizing, Frederick William overcame his doubts and allowed himself to be persuaded by the Gerlach brothers to appoint him as representative to the Bundestag; the Prince of Prussia contented himself with a few disparaging remarks about a jumped-up 'Landwehr lieutenant'; the Liberal press jeered a little; and Bismarck, with no diplomatic training whatsoever, and generally regarded as no more than a reactionary politician from the backwoods, found himself at thirty-six in a key diplomatic post.

It was stipulated that he should serve three months as deputy to the outgoing minister, Theodor von Rochow. And he knew that in those three months he had to prove himself. He was elated. To Johanna and her mother he wrote in jubilation: 'You people have often complained that nothing was ever done for me by those above me. Now, beyond my wildest expectations or desires, comes this sudden appointment to what is at this moment the most important post in our diplomatic service.'[2] But he knew that Johanna would be less well pleased (as in fact was the case), that she would dread having to follow her husband abroad, shrink from the idea of mixing with cosmopolitan high society, prefer by far to have him in a ministerial post at home, with everyone bowing down to him (and her), even if his real power were insignificant.

Johanna's complaining at times verged on the lachrymose, but her husband suppressed the irritation he must sometimes have felt. Years later he was to answer her back fairly briskly: 'What is the use of peaking and pining?' he once exclaimed when she was grumbling away about uprooting herself and following him to St. Petersburg. 'What must be, must be!'[3] But now, he was on the defensive. In this same letter he did his best to convince Johanna and anyone else who would listen that the position was unsought by him, that he had not lifted a finger to secure it, that he had no choice in the matter. 'I have not sought it. The Lord has willed it, or so it would seem, and I must obey, although I can see it will be an unfruitful and thorny office, wherein with the best intentions I shall forfeit the good opinion of many people. It would be cowardly, however, to refuse.'[4]

He was to go on like this, repeatedly. But in fact, he appears at this time, and in his early days at Frankfurt, to have been torn as he was never to be torn again between the irresistible attractions of public life and power and his profound love of the countryside; between his need for a quiet, still domestic centre of the kind that Johanna could provide and the excitement and stimulus of the world of affairs. Some of his letters show him almost ill with homesickness. It has often been said that his profound longing for country life should not be taken too seriously in view of his repeated refusals to lay down his office when he had the chance. But it was clearly as genuine as his early love of poetry, his love for Johanna, his later love of solitude. When a politician publicly lays his hand on his heart and declares that all he wants in life is to abandon responsibility and retire to the country, asking to be admired for his great sacrifice, he need not be believed and he should not be trusted. Bismarck was not like this at all. He displayed his longing only in letters to his wife and family; he demanded in this particular no sympathy from anyone. But his love of country life has to be understood as one important element in an extremely complex nature.

'I can hardly hold out against the longing to be with you, and feel so homesick for you all and for the green spring and for life in the country, that my heart is heavy indeed' he wrote on the eve of his departure for Frankfurt. 'Today . . . I was at General Gerlach's, and while he was droning away about treaties and monarchs I looked out at the chestnut and the lilac blossom . . . underneath the windows tossing in the wind, and heard the nightingales and imagined myself standing with you at the windows of the panelled room looking out onto the terraces, and I did not know what G. was talking about.'[5]

Nor was this a passing mood. For years to come, new landscapes filled him with delight. He might be on a hunting expedition in southern Sweden: 'Roebuck are stronger here than anywhere I have ever seen them, and this region is far more beautiful than I had imagined. Magnificent beech woods, hilly, and walnut trees in the garden as thick as a man.'[6] Whether he is taking time off for a midnight swim in the Rhine (he had an enduring passion for swimming in all waters at all times, as for shooting): 'There is something strangely dreamlike in thus lying in the water on a warm quiet night, carried gently along by the current, seeing only the sky with moon and stars, and, to each side wooded hill-tops and castle battlements in the moonlight, hearing nothing but the gentle splash of one's own motion. I should like to swim thus every evening.'[7] He had the painter's eye and the poet's command of words, whether he was evoking the great sweep of the Pyrenees or describing in a fascinating series of letters the people and the cities and the plains of Hungary.

Listen to this, one letter of many from his Hungarian tour in 1852 (he is travelling with armed escort through brigand country): 'After a comfortable breakfast under the shade of a magnificent lime tree, I climbed into a very low open-frame waggon, with straw sacks drawn by three steppe-

horses; the lancers loaded their carbines, took their places, and away we
went at a tearing gallop. Hildebrand sat on the front sack with a hired
Hungarian servant and for coachman we had a dark-brown peasant with a
moustache, broad-brimmed hat, long black hair shining with grease, a shirt
that stopped short of his stomach, leaving a visible dark brown band of his
own skin about the breadth of a man's hand between it and white trousers,
each leg wide enough for a woman's skirt, reaching to the knees where the
spurred boots begin. Imagine firm grassland, level as a table, on which for
miles around, as far as the horizon, there is nothing to be seen but the tall,
bare poles of the beam-wells, dug for the half-wild horses and cattle. We
passed thousands of white-and-brown oxen, timid as deer, with horns as
long as a man's arm; shaggy, ugly-looking horses herded by half-naked
herdsmen on horseback with long staves like lances; endless droves of pigs
always with a donkey, to carry the herdsman's sheepskin (*bunda*), and
sometimes himself; great swarms of bustards, rabbits, marmot-like *susliks*;
occasionally wild geese, ducks, lapwings got up from a brackish pond as we
passed. . . .'[8]

Bismarck could be no less discerning and aware when it came to people.
Here is old Meyer Amschel Rothschild at home in Frankfurt: "He is a little, thin, hoary imp of a man, the patriarch of his tribe, but a poor man in
his palace, childless, a widower, cheated by his dependents, and treated
shabbily by refined, Frenchified and Anglicized nephews and nieces, who
will inherit his treasures without gratitude and without love.'[9]

His letters from Frankfurt in the spring of 1851, however, show more
than sadness at the thought of a lost Schönhausen summer, more than the
nostalgia of a born countryman confined by city streets. There is also a
strong sense of destiny, almost of fatality. At last he had achieved the sort
of position he wanted (although he denied this repeatedly, not only to Johanna, but to others too), an important and responsible place in the great
world of affairs. Ambition was thus for the moment satisfied; but ambition
would, he knew, demand its price. 'I feel,' he wrote on May Day, 'as
though we were emigrating to America, taking leave of our dear old
ways, for who knows when the wheel now catching us up will let us go
again? . . .'[10]

Two days later he is even more obviously preparing Johanna (himself as
well, it seems probable) for the final and total break with the past:

'My sweetest, dear heart—Why so sad? For it is pleasant in foreign
lands, but I can hardly keep back my tears when I think of the quiet country life with you, and all that goes with it. . . . Why do you talk of a long

separation, my angel? Do get used to the idea that you must go out with me into the winter of the great world; how shall I warm myself otherwise? It is possible, even probable, that for long years to come I shall only be a fleeting visitor on home-leave; we cannot and must not be separated for so long. Weigh the anchor of your soul, and make ready to leave the safe harbour of home. I know by my own feelings how painful the idea is for you, how sorrowful the prospect for the old ones.'[11]

He might, one feels, have been a soldier preparing to go to the wars— and, then, lo and behold, out it comes: 'But I repeat, I have not at all desired, or even contributed with a syllable to what has come about; I am God's soldier, and whither He sends me, thither I must go, and I *believe* He sends me, and that He shapes my life as He needs it.'[12]

Thorny the new job may have been, but unfruitful it was not. Bismarck got a great deal out of it: indeed, it made him. No statesman ever received a better education in the makings of diplomatic manoeuvre and political intrigue.

The most obvious benefit was the immediate widening of his field of vision. Until now practically all his dealings had been with fellow-Junkers, professional soldiers, courtiers—all members of rather highly specialized classes—and the peasants of Brandenburg and Pomerania. In the Prussian assembly he had encountered for the first time (and collided heavily with) the new bourgeoisie and with Catholics from the Rhineland, aristocratic as well as middle class. But he knew next to nothing about these; and about Austrians and fellow-Germans outside Prussia he knew nothing at all.

Frankfurt brought him into touch with people and a culture very different from the Prussian. The city itself, proud and rich, one of the last of the great free cities, a part of the main stream of European history, impressed him almost against his will. There, for example, and on the Rhine not far away, he made the acquaintance of two men of widely differing backgrounds and ideas but each supreme in his own field and strong and gifted enough to compel in this self-willed, self-consciously gifted Junker the sort of admiration and respect which, until now, he had felt for no man. The one was the doyen of the Rothschild family, old Meyer Amschel, who lived in Frankfurt without show, who impressed him with his pride of race and his lack of all pretension. (This meeting was to influence him in his own choice of financial adviser in years to come, to his own great profit.) The other was no less than the oldest of all elder statesmen, Metternich himself, now spending a few months on his Rhineland estate on his way back from exile in Brighton to his final resting place in Vienna. Together the old wizard and the young genius found common ground in their astringent attitude towards the follies of mankind and their delight in the superb and celebrated Johannisberg wine from Metternich's own ancestral vineyard.

The drawback of the Frankfurt appointment, seen as a crucial stage in the education of a statesman, was that it focused Bismarck too soon and too exclusively on foreign politics. He knew a little about finance, but next to nothing about industry and trade, and he had no idea at all of the tremendous power which the development of railways, of mining and manufactures, above all of coal and steel and chemicals, was in the process of bringing to the Prussian state, which he still thought of (and was to go on thinking of for years to come) as poor and backward, weak relative to Austria. He failed to understand the men who were the driving-force behind the industrial explosion: he did not know who they were. Frankfurt, though broadening his vision of Europe, at the same time blinkered it by confining it to diplomatic struggle and manoeuvre. He had no occasion to think about Prussia as a living organism, developing in response to the spirit of the industrial age. Prussia for him was Brandenburg and Pomerania with their forests and sandy wastes; it was Hohenzollern; it was the army that upheld the throne. It also included a pack of black-coated Liberals trying to drag it down. For the rest it was a concept, an abstraction. Frankfurt did nothing to bring it to life.

What he was about to discover, without much repining, was that there could be no future for Prussia as he understood it, within the Confederation: if Prussia was to take what he considered to be her rightful place among the powers she must find allies outside Germany, not, as he had hitherto imagined, by developing a special relationship with Austria, now clearly seen to be impossible. For Schwarzenberg, in charge of a resurrected Austrian Empire, had abandoned Metternich's established policy of co-operating with Prussia, consulting her in advance of the rank-and-file members of the Confederation, and at least appearing to treat her as an equal. In the new Confederation Austria was permanently in the chair, as was fitting, an echo of her centuries' old imperial position. Below the chair, as far as Schwarzenberg was concerned, there was nothing to choose between a dozen states, most of whom were entitled to one delegate each, whether kingdoms like Prussia or Bavaria, or duchies like Anhalt (some twenty of the smaller states had five delegates between them).

Count Leo von Thun-Hohenstein, the Austrian chairman, belonged to a great Bohemian family with vast estates and rich palaces. He exemplified the casual arrogance of the somewhat overbred Austrian 'first society,' treating fellow-members of the Diet not as his colleagues, which they theoretically were, but as born inferiors. And most of these, although they could combine against Austria in any matter seeming to affect their vital princely interests (as in effectively blocking Schwarzenberg's attempt to include all the non-German parts of the Habsburg Empire within the Confederation), in social matters they deferred to her. Bismarck seems to have taken one long look at Count von Thun and decided that co-operation with Austria through gentlemanly persuasion was a hopeless dream. Schwarzenberg was giving in to his personal emotions when he should have calculated coldly. It was pleasant to humiliate the heirs of Frederick the Great, who had so treacherously and irreparably damaged Austria. But, as Metternich had seen, it was impossible for Austria to treat Prussia as one small German state amongst others. Vienna *needed* Berlin. If Schwarzenberg failed to see this, the Austrian chairman of the Bundestag was even blinder.

Very well, said Bismarck in effect, if he could not extract Austria's acknowledgement of Prussian equality, at least he had a powerful nuisance value and could make it very difficult for Vienna to get her way in all sorts of matters. In his own vivid phrase: 'When Austria hitches a horse in front, we hitch one behind.'[13] Travelling laboriously from court to court in southern Germany, he worked to influence the rulers and their ministers over the heads of their representatives at Frankfurt, cajoling, flattering, bribing, playing one against the other, sowing distrust of Austria, sometimes threatening.

Too much has been made of the personal hostility Bismarck felt towards Count von Thun. This existed, of course. From the start he felt himself slighted by this aristocrat who, as he saw it, concealed the morals of a card-sharper behind an air of false amiability.[14] He may well have felt some jealousy of a dazzling magnate who came of a family rich beyond the dreams of any Junker and represented a culture no less superior to anything Brandenburg or Pomerania had to offer (the Thuns had been generous patrons of Haydn, Mozart, Beethoven). The count, moreover, was a master of that casual, offhand, gratuitous offensiveness, as much a mark of Austrian officialdom as was its unreliability and idleness—the notorious *Schlamperei*. Bismarck was never casual, and he never broke a promise by accident or out of slackness. He did not cheat unconsciously, and he held in especial contempt those who cheated without clearly realizing what they were doing. With his downright aspect he brought a note of foreboding into his relations with the Austrian representative.

Fifteen years later it was to end in armed conflict; but not for a long time did Bismarck begin to feel that war between Prussia and Austria was inevitable. Inevitability was a concept he instinctively rejected: the lives of nations as well as of individuals were so full of accidents. His understanding of this was an important element in his genius. Equally certainly, even in his first brushes with the Austrians he saw, looking far ahead, that war must be considered as a possibility: the greatest service a statesman could do was to keep his mind open to all possibilities.

Although he was certainly irritated by Austrian ways and pretensions, he was also kicking against the constraints of official protocol and the extreme tiresomeness of having to treat fools gladly. His celebrated demonstrations against Count von Thun—lighting a cigar at meetings where by custom the count was the only man to smoke; pulling off his own jacket when the count held court in his shirt-sleeves; refusing to wait when the count was not ready to receive him at the time agreed—all these trivialities and more besides were protests against fate at least as much as they were demonstrations against Austria. They were also in part directed against some of his colleagues, whose self-importance and pomposity made him nearly ill: 'men,' as he wrote to his friend Hermann Wagener, editor of the *Kreuzzeitung*, 'who put on solemn professional airs when all they want is to ask you for a light or the key of the lavatory.'[15]

To dwell too much on the surface of Bismarck's encounters with the Austrians and his colleagues from all the Germanies is to miss what was going on underneath. There were two distinct movements, each concealed from all but one or two intimates, each very strong; the one a deep psychological conflict, the other an intellectual leap forward of a kind that at once put this strange creature, who had not been in diplomacy for more than a few months, head and shoulders above his contemporaries, and into the class of the great masters. The volume and detail of his letters and dispatches are the biographer's delight and also his despair. It is fascinating beyond measure to watch this mind, largely untrained, coming to grips with Europe and appropriating that continent to itself. It is no less fascinating to view this process against a private drama hidden from the world behind a front of contemptuous superiority and an immense physical presence—nothing less than a crisis of the spirit.

Many writers on Bismarck have found it hard to credit the sincerity of

71

some of his more pious declarations, notably the 'God's soldier' letter, quoted earlier: it has sometimes been concluded that he was writing to impress Johanna, still more her mother. The same has been said of a very strange outburst in a long letter to Johanna, written two months later, on 3 July, when to all appearances he had quite settled into his new life at Frankfurt. 'The day before yesterday,' he wrote, 'I dined at Wiesbaden . . . and there with a mixture of sadness and mature wisdom contemplated the scene of past follies. May it please God to fill with his strong, clear wine this vessel in which the champagne of a twenty-one-year-old youth so uselessly foamed, leaving stale dregs behind. Where and how are Isabella Lorraine [-Smith] and Miss Russell living now? How many of those with whom I flirted, tippled, and diced are dead and buried? . . . ' And so on, until a celebrated passage about living without God:

'I cannot imagine how a thoughtful person who, nevertheless, knows nothing or wishes to know nothing of God can endure the despicable tedium of life, a life which is fleeting as a stream, as a sleep, even as a blade of grass that soon withers. . . . I do not know how I endured it in the past; if I should live as I did then, without God, without you, without the children, I should not in fact know why I should not cast off this life like a dirty shirt; and yet most of my acquaintances are thus, and they live.'[16]

It is easy enough to understand a certain scepticism on the part of the reader today when he encounters this echo of the 'conversion' letters to Johanna and her father four years earlier—until scepticism is confounded by an agonized passage from a remarkable letter written from Frankfurt on the following day, not to Johanna, but to Hans von Kleist-Retzow, a trusted friend of staunchly reactionary views. Suppressed for over a hundred years, these words are vital to an understanding of the man; they open a secret window.

'The chief weapon with which evil assails me is not desire for external glory but a brutish sensuality, which leads me so close to the greatest sins that at times I doubt whether I shall ever gain access to God's mercy. At any rate, I am sure that the seed of God's word has not found fertile ground in my heart, laid waste as it has been from the days of my youth. Were it otherwise I could not be, as I am, the plaything of a temptation which even invades my moments of prayer. Whenever I am alone and unoccupied I have to struggle against visions of an abyss, the product of a depraved fantasy which leaps with astonishing agility from the consoling image of Him who suffered for our sins to new sinful thoughts. . . . I am often in hopeless despair over the ineffectiveness of my prayers. Comfort me, Hans, but burn this without speaking of it to anyone.'[17]

He was not often alone and unoccupied. Soon after that cry from the dark Rochow was recalled and Bismarck was confirmed as his successor. Now he is looking for a house, preferably one with a walled garden, and within a matter of months Johanna and the children have joined him. His way ahead is becoming clear and he has little time to think of anything but forwarding his own career and working Prussia into a dominant position (the two are interdependent). The pattern of his life is set. Against a cosily domestic background, encouraged in his gargantuan appetite for food and drink by an adoring wife (not that he needed any encouragement), an internal life marked by waves of intense cerebration, often of a revolutionary kind, concealed—by all the arts of a politician who has decided that brutal frankness and rudeness pay but knows how to charm and delights in deviousness—a public image illumined every so often (but not for yet another ten years) by the dazzle of a spectacular master-stroke.

A picture of his domestic life in the 1850s (enlarged by the advent of a third child, always known as Bill, in 1852) is supplied by his old university friend John Lothrop Motley, who visited the Bismarck family in Frankfurt in the summer of 1855:

'It is one of those houses,' Motley wrote to his wife, 'where everyone does what he likes. The show-apartments, where they receive formal company, are in front of the house. Their living rooms, however, are a salon and a dining room at the back, opening on the garden. Here are young and old, grandparents and children and dogs all at once, eating, drinking, smoking, piano playing, and pistol shooting (in the garden), all going on at the same time. It is one of those establishments where every earthly thing that can be eaten and drunk is offered you—porter, soda water, small beer, champagne, burgundy or claret are about all the time—and everybody is smoking the best Havanas every minute.'[18]

In spite of all this heart-warming openness ('I can't express to you how cordially he received me. If I had been his brother, instead of an old friend, he could not have shown more warmth and affectionate delight in seeing me'), it is interesting to observe, Bismarck found himself driven to dissemble, to deny his ambition, even to one of his two oldest friends; and the future historian of the Dutch Republic was quite taken in: 'He is a man of

, and of very great powers of mind,' he very fairly observed,
prominent place which he now occupies sought *him*. He
r any other office.'[19]

...g, indeed, could have been more misleading than this picture of
relaxed domesticity. Bismarck was already obsessionally caught up in the
business of high politics and diplomatic intrigue, pretend as he might that
his duties were repellent and his appointment unsought. Even when he is
opening his inmost heart to Kleist-Retzow, immediately after the cry from
the pit he switches back in the same letter with all his natural verve and
venom to the business of the day. So away he goes in the next breath with
the already familiar charges: 'The Austrians invariably cheat at cards and
always will. With their measureless ambition I do not see how we can expect ever to make an honest alliance with them.'[20]

By the time of Motley's visit to Frankfurt in the high summer of 1855
Bismarck had come a long way towards crystallizing out into the figure the
great world was to know. In the four years since his appointment to
Frankfurt he had been astonishingly transformed into a diplomatic
schemer of extreme subtlety and deviousness, who, unlike most diplomats,
had also the makings of a natural master of men.

The Frankfurt period has been seen too much in terms of Bismarck's
private quarrel with Austria and too little as a source of light on the growth
of the great man's skill and judgement. No time of his life is more elaborately documented. He was an irrepressible talker and correspondent, and
this period was the heyday of his letter writing. Above all in his formal dispatches and private letters to Otto von Manteuffel, his chief in Berlin, and
his less frequent but sometimes immensely long and circumstantial letters
to his old friend and sponsor Leopold von Gerlach (usually intended also
for the eye of the king) it is possible to follow the movement of his mind
week by week, sometimes it seems almost hour by hour. The judgement is
sometimes astonishingly wild, the passions uncontrolled, but the penetration of the eye, the workings of a swift and powerful brain applying itself
for the first time to world affairs, are fascinating to watch.

Most rare and wonderful of all is the revelation of the free mind and eye
of an artist in the proper sense of that word. It is, of course, a truism that
politics is an art and not a science. Bismarck himself used to talk in those
terms ('Politics is less a science than an art. It is a subject that cannot be
taught, one has to have the gift.' Again: 'Because they have yet scarcely
outgrown the political nursery, the Germans cannot accustom themselves

74

to see politics as a study of the possible').[21] But this is hackneyed, superficial, a pointer to Bismarck's failure as a leader (as distinct from a master) that he found it necessary to state the obvious in this context with the air of a discoverer.

In speaking of the free mind and eye of the artist I am thinking not of the instinctive quality which may emerge in apparently effortless mastery of all sorts of skills—from flexibility and timing in politics to 'hands' in horsemanship—but, rather, of the eye of the small boy who calls out that the emperor has no clothes; the rare sort of eye that takes no account of accepted conventions, prejudices, pretences, received ideas, established patterns, or hallowed associations. In the context of a Prussia engaged, almost without knowing it at that time, in making a bid for the mastery of Germany, the effect of that mind, that eye, may best be summed up not simply as the turning upside down of the established system (a trick well within the capacity of any idiot revolutionary who prides himself on being sufficiently literate to read the warning, Fragile—this side up!), but, rather, as the detachment of Prussia from all traditional ties (to say nothing of solemn and binding agreements) in order to win perfect freedom of action; or, put another way, an open-eyed rejection of the time-honoured European pattern, so that the pieces, once dispersed, might be reassembled at leisure in a form more favourable to Berlin.

From quite early on he was seized with two dominant imperatives. The first was to harness the spirit of German nationalism to the Prussian cause, specifically by appealing to the material interests of the new bourgeoisie in the lesser states as opposed to the dynastic interests of their princely rulers. This meant, of course, an appeal to a spirit he despised and to the Liberals who nurtured it and who, only a few years earlier, he had seen as treasonable rebels to be destroyed. When he first started thinking seriously along these lines it was in terms of a calculated deception: for example, in 1853 he wrote to the Prince of Prussia suggesting that recourse might profitably be had to 'parliamentary liberalism' as a temporary means to promote Prussia's influence over the German states, to be jettisoned when its work was done.[22] This kind of deception which was later to be adopted in another context and with considerable effect by the Russian, Lenin, was no more than elementary Machiavellianism, if of a rather histrionic kind: it might be called second-degree Bismarckianism. First-degree Bismarckianism, towards which our hero was only groping in the mid-1850s, was more subtle. There is an early hint of it in his startling observation to the Liberal deputy Victor von Unruh in the summer of 1859. Any hope, he said, of

75

Prussia finding a reliable ally among the great powers was foredoomed. 'Prussia is completely isolated. There is only one truly reliable and enduring ally, to be won if tackled in the right way: the German people!' Enjoying the dazed look in Unruh's eyes at this apparent volte-face of a reactionary and anti-Liberal aristocrat, Bismarck expanded: 'I am just the same Junker that I was ten years ago . . . but I would have to be blind or imbecile not to see things as they really are.'[23]

The second, and for some time by far the most important, imperative was precisely that need to find a powerful ally outside Germany which he was later to tell Unruh did not and could not exist. This search led him to discard all accepted ideas about traditional loyalties, affinities, enmities. In the course of it he showed the quite extraordinary rapidity with which, at his best, he could recognize his own misconceptions and make a new start.

As early as 1853, having decided either that Austria would never allow Prussia to share the mastery of Germany on equal terms or else that such a sharing, even if by patient diplomacy it could be achieved, was not enough, that Prussia must be first, he was concluding in his reports and letters that since Prussia could not survive, let alone grow, without a powerful ally, and since the official ally, Austria, was determined to frustrate her and cut her down to size as a junior partner, Prussia must look elsewhere. Or—an early example of Bismarckianism of the second degree— at least *appear* to be looking elsewhere. For only by frightening the Austrians into believing that Prussia might ally herself against them could she hope to achieve the standing she deserved.

There was only one potential ally of the calibre required, and that was France of the Second Empire, which had been inaugurated with the coronation of Napoleon III on 1 December 1852. Russia was out of court: she still looked to Austria as her chief partner in the Holy Alliance against the forces of subversion and revolution. And the blood ties between the Hohenzollerns and the Romanovs, close as they were, had counted for nothing in the great confrontation between Prussia and Austria at Olmütz, when Nicholas I had threatened to march on Berlin unless Prussia gave way. England, behind her barrier of sea-power, with her habit of paying other lands to do her continental fighting for her, did not enter into any serious calculation. This left France, a pariah, still untouchable after Louis Napoleon's recent usurpation, still regarded as a revolutionary force, abhorred and feared by all legitimists like the Gerlachs in Berlin, but a nation desperately anxious to get back into the European power-game. Logic therefore pointed to a rapprochement between France, with her still supposedly incomparable army, and a Prussia which had nothing to lose and everything to gain by cutting free from the system into which she had been locked since 1815.

This was the sort of thinking that Bismarck unfolded, discreetly at first, to Manteuffel (prime minister as well as foreign minister) and Leopold von Gerlach. It was as original in its way as the thinking of Maria Theresa's great chancellor, Kaunitz, a century earlier, which produced the spectacular reversal of alliances on the eve of the Seven Years War, for the first time joining Austria with France, her hereditary enemy, against Prussia and England. And in spirit it belonged to that epoch, not to the modern world at all.

But it was still only thinking. Bismarck had no power. He could see with perfect clarity that if Austria was to be opposed with anything but pinpricks Prussia would first have to put an end to her awkward sprawl, which was a strategic as well as an economic limitation; then find an outside ally. He could see, but he could not act. And this sense of frustration must have been at least a part of the cause of his almost malignant vilification of the Austrians. His abuse, his obstructionism, his legalistic pettifogging became so outrageous that poor Baron Prokesch-Osten, Thun's successor, was driven almost to despair. It was one thing to give the Austrians as good as he got, quite another to blind himself, or at least to seek to blind his masters, by absurd distortions, slanders, lies. It was one thing even to call the Austrians a nation of card-sharpers, quite another in all apparent sobriety, to characterize Prokesch-Osten, a quiet, scholarly poet, a historian of distinction, as an Armenian pedlar of mousetraps.

This sort of self-blinding, coupled with barrack-room coarseness of abuse, soon came to be a feature of Bismarck's career. Thus he could underrate the Russian ambassador to Frankfurt, Prince Alexander Gorchakov, dismissing him as 'a solemn and misguided fool, a fox in wooden shoes' for no reason at all other than anger at the Russian's quite proper attempt to get him to recognize that the Austrians were human too—Gorchakov, soon to succeed old Nesselrode as foreign minister, was certainly cunning as a fox, vain as a peacock, too, but also a talented and tenacious antagonist, quick on his feet, and destined many years later to become an object of obsessional hatred on the part of Bismarck.

His reports and letters of this period make astonishing reading: one has constantly to remind oneself that Bismarck had no power, that he was simply Manteuffel's envoy, the Prussian representative in the Federal Diet, representing a king who believed in the Confederation. One has to remind oneself also that Austria was still very grand. To all but this terrible Junker her pre-eminence in Germany was self-evident. Prussia had gone back in the world since Frederick's great leap forward with the rape of Silesia and the perfection of the Prussian army as a powerful fighting machine a century before. Austria was still great. The attitude of the other German states was equivocal. Prussia served a useful purpose in so far as her existence helped them to withstand inordinate demands from Austria; but she was an ever present danger in the pursuit of her own ambitions, most immediately to the smaller, northern states. Bismarck was aware of this, just as he was aware that sooner or later Prussia to hold her own with Austria would have to absorb the territories of at least some of her neighbours. But it was not his place to make policy. He had one immediate over-riding and prosaic task: while keeping on terms with Austria, to work for her continued exclusion from the German Zollverein, or Customs Union.

It is not too much to say that at this time the Zollverein formed the real basis of Prussian power, which was thus not military but economic. Through the Zollverein she was able to spread and intensify her influence throughout Germany and to exploit the swiftly accelerating industrial revolution in her favour. This most effective institution had started modestly as far back as 1818 as an exclusively Prussian domestic convenience designed to knit together the pre-Napoleonic Prussia of Brandenburg, Pomerania, Silesia, etc., with the new acquisitions in Saxony and the Rhineland. It was urgently needed, for the new, enlarged Prussia embraced sixty-seven different tariff areas and nearly three thousand categories of trading goods liable to excise duty.[24] Once the required domestic unification was accomplished, the next obvious step was to persuade neighbouring states to join in. Metternich's Austria, of course, had her own customs system, separating her rambling, polyglot empire from the rest of Germany. Some of the southern states of Germany, excluded from the Austrian system by Metternich for what seemed to him good reasons, and not relishing the idea of closer ties with Protestant, overbearing Prussia, tried to develop their own union; but in the end this fell apart. By 1834 all the states had joined the Prussian system except for Hanover (which was not finally separated from Great Britain until 1837) and one or two very minor northern states; Hanover finally yielded in 1851. By that time Schwarzenberg and his Austrian government-of-all-the-talents had hammered its various parts into a tightly centralized state which ran from Polish Galicia, hard against the Russian Empire in the east, to the Swiss border in the west, from Lake Constance to Lombardy and the Adriatic. It was Schwarzenberg's minister of commerce, Baron Bruck, the founder of Austrian-Lloyd and the creator of Trieste as a great port, who conceived the dream of 'an empire of seventy millions.' And this dream was to be achieved by the enlargement of the German Customs Union to embrace all Austria with her polyglot population of Croats, Czechs, Italians, Magyars, Poles, Serbs, Slovaks, Slovenes, Wallachs, and others, all ruled by the German-speaking house of Habsburg, the head of which thought of his peoples not in terms of national patriotism but only in terms of 'patriots for Me.'

Had the whole of Austria been able to enter the Customs Union, of course, it would have meant the end of the Prussian challenge to Austrian predominance. Frederick William IV, left to himself, might have let it happen, but it is safe to say that no other Prussian would have agreed, neither the Gerlachs with their mystique of Hohenzollern divinity nor Manteuffel with his down-to-earth, unimaginative, bureaucratic conservatism, nor Bismarck who was already beginning to equate the aggrandizement of Prussia with the development of his own career.

He did not, of course, immediately urge warlike solutions upon his government in Berlin; but from the very beginning he showed an independence of mind that startled even those of his superiors who had encountered his boldness earlier. Neither his official reports to Manteuffel nor his semi-official commentaries to Leopold von Gerlach were the dispatches of an obedient envoy: they were the polemics of an impatient man on the spot convinced that he knew better than his masters, urging upon them with every device of rhetoric and casuistry a favoured line of policy.

Objective reporting was not beyond him. He could describe exactly enough, as is clear from letters to Johanna; and his character sketches of his colleagues, when these are not made valueless by anger or pique, are brilliant and penetrating. When he was sent to Vienna for a few months in 1852 to take the place of the Prussian ambassador who had fallen ill almost immediately after the death of Schwarzenberg, he was able to report lucidly and reasonably on the young emperor, who impressed him, and on the new prime minister, Count Karl von Buol-Schauenstein, who did not. But he was not seriously interested in reporting as such, and the real weight of his dispatches and letters was concentrated on the more important business of educating his superiors, above all by trying to argue them into changing their attitude to Louis Napoleon's France.

This protracted and obstinate campaign was inaugurated in the early

79

days of 1853, only a month or two after Louis Napoleon was proclaimed emperor. On 27 January, in a letter clearly intended to be seen by the king, Bismarck took exception to an extravagant attack on Napoleon carried by his old newspaper, the *Kreuzzeitung*. Here he sowed the first seed of his new doctrine. For heaven's sake, he said in effect, stop treating Napoleon like an outcast: by alienating him we are throwing away our best weapon against Austria. He knew that neither the king nor anybody else in Berlin saw the future in terms of a deadly struggle with Austria; they merely wanted an acknowledgement of Prussia's standing as a power superior to the rest of Germany outside Austria. So Bismarck had to be careful, adapting himself to his audience and making it appear that he was advocating no more than the seizing of any possible means of softening the Austrian attitude and gaining support among the German states rather than the struggle for mastery which he envisaged. It should not be thought, he protested, that he was advocating an actual Franco-Prussian Alliance. All he asked was that by treating France in a respectful and civilized manner and entering into decent relations with her Prussia should give the impression that she *might* in certain circumstances be compelled to join forces with her.

Why, he asked, should we insist on telling all the world that we would never on any account turn to France? 'Let us at least not burn our boats *in public!*'[25] And to Manteuffel on the same day he urged that even if no approach was ever made to France, Prussia should be careful to do nothing to discourage the Austrians from thinking that 'in certain circumstances' Prussia might choose France as 'the lesser of two evils.'[26] And not only the Austrians: he wanted the smaller German states too to contemplate with quaking hearts the dire possibility of Prussia and France joining hands in an unholy alliance to carve up their territories between themselves.

There were a number of striking features about this first Bismarckian excursion into high diplomacy. The first was that a very raw ambassador to the Bundestag was speaking out of turn: he had been sent to Frankfurt to carry out instructions from Berlin and keep his masters informed about developments in Germany and Austria, not to make policy. And he was not censured. Instead, while Manteuffel fumed, convinced quite justifiably that Bismarck had designs on his job, the king and Gerlach were continually sending for him to come to Berlin to argue his views or support them in theirs.

The second feature was his almost instant conviction that Austria had to be reduced. This meant denying the validity of the German Confederation, which it was his duty to uphold.

The third feature was the rapidity with which Bismarck, who then knew very little about France or the world in general, summed up a rapidly changing situation. Whereas in the eyes of every proper conservative throughout the length and breadth of Europe France was still a cess-pit breeding revolution and the new emperor a usurper and potential aggressor in the style of his uncle, Bismarck, almost alone, saw Napoleon III as he really was.

The fourth feature was the very curious unreality of Bismarck's recommendations, given the circumstances of the hour. The legend of his infallibility has been so firmly implanted, not least by Bismarck himself, that it is the easiest thing in the world to overlook his tactical and strategic errors, or at least discount them. But his errors were to be many and sometimes grave. On this occasion he showed a brilliant flexibility of mind in urging his superiors to cease cold-shouldering France. But for a Foreign Service official even to suggest early in 1853 that a Franco-Prussian *rapprochement* might frighten Austria was not only to fly in the face of reason but also to make his superiors question his judgement and his fitness for office, as well as to stiffen them in their anti-Napoleonic stance. The fatal flaw was that as long as Russia and Austria stood together any move by Prussia directed against either of these powers would be knocked on the head at sight—as had in fact happened at Olmütz.

If this man with the eye of an artist could make errors of judgement he had unlimited courage and he also had luck, that prime requisite of a successful politician, soldier, or entrepreneur of any kind. At almost the very moment when he was puzzling Berlin with his premature suggestions about France those suggestions were suddenly not premature at all. Far, far away, far indeed beyond the horizons of Bismarck, Manteuffel, and Frederick William IV, Nicholas I of Russia had been goading himself into a state of extreme irritation about Turkey. Refusing to take no for an answer, for years past he had sought to engage the powers, above all Britain and Austria, in schemes for the orderly dismemberment of the Ottoman Empire which, he insisted, was on its death-bed. All he succeeded in doing was to arouse their suspicions. Britain, with a shiver, saw Russia in Constantinople, cutting her communications with India; Austria saw the Balkans, moribund under Turkish rule, menacingly transformed into a base for future Russian expansion.

Thus the pot simmered, but, ironically, it was heat from France that caused it to boil over—ironically because, to put it bluntly, Napoleon was doing no more than strike attitudes on the edge of a problem that had nothing to do with him. He had been seeking a pretext to show the French he could bring them glory, and now he found it, though not in the way he had anticipated. He had only wanted to make a noise in the world, to show that France was once again a power to be reckoned with. And he saw an easy chance in the sudden flare-up of the habitual quarrelling and bickering between the two sets of monks, Latin and Greek, Roman and Orthodox, who stood guard over the holy places in Jerusalem and Bethlehem, marooned in tiny enclaves in the heart of Islam. When they started throwing down each other's altars and actually coming to blows in the sanctuary Napoleon put himself forward as the champion of the Catholic faction, winning certain concessions from the sultan which outraged Nicholas when he heard of them; for Nicholas was the self-appointed protector of *all* Christians under Turkish rule. In face of belligerent Anglo-French warnings (Britain, as always, obsessed by the Russian 'threat' to her imperial trade-routes), on 2 July he sent his troops across the River Pruth to occupy the principalities (Moldavia and Wallachia, forming most of latter-day Rumania; then under Turkish suzerainty). For the next three months diplomats of all the powers fussed and struggled to avert impending war. But Turkey knew she had the Maritime Powers, England and France, on her side, and on 8 October finally declared war on Russia. The other powers held off. But on 30 November Admiral Nakhimov caught the Turkish fleet in harbour at Sinope and sent it to the bottom. Popular indignation in London and Paris was now irresistible. In January 1854 the British and the French sailed through the Bosporus, and on 21 March declared war.

The development of that war, the ineptitude displayed by both sides, concerned Prussia as a sovereign state only indirectly. Bismarck insisted that she was not interested in the Balkans or the Straits. But Prussia was part of a confederation which included Austria, and Austria was deeply concerned, and Bismarck's almost obsessional fear was that Austria would become embroiled in the war and drag Prussia after her. In fact there was little risk of this. Frederick William found himself in one of those situations he most enjoyed, so energetically assailed by conflicting advice from different quarters that he could bask in the sensation of decision-making while in fact simply allowing his advisers to cancel each other out. Thus Manteuffel clung to the Austrian alliance sealed after Olmütz, and actually succeeded in getting it renewed in April 1854 to the accompaniment of cries of woe from Bismarck in Frankfurt. As early as February he had despatched in vain a characteristic warning to Manteuffel: 'I should be alarmed should we seek protection from a possible storm by tying our trim and seaworthy frigate to the ancient, worm-eaten Austrian man-o-war.'[27] Leopold von Gerlach, on the other hand, passionately believed that Prussia's place was by the side of Russia, the senior partner in the Holy Alliance and Prussia's ally in face of Bonaparte. Other advisers, most notably the prince of Prussia himself and the king's gifted but eccentric friend Baron von Bunsen, the long-established Prussian ambassador to England, urged an alliance with the Maritime Powers. As for Frederick William, Tsar Nicholas I, who had more humour under that coldly forbidding exterior than is generally realized, summed up his state of mind when he exclaimed: 'My unfortunate brother-in-law goes to bed a Russian and wakes up every morning as an Englishman.' He did nothing, for which Nicholas was duly grateful. Bismarck, who demanded neutrality, could have saved his breath: there was never any serious danger of Prussia's going to war.

Austria, on the other hand, muddled her admittedly delicate situation, with the result that when it was all over she was hated by both sides. Nicholas had taken Austria's support for granted, and was shocked almost to the point of illness when his brave young protégé, Francis Joseph, who owed him the crown of Hungary and was in any case the heir to the Holy Alliance, was so disturbed by the Russian advance into the Balkans and the prospective removal of Turkey as a buffer state between the two empires that he would not be contented with Nicholas's verbal pledges. There might have been ways round this difficulty if the tsar had been quietly made to see that his southward plunge was in fact a grave disturbance of the European balance; but Buol-Schauenstein blundered into the deepest water when he decided that here was a chance to head Russia off from the Balkans for ever. He demanded not only the Russian evacuation of the Principalities but also that Austria should move in to take Russia's place. The presence of a powerful Austrian army along the south-eastern frontier tied up 200,000 Russian troops which might have been used to reinforce the Russian army in the Crimea. And it was the Austrian ultimatum in 1856 which finally caused Alexander II, Nicholas's successor, to give up the fight. Austria's ingratitude, he said, had killed his father.

Austria, of course, was trying to swing the rest of Germany behind her and for once Bismarck in Frankfurt found himself speaking for a majority of states in the Confederation when he resisted her demands. What is most fascinating is the way in which, even while he was opposing any involvement with all his might, he could see ways and means of exploiting in Prussia's favour the very situation he wished to avoid. Thus, when the Austrian Alliance was renewed in April 1854 Prussia agreed that should Austria become involved in war the Berlin government would mobilize 100,000 troops to stand on the eastern frontier with Russia. (It was this pledge that gave Buol-Schauenstein the muscle to demand the evacuation of the Principalities.) Bismarck, who characteristically expressed his opinion of Austria's Balkan policy in the jibe that her only interest was 'the obtaining by trickery of a few stinking Wallachians,'[28] also had this to say: 'Great crises are the very weather for Prussia's growth, if we take advantage of them fearlessly and, perhaps, very recklessly.'[29] His idea of fearless and (perhaps?) 'very reckless' action was contained in his advice to the king once the treaty of alliance had been renewed: if Austria called on Prussia to mobilize in accordance with the treaty she should by all means do so; but she should so concentrate her troops that they would be in a position to advance against either Russia or Austria as the interest of the moment suggested. 'With 200,000 men, Your Majesty would at one stroke become the master of the entire European situation, dictate the peace and secure for Prussia a worthy position in Germany.'

'A man of Napoleon's sort,' Frederick William commented, 'can commit such acts of violence, but not I.'[30]

Politics as the art of the possible . . . Did Bismarck know that there was no chance of such ideas being accepted? Did he decide to put them forward simply to keep his name and person to the front? Or did he really believe that Frederick William, to say nothing of Manteuffel, might be persuaded to act in this sense?

With Austria and Russia at loggerheads, the European situation was turned upside down. The Crimean War was one of those climacterics that seem to occur perhaps twice in most centuries—after which nothing is ever the same again. It finally laid the ghost of the Holy Alliance and, more practically, tore to pieces the fabric of post-Napoleonic Europe so laboriously stitched together by Metternich and somehow patched up in the aftermath of the 1848 explosions. With Austria and Russia glaring at each other in a state barely short of war, the great barrier to a Franco-Prussian *rapprochement* was down and Bismarck's urging that Prussia should reach an understanding with France quite suddenly made sense. Now he went further. To his uncomprehending masters in Berlin he began to advocate a triple alliance of France, Russia, Prussia against Austria. . . . But France is at war with Russia! And Austria is our ally! they objected. Never mind, he retorted, in effect: soon Russia will be forced to ally herself with France; Prussia should be in with them both, making a firm front against Austria, who was ever faithless and ever concerned with reducing Prussian power. Russia, he insisted, would be eaten up with desire for revenge for Austria's betrayal, but she had no hard feelings against France. And the French, though at war with Russia, had no feeling of hatred against her.

He was speaking from special knowledge. In August 1855, while the war was in full swing, he decided that the time had come to visit Paris and see for himself what Napoleon was made of. His journey was unofficial and he used as his pretext a visit to the great exhibition which drew all the world to Paris at that time, but which did not interest Bismarck in the least. It coincided with Queen Victoria's state visit to France in return for Napoleon's state visit to England in April, and Paris blossomed into a scene of such splendour that the English queen as well as Bismarck was all but overwhelmed. At a great ball in the Tuileries Bismarck was presented to Napoleon and Eugénie as well as to Victoria and her prince consort. He was properly responsive to Eugénie's grace and beauty 'more beautiful than any of the portraits I have seen': the empress, he told Johanna, was in general style not unlike his sister, Malwine, though her face was longer and narrower and her eyes and mouth more beautiful.[31]

He did not learn much from Napoleon on this visit. But he was immensely impressed by the richness, brilliance, and variety of Paris—by its sheer size too—which was already being remodelled by Baron Haussmann to form a city of great boulevards. He was enchanted with the surrounding countryside and revelled in one of those great ritual stag-hunts in the forest of Fontainebleau. Above all he had long conversations with Napoleon's half-brother, the duc de Morny, and with the comte Alexander Walewsky, Bonaparte's natural son, now the new emperor's foreign minister. Both were pro-Russian and against the war.

About his impressions he did not write much except to Johanna, to whom he gave an ecstatic account of the city and his own reception by the count. But from Frankfurt, on his return, he reported at length to Manteuffel, not only stressing the general lack of interest in the war displayed by those Frenchmen he met (they usually shrugged their shoulders, he said, when asked about it) but also exposing with chapter and verse the fearful strain it was placing on France's military resources: most of the garrison towns were empty of troops; he gave figures for such vitally important strategic centres as Metz and Strasbourg—though where he got these he did not say. Morale in the army was bad, chiefly because of the way the press, above all the emperor's own paper, *Le Moniteur*, was minimizing the losses in the Crimea.[32]

All in all he returned with ammunition to continue and develop his thesis that France would soon be in the arms of Russia and that any Austrian understanding between Paris and Vienna was tenuous in the extreme. In Louis Napoleon he saw nothing to contradict the impression he had confided to Manteuffel several months before he had so much as set eyes on the man, when he had written that his 'itch to achieve the unexpected amounts to a disease, and it is nourished by the empress.'[33] He was speaking then in the context of a fantasy of his own conjuration: namely that Napoleon, frustrated by the long resistance of Sevastopol, might at any moment abandon the Crimean campaign, take all his troops (together with new reserves recently called up), and establish himself as lord of the Bosporus. And he continued: 'Even if the creation of a Latin imperium might not be an immediate consequence, at least such a situation would be rich enough in possibilities to enable the French to forget the failure of the Crimean enterprise and at the same time give expression to an element of adventurous romanticism which is even stronger in the empress than in her husband. Foolhardy and baroque such a policy would be, but it is precisely because of these qualities that certain individuals close to the imperial couple are inclined to give it credibility.' Admittedly, he continued, such a 'supremely Quixotic' action could not be undertaken without allies. England would obviously be no party to it, but Austria might be tempted, and it was conceivable that in certain circumstances even Russia might support it. . . .[34]

'Foolhardy and baroque' such a plan on Napoleon's part assuredly would have been. As a product of Bismarck's imagination it was in detail a fantasy of a rather silly kind; and yet at the same time it was uncannily prophetic. The absurd scenario of the French managing to occupy Constantinople without plunging Europe into war was an example of that irresponsibility which was not only to win Bismarck the distrust of his superiors but also, when translated into practice at the height of his career, to lead to trouble on a number of occasions. On the other hand the profound insight into Napoleon's character, months before he met the man and years before he seriously conversed with him, was illustrative of his almost perfect freedom of approach and depth of penetration. (For the time was to come when Napoleon did in fact embark upon a venture no less 'baroque' and no less foolhardy than the one sketched out for him by Bismarck. This was when, in 1863, he persuaded Francis Joseph of Austria very reluctantly to permit his brother Maximilian to accept at Napoleon's hands the doomed and fantasmal crown of a nonexistent Imperial Mexico.)

It was not until a second visit to Paris in 1857 that Bismarck got to know Napoleon well: indeed he then attained to a sort of intimacy rare between a ruler and an envoy from another land (no doubt it was the adventurer in Napoleon—as also, later, in the Socialist leader Ferdinand Lassalle, that appealed to the adventurer in Bismarck, which was very strong).

This relationship was to have important consequences in later years; but at the time its chief fruit was a remarkable series of letters to Leopold von Gerlach in which he not only pushed his demand for a French understanding harder than ever before but also laid bare the essence of the political philosophy which he had been hatching for years past.

The real purpose of these letters was twofold, first to ram home Bismarck's views on France and Napoleon III, then to display his rejection of all such concepts as holy alliances, dynastic loyalties, the natural collaboration between like-minded states and the rejection of others. In the end this strange man, who lashed himself into a genuine fury at what he considered Austria's perfidy and selfishness and unreliability (he meant, of course, her antagonism to Prussian expansionism), established himself as the prophet and champion of the self-centred state, concerned only with its own security and growth. Prussia is all that matters and every state outside Prussia is a potential ally or a potential enemy according to circumstance and regardless of its system of government or the nature of its ruler.

'When I have been asked whether I was pro-Russian or pro-Western powers I have always answered: I am Prussian, and my ideal in foreign politics is total freedom from prejudice, independence of decision reached without pressure or aversion from or attraction to foreign states and their rulers. I have had a certain sympathy for England and its inhabitants, and even now I am not altogether free of it; but they will not let us love them, and as far as I am concerned, as soon as it was proved to me that it was in the interests of a healthy and well-considered Prussian policy I would see our troops fire on French, Russian, English, or Austrians with equal satisfaction.'[35]

Again: 'For me France, regardless of whoever stands at her head, is only one piece—though an essential one—in the chess game of politics—a game in which my duty is to serve only my king and my country. I cannot as a Foreign Service official justify the harbouring of sympathies or antipathies towards foreign powers either in myself or in others. Such a concept contains the embryo of disloyalty to the sovereign or the country. . . . In my view even the king himself has not the right to subordinate the interests of the fatherland to his feelings of love or hatred for foreigners. But he must answer to God, not to me, so I will say no more on this point.'[36]

As for the fight against revolution, and the image of Louis Napoleon as conqueror and revolutionary modelled on his uncle, in the first place there is no difference between an aggressor descended from a long line of kings and an aggressor come to power as the result of a revolutionary upheaval. 'A legitimate monarch like Louis XIV is just as hostile an element as Napoleon I.'[37] As for Gerlach's view of Louis Napoleon as the inevitable agent of revolution, it was hopelessly wrong. It was wrong to think even of Napoleon Bonaparte as a product of revolution: revolution had merely served his ambition. And Louis Napoleon was very different. He was not so clever as people imagined, and he was not a conqueror. By all means let us fight against revolution in principle. But why harp on the French Revolution as a special case? Think back a little, and it will be seen that every monarch in history, including the German princes, has owed his throne to some sort of revolutionary upheaval. There was no such thing as a legitimate monarch, he said, in effect, and there never had been.[38]

Although Bismarck's arguments were sound and sensible, Gerlach had some reason on his side. Napoleon III was bound to be a disturbing influence by the very fact that the nature of his rise made him dependent on mass opinion: he would be forced to show off. Bismarck himself had seen this when he wrote that Napoleon would have at all costs to keep moving. He was convinced, however, that the parvenu emperor would go where conquest was easy: he had his eye on Italy, not Germany; and Italy was Austria's responsibility. There was nothing particularly revolutionary about conquest as such. 'The drive to conquest is no less present in England, North America, Russia, etc. than in Napoleonic France; and as soon as might and opportunity present themselves moderation and justice do not easily set bounds, even for legitimate monarchs. But in Napoleon III this instinct does not seem to be dominant; he is no war-lord, and in a great war . . . the French army would look more to a lucky general than to the emperor. He will therefore turn to war only if he feels compelled by *internal* necessity.'[39]

Again and again the future chancellor argued the folly of reducing the area of choice for a modern ruler who must be free to move in any direction and pick any ally. 'So long as any of us is convinced that any part of the European chessboard remains closed to us of our own will, or that we tie one hand behind our backs on principle, while others to our undoing use both, so those others will exploit our good nature without fear and without thanks.'[40]

The astonishing thing is that Frederick William, with his illusions of divine right, and Gerlach, his soldierly friend and adviser, continued to tolerate, and encourage, their iconoclastic protégé.

CHAPTER VI

COLD STORAGE
ON THE NEVA

By now many believed that Manteuffel's days were numbered and that the prodigy from Schönhausen would soon take his place. It is impossible to tell whether Frederick William would have gone so far. In October 1857, the king was smitten by a heavy stroke and his brother William, Prince of Prussia, took over the effective government of the country. He was sixty. Barely a year later the king's mind gave way and William was appointed regent. The next four years were to be frustrating years for Bismarck. He had shown a notable error of judgement in failing to apply himself to the wooing of the prince, who had every chance of succeeding his childless elder brother.

This was the kind of mistake Bismarck was liable to make. Hypersensitive as he was in some ways, in his human relations he could be so insensitive that only the overwhelming force of his personality, together with his almost magical powers of persuasion once he set himself to use them, could compensate for the absence of sympathetic awareness. He himself once remarked, as a not particularly interesting or significant fact, that his capacity for admiration of his fellow-human beings was 'only moderately developed.'[1] He might also have said that he did not understand people and was incapable of entering into their feelings or the workings of their minds; but this, of course, he was temperamentally debarred from knowing: he thought he understood them perfectly, and was convinced that, with the rarest exceptions, they were venal or stupid or cowardly, or all three. He understood their weaknesses and nothing else.

This was such a disastrous deficiency in a politician or a man of affairs that it is hard to understand why historians have passed it over as of secondary importance. The fact that it has been shared by other men of commanding eminence does not lessen its importance. On the contrary: the fruits of Lenin's fathomless contempt for almost the entire human race lie before us. Bismarck liked Motley and Keyserling: they were far away and had no connection with his world. He was somewhat drawn to Napoleon III and Lassalle. He respected Disraeli. But almost all his fellow-countrymen he despised. (Later on he developed a certain grudging respect for the Liberal Rudolf von Bennigsen, but this did not extend to establishing the sort of relations which might have induced a self-respecting person to respond to his overtures when, in the 1870s, he decided he needed a Liberal in his cabinet.) After Vincke in his early days there was only one man in the whole of Prussia whom he saw as someone to be seriously reckoned with. This was the hunchbacked Catholic and Hanoverian loyalist Ludwig Windthorst, a man with a first-class brain and the sharpest of tongues. As one of the very few men in Germany fit to work with him on equal terms, Bismarck did him the honour of hating him. He saw nothing odd about hating. 'A lying rascal,' this accomplished liar called his most upright opponent. And: 'Hatred is as much an incentive to life as love. Two things maintain and order my life, my wife and Windthorst; the one for love, the other for hate.'[2]

This he confided to his assistant, Tiedemann, in 1875, when he was sixty and virtual dictator of Germany. Even later still he could still be kept awake at night by a sudden overwhelming effluxion of hatred and resentment against his Berlin schoolmasters of nearly seventy years before.[3]

It is so easy to be carried away by Bismarck's virtuosity, to be ravished by his charm, stimulated and refreshed by his outspokenness; this makes it all the more essential to grasp the darker and more questionable aspects of his nature from the beginning. The savagery and disingenuousness of his verbal campaign against his Austrian colleagues in Frankfurt were to be duplicated and repeated in varying contexts throughout his career, with all the more effect as he grew into power. Sometimes they would be directed not at the enemy, real or imagined, outside the gates, but against his own side—or what was supposed to be his side. Thus, even while he wrestled at long range with Manteuffel and Gerlach, struggling to convince them that he was right about Austria, about Napoleon III, about France (but nevertheless pledged as a servant of the king of Prussia to carry out his master's wishes and cooperate with his ally, Austria), he was also labouring to undermine his government's policies. He went so far as to approach the Russian chargé d'affaires at Frankfurt in 1854 and show him his own confidential memoranda to his superiors in Berlin, memoranda vilifying the Austrian ally and urging a new alliance against her of Russia, France, and Prussia. When the Russian asked incredulously whether there was even a faint chance that Frederick William might entertain such a scheme, Bismarck replied in words that reflected his nature to perfection: 'If your government wishes to entrust me with the task of prevailing upon the king, I guarantee its success.' And he went on to urge swift action so that Austria might be assailed with overwhelming force before she realized what was happening and could concentrate her troops.[4]

In later years the iron chancellor was to become notorious for the furious severity with which he demanded and enforced total obedience from his underlings. 'My ambassadors must wheel into line like soldiers!" was one of his best-remembered sayings.[5] Woe betide any of them who spoke or acted out of turn.

But with Manteuffel and with Frederick William, he played fast and loose. It is interesting to compare his dispatches to Manteuffel with his letters on the same subject to Leopold von Gerlach. Long passages are virtually identical, but the general sense and emphasis is nicely directed in the one case against Manteuffel's unprincipled pro-Austrianism and in the other against Gerlach's faith in Russia and almost mystical belief in the divinity of kings. Bismarck was far from being the first or the last politician or diplomatist to hold his master in contempt: public servants may be expected to work, even to intrigue and cheat, for the adoption of policies in which they passionately believe—at least those among them who believe in anything at all. Between Bismarck and his sovereign, however, there existed, or was believed by the king to exist, a special relationship, and it may be thought that Bismarck's approach to the Russian diplomat exhibited a disturbing unawareness of any sort of a dividing line between the permissible and the insupportable.

Life was to be difficult for him once Frederick William was out of action. He was spoiling to emerge from the ante-rooms of power and take command. He had believed that at any moment the king would get rid of the inferior Manteuffel and put him in his place. There may or may not have been some justification for this belief. There was none for his evident conviction that under the prince regent he would continue as before. It soon became apparent not only that Prince William had a long memory but also that he thought nothing at all of Bismarck's political ideas, 'the politics of a schoolboy' he had called them some time earlier. And matters were not improved when Bismarck pulled himself together and early in 1858 produced, especially for the delectation, enlightenment, and instruction of the prince, an immensely long memorandum in which he analysed Prussian policy since the failed revolution of 1848 and laid down a programme for the future. This memorandum, which came to be known as Bismarck's 'Little Book,' was a perfect exposé of his mature political wisdom and a guide to his actions for years to come.

But even though he was circumspect about Austria, he could not carry Prince William with his general argument, which ran like this:

Of course Prussia must behave like a loyal member of the Confederation by fulfilling her statutory obligations; but for Austria, primarily a non-German state, to be allowed to dominate that Confederation by sheer weight of numbers, when most of her millions were not Germans at all, was an absurdity. Prussia must champion the spirit of Germany and win to her side the lesser states by appealing to German nationalism.[6]

Prince William saw no reason why he should turn against an old ally to please Herr von Bismarck. He also objected to what he took to be Bismarck's pro-Russian bias. As for France and the wretched Napoleon! . . . No, there was another answer, the answer provided by what had come to be known as the *Wochenblatt* party (called after its own newspaper) in opposition to the *Kreuzzeitung* party. The one represented Prince William, who had moved away from the *Kreuzzeitung* circle, as the other represented his brother's court. And it had what can only be called a 'Westernizing' bias: the natural alliance, it urged, was between Prussia, Austria, and England.

Bismarck in Frankfurt had made a mistake in not treating this party seriously, and now he made things worse *vis-à-vis* Prince William by the reckless way in which he denigrated Austria to almost anyone in Frankfurt and elsewhere who cared to listen to him. It had been one thing for him in confidence to argue with Gerlach and Manteuffel that 'The policy of Vienna being what it is, Germany is clearly too small for the two of us'; that 'failing an honourable agreement concerning the influence of each, we shall both plough the same disputed acre and Austria will remain the only state to which we can permanently lose or from which we can permanently gain'; that 'For a thousand years off and on . . . the German dualism has regularly adjusted the reciprocal relations [Austro-Prussian] through full-scale civil war'; that yet another war would be called for 'in this century'; that 'in the not far distant future we shall have to fight for our existence against Austria.'[7] Here it could be held that he was stating a legitimate point of view, and exaggerating sharply to make his point among friends —although, in fact, remarks of this kind had been getting back to Vienna since early 1855. But in 1857 he started saying the same sort of thing outright to the Austrian representative in Frankfurt, Prokesch-Osten's successor, Count Johann von Rechberg. The existing situation, he declared, cannot continue but must lead either to an understanding or a decisive break.[8] Furthermore, he said, it was a delusion for Austria to assume she could count on Prussia in the event of war; indeed, he went so far as to predict that if no 'settlement' was reached, Vienna would find Berlin in the enemy ranks, and so on—all without the least authority from the Berlin government and in direct contravention of official policy.

When this sort of thing got back to Berlin, as it did, Bismarck could hardly be surprised if he found himself even more out of favour with Prince William than before, but surprised he was. It was clear to him that, quite apart from his personal difficulties with the regent, he had lost his favoured position at court. In November 1858 Manteuffel, whose venal, negatively repressive bureaucratic regime, a product of the post–1848 reaction, had long affronted Prince William, was sacked. His place as chancellor was taken by the comparatively liberal Prince Charles Anthony of Hohenzollern-Sigmaringen, as foreign minister by Alexander von Schleinitz, neither of whom liked Bismarck. Schleinitz in particular was a favourite of Augusta's. The new policy was to work for an alliance with Austria and England against Russia: Prince William was a great respecter of Austrian seniority, but he could not forgive the tsar for backing Austria against Prussia in the Olmütz crisis of 1850. Since Bismarck had then favoured Austria and was not intriguing almost recklessly against her and in favour of France, it is not really to be wondered at that William should have dismissed this awkward official's 'argufying' (for this is how he would have seen the beautifully presented justifications of his envoy to Frankfurt—in his eyes a clever but tiresome sea-lawyer, rather than a dutiful public servant). The prince regent, by no means slavishly pro-Austrian, was convinced that Prussia was destined to lead Germany in unity; but there was no hurry about this, and he imagined that his goal could be reached by agreement, compromise, intelligent legislation, and the cool exploitation of economic forces. Nobody was sure whether Bismarck really wanted war with Austria or not, but it was reasonable for the men round the prince regent to conclude that he did. He himself freely admitted that he advocated a policy of threats and coercion, with war only as a last resort. Obviously he would have preferred to get from Austria all he desired without fighting. But if war should be needed, he was ready to provide it. And so he did. Is the highwayman who relieves you of your money at pistol point any different from the highwayman who shoots if you resist?

More important to Bismarck even than the fall of Manteuffel was the immediate loss of influence of the old Court Camarilla, including the Gerlach brothers and the *Kreuzzeitung* party as a whole with their profound faith in Russian absolutism. The general line of Bismarck's thinking until now had been to use Russia on the one hand and France on the other to strengthen Prussia in her demands on Austria. The new royal policy was by all means to augment Prussia's power and standing, but in agreement with Austria, and then, with a combination of the re-formed armies of Prussia and the armies of the Confederation, to have ready for action a most formidable force divided into two commands, Austrian and Prussian, supported by the British fleet in control of the seas. It was not a very realistic plan, but then neither Prince William nor Schleinitz laid claim to political infallibility. Bismarck, whose earlier recommendation that Prussia should ally herself with France against Austria *before* Russia turned against her was no less silly, was a genius. But a genius of what?

More and more it was beginning to appear that his particular genius was opportunism. The remarkable change of tactics represented by the 'Little Book.' was less a stage in the organic development of his thinking, than a new throw of the dice. The angry Junker particularist, the burgeoning statesman who had played with the idea of international alliances in his personal campaign to break the supremacy of Austria, the man who had regarded German nationalism with irritable contempt, suddenly decided that alliances were less important than internal solidarity in the struggle against Austria. He announced in effect that what was good for Prussia was good for Germany, that German public opinion must be mobilized in support of Prussia, the shield of all honest Germans everywhere. To what extent he produced this line in 1858 because he thought it would appeal to Prince William, to what extent he had in fact come to think that the key to the future lay in the manipulation of German nationalism, it is impossible to say. And, indeed, it is by no means clear what he understood by the future at this stage—i.e., how far ahead he was seeing. What is certain is that for whatever reason he was now advocating *formally* and for purely tactical reasons an appeal to motives and emotions which he regarded with contempt.

95

*   *   *

In October 1858 there could be no pretending that King Frederick William might one day recover. With the proclamation of the regency and the dismissal of Manteuffel, the new chancellor, Prince Charles Anthony, presided over new elections to the Diet. The conservatives were over-whelmed by a landslide victory for Vincke's moderates, who took 210 seats, leaving only 59 to the old guard. All over Prussia, and over much of Germany too, people rejoiced at what they took to be the promise of a lib-eral 'New Era.' But Bismarck, who was pleased to see Manteuffel go, seems not to have read the signs. He somehow convinced himself that the scales had been removed from the eyes of not only the prince regent but also his wife, Augusta, who had at last begun to appreciate him at his true worth.

It was a curious misreading of the situation. Even while he was dilating in a letter to Johanna on the favour in which he was now held at Potsdam and Berlin,[9] the official machinery was set in motion which was to replace him at Frankfurt. Nine days after that euphoric letter he was dumb-founded to learn that the very man about whose pretensions he had been rather coarsely jeering, Count 'Guido' von Usedom, was to take his place—above all because he could be trusted to get along with the Aus-trians. It was a complete and demonstrative rejection of his advice, exhorta-tions, agitation, and intrigue over the past eight years. For Austria was now in trouble, and in Bismarck's eyes Austria's crisis was Prussia's opportunity.

In Turin, Count Camillo Cavour, the only statesman of the age to compare with Bismarck, was approaching the climax of years of scheming and manoeuvre to harness France or Britain, or both, to the destruction of Austrian power in Italy. In July 1858 Cavour had secretly met Napoleon at Plombières, in the Vosges, the emperor's favourite spa, and obtained from him a firm promise to help the Piedmontese throw Austria out of Lom-bardy and Venetia as a prelude to the unification of Italy under Victor Emmanuel of Sardinia—France to have Nice and Savoy in return. On 1 January 1859, at his New Year's Day reception in the Tuileries, Napoleon rested those clear, grey conspirator's eyes upon the Austrian envoy, Count Joseph Hübner, remarking for all the world to hear: 'I am sorry that our relations are not so good as they were, but I beg you to write to Vienna that my personal sentiments for the emperor are unchanged.'[10] It was a cataclysmic statement. No declaration of intent could have been clearer. It meant that Cavour could now safely do his utmost to provoke Austria into declaring war in Piedmont. All the world saw that Austria had only one course: to refuse absolutely to allow herself to be provoked. But the man in charge in Vienna was still Count Buol-Schauenstein, who had muddled his country into the worst of both worlds over the Crimean War; and his young emperor was still too inexperienced to sack Buol or control him. On 18 April 1859, against the urging of Austria's well-wishers and all those who regarded the new Napoleon's rising star with extreme unease, Buol allowed himself to be exasperated into dispatching the ultimatum which Cavour desired.

It was the Bavarian minister to Berlin, Baron Ludwig von der Pfordten, who made the classic remark about Buol: 'He is like a locomotive which does not know where it is going and, when asked, answers only with steam and whistling.' Where Buol was heading was in fact for Austria the beginning of the end. The ageing Metternich (who, alas, had himself recommended Buol to Francis Joseph) said much the same thing: 'The consequences of any and every action are hidden from Count Buol. He sees what is right in front of him; of what is coming he sees nothing.' What was coming was the defeat of the Austrian army by the French and Piedmontese at Magenta and Solferino, and the consequent loss of Austria's richest and most cherished province, Lombardy, with the great city of Milan and the fertile valley of the Po.

It was a situation ready-made for Bismarck, had Bismarck been in power: Austria grappled for her life with France, while Russia, bleakly vengeful, looked on. But Bismarck was very far from power, further, indeed, than he had been for some years past. His new appointment as ambassador to St. Petersburg he regarded as a humiliation (contrary to normal usage he was not even accorded military rank as a general, but remained a Landwehr major). At the end of March 1859 he was off on the long, cold, exhausting journey by coach and sledge, leaving Johanna and the children behind until he could find a place for them to live in St. Petersburg. And it was from Russia that he had to watch, at times almost choking with rage, while Prussia, instead of exploiting Austria's misfortune for the benefit of her own aggrandizement, mobilized six army corps to go to the aid of Francis Joseph. But this action was too hesitant, too slow, too late, to win Austria's gratitude, even though it made Napoleon wind the war up quickly after Solferino, for fear of what the Prussian armies might do across the Rhine.

Bismarck's only pleasure at this time was the depth and intensity of hatred for Austria displayed by the Russians—and the fuss they made of him, from the tsar downwards, as a Prussian envoy known to share this hatred. He commented on the prevailing 'war-fever' with warm approbation.

As early as 4 May, on the very day that the hopelessly incompetent old Austrian general, Field-Marshal Franz Guylai, at last crossed the River Ticino into Piedmont and started his laborious copy-book deployment in the Po valley marshes, Bismarck was writing to the regent's aide-de-camp, General Gustav von Alvensleben, a letter combining an elegant and exact appreciation of the mechanics of the situation with a total absence of feeling for the underlying reality—an interesting variation on the lack of feeling that so recently had led him to believe that he was loved by a regent who was merely being polite: 'We shall have the winning ticket in the lottery, if only we let the Austrians get deep into their war with France and then march south with our whole army, carrying our frontier-posts in our knapsacks and setting them up again on the shores of Lake Constance, or as far as Protestantism extends.'[11]

He did not really believe this advice would be taken, for he went on to say that if this policy was 'too adventurous,' at least Berlin should seize the opportunity 'either to change our relationship with the Confederation, or to leave it.' And 'privately' to Schleinitz a week later he also urged the dissolution of the Confederation.[12] In both these letters he floated for the first time the idea of turning 'the kingdom of Prussia' into 'the kingdom of Germany.' And in his letter to Schleinitz he foreshadowed the phrase about blood and iron that three years later was to echo round the world: 'I regard our connection with the German Confederation as a sickness of Prussia that will have to be cured sooner or later *ferro et igne*, unless we take treatment for it at a favourable opportunity.'[13]

Nobody paid any attention to him. For all practical purposes he had been rusticated. But although he did not really believe that Prince William would resort to arms to bring the northern German states under command of Prussia, he seems still to have had no conception of the mistrust, the apprehension, the alarm, which such radical talk aroused. When, after Magenta, Prussia mobilized to go to the help of Austria instead of threatening her, his venomous indiscretions became the talk of St. Petersburg: this envoy extraordinary, far from representing his royal master's policies in the best light to the Russian tsar, made no bones about exhibiting his contempt for them. For a moment it looked as though he had at last gone too far and put his career at risk. Prince William was indignant when the news of this remarkable behaviour reached Potsdam. Should he dismiss this disloyal servant or simply reprimand him?[14] But even while he was trying to decide, the tension went out of the international situation, as the two emperors, Austrian and French, sick of the bloody reality of war, and fearing the consequences of its prolongation each for his own reasons, almost threw themselves into each other's arms to conclude the peace of Villafranca. At the same time, Bismarck himself fell seriously ill.

It is clearly impossible to decide how much the illnesses of any figure of the past (or of the present, too, for that matter) were psychosomatic, how much 'real.' Bismarck's illnesses were to punctuate his career in a fairly expressive manner, and obviously the psyche played a great part in their nature and their timing. This seems to me to tell us nothing except that our hero was likely to fall ill, sometimes catastrophically, when frustrated, thwarted, or made angry. All these things happened frequently and violently, so his illnesses were frequent and violent to watch. He was, as must be already apparent, neurotic to a degree. But the punishment to which he subjected his immense frame provided his body with instant pretexts for going wrong under strain. For example, he was a fearless but by no means highly accomplished horseman (he had difficulty in following the movement of the horse), and in his Schönhausen days, before his marriage, he suffered many falls, which he shrugged off, even though on three separate occasions he suffered from concussion. In 1858 he fell again and broke three ribs. He exposed that same frame to heavy ordeals in his shooting expeditions. And he punished it all the time with a huge and uncontrolled appetite for food and drink, an appetite he indulged until it nearly killed him. When he was in his late sixties a favoured visitor to the Bismarck country estate at Varzin was astonished to see how Johanna, far from trying to persuade her husband to eat and drink more sensibly, constantly pressed him to second helpings of even the richest dishes.[15] Presumably she had been behaving in the same way all their married life.

The first sign of bodily rebellion had occurred during those weeks of frustration, with a strong undertone of humiliation, when Bismarck was waiting for the regent to confirm his appointment to St. Petersburg, which filled him with resentment. His left leg began to play up with what seemed to be rheumatic pains. In fact he had injured that leg two years earlier on the hunting expedition which found him falling in love with the landscape of southern Sweden, and it had not been properly treated, so eager was he to get on with his shooting. Now, within three months of his arrival in St. Petersburg, the leg had become a deep-seated affliction, affecting his whole body and bringing him dangerously low. On 29 June he wrote from Peter-hof to his beloved sister, Malwine: he had been on his back with rheumatic pains for some weeks, he said, and more recently the combination of worry, climate, and a bad cold brought things to such a pitch that he could breathe only with the most painful effort: 'After being made to feel half-way to a better world, I succeeded in convincing the doctors that eight years of unbroken worry and constant excitement had weakened my nerves and that further letting of blood would only bring on typhus or idiocy.'[16]

Johanna was on no account to be told that he had anything more than a touch of rheumatism, and indeed his condition was improving when a German quack-doctor with a big practice in St. Petersburg mismanaged a poultice and burnt a deep hole in the soft flesh under the left knee. Soon the limb was in such a state that there seemed no hope of saving it. But Bismarck was not the man to suffer meekly the amputation of a little finger, let alone a leg. He had himself taken back to Berlin, even though his sufferings on the long, rough journey were acute, and there Johanna arrived from Reinfeld, full of high spirits, to find the wreck of a man, almost, it seemed, without the will to live, prostrate, racked with a high fever, his great frame ravaged and exhausted.

But Berlin doctors pulled him through and the leg was saved, to heave its owner across the roughest country on many more shooting days. And the remarkable thing was that once he had recovered from the journey, even as he lay waiting for the doctors to make up their minds how best to set about the cure, he plunged head-first into politics, choosing this of all moments to put himself forward as a prophet of German nationalism to a wider public than the regent and his ministers. For it was now that he made that remark, already cited, to the Liberal industrialist Viktor von Unruh, that the only proper ally for Prussia in her isolation was the German people. . . .

The catalyst was the discovery (from the newspapers) a day or two earlier that a formal nationalist movement was taking shape and gathering weight and momentum: a number of German Liberals led by the gifted Hanoverian politician Rudolf von Bennigsen, were incubating the idea of an all-German association to be called the Nationalverein, a National Union, to propagate the dream inherited from the Frankfurt Parliament of a strong and united 'Little Germany' that would look to Prussia for leadership and stiffening, perhaps discipline too. Bismarck's observation was so apposite that in no time at all the leaders of the new association decided that they must capture him for themselves. The Nationalverein was publicly launched in Frankfurt on 15 September 1859. Three days before the first meeting Unruh was authorized to write to Bismarck (now convalescing in Wiesbaden) to explain that the association would look to Prussia to champion the cause of German unity in face of Austrian opposition. Furthermore, he added: 'We, and this includes Herr von Bennigsen, would be sincerely gratified if you should be appointed minister for foreign affairs.'

Bismarck, when it suited him, could be as correct in his conduct as any diplomat: he journeyed from Wiesbaden to Baden-Baden to discuss this remarkable initiative with his chief, Schleinitz, whom he was thus being invited to supersede. Schleinitz took it well and tacitly authorized him to continue his conversations with Unruh, even though Schleinitz himself was dominated in his imagination by the menace of France, still more of a France in alliance with Russia: for him the only security still lay in a firm understanding with Austria. Bismarck had a further meeting with Unruh, who made it clear that in spite of some resistance from the southern states, the sense of the Frankfurt meeting favoured Prussian leadership, even to the point of some sort of temporary military dictatorship.

It was on this note that, in October, Bismarck started back to St. Petersburg. He did not get very far. For part of the way he was required to accompany his royal master on a state visit to Warsaw to meet Tsar Alexander II, and he drove himself too hard, with gruelling days in the saddle on top of wearisome official functions and a surfeit of feasting. At Hohendorf, in Pomerania, he collapsed, could not breathe, thought he was dying. This time it was pneumonia (in those days, and for a long lifetime to come, a killer illness). He was lucky to survive, and for some months he was sure that he would never be strong enough to take up his career again. . . .

Until, in March 1860, came the rumour that William had at last had enough of the indecisiveness of Schleinitz and was looking for someone to replace him. The rumour was enough to shake Bismarck out of his apathy and send him straight off to Berlin, where he lost no time in drumming up supporters and, in the words of the sometimes malicious diarist (and later, influential contact-man) Theodor von Bernhardi, went about 'telling everyone who would listen that he was misunderstood and even the victim of slander, really a Liberal at heart'.[17]

The whisper was in fact half correct. But the times themselves seemed to be moving away from Bismarck. With Garibaldi in Sicily and Naples, the 'revolutionary spirit' was on the march once more. Buol had gone from Vienna, replaced by Rechberg, who was working hard to resurrect the Holy Alliance of Austria, Prussia, and Russia against the spirit of revolution and subversion. Prince William, no less than Schleinitz, was ludicrously sure that Napoleon and Russia were working hand in glove together for the undoing of Prussia, Napoleon living only for the day when he could regain his uncle's German conquests and restore under French sovereignty the Confederation of the Rhine. Schleinitz's main task was still to work for an alliance with Austria and England. This was something Bismarck could not, would not, do.

His rejection in April 1860 was the climax of a year of disaster, the low point of his career. 'William has refused to give the billy-goat the job of gardener!' exclaimed Prince Charles Anthony, making one of the all-too-few jokes that enliven German history.[18] To Bismarck it was not a joke at all.

At this point it is worth having a look at the forty-four-year-old envoy through the eyes of one who was seeing him very close, Kurd von Schlözer, an extremely intelligent second secretary at the Petersburg embassy, a man of considerable culture and strength of character, if a little self-important and touchy and inclined to stand on his dignity. This honest public servant was appalled by Bismarck's manners when he took up his appointment in April 1859:

'My new chief,' he wrote, 'is a man with no consideration for others, a man of power who dreams of dramatic gestures, who is anxious to shine, who knows everything without having seen it and affects omniscience although there is much that he does not know. At Frankfurt he was used to very young attachés who stood to attention and trembled when he approached.'[19]

Schlözer, another protégé of Queen Augusta, which gave piquancy to his relations with Bismarck, was determined neither to capitulate nor to lose his temper. He resisted politely but stiffly his new master's attempts to use him as a cross between an errand boy and a stenographer, and did his best to make an objective study of this strange creature who sulked because he took against the imposing embassy residence and established himself in a far from imposing hotel, making the clerks and cipherers come to him; but at times he found him unbearable: 'This perpetual harassment by an unscrupulous, neurotic chief who thinks all other men are weaklings, who veils his own plans in darkness or suddenly tries to astound his *vis-à-vis*, who trusts nobody in the world—none of this is very pleasant. . . .'[20] Even so, a few weeks later he is having to acknowledge his new master's genius, 'his surpassing intellectual power,' and to confess that an inner voice tells him that 'there is something in him that I might call master—but not yet!'[21]

And now the long illness intervened. Bismarck was away from his post for eleven months, from July 1859 to June 1860, but within weeks of his return he too is having second thoughts about his prickly subordinate, and being big enough to admit it; and it was not long before Schlözer himself realized that he had won the confidence of this terrible man, and that it was worth having. He had secured a powerful patron, one of the very rare examples of a man standing up to Bismarck and winning his respect: for like most bullies, contrary to popular belief, Bismarck did not enjoy being answered back.

Even then, however, Schlözer found the ways of his 'giant Bismarck' frequently impenetrable: 'He is the devil himself, but where is he going?'[22] And again: 'I dine with Bismarck every day and there is no more trouble between us. He is the wholly political man. His whole being is a ferment of impulses and desires to be expressed, manipulated, shaped. He is determined to command the political arena, to master the chaos in Berlin, but he does not yet know how.'[23]

That was in October 1860.

A month later both he and Bismarck sense that some sort of a climax is approaching. And yet still nothing happened: 'My Pasha is now in a state of painful agitation. His Berlin visit and the sight of the confusion and indecision there have fired his blood. It seems that he thinks his hour has nearly come. There will be a violent conflict in the chamber. Schleinitz will lose his temper and offer his resignation—and then Pasha will take over. The big question is "Will he suit Prussia? Will Prussia suit him?"— This violent spirit suddenly bursting out on to such a narrow and limited stage . . .'[24]

But the hour was still not struck and Bismarck waited in growing misery. 'Meanwhile Bismarck receives no news from Berlin—that is to say, the Wilhelmstrasse [the Ministry of Foreign Affairs] simply does not write to him. They don't like him there and they behave as though he does not exist. So he conducts his own political intrigues, does no entertaining, complains incessantly about the cost of living, sees very few people, gets up at 11 or 11:30 and sits about all day in a green dressing-gown, not stirring except to drink—fulminating against Austria.'[25]

In fact, for the first time in his career, throughout that summer of 1860 Bismarck had been rattled, and showed it. The agitation commented upon by Schlözer was not far from panic. Before his return to St. Petersburg he had argued rationally enough his conviction of the imperative necessity for Prussia to achieve some sort of an understanding with France: Napoleon's annexation of Nice and Savoy in return for services rendered to Cavour and Sardinia did not mean that his next move would be towards the Rhine. Bismarck still believed, correctly, that Napoleon was the most unwarlike of men. With Gerlach he had gone over all the old ground once more: 'To me France would be the most dubious of all allies, but I must hold open the possibility of such an alliance because one cannot play chess if sixteen out of twenty-four squares on the board are out of bounds.'[26] On the other hand, he outraged the regent and Gerlach by welcoming the rise of the House of Savoy. 'It must be beneficial for Prussia to have a strong Italian state in the south between France and Austria.'[27] A few months later, urging official recognition of the Italian state, he wrote: 'We should have had to invent the Kingdom of Italy, had it not come into existence on its own.'[28] When it came to his own career, however, isolated in St. Petersburg, his coolness for once deserted him. The persistent reports that he had advocated the surrender of part of the Rhineland to win Napoleon as an ally, false as they were, gained more and more believers, and the leaders of the Nationalverein began to think twice about his usefulness. To whom could he now turn? There was nobody, not a living soul, who was worthy of his trust: 'One ought not to rely on men,' he wrote. 'I bless every impulse which drives me back within myself.'[29]

And so it went on through the autumn and the winter. The young Friedrich von Holstein, later to play so far-reaching and controversial a part in Germany's destiny, and to be credited, erroneously, with the main responsibility for the 1914 war, arrived as a junior attaché in St. Petersburg in January 1861, and years later described the first impression made on him by Bismarck: 'Never gay, even when telling amusing anecdotes, a thing he did only occasionally, in particularly congenial company. Total impression one of a dissatisfied man, partly a hypochondriac . . . partly a man insufficiently reconciled to the quiet life led in those days by the Prussian representative in St. Petersburg. I have scarcely ever known anyone so joyless. . . . His laughter was always at someone else's expense.' And he goes on: 'His every utterance revealed that for him action and existence were one and the same thing.'[30]

Two months later Bismarck would himself confirm his isolation in a letter to Malwine: 'King's messengers no longer seem to travel. For months I have received no dispatches from the ministry by courier, and whatever comes by post is tedious.'[31] He had enjoyed a certain amount of shooting that winter, including several bear hunts, but he turned his back on grand society and now did his best to give the impression of a man resigned to living out a life of reasonable distinction in reasonably affluent obscurity.

It is doubtful whether Malwine was deceived. Certainly Bismarck had for once given himself away not only to his Berlin colleagues but even to the Russians. Letter after letter was sent off to Berlin, self-justifying, denying Napoleonic sympathies, invoking witness of the soundness of his views here, there, everywhere. It was a tone that was never to be heard again from him, and it must have made those enemies of his who heard it rub their hands with delight. To crown it all he asked Gorchakov to issue an official denial that he, Bismarck, had ever suggested a Franco-Russian-Prussian alliance against Austria *involving the cession* of German soil. Gorchakov, wisely, would have nothing to do with a tactic so inept; the old fox must on occasion have remembered this act of desperation when, in later years, he found himself again and again faced with Bismarck at the summit of his career and in his most overbearing mood. '*Qui s'excuse, s'accuse*,' he reminded his young colleague on this particular occasion. At the same time he gave utterance to one of the key remarks of nineteenth-century diplomacy. With particular reference to Russian resentment at the Straits provisions of the Treaty of Paris which forbade Russian warships to pass the Dardanelles, he observed: 'Russian policy for the time being must be "enigmatic." '[32]

But now, at last, the great change was impending. The death of Frederick William in January 1861 seemed to make no difference to the political situation: there was no reason why it should, since Prince William had enjoyed full powers for three years past. Bismarck was now almost ill with frustration, and if things had gone on much longer without a change there would almost certainly have been another breakdown. In April Johanna wrote to the faithful Keudell saying that her husband had suffered several small rheumatic seizures 'which probably aged me more than they did him'; further that 'his nerves are always in such a pitiful state that it is impossible not to worry.'[33]

Then, suddenly, there was a crisis in Berlin. It soon turned out to have been an unnecessary crisis, but, without anybody realizing what was happening, it prepared the way for victory in the autumn of the following year.

CHAPTER VII

THE CALL
TO ACTION

Throughout almost the whole of his Russian interlude Bismarck's main preoccupations were almost ludicrously far removed from the most deeply felt concerns of his sovereign in Berlin. When he came to the throne at sixty-three the new king was set in his ways. They were honourable but very narrow ways. He was determined to uphold the glory of Prussia as one of the two senior German powers. Since, as we have seen, he was quite sure that Louis Napoleon, like his uncle before him, was a potential aggressor on a continental scale, and since Russia appeared to be flirting with him as a desirable ally against Austria, then the sensible thing for Prussia was to join forces with Austria and England. But there was no real drive behind this idea: William did not think naturally in terms of foreign politics. He asked no more than a safe, quiet life.

At home he was even less dynamic: all he knew about domestic politics was that he had sworn to uphold the Constitution of 1848–50 and was determined to carry out this tiresome duty, regardless of the urgings of his more impetuous advisers who wanted him to abolish it. The trouble was that he did not understand the Constitution and was liable at any moment to breach it without realizing his offence—as when he created a first-class crisis by deciding that it would be splendid idea for representatives of all the estates (which did not in fact exist) to swear a medieval oath of fealty at his coronation in Königsberg.

Away from the mysteries of representative goverement he was, however, shrewder than many historians have recognized, and there were two things he understood well: one was gentlemanly behaviour (honesty and human decency); the other was the army. Gentlemanly behaviour he took for granted, which put him at a disadvantage when dealing with a Bismarck; the army, its welfare and development, engaged his whole interest and attention. The Liberal politician Ludwig Bamberger put it very exactly when he observed that for William 'the state consisted of soldiers and the soldiers were the king's.'[1] The soldiers, moreover, were most emphatically not to be used for aggression: they were to uphold the dignity of the realm and secure the safe, quiet life to which this king so modestly aspired. But to do its job the army had to be brought up-to-date, and for a long time, first as Prince of Prussia, then as regent, William had been thinking about little else.

Thus it was that during the years when Bismarck in St. Petersburg was thinking about nothing at all (apart from his own future) but Prussia's position in Germany and the world, William, his government, and then parliament itself, were thinking and quarrelling about the army, its size and composition, its place in society, its special relationship with the crown. Unfortunately, although stubborn to the point of pig-headedness, when it came to what he conceived to be a point of principle William was unsure at heart and weak. He needed a strong man to lean upon. He was given to sudden outbreaks of hysterical self-pity, ending in tears.

The soldier upon whom William leaned most heavily in his early days was Albrecht von Roon, six years younger than the king and twelve years older than Bismarck, over whose career he had watched from its first beginning. Roon was, indeed, the only man who recognized Bismarck's genius at sight and never wavered in support of him. Roon had a rough edge to his tongue, to put it mildly, and it amused him to play the bluff soldier—so much so that most people took him at his face value. In fact he had a keen and subtle mind and was widely and deeply read. In 1860 William promoted him to full general and made him minister for war. Two years later he was made also minister for marine. He held both posts until the end of the Franco-Prussian War and it was he more than any other who made the Prussian army into the finest fighting machine in the world. Without Roon, Bismarck would never have been chancellor: it was a superb achievement to have provided the two great strategists, political and military, Bismarck and Moltke, with the means to realize their dreams. Like his great protégé, Roon was perfectly unscrupulous—of course, from the highest motives—and it was symptomatic that his army reform started off with a lie.

The belated mobilization in support of Austria in 1859 showed up so many shortcomings in army equipment and organization that the king and

Roon had the pretext they needed for introducing root-and-branch reforms. Even those deputies who most distrusted the army and deplored its political and social influence were agreed on the need to strengthen it and were ready to vote supplies to that end. They knew, for example, that since the Vienna Congress the population of Prussia had nearly doubled itself, from 10 to 18 million, while the annual recruitment quota had remained unchanged at 40,000. They agreed that the army must be enlarged. The conflict arose over the means.

Roon, in common with practically the whole of the officers' corps, was determined to use the occasion of army expansion to force through a complete reorganization along lines he had already indicated when William was still Prince of Prussia and he, Roon, his military adviser. It was a reorganization designed to alter completely the character of the army as determined by the great reforms of Stein, Scharnhorst, and Boyen and to take it back in spirit to the era of Frederick the Great. This was to be done by reducing the size and importance of Stein's celebrated Landwehr, or militia, in favour of a return to that exclusive and aristocratic professionalism which had been Frederick's obsession. The exorbitant demands of the Seven Years War had forced Frederick to allow the commissioning of commoners. But as soon as the fighting stopped, instead of recognizing that men without a 'von' to their names had proved their ability, their loyalty, and their readiness to fight and die for their king, that very strange monarch at once reverted to the old system, narrowing the field from which officers might spring, shutting out the talented in favour of aristocratic imbeciles; and securing once more for the army a separate and privileged existence living by its own rules, creating its own ethos, and looking down from a great height on civilian life. Thus it was that the armies of Napoleon, led by the sons of innkeepers and coopers, were able to break into small pieces a Prussian army which enjoyed no popular standing and was commanded by elderly Junkers with unimpeachable antecedents and too often very little else.

It was in response to this débâcle that the Landwehr was born, a citizen army to fight alongside regular units—two years with the colours, seven years in first reserve, seven years in second reserve. At Leipzig in October 1813, the Battle of the Nations, the new army covered itself with glory, and the shame of Jena was avenged. The dream of Stein and Scharnhorst had been to inject into the standing army a leavening of civilian values; indeed, to anchor that army firmly in the hopes and aspirations, the pride as well, of the society it was created to defend. It was precisely this conception that generations of Junker officers most contemptuously rejected: civilian society to them meant nothing at all but the supplier of conscripts and funds and services for the army, which alone was the body and *raison d'être* of the state.

So long as Frederick William IV, with his real if unstable intimations of enlightenment, was on the throne the Landwehr was safe. But the reluctance of certain units to fire on civilians when called upon to help put down the final defiance of the revolution in Baden and Württemberg in 1849 gave point to the view well expressed nine years later by Roon himself in a celebrated memorandum: the Landwehr, he argued, was 'militarily as well as politically a false institution.' The militiaman was a civilian first and foremost, lacking proper discipline or the true spirit of soldierly subordination and self-sacrifice. 'Every Landwehr man has become a voter, thanks to our present parliamentary system of government.' There could be no hope for the army unless it functioned as the personal and unthinking instrument of the royal will, politically neutral.[2]

The remarkable thing is that the Landwehr lasted in its unreconstructed form as long as it did. Even in the days of Frederick William III the great reforms were regarded apprehensively not only by Prussian Junkers but also by foreign observers. Then the citizen army was seen by Austria, by Russia, even by England, as a disturbingly revolutionary force bent on exalting German nationalism at the expense of Austria.[3] How odd that the names Scharnhorst and Gneisenau, which were to be seized upon and exploited for their own purposes by German militarists almost infinitely far removed from these men in character, intentions, and ideas, should have been regarded as dangerous revolutionaries by the Congress powers and increasingly as subversive by the dynasty they had saved.

Roon was not interested in politics, unless as a deep, instinctive conservative. He was later to insist that his proposals for army reform were inspired by technical considerations untouched by politics, and he may be believed. It depends on what is meant by politics. Putting the army at the exclusive service of the king was not in Roon's eyes a political activity at all: it was a self-evident necessity. So self-evident that it never occurred to him that his actions might cause a serious political upheaval. Nor did it occur to William, whose first impulse on his accession was to start realizing his dreams.

There was still to be conscription. Neither Roon nor the king thought of returning to a closed, purely professional army. On the contrary, although the Landwehr was to be reduced, universal military training was to be extended from two years to three. For Roon neatly reversed the Scharnhorst-Boyen dream: instead of bringing the civilian spirit into the army, civilian life was to be injected with the military spirit; conscripts were to be given an extra year in which they might be imbued, indoctrinated, with the military idea in its purest form, uncontaminated by the temptations, expediency, and compromises of civilian life.

William and Roon have been decried for this, Roon above all. But they were doing no more than giving expression to the deepest instincts of the Prussian ruling class. The constitutionally minded, popular and very decent General Eduard von Bonin, who had been brought back as minister for war with the 'New Era' government of 1858, was entirely correct when he insisted that if Roon's proposals were adopted the country would be separated from the army, less correct when he went on to say that this would mean the 'loss of the essential condition of her existence,'[4] which was the confidence of the people in the army. How delicate a plant this confidence was had been shown only ten years before when the army had been reviled as a foreign body in the state, an instrument of reaction and tyranny.

Bonin, alas, was fighting a battle that was already lost. The Liberals had had their chance to 'constitutionalize' the army, like the kingdom itself, in 1848, but had drawn back from decisive action in their shrinking from the excesses of the revolutionary mob. Now, more than thirteen years later, in spite of their vested interest in the Landwehr, it is safe to say that those who took an active pride in this institution were those to whom precision drill, parade-ground discipline and barrack-square manners most deeply appealed, while the anti-militarists wanted no part in it, thus defeating the purposes of the Landwehr as a leaven. Roon may not have recognized soon enough that he was on a collision course with the parliamentarians, but Bonin on his side showed an equally faulty appreciation of reality: the king was a fact of life no less real than parliament and a good deal more effective; the 'essential condition' of Prussia's existence was at this time in reality mutual confidence between king and army. The 'New Era' administration was caught between the parliamentarians and the king, and Bonin was only the first to find his position intolerable. He resigned in November 1859, the first major casualty in the battle for parliamentary rule in post-1848 Prussia; Roon took his place.

It has often been said that Roon's determination to reduce the Landwehr had more to do with class-warfare than with military efficiency, and, of course, his action did in fact strengthen the throne and the aristocracy,

Prussian Junkerdom, in face of parliament and the bourgeoisie. But that this was incidental to the genuine search for efficiency (depending, as he saw it, on instant obedience and subordination to a directing will) may be seen at once by comparing Roon's attitude to the attitude of his flamboyant, ambitious, and fanatically reactionary brother officer and rival, General Edwin von Manteuffel, cousin of the ex-prime minister of that name.

If Roon was responsible for Bismarck's elevation, he was also responsible for pushing General Manteuffel to one side. An able soldier, a dreamer by temperament, Manteuffel was a fine specimen of what came to be regarded as a peculiarly German type: the romantic militarist. In 1859 his position was strong indeed. As quite a junior officer he had been prominent among those who had urged poor Frederick William IV in 1848 to slip out of Berlin and allow the army to blow the revolutionaries out of the city. He had moved far since then and for five years had been head of that strange institution the military cabinet, a group of officers appointed by the king personally as his personal advisers. The head of the military cabinet had a base in the Ministry for War as head of the personnel department, but he also had direct access to the king, by-passing his technical superior the war minister himself.

Manteuffel clearly saw the logical conclusion of the military cabinet system, with himself in closest communion with the monarch at its head: the wretched Constitution and the Landtag with it, must be swept away; an absolute monarchy must rule through an effective military dictator— for which apotheosis he, Manteuffel, with total dedication, had been humbly preparing himself from his youth.

He was the sort of man who thinks in magniloquent terms and by sheer force of example compels others to do the same. Thus Lothar von Schweinitz, a notably sober-minded soldier-diplomat, could eulogize him in these terms: 'A burning love for his country, true piety, enthusiasm for the noble and sublime, filled this true Prussian; Christian humility and classical greatness of soul were united in this man and made him, by natural inclination fanatically inclined, a model of those virtues upon which Prussian greatness is founded.'[5] It was a tone set by Manteuffel himself. As a young officer in attendance on the king in the stormy days of 1848, he was taken to task by one of his seniors for speaking out of turn in urging Frederick William to fight: 'Manteuffel! What responsibility are you taking on yourself?' And he replied with a flourish: 'All responsibility before God and man, where nobody else has any advice to offer and it is a matter of the king's security.'[6]

One is reminded of the young Bismarck's romantic excesses in Berlin and Potsdam in those critical days. The difference was that Manteuffel went on talking like that all his life, inspiring dangerous rhetoric in others. In 1859 he had only one desire; for the king to dissolve the Landtag, abolish the Constitution, and start ruling by decree, even at the cost of bloody civil war. Bloodier revolution, he was convinced, would otherwise befall. It had been just round the corner since 1849 and the Landtag's refusal to let the king have his way with the army made it inevitable. He was not alone in this. Even though the 1848–50 Constitution represented so timorous a step towards liberalization, to ministers of the old era it was the next thing to anarchy. Uneasy consciousness of the power of the mob was ever present in their minds. Most of the men close to the king, including Roon himself, supported Manteuffel in his determination to make parliament back down. But for many reasons, some good, some bad, some to do with concern for the state, some to do with concern for their own careers, all except a handful resisted the logical conclusion urged by Manteuffel. Neither the king, nor Roon, nor anybody else could envisage with enthusiasm this bellicose Don Quixote as effective dictator, ruling in the name of the king; and the king, especially, would have nothing to do with the risk of a civil war that would tear his country apart and ruin his beloved army.

So it was that after much coming and going William, in April 1862, began to speak of abdication. It was late in the day. At this very moment Manteuffel was sure that his hour had come. For some time now he had been deliberately trying to provoke the Liberals into taking some action that might justify a military *coup* to put them down. In 1860, he had encouraged Roon to cheat the Landtag. When the army reform bill was thrown out, the government made a provisional grant of funds in return for a promise from Roon, as the new minister for war, not to use them for any purpose but the strengthening of existing army units. In fact they were used to finance the new regiments desired by William, then still prince regent. The Liberals turned a blind eye to this challenge, which they should have met head on. In the following year, 1861, General Manteuffel went out of his way to provoke the Liberals yet again by persuading William, now king, to dedicate the standards of these illegally established regiments at the tomb of Frederick the Great. His attitude towards the Landtag was perfectly expressed in his remarks to a ministerial deputation headed by Rudolf von Auerswald (a personal friend of the king and appointed by him), who entered a legitimate protest against this piece of theatre: 'I do not understand what Your Excellency desires. His Majesty had ordered me to organize a military ceremony. Am I to decline because of a number of people sitting in the Dönhoffplatz and calling themselves a Landtag who may be displeased with this ceremony? I fail to see in what way these people concern me. As a general officer I have received no order to take my instructions from these people.'[7]

The colours were dedicated, the regiments formally established. Parliament raged and the 'New Era' ministry trembled with impotent frustration, but still no solid and consistent opposition was forthcoming. Manteuffel was more *tête montée* than ever. He saw himself as the rock upon which the monarchy was founded. If the monarch was brought down, then he, the Strafford of Potsdam, would gladly, proudly die. Indeed, he seems to have been torn between hankering for a martyr's death and the lure of a triumphant career as a nineteenth-century Wallenstein— so muddled was this strange but desperately loyal man that he saw in this most self-seeking and disloyal of the great captains of history an ideal of self-sacrificial service. His admirers have presented him as a sort of Prussian Bayard, but his passionate concern with self makes this a false comparison. There was, by all means, an element of Quixotry. He would indeed have died for his master, though he would have preferred to stay alive (and did so), and he was quite certainly keen to prove himself in prison. It was in character, however, that when he did find himself behind bars there was an element of farce in the proceedings.

He was sharply attacked in the spring of 1861 by a stubborn and courageous Liberal city councillor and Landtag deputy, Karl von Twesten. In a pamphlet designed to warn king, government, and people Twesten argued passionately against the elevation of the military cabinet, which, he prophesied, would end up by separating the army from the people and producing a reversion to the 'atmosphere of distrust and hostility between military and civil society' as had existed before the post-Stein reforms. Manteuffel himself he characterized as an evil genius, 'an unwholesome man,' who should at once be removed from 'an unwholesome position.'[8] The general, as might be expected, responded with a challenge, but lost much sympathy by insisting that Twesten withdraw not only his personal imputations but his whole thesis about army control and the Landwehr. In the consequent duel Twesten was hit in the arm. Manteuffel insisted on being punished and was sent to the guardhouse for two weeks, full of a sort of lunatic, martyrized self-pity. Twesten, he was convinced, was the instrument of a secret society set on overthrowing the state. But the height of the farce was William's hysterical reaction. In a letter to Roon he was beside himself: 'To be deprived of Manteuffel's services at this of all moments, to have him hunted out of my presence by the triumph of democracy—the upset this event will cause in my own intimate circle—these are things that can drive me out of my mind because they impress still another woeful stamp upon my reign.'[9]

Although Manteuffel was to settle down to a routinely distinguished career, proving himself as a field commander in the wars with Austria and France, undertaking many diplomatic missions (oddly enough, this highly emotional man was considered a skilled negotiator), and finishing as governor of Alsace-Lorraine, the strong flamboyant streak in him exacerbated, or encouraged, the unstable elements in the character of the king. He rejoiced in his absurd prison sentence not only because, as he observed to Roon, 'The more severe the king seems to be to me here, the better position he and Your Excellency will be in to be severe to the other side.'[10]

And, indeed, for a moment in the winter of 1861 it did look as though events were playing into Manteuffel's hands. The formation of the new German Progressive Party (Deutsche Fortschrittspartei) and its sweeping gains in the December Landtag elections was the signal for more radical demands for reform and renewed determination to resist the third year of military service. Manteuffel was not alone in believing that his hour was at hand. Roon and other sober Conservatives were also beginning to think that it was high time to get rid of the Landtag and make an end once and for all of democratic encroachments on the crown's prerogatives. In January William finally agreed to adopt Manteuffel's plan to put Berlin into a state of readiness for a counter-revolutionary coup; 34,500 infantry, 16,000 cavalry, and 100 guns were to be deployed under sealed orders. All Manteuffel had to pray for was a revolt to put down; and this he was determined, if necessary, to provoke. He had the king and Roon in his pocket—Roon committing himself to the belief that if the next elections were unfavourable to the government, 'then it would have to be force.'[11]

Then, when feelings were running higher than ever before and it seemed only a matter of days before the shooting must start, the king himself wavered. He could not bring himself to be party to a civil war: he must, he declared, either give way or abdicate. Manteuffel's only reply was that there must be no question of concessions: Very well, then, said the king, I shall abdicate. That was in September 1862, and Roon, seeing that the king wanted to compromise, seeing that the Progressives, confident in their new and increasing strength, were also in a mood to accommodate him, decided to take action.

His secret weapon was Bismarck, and it was against this background of incipient civil war, or at least the destruction of parliament in any form, that Bismarck came to power. He had not only the Liberals to deal with; he had to neutralize the Manteuffels as well.

Nothing could bring home more sharply the extraordinary quality of Bismarck's mind and character than his conduct throughout this protracted crisis: he behaved as though it did not exist. From June 1861, when William announced his intention of having himself crowned like a medieval sovereign, until September of the following year, when Bismarck, on leave in southern France, responded to Roon's famous telegram of recall (*Periculum in mora: Dépêchez-vous*), he displayed not the slightest visible interest in the nature of the domestic strife convulsing Prussia and kept his eyes firmly on the world outside her borders. It was as though he had made his final wager in a game for the highest stakes and had set himself down to wait, letting others do the agonizing. This was made easier by the fact that the technicalities of army reform (as indeed the reform itself) did not interest him—and also by the conviction, at least from July 1861, that events were at last moving his way, if much too slowly.

It was Roon who brought his old protégé back into the picture at the height of the coronation crisis in June 1861: for a moment it looked as though the new administration would either resign or split hopelessly over the king's obstinate whim, and Roon wanted Bismarck at hand to help him defeat the Liberals and keep them defeated. By the time Bismarck arrived in Berlin on leave from St. Petersburg in late June William had given way and the crisis was over; but the journey was not in vain. For William had other matters on his mind besides the army question: the interminably nagging problem of the government of Germany, of unification, of Prussia's relations with Austria and the smaller states. These were now beginning to call urgently for some sort of solution: the initiative was moving away from Prussia.

In July the king went to stay with the grand duke Frederick of Baden, his liberally inclined son-in-law. There, two things happened: William was shot at and slightly grazed by a young German nationalist, called Becker, because he had failed 'to do enough for German unity'; at the same time the grand duke's foreign minister, Baron Franz von Roggenbach, produced a plan for the federal union of a Little Germany with a national parliament and a Prussian executive (echoes of the Nationalverein) formally committed to the support of the Habsburg Empire in its entirety. This was the plan on which Roon asked Bismarck to comment.

The result was the so-called Baden-Baden Memorial. Here Bismarck put all his weight of intellect behind the argument he had already outlined in the 'Little Book' of 1858: Prussia must harness German nationalism to her own ends; the Confederation must go; Prussia's position in an organization of this kind did not and could not reflect her importance as its chief defender. Further, the only way to respond to the spirit of German nationalism and bring the many kingdoms and principalities to a common outlook was to establish some sort of 'national assembly of the German people,' its members to be chosen from the state legislatures. Since, however, Austria was bound to object to such a solution, and would carry some of the lesser states with her, another way might be taken to reach the same goal. This was to work through the establishment of an apparently innocuous 'Zollverein Parliament' through which Prussia could bring pressure on weaker members in matters other than trade, working towards a common military command and a representative assembly empowered to lay down the law on tariffs, trade, and commerce in general.

This arrangement, with its direct challenge to Austria and its uncanny pre-echo (on a purely German stage) of the essential arrangements of the North Atlantic Treaty Organization and the European Economic Community a century later, was (not surprisingly) too much for William. When all was said, he was then locked in stubborn conflict with his own parliament, the pretensions of which were as much as he could bear—perhaps, more indeed. And how here was Bismarck, supposedly a conservative Junker, asking him to give his blessing to yet another parliament, and one, moreover, conceived as a direct challenge to his fellow-monarch, his imperial brother, in Vienna.

So Bismarck found himself being returned to cold storage. In September the Roggenbach scheme was agreed to, with certain modifications. (Even this came as a severe shock to the Austrians, who had imagined that with the throwing out of the Radowitz plan ten years earlier Prussia had abandoned her dream of setting up a union of northern states to dominate the Confederation.) At the same time Count Albrecht von Bernstorff, a neutral, decent-minded diplomat, was made foreign minister of Prussia, Roon's recommendations notwithstanding. But Bismarck at least knew that there was movement in his favour. Bernstorff, who had never aspired higher than an embassy to Paris or London, understood that he was no more than a stopgap. The king knew, though he still resisted: he knew that

Augusta, his wife, and Frederick, his son and heir, rejected Bismarck, as did all the moderates in the Landtag. He might well have to fight the Liberals, but this would be a job not for Bismarck but for Manteuffel and his army. And yet, how much longer could he keep this able and stupendously self-confident man out of the driver's seat? Bismarck may have been sulking in St. Petersburg, but when he set his mind to it he could still display his genius. Some of his dispatches in the blackest days of despondency show that the marvellously attacking intelligence, the humour too, still lived under the dark mood of boredom, frustration, disillusion.

On the face of it he was defeated. But when in November 1861 he returned to St. Petersburg after nearly six months in Germany he found the atmosphere changed. The Russians had come to see that they need not take seriously the fashionable, unsettling talk about the dawn of a new age in Prussia: William was clearly a conservative like his brother, and likely to prove more reliable. No less convinced of the divine right of kings, he had placed the crown on his head with his own hands in the ceremony at Königsberg to show that he derived his authority directly from God, and not from any prelate purporting to act in God's name. The Russians had also obtained from their Berlin embassy a lively appreciation of Bismarck as the coming man, whether the king liked it or not. Only that summer he had been virtually cold-shouldered in St. Petersburg; now, on his return, he found himself being made much of, particularly by Gorchakov, well-established as foreign minister and soon to be chancellor, who set to work to win his confidence.

That was in November 1861. It was to be a very different winter from the previous one. While the king in Berlin wrestled with parliament, while Manteuffel planned his glorious future as a man of destiny, which involved not so much cleaning the Augean stables of liberalism as razing them to the ground and running up a barracks in their place, Bismarck waited and quite often enjoyed himself. He grumbled at the waste of time and energy entailed in his new popularity, but he had come to life again, and that winter he had some of the finest shooting in his life—one expedition involving a highly adventurous encounter with a wolf pack. In January 1862 Johanna reported with satisfaction: 'After several days away shooting he came home very happily yesterday having shot a bear and a gigantic elk —heaven be praised in the best of spirits in spite of so much exhausting exercise.'[12]

Bismarck had got himself in hand. There were to be no more agonized self-justifications (when next he complained to Roon, the tone was to be that of a king's first servant complaining of his master's shortcomings). Only Roon and one or two others knew how desperately he cared and hungered for power. To the rest of the world, even including his beloved sister, he presented himself as something of an elder statesman, a sort of Prussian Cincinnatus (it was good practice for the future), ready to answer the call of duty if needs must, but asking no more of a life too full of strife than a mellow eventide of peace. Thus a fortnight after that successful and exultant shooting trip he was writing to Malwine like an old, old man, forgiving and serene (he was forty-six): 'Since my illness my mind has become so dull that I no longer have the energy for any serious activity. Three years ago I should still have made a useful minister, but now I am like a worn-out trick-rider called on to go through his paces yet again.'

He went on to discuss the advantages of settling down to run Schönhausen or Kniephof when their leases expired in three and five years' time respectively. Where to live if he decided to retire before then? 'Meanwhile the present reshuffle of appointments leaves me cold: I have a superstitious dread of asking anything for myself, in case my wish is granted and I live to regret it. I could go to Paris or London or stay on here without repining and without gladness, as it may please God and His Majesty—but it will make no difference to the country or to me whatever is decided. . . . Johanna hankers after Paris because she thinks the climate would be better for the children, but illness may strike anywhere, accidents too, with God's help one comes through or bows in submission to His will. . . . I should show myself ungrateful to God and man if I pretended that things were going badly for me here or that I was desperate for change. I dread the ministry as I shrink from a cold bath. I would far rather have any vacant post in the Foreign Service or go back to Frankfurt, or even Berne. . . .'[13]

He did not have to keep up this pretence of indifference much longer. His formal recall came in March 1862, and it took some weeks to pack up and hand over. On 10 May he found himself back in Berlin and compelled to pay some attention to the crisis that now gripped Prussia. The Liberals had done well in the elections and at last stood firm against the king, who promptly dissolved the Landtag. There had been fresh elections, bringing a Liberal landslide. It was not only Manteuffel now who feared bloody revolution, but Manteuffel was the only man who was quite sure he knew how to deal with it. To him it looked as though the great day had arrived. The sealed orders issued months before would soon be opened to acquaint the army commanders with a detailed and elaborate plan for the methodical reduction of Berlin, fighting street by street.

Only two things were missing. In the first place parliament had not the least intention of staging an insurrection. Anyone with a clear eye would have seen that the swing to liberalism in the country and its strengthening in the Landtag did not mean that the Liberal deputies were spoiling for a fight: they might detest the army, but they were terrified of the mob and they were looking for compromise. In the second place, it was not in the king's nature to meet his people head on and spill their blood. It was to William's credit that in the end he saw through Manteuffel's political pretensions to his essential irresponsibility. He was not going to allow Prussia to be riven and perhaps ruined by civil war nor was he prepared to put himself under an obligation to the army as a political force. The army was his to command, and if he could not win the confidence of his people, then it was time for him to make way for one who could.

Very well, then, said Roon in effect, in that case it will have to be Bismarck. William resisted. He wanted to use Bismarck but shrank from giving him his head. Bismarck for his part was prepared to go on waiting. To Johanna he wrote from Berlin saying that he would refuse the premiership unless he was given absolute control of foreign policy: 'On Sunday I shall have been here fourteen days, then I shall explode and demand a post or my release.'[14] He was already dreaming of transforming Prussia into a power as strong as any in the world, and he knew that this would have to be done with the authority of a reluctant monarch. There is no other explanation of his behaviour at this moment: it had to be all or nothing. If he had simply hankered after power for its own sake, he could have entered the ministry, knowing that he could outshine and outmanoeuvre all his colleagues. But he would still have been dependent on the king. It is clear that by the spring of 1862 he had understood that to get his way he must make the king dependent on him. And the first step towards this must be for the king to realize that he desperately needed him—not simply as one able minister among others but as the only man who could save the country.

There was still some time to wait. With the Liberals in the new parliament so strong that they could offer compromise, the grim choice between Manteuffel and abdication had receded, and with it the need for another strong man. But what to do with Bismarck? The solution was to pack him off to Paris: this got him out of the way yet kept him fairly close at hand in case of need.

Bismarck was irritated beyond measure. Would his wretched monarch never make up his mind? He seems to have been oblivious to William's natural reluctance to offend his own family by handing over the government of Prussia to the man detested above all others. What is equally remarkable is Bismarck's own certainty that, barring accidents, he would soon be called, and on his own terms.

So while William on the one side wrestled with parliament and on the other helped the proponents of 'Little Germany' to push through the Roggenbach programme more or less as it stood, defeating a strong counter-proposal from the Saxon prime minister, Count Friedrich von Beust, Bismarck, aloof from such mundane trivialities, trundled off to Paris, more exasperated than depressed. He enjoyed meeting Napoleon again, fatter and softer but still mentally alert, and found Eugénie more beautiful than ever. But he chafed incessantly for action: 'In the heart of great Paris I am more lonely than you in Reinfeld and sit here like a rat in an empty barn,' he wrote to Johanna.[15] Napoleon, however, treated him as the coming man and sounded him out, as the known champion of an understanding with France, on the possibility of an alliance. He behaved, indeed, with an extreme lack of discretion, evidently deciding that the best way to deal with this Pomeranian prodigy was to take a leaf out of his own book and adopt an approach of shocking candour. It was characteristic of Bismarck that he missed the point and did not realize that Napoleon was parodying him. In the enchanted garden at Fontainebleau, against the ravishing harmonies of the most pleasing of all palaces, with the great carp lazing in the artificial lake, with the ornamental canal stretching away, straight as a die, to nowhere, emperor and envoy paced the gravel side by side, the little plump man with the imperial, the enormous Prussian attentively bowing his great height.

'Do you think the king would be disposed to enter into an alliance with me?'

Coolly and very quickly, Bismarck countered: he was sure that King William had nothing but good-will towards France, but for an alliance there needed to be 'a motive, a specific purpose.' The emperor did not rise: 'Not at all,' he replied; it was a matter of two people being naturally drawn together. What he had in mind was an intimate and lasting understanding based on common interests ... not an adventure of any kind. And he added, coming to a stop: 'You cannot imagine what singular overtures the

Austrians made me a few days ago.' Austria, he went on to explain, seemed to have panicked at the very first hint of Bismarck's nomination to Paris. The Austrian ambassador (Prince Richard Metternich) had confided to him that he had received instructions which went so far that he found them frightening: he had been given full plenipotentiary powers to promise anything and everything in exchange for an understanding with France.[16]

All this was excellent fun, but Bismarck knew how to be circumspect when he saw a noose dangled in front of him. He was careful in reporting his conversation with Bernstorff in Berlin to make a joke of it, presenting himself as a Joseph resisting seduction by Potiphar's wife. Even so, that report revived William's unease. 'Tell him,' he instructed Bernstorff, 'that I shall never consent to an alliance with France.'[17] Bismarck felt ill-used. He had been very careful indeed to dissociate himself from the idea of an alliance, or any sort of formal agreement, whereas William himself had relaxed his distrust of France sufficiently to have embarked on a state visit to Compiègne the year before.

And Austria was indeed showing signs of desperation. This was due less to Bismarck's appointment to Paris than to Prussia's foiling of all her very active attempts to achieve a Greater Germany under her own leadership (she was prepared to contrive an administrative division of her empire which would exclude Hungary), failing that, a reorganized Zollverein (in three years' time the whole question of her membership in the Zollverein would come up for review). What Vienna saw as the most damaging Prussian blow, far more than William's visit and the appointment of Bismarck to Paris, worrying as these were, had been the signing in March 1862 of a trade treaty between Prussia and France, which effectively opened up the Zollverein to free trade in spite of much grumbling from some of the smaller states. This created a revolutionary economic situation and made it impossible for Austria, who could not conceivably open her own empire to free trade at this epoch, to realize her urgent wish of entering the Zollverein. Seeing Prussia on the ascendant in Germany and now moving closer towards France; seeing France as she firmly believed, moving closer to Russia and abetting Russia's pro-Slav, anti-Austrian manoeuvres in the Balkans, no wonder the Austrians were desperate.

In his present mood Bismarck viewed these developments as from a great distance. He had been sure when he came to Paris that it was only for a day. But after some weeks he was no longer so sure. In Berlin compromise was still in the air, reflected in Roon's letters in answer to his increasingly irritable enquiries. Roon himself (but not the king) was prepared to give up the third year of military service in exchange for the voting of supplies by parliament. All Bismarck wanted now was a decision one way or another. He was sick and tired of not knowing where he stood or what would happen next. The strain of his self-imposed waiting game was beginning to tell.

This did not prevent him from talking to Napoleon less as an ambassador than as an elder statesman. Nor did it prevent him from taking a trip to London at the end of June to test the temperature there, and letting everyone understand that he was the future prime minister of Prussia. It was on this occasion that he met Disraeli, then in opposition, to whom he is supposed to have declared: 'I shall soon be compelled to undertake the conduct of the Prussian government. My first care will be to reorganize the army, with or without the help of the Landtag. . . . As soon as the army shall have been brought to such a condition as to inspire respect, I shall seize the best pretext to declare war on Austria, dissolve the German diet, subdue the minor states, and give national unity to Germany under Prussia's leadership. I have come here to say this to the queen's ministers.'[18]

It is to be doubted whether Bismarck did say all this, although it has been repeated as gospel by many biographers, but he may well have conveyed the sense, and he was certainly capable of telling anyone who cared to listen that he would soon be chancellor and that he proposed to start a revolutionary and fratricidal war to drive Austria out of Germany—as, in fact, five years later he did. Nobody in his lifetime was ever able to establish just what Bismarck said and what he did not say in private—as a rule because at one time or another he said everything, usually with an air of almost childlike candour, contradicting himself when he was moved to do so without a tremor of an eyelid.

An unexpectedly vivid insight into Bismarck's mentality at this time is provided by the very shrewd Russian ambassador to St. James's, Count Philipp Brunnow. Brunnow was very much at home in London and put himself out to help the Prussian visitor find his way about. He laboured in vain. Reporting to Gorchakov when Bismarck had gone back to Paris, he gave it as his view that the idea behind the visit had been unsound and the visit itself a failure. 'Four days,' he wrote, 'are not enough to get to know the statesmen who are at the helm of affairs in England. On principle they discuss only those questions which they are under the necessity of settling;

they are neither accustomed nor inclined to aimless and unnecessary conversation.'

After that discerning comment, he went on: 'The reserve which M. de Bismarck has met with in London has astonished him all the more since he believes himself designated to replace Count Bernstorff shortly at Berlin. He thought the English ministers . . . would attach more importance into entering into direct relations with him. Disappointed in this expectation, he felt a touch of annoyance at it, which he in no way tried to conceal from me. This dissatisfaction has prevented him from bringing to the appreciation of men and things in this country the degree of concentration and determination which I have noted in him everywhere else.'[19]

After London, Bismarck simply went away, taking a month's leave because there was nothing else to do. Nobody realized that he was establishing a pattern for the future by withdrawing to a far place, going into retreat, as it were, when critical decisions had to be taken and he felt he had done all he could to influence them. He went first to Trouville, which he found insufferably dull, then south to Biarritz, where the Pyrenees sweep down to the Atlantic. And it was at Biarritz that he fell in love with the twenty-two-year-old wife of an old acquaintance, Prince Orlov, Russian ambassador to Brussels.

That he was bowled over by Katharina Orlov, a Princess Trubetskoi, as he had not been bowled over by any woman since Marie von Thadden, perhaps since Isabella Lorraine-Smith, there has never been any doubt. They went bathing together, climbed mountains together, picnicked together, and Kathy played Beethoven, Schubert, Mendelssohn, unendingly. The prince seems to have smiled on this idyll of his much younger wife and his much older colleague. It seems most unlikely, given all the circumstances—the conventions of the time, and the noted capacity of virile nineteenth-century males to allow themselves to be swept along by strong emotions without being carried finally away—that the affair was ever consummated. But serious it was. He was covered with sea salt and sun, he wrote to Johanna. He prayed that he would not be called back to Berlin. He was feeling quite wonderfully restored. And why? 'Invisible to all the world, hidden in a steep ravine cut back from the cliffs, I gaze out between two rocks on which the heather blooms at the sea, green and white in the sunshine and the spray. At my side is the most charming woman, whom you will love very much when you get to know her; a little like Marie

Thadden . . . but with a personality all her own—amusing, intelligent, and kind, pretty and young.'[20] To Malwine he wrote: 'Since the Orlovs arrived I have been living with them as though we were alone in the world. . . . I am a little in love with the enchanting Principessa.'[21]

Johanna, far away that August with the children in Pomerania, showed herself at her best in a way that helps to explain how Bismarck found in her the indispensable quiet centre of his turbulent existence, regardless of her many faults, which intensified with age. To her old friend Robert von Keudell (soon to rise high in her husband's train) she wrote: 'Were I at all inclined to jealousy and envy I should be tyrannized to the depths now by these passions. But my soul has no room for them and I rejoice quite enormously that my beloved husband has found this charming woman. But for her he would never have found peace for so long in one place or become so well as he boasts of being in every letter.'[22]

It was his last fling. We remember how, eleven years before, he had written to Johanna from Berlin about his appointment to Frankfurt, telling her how he had watched the lilac and the chestnut blossoms tossing in the wind while Leopold von Gerlach droned on about treaties, torn between elation over his appointment and sadness at leaving for ever perhaps the delights of country life. Now, in the deep south with his enchanting companion he deliberately cut himself off from Berlin, half praying never to be recalled, half putting his fate to the test by standing, as it were, outside the arena while the great decisions were being taken. He himself could not have said how much it was flight, how much challenge. He was committed enough, in a faint echo of his pursuit nearly thirty years before of Isabella Lorraine-Smith, to accompany the Orlovs as they moved across France, instead of returning to Paris from his leave as he should have done. But the dream had to end. And in Toulouse on 12 September he pulled himself together to compose a long-overdue reply to a letter from Roon, and in the course of it to deliver a sort of ultimatum. He must know where he would be spending Christmas. That at least! Uncertainty had gone far enough: 'My furniture is in Petersburg and will be frozen up there, my carriages are in Stettin, my horses at grass outside Berlin, my family is in Pomerania, and I am on the road.'[23]

Two days later, at Avignon, he said good-bye to the Orlovs, who were going on to Geneva. Next day he was back in Paris, while the conflict in Berlin about the three-year term of military service and the army estimates came to its climax. It must be three years or nothing, declared King William; if he could not lay down the law for the army he himself was nothing. If the Landtag would not agree, then abdicate he must. Roon was still hoping to persuade him to compromise, but he was firm. Bernstorff on 16 September wired to Bismarck advising him to return to Berlin at once. Bismarck did not reply. He appeared to be playing hard to get, and in a way he was. But the reason for his failure to reply was that he did not receive the telegram when it arrived: he had driven out to Fontainebleau to pay his respects to Kathy Orlov's mother, a Princess Trubetskoi, and make a sentimental pilgrimage to Kathy's childhood home and the park in which she used to play. This was his final act of freedom. Next day, 17 September, Roon at last realized that he had quite failed to persuade the king and himself decided that it was high time for Bismarck to come home. So the famous telegram was sent: 'Delay is dangerous. Hurry!' On Saturday the twentieth Bismarck was back in Berlin.

'In these next few days,' wrote Johanna to Keudell, 'our fate will be decided, perhaps is decided already. After his return from the delights of mountain and sea Bismarck was called urgently to Berlin by two telegrams. From there he has written, still well and gentle but very uneasily, because once again he finds everything at sixes and sevens and is desperately afraid that nothing will ever, ever be finally settled but will be left hanging in the air, the thought of which makes him shudder as it does me. Let God dispose of us as He thinks best—after all the endless dilly-dally one finds oneself quite drained of will and I only pray most urgently that all will come right for Bismarck and the children—I am really very unimportant and always content if only those four are happy and well. . . .'[24]

What Johanna did not know when she wrote on 24 September was that her husband had in fact achieved his goal and was already embarked on the course which would carry him to the mastery of Europe.

The final act had been the critical audience at Babelsberg on Monday, 22 September. William had been quite determined to abdicate. It had already been touch and go when Bernstorff had telegraphed Bismarck in Paris. Only the stubborn refusal of the crown prince to accept the crown had stopped it happening. Frederick, at thirty-one, had a generous heart and strongly liberal inclinations, encouraged and fortified by his wife, Queen Victoria's eldest daughter, Victoria Louise, the Princess Royal, to whom he had been married for four years. For the supreme desire of Vicky's heart, inherited from her adored father, the late prince consort, was to help her husband introduce into her adopted Prussia something like the British parliamentary system, thus opening the way to a liberal and united Germany under Prussian leadership. She was now strenuously urging Frederick to do his father's will and accept the crown, declaring with perfect foresight that if he did not seize this opportunity he would one day regret it bitterly.

But Frederick, liberally inclined as he might be, was also a Hohenzollern and a dynast. He had no intention of receiving the crown as a gift from a rebellious parliament. Of course he wavered a little: he knew that he could carry Prussia forward as his father could not; but there was plenty of time, and he could not have imagined for the moment that William, already creaking at the joints at sixty-five, would live and reign for twenty-six more years. There was only one thing that might have made Frederick change his mind, and that would have been the projected appointment of Bismarck as prime minister. But William had solemnly promised both his consort and his eldest son that he would never on any account appoint Bismarck, and right up to the third week in September, he had every intention of keeping that promise.

But when on Saturday, 20 September, he was still threatening to abdicate and countered Roon's arguments with the flat statement that there was nobody who could bring parliament to heel—nobody except Manteuffel by military action, which he was not going to have—he had no answer ready when Roon announced that Bismarck was already in Berlin and willing. Further, that he had already seen the crown prince. It was clear that he himself must agree to receive the dread Junker the next day. The matter was not finally clinched, however, until Roon made a direct appeal to William's 'soldierly spirit': it was his simple duty to sustain his burden as long as he could find a servant to act as his strong right arm, and this Bismarck could do. The king responded to the bugle call of duty.

And so, on Sunday morning at Babelsberg, on the River Havel near Potsdam, there took place the first of a long and increasingly weary series of arguments between the monarch and his most formidable subject that were to make the king's life an intermittent purgatory over the years to come.

Nobody knows exactly what took place at Babelsberg, but Bismarck's own over-colourful account is probably near enough to the truth in essence. There on the table lay the deed of abdication, ready for the king's signature; there, also, was a long memorandum presented by the king for Bismarck to read and digest as they took a walk together in the park: in it the duties and opportunities of a first minister of Prussia were elaborately detailed and hopefully circumscribed. The king announced that he saw no way to reign with dignity if he were to be subject to the will of parliament. Bismarck replied in effect that he could manage parliament, that he could form a ministry and put through the army reforms, if necessary in defiance of a parliamentary majority. If that was really so, the king replied, then it would indeed be his own duty to fight on.[25]

It says everything both for Bismarck's charm and almost hypnotic intensity of will that William, who feared and distrusted him, who knew both from his own experience and the tales told him by Augusta and his ministerial advisers just how reckless, insolent, and at the same time profoundly devious he could be, so easily succumbed. The memorandum with its limiting conditions was ignored by the subject and forgotten by the sovereign. William did not have to ask how Bismarck proposed to manage his *tour de force*. It was clearly a matter of will-power and drive, and his new champion had both. Bismarck on his side well understood the significance of a peculiarity in the Prussian Constitution (the king, unable even to imagine a responsible ministerial collectivity, took it for granted without, apparently, realizing its implications) which rendered ministers responsible not to parliament but only to the king: ministers could not be members of parliament; they were the representatives of the monarch *in face* of parliament, which they went down to address, as it were, *ex cathedra*. Parliament's only effective sanctions were moral and financial. Confronted by a prime minister who was not susceptible to moral pressure and was prepared to live and act in a crisis situation for as long as was necessary to wear the opposition down, there was nothing it could do provided the minister retained the confidence of the king—short of overthrowing the king.

When Bismarck emerged from that audience—and all unknown to Johanna, waiting anxiously in Schönhausen until she read the news in the papers two days later—he was acting chief minister and minister-president and foreign minister–designate. It had been a close-run thing. Had William abdicated, the name of Bismarck would never have been heard of outside Germany. Thus the third week of September 1862 may be seen as one of those turning points in history, silent, unnoticed, but almost infinite in their consequences.

Within eight years this extraordinary man, cajoling, ruthlessly driving, bullying, cheating his ever reluctant sovereign, had embroiled his country in three calculated wars, significantly enlarged his master's realms, beaten Austria out of Germany, destroyed the empire of Napoleon III, and united all Germany, with Alsace-Lorraine added (and lacking only the German-

Austrian provinces), under the Prussian king, now German emperor, to make the most formidable power in Europe. After that, with France beaten, humbled, and thirsting for revenge, with Austria driven to adventures in the Balkans, this strange neurotic genius, still only fifty-six years old, set himself up as a wise and moderate elder statesman concerned only with maintaining the peace. So successful was his impersonation that when after thirty-two years of almost absolute power he was driven from office by a brash new emperor, his passing was marked as a calamity by the Europe which had once reviled his name and was still oblivious of the dragon's teeth. These he had begun to sow only a matter of days after his assumption of office.

PART TWO

ACHIEVEMENT

I am not afraid of war, on the contrary;
I am also indifferent to the labels revolutionary or
conservative, as I am indifferent to all phrases.
You will soon convince yourself that war is a part
of my programme as well.
—BISMARCK, 1865

There is a new element in politics, a deepening,
of which earlier victors knew nothing or at least made no
conscious use of. One is trying to humiliate the loser as much
as possible, so that in future he will hardly dare to move.
—JAKOB BURCKHARDT, 1871

The unification of Germany by the now defunct and almost
forgotten Kingdom of Prussia was at once inevitable
and absurd, artificial and harmful.
—GOLO MANN, 1971

CHAPTER VIII

ONE MAN AGAINST THE REST

The Bismarck who now appeared on the world stage which he was to hold and dominate for three decades was not the hugely looming, unmovable figure of his later image, a growling giant, invulnerable, in a floppy hat and an overcoat down to the ground, accompanied by crop-eared mastiffs as surly-looking as their master—or even the commanding uniformed figure in Prussian blue, spiked helmet and jack-boots who presided over the destruction of Napoleon III and the Second French Empire. He was tall and very pale, already rather paunchy, his voice high-pitched and a little uncertain as he rose to speak for the first time in the Lower House of the Landtag, a fine-drawn look about those strange eyes which seemed to be looking sideways; it was only with the habit of power that they became terrible in their penetration. He made no very firm impression. Indeed, it could have been said that he hardly knew why he was there. And this in a sense was just. He was still not interested in the army question, to which he owed his elevation. He seems to have convinced himself that once installed in office he would be able to persuade William to give up his demand for a third year and make his peace with parliament. Nobody except Roon and the king himself took him very seriously. Most believed that he was rather an absurd figure, dangerous while he lasted, but too big for his boots, who would soon find himself in trouble and vanish from the scene unmourned.

His survival was all but miraculous. He had no ministerial experience, he had no position in the country to use as a power base or to make his name widely known. Where domestic policies were concerned his mind was a beautiful void. Politicians knew him from his early explosive appearances in the Landtag and from stories about his behaviour in 1848; diplomats knew that he had turned his tour of duty in Frankfurt into a one-man campaign against Austria. To liberals and moderates, in spite of his brief flirtation with the Nationalverein, he was a reactionary Junker all through. The old romantic monarchists of the *Kreuzzeitung* circle had long come to distrust him because of his attitude to France and Austria, to say nothing of a deviousness which seemed rather perplexingly at odds with his frequently brutal candour. Even those who most feared him, like the crown prince and his English wife, never thought of him at first as an enduring threat to all their ideals: he was a temporary disturbance, to be resisted and deplored, but not built to last: 'People will immediately smell reaction,' wrote Prince Frederick in his journal. 'On all sides there will be distrust and poor Papa will cause himself many difficult hours through this dishonest character.'[1]

It is hardly too much to say that in the autumn of 1862 Bismarck was the most lonely man in the kingdom. Roon was his only true friend and reliable supporter, but he knew that he was in a sense Roon's instrument. The king would stand by him as long as he was needed to do battle with parliament on the army question. Bismarck himself, who liked solitude and time to mature his long-term plans, can scarcely have had time to think in those last days of September and thus had to rely on his other weapon, which was double-edged, the inspired boldness of a blindfold tight-rope walker; he had at all costs to keep going; if he faltered, wavered, he was lost. But for the moment he did not know where he was going.

For ten years now his one devouring preoccupation had been the elevation of Prussia to a position of at least equality with Austria. If Austria refused to admit this equality—formalized by Prussian hegemony over all Germany north of the River Main—then she would have to be coerced. Like so many men of action who have never worked as a part of a team, he had no conception of the negative power of inertia. Thus, he knew what had to be done to cut Austria down to size; all that was lacking, he thought, was the vision, the will, and the authority to use them. He had always had the vision and the will, and he now possessed the authority, provided only that he could keep the king on his side. He hoped in those first days to make his peace with parliament and induce the king to compromise. It would then, he seems most erroneously to have thought, be a simple matter for him to carry both king and parliament with him on a course which needed only to be understood to be adopted. Thus it was that his first speech in the Landtag was conciliatory and his second, in his eyes, exploratory. It was necessary to acquaint his fellow-Prussians with his thinking, developed in solitude over so many years. And the crux of his line of thought was the point he had reached in his correspondence with Schleinitz three years earlier, when, writing from St. Petersburg, he had recommended the swift exploitation of Austrian difficulties in the war for Italy or, failing that, the adoption of a policy designed to make an end of the German Confederation: 'I regard our connection with the German Confederation as a sickness of Prussia that will have to be cured sooner or later *ferro et igne*, unless we take treatment for it at a favourable opportunity.'[2]

Now, on the last day of September 1862 he offered an elaboration of this thought to a larger audience—to the Landtag in Berlin, to Germany, to Europe, to the world. Dutifully fulfilling his obligations to the king, he was explaining to parliament why it must be prepared to spend more money on the army. The army was not a luxury, he said in effect; for the survival and development of Prussia it was a necessity. Prussia 'must gather together her forces, conserving her strength for the favourable moment which has been missed several times already. Prussia's frontiers as drawn by the Vienna Treaty do not favour a healthy political existence. The great questions of the day will be decided not by speeches and majority votes—that was the great mistake of 1848 and 1849—but by iron and blood.'[3]

Thus was the legend born. How unfair, many historians have protested, that Bismarck should have been labelled for life and all eternity as a self-confessed man of violence on the strength of a single remark, misunderstood, torn out of context.

It was not unfair at all. When a prime minister starts talking with relish about iron and blood (the phrase was later—perhaps for euphony—turned round to read 'blood and iron') in his second speech in office and in connection with the rectification of his country's frontiers it is only fair to take him seriously. And when within eight years of making that speech he has personally manoeuvred his country into three brilliantly successful wars, it must be clear in retrospect that the possibility or probability of war, or wars, of Prussian aggrandizement was in the forefront of his mind from the beginning. On another occasion he committed himself to the popular fallacy that a state must either expand or dwindle; there can be no standing still. But how rectify frontiers, how expand, how upset the boundaries drawn at the Congress of Vienna without war? Bismarck was at pains always to insist that war for him was only a final resort, to be avoided thankfully if the desired result could be achieved by other means. On a number of occasions he spoke very movingly about the fearful responsibility of sending men to be killed or maimed on the battlefield. On the other hand, at no time, so far as is known, did he ask himself whether the very fact that his aims could be achieved only by war did not put a question-mark against those aims.

What, in the autumn of 1862, was it that he wanted to achieve? It is doubtful whether at this stage he had any more specific or distant aim than reducing Austria's pretensions to the leadership of Germany, and setting up some sort of a North German union dominated by Prussia—the very arrangement he had spoken of with such contempt twelve years earlier when poor Radowitz had been savaged by Schwarzenberg with the backing of Tsar Nicholas I.

Bismarck was to pretend that he had not been thinking of war when he spoke of iron and blood. But he pretended so many things on so very many occasions. Even Roon thought his protégé was asking for trouble and reproached him for it; and of course the whole of liberal Germany cried out in indignation. King William was at Baden-Baden enjoying a family party for his wife's birthday. He had not made Bismarck prime minister to provoke a revolution. Deeply perturbed, he decided that he had better get back to Potsdam and have it out with the wretched fellow, perhaps in the end to be forced to admit to his family, to all those tiresome parliamentarians, that he had been wrong. Bismarck, when he heard that the king was coming, understood what was in the wind. William had already demanded an explanation and received the improbable reply that by the phrase 'iron and blood' he had meant no more than that the army must have more guns and more soldiers—a fantasy which, interestingly enough, Bismarck was to cling to in his memoirs thirty years later.[4] Obviously that excuse would not wash, and Bismarck decided that his best hope was to meet the king before he reached Berlin and could be got at by his enemies.

And so, on 4 October, transpired the extraordinary scene on Jüterbog station. Jüterbog, fifty miles to the south of Berlin, was a new junction at which the king's train must stop. The station buildings were still unfinished (so new was the railway) and the platform littered with planks and ladders, piles of bricks, and timber balks. There, amid a mob of third-class passengers and workmen, the king of Prussia's first minister, not an inconspicuous figure, waited solitary in the autumnal dusk, seated on an upturned wheelbarrow, for the interview that might bring to an end his political career before it had started.

The omens were not good. When the train drew in Bismarck had difficulty in locating his sovereign, who was alone in an ordinary first-class carriage. The king did not smile when Bismarck asked permission to ride with him back to Berlin. He was, Bismarck himself later wrote, 'visibly cast down and still under the influence of his wife.' He interrupted his minister abruptly and gloomily: 'I can see in advance just how all this will end. Out there in the Opernplatz under my windows they will cut off your head and soon afterwards mine.'

Bismarck guessed that he had been brooding on the fates of Polignac, Strafford, Louis XVI. He broke into the royal silence: ' "And after that, Sire?" "After that we shall be dead." "Yes," I retorted. "After that we shall be dead, but we all have to die sooner or later, and what better way than that? I myself fighting for the cause of my king and Your Majesty, in sealing your royal prerogative by the Grace of God with your own blood, whether on the scaffold or the battlefield. . . ." '[5] And so on, and so on. . . . This extraordinary performance was kept up relentlessly in the closed carriage as the train clattered on through the darkness, until William was once more dazzled into acceptance of his own heroic role. By the time journey's end was reached he was Bismarck's unprotesting captive.

It is revealing to juxtapose Bismarck's own account of this interview, written with marked self-satisfaction in his seventies, with the entry in Kurt von Schlözer's diary for 5 October (Schlözer had been recalled to Berlin from St. Petersburg to wait for a new posting, and he and a colleague dined privately with Bismarck on the eve of the Jüterbog excursion). After describing how Berlin was still in full crisis, with 'Bismarck play-acting in all directions,' trying to bring king and the various parties together, he elaborates: They drank a great deal of champagne, 'which loosened still further a tongue loose by nature' and Bismarck in this unbuttoned mood proceeded to explain to his two subordinates just how clever he was, 'delighting in the way he is throwing dust into everybody's eyes from the king's downwards. Carefully he explained how he hoped to persuade William to accept the two-year term of service, while at the same time making all the parties believe he was really one of them: to the Upper Chamber he presented himself as a reactionary so black, he declared, that the reactionaries themselves were horrified at the lengths he pretended he was prepared to go; to the Lower House he showed himself now very rigid, now as a man honestly in search of compromise; while to the German states he put it about that the king had the utmost difficulty in restraining his "Cavourism." '[6]

* * *

Bismarck had deployed his talents as a deceiver and got as far as he could with them. Almost at once he discovered that there was no moving the king on the three-year military service issue, and he was now, willy-nilly, forced to exercise his talents as a bully—hitherto, for lack of opportunity, confined to the small world of an embassy staff. Now he had parliament and all Germany at his feet. He had gone to the trouble of sounding out a number of liberals to see if they would join his government—among them even that Karl Twesten who had fought a duel with Manteuffel. The prime objective here was to explore the possibility of splitting the opposition. But it is hard not to believe that by asking Twesten to consider serving under him Bismarck was more interested in infuriating Manteuffel than in enlarging the bases of his administration. After all, even the not very liberal but decently enlightened members of the 'New Era' government, Bernstorff as foreign minister and August von der Heydt as minister of finance, had resigned rather than offend against the Constitution. And once it was inescapably clear that the battle was to be fought out on the army estimates there was no conceivable place in the administration for any moderate.

Bismarck did not even chose the best die-hards. Apart from Roon, his government consisted of third-raters whom he could use and discard as it pleased him. Many years later the foreign minister of Baden, Franz von Roggenbach, was to say of him that it was useless for any party to try to cooperate with Bismarck and to influence him; there was nothing between outright war and total submission. The same could have been said of individuals. As he strengthened his hand Bismarck was able to tolerate a very few colleagues of outstanding ability: his general rule was to surround himself with mediocrities—at no time did he seriously try to harness brilliance to his cause or to bring on younger men. For thirty critical years in the development of Prussia and all Germany—years during which Berlin was being transformed almost behind the back of its great leader from the capital of a poor, agrarian province, into the headquarters of the dominant power in Europe, a unified German empire, its industrial might surpassing all except Britain's—Bismarck consistently prevented his fellow-Germans from developing a political sense and a breed of politicians competent to preside over the tremendous machine which the German industrialists and the German bankers had created for him to order. But why did his contemporaries let this happen?

Here he was now, at forty-seven, himself totally inexperienced in political life, though by now highly skilled in the technicalities of diplomacy, acutely aware of nationalism as a popular force, aware of the political power he could release by granting political rights to the masses (but congenitally incapable of appreciating the real meaning of nationalism and lacking the imagination to understand what was bound to happen if he gave the down-trodden workers a voice)—here he was, with nothing but himself, standing up in the Prussian parliament and laying down the law, as he was to go on laying it down for another thirty years.

For the next four years, nevertheless, he lived on the edge of extinction. Paradoxically, for his most critical initial period he was sustained by one thing and one thing only, the king's determination to secure the three-year system. If in these first weeks as prime minister Bismarck had been able to persuade William to drop his demand, as he had at first imagined he would be able to do, there would have been no further need for him and William would never have sustained him in face of the acute dislike and unease he inspired almost universally. As it was, with the king behind him, he was able to dissolve parliament when he felt like it, refuse to have anything to do with the amended budget, and rule without the consent of the Lower House.

In October he prorogued the House, which was not recalled until January of the following year, affording an interlude which gave him time to take his first curiously clumsy and uncertain steps in the making of foreign policy. The new chamber, refreshed and emboldened, faced him with an address to the crown that was in effect a denial of his right to act as he had done and an attempt to lay the foundations of constitutional government as understood in the West. In return Bismarck counter-attacked with all guns blazing. The date was 27 January 1863. It was the first fighting speech of his career as a statesman and it set the tone for the future. In language that stung he poured scorn and contumely on the perfectly reasonable demands of the parliamentarians. He denied parliament the rights it claimed. To concede them would be to grant it full and final powers. 'This Address,' he declared, 'claims to deprive the House of Hohenzollern of its constitutional rights of government and to transfer them to a majority of this House.' He went on to give a child's guide to the difference between the English and the Prussian system. 'An English ministry, whatever it may call itself, is a parliamentary one, a ministry of the majority in parliament; but we are ministers of His Majesty the King . . . you are contesting power in this country not with the ministry but with the crown.' And, after a great deal more, he wound up: 'The Prussian monarchy has not yet fulfilled its mission, it is not yet ready to serve as a mere ornamental feature of your constitutional edifice or to become a superfluous cog in the machinery of government.'[7]

This assertion of the integrity of the monarchy was Bismarck's trump-card. For how could the deputies attack him without seeming to attack their king, to whom even the most liberal were inalienably loyal, deploring only his refusal to allow them any say in the control and management of the army? But the passage which caused the most unease contained words which, looking back, may be seen as the first statement of a theme, which was to gather sinister resonance throughout the next half century: 'A statesman wise in constitutional matters has said that all constitutional life is always a series of compromises. If compromise is made impossible . . . the series of compromises is broken and is replaced by conflicts. Since the life of a state cannot stand still, conflicts become questions of power; whoever has the power in his hands then proceeds according to his will.'[8]

These words were picked up by Count Maximilian von Schwerin, an aristocrat of ancient family, a moderate Conservative, who had held a post under the king in the New Era ministry. Unfortunately he got them wrong and thus spoilt his opportunity. 'The sentence in which the speech of the Prime Minister culminated in the statement that "Might comes before Right," that "you may talk as you like, we have the power and will therefore force through our view"—this is not a sentence that can support the dynasty of Prussia in the long run. The sentence on which the greatness of our dynasty and of our country rests, and the reverence which Prussia's sovereigns have enjoyed and will enjoy for ever, is quite the reverse: "Right before Might." '[9] In fact Bismarck had not said just that—although he had clearly meant it. He was able to intervene at the end of the debate, contradicting Schwerin, and also the spirit of his own speech, by stressing the letter. In so far as might in the last resort is what counts in politics, Bismarck was enunciating a truism. But there is all the difference in the world between acknowledging a regrettable fact of life and glorying in it. As Heinrich von Sybel (then Speaker of the Committee of the Lower House, later to become the great patriotic historian of the First Reich) observed at the time: 'The ministers and the majority of this House speak different languages; their thoughts are ruled by a different logic and their actions by different moral laws.'[10] He meant Bismarck, and nobody but Bismarck.

The Schwerin episode was somehow typical and prophetic of the amateurishness of so many German liberal politicians. And it is a measure of Bismarck's success and of his effect on Germany that within a very few years Sybel himself was transformed into one of his most fervent supporters when the results of his thoughts and actions were demonstrated so triumphantly—with iron and blood.

This defiance of the reconvened House was a climacteric. The next day Bismarck sat down to give his version of it to Kathy Orlov, bewailing the tedium of parliamentary speech-making and the sad obligation to attend and listen for any point that might seem to require an answer as well as to keep his ministerial colleagues up to scratch. Of his own critically important speech he was content to observe: 'Yesterday I made a little speech to the deputies, dry and courteous, which was like a slap in the face at the very moment when they thought they had us on our knees. It was very amusing; but one wearies of these barren entertainments. They take place on a level where only quarrelsome professors or dry-as-dust lawyers are comfortable.'[11]

So much for Count Schwerin—to say nothing of a number of his gifted colleagues of all parties, condemned to oblivion by the arrival on the political scene at a most critical moment in the history of Germany of a man who begins at last to take clear shape as a Nihilist of genius.

His rise was a phenomenon unique in recent times. There have been plenty of dictators, but Bismarck was the only dictator to establish himself without any base in the country. Bonaparte found his following in the revolutionary army; Lenin commanded a secret society of conspirators which, with false promises, attracted a following just large enough to destroy the Kerensky government; Mussolini marched and counter-marched his way to power at the head of a frightening band of regimented thugs; Franco had the Spanish army at his back; Hitler was able to build up a private army and a major political party before he came to power. Bismarck had nobody but the king—the elderly monarch who distrusted him and feared him, but found him temporarily indispensable. He succeeded by persuading, cajoling, frightening, bamboozling the king into believing that he was permanently indispensable.

It was a strange weakness in this very strong character that he felt compelled to dramatize his own superiority. To his old friend Motley he wrote less than a year after coming to power, 'Here in the Landtag, while I am writing to you, I have to listen . . . to uncommonly foolish speeches delivered by uncommonly childish and excited politicians, and this gives me a few moment of involuntary leisure. . . . These chatter-boxes cannot really rule Prussia . . . they are fairly clever in a way, have a smattering of knowledge, are typical products of German university education; they know as little about politics as we knew in our student days—no, less! As far as foreign politics are concerned they are, taken individually, children; in other matters they become children as soon as they meet together *in corpore*.'[12] It did not occur to him that it was his responsibility to bring these 'children' out and lead them. Instead, he used them, deceived them, crushed them.

Self-isolated, thus, he stood up before parliament and laid down the law, exhibiting a confidence in the rightness of his own judgement unsupported by any practical experience of governing. In all Prussia he was the only man in step. And yet with all this, a man of powerful intellect, he had very few ideas. This, perhaps, is the most remarkable feature of all. Indeed, it is not too much to say that from 1851 when he went to Frankfurt, until the great victory over Austria at Königgrätz (Sadowa) in 1866, he had only a single idea: the elevation of Prussia at the expense of Austria. All other activities were subordinate to this end.

How tremendous, then, must have been the power of his personality—a combination of personal magnetism, charm, menace, rudeness, arrogance, irony, delicacy, brutality, humour, deceitfulness, and openness, of gentle candour and deepest-dyed cynicism—to overcome his isolation and to convince the world that he did not make mistakes. These qualities were underpinned, of course, by the one quality which all dictators, all the so-called great men in history, have held in common—the gambler's recklessness—the conjunction of passionate boldness and ice-cold calculation in the heat of action. It seems altogether too much that a man of such remarkable qualities should also be good, humane, far-seeing, wise: such a man, indeed, must be a god. Bismarck could look wiser than anybody in the world; he could appear far-seeing; there were moments when he managed to appear good. But he was none of these things.

CHAPTER IX

NEW MANNERS;
NEW WAYS

By the late 1850s it was obvious that the drive towards closer union among the Germans could never be reversed: the cultural, linguistic and military impulses were now powerfully reinforced by the needs of industry and trade, which turned out to be the critical factor. A fragmentation which had been tolerable in the first half of the century, when transport was limited to bad roads and inland waterways and when a vestigial sense of allegiance to Vienna, as headquarters of the ancient empire, supplied a common focus, became insupportable when the railway system swiftly developed from a matter of odd bits and pieces into an elaborate network bringing all the German states within a short day's travel from each other. When German visitors to London contemplated the handiwork of their countrymen on show at the Great Exhibition in Paxton's Crystal Palace in 1851 even the most stubborn particularist saw the absurdity of the situation which allowed no unified *German* contribution to compete on an equal footing with the exhibits of the major powers. There were in fact German exhibitors from the various German states, and at the last minute their exhibits, with some exceptions, were coordinated by the Zollverein, but the Zollverein was not a country. As Prince Chlodwig Hohenlohe-Schillingsfürst put it, no man could stand up in a foreign land and say, 'I am a German.'

Absurdity was compounded by the fact that one of the most impressive items in the whole exhibition, prophetic of the future, came from an iron-master of Essen, Alfred Krupp, who showed a miracle piece, a flawless cast-steel ingot weighing two tons: this had been heard about (it had been cast nearly four years earlier), but nobody quite believed it. Herr Krupp also showed a six-pounder field gun with an all-steel barrel. (It is an interesting fact that Krupp was driven to selling his cast-steel barrels abroad—to Russia and to Egypt—before he could interest the Prussian War Office in them.)

What was happening was the fulfillment of an important part of the dream of the brilliant economist Friedrich List, who in 1819, long before the first railways, had urged a system of internal free-trade within the German Confederation, the first beginning of the Zollverein, and in 1841 published his masterwork, *The National System of Political Economy.* List, of course, saw the way ahead too soon, like all pioneers, but life was now catching up with him. To help the German economy develop he had preached the need for protective tariffs against the outer world. But German industry was stronger now. It had come through the depression years 1847–49 and was ready to participate in the great revival of European trade stemming not only from the stabilizing influence of counter-revolutionary governments, which had learned a few lessons from the revolutionary upheaval, but also, perhaps even more, from the sudden, almost breathless expansion of global trade. The English were strengthening trade-links with an already far-flung empire; the French were opening up Algeria; the Russians penetrated to the River Amur and established bases on the Pacific, hard up against China; the Japanese were moving into the international arena after centuries of self-imposed isolation. Even more importantly, the discovery of gold in immense quantities in Australia, in the United States, and in Russia too, created vast new markets for European products, as well as injecting great sums into the European monetary system. In the words of a distinguished economic historian: 'The sudden influx of gold to Europe from the United States and Australia had consequences as significant as those that followed the Spanish exploitation of the Potosí silver-mines in the sixteenth century.'[1]

Germany in general and Prussia in particular were well-poised to benefit from this movement, which itself touched off a banking boom of a kind which might have been positively designed to favour the swift channelling of money into manufacturing industry. For the new German banks, as distinct from the old-established banking houses of the kind exemplified by the Rothschilds, were far more speculative in character than their staider forerunners in England, less interested in safeguarding their funds than in swift returns on investment. Their inspiration, indeed, was the celebrated French invention the Crédit mobilier, the special function of which was to deal in the shares of new companies—buying blocks of these and placing them with individual customers, or clients. This intimate association of banking and industry provided a new sort of dynamism, which was splendid while it lasted. Like all good things, like the railway boom in England for example, it was bound to be taken up too enthusiastically by too many people. It was bound to end in tears when pretty well every town in Germany had its own credit bank. And so it did. But not before it had given a tremendous fillip to the economic growth of Germany when it was most needed. And not before it had multiplied and fortified the solid bourgeoisie, looking to their own efforts for advancement rather than to governments and kings.

Thus, in the ten years 1850 to 1860 the German railway network almost doubled (3660 miles to 6930 miles), while coal production was nearly trebled in the six years 1851–1857 (5,800,000 tons to 14,800,000 tons).[2] Iron and steel, textiles as well, increased in proportion. And in all cases the chief beneficiary was Prussia. When Frederick the Great in 1741 had set his heart on wresting Silesia from the young Maria Theresa of Austria he knew it was a rich land, but he had no conception of the future importance of its textile industry and he had no idea of the vast extent of the great Silesian coalfields. Even when the coal began to be seriously worked towards the close of the eighteenth century there was nothing much to be done about it: Silesia was too far away. But with the growth of the railways the situation was dramatically changed. And with Silesian coal added to the coal of the Saar and the Ruhr, which had come to Prussia through the Treaty of Vienna, the Prussian economy, for long the strongest in Germany outside Austria, was now overwhelming; and the growth of Prussia made it all the more desirable for the manufactories of other states—chief among them Saxony, Bavaria, and Württemberg—to be linked by more than the ties of the Zollverein with Berlin.

The movement towards closer union, then, was gathering an irreversible momentum. It was a question of what sort of union, federal or centralized? And where would Austria fit in? And what would the rest of Europe say, what would France in particular say, to the establishment of a powerful new state in the very heart of Europe? Bismarck has been called again and again the 'regenerator of Germany.' But the regenerator of Germany was not Bismarck, it was the industrial revolution. Bismarck, after a false start, found the way to ride that wave. But to what end? And was it the only way?

* * *

The most striking features of Bismarck's first year as prime minister were the irrelevance of most of his actions, his apparent lack of understanding of the real forces at work in Prussia, in Germany, in Europe, and the manic fury with which for a time he thrashed about in a net of his own devising. The pent-up energies of a decade and more could no longer be restrained. The wild man of the old Schönhausen days was rampaging over half Europe instead of a few square miles of Pomerania. It was no wonder that so many contemporary statesmen and diplomats came to regard the new chancellor as a fantasist and joined with his enemies in Prussia in waiting for the day when he would overreach himself and fall.

Indeed, in that first year Bismarck scarcely put a foot right, and the wonder is that he did not fall, never to rise again. The moment he had dissolved his first Landtag and had time to look at his supreme interest, foreign affairs, he threw himself into the immediate realization of his *idée fixe*, the reduction of Austrian pretensions and the assertion of Prussia's equality; and he set about it by the means he had always preached, an understanding with France and perhaps an *ad hoc* alliance with France and Russia. But now it was the end of 1862, and he had failed to notice important changes in Austria, in Germany, in France, in Russia, since he had made his original analysis.

The first change was that Austria, recovering from her Italian débâcle of 1859, was once more on her feet. She was now presenting herself, not unplausibly, as a seat of enlightenment and progress, dazzling the eyes of German liberals with her movement towards constitutionalism. This would not last, but it made a powerful impression at the time. After the humiliation of Magenta and Solferino, the emperor Francis Joseph had digested his lesson: autocracy was no longer enough. Even under the harsh rule of Schwarzenberg more than a decade earlier, Austria had moved far away from feudalism, the last traces of serfdom being abolished and the hereditary nobility pushed aside in favour of the quasi-Jacobin dictatorship of Schwarzenberg himself acting in the young emperor's name. With Schwarzenberg prematurely dead, the too-young emperor had tried to be his own dictator and come to grief at the hands of incompetent ministers whom he did not know how to control and inferior generals whom he did not know how to dismiss. Now, bitterly defeated at the head of his own army by the upstart Napoleon III, he decided that the time called for at least the appearance of constitutional rule, and the upshot, known as the February Patent of 1861, gave the new Austrian parliament a far stronger voice than was enjoyed by the Prussian Landtag. This new look in Vienna was enough to make a very considerable appeal to the liberals in the German states, setting up a counter-attraction to Prussia and promising a new life to the Confederation which Austria was now by every means seeking to revive.

Another change was that Napoleon was no longer, as it were, immediately looking for trouble, or even for a pretext for pushing his frontiers up to the Rhine. The Crimean War and the war with Austria for the liberation of Italy had given him all the glory he needed for the time being and (again for the time being) he was no longer the restless head of an unsettled power who might be conveniently hard-pressed to any nationalist cause.

The third change was that the warmth had gone out of the Franco-Russian *rapprochement*, the idea of which had been central to Bismarck's thinking. Here, he had argued, were two unsatisfied powers thirsting for a re-drawing of the frontiers of Europe. But while Napoleon had done enough for the time being to wipe out the humiliation of his uncle's final catastrophe, so Alexander II in Russia was far too busy with the consequences of his first great reform, the emancipation of the serfs in 1861, and preparations for others (the reforms of the army and the judiciary), to pursue an active foreign policy (again for the time being). In any case, he had only one obsessive aim: to erase that article of the Treaty of Paris which forbade Russian ships the freedom of the Straits, bottling up the Russian fleet in the Black Sea.

Bismarck showed one other failure of perception. He badly misjudged England. Of course he knew that England had a particular interest in the Mediterranean and the Aegean, that French and Russian policies were affected by this interest; but he was never to appreciate the degree of the tension thus engendered. One result of this short-sightedness, which was shared to a much lesser degree by the Austrian Foreign Ministry, was that he did not see Russia and France quite so clearly as he thought he did: he did not appreciate the multifold consequences of the strained preoccupation of those two powers with Britain. More obviously, he did not understand how London saw first Prussia, then the new German Reich. He could not penetrate his own suspicion of English interference in Prussia's internal affairs through the crown princess, and, indeed, the whole Coburg clan, now headed by Queen Victoria's second son, Alfred Ernest Albert (duke of Edinburgh until he surrendered his title to become duke of Saxe-Coburg-Gotha). Instead of exploiting the crown prince and his English

145

wife to Prussia's advantage, he set his face against them. Perhaps he never quite got over his failure to engage the interest of Palmerston and Russell on his swift visit to London in the summer of 1862. 'The English ministers know less about Prussia than about Japan or Mongolia, and they are no cleverer than ours,' he had then written to Johanna.[3] But what, until he himself was in the saddle, was there in Prussia worthy of an English minister's detailed attention?

Blinkered, thus, by his own preconceptions Bismarck threw himself head-long into the task of swiftly achieving what he had dreamt of for so long: he believed, moreover, that the best guarantee of his own future would be a brilliant performance in the international arena. But it was not to be. He continued to irritate, amuse, or alienate the world by his restless changes of front and his extraordinary lack of discretion. Now he was playing fast and loose with Austria, so that after some months Count Alois Károlyi, the Austrian minister in Berlin, could report that he found it 'truly astonishing with what rapidity Herr von Bismarck goes from one extreme to another diametrically opposed.'[4]

Thus, in Paris in October, believing that he had secured from Napoleon assurances of neutrality in the event of conflict with Austria, he had immediately started to put pressure on Prince Richard Metternich, the Austrian ambassador to France. He thought it desirable, he announced to this startled envoy, to make it clear that his purpose was the establishment of Prussian leadership in northern Germany. He hoped to achieve this purpose in close accord with Austria, but if Austria opposed him he would treat her as a hostile foreign power.[5] A little later, back in Berlin, he summoned the Austrian ambassador, Count Károlyi, ostensibly to complain against the persistent hostility of the Austrian press, in fact to elaborate on his message to Metternich junior. It was now that he made the ominous suggestion, which was also a threat, that Austria would do well to forget about Germany and, looking east, base her centre of gravity on Hungary. Then Prussia and Austria could happily and profitably unite in a 'firm alliance.' Prussia would unconditionally support Austria in her remaining Italian interests and (recklessly foreshadowing the catastrophic guarantees of his successors on the eve on the 1914 war) in eastern Europe too. At the very least he expected Austria to stand by while Prussia used strong-arm methods to bring her unfortunately placed neighbours, Hanover and Electoral Hesse under her control.[6]

Károlyi was very cool. Reporting to Vienna, he suggested that the threat of war was 'highly speculative,'[7] but he was quite sure that Bismarck meant what he said about Hanover and Hesse.

He did indeed. And now, with Austria going ahead with her latest plan for the reform of the Confederation and looking forward with some confidence to a majority vote in the Diet, he went so far as to prepare for war and ask France what she would do 'if things heated up in Germany.' And Bismarck was dashed, though he did not show it, when he was told by the French ambassador, Baron Charles de Talleyrand-Périgord, that if the conflict was localized, the emperor would simply look on, but that if the Confederation itself was threatened, with a consequent shift in the balance of Europe, then he would 'seek that combination offering the best guarantee of the security of the state and the peace of Europe.'[8] That was in December 1862.

Almost immediately afterwards there was another setback. Once more forcing the pace, Bismarck asked France for a formal declaration that she would refrain from entering into separate trade treaties with any state in the Zollverein other than Prussia: Prussia was to control the European trade of all the lesser members. Not unnaturally this preposterous demand was rejected. And it was this double rebuff that drove Bismarck to make new overtures to Austria, but always alternating his blandishments with menaces in bewildering confusion. Prussia needed Austria and Austria needed Prussia, he urged; no, Prussia did not need Austria at all—she was wholly self-contained, could look after herself and grow, whereas Austria had made enemies of half Europe; surely emperor and king should get together to defend legitimacy in face of imminent revolution? On the other hand, Austria had better look out: old, decaying powers were threatened by revolutionary forces which Prussia knew how to harness.[9] And, indeed, he was soon to show that the king of Prussia's first minister was not at all above calling Hungarian and Polish revolutionaries in aid against the emperor of Austria.[10]

Nobody took him seriously enough. From the Austrian point of view the tragedy was a division of power in Vienna between the new imperial chancellor, Ritter Anton von Schmerling, a strong man who was determined to keep Prussia in her place but knew enough to respect her, and Count Johann von Rechberg, as foreign minister. Rechberg knew a great deal about Bismarck, but still thought of him as a diplomatic tyro, to be patronized: 'If Bismarck had had a proper diplomatic training, he would be one of the first of German statesmen, if not *the* first. . . . He is courageous, resolute, and ambitious, but incapable of sacrificing a prejudice or a party view to any higher consideration. He has no real political sense; he is a party man in the strictest sense of the word.'[11] It is impossible to imagine a more fumbling or muddled judgement from an intelligent diplomat who had faced Bismarck time and time again across the table in Frankfurt.

Too often the mistakes of great historical success figures are forgotten or brushed aside by historians as irrelevant, just as the successes of the losing side are also forgotten. To attempt to restore the balance is to risk being accused of sentimentality. It is nothing of the kind. Leaving on one side the very large and fascinating question of the might-have-beens of history, or the spectacular consequences of quite trivial accidents, it is impossible to understand what a man was really made of, even to appreciate his virtues, unless due regard is paid to his mistakes. Thus, for example, Bismarck's odd behaviour in Berlin and Potsdam in 1848 tells us a great deal about his impulsiveness, a quality which in his successful actions gave an extra and almost irresistible acceleration, like the reheat of a jet engine, to his more obvious boldness: he could move very fast indeed, although by no means invariably in the right direction.

One of the most dangerous mistakes of his life came very near to putting an end to his career even while he was still busy threatening Austria in the matter of the Frankfurt vote (which, as it turned out, ended in a narrow defeat for Austria, thus enabling him to defer his promised action of forming a German parliament as a 'counterweight' to the Diet of the Confederation). Since 1861 the cause of Polish nationalism had been building up a new head of steam in Russian Poland, which had been relatively quiescent since the bloody failure of the 1830 uprising—a disaster in memory of which many Polish women of gentle birth still went about demonstratively in mourning. Bismarck had been in St. Petersburg when the trouble started. With a characteristic mixture of apprehension, irritation, and contempt he had been watching the efforts of the Russian liberals, headed by the tsar's younger brother, the grand duke Constantine, to win the loyalty of the tsar's Polish subjects by ameliorating the rigidities and harshnesses of Russian rule. It was with satisfaction that he saw these efforts rejected in a wave of contumely and bitter violence that broke the heart of the decent old Field-Marshal Gorchakov (cousin of the foreign minister, and uncle of the novelist Leo Tolstoy) and led to the installation of General Sukhozanet, a martinet of the first order, as his successor. Sukhozanet placed the

Otto von Bismarck at
the age of eleven. Drawing
by Franz Krueger

Schönhausen, the Bismarck
family estate

Johanna von Puttkamer,
Bismarck's wife.
Portrait by J. Becker

Princess Katharina Orlova

Bismarck in 1863

Frederick III as Crown Prince,
with his wife Victoria, daughter of
Queen Victoria of England

King Frederick William IV of
Prussia, photographed in 1855

Albrecht von Roon

Helmut von Moltke

Napoleon III, Emperor of France. Portrait by J. H. Flandrin

The meeting of Bismarck
and Napoleon III after
the Battle of Sedan.
Mural by Carl Sellmer

Francis Joseph I,
Emperor of Austria.
Portrait by
Philip de László

The morning after Königgrätz: All that was left of a battery of the
Austrian Army Reserve Artillery. Painting by Rudolf von Ottenfeld

country under martial law, ruling by terror, and inflicting brutalities on women and children as well as men.

That was in 1861, and Bismarck, writing to his sister (in that same letter in which he unconvincingly announced his renunciation of all ambition), commented as follows: 'Hammer the Poles until they wish they were dead; of course I'm sorry for them, but if we want to exist we have no choice but to wipe them out: wolves are only what God made them, but we shoot them all the same when we can get at them.'[12] More officially, he wrote to Bernstorff a little later: 'Every success of the Polish national movement is a defeat for Prussia; we cannot carry on the fight against this element in accordance with the rules of civil justice, but only in accordance with the rules of war.'[13]

It is impossible to understand Bismarck, Prussia, and therefore Germany without keeping Poland firmly in view. To most English-speaking historians 'a far-away country of which they know little' (to paraphrase the disastrous words of a British prime minister speaking of Czechoslovakia in 1938), to Bismarck its reconstitution as an independent state was an ever present menace, indeed, a problem more immediate for him than the Austrian one. It occupies so small a space in his biographies only because he did not write and talk about it much, but it occupied a large space in his mind. He did not write and talk about it much because the king and all the conservatives felt as he did: he did not have to argue or persuade.

This hostility towards Poland, exaggerated almost to the point of insanity, was a product of Prussian history. It played a large part in the shaping of the Prussian state and also the Prussian mentality, and thus, in later years, in distorting the orientation of the *German* state and the *German* mentality, to which, by then, it should have been peripheral. Germany had no obvious frontiers in the north-east. Teutonic knights had fought interminably over the barren heaths and the forest lands and marshes that later formed part of the mighty kingdom of Poland. The western and southern German lands, fragmented as they were, made at least some cohesive sense, looking to the Catholic emperor in Vienna. But the Protestant north looked east into the unconquered wilderness, and the piecemeal absorption by the Hohenzollerns of all the lands up to Königsberg provided no political cohesion except the crown itself.

After the three partitions of Poland in the eighteenth century those frontiers seemed secure. Catherine II of Russia took her share partly to subdue a tiresome neighbour, mainly out of greed; Austria took her share reluctantly as far as Maria Theresa was concerned (she saw no good coming out of the sort of dynastic banditry from which she herself had suffered at the hands of Frederick the Great, but submitted to the ambition of her son the Emperor Joseph II); Frederick himself took his share for the aggrandizement of his kingdom and the securing of more distant frontiers.

Bismarck knew the Poles. He knew their language and urged the crown prince to learn it too. He knew the Polish peasants of East Prussia and liked them; he knew the Polish nobles and bourgeoisie and feared them: in his eyes they were Slav barbarians got up in a parody of Western elegance and irredeemably corrupted by revolutionary intellectuals. He applauded Nicholas I of Russia, who had ruthlessly crushed his Poles in 1831. He was highly suspicious of Alexander II, the reforming tsar, the tsar liberator, who, not content with abolishing serfdom, was treating the Poles too kindly, having replaced the tyrant Sukhozanet with his brother, the grand duke Constantine. He had no words for the Austrians, who treated the Poles of Cracow and Galicia very kindly indeed, having won over their mobility by allowing them to oppress their own peasants (Little Russians and Ruthenians more than Poles) and enter into the government and the highest society of Vienna.

Thus it was when in February 1863 the people of Russian Poland rose and stormed Constantine's palace, killing his chief of staff, and Alexander felt at last compelled to hit back hard, Bismarck, thinking very fast but not very deep, saw what he took to be his chance to put Russia under an obligation and at the same time repay the French for their recent coolness. For Napoleon, as befitted a monarch who put himself forward as the champion of small nations, the prophet of self-determination, was driven to throw away his growing *rapprochement* with Russia by protesting vehemently against the Russian action. In this he was joined by England. There was wild talk of war. Bismarck promptly seized the opportunity to show his solidarity with Russia and assert himself against France. He mobilized four army corps and dispatched an emissary to St. Petersburg, General Gustav von Alvensleben, a member of the military cabinet. His task was to offer joint action. Alexander, who was in despair over the need to fight the Poles whom he had hoped to appease by withdrawing Sukhozanet, did not want any joint action, but neither did he wish to offend the king of Prussia, his uncle. The result was the signing on 8 February of the notorious Alvensleben Convention, a treaty worthy of an age less hemmed about by scruple than the mid-nineteenth century (indeed, a little more than seventy years ahead of its time), which stipulated that Prussia would hand over to the Russians any Polish rebels who took refuge on her territory.

Instead of pleasing Russia, all Bismarck succeeded in doing was to irritate Gorchakov and divert Western anger and disgust from St. Petersburg to Berlin. More than this, he saved Napoleon from the necessity of challenging Russia too sharply and gave him the chance to turn the righteous indignation of the French against Prussia, an easier target by far. Finally, Austria, partly in pursuance of her wooing of the German liberals, partly tempted by the mirage of a re-creation of the Crimean coalition which would keep Russia in her place and neutralize Prussia, rather feebly put her name to a joint protest to Berlin.

For a moment Bismarck was terribly exposed. Himself isolated in his own parliament, he had now succeeded in isolating Prussia in Europe. He was reduced to pretending that the convention did not in fact exist because it had not been ratified. The tsar was not impressed by this performance. It was widely expected that Bismarck would resign. But he did not resign. Neither France nor England had any intention of going to war with Russia, and by Easter the tsar was ready to offer the Poles an amnesty if they laid down their arms. They replied that they could not trust the honour of a Russian tsar; savage guerrilla fighting dragged on for another year. By the time it was all over, the minds of Bismarck and of everybody else in the West were elsewhere. King William, who had been appalled to find Prussia the target of universal loathing, had said in effect to his new chancellor, You got us into this mess, now you can get us out again.

It was England who managed this for him, by re-directing the condemnation towards Russia, where it was most deserved. And when the balance sheet of the crisis was drawn up it was found that Prussia had come out of it a good deal better than she could have expected. The Franco-Russian *rapprochement* was in ruins; Francis Joseph of Austria, for the second time, had profoundly offended a Russian tsar, and this time the rift was final. Bismarck's nightmare of a Russian-Austrian-French coalition was exorcised. Further, although Russia had been irritated by Bismarck, the fact remained that for the moment he was her only friend. This meant that if all went well Prussia could count on Russian neutrality in the event of war with Austria or France. To his powers of persuasion and deception, to his immense self-confidence and force of character, to his iron fist, Bismarck now added the supreme quality of luck: he was one of the elect for whom the gods labour by turning their defeats into victories, their errors into master-strokes. He himself, of course, never admitted error.

There was one other aspect of his Polish witch-hunt. Since 1848 Prussian liberals had in a fairly half-hearted way taken up the cause of the Poles, rather sickened by their fate at the hands of the Russians, yet not unnaturally afraid of advocating their liberation. By turning his most brutal face towards them Bismarck hoped to goad the liberal Opposition into indiscretion: this would irritate the king into backing his difficult prime minister at a moment when his faith in him had reached a very low level.

It had been a narrow squeak, but nothing could dent that self-confidence. Bismarck had been in office for barely six months, in constant conflict with the opposition and variously at odds with the sole source of his authority, the king. The parliamentary row about the army estimates dragged on. At every vote the opposition grew stronger. There came a time when it embraced virtually the whole of parliament. On one occasion in May the vote against a ministerial proposal was 295 to 5. Virtually the entire House was protesting against a flagrant infringement of its right to interpellate a minister. This meant that Bismarck had made himself effectively dictator. On 27 May he dissolved the House once more and on 1 June proclaimed his notorious Press Decree, banning all publications calculated to bring crown, state or church into disrepute. He had already started ridding the civil service of all known supporters of the parliamentary opposition, promoting Count Friedrich zu Eulenburg to be an obedient minister of the interior, who at once made it clear that the first duty of all officials was unconditional and unquestioning support of the crown—i.e., Bismarck. He had tried in vain to introduce the concept of political loyalty into the judiciary. In later years he more than once insisted that nothing could be further from the truth than to think of him as a reactionary. For example, to the Hungarian Count Seher-Toss he explained that he had been play-acting: 'At court the king was for ever being told that I was a democrat in disguise. I could win his complete trust only by showing him that I was not afraid of the Chamber.'[14] Obviously he exaggerated his Junkerdom at times, but the chief reason for this was to conceal from conservatives that he was not one of them but a revolutionary—the revolutionary leader of a revolutionary party of one. It may have been useful for him to show the king how boldly he defied the chamber, but he would have defied it anyway. What he was doing was getting his own way, and his own way could be devious as well as blunt.

An outstanding example of his flexibility, his deviousness, his carelessness of principle, is offered by his very secret dealings with the brilliant and flamboyant Socialist leader, Ferdinand Lassalle. In May 1863, Lassalle had founded the General German Worker's Association together with Karl Marx (who soon turned his back on it). All through the spring and summer of that year the new prime minister, the first servant of the Prussian king, received him privately to pick his brains, to plan ways and means of using his attraction for the workers in his campaign to split the liberals (above all to destroy the Progressives). Universal suffrage, said Lassalle, was the answer: the workers would swamp the bourgeois liberals, who profited by the existing electoral system. Failing that, a *coup d'état*. He was seeking to use Bismarck as Bismarck was seeking to use him. Their conversations continued while all the time Bismarck was assailing in his public speeches as well as his police measures everything Lassalle stood for . . . until, in August, they parted for ever. Each had been fascinated by the other: adventurer spoke to adventurer; Lassalle succumbed to the magnetic attraction of power, while Bismarck was attracted by Lassalle's so enviable irresponsibility. (Before a year had gone by Lassalle was dead, killed in his duel with the husband of Helene von Dönniges; and that was that.)

In 1862 the liberal press in Prussia reflected the composition of the Landtag. It has been estimated that it ran off 250,000 copies of various papers a day, with a readership of one and a quarter million, while the conservative press could only manage 40,000 with a readership of 200,-000. This included the celebrated *Kreuzzeitung*, edited by one of Bismarck's early supporters, Hermann Wagener. Although bribery and corruption in those early days reached nothing like the wonderful scale achieved when Bismarck had won his second war and had laid his hands on the private fortunes of the king of Hanover, he made a useful beginning by purchasing in secret a very serious paper, the *Norddeutsche Allgemeine Zeitung*, founded in 1861, which was to become his chief organ and increase its circulation simply by virtue of the news it got from him and the brilliance of the articles which he either corrected or himself dictated.

The most interesting fact about this newspaper, and one which helps a little to explain Bismarck's rather imperceptibly poor opinion of the human race, was that its editor, August Brass, had been a prominent revolutionary in 1848.[15] Now, returned from exile, Brass was happy to allow his left-wing newspaper to be secretly subverted, even though his most distinguished colleague, Wilhelm Liebknecht, already embarked on a lifetime of revolutionary struggle, exile, and prison, resigned in disgust when he discovered the source of his editor's new-found affluence. Already at Frankfurt Bismarck had shown a lively awareness of the advantages of buying journalists on behalf of his government (the eagerness of all too many to make a sale was an invitation to contempt) as well as a swift mastery of the requisite techniques. But Brass of the *Norddeutsche Allgemeine Zeitung* was his first personal capture; and although in later years, when he had much more money at his disposal, he was to spread his network of corruption far and wide, Brass and his paper were to remain his chief instruments for disseminating deliberate leaks, slanders, lies, and for whipping up a fever of hatred, exploiting the basest emotions when required for whatever purposes—a process so innocently documented in his memoirs by the great man's own press officer, Moritz Busch, who had no idea that his own sycophancy, Brass's venality, and their master's corrupt exploitation of their corruptibility was in anything but the very best of taste.

Even so, Brass and his paper in 1863 were inadequate as an answer to the overwhelmingly liberal press. Bismarck was not the sort of man to put up with public criticism: if as minister-president he could not silence the opposition, what was the use of being minister-president? He proposed one shabby expedient after another designed to suppress the free expression of opinion without introducing formal government censorship, only to listen with scarcely comprehending impatience to the careful explanations of his by no means over-scrupulous colleagues as they earnestly sought to convey to their difficult master that there must be limits not only to unconstitutional behaviour but also to plain crookedness. What was the good of being minister-president if your subordinates, who owed you their careers, would not let you do as you liked? What indeed? . . . But for a time he contented himself with Brass and with dispensing large sums from the public purse for the promotion and expansion of local party newspapers.

The Press Decree of 1 June was a catch-all device on a grand scale. It exploited a section of the Press Law of 1851 which, in spite of the formal abolition of censorship under the new Constitution, gave the government of Prussia extraordinary powers. It could confiscate and impose heavy fines for incitement to hatred and contempt, for slander, for publishing false information (a fairly fine-meshed net); more, it could legislate for any other restrictions that might come into its head. What came into Bismarck's head was to introduce a new statute under which a newspaper could be banned not simply for printing a specific article which might be regarded as offensive but also for exhibiting a 'general attitude' that might be held to jeopardize the public welfare. This was blanket censorship by another name, without even the bureaucratic safeguard of an official censor's department.

The king did not like it. Just as in his innocence William was capable of breaching the Constitution while believing that he upheld it, so now, no less innocently, he thought the new law he was required to sanction clearly offended against the spirit of the Constitution. Bismarck managed to persuade him he was wrong, and William put his signature to it rather unhappily, convinced by his difficult mentor that this was a necessary act to check the corruption of the politically naïve by evilly disposed revolutionaries. . . . Bismarck had won yet again.

It was an expensive victory for Prussia and all Germany. Its most immediate consequence was to confirm the breach between Bismarck and the crown prince, Frederick. Frederick and his English wife, Victoria Louise, stand high among those losers to whom history is unkind for no other reason than that they lost. In their lifetime the object of Bismarck's most unscrupulous intrigues and slanders, after death they have been commonly written off as ineffectual. But Vicky, the eldest and favourite daughter of Queen Victoria and Albert, was very far from ineffectual. Given his chosen line of policy, Bismarck was right to fear her; but had he so decided, he could have used this royal marriage as a means for establishing a lasting bond with England which might well have changed the course of history. He did not so choose. Without understanding England, and without knowing why, he felt inferior and uneasy, as it were, in her presence. In spite of her all too obvious weaknesses and follies, England had achieved and maintained a position of grandeur out of all proportion to her size. Her diplomatists were widely believed to be the cleverest and most devious in the world, and this little fact alone was enough to fill with bafflement the heart of a man who was quite deliberately setting out to surpass all others in cleverness and deviousness. The English were superior, obviously, and so was he, Otto von Bismarck-Schönhausen: but the English made light of their superiority, or denied it, while he, Bismarck, rarely stopped boasting about his—a mark of inferiority which he must have at least dimly perceived. He was not his best with Victoria Louise.

It is not necessary to document her detestation of Bismarck. Her letters to her mother are full of his corrupting influence on the king, his hostility towards the crown prince, and the consequent harm done to Germany.[16] But it was not an unreasoning hatred. Even as late as 1887, after twenty-five years of unremitting persecution, she could write: 'He has done very grand things and has unequalled power and unrivalled strength at this moment. Oh, if they were but used for the good cause, always one would be ready to admire and to bless him. He has made Germany great, but not loved; neither has he developed her immense resources for good. Despotism is the essence of his being.'[17] 'That wretched B,' Vicky had written furiously in what she would one day look back upon as the carefree days of the early 1860s, 'will not stop his mad career until he has plunged his king into ruin and his country into the most dangerous difficulties.'[18]

How often prophets are nearly right. William was to live and reign for another twenty-six years, with Bismarck leading him as one leads a nervous horse, and to die with honour, imperial head of a united Germany. But in the sense that he was corrupted, Bismarck had ruined him. He had ruined the life of the crown prince. But in the end he himself was destroyed, and through the manner of his destruction Vicky had her posthumous revenge; for he was destroyed by her own son, the emperor William II, whom he had set against his mother and encouraged in his excesses, and who went on to destroy the Germany that Bismarck had created. So ruin came, rather later than Vicky had foreseen, and rather more tortuously, but for the reason she gave: the character of Bismarck.

As already observed, it was the Press Law which formalized the breach between minister and crown prince. In the late spring of 1863 Frederick had repeatedly complained in private and in the State Council about Bismarck's high-handed and unconstitutional ways, and been ignored. But on 5 June he made his public bid. He was angered by the publication of the Press Decree in his absence.

In Danzig to attend a military review he learned something of the strength of popular opposition to his father's new minister-president. The mayor of Danzig stood up to welcome his Royal Highness and, greatly daring, explained that he would have found the ancient city a great deal more en fête but for the gloom cast by the Press Decree. Frederick responded. He announced that he had no part in that government decision and publicly deplored it.

That night he wrote in his diary: 'I have openly acknowledged myself an opponent of Bismarck and his disastrous theories and thereby shown to the world that I have not accepted or indeed agreed with his policy.'[19]

Frederick's stand caused a major sensation. Here were father and son at loggerheads in the grand Hohenzollern manner. (The young Frederick the Great, it was remembered, had been imprisoned by his father for less than this, and his friend Katte executed before his eyes—though anyone less like Frederick II than his kindly, large, blond, comfortably uxorious great-great-grand-nephew it would be hard to imagine.) Edwin von Manteuffel as the king's chief military adviser, at once argued the importance of publicly demonstrating that the officer's code of loyalty must apply no less to an heir to the throne than to the most humble ensign; and he welcomed the opportunity to give Frederick's liberalism a knock-out blow. The crown prince had disobeyed his commanding officer, the king, and must be punished in the prescribed manner: he must be court-martialled and imprisoned. The daughter of Queen Victoria looked on aghast as she saw her husband on the verge of being steam-rollered by everything in the Prussian system and character which seemed to her (and him) most idiotic, ludicrous, and vicious: the code of the cadet barracks, the popping eyes, the rigid, elbow-straining salute, the clicking heels, the sabre slashes on the cheek, colonels who behaved like sergeant-majors, and sergeant-majors who behaved like gods. . . .

It was Bismarck who stopped that particular nonsense. He would have liked nothing better than to have seen Frederick confined to a fortress for life and Vicky sent home to her mother. But, as usual, he saw farther than his nose. He did not want a royal martyr as a rallying point for all the Liberals in the land, and he was pretty sure that Frederick, having protested in vain, would soon quieten down. So he urged William to be lenient and content himself with a formal reprimand.

From now on the battle-lines were drawn, but from now on Bismarck had the upper hand. The moment was coming near when he would be able to exploit his power to some purpose.

CHAPTER X

SERVANT INTO MASTER

Paradoxically, it was an Austrian initiative that gave Bismarck his first great chance. Francis Joseph in Vienna, aware that time was running out, and determined to make the most of Austria's revived authority while Prussia floundered in the shallows of her own internal crisis, decided to make a supreme bid to reassert his leadership of a reinvigorated Confederation. The only thing to do, he thought, was to forget about popular movements and deliberately rally the German princes: if they would formally declare themselves for a revised Confederation under Austrian presidency he could see to it that the king of Prussia was kept in a perpetual minority.

It was important that William should not be given longer than was absolutely necessary to ponder the matter. Accordingly, at the beginning of August, Francis Joseph in person approached him while he was taking the waters in Bad Gastein, on Austrian soil, confiding to his much older brother-monarch his decision to invite all the German kings and princes to a special congress in Frankfurt a fortnight later. He counted on William to lend his dignity, his prestige, his seniority to the occasion. William was flattered. He half-promised to attend, but asked for time to think it over.

Bismarck was also at Gastein. After the unsettling events of the past three months he was sticking as close to his master as he decently could, not pushing himself into the foreground, but ever watchful in the shadows. While he waited and enjoyed the fine mountain air and the everlasting murmur of rushing waters, he knew that there was something in the wind, but not just what it was. On 2 August he found out. 'At Gastein on 2 August 1863,' he wrote many years later, 'I was sitting under the fir-trees in the Schwarzenberg Gardens above the deep gorge of the River Ache. Over my head a pair of tom-tits had made their nest, and I sat there with my watch in my hand to discover how many times each minute the parent birds brought a caterpillar or some other grub to their nestlings. While contemplating the useful activity of these little creatures I noticed that on the far side of the gorge, on the Schillerplatz, King William was sitting by himself on a bench. When it was time to get ready to dress for dinner with the king I went back to my lodgings and there found a note from His Majesty saying that he would wait for me on the Schillerplatz because he wished to speak to me about his meeting with the emperor. I hurried as fast as I could, but by the time I reached the king's apartments a conversation had already taken place between the two sovereigns. If I had spent a little less time observing nature and seen the king sooner, then perhaps the first impression made on His Majesty by the emperor might have been rather different.'[1]

And if Bismarck had told us how many times a minute the tits carried food to their late-summer brood we might hve been more inclined to see in this pretty little idyll more than a calculated softener for the rough stuff to come. For even on Bismarck's own showing, it was very rough indeed. Poor William was chivvied, coaxed, harangued, brow-beaten, battered into declining the emperor's invitation.

The process started that evening: was it conceivable that His Majesty had not understood the deliberate insult offered by the emperor in issuing his invitation at such short notice? Bismarck thought he had won his master over, but he could not be sure. He decided to stick closely to him, accompanying him a few days later on the long mountain journey across Austria to Baden-Baden deep in the Black Forest. There, William was to stay with his son-in-law and daughter, visiting his sister-in-law the Dowager Queen Elisabeth at Wildbad on the way. Elisabeth at first insisted that the king must accept as a gesture of solidarity with his fellow-princes. Bismarck took her to one side and quietly threatened her with that heavy courtesy of which he was a master: if the king accepted the invitation, very well, he, Bismarck, would dutifully accompany him to Frankfurt and see to his business, but when he returned to Berlin it would not be as minister.

Elisabeth prudently reversed her attitude. But worse was to come. To Baden-Baden, even while his fellow-princes were assembling with their retinues at Frankfurt, came King John of Saxony, an admired, respected friend of William's. He presented himself as the emissary of the emperor and all the German rulers to beg William to reconsider.

'My master found it hard to resist this move,' wrote Bismarck. Over and over again he repeated, as though hypnotized: 'Thirty reigning princes and a king as their courier!'[2] How could he resist this stupendous honour? But Bismarck stuck it out. He was determined at all costs that the ascendancy over his king he had half secured at Babelsberg less than a year before, and strengthened in the aftermath of the crisis over Poland and the rebellion of the crown prince, should be finally confirmed. He argued interminably, using all his marvellous powers of persuasion. The king, wearied to the point of exhaustion, torn between his dynastic instincts, his appreciation of the unparalleled gifts of his new chancellor, and his profound distaste for Bismarck's methods, lay on a sofa. As always, the argument that told in the end was the fate of his beloved army. Here we are, said Bismarck in effect, in the middle of a stubborn fight between Your Majesty and parliament for control of the army, the army of Prussia, the army of Frederick the Great—and Your Majesty would see that whole army degraded, his historic regiments thrown into the common pool with the rag-tag from all over Germany and under the control of a committee! On and on he hammered until, just before eleven o'clock, the king burst into tears and gave in. Bismarck, himself, hurrying off to impart the news to Count Beust, the Saxon minister in attendance on his king, was so worked up that he slammed the door behind him, pulling off the handle in an access of nervous violence. Later, when he reached his own apartments, he picked up a glass jug and hurled it to the floor.

He had already come very near to smashing poor Count Beust, from whose memoirs we hear for the first time the authentic tones of a Bismarck not trying to charm his monarch or a foreign diplomat, but in a choking rage:

'You have come to ruin us!' were his first words. 'You will not succeed!'

He then went on to deliver his master's formal note of refusal to King John.

In that case, Beust replied, King John would wish everyone to have time to think again. He, Beust, would take it upon himself to cancel the special train standing by to carry his master back to Frankfurt.

Bismarck exploded: 'I swear to you that if the special train with King John has not left by six tomorrow morning, then by eight o'clock a Prussian batallion will move into Baden from Rastatt, and before my king is out of bed, King John's house will be surrounded by troops with only one order—that no Saxon is to be admitted.'

Beust, hardly believing his ears, nevertheless responded quickly: Prussia, he said, had no right to march troops into Baden in peacetime: such an action would be a direct breach of Confederal law, a breach of the peace. To which Bismarck replied: 'Breaches of law and the peace are matters of perfect indifference to me. All I care for is the well-being of my king and my country. Today you have made him quite ill. Tomorrow he must have rest.'[3]

To this extraordinary outburst was added another, when he told another member of King John's suite, Prince Kraft zu Hohenlohe-Ingelfingen, an artillery officer of distinction, that if King William had decided to go to Frankfurt he, Bismarck, would have gone with him as his amanuensis, but not as his first minister. And never again would he have set foot on Prussian soil, for he would have known that King William had been guilty of high treason, so sure was he that this step would led to Prussia's ruin.[4]

The whole of Bismarck's character is in these interviews. The passionate and overbearing wrestling to subdue the king to his will, and the nervous hysteria that ended in the pulling of handles off doors and the smashing of glass figure in every biography and tell us a great deal about the man. But the interviews with Beust and Hohenlohe tell us a great deal more. Regardless of the rights and wrongs of the quarrel with Austria, what sort of a man is it who will implicitly accuse his king of being on the verge of committing high treason (against himself? against the state?) because he will not do as his chief minister tells him? And what sort of a man is it who would take it upon himself to call up troops to invade a friendly principality in order to prevent one well-disposed monarch from appealing to another? The events of this single evening, the evening of 16 August 1863, are sufficient to make redundant, indeed absurd, a great deal of the unending debate about the character and motives of Bismarck.

He had broken the will of the king, and besides smashing glass, he had smashed the Confederation for ever. He had also ensured that in any sharp conflict with Vienna King John in Dresden would certainly be on the side of Austria. Bismarck had had his triumph. He was master of Prussia, but a Prussia dangerously isolated, at odds with the rest of Germany, and bitterly divided against herself. In fact by smashing the Confederation he had cleared the ground for Prussia's primacy; but it did not look like that at the time. The Congress of Princes made a tremendous show. All Europe was impressed by the revival of Austria's fortunes and her apparently effortless resumption of her authority. Prussia was in the shadows. Queen Victoria happened to be staying with the Coburgs, and Francis Joseph on his way back to Vienna from Frankfurt took his opportunity to wait upon her. She was deeply perturbed and allowed herself to protest at the apparent snubbing of Prussia. Was not Vienna pushing Berlin too hard? She hoped very much that 'there was no disposition to lower Prussia.' Francis Joseph assured her there was nothing of the kind, 'no one dreams in Germany of lowering Prussia, which was an impossibility, but that, at Berlin, great pretensions were raised. . . .'[5]

Francis Joseph, on the face of it, the hero of the hour, was perhaps the only man beside Bismarck to realize the extent of his defeat: the Congress without Prussia had no meaning. Behind his cool exterior, behind the reserve that fatally forbade him to explain himself even when invited by the English queen to do so, he was in a turmoil of frustration. Without knowing which way Berlin was going to jump, even the most pro-Austrian princes refused to commit themselves. 'All the time,' the young emperor wrote to his mother, 'we had to struggle with suspicion, cowardice and bottomless stupidity, so that our nerves were stretched to the breaking point.'[6]

He would have been grimly amused to know that Bismarck too was feeling close to desperation—drained of energy, master of his king but only by fighting every inch of the way and thus denied the fluent exercise of power, and even then dependent utterly on the submission of a monarch who need not submit, who might at any moment rebel and throw off the unnatural yoke, or even die—thus delivering him into the hands of his enemies, the crown prince and his wife. With all this he was condemned to everlasting bickering with a hostile parliament which he despised so much that it sometimes made him almost ill to have anything to do with it. He was indeed physically and mentally played out. He had called Johanna's old friend and familiar, Robert von Keudell, to Berlin to act as his secretary, and at their first meeting Keudell was shocked by the great man's pallor and evident weariness. He sat for some staring at nothing and then said: 'I feel that I've grown fifteen years older in this one year. People are even more stupid than I had thought.'[7] It was 20 October 1863, eleven months to a day after the critical interview at Babelsberg. He was plunged into the first of those profound depressions which were to punctuate his ministerial career on the pattern long established in his private life.

Within a month all was changed. 'I am sure you will feel much younger again as soon as we see some great new turn in foreign affairs,' Keudell had responded fatuously, but accurately all the same, to his new master's tale of woe.[8] He was lucky not to have had his head bitten off. 'What new turn?' Bismarck might well have demanded. The outside world seemed to be getting on very well without Prussia: it was hard to envisage any probable development that could benefit her immediately. But almost at once the miracle occurred.

The twin duchies of Schleswig and Holstein had been under Danish rule, declared 'inseparable to eternity,' for just over four hundred years. It was an arrangement that had survived the remaking of Europe at the Congress of Vienna, in spite of a remarkable anomaly; for although under the Danish crown, Holstein, with its almost wholly German population, had been part of the Holy Roman Empire and so was now a member of the German Confederation, while Schleswig, with a mainly Danish population in its northern part and a preponderant German element in its southern part, was not. With the rise of nationalism all over Europe the situation in the duchies became a highly emotional issue on which all patriotic Germans could feel as one, and in the revolutionary year of 1848 when the Holsteiners rose against the Danes, Prussian troops marched in to their succour with the noisy approval of the Frankfurt Parliament. They did not have to march very far, for the Holstein boundary came down to the suburbs of Hamburg; with its rich pastures and celebrated black-and-white cattle it habitually looked towards Germany rather than Denmark. But the dream of union was most abruptly shattered when Russia intervened and made it clear that she was not going to have a revolutionary Germany advancing deeper into the Baltic: the Prussian troops retired in ignominy.

This was not the first time there had been trouble over Schleswig-Holstein, and the powers decided now to put an end to it. In 1852 plenipotentiaries from Austria, Britain, France, Prussia, Russia, and Sweden conferred in London and came up with a formal joint guarantee of the integrity of the Danish monarchy on condition that it did not encroach upon or diminish the ancient rights and privileges of Holstein, with which was included the tiny adjoining Duchy of Lauenburg. They went further. Because Frederick VII of Denmark was the last of his line, they engaged themselves in the Treaty of London to underwrite the succession of Prince Christian of Glücksburg, whose claim rested on his marriage with the king's first cousin. But that claim was contested by the Schleswig-Holsteiners, who insisted that the duchies, unlike Denmark proper, had always recognized the Salic law which forbade inheritance through the female line. Their own candidate was Prince Frederick of Augustenburg, a direct descendant of one of the sixteenth-century Danish kings. Augustenburg was widely popular throughout Germany, in part because the Holsteiners wanted him, in part because he had spent most of his life in Germany, attending the university at Bonn, making a particular friend of the Prussian crown prince and through him endearing himself to the king and queen. Although the Treaty of London should have settled the matter for ever (Augustenburg being paid a considerable sum to renounce his ducal rights), it did not. The quarrel rumbled away, every so often breaking surface, the Holsteiners in a state of profitless unrest egged on by their German brothers across the border—until in March 1863 King Frederick decided to put an end to this eternal divisiveness by proclaiming a unitary constitution: all special rights and franchises and privileges of any kind were done away with and the duchies placed on a level with the rest of Denmark. In doing this, of course, he breached the Treaty of London.

In Germany the nationalists raged. Bismarck, who was running himself in as minister-president and had his hands full, was quite happy to allow them to do so. If anti-Danish frenzy diverted the popular mind from difficult problems nearer home, so much the better. For the moment it was enough for him to note with satisfaction that Denmark had put herself in the wrong: it was the sort of situation he knew most instinctively how to exploit. There was no need to do anything in the spring of 1863. Much earlier, seven years earlier indeed, during one of the recurrent crises over the duchies, he had written from Frankfurt advising his government to keep its powder dry: the proper course was to go through the motions of defending German honour without in fact doing anything: there would be time for action when, sooner or later, Prussia could see her way to extract 'some practical gain.'[9]

He saw it like that still. What he was to call a little later 'the beer-hall enthusiasm' of German nationalism might well come in useful one day, but it was not a thing to be guided or diverted by. He himself cared no more for the Germans in Holstein than he cared for the French or the British or the Bavarians or Saxons—or, one may say, the Prussians themselves. In his own characteristic words: 'Whether the Germans of Holstein are happy or not is no concern of ours.' Thus, throughout that noisy spring and summer, through the unending conflict with the Diet, the Polish crisis, the row with the crown prince over the Press Decree, the struggle with King William over the Congress of Princes, he paid minimal attention to the outcry over Schleswig-Holstein, even though it was violent enough to shake the Danish king and make him put off ratifying his own constitutional reform. But then, suddenly, on 15 November, came the news that the king was dead. Prince Christian immediately acceded to the throne under the terms of the Treaty of London—and three days later put his signature to the new Constitution in breach of the treaty. A new and promising situation was in being.

The first move came from the Holsteiners who demonstratively refused to swear allegiance to the new king and apealed directly to the Frankfurt Diet to recognize Augustenburg as ruler of an independent Schleswig-Holstein-Lauenburg. The whole of Germany was straining to march in their support. The ferment was such that even Bismarck at his coolest could no longer ignore it. All Germany clamoured for war: something had to be done, and done fairly quickly. Bismarck had no objection to war in general or to war with Denmark in particular. But we remember his insistence in his notorious defence of Prussia's climb-down in face of Austria at Olmütz thirteen years earlier at the very outset of his political career: 'The only healthy foundation for a large state—and this is what marks it off from a small state—is state egoism rather than romanticism, and it is unworthy of a great state to fight for something which does not concern its own interest. . . . Gentlemen, show me an objective worthy of war and I will go along with you. . . .'[10]

More recently, in his first weeks as minister-president, he had written specifically about war with Denmark to his envoy at the court of King Charles of Württemberg: 'I have not the least doubt that this whole business of Denmark can be settled in a way desired by us only by war'; but he was not, he went on to say, prepared to fight a war simply 'to set up a new archduke in Schleswig-Holstein to vote against us in the Confederation.'[11]

What, therefore, to do? There was not much time. As early as 18 November the Hanoverian Liberal leader Rudolf von Bennigsen called the executive committee of the Nationalverein to Berlin, and the outcome of its deliberations was an inflammatory manifesto calculated to touch every German on a tender nerve: failure on the part of Germans everywhere to march to the aid of their brothers in the north would be nothing less than rank betrayal! Never again a disgrace like the loss of Alsace-Lorraine to France in 1648! Rather, Schleswig-Holstein must be recovered from Denmark as East Prussia had been recovered from Poland, Pomerania from Sweden, the Rhineland from France. . . .

Faced with this sort of mood, Austria as the first Germanic power had to do something too. But what? The last thing imperial Vienna wanted was to place itself at the head of a popular movement and embark on a crusade under the banner of nationalist self-determination. What would Austria's own nationalities have to say to that?

It was Bismarck, the old enemy, who took her by the hand and showed the way—which was also (how clearly did he realize this?) the way to her own ruin.

For in Berlin one of those comic situations, all too common in the history of liberalism, was swiftly taking shape. The Prussian liberals who wanted to march to the aid of their 'northern brothers' were stricken by the awful thought that in this noblest of causes they were demanding military action from the very man to whom they were so furiously denying the means of military action. . . . While Bismarck for his part had no intention whatsoever of inaugurating the sort of military action they had in mind; he had developed, very fast and secretly, quite a different plan.

In later life, looking back on his great triumphs, he was to say that of all his diplomatic achievements the affair of the duchies was the one of which he was most proud. It was indeed a vrituoso performance; quite suddenly, as though by magic, all the contradictory qualities of this extraordinary man came together and combined to dazzle and overwhelm. To admire it is not necessary to believe that every move was foreseen and calculated in advance. Much of the beauty of the performance lay in the dizzily swift improvisations on a simple theme, none the less clearly stated for being hidden. The theme was aggression. The interesting thing was that to Bismarck at the summit of his glory it was a performance to be looked back upon with pride.

There is no need to follow step-by-step the elaborate manoeuvring whereby Bismarck exploited the Schleswig-Holstein crisis in the exclusive interest of Prussia. From the moment of King Christian's proclamation of the unitary Constitution a situation began to develop which, handled cleverly and very boldly, could lead to the acquisition by Prussia at least of Holstein with the deep-water harbour of Kiel. But there were many good reasons why Prussia could not act on her own. And if she acted with the rest of Germany it would mean surrendering the duchies into the hands of Augustenburg. This left Austria as a possible ally. The fact that since the abortive Congress of Princes Vienna had hardly been on speaking terms with Berlin did not worry Bismarck in the least; Austria, he was sure, was no less reluctant than Prussia to engage in a nationalist crusade—though for very different reasons. And there was a very strong card to play. Austria more than any other power had a vested interest in the sanctity of treaties: the past development and continued existence of her remarkable empire were based on the strict observance of international agreement. She might thus be expected to respond to an appeal by Prussia to join her in upholding the Treaty of London. But would Francis Joseph be able to swallow his pride and make a common front with the Prussia which had so lately wrecked his princely congress? Would the new spirit of constitutionalism in Austria stand in the way and force Vienna to align herself with the Confederation in demanding that Christian of Denmark should renounce his own new 'illegal' Constitution under pain of what was picturesquely termed a Federal Execution—i.e., armed intervention by the united forces of the Confederation against an offending member, viz. King Christian, in his capacity of duke of Holstein?

Bismarck need not have worried. Rechberg was delighted and surprised by Prussia's unexpected bid for Austrian favour. And yet not surprised: for he had never relinquished the illusion that in spite of his perversities and his overbearing manners, Bismarck was at heart a rock for the conservative cause in both Germany and Austria to build on. As for Francis Joseph, he was already tired of playing at liberalism: the more you gave the more people asked. And thus it was that on 28 November the world was astonished by the news that Austria and Prussia, who had gone to bed in a state of spluttering hostility, had woken up the best of friends, their differences apparently vaporized overnight; they now stood shoulder to shoulder, the self-righteous embodiment of law and virtue. Even King William in Berlin was shocked, bewildered (as so often in years to come) by his chief minister's sudden change of front: it had been only in August that Bismarck had put him through that terrible ordeal in the middle of the night at Baden, persuading him against his better judgement that Austria was bent on his destruction; and now, in November, here he was declaring that the peace of Europe and the honour of Prussia depended on the intimate alliance of Habsburg and Hohenzollern. He pleaded so well that not only William himself but also the old conservatives were convinced that the minister-president had woken up to the error of his ways and at last perceived his proper duty as a defender of legitimacy. Rechberg was convinced of it too. And so was the Austrian ambassador in Berlin, Count Károlyi, whose attitude towards Bismarck hitherto had been coolly sceptical. Within a matter of weeks he was informing Vienna, almost starry-eyed, about the minister-president's 'openness and candour.'[12]

The charm of entering into an *ad hoc* alliance with Austria was manifold: it would prove to the world in general and Vienna in particular that past misunderstandings did not mean that Prussia was determined to bring Austria down; it would worry Louis Napoleon in Paris, who was beginning to take Bismarck's hostility to Austria a little too much for granted; more substantially, it would imply acceptance by Austria of the principle of what would nowadays be called a 'special relationship' between Berlin and Vienna within the Confederation—a return to the Metternich understanding that Austria should treat Prussia if not as an equal at least as a power in her own right, not simply as one among many German states: after such a demonstration it would at least be difficult for Austria to maintain her refusal to countenance Prussian hegemony north of the River Main. It would also afford Bismarck himself the secret amusement of the successful confidence-trickster. He could never have too much of this. The very astute Saxon minister, Count Beust, recounted how when he commented admiringly on the cleverness of Austria's new policy, 'Bismarck merely smiled.'[13]

He had bound Austria to his side. He knew that Russia was in no mood or state to intervene. He feared English intentions, but believed that if he looked after France England could not possibly act without a continental ally. In fact it is doubtful whether he realized quite how far apart France and England at that moment were. For Napoleon, partly out of genuine concern for peace, partly out of a restless drive towards prestige and the restoration of French influence, had recently proposed a grand congress of the powers, in effect a disarmament conference, to discuss outstanding differences and re-establish a genuine European concert. None of the powers would agree to an unrestricted conference, but only Lord John Russell in London turned down the idea absolutely in terms that amounted to a snub. Napoleon was hurt and angry and thus for some time to come far from feeling kindly towards England.

He was also uneasy, as was intended, about Prussia's apparent *rapprochement* with Austria. To make doubly sure of Napoleon (it may not have been necessary), Bismarck put himself out to scatter heavy hints about the possibility of the accession to France of the left bank of the Rhine. When Napoleon's special envoy, General Emile Fleury, turned up mysteriously in Berlin shortly before Christmas, Bismarck was at pains to confide the reason for his objection to a general congress: it would necessarily have raised the Polish question, he explained, and this he would not have: 'Rather die than permit discussion of our possessions in Poland! I would rather cede our Rhenish provinces.'[14] He went on about this to Talleyrand too. At this stage, in fact he was over-insuring against trouble from France. He does not seem to have realized that any action which led to dissension within the German Confederation, up to and including its break-up, would be pure gain in Napoleon's eyes. He seems also to have feared, at least with part of his mind, that England might tempt France to act with her against Prussia by similarly promising Napoleon the left bank of the Rhine. He was intent on convincing the French that for any revision of the 1815 treaties they must look to Prussia. As he observed to Antoine, duc de Gramont, the French ambassador in Vienna when the Danish War was over: 'We can march with France better than anybody else, for as a start we can give her what other powers can only promise.'[15]

It is safe to say that in those December days of 1863 nobody knew Bismarck well enough to understand that he was playing a game. It was a brilliant and marvellously complex game, but it is also safe to say that even he himself did not know how it would develop. He used to swing between a bland insistence that his successful manoeuvres were long foreseen and planned in detail and a very proper acknowledgement that no statesman can control events, but can only ride them as a surf-rider rides the waves. Or, to take one of the more picturesque of his many observations on the subject: 'This trade teaches that one can be as clever as the cleverest in the world and still at any moment finds oneself walking like a child in the dark.'[16]

Compare this gleam of genuine humility with his swaggering, as reported by the Hessian minister Reinhard von Dalwigt, when Denmark had been fought and conquered: 'Bismarck boasted with the candour peculiar to him of how from the beginning he had conducted the Schleswig affair in accordance with Prussian interests. He had posed conditions to the Danes which he knew they could not possibly accept. At the same time he had by indirect means encouraged them to active resistance. Through his secret agents he had put before them the certain prospect of English assistance, while he had assured himself in advance that France did not want to go to war and therefore England had to keep her sword in the scabbard. . . . His own aim is the annexation of the duchies; the difficulty is to bring the king to act.'[17]

Prussia could only live if she grew, Bismarck had said. He had made it clear that sooner or later she would have to absorb Hanover and Hesse, the states that stood between old Prussia and the new Prussian Rhineland. As for Schleswig-Holstein, he raised the matter of annexation as early as January 1864, when, quite unnecessarily, he informed Károlyi that there was a great deal of talk about annexation in Berlin, but that he himself was firmly against it.[18] And such was his charm, his apparent candour, his extraordinary capacity for carrying conviction, that even the sceptical Hungarian believed him. In fact, there was no such talk among people who mattered. Nothing was further from the thoughts of both the king and the crown prince. It was not until the Crown Council of 3 February that Bismarck for the first time threw out the idea of annexation, partly to discover how people reacted, partly to start getting them used to the idea.

One of the few diplomats who saw which way the wind was blowing was Sir Andrew Buchanan who, as early as 12 December 1863, reported back to Lord John Russell that he would be surprised if 'M. de Bismarck did not seek to obtain more solid advantages for Prussia in return for the losses and sacrifices which the country will have to suffer in the event of war than the honour of having placed a prince of Augustenburg on the ducal throne of a Schleswig-Holstein state.'[19] And yet even this shrewd Scot found himself a week later convinced that Bismarck stood for peace against a belligerent Germany. Just after Christmas he had complained to him on behalf of the British government after the warlike posture of the Confederation and sought Prussia's help to counter it. Bismarck, who knew that in a few days Holstein would be invaded, responded to Buchanan with an extraordinary proposition. The language of the British protests was not strong enough to deter hot-heads, he insisted, with the result that the impression had got round that Great Britain would not act in defence of Danish integrity: he suggested that it would be a good plan for Britain to threaten the Confederation with a British naval blockade if they moved against Denmark.[20]

There was only one conceivable reason for this suggestion: to push Britain into making the Danes believe that she would come to their rescue, thus stiffening their resistance. Bismarck wanted them to fight. It is easy to say now that there was no chance of Britain acting, but it was by no means so certain at the time. The eighty-year-old Palmerston was passionate to act; Lord John Russell was sorely exercised. A little later it was indeed touch-and-go—a majority decision in the Cabinet, above all the queen's deep-rooted pro-German inclinations. But there was some high feeling.

It was not a Continental writer but a future British foreign secretary and prime minister, Lord Salisbury, who was to publish in *The Quarterly Review* of April 1864 the most bitter and vehement condemnation of Britain's too habitual appeasement of the strong and betrayal of the weak, winding up in words apposite to so many subsequent occasions: 'The people whom she [Britain] affected to befriend are in danger of being swept away. One of the most wanton and unblushing spoliations which history records is on the point of being consummated. But as far as effective aid goes, England stands aloof. . . . Her pledges and her threats are gone with last year's snow, and she is content to watch with cynical philosophy the destruction of those who trusted in the one, and the triumph of those wise enough to spurn the other.'[21]

Salisbury was writing when it had become clear that Bismarck's championship of the London Treaty had been only a pious fraud, cover for a deeper game. The Confederation had served its purpose. Disoriented and shocked by the defection to the side of Prussia of their accepted leader, Austria, its members, meeting in Frankfurt, still could not find the strength and unity among themselves to outvote Austria and Prussia, stand against the Austro-Prussian threat to act on their own, and insist on their support of Augustenburg. Instead, by one vote, they accepted the London Treaty as the basis for their action, and on 1 January Saxon and Hanoverian troops entered Holstein and Lauenburg, only to find that the Danish army was retiring without putting up a fight. They would, however, advance no farther and the Austro-Prussian armies moved, as it were, across the bows of the Hanoverians and Saxons and into Schleswig. They were quite ready if necessary—Bismarck cheerfully, Rechberg fearfully—to fight the Confederate troops as well as the Danes, who now made a gallant stand.

As far as Bismarck was concerned, it was all done with mirrors. The hardest task was poor Rechberg's, who had to face the Austrian parliament and carry his emperor with him. And this was done in the teeth of the German-Austrian deputies from the German heartland of the multinational empire who were upholders of the Confederation to a man. 'Why are we acting with Prussia?' one of those deputies cried out from his heart. 'Is Prussia anywhere our friend? Does she not denounce Austria as the arch-enemy of Prussia? Prussia has scarcely digested Silesia, and now she is stretching out her claws to the duchies, while we are leading her into them to the music of our own good regimental bands. What tune must we play to get her out again?'[22]

If it seems extraordinary that this very just estimate of the situation was lost on Francis Joseph, it has to be remembered that the German Austrians were nationalists who exalted their own nationality above the needs of the multinational empire, which the supranational emperor regarded as his sacred trust. The situation was complicated by his obsessive suspicion, fear indeed, of Napoleon whom, in the bitterness of his defeat in Italy, he had come to regard as an unprincipled scoundrel: he had no idea of the strange, uneasy collaboration between the conspiratorial adventurer in the Tuileries and the conspiratorial bully in the Wilhelmstrasse.

His considered attitude, which was to lead to the undoing of the Habsburg monarchy and the triumph of Prussia, is expressed in a letter to one of his few close friends, Prince Albert, the crown prince of Saxony: 'I am only sorry that you are not bringing your Saxons into the battlefield, just as I am sorry above all that Germany is split into two camps and that we must see you opposed to us. . . . One foresees all too clearly the coming of a European war in which Austria and Prussia will have to come to your help against their will in face of the man in Paris who, in the last analysis, is the chief enemy of us all. . . . I do not want to go into what Bismarck may or may not have said. He has his great faults, which we had reason to know all about in earlier times; and one of those faults is that he speaks all too recklessly and exaggeratedly, trying to frighten people with words. In the proceedings in Holstein the Prussians have admittedly been wrong in form, but in essence, in my opinion, they have been correct. . . . In this alliance the position and steadily maintained objectives of Austria are enough to protect you against any further designs the Prussian may have. . . .'[23]

Francis Joseph was writing on 15 February 1864, a fortnight after the Austro-Prussian invasion of Schleswig. Had he been able to read a letter written six weeks earlier by Bismarck to his recalcitrant envoy in Paris (who saw himself as his rival), Count Robert von der Goltz, he would have thought differently. Bismarck, too, was writing to explain why the Austro-Prussian alliance was desirable.

'You do not trust Austria. Neither do I. But I consider it the correct policy at present to have Austria with us. Whether the moment of parting will come, and on whose initiative, we shall see. . . . I am not in the least afraid of war, on the contrary . . . you may very soon be able to convince yourself that war also is included in my programme.'[24]

When the Danes fought back in Schleswig they should have been crushed at once: a little army of 40,000 was opposed to all the might of Austria and Prussia. But the brilliant plan of campaign designed to capture the whole Danish army on the first day, devised by General Helmuth von Moltke (who, ironically, had started his career in the Danish army), was muffed by the Prussian commander-in-chief, General Friedrich von

Wrangel, a veteran of Napoleonic wars, whose chief glory had been the re-conquest of Berlin for Frederick William IV. It was left to the Austrians to save the day, and they did this with such effect and with such a marked superiority in attack, that it gave them (and Europe) an altogether too elevated idea of their military capacity—and caused them to underestimate correspondingly Prussia's real strength. Nobody seems to have noticed that, despite wretched leadership in the field, the Prussian infantry were much better than the Austrian, and for the simple reason that they were better officered: the most gifted of the Austrian officers corps went into the cavalry, considering the infantry beneath their dignity. Nobody paid sufficient attention to the effect of the great Prussian weapon, the breech-loading needle-gun, which could be re-loaded lying down behind cover and which fired five rounds to the conventional muzzle-loader's one. The Austrians were so embarrassed by the failure of the Prussian generals that they went out of their way to give them a victory of their own. The chance of the Prussians came when the unfortunate Danes were forced back to the lines of Düppel, a historic, but not very imposing system of earthworks between Flensburg and Sonderborg which formed the key to North Schleswig. The storming of Düppel was thus the first victorious appearance of the Prussian army on a battlefield for just on half a century. Prussian blue had arrived.

It was mid-April. The progress of the Austro-Prussian forces was making Europe a little edgy. Britain in particular had not liked the invasion of Schleswig but had settled for a promise that the Danish monarchy itself would not be violated. With the Prussians now on the threshhold of Denmark proper, something had to be done to stop the situation getting out of hand. Lord John Russell called a conference of the signatories to the treaty of 1852 to freeze the situation—as he saw it, that is, to return the duchies to the Danish crown and to restore their ancient rights to the peoples of the duchies—i.e., to restore the *status quo*. Nothing, of course, was further from Bismarck's mind. To provoke the Danes into resistance to this scheme he demanded ever higher terms—an operation he conducted at long range, preferring not to go to London himself but to manoeuvre from Berlin and keep the French close to him. The upshot of the consequent deadlock was that in May the conference was suddenly presented with something like an ultimatum: since the Danes would not agree, Austria and Prussia would have no choice but to join the rest of Germany in support of the Augustenburg claim.

This initiative came from Rechberg, who had begun to smell a very large rat: belatedly suspecting Bismarck's designs, he made a supreme effort to ensure that there would be no gain for Prussia. But Bismarck reacted instantly. Of course he would back Augustenburg, he declared, hand on heart for all the world to see—but in no time at all he then set to work with grim diligence to make it impossible for Augustenburg to accept. The unfortunate duke had already made heavy concessions to William: Holstein to enter the Zollverein; the creation of a Prussian naval base at Kiel and the digging of a ship canal; the army to be equipped and trained on the Prussian system. To no avail. On the evening of 1 June, when all seemed settled, bar matters of minor detail, the ill-fated ruler went full of confidence to his fatal meeting with Bismarck in Berlin and at last discovered what he was up against. He emerged broken and despairing. For Bismarck set out deliberately to humiliate him by inviting him to become an obvious puppet ruler; a puppet who would be compelled to abandon his own liberal principles of government in favour of a conservative style dictated by Prussia; a puppet, moreover, who would be compelled to hand over considerable areas of his estate as 'compensation.' The duke knew defeat when he saw it and walked out into the night. His side of the story never reached the ears of the king and the crown prince, who were shocked when Bismarck informed them that he had rejected the terms which everyone believed he had accepted. It was good riddance, Bismarck commented; the duke had been so arrogant in his demands, so lacking in gratitude for all that had been done for him, above all by King William, that it was out of the question to support his claim any further.

In a spirit of suicidal desperation the Danes took up their arms once more. Austria still stood embattled shoulder to shoulder with Prussia; but to what end? She was now fighting quite without a cause and (it was obvious now) against her own interest. Bismarck was surprised that she had not realized this sooner. Even as he travelled up to Schleswig after the storming of Düppel in April he had remarked to Keudell that it was hard to see 'why the Austrians have come all this way with us when they cannot possibly stay here.'[25] But no doubt, he went on, they were afraid Prussia would grow too strong in Germany if she were left to deal with the Danish question on her own. Yes, indeed: but what was to be done? We recall that cry of outrage, and anguish from the Vienna parliament a bare six months before: '... now she is stretching out her claws to the duchies, while we lead her into them to the music of our own good regimental bands. What tune must we play to get her out again?'

There was no such tune. In less than two months the horribly battered

Danes were suing for peace and Bismarck was in Vienna, making sure in his inimitable manner that Prussia would stay in the duchies. He had broken the Danes; he had broken Augustenburg; he had defied the German Confederation; he had held off Britain and France; he was now to turn the screws on all those in Vienna who still hoped for a peaceful accommodation with Prussia—and to go on turning them until the victims bit back in desperation. What could be easier for the man who could boast that at the London Conference he had yoked the Augustenburg ox to the plough, and, as soon as the plough was moving, unharnessed him and cast him loose?[26]

CHAPTER XI

OPPORTUNISM AS
A FINE ART

The moment at which Bismarck clearly saw that he could use the affair of Schleswig-Holstein as a means of forcing Austria out of Germany is impossible to determine, just as it is impossible to point to the precise moment when he decided that it had to be done by war. Both uncertainties of this kind are unimportant, and to worry about them is to miss the way his mind worked. Nothing could be further from reality than the 'either–or' approach (either Bismarck was determined on war with Austria or he was not; either he deliberately forced the war with France in 1870 or he did not). All that matters is that once he had defined a goal nothing was allowed to stand in his way. The almost infinite complexity of his thinking *and feeling* is beyond analyzing—his pursuit of apparently conflicting ends, his skill in keeping open any number of choices until the last moment. Rudolf Stadelman has spoken of his 'diabolical simultaneity'; Otto Pflanze has discussed at length what he calls his 'strategy of alternatives'; but even here, although complexity and ambiguity are apprehended, still too much weight is given to conscious mental processes, to deliberate, calculated planning.

In an earlier chapter reference was made to Bismarck's possession of (or by) qualities more usually found in the creative artist. Fritz Stern happily supports this suggestion by calling in aid Keats's celebrated concept of 'negative capability' as applied to great artists in general and to Shakespeare in particular: 'a man is capable of being in uncertainties, mysteries, doubts, without any irritable reaching after fact and reason.' And a crucial fact about Bismarck is that his thoughts were indeed capable of existing in a state of something very like suspension, to borrow an image from the chemists, with all the ingredients hovering invisibly in solution until the right temperature is reached, the right catalyst introduced, to crystallize them beautifully out.

A man, nevertheless, needs certainties to drive him. What may be isolated as the irreducible minimum of Bismarck's certainties?

We have seen enough of him now to understand that his determination to be his own master was absolute, was, indeed, the only absolute for him, and therefore governed his conduct. The complicating factor was that he was also possessed by ambition, and thus shut off from the usual escape routes of those who will not be ordered about—either to some degree to contract out of society and live in obscure independence or else to seek a way out in what may be called spiritual absenteeism. Bismarck, tortured by ambition, was nevertheless precluded from taking part in the usual round of competition for place. He had to pretend not to want it; he had to dare recklessly by flaunting his independence in the faces of men who were strong enough to break him; he had to acknowledge one master because he no longer lived in an age when a born master of men could build a castle, raise an army, and subdue a kingdom to himself. That master had to be the hereditary monarch to whom he could formally bow, but who must be made to obey his servant's will. The king of Prussia might be content with sovereignty over a minor power, patronized by Russia, treated by Austria as rather less than an equal, but if Bismarck was going to serve him this was not enough: Prussia must also be great, if only to be worthy of his service. And even then that service required a divine sanction. Let us refer again to that remarkable monologue recorded by Moritz Busch so soon after Bismarck shattered France and transformed his master the Prussian king into the German emperor. 'If I were no longer a Christian I would not serve the king another hour. . . . Sever my connection with God and I would pack up tomorrow and be off. . . . If there is no Divine commandment, why should I subordinate myself to these Hohenzollerns? They are a Swabian family, no better than my own, and in that case no concern of mine. . . .'[1]

He did not believe in absolute monarchy, he was by nature a republican and a Jacobin. He did not believe in absolute monarchy because he was quite clear about the abuses inherent in it; but he was afraid of revolution and the mob. So the safest thing was a king as God's anointed, a parliament that could be bullied in the name of the king or flattered in the name of whatever cause was fashionable (for the time being, German nationalism), stirred up, if necessary, against the king himself, manipulated always by a strong man who knew what was good for the country and who also had a private arrangement with God.

There was one more driving force, barely glimpsed so far, but soon to become very strong, perhaps even dominant: paranoia.

Bismarck's mind was so incomparably subtle in its expedients and in its perceptions of power relationships that it is easy to overlook a very simple fact: namely that the ends to be served by this dazzling apparatus were primitive and crude. There is a revealing little story in a letter from Disraeli attending the Congress of Berlin in 1878. As part of the Berlin settlement Britain had managed to get Cyprus from Turkey, and Bismarck, who had succumbed to 'the old Jew's' magic, seemed to be as pleased about this as about any stroke of his own: 'When he heard about Cyprus,' Disraeli confided to Queen Victoria, 'he said: "You have done a wise thing. That is progress. It will be popular; a nation likes progress." ' And Disraeli added: 'His idea of progress was evidently seizing something.'[2]

Now, in 1864, he was on his way to seizing the duchies for Prussia. And he knew just what he was doing. It was not at all a case of the overbearing Junker in his boreal innocence having no idea that he might be offending against anyone's code of decency or notion of propriety. On the contrary. Bismarck's great problem (as so often in future enterprises) was his master the king, who knew that he had no title to the duchies and was appalled by the idea of seizing them. Much of Bismarck's activity for some time after the Danish surrender was bent on convincing William that stealing was not theft. Once this had been achieved after a hard struggle (for William prided himself on his honesty) he moved on naturally to the next stage, which was to convince him that Austria meant war.

The man to whom Bismarck talked most freely during this most critical period of his career, from the conclusion of the Danish War with the signing of the Peace of Vienna in August 1864 to the declaration of war on Austria in June 1866, was, of all people, Napoleon's ambassador to Prussia, a rather solemn and self-important little Corsican of Greek origin, comte Vincente Benedetti. He talked to him now partly because he liked him (although he was quite cheerfully to break his heart a few years later), partly because he always enjoyed thinking at least some of his thoughts aloud—to tease, to surprise, to shock, to coax, even perhaps to hypnotize, as well as to relieve the pressures which built up in his own mind during those long, sustained periods of brooding in total withdrawal which preceded every powerful explosion of activity. More particularly in the case of Benedetti, however, he needed to keep his finger on the pulse of France, to bind her to him, to appear to take Napoleon into the innermost heart of his confidence, to make sure that there should be no *rapprochement* at this time between Paris and Vienna. Thus it was to Benedetti that he said in 1865:

'If Prussia has not burnt her boats yet, they are at any rate smouldering,'[3] and, a year later, more circumstantially: 'I have succeeded in persuading a king of Prussia to break off the intimate relations of his House with the Imperial House of Austria; to make an alliance with revolutionary Italy; to make arrangements, for a possible emergency, with the French Emperor; and to propose at Frankfurt the revision of the Federal Act by a popular parliament. I am proud of my success. I do not know whether I shall be allowed to reap where I have sown; but even if the king deserts me I have prepared the way by deepening the rift between Prussia and Austria, and the Liberals, if they come to power, will complete my work.'[4]

Even more remarkable were his relations with the survivors of the Hungarian revolt against Austria, whom he was actually wooing—exiled revolutionaries to be harnessed to the Hohenzollern cause to destroy the Habsburgs. In June 1866 on the very eve of the war he declared to the Hungarian rebel General Stefan Türr: 'I have not yet succeeded in convincing the king that war is immediately necessary, but never mind! I have put the horse at the ditch and he must jump.'[5]

Who did he think he was? Ignoring for the moment the characteristic boasting (which was to increase rather than diminish with the years), what image of himself did this extraordinary man sustain in his own heart? Where did he discover the sanction which permitted him to harry and deceive his own countrymen from his sovereign downwards and drive and manoeuvre them into a war against fellow-Germans which was nothing but a war of national aggrandizement on behalf of a people he despised? We face again the lack of inner coherence, the pyrotechnical display of talent that conceals a void.

We remember that revealing letter to his American friend Motley, written in April 1863, so early on in his conflict with parliament: 'Here in the Landtag, while I am writing to you . . . I have to listen to uncommonly foolish speeches from the mouths of uncommonly childish and excited politicians. . . .' Taken out of context, it would be easy to feel sympathy for the writer of that letter—a great man beset by the irrelevant and silly chatter of a bunch of nonentities, clerks and intellectuals with provincial manners and no political experience or sense. One might ask why the great man should find it necessary to spell out, like a schoolmaster, his sense of his own superiority. . . . And then one might reflect that of course, what he says is true of every elected parliament that ever was or ever will be: the light depends on the few, and the function of the many is above all to keep an eye on the few, who too easily get above themselves. And then one asks, who were Bismarck's 'few'—and realizes that they did not exist. To Motley, after barely six months in office, he is delivering a blanket condemnation of every living soul in the Prussian Lower House: *all*, without distinction, were in his eyes beneath contempt.

So there was something wrong with those eyes. A reference to the record to discover what was going on in the Landtag while Bismarck communed with his distant American friend is revealing. The sort of chatter which he was here dismissing so loftily was in fact a very determined and sometimes quite ably mounted onslaught on the detested army bill. The attack was led by Karl von Twesten, one of the few liberals prepared to stand up seriously to Bismarck. The context was the crisis arising from the proclamation of the new Danish Constitution by King Christian, and it was Twesten's flat declaration that if there was war with Denmark the House would refuse to support the government in protest against the army bill that stimulated Bismarck to the celebrated retort: 'Let me assure you and also the world,' he rapped out, 'that if we find it necessary to carry on a war we shall do so with or without your consent.'[6] And it was during the ensuing uproar that he turned his back on the chamber and walked out to write to Motley.

Bismarck liked to pretend that he was above the battle. Far from it: he was in the thick of it. He was at war with the Landtag. The thought of trying to lead it along the way he intended to go did not enter his head. A few weeks earlier the Speaker had called him to order for accusing the Opposition of traitorously siding with the enemy when his Polish policy was being questioned, and he had flung down the glove: neither he nor any other minister was subject to parliamentary discipline, he declared.[7] And, such was the 1848–50 Constitution, this in fact was true, though not a matter to come out with bluntly.

Quite soon he was going to need the Lower House, but even when that time came and he was building on it he never sought to reason, to persuade, to lead: he bamboozled it, flattered it, cheated it, blackmailed it, bullied it. He saw himself not as first among equals but always as immeasurably superior—which, of course, in all but humility, decency and kindliness he was: but was it for him to say? He was the master of a pack to be whipped into obedience, sometimes to be rewarded, sometimes punished. The image was one he himself once used: when he was stirring up a mood of nationalist hysteria at a certain stage in the Schleswig-Holstein affair, he wrote to the Prussian high commissioner, Baron Konstantin von Zedlitz: 'We must let the whole pack howl.'[8]

The tragic Bismarckian paradox was that this great hero of a people who liked to be led was not a leader at all. He was a manipulator. He manipulated everyone and everything, from the king downwards to junior civil servants. He manipulated his followers and he manipulated his opponents (those whom it was not safe or politic to destroy out of hand): he manipulated the rulers of the German states and the forces of German nationalism as he sought with varying success to manipulate France, England, Russia, Italy, Austria—and play them off against each other. The consequence in the international sphere of this terrible and conscienceless superiority was that he destroyed all trust.

Worse than this, so overwhelming was his own authority, so superior the formulations of his political ideas, that Bismarck managed to impose those ideas almost absolutely on Prussia and to a deplorable degree elsewhere. Yet it is wrong to speak of ideas. He had only one idea, the idea summed up by the term *Realpolitik*, the exaltation of the *Staatsrecht*, the right *and duty* of the state to pursue its own advantage regardless of any other consideration and by whatever means comes to hand, coldly excluding morality, decency, honour. By his own unexampled display of *Realpolitik* he brought back into the mid-nineteenth century, poisoning it, that barbaric concept, the state above all morality, which was being so painfully discarded. Why did so many so eagerly believe him when he declared that *Realpolitik* must be the basis of all international relations? He never argued the case, or even attempted to; he simply stated it, as one states a self-evident truth. But it was not truth at all. Behind the crisp economy of his words his thinking here is no less muddled than the thinking of the conventional liberal-minded moralizer. We recall the first of all his speeches—on the 'humiliation' of Olmütz in December 1850: 'The only healthy foundation for a large state . . . is state egoism rather than romanticism, and it is unworthy of a great state to fight for something which does not concern its own interest. Gentlemen, show me an objective worthy of war and I will go along with you.' How many questions are begged in those few words! The only thing to be said for them is that they avoid hypocrisy. But it takes more than an absence of hypocrisy to make a useful political philosophy. And it is clear that from the beginning to the end of his career Bismarck never asked himself the elementary question: Where does the true interest of Prussia lie? He took it for granted that it lay in the accumulation and the exercise of power, and that to augment her own power Prussia was justified in falling upon any neighbour who might conceivably at some future date curtail her perfect freedom of action. It is true that Bismarck showed himself moderate in his ambitions once he had established the power he thought Prussia needed, but he was not at all a moderate in the manner generally supposed, and he brought to the maintenance of his power deceit as well as threats on a grand scale. It did not occur to him that the interest of Prussia might best be served by working for understanding with Austria, or that the subduing of Prussia to the concept of a larger, unified, or federated Germany to be arrived at slowly by peaceful and organic means might serve the interests of the Prussian people better than ruling the roost. He was not interested in the people; he thought purely in terms of the dynasty, which he used while nominally serving it, which meant that he thought purely in terms of his own power.

It is easy to see how so many historians, wearied by the evasions and the cant of so-called democratic politicians who could not tell the difference between the truth and a lie if their lives depended on it, find the clear-cut certainties of this most unspeculative of men: 'Most statesmen,' writes A. J. P. Taylor in a passage unworthy of his brilliance, 'seek to show that they have acted from high-minded motives, but have failed to live up to them. They do not plan wars; they drift into them and think it an adequate excuse to plead that this was unintentional. Bismarck aspired to control events. He would go to war only "when all other means were exhausted" and then for "a prize worthy of the sacrifices which every war demands." This may shock those who judge by motives instead of by results.

'But Bismarck's planned wars killed thousands; the just wars of the twentieth century have killed millions.'[9]

Bismarck's thinking was better than that. Leaving aside the philosophical implications of motives versus results, the statement is nonsense if only because 'results' are not limited to the winning or losing of a war. The results of Bismarck's policies are with us still: those policies helped to produce wars far more terrible than any war Bismarck ever visualized or would have permitted to take place in his lifetime, the very wars, indeed, into which lesser statesmen were to drift. Of course he was far from being solely responsible for the disasters of the twentieth century, but he had more indirect responsibility for them than most. Of course he was not the only nineteenth-century statesman to believe that war was a reasonable way of carrying on, but he was the only one who actively stirred up war-hysteria to make people eager to fight when it had never crossed their minds to do so and for a cause in which they did not believe. This is what Bismarck was to do between the capitulation of Denmark in 1864 and the war with Austria and the rest of Germany two years later. The Prussian people, who would have been pleased to join the rest of Germany to fight for German nationalism and Augustenburg against Denmark, had to be most carefully conditioned to fight for their own territorial gain against fellow-Germans not only in Austria but also in Hanover, Hesse, Saxony, Baden, Württemberg, and Bavaria.

Time was not on Bismarck's side. The image of the leisurely schemer and weaver of spells which he contrived to establish in his later years has obscured the urgent, the almost frenetic intensity of purpose he exhibited in the years of struggle. From 1862 to 1866 his entire career, his very existence, depended, as he saw it, upon his ability to conquer public opinion in Prussia before there was another revolution or before the king lost patience and allowed General Manteuffel and his friends to do away with the Constitution once and for all. There was only one way to win public opinion while retaining existing royal prerogatives and that was to present an excited and awe-struck people with a prize in the shape of territorial gains—through diplomacy, purchase, war, or all three. He expected it would have to be war, but he was determined to go as far as he could without war. He was not yet sure of Italy and France, and he was by no means sure that he could find the cash to fight a major campaign.

Time and time again in the early days of the Schleswig-Holstein crisis the liberals allowed themselves to exult in the prospect of Bismarck's imminent dismissal. In the closing weeks of 1863 a parliamentary resolution in support of Augustenburg was proposed by none other than the celebrated pathologist Rudolf Virchow, who was also a prominent liberal deputy. It was carried with a resounding majority. Since it was widely known that the king and most of the members of his family were also in favour of Augustenburg, the hopes of Bismarck's enemies rose high. But he survived, as months earlier he had survived the fiasco of the Alvensleben Convention, and as very soon he was to survive a crushing government defeat (275 votes to 50) when the finance minister, Karl von Bodelschwingh (who had succeeded von der Heydt in 1862), requested a 12-million-thaler credit to pay for Prussia's share in the Federal Execution against the Danish king.

This was when Bismarck threw out his contemptuous challenge, 'we shall take the money where we find it,' and Karl von Twesten made his dramatic appeal to William:[10] the Liberals, he said, would support any other ministry, even a Conservative one, if only it pursued a truly national policy—as opposed to the so-called European policy which the minister-president, by his adherence to the Treaty of London, was supposed to be favouring (since this is precisely what he said he was doing, for the purpose of luring Austria into his net and putting England and France in check, he had only himself to blame if his own countrymen were deceived as well).[11] At the end of January 1864, with Prussian and Austrian troops poised for their invasion of Schleswig, the Landtag carried a resolution stigmatizing the expenditure of public funds without parliamentary approval as a breach of the Constitution. Once more the unfortunate chamber was prorogued for its pains.

Now, however, what was beginning to look like a serious and concerted effort by liberals of every kind to force the issue began to crumble in face of intimations of military glory. Already there were some who forecast that the first Prussian victory would swing the opposition into line behind Bismarck, and in fact the storming of Düppel swelled every Prussian breast with pride. If Bismarck called an election at that moment, Bernhardi commented, he would win a hundred seats.[12] Some members of his government wanted to do just this, but the last thing Bismarck desired was any kind of political distraction. He saw a difficult time ahead, and the longer he could keep parliament in the background the better. The Landtag, prorogued on 25 January 1864, did not meet again until a year later, and in that time a good deal happened, not least the development of a carefully contrived agitation for annexation of the duchies; not least the growth of Prussian patriotism, for the lack of which Bismarck in the last days of the old session had taunted the Opposition; not least the intensification of all sorts of pressures and sanctions on opponents, or suspected opponents, of Bismarck's policies, and all associated with them.

At a time when the rest of Europe, including most of Germany (Baden, Württemberg, Bavaria, Saxony), the great Austrian Empire, even Russia for a brief spell, was moving towards greater individual freedom, a deeper sense of individual dignity and a new understanding of the constructive forces latent in those who were not born to rule, Bismarck was systematically transforming Prussia into a police state. And he operated thus not in the spirit of a Nicholas I of Russia, who regarded his realm as a holy trust, his people as wayward children to be disciplined for their own good and protected from their baser selves—Bismarck had no such claims to be above the law (or, rather, to be the law itself) and he was not in the least moved by paternal affection for his people. He operated thus with one purpose only—to subdue the Prussian people for the enlargement and glorification of the Prussian state.

Thus, after the 1863 election he shocked the nation by the savagery of his assault on all who had exposed themselves by speaking out against his policies. Parliamentary deputies of distinction, as well as unsuccessful candidates, were heavily fined for attacking the government in their election addresses. Manufactories and businesses connected with opposition politicians were subjected to sanctions and deprived of government contracts; civil servants were dismissed; professional men with a liberal cast of mind were excluded from government appointments. A very important landmark was passed in May 1864 when the king reluctantly agreed that judges should be advanced not on grounds of seniority but in recognition of their political soundness. The liberals fought back but Bismarck rode them down, using the bureaucracy as though it was a private police force; senior civil servants carried out his command in a spirit of obedience that was very close to servility. Thus, when a liberal was elected mayor he would find the government refusing to confirm his appointment, a government agent being set up in his place. Most of the lower courts were presided over by liberals, but virtually all high court judges were conservatives, able and eager to overrule the lower courts in every case which had a political aspect. When the minister of justice himself, Count Leopold von Lippe, protested against this suborning of the judiciary Bismarck retorted as a matter of course that it was the business of the government to reward its friends and punish its enemies.

By 1865 things had gone so far that he felt strong enough not merely to talk down, override, or simply ignore the most articulate of the parliamentary objectors to governmental lawlessness but actually to prosecute two distinguished deputies of the Lower House, Twesten and John Peter Frentzel, for protesting, *as deputies*, in the Chamber itself, against the erosion of constitutional rights. One of the staunchest of the liberal deputies, the Progressive Party leader Baron Leopold von Hoverbeck, who had been in the van of the fight against the Army Bill, predicted that the will of the reformers would be steadily undermined, sapped by Bismarck's relentless pressure, to the point when all opposition would simply fade away. Better, he declared, have an openly absolutist system, under which everyone knew where he was and could see the enemy for what he was.[13]

It was an extraordinary performance on the part of this very extraordinary newcomer. It was made possible in part because most conservatives still imagined, until it was too late, that Bismarck, in spite of his notorious vagaries, was at heart a conservative like themselves and therefore on their side; in part by the sheer lack of experience in political responsibility to be found in liberal (or any other) circles; in part by the running for cover of civil servants too long accustomed to quasi-military subordination; in part by a king who thought of himself as a soldier above all, upheld by a military caste which traditionally took the concept of the army as a political force entirely for granted. What happened was that in the course of three years the newcomer, by deliberately emphasizing all the most backward aspects of the Prussian ethos, so demoralized his Prussia (as later all Germany) that she was led ever further away from the mainstream of west European development. And the most extraordinary thing of all was that he managed to impose his own rule without formally destroying the Constitution and without returning to monarchical absolutism. By the time he had at last won the acclaim of his countrymen by giving them a great victory, the society over which he then presided for another twenty-five years had stopped growing: he himself had stopped it.

It is easy to be hard on the Prussian liberals. But they were caught between the hereditary conservatives on the one hand and the peasantry and the growing proletariat on the other. The army was their great enemy, but the king loved the army and they valued the monarchy. They were not republicans—why should they have been in that epoch when the French Revolution was still so close in time? And they had had their own failed revolution of 1848 to remind them of the horrors lurking in the abyss. The liberals, like good bourgeoisie, were highly nervous of the mob, which so easily threatened to destroy all they had built up with their own toil and their own brains. Bismarck, on the other hand, planned to unleash the mob and control it, in the belief that the peasant vote under a system of universal suffrage would uphold the prerogatives of the crown. Again, the liberals condemned war; but their very liberalism was rooted in a new sort of national pride: Prussia within Germany, Prussia leading Germany in unity. And when Bismarck, who had no national pride, beat the drum for them and sent them into battle and on to victory, it was national pride that triumphed and delivered them finally into the hands of the great manipulator. So that in time they came to glorify his *Realpolitik*, not realizing that he could be as woundingly impersonal towards his fellow-countrymen as he was towards the governments of foreign lands; not realizing that the accomplished practitioner of *Realpolitik* would apply to his own people the techniques they so admired when applied to the undoing of foreigners.

Compared with Bismarck and the small forces he commanded the liberals were numerous but wretchedly fragmented. They aspired not so much to take a share in government as to watch over it and keep its activity under some control. Some of the most gifted, like Bennigsen, came from outside Prussia. Others, deputies from the Rhineland provinces which had been part of Prussia for only a single generation and enjoyed age-long traditions remote from the Junker traditions of the lands beyond the Elbe, were hard put to it to understand Berlin. The bulk of the Prussian deputies were professional men—doctors, lawyers, teachers—and business men from the larger towns or the swiftly expanding industrial centres.

In the 1862 parliament the Liberals were in an overwhelming majority. Out of 352 seats only 11 were held by true-blue government supporters. The Catholic Centre Party (mostly from the Rhineland) and the Polish deputies, 56 in all, would sometimes vote with the government, sometimes against it. The Liberals themselves had 285 seats, 135 of them controlled by the new and radical Progressives led by Hoverbeck, whom we have already encountered, and Max von Forckenbeck, who was in the forefront of the attack on the Army Bill—both respected members of the East Prussian squirearchy. But the Progressives themselves were divided. They included a small, very radical wing led by Benedikt Waldeck, who had sat in the notorious National Assembly of 1848 and looked back to that year of revolutions for his inspiration. To the right of the Progressives but still slightly left of centre, were 103 moderates, and still to the right of these some 47 'Constitutionalists.' The whole contained some very able men. They were beginning to understand how to work together and to enjoy the new sense of responsibility laid upon them by their office. Given a fair wind, the Lower House would have developed into a useful forum, teaching itself how to govern and working to bring the king to an understanding of his constitutional position, which is all most of them ever aspired to. But a fair wind was the last thing they got. It was a tragedy of a very high order, and yet characteristic of the muddle in which Prussia found herself, that in the very first days of the new reign King William had to be questioned and opposed on the one matter (the conduct of the army) which he regarded as

inalienably and absolutely his own prerogative; and it was a blow of fate
that in this moment of crisis the one man who was ready and able to defy
parliament without formally abolishing the Constitution should have been
waiting and ready in the wings. The alternatives were abdication in favour
of a liberally inclined crown prince, or military dictatorship at the hands of
General Manteuffel. It might have been better for Germany, and therefore
for Prussia, if Manteuffel had prevailed. Sooner or later there would have
been another popular revolt against absolutism; and certainly the southern
states of Germany would never have allowed themselves to be unified and
dominated by an openly absolutist Prussia.

Bismarck was skilled enough as a parliamentarian to kill the Lower
House as an effective body, while, as a natural dictator, he was skilled
enough to hide behind the sacred figure of the monarch, borrowing authority from the king when he needed it, rejecting it when it did not fit in
with his plans. Thus it was that throughout the 1860s the Prussian Liberals, who like all German Liberals wanted unity not only for nationalistic
reasons but for trade and commerce and air to breathe and an end to
small-court nonsense, were left to their devices by the great leader, who
preferred to stake his appeal for unity on force and on the nationalist emotion to generate that force, while he occupied himself with diplomatic exercises directed to his own greater glory. Industry for him meant the sinews
of war. Before opening the second phase of his offensive against Austria, he
decided it was time for him to make himself known in the Ruhr. On his
way back to Berlin from Paris at the end of October 1864 he spent some
time seeing what 'Krupp's cannon foundry at Essen' had to offer.[14]

CHAPTER XII

TO THE BRINK— AND OVER

The conference on what to do about about the duchies which took place in Maria Theresa's great summer palace at Schönbrunn on the outskirts of Vienna was beautifully indeterminate, and the fact that historians are still arguing about what Bismarck meant in August 1864 is a high tribute to his impenetrability. How could Francis Joseph and poor Rechberg be expected to have known what was going on behind that baggy and unsettling gaze when the brightest spirits of all the history schools of Europe and America argue about it to this day? Is it *lèse majesté* to suggest that Bismarck himself did not know? Why should he have known? When you are waiting to see which way a cat will jump you pretend to be very busy.

Bismarck pretended to be very busy. He wanted the duchies for Prussia: it was simply a question of how and when. In conversation with Rechberg he suggested that in return for the duchies Prussia might underwrite Austria's position in Italy. Rechberg was sensible enough to demand more than a vague verbal promise and no doubt congratulated himself on his prudence when Bismarck backed away from the carefully prepared draft agreement which embodied the Austrian proposals—Prussia to receive Schleswig in exchange for her support of Austria in Venetia; and Holstein if and when Austria regained Lombardy. Free and loose in his talk as he was, Bismarck was as circumspect as any Russian when it came to committing himself on paper. What Rechberg failed to realize was that by reacting with such transparent eagerness to a deliberately vague proposition he had risen to the fly and told Bismarck what he wanted to know: namely, that Austria had no objection in principle to Prussia's eventual annexation of the duchies. All that remained, therefore, was the question of when and how.

With this in mind Bismarck once more put his own royal master through the hoops. The still young emperor and the elderly king sat facing each other in that great palace amid the marvellous and airy arabesques of rococo fantasy with Rechberg's draft agreement between them. Francis Joseph, who was at last beginning to learn about diplomacy, asked William outright whether he wanted to annex the duchies or simply to secure certain rights in them. Bismarck made no move to help his master out but left him to answer alone, which he did, halting, reluctant, visibly wrestling with his conscience. No, he declared, he had no right to the duchies and therefore could not claim them.[1] Since that put an end to any sort of a deal between Austria and Prussia, Bismarck was now at liberty to find ways and means of obtaining the duchies for nothing.

The means he chose was a war of nerves. But first he needed to steady his own raw nerves. For two years now he had been fighting with no help from anyone at all except for Roon, and usually against his king's objections on the one hand and parliament on the other. He was for the moment exhausted. It was time for Biarritz—and Kathy Orlov once again. So off he went once more on official sick-leave, knowing that the Orlovs would be paying their annual visit. And at once he was transported: all his old delight came flooding back from oblivion. So that to Johanna, left behind with the childen in Berlin, he wrote: 'It is like a dream for me. There lies the sea in front of me, while Kathy works away at her Beethoven overhead, such weather as we have not had all summer, and not a drop of ink in the house.'[2] Nobody knows what Kathy Orlov really made of him. They were to write to each other for the remainder of her all too short life (she died ten years later, in 1874, at thirty-five), but they never came together again.

Now, however, he found in her his return to innocence—or, if not innocence, at least a light-heartedness almost quite forgotten. Not innocence, because even as he rejoiced in her company he was engaged in one of those tactical withdrawals whereby he removed himself from the centre of affairs when some crisis, large or small, was brewing. This time the crisis centred on Vienna, not Berlin, and it concerned the future of Rechberg, who was in deep trouble with his political opponents for failing to stand up to Prussia—or, rather, for misreading Bismarck's character and convincing himself so disastrously that he was a fellow-Conservative above all concerned with maintaining the old order. To stay in office, Rechberg had to produce some sort of a rabbit out of his hat, and quickly. The only available rabbit at short notice was yet another promise from Berlin to take Austria into the Zollverein at some future date. It would not have been a very impressive trophy, but it would have helped. Bismarck recommended that the promise should be given, but his trade and finance ministers raised technical objections. He had gone off to Biarritz leaving the matter unsettled, but he could have struck like Jupiter from afar had he really wanted to save Rechberg. The very fact that he did not do so and then, years later, made a great to-do about the unhappy consequences of Rechberg's fall (Austrian anti-Prussianism, leading to war) suggests very strongly that this was one of those occasions on which he preferred not to take the obviously decisive action himself but to leave the last move to others, knowing that there would be advantages to be won from every possible move—or, that if at the last moment he found he did not like the decision, he could take swift action of his own to counter it.

On this occasion there were advantages to be had both from saving Rechberg and from letting him drown: that upright and unsubtle man had staked his reputation on the Prussian alliance, and for as long as it was convenient for Bismarck to preserve it Rechberg was the best man to have in Vienna. On the other hand, since it was clear that Prussia must soon be shifting her attitude towards Austria, it might be easier to let Rechberg go now in order to establish a more distant relationship with his successor.

And this is what happened. There was one man in Austrian service, Maximilian Biegeleben, a departmental official, who had the clearest possible view of Prussian aims and did his level best to urge a formal confrontation. But it was beyond the powers of a civil servant to move Rechberg from his course or later to influence the honest and well-meaning diplomat, Count Mensdorff-Pouilly, who succeeded him. For Mensdorff was too much of a gentleman to fathom the schemings of a Bismarck. And Biegeleben was too unimaginative to understand that no pin-pricks, however painful, would move a Bismarck from his course, once he had decided on it; further, that all such jabs would be turned against Austria with interest.

In fact Mensdorff was scarcely less eager to appease than Rechberg. The process of isolating the future of the duchies and their removal from the jurisdiction of the Frankfurt Diet continued. By the end of November 1864 Austria acted in concert with Prussia in forcing through a vote to remove the Confederate troops from the duchies, which left the two powers in sole command. Since this situation was absurd from Austria's point of view, Mensdorff, who never understood the true inwardness of the affair of the duchies, suggested alternative propositions, which removed the situation entirely and visibly from the world of principle to the world of naked power, thus marking the final retreat from legitimacy on the part of Austria, the champion of legitimacy.

From now on she was meeting Bismarck on his own ground: the ground of might, of *Realpolitik*. If Prussia would not agree to the creation of a new principality under Augustenburg, one alternative was for her to annex both duchies in return for compensation in the form of various small parts of Württemberg and Silesia. Bismarck now showed himself a master of infinitely pettifogging objections, driving poor Mensdorff nearly out of his mind with frustration and exasperation. But in the middle of all his lawyer's nonsense (which included a formal examination of the claims to the duchies of his own king as ruler of Brandenburg) one hard point emerged. From November onwards Bismarck had been talking with his grandest vagueness about Prussia's 'special rights' in the duchies—rights which would have to be satisfied if, hypothetically, she gave up the idea of annexation. In February 1865, under extreme Austrian pressure, he at last produced a definition of those special rights, which came to be known as the 'February Conditions': the army and navy of Schleswig-Holstein were to swear allegiance to the Prussian king and become part of the Prussian armed forces; coastal bases were to go to Prussia, who could also build a canal across the isthmus; the duchies were to enter the Zollverein; Prussian troops would garrison a Confederate fortress. . . .

The conditions were instantly rejected, as they were meant to be. They were 'without precedent in all history', Mensdorff declared. In fact, Bismarck had simply resurrected the impossible conditions he had sought to impose on Augustenburg himself the previous summer. Now there was nothing to be done but continue with the joint administration, but at least Mensdorff knew that Austria must cease giving way. Too late. Bismarck had already embarked on a policy of extreme provocation, which could be met only by retreat or ultimatum. On his way back to Berlin from Kathy and Biarritz the previous autumn he had called on Napoleon and his foreign minister Edouard Drouyn de Lhuys and satisfied himself that for the time being Austria would find no help from France. He now felt safe enough to press hard. The Prussian commissioner in Schleswig, Zedlitz, was already behaving like a viceroy, and Mensdorff at last decided to open a counter-offensive. He encouraged Bavaria to raise the Augustenburg issue in the Diet and he encouraged Baron Ludwig von Gablenz, the Austrian commissioner in Holstein, to allow pro-Augustenburg demonstrations. Bismarck replied by demanding that Austria should expel the duke from Holstein. Austria refused, whereupon Bismarck formally charged her with breaking the terms of the alliance.

This was getting very close to war. One of the few politicians of flexibility and vision, the Saxon Beust, urged upon Austria the unheard-of recommendation that she should herself convene a German parliament elected directly by the people. His argument was that with Prussia determined to challenge Austria at every turn, the Confederation as then constituted could no longer answer the needs of the day. Bismarck was embarked on a course which would lead inevitably through the annexation of the duchies to the mastery of Germany. This could not, however, be achieved by a simple war of conquest, which meant that Bismarck would have to get the people of Germany, or the mass of them, on his side by promising them the realization of their dream of unification. *Let Austria pre-empt him and turn the tables on Prussia in the only decisive way, while there was still time:* she would have Saxony and all the southern states behind her.[3]

But there was nobody in Vienna to echo Beust's words, if only to the extent of exploring new lines of action and thus taking the initiative away from Prussia. And Francis Joseph himself had no thought at this moment for anything but survival. He was beset on every side, in his private as well as his public life; the Hungarians, for ever ungovernable, were pressing hard for their independence; his adored empress, Elisabeth, was moving further away from him than ever; his brother Maximilian was already deeply embroiled in the tragi-comic Mexican adventure which was to end in front of a firing squad in an alien and unconquered land; the empire itself was bankrupt. Within two years, when he had lost to Prussia the leadership of Germany and been forced to concede to Hungary all the advantages and none of the disadvantages of independence as equal partners with Austria in a Dual Monarchy, he was to come to terms with reality, but now all he could do was try to keep his end up with Prussia while at the same time avoiding war.

For a time this situation suited Bismarck too. His plan, as Beust saw, was to obtain the duchies and then from this larger Prussia establish control of all Germany north of the River Main. If this could be done without a war, so much the better, but it had to be done fairly soon, because time was not on his side.

Well over a century was to pass before the brilliant researches of Professor Fritz Stern into the life of Bismarck's personal banker and financial adviser, Gerson Bleichröder, showed (among many other larger matters) how the Austrian war was paid for and the money obtained. In so doing he also demonstrated that the need for hard cash played a part as important as diplomacy in Bismarck's manoeuvring before the final clash, his blowing now hot now cold, his apparently inexplicable hesitations.[4]

The first of these was the occasion of the Crown Council of 29 May 1865. Feeling had been flying very high since the Bavarian move at Frankfurt on the one side and, on the other, Roon's announcement in early April that the headquarters of the infant Prussian navy were to be moved from Danzig to Kiel, in Holstein. Protest and counter-protest poisoned the atmosphere in Berlin and Vienna alike. Before the month was out Bismarck had made his sombre pronouncement: 'We are reaching a parting of the ways: unfortunately our tickets are for different lines.'[5]

He was also winning his battle with the conscience of King William. The thing that carried the day was the outcome of his appeal to a reactionary and anachronistic court known as the Crown Syndics, which came out with the verdict that King Christian had in fact been the only lawful ruler of the duchies and that since in the previous August he had ceded all his rights in Schleswig-Holstein to Prussia and Austria by the Peace of Vienna, it was within the province of the rulers of these countries to dispose of the duchies as they saw fit. This remarkable ruling, which contradicted the whole case for the Danish War (that the Danish king had forfeited his rights in the duchies by flouting the Treaty of London) was regarded with derision outside Prussia, but it served Bismarck's purpose by giving comfort to William.

All seemed to be set for the final confrontation. William himself was now enthusiastic for annexation and was ready to risk war; Roon too. But it was now, at the critical Crown Council, that Bismarck, as so often, produced a surprise. There would have to be war sooner or later, he explained, but not yet, and not simply a war for possession of the duchies. Let us soften the most provocative items in the February Conditions, he went on. Provided the Prussian army effectively controls the armed forces of Holstein it does not matter whether this control is formalized or not. And so on. This sort of issue was not in itself worth a war—war, when it came, must be fought for some 'higher aim.' What he meant by a 'higher aim' in this context was the establishment of North German union controlled from Berlin.[6]

Thus, at the very moment when he had the king on his side and ready to fight for the duchies he said in effect: Not enough; what we have to fight for is Prussian mastery of North Germany. William was now being invited to take another giant step forward. He was being invited to accustom himself to the idea of fighting not only Austria but all the states of the Confederation who would ally themselves with her. And the war aims would not be limited to the return to Germany, or Prussia, of the long-lost Holsteiners, but would extend to the conquest by Prussia of peaceful members of her own German family.

The task now was to rattle and provoke the Austrians into making mistakes—but at a tempo carefully controlled. Everything possible was done to harass, exasperate, confuse the Austrian authorities; every complaint the Austrians made was received with a great display of injured innocence. It was Bismarck at this period who originated and brought to perfection a technique which, widely adopted by his successors, was to develop into one of the more unfortunate characteristics of German official behaviour: stamp on your neighbour's foot and when he complains or stamps back look aggrieved and ill-used. (Bismarck, of course, knew just what he was doing; others, who tried to copy him, did not.)

The first crisis came at the end of July. By refusing to abate any of the February Conditions, William made it impossible for Bismarck to sustain the ideal flexibility he sought in all his dealings. Roon was quite sure that the army was ready. Bismarck was not. Nor was he yet sure what France and Italy would do in case of war. Above all he lacked money. Money was on the way, but he needed it under his hand. Gerson Bleichröder, the gifted and ambitious Jewish banker whose agency for the Rothschilds and whose wide international connections made him so invaluable to Bismarck, had already negotiated on his behalf the sale to private interests of the Prussian government's rights in the Cologne-Minden railway. But the cash was not due until July 1866. Furthermore, Bismarck knew that he had no right to dispose of state property without parliamentary approval. Roon on the other hand regarded the fruits of this dubious and rather desperate transaction as money in the bank. 'We have money enough to give us a free hand in foreign policy,' he wrote, 'enough, if need be, to mobilize the whole army and pay for an entire campaign. This gives our stance vis-à-vis Austria the necessary aplomb so that we may hope that they will give in to our reasonable demands without war, which none of us wants. . . .

Whence the money? Without violating a law, primarily through an arrangement with the Cologne-Minden railway, which I and even Bodelschwingh consider very *advantageous*.'[7]

(The recipient of this confidence was Moritz von Blanckenburg, now a Conservative leader in the Landtag, once, eighteen years before, the man who had striven to bring Bismarck to Christianity: the husband of Marie von Thadden.)

But in fact the law was broken, and Bismarck knew it. He also knew, or believed, that Austria was so desperate for cash that she dare not risk a war: his best information on this matter came, like so much of the same kind, from Bleichröder, although nobody but Bismarck knew, and Bismarck never publicly acknowledged, the great services he rendered. Bleichröder believed that because of her appalling financial situation Austria would be prepared to yield still further concessions, and he was right.[8]

August 1865 and Bad Gastein once again—not even the prospect of imminent war with Austria could keep William away from his favourite and enchanting Austrian spa. Bismarck went with him. Francis Joseph decided to try one more appeal, instructing Count Blome, his minister to Württemberg, to go to Gastein and sound out the Prussian king. Francis Joseph could not have made a worse choice of envoy. Blome was determined to reach a settlement no matter what it cost Vienna. The result, signed and sealed at Salzburg in the archbishop's palace, where the young Mozart had once lived and worked like a servant, was from the Austrian point of view calamitous. The 'eternally inseparable' duchies were to be divided for all purposes of control and administration (but with nominal joint sovereignty), Holstein to Austria, Schleswig to Prussia. Austria had lost the last vestige of her moral propriety, by which she set great store. She had also placed herself in an untenable position, presiding over an enclave entirely surrounded by Prussians. 'I never imagined,' Bismarck exclaimed, 'I should find an Austrian diplomatist who would put his name to such a document!'[9] To Eulenburg at the Ministry of the Interior in Berlin he wrote that he had been playing for time to get money and to neutralize France. He was looking for a stop-gap arrangement 'tolerable for us . . . with which for the time being we can live with honour without the possibility of war running away from us.'[10] On a more personal note, he also asked Eulenburg to tell Bleichröder not to unload for fear of war any of his, Bismarck's, personal securities that he might still hold. . . . This one letter to Eulenburg, only very recently brought to light, provides a direct insight into Bismarck's public and private morality which in itself makes nonsense of a whole library of apologetics.

The Gastein Convention for Bismarck was, to use his own phrase, a 'papering over of the cracks.' But for Austria it was hardly even that. Holstein was now an open wound which Bismarck was determined to keep open. There was a moment when it looked as though Austria might be ready to sell Holstein to Prussia, as she had sold Lauenburg; Bleichröder was active in raising funds for this; Bismarck was ready for it. It meant putting off the final confrontation with Austria yet again, but there was a good deal to be said for that: Austrian finances and Austrian armaments were not improving. Prussia, on the other hand, was now beginning to profit from the army reforms carried through in the teeth of parliament. But France was still a worry, and as after Schönbrunn, so now after Gastein, Bismarck went out of his way to reassure the French, who read into the Convention a new *rapprochement* between Prussia and Austria. Drouyn found fresh confirmation of his extreme distrust of Bismarck, which his master Napoleon did not share. When Drouyn heard news of Gastein he lodged a formal protest: 'We regret to find no other foundation for the Convention than force, no other justification than the reciprocal convenience of the co-sharers. This is a mode of procedure to which the Europe of today has become unaccustomed, and precedents for it must be sought in the darkest ages of history.'[11] It is not clear whether Drouyn saw the Bonapartist era as one of those 'darkest ages' or whether he thought the sort of force used by the first Napoleon was different from the sort of force now employed by Austria and Prussia. Be that as it may, the naked cynicism of the joint annexation by the two powers who had gone to war to protect the integrity of the duchies they were now absorbing did undoubtedly shock their neighbours. In the words of Lord Russell whose own feeble policy, nevertheless, had invited the final result: 'All rights old or new . . . have been trodden underfoot by the Gastein Convention, and the *authority of force* is the only power that has been consulted and recognized.'[12]

One unfortunate consequence of the Gastein Convention (unfortunate for Germany and the world: fortunate for Bismarck) was the way in which Austrian complicity blurred and partly obscured the truth about Bismarck's own design. Austria, on the face of it, had allowed herself to be tempted into corruption for the sake of territory which she did not want, which was of no conceivable use to her, and the possession of which was bound to bring her into conflict with the tempter. Perhaps the cleverest, most subtle, most malignant passage in Bismarck's handling of the whole affair of the duchies on which he was to pride himself was the way in which he manoeuvred Austria into sharing his iniquity, thus softening the stark black outlines of his own behaviour.

Even so, he still had reason to fear France's reaction to Gastein. While he instructed his newspapers to attack France and England with venom unrestrained, he did what he could to reassure Napoleon at long range, and then in October headed for his beloved Biarritz, where he knew the emperor would be spending some time with Eugénie. But of course he was also looking forward to Kathy Orlov, and this time he took with him Johanna and their daughter, Marie, who had been unwell.

It must have been a somewhat bizarre excursion: Bismarck, his nerves in shreds after pulling off his coup at Gastein, preparing himself for an elaborate sparring match with Napoleon, and for the first time carting off Johanna to join in a jolly family party with the Orlovs. It was even more bizarre when the Bismarck entourage arrived to find no Kathy. She had changed her plans, they were told, cancelled her reservations at the last moment, and gone off with her mother to Torquay on the south coast of England. Almost at once a letter arrived from England explaining that Mama had been alarmed by news of a cholera outbreak in Bordeaux and would not allow her to travel south to the Pyrenees.[13] Bismarck took it hard. He sent off an extremely stiff and stuffy reply, suggesting that Kathy could have done him 'a very great service' had she been able to bring herself to inform him of her changed intention at the same time as she had written to the proprietor of her Biarritz hotel.[14] After ten days he had decided to forgive her, but was still deeply upset. 'Biarritz,' he wrote, 'is a truly miserable place for a holiday, and it is highly improbable that I shall ever come here again. So long as I was with you I was able to overlook or quickly forget all the inconveniences, but now I have been cured of my illusions and nothing remains but boredom and vexation.'[15] Now, without Kathy, for the first time he was noticing that the wine was bad, the drinking water stale, the beds damp and too short. 'If we eat in our room the service and the food is bad; but if we eat downstairs in the dining-room the company is bad. . . .' 'I came in search of the fountain of youth and I have aged ten years; that makes me just sixty. . . .'[16] And so on. He does not say how Johanna was managing.

There is no direct evidence to show just why Kathy Orlov ran away. We do know, however, that she and Bismarck had been corresponding about a meeting earlier in the summer, that it was not until late in September that he wrote to Kathy about hotels and told her he would be bringing Johanna and Marie, that he arrived in Biarritz on 3 October and there discovered that she had cancelled a week earlier. It seems a fair presumption, therefore, that Kathy decided that Otto *en famille* was not what she had bargained for—and that he himself guessed as much, and also felt in his bones that here was the end of a chapter. They still went on writing to each other, but they never met again. There was to be no further mellowing influence in Bismarck's life.

Not that Kathy would have made him behave differently in either the short run or the long. He was now fully wound up and undeflectable, proceeding like a huge and irreversible mechanical juggernaut, until he ran at last, after twenty-four more years, into an immovable object and overturned, wheels racing. The immovable object was vanity, the vanity of William's grandson, the Kaiser William II. Vanity was that tiresome ruler's only strength. The fact that all Bismarck's own protean strength could not overcome it raises questions about the nature of that strength. This is to gallop ahead of time; but I do not think it is helpful to contemplate this great figure as he approaches his first major triumph without bearing in mind what happened to him in the end: he was destroyed by a monarch so manifestly his inferior that it did not even occur to him that he was threatened. What made him so vulnerable?

He is certainly vulnerable now as he sits in Biarritz glooming about Kathy Orlov, because he is pushing his luck very hard. The very day after his arrival he has had a long conversation with Napoleon, and soon he is to have another—followed by yet another at St.-Cloud on his way home (St.-Cloud, the Imperial Palace, to be burned to the ground by Prussian troops only five years later). And he has decided that Napoleon is a spent force, an ailing man who has used up all his vitality and is now simply hanging on. This did not mean that he could make no more trouble; it did mean, Bismarck thought, that there was no danger of an active coalition between Austria and France for the undoing of Prussia. And although nothing came out of the Biarritz and St.-Cloud meetings, they gave Bismarck a chance to frighten Vienna by investing the occasions with a deep mysteriousness that boded unknown terrors. At least he was able to report in characteristic style a little optimistically, but in the main correctly, that Napoleon was still favourable to Prussia: he was, he said, ready 'to dance the cotillion with us, without knowing in advance what the steps will be or when it will start.'[17] In fact, Napoleon, in his own personal style, was playing the game as Bismarck was playing it in his: each was determined to use Austria as a lever against the other. One consequence of this was that at the very moment when Bismarck had hoped to persuade Vienna to surrender Holstein for desperately needed cash, French bankers came to her rescue with a massive loan.

But, of course, it was not a rescue. Had Austria got rid of Holstein for cash and then sold Venetia to Italy, which she could also have done at this time, the face of history would have been changed. For Bismarck would have had no excuse to go to war and no Italian ally if he did so.

The refusal by Austria of the cash offers from Prussia and Italy was a disguised climacteric. In one of his conversations with Benedetti Bismarck remarked: 'If the king is to be persuaded to demand his rights, he must first be convinced that somebody is disputing them. But when once he believes that his authority is being challenged, he will concur in the most energetic measures.'[18] To keep the quarrel going now Austria had to be provoked into seeming to do just this. And so it happened. Austria was doomed. It was not merely that under internal strain, above all induced by the Hungarians, Francis Joseph could not think straight about Germany; even while Vienna blundered from one mistake to the next the outside world rejoiced in the tribulations of a proud and rival power. Nobody wanted Austria brought down; everyone was pleased to see her suffer. Russia had never forgiven her the 'betrayal' of the Crimean War; Napoleon assumed that she was far stronger than in fact she was, so that sooner or later Bismarck would have to turn to him for help—at a price; England, traditionally far removed from Catholic Austria, still highly sympathetic towards Prussia (even though Bismarck personally was regarded with increasing distaste and distrust), had turned her back on the Continent: she had publicly disgraced herself twice in the course of the year, betraying her principles and her friends, first in the matter of the Polish revolt, then in the matter of the duchies. Palmerston was finished, and the Russell-Gladstone combination had taken over.

Thus it was that Austria was alone, while nobody understood that she was drowning. Francis Joseph's supreme mistake, once he had made up his mind that he would not surrender his position to Prussia within Germany, cost what it might, was to refuse the life-line flung from Italy almost immediately after Gastein, when La Marmora offered 500 million francs as the purchase price for Venetia. This would not only have got rid of the enemy on the southern flank, leaving Austria to face Prussia only, but also broken up the dangerous partnership between Napoleon and Victor Emmanuel, who could then have freed himself from dependency on France. It would also have been a source of quite desperately needed cash for the restoration of the Austrian army which, even while Prussia threatened, was being steadily reduced in material and men. But Francis Joseph was too proud.

Bismarck, of course, was beside himself with delight—and also contemptuous. What idiots those Italians are, he exclaimed in effect, to throw away 500 million francs—why, for 300 million they could have had a war!

All through the autumn and winter of 1865–66 the goading went on, with Austria trying desperately now to avoid the least suggestion of provocation—and Gablenz in Holstein doing everything in his power to damp down agitation on behalf of Augustenburg. But Bismarck, with an eye like a hawk's, responded to every move, every word, with an immediate show of righteous indignation—mainly for the benefit of the king and to prove to the Prussian people that when war at last came Austria, not Prussia, would be the aggressor.

In January 1866 Austria was given what looked like another chance—by Bismarck himself. Nobody knows whether it was a genuine offer, or simply a deception: surrender to us the primacy of North Germany and we will help you to reconquer Lombardy. But Francis Joseph refused to consider the matter: he still believed he could manage a two-front war if only Russia and France kept out of it.

At Potsdam on the last day of February 1866 there took place an especially important Crown Council. Generals Moltke, Alvensleben, and Manteuffel (called in from Schleswig) were all present, and so was the civilian Count von der Goltz, summoned from the Paris embassy. War with Austria was the subject under discussion, from which various consequences flowed. Moltke, as chief-of-staff, insisted that there could be no question of fighting Austria without an understanding with Italy. Bismarck argued that the movement towards war should not be allowed to go any further without some sort of guarantee from France. Thus, in March Prussia signed a secret treaty of alliance with Italy with a life of only three months: Italy would fight Austria on Prussia's side if she went to war within those three months. In March also William agreed to send Goltz back to Paris with a personal letter suggesting an 'entente intime.' This did not work so well: Napoleon was feeling that he could achieve more by waiting. France would be neutral, he replied, but ready to act in her own interests if the European balance was threatened. In March finally, Francis Joseph, alarmed by reports from his generals of the inadequacy of Austria's defences in Bohemia, agreed to move a few regiments to face the threat from the north. He did this despite agonized warnings from Mensdorff and others that a few regiments would be of little help in war, but would give Bismarck a first-class opportunity to charge Austria with warlike intentions.

This is what happened. Bismarck rent the European air with cries of outrage. Accusations of bad faith accompanied by unscrupulous exaggerations flew like confetti. William himself was pushed by the end of the month into giving the order for the strengthening of his own frontier fortresses. At last Bismarck was getting Austria where he wanted her.

But he was also creating much alarm and despondency in Europe. When Mensdorff offered a formal declaration of Austria's peaceful intentions and invited Prussia to do the same Bismarck was very hard pressed. He had not only the parliamentarians against him but now the old Conservatives too, and even more disconcertingly, senior members of his own Foreign Office—Goltz (who coveted his master's post); Bernstorff, his old chief; Schleinitz, now minister for the court and very much a favourite of the court. Between them they organized what became known as the Coburg intrigue when Mensdorff, who was related through the Coburgs to half the royalty of Europe (he was a cousin of Queen Victoria), played his last card by persuading Victoria herself, with the duke of Coburg and almost the entire Prussian royal family from the queen and the crown prince downwards, to bring their influence to bear on King William—who actually did go so far as to prevail on his first minister to moderate the tone of his dispatch of 6 April in reply to Mensdorff's challenge. Even so, that dispatch was still far too peremptory and demanding, and it gave the opportunity to Biegeleben, the only man in Austria who was determined to have war, to reply in kind, so that all the soothing of William's ruffled feelings by the Coburgs and others was undone. Biegeleben has to be given credit for being the first Austrian to perceive that Bismarck was determined on the humiliation of Vienna, but his action was irresponsible all the same: it was the irresponsibility of the permanent official who pushes his country towards a war when he quite lacks the means of influencing armaments or strategy.

Now it was simply a matter of time. All the same, in late April Bismarck was to suffer a nasty moment. At one of those brilliant occasions, a ball at the Tuileries, which Napoleon used so often as the setting for his more ominous pronouncements, the emperor took Goltz on one side and embarked on a little gentle blackmail. It was his 1862 conversation with Bismarck himself all over again, but this time the atmosphere was heavily charged with the sense of imminent war. Vienna, he confided, had been holding out the most tempting offers to France, and this was something he could not be expected to ignore. Since no comparable offers had come out of Berlin he would probably have to close with Vienna. 'The eyes of the whole country,' he went on, 'are on the Rhine.'[19] A few days later, on 6 May, he startled all the world by publicly denouncing the 1815 settlement, the fruits of the Congress of Vienna.[20]

No wonder the rest of Europe was on edge. It has to be remembered that the first Napoleon's terrible fighting machine was still a living memory. The French army, which had swept all Europe, was still regarded as the most formidable on the Continent, while the new Napoleon himself was seen as a natural predator like his uncle before him. With the British he had beaten Russia in the Crimean War, with the Piedmontese he had beaten Austria in north Italy. Not all his waverings at the time of the Polish crisis, or the humiliating fiasco of his Mexican adventure, or his failure to exploit the Danish War in the interest of France, had been enough to dispel this illusion of military superiority, which was shared by many of those closest to the emperor himself—by Eugénie above all, but scarcely less by Drouyn at the Foreign Ministry, to say nothing of lesser figures such as Gramont, then French ambassador in Vienna, who, only four years later, was to hurtle the empire itself into ruin, and his emperor with it.

Now, in 1866, there were times when Napoleon himself seemed to be the only man in all the world to realize that he had no clothes. He was only fifty-eight, but ill and in constant pain, tired and prematurely worn out by all the strains and stresses of the adventurous and hectic life he had forced himself to live. He was a conspiratorial dreamer who had been impelled into furious activity by birth, pride, ambition, and, as a consequence, given all France to play with. Bismarck almost alone among statesmen had a proper understanding of the man: he saw through to the back of those tranquil, grey, inscrutable eyes—as he saw through to the back of everything that had no moral force behind it. He knew that Napoleon, greedy for the old frontiers, driven by Eugénie and his excitable compatriots, was being pushed to do something, anything, and yet could not make up his mind whether to go for Belgium, Luxemburg, the Palatinate, or the Rhineland. Many years earlier, when Queen Victoria had expressed concern to Eugénie about Napoleon's avowed intention of proceeding to the Crimea to assume command she, Eugénie, had replied: *'il faut étonner les Français; il ne faut jamais leur laissez le dernier mot; c'est ainsi que l'empereur a toujours fait.'*[21] And it was thus that the emperor was doomed to continue to the end. Bismarck had an inkling of this and could not be sure that Napoleon's manifest desire for peace would prevail.

In fact, once Napoleon had made his challenge to the 1815 frontiers he relapsed into enigmatic silence, either waiting to see which way the cat would jump or a little shaken by his own recklessness. Not, however, before Bismarck had taken out an insurance policy. The Coburg initiative had come to grief, but Bismarck had been alarmed by the possibility of his sovereign's mind being turned against the course upon which he had seemed so safely set by dynastic loyalties. Fury and frustration on this account now brought on his old physical troubles—aggravated by too much food and drink and no exercise at all. He would have to give up, he exploded to Roon. This 'awful friction' had become more than he could bear. The great man was still only fifty, and yet there he lay propped up on a sofa all day, an exhausted hulk complaining of unendurable pain, 'a wounded boar' reported Károlyi at this time, wounded and the more dangerous because of that.[22]

Károlyi was himself seriously perturbed. He had watched with profound apprehension the comings and goings of the Italian generals in Berlin. But Bismarck held back. He was determined to fight Austria to the death should it prove necessary to achieve his end, but if that end could be achieved without a war he was still prepared to do without one. And at this moment one of those strange little might-have-beens of history, soon hurried into oblivion by the flood of real events, was taking shape. There were two brothers Gablenz, Anton and Ludwig, both imperial knights owing their allegiance to the old, dead empire. Anton had entered the Prussian service, Ludwig the Austrian. Both were serious, upright, and distinguished. It was Ludwig, as Austrian commissioner in Holstein, who had been the target of much scurrilous Bismarckian propaganda. Now, as the two camps drifted further and further apart the brothers came together and concocted a peace-plan.

To them it was the most natural thing in the world that they should find themselves in the service of different monarchs. It was also inconceivable to them that the monarchs should fight each other. They still belonged to

the world in which a Metternich or a Beust could move from the Rhineland or Saxony to Vienna, in which Bismarck's own maternal grandfather
could move from Saxony to the Prussian service; in which the composer
Brahms from Hamburg, like Beethoven from Bonn before him, could
move to live out his life in Vienna—that world which was to be swept
away by blind nationalism, born, fairly enough, in response to French revolutionary aggression, but all too easily degraded to an intolerant and hysterically strident chauvinism.

The Gablenz plan had its impracticabilities, but Bismarck gave it his
blessing all the same, whether because he knew it would come to nothing
and yet would make him appear conciliatory, or whether because he still
wanted to avoid war if he could drive Austria out of Germany by other
means it is impossible to tell. Under the plan Schleswig-Holstein was to be
reconstituted as an independent principality, but ruled by a Hohenzollern
instead of Augustenburg. Prussia would secure the most important of the
special rights she was so loudly demanding; Austria would have her war
expenses paid by the duchies. Germany, with the several kingdoms and
principalities keeping their sovereignty, would be divided into two military
commands, North and South, with the River Main between them. Each
army command would reinforce the other against France and Italy. All
through May the brothers were as busy as bees, hurrying from chancellery
to chancellery with hopes flying high. But at the end of the month the
whole plan was neatly torpedoed by Francis Joseph: he would only adopt
it, he said, if it were backed by at least one of the medium states, e.g., Saxony or Bavaria. Since none of these was ready of its own free will to surrender its destiny absolutely into the hands of Austria or Prussia that was the
end of the Gablenz dream.

Bismarck now had to work hard and fast to make sure of Napoleon. But
what did Napoleon want? Did he himself know? And how much was Bismarck prepared to offer? Almost certainly some Prussian territory, if only
he could get the king to agree; probably the upper Moselle, with Luxemburg. But he knew very well that William would never consent to give
away any part of his inheritance. In the end he had to move without any
agreement with Napoleon.

There was only a month to go. Both sides were now manoeuvring to
gain the support of the lesser states. Bismarck tried cajolery, flattery, and
bribes; then, when they did not work, threats: *vae victis!* These did not
work either: when it came to the pinch, fear and resentment of Prussian
domination drove even the waverers into the Austrian camp. Saxony had

been with Austria from the beginning. Hanover and Hesse-Kassel, more immediately under the Prussian guns, took a long time to decide that their best hope of survival lay with the Confederation. Baden, Württemberg, and Hesse-Darmstadt favoured Austria, but were extremely limited in their usefulness without Bavaria behind them. And it was now that the equivocal relationship between Vienna and Munich was most severely felt.

The Wittelsbachs were even more ancient than the Habsburgs but they had not done so well. In the eighteenth century they had made a strong effort to expand at Austria's expense. When the wolves gathered in 1741 to savage the young and inexperienced Maria Theresa, Charles Albert, as Elector of Bavaria, allied himself with France and the Prussia of Frederick the Great. He actually got as far as having himself crowned emperor in Prague, but on that very day his own capital, Munich, fell to a brilliant counter-stroke, and soon Charles Albert was undone and dead and the imperial crown firmly back in Vienna. More recently, Bavaria had changed sides and fought with Napoleon Bonaparte against Austria (against Prussia too): it was as a reward for this that Napoleon allowed the elector to call himself king.

With this sort of background nobody could ever be sure which way Bavaria would move. It made no difference to the Bavarians that the Austrians were fellow-Catholics: the great game was to play off Austria against Prussia without being swallowed up by either—and to back the winner in the last resort. The position in 1865 was all the more unpredictable because the twenty-year-old king, Ludwig II, was a non-ruler, sublimely unconcerned with affairs of state. He was a fantasist and a musician, lavishing all the country could afford and more on his madly extravagant architectural follies and his support of Richard Wagner at a most critical stage in his career, putting on his operas in Munich and in due course building for his exclusive use the first model opera house, the Festival Theatre at Bayreuth (a little town that had belonged to the Hohenzollerns until 1791). The foreign policy of Munich was thus effectively in the hands of Baron Ludwig von der Pfordten, whose dullness and lack of imagination in general was not compensated for by his occasional amusing remark. In the event, he allied himself with Austria, but without conviction and, as will be seen, with dire consequences for Francis Joseph when it came to battle.

On 20 April frightening reports reached Vienna from north Italy: the Italians were mobilizing all along the frontier with Venetia. It was later found that they were doing no such thing, and some believed that the reports had been put out by Bismarck himself to drive the Austrians into an indiscretion. If so he succeeded in his aim. For Francis Joseph felt driven to order the mobilization of the southern army in direct contravention of the joint agreement of the two powers to return their armies to a peacetime footing. Bismarck was suddenly well again. In private he exulted. In public he fulminated. Vienna had committed an act of aggression, he roared. Nonsense, replied Vienna. This mobilization was purely defensive and directed against Italy alone. It had nothing to do with Prussia: the position on the northern front remained unchanged. And to that Bismarck replied very stiffly that the Prussian general staff could not possibly distinguish between regiments called up to move south and regiments called up to move north. He was riding Austria very hard indeed, and William, furious now with what Bismarck assured him was Austrian perfidy, had quite lost all sense of monarchical solidarity. Bismarck was free to behave as insolently as he liked.

Meanwhile the Frankfurt Diet was making its voice heard for the last time. Saxony took the lead in a concerted attack on the Prussian position, winning a two to one majority for a resolution demanding from Prussia an explanation of her mobilization. On the last day of May, desperate with frustration, while Bismarck watched and waited, Austria formally breached the Gastein Convention and placed the fate of the duchies firmly in the hands of the Confederation, whence they had been abstracted so many weary months before. Prussia promptly invaded Holstein, but even now Austria drew back, taking her troops into Hanover without making contact with the Prussian forces. Bismarck had to try again. It was now his turn to put up a plan at Frankfurt: the Confederation was requested to adopt the idea of a German union without Austria. Under this extreme provocation the Austrian delegate, breaking all the rules of the Confederation, called for the immediate mobilization of all the member states apart from Prussia. Prussia made the obvious retort and declared the Confederation dissolved. On 15 June the Prussian envoys to Saxony, Hanover, and Hesse-Kassel delivered ultimatums: Prussia would be marching through their territories to get at Austria; resistance would mean war.

And march she did. On 17 June Francis Joseph told his people that war was unavoidable. It had already started. Prussia had, in effect, declared war not only on Austria but on the whole of Germany too.

CHAPTER XIII

GERMAN AGAINST GERMAN

Most people expected Austria to win, not an annihilating victory but one decisive enough to put Prussia in her place and re-establish the German Confederation firmly under Austrian control. Francis Joseph himself took victory more or less for granted: he did not want war; he knew it would be costly—indeed, all but insupportable at a time when his realm, always hard up, was very close to bankruptcy. And he needed all his energies to deal with the ever growing Hungarian threat to the unity of that realm. Napoleon also overrated Austria's strength. Certainly she had lost the war in Italy to him only six years earlier, but he knew, none better, how nearly it had gone the other way: at Magenta, indeed, he thought he had lost the battle until it was suddenly, astonishingly, discovered that the Austrians were in retreat. And after Solferino he exclaimed that he had had enough of war: it was too chancy ('*Le hasard joue un trop grand rôle*').

The German states also believed that Prussia was inviting trouble. Bismarck found them obdurate, not to be won over by any means in his power. Now that he had at last engineered the great collision, he was far from confident. He had done all he could to give the generals their best chance of victory and his future was in their hands. Years later he was to refer to these critical days as the time 'when I was almost as close to the gallows as to the throne. . . .'[1]

This was scarcely an exaggeration. All through that spring of 1866 it had every day been growing clearer to him that with the best will in the world he could not survive as first minister without a victorious war. It was his only hope. In the eyes of the people it was one thing for Prussia to stand up to Austria and insist on being treated as an equal, quite another to go to war with her. Indeed, it was unthinkable, and the realization that he was willing the unthinkable and doing his best to provoke Austria into declaring war filled the nation as a whole with revulsion. At the same time he was alienating King William, as when he produced a revolutionary plan to win popular support for Prussia throughout Germany by introducing a federal scheme for universal suffrage.

He was twisting and turning now and trying to rattle the Austrians with every expedient—by, for example, staging demonstratively conspiratorial assignations between his own agents and subversive elements and rebels in all the capitals of the Austrian Empire—and in Belgrade and Bucharest for full measure. He was so generally detested that even when in early May he was shot at twice as he walked down Unter den Linden and showed his courage and immense strength by seizing the would-be murderer, a left-wing student who committed suicide under arrest that night, and holding him until two guardsmen rushed up and disarmed him, there were plenty who wished the young man had shot better (one of the bullets penetrated Bismarck's clothes but only scored and bruised his ribs). Even his staunchest well-wishers were attacking him, not for wrong-headedness but for wanton and reckless irresponsibility. When his old patron Ludwig von Gerlach (Leopold, his brother, had died in 1861) wrote in the *Kreuzzeitung* to this effect it says something about Bismarck's state of mind that he felt betrayed and deeply wounded, although Gerlach had long been reproaching him in private for the policies which were now coming to fruition.

Gerlach's own description of his one-time protégé in this moment of supreme crisis is revealing in another way. The grand old man, not content with flaying Bismarck in print, felt it his duty to appeal to him in person. And he reported on the meeting thus: 'He was tense and passionately worked up. I warned him against so deeply disastrous a war, reminding him that Olmütz had been in part his own achievement, and I pleaded with him to continue our personal relationship, a plea he ignored. There was an air of restless desperation about him. He spoke of God and of prayer: the matter was one between God and himself, not between friends and political associates.'[2] By God he meant destiny.

That was the end of a chapter, the breaking of Bismarck's last links with his old life. And it was in that mood that he went to war. Bismarck's diplomacy, Krupp's steel, Roon's military machine, Moltke's strategic genius were about to transform the face of Europe. It was now up to Moltke above all.

Very few people knew anything about Moltke. Bismarck himself did not at all understand the depth and range of his genius. When he rode off at the side of his monarch and, in the uniform of a major of the Landwehr, quite overshadowed by the field-marshal and his staff, Bismarck knew that he had embarked on the greatest gamble of his life. 'If we are beaten' he had told the British ambassador, Lord Augustus Loftus, 'I shall die in the last charge.'³ That was in the Chancellery garden in the Wilhelmstrasse as the clocks struck twelve on the night of 15 June. Moltke's columns at that very moment were starting their march into Saxony, Hanover, and Hesse-Kassel. Two weeks were to pass before the king and his entourage, Bismarck with them, entrained to join the Prussian First Army under Prince Frederick Charles on the Bohemian frontier. And enough had happened by then to make Moltke quite sure that he would win, and to bring the reality of Prussian might suddenly alive to Germany and all the world. But still Bismarck was far from sure.

The failure of Austria was a failure of the high command; the success of Prussia was a success of the high command. The troops and the field commanders on both sides fought with quite extraordinary gallantry and tenacity, but on the Prussian side they were trained, led, and commanded by a genius, and on the Austrian side they were not.

Moltke was a model staff officer who, when opportunity offered late in life, suddenly revealed himself as a natural commander-in-chief (the king, of course, was nominal commander-in-chief; but it was Moltke who drew up the plans). Born in 1800, a Mecklenburger brought up in Holstein, he started his military career as an officer-cadet in the Danish army, which he was later to destroy. At twenty-two he resigned to enter the service of Prussia. For the next twenty-six years he was the perpetual staff officer, mostly in Intelligence, either in Berlin or on detachment to help with other armies, most notably the Turkish army. He travelled incessantly, mapping wherever he went, analyzing past battles, finally undertaking major historical studies. At forty-five he married Mary Burt, an English teacher. At forty-eight in 1848, the year of revolutions, on the edge of retirement as a corps commander, he was called into action to help put down the Berlin rising. At fifty-five he was appointed personal adjutant to Frederick, the crown prince, who was himself a very good soldier. And two years later he was picked by the prince regent, soon to be William I, to be chief of general staff.

He was, thus, fifty-seven, lean, fine-drawn, but very tough, when he embarked with the new war minister, Roon, on a complete reorganization and re-training of the Prussian army. But he still found time to write in the busy years that followed—about the Austrian campaign of 1859 in Italy, about the Danish War. At the same time he was working on an entirely new manual of training, embodying tactics to exploit the celebrated breech-loading rifle, the needle-gun. The Prussian army had had this weapon (rejected by Austria on the grounds of expense) for a number of years, but had not yet worked out how to take best advantage of its marvellous rapidity of fire, to say nothing of the fact that it could be fired lying down—five shots lying down, to one standing up from the old muzzle-loaders. . . .

Above all Moltke was the first chief-of-staff to appreciate the way in which the problems of logistics, the movement and supply of armies, had been transformed by the advent of the railways. He and Roon between them had based the organization of the enlarged and improved Prussian army on the new and still growing Prussian railway network. Elaborate time-tables were drawn up to govern the hypothetical movement of troops and guns and horses wherever they might be needed. And superimposed on the railway network was the Prussian system of territorial organization. The country was divided into fixed areas, the *Kreis*, each with a corps HQ. Regiments were raised locally and garrisoned locally and combined in divisions belonging to the *Kreis*, so that on mobilization complete formations of regulars and reservists could be called up immediately, equipped, paraded, and entrained as fighting formations, ready to step off the train and go into action. Whereas in Austria nobody had paid serious attention to the development of strategic railways, and mobilization took up to four times longer because it was imperial policy to station regiments in peacetime far from their home depots in order to preclude the possibility of garrison troops of a given nationality becoming contaminated by possible disaffection among their civilian kith and kin.

With all of this, the name of Moltke was very little known. As chief of general staff, an unknown quantity in an untried organization, he had perfected his great plan for the Austrian war in obscurity and secrecy. Not even his generals understood that he was in effective command of the entire operation. He had four armies, all moving independently under remote control from Berlin. General Falckenstein in the west was to destroy the Hanoverian army and the forces of Hesse-Kassel, and then neutralize the Bavarians, the Württembergers, and the Badeners. (It was in this connection that Bismarck the civilian first came into conflict with Moltke the soldier: learning from his own diplomatic sources of the conference in Bavaria, he took it upon himself, without consulting the high command, to order Falckenstein to by-pass the Hanoverians and go straight for Munich. Moltke was first incredulous, then wrathful.) But the main campaign called for three separate armies to converge on Bohemia and defeat the Austrians on their own ground: the Army of the Elbe under Herewarth von Bitterfeld and the First Army, under the king's nephew Prince Frederick Charles, advanced more or less directly, while far to the left the Second Army under the crown prince came round through the mountains of Silesia to join them. All three armies were on Austrian soil, in Bohemia, within five days of the declaration of war. There followed a brilliant series of attacking engagements as the advancing Prussians shattered the Austrian outposts, causing very heavy casualties and meeting with only one serious setback, when the crown prince suffered a sharp repulse at Trautenau on 27 June.

Everything was going Moltke's way. Francis Joseph put the wrong commander in charge of the northern front—a splendid lion of a fighter, a hero to his country and his men, the only general on the Austrian side who had done well at Solferino, Ludwig von Benedek. Benedek pleaded for command of the Italian front. There, he knew every bush and every ditch; he knew nothing of Bohemia. He also knew, though he did not say so, that magnificent as he was as a corps or even an army commander, he was not a commander-in-chief. But the emperor sent his uncle, the archduke Albrecht, to Italy, to win an easy victory, while poor Benedek was called to face the unknown menace in the north. This was Moltke's first great advantage, apart from the man-made advantages of railways and the needle-gun.

The second was the behaviour of Austria's allies. Hanover made a stand, but was defeated at Langensalza on 27 June. Hesse offered very little resistance to the Prussian advance. The only heroes were the Saxons; and here the King of Saxony's steadfastness and loyalty had a tragic issue. With quite remarkable unselfishness he ordered his army to march east to join with Benedek's forces, leaving their homeland and their capital, Dresden, vulnerable. It might have been expected that the Bavarians, for their part, would adapt themselves to this plan by throwing troops out eastwards to cover Dresden. But they failed in their duty, partly from pusillanimity, partly as a result of almost unbelievable muddle, so that not only their own forces but also those of Baden and Württemberg played virtually no part in the war, being tied up by Falckenstein after he had swept the Hanoverians out of the way. On the eve of war King Ludwig had slipped off to Switzerland, secretly, for a meeting with his idol, Richard Wagner. When war broke out he made himself inaccessible to his ministers for several days, treating himself to firework displays on an island in the Starnbergersee (where twenty years later, he was to drown).

Moltke's three main columns thus proceeded relentlessly. The Army of the Elbe and the First Army effected their planned junction on 30 June and the stage was now set for the head-on collision of the two great forces. Benedek, after fearful hesitation and numbed with shock at the series of defeats which had already cost him 30,000 men without a pitched battle, had been on the edge of retreating across the Elbe and falling back on Olmütz to turn there and fight another day. But it was too late, and now he had decided to make a stand in front of the little village of Königgrätz, or Sadowa, with his back to the historic river. The crown prince was still fighting his way through the Silesian mountains, but Moltke could wait no longer. The king with his vast retinue, six special trainloads of them, including Bismarck, had arrived at GHQ on 1 July and was formally in command. Moltke believed that the crown prince could be relied upon to march to the sound of guns and effect his junction on the battlefield itself. And so it was. On the night of 2 July, in streaming rain that turned the ground into a morass, the troops moved up into position, and at dawn the next day two great armies met.

Königgrätz was a decisive battle in every sense of the word, and it also pulled in more troops than ever before in history had clashed in one single encounter: nearly half a million men and 1500 guns. It was also an extremely bloody battle, and each side, fighting up to and beyond the limits of human endurance, honoured the other. At the end of that terrible day the magnitude of the Prussian victory was such that the courage of the Austrian soldiers and the narrowness of their defeat were forgotten. There was nothing to choose between the fighting men. At one stage of the battle the 27th Prussian Infantry Regiment advanced to clear a wood with 90 officers and 3000 men: when it had won through it had 2 officers and 400 men. On the other side, the last Austrian reserve formation was I Corps which had already been severely battered in the fighting of the past week.

Now at the end of the day it marched forward in close formation with flags flying and drums beating and to the tune of a regimental march. In twenty minutes it lost 279 officers and 10,000 men, just half its effectives.[4]

The day was saved for Prussia by the crown prince and his Second Army. The First Army, under his cousin, was on its last legs. Prince Frederick Charles had pulled all his infantry out of the battle and gathered his cavalry to screen them in retreat if the Austrians advanced. But the Austrians did not advance. At 3:30 in the afternoon Moltke's plan paid off and the crown prince with his comparatively fresh Second Army moved straight into the attack. It was then that the Austrian I Corps marched to its destruction, after the Austrian gunners on the right, who had taken the full impact of the fresh Prussian army, had been killed almost to a man beside their guns.

Major Otto von Bismarck-Schönhausen, immense with spiked helmet, cavalry jack-boots, spurs, rode beside his king. They had moved up long before dawn in the cold, driving July rain; and it was to be a hard day. At the end of it the minister-president discovered that nobody had found him anywhere to sleep. Stumbling about a farmyard in the dark he fell into a midden, but at last found shelter in a barn.

To Johanna a few days later he wrote from Zwittau in Moravia: 'At Königgrätz I rode the big chestnut, 13 hours in the saddle with no feed. He stood it very well, and was not put off by shell-fire or corpses on the ground, ate rough grass and the leaves off plum-trees for preference at the most awkward moments, and stayed lively to the end, when I was wearier than the horse. . . .'[5]

He was deeply moved by the sights he saw, as well he might have been. A great deal of the fighting was in fir woods, and the wounds inflicted by the splinters of the shattered trees were often worse than those made by jagged steel. When Prince Frederick Charles's cavalry at last swept into action, not now to cover a retreat but to attack, the ground was so thickly strewn with the dead and wounded of the Austrian I Corps that a terrible scream went up as the drumming hooves came nearer. Did Bismarck hear that scream? Certainly he was pursued by the nightmare thought that his son Herbert might have been lying, mangled, in that field.

He was to advert to the horrors of war again and again, and by no means with only the conventional politician's conventional regrets. He allowed his imagination to be touched. Thus, for example, in the spring of 1867, he is discussing the possibility of war with France with the Free Conservative leader Count Eduard von Bethusy-Huc, who had been deputed to interrogate him on behalf of his party. Preventive war he condemns out of hand, and goes on to say: 'If foreign ministers had always followed their sovereigns to the front history would have fewer wars to tell of. I have seen on a battlefield—and what is far worse, in the hospitals—the flower of our youth carried off by wounds and disease; from this window I look down on the Wilhelmstrasse and see many a cripple who looks up and thinks that if that man up there had not made that wicked war I should be at home, healthy and strong. With such memories and such sights I should not have a moment's peace if I had to reproach myself for making war irresponsibly, or out of ambition, or the vain seeking of fame.'[6]

It seems reasonable to suppose that he was closely affected by what he saw at Königgrätz and after; but his response was not, as it might have been with a lesser man, to vow to move heaven and earth to avoid future wars. On the contrary, since the only possible justification for war was historical inevitability (a phrase to be made familiar by another nineteenth-century German, Karl Marx), and since he had in fact made a war and might have to do so again, then it was clear that he was history personified. And thus a new and more solemn note is heard: Yes, I made the war of 1866 in painful fulfilment of an imperative duty, because otherwise Prussian history would have stood still.

It is not too much to say that he entered the war of 1866 as a gambler and emerged from it a man of destiny. And the irony was that now, as before, he was apart from almost all his countrymen. Just as in the months before the war his name was cursed by those who were horrified at the thought of civil war, 'a war between brothers,' so now in the intoxication of victory he had his work cut out to kennel the dogs he himself had unleashed.

And so what appeared to be yet another side of this extraordinary nature now presents itself; but in fact there is nothing new.

With Vienna at his feet, with a fifteen-year-old dream realized so brilliantly and completely that it must have seemed to him like a miracle (although, of course, he affected to take this triumph casually for granted), the fomenter of conflict now appears as the counsellor of prudence, moderation, reconciliation.

Almost at once after Königgrätz he was embroiled with the generals and the king in one of the hardest fights of his career: to stop his triumphant warriors in their tracks and prevent them from marching on Vienna to dismember the Austrian Empire: he was going to need a strong Austria and he was afraid of France. Moltke wanted to pursue Benedek's army and destroy it—and destroy also the Austrian Army of the South if it moved up from the Po to the Danube to do battle. William, sober as a rule, but now much over-excited and flushed with the glory of Hohenzollern, was intent on the formal occupation of Vienna, with a victory parade and the signing of the peace at Schönbrunn in emulation of Bonaparte. (Where now was his sense of dynastic solidarity?) Prince Frederick Charles, carried away by his success as commander of the First Army, produced a grandiose plan for storming the fortifications of Florisdorf on the left bank of the Danube opposite the city and commanding the direct river crossing.

Bismarck argued, pleaded, jeered, raged, as day after day the army fanned out over Moravia, fighting one or two sharp but minor actions on the way, while GHQ moved down to Zwickau, past the grim old fortress of Olmütz (where Benedek, a tragic figure, had hoped to make his stand), down to Brunn, with its bitter memories of Austerlitz—until finally, on 27 July, an armistice was signed in the great castle of the Dietrichsteins at Nikolsburg, when the First Army advanced patrols were only four miles short of the Danube.

By that time William had got the bit between his teeth and discovered that it was his duty not only to occupy Vienna but also to insist on important territorial gains at the expense of Austria and her allies, above all of Saxony. To begin with he would have been satisfied with the reform of the Confederation under Prussian leadership, the formal acquisition of Schleswig-Holstein, and the annexation of that part of Silesia which Maria Theresa had managed to defend from Frederick the Great. He also demanded the abdication of the rulers of Hanover, Hesse-Kassel, Meiningen, and Nassau who had fought against him in favour of their heirs apparent. But soon he was insisting on Prussia's outright annexation of Hanover and Hesse, of parts of Saxony, and, in an access of dynastic romanticism, the recovery of the old family properties (going back to the days before the Hohenzollern move from Swabia to Brandenburg) in Franconia, including Bayreuth and Ansbach.

To all this Bismarck said 'No!' And in the end he had his way, inducing the king to accept the terms he had worked out with Francis Joseph through the mediation of Napoleon. His final victory he owed to the crown prince, to whom he appealed for help when his father seemed to be immovable. Napoleon and Francis Joseph had conceded almost everything, far more than Bismarck had expected, but on one point, Francis Joseph stuck: he refused, cost what it might, to desert his faithful Saxon cousin; and it was precisely Saxony on which William had now set his heart.

During the previous three weeks Bismarck had deployed every argument he knew—fear of immediate intervention from Napoleon (We will destroy him, said Moltke); fear of future hostile coalitions between a bitterly resentful Austria and France or Russia or both, to undo a Prussia that was growing too fast (Moltke seemed unable to take this political argument in, and the king brushed it aside); fear of the immediate consequences of pursuing the Austrian armies into the unknown. They would not stand still to be destroyed, he argued; they would melt away into the vastnesses of the Hungarian plain, leaving the Prussian army marooned in Vienna. He gave the soldiers a lesson in military geography (to Moltke, the supreme map-maker!): The Danube is a very broad stream, he said in effect, you can't simply ride across it on horseback. If we cross to the right bank we shall have to stay on that side—with no rear communications. In that case the most sensible course will be to march on to Constantinople, where we can found a new Byzantine Empire and leave Prussia to her fate.[7]

Bismarck's nerves were getting a little frayed. So were the nerves of the generals and the king. He was exasperated by their political ineptitude. He was worried about Napoleon, who was making tiresome demands. As early as 9 July he had written to Johanna: 'Things are going well for us in spite of Napoleon; if only we don't push our demands too far and think we have conquered the world we shall get a peace worth having. But we allow ourselves to be carried away as easily as we fall into despair, and I have the thankless task of pouring water into the sparkling wine and trying to make it plain that we are not alone in Europe but have to live with three other powers who hate us and envy us.'[8]

Up to the very last minute he thought he had lost (he was still gambling— or, rather, the great gamble had not been rounded off by König-grätz). It reached the stage one evening at Nikolsburg, where the peace was to be signed, when he felt it hopeless to go on arguing. He turned his back on the company and made his way upstairs. Years later, in a rather highly coloured account of that crisis, he wrote that he had half decided to ask the king to allow him to resign and rejoin his regiment; when he reached his own room on the fourth floor he thought seriously of throwing himself out of the open window, to death in the summer night. But as he sat, despairing, with his head in his hands he heard a footstep behind him. It was his old enemy, the crown prince, who laid a hand on his shoulder and said 'You know that I was against this war. You considered it necessary, and the responsibility for it lies on you. If you now think that our end is attained and that it is time to make peace, I am ready to support you and defend your views against my father.'

In a short time his deliverer was back: 'It has been a very difficult business, but my father has consented.'[9]

Twice Bismarck was thus saved by the man who most distrusted his policies and whom he himself was later to treat so badly: once on the battlefield when his army had arrived in the nick of time to turn the tide at Königgrätz, now in the highest council of the land. William gave in, but he was very bitter: 'At the gates of Vienna,' he wrote in his own hand in the margin of Bismarck's last memorandum, 'the victor must bite into this sour apple and leave posterity to be the judge.'[10]

Nothing has contributed more to the legend of Bismarck's statesmanlike moderation than his fight, even to the point of tears and resignation, to keep defeated Austria intact as a future ally. The mistake has been to equate moderation with native virtue. Moderation is a quantity, not a quality: it may co-exist with a perfect lack of generosity, with a very black heart. For example, the most accomplished blackmailers are moderate in their demands. Bismarck's moderation had this calculating quality; and the dynamics behind each display of moderation were the same driving force that pushed him into his most extreme and violent attitudes, gestures, actions.

Thus, at the very time when Bismarck was affronting king and high command alike by his softness towards Austria and her German allies, he was conducting a separate but related operation vis-à-vis Russia and France. At all costs those jealous powers had to be held off while he was locked in his domestic struggle. This meant bombarding St. Petersburg with messages of earnest reassurance and subjecting Napoleon in Paris to a by-now-familiar mixture of half-promises and scarcely veiled threats. Only when he had the peace treaty with Austria in his pocket did he show his real nature, suddenly turning on both Russia and France with savagery undisguised.

From the very beginning he had feared intervention by the neighbouring powers alarmed by any dramatic shift in the European power balance. And in fact Napoleon made himself felt only two days after Königgrätz, on 5 July. The emperor in Vienna, he announced, had asked him to mediate between Vienna and Berlin. This was sooner than Bismarck had bargained for (Mensdorff had sent a desperate telegram to Napoleon on 2 July, *before* Königgrätz, when Benedek for a moment lost his nerve and begged Francis Joseph to sue for peace immediately). He also found that there had been a secret agreement between Napoleon and Francis Joseph, concluded on the very eve of the war, assuring Vienna of French neutrality in exchange for the cession of Venetia, which Napoleon was intent on presenting to the Italians as a gift from himself. This meant that there was nothing at all to hold the Austrian Army of the South any longer in Italy: it could move up and face the Prussians. If secret agreements of this kind could exist without his, Bismarck's, knowledge, a situation which affronted him unbearably, he had to be very careful indeed.

He was also very angry in his grimmest manner: 'The day will come when Louis will be sorry that he came out against us; it may cost him dear!'[11] he growled.

He was determined that Napoleon should get no credit for peacemaking, and yet peace must be made quickly before France, Russia, even England, decided they must act to undercut Prussian pretensions. To Alexander in St. Petersburg he sent a placatory message: the tsar was not to worry; there would be no drastic change in the map of Europe, since all that Prussia asked was a reform of the Confederation with the expulsion of Austria from Germany, and a final accounting in the matter of the duchies (he did not say how). Through the French ambassador Benedetti (who had exasperated him by turning up, an unwanted foreign civilian at Prussian GHQ) and Goltz, his own ambassador in Paris, he kept Napoleon most skilfully in play—an operation made easier by the emperor's debility and extreme indecisiveness. He used Napoleon as a bogey to frighten King William—and then turned round and used William as a bogey to frighten Napoleon: his king, he assured the emperor of the French, was straining at the leash to punish France for daring to intervene in his personal quarrel with Austria.

As things turned out, Bismarck was agreeably surprised to discover that Napoleon was ready to tolerate Prussian hegemony in North Germany, and by 19 July Benedetti had returned from Vienna with a cut-and-dried plan, arrived at in agreement with Austria, which was very close to Bismarck's own idea, though far removed from William's: Venetia to go to Italy (but Italy had already moved in with her own troops, without waiting for French permission); exclusion of Austria from any German union; a North German confederation to be formed under the aegis of Prussia; the German states south of the River Main to pursue 'an independent national existence' (meaning that they would be free to fall under the influence of France, as in earlier days); finally, Schleswig-Holstein to go to Prussia, and Austria to pay a war indemnity.

From Bismarck's point of view the only serious objection to this outline was that nothing was said about Prussia's outright annexation of certain parts of Germany. While he held off the king with one hand, he set about putting this matter to rights. He found that Napoleon was even more cautious than he had imagined. Eugénie and Drouyn were urging him to fight while Austria still had an army and while the Prussians were tired and on the wrong foot after the Bohemian campaign. But Napoleon knew better than his empress and his foreign minister that France could not then fight a war. The army was far from ready; both it and the economy were badly overstrained by his absurd and calamitous attempt to set up an empire in Mexico. The artillery particularly was in very bad shape, and there was a serious shortage of horses. To cut a long story short, Napoleon agreed in principle to Prussian annexations but without insisting on precise definition beforehand—and without demanding specific 'compensation.' It was then that Adolphe Thiers made his accurate and sombre prophecy: 'It is France who has been beaten at Sadowa.'

In less than four weeks the face of Europe had been changed. The capital of central Europe had moved from Vienna with all its brilliance to the backwoods city of Berlin. And it was not until it was all over that the enormity of what had happened dawned on Russia and France. Then there was urgent talk of a European congress: if the Continental order established by the Congress of Vienna was to be replaced by a different system, then the signatories to the Treaty of Vienna must meet to sanction the changes—or to forbid them. Napoleon was also having second thoughts. He sent Benedetti once more with new demands. And this time Bismarck, the man of moderation, snarled almost shockingly and showed his teeth. More, he displayed all that old recklessness of the wild man of Schönhausen, of the year of revolutions, of the revolutionary dispatches from Frankfurt and St. Petersburg in the 1850s, of the head-on collision with parliament in 1862. But now he was operating not in a domestic setting, or as a critic without power of action; he was the minister-president of a Prussia which had just revealed herself as the military superior of Austria and almost certainly of France as well. Just as during the run-up to the war with Austria he had conspired with Hungarian, Slav, and Italian revolutionaries and rebels for the undoing of the Austrian emperor (an activity which would have horrified and shocked into angry protest his own sovereign had William known of it), so now he showed that if Prussia could not get her own way (meaning his, Bismarck's, own way), he was ready to plunge all Europe into revolutionary violence.

Even while the original negotiations were going on he had angrily, if rather implausibly, threatened Napoleon with the spectre of 'a national uprising' uniting the whole of Germany. To this end he would, he declared, invoke the spirit of the Frankfurt Parliament of 1848, which he had so contemptuously denounced at the time. Now Prussia would know how to effect 'the complete ignition of the national spirit' and bring the *furor teutonicus* to bear on France. [12]

He was talking like this even while in another tone of voice he was tempting Napoleon with imprecise suggestions of possible 'compensation' on the Rhine—i.e., an accession of territory to set against the aggrandizement of Prussia in Germany. Napoleon dithered, and it was not until after the peace between Austria and Prussia was signed on 26 July at Nikolsburg that he pressed hard for specific gains—the 1814 frontier on the Rhine and the removal of Prussian influence from Luxemburg and Limburg (both of which had been part of the German Confederation, though under Dutch sovereignty). It was too late. Bismarck no longer had to tempt or promise. He could be brutally frank at last, a situation in which he always felt most happy. And, without talking about revolution, he managed to persuade William that his rights were being challenged by Napoleon. 'If you want war,' he told Benedetti, 'you can have it. We shall raise all Germany against you. We shall make immediate peace with Austria, at any price, and then, together with Austria we shall fall on you with 800,000 men. We are armed; you are not.' Napoleon had better look out, he went on; once war broke out it would be found to have 'revolutionary features'; and in a revolutionary situation Napoleon might find his throne a good deal less secure than the thrones of German princes. [13]

He lashed out at the Russians, too. When they heard the final peace terms, the tsar and Gorchakov were quite determined on a European congress. Bismarck threatened them. The Russian government would be wise to take care, he said in effect, or it would find itself up against a united Germany in arms, and not only a united Germany, but an insurrectory Poland too. Prussia would be forced 'to unleash the full national strength of Germany and the bordering countries.' And when Alexander ventured to object to this revolutionary attitude, Bismarck went to the limit: 'Pressure from abroad will compel us to proclaim the German constitution of 1849 and to adopt truly revolutionary measures. If there is to be a revolution, we would rather make it than suffer it.'[14] A great many people forgot these words; Alexander and the Russian government never did.

In conversation with the Italian general Govone he was even more specific. If France came to an arrangement with Austria or Russia he would launch 'a war of revolution' to break up the Habsburg Empire: 'We would initiate uprisings in Hungary and organize provisional governments in Prague and Brunn.'[15]

It has to be remembered that the Bismarck who threatened the tsar of Russia and the emperor of the French with war and red revolution, the Bismarck who brought the Habsburg Empire to its knees, was the Bismarck who had achieved high office only four years earlier and who a bare month before had been quite alone in challenging the settled *status quo* of Europe. He knew what he was doing. In an important and revealing interview with the old 1848 radical Carl Schurz, who, exiled for a time, had made a new life in America (this was in the winter of 1867–68, and Bismarck was recollecting emotion in relative tranquillity), he expatiated on his arrangements with the European revolutionaries: if France had gone to the help of Austria 'we should have been forced to spring every mine.' This would have meant the destruction of Austria and the erasing of the Habsburg Empire from the map. What Prussia would have done to fill the vacuum he confessed he did not know; but something would have had to be done to fill 'the great empty space' which 'would have opened up between Germany and Turkey.' Something, he did not know what, would have had to be done to succour the Hungarians, without whose help this apocalyptic vision would have been unrealizable.[16] The crux of the matter was that though determined to push to the end for a diplomatic solution of the Austrian problem, in the last resort he would indeed have sprung his mines, deliberately setting off a chain reaction he knew he could not control. Nothing, *nothing* must be allowed to come between him and his objective—neither parliament nor king, neither old friends nor new enemies.

In the event, he succeeded without springing his mines, but how, in the light not merely of his conversation with Carl Schurz but also of the official record of his instructions to Goltz, his ambassador to Paris, and others, it is possible to maintain that Bismarck was moved by statesmanlike moderation it is very hard to imagine. In all the panoply of prime-ministerial responsibility, the Bismarck who had broken Austria in 1866 was the Bismarck who, without responsibility, and many years earlier, had urged his government to march on Austria, while she was facing east at the time of the Crimean War, and set up its frontier posts at the limits of Protestant Europe—and the Bismarck who had secretly urged the Russian chargé d'affaires in Frankfurt to suggest to the tsar that Prussia might join him in falling upon an Austria which was at that time Prussia's ally.

CHAPTER XIV

'I HAVE BEATEN
THEM ALL!'

In a matter of weeks the most hated man in Prussia had become a national hero. Only God-fearing Conservatives, like Gerlach, and the more stubborn liberals, like Virchow, regarded the upshot of the war as a disaster. The rest might have echoed in rousing chorus Wordsworth's lines: 'Bliss was it in that dawn to be alive. . . .'

Men who had regarded Bismarck as a monster saw in him now a mixture of Moses and Young Siegfried. The respected Prussian jurist Rudolf von Thering had been disgusted by his behaviour on the eve of war: 'I doubt whether a war has ever been provoked so shamelessly and with such horrifying frivolity,'[1] he wrote just over six weeks before the explosion. 'My innermost feelings are revolted by this violation of every legal and moral principle.' But six weeks after Königgrätz he could write to another friend in 'an ecstasy of happiness such as my heart has never known': 'I bow before the genius of Bismarck, who has achieved a masterpiece of political planning and action that have few parallels in history . . . I have forgiven the man everything he has done up to now; more, I have convinced myself that it was necessary: what seemed to us, the uninitiated, to be criminal arrogance turns out to have been the indispensable means to the end.[2]

'. . . I have convinced myself that it was necessary. . . .' How often those words, or variations of them—meaningless incantations to hallow some of the vilest actions of our epoch—were to be heard all over Prussia and beyond. 'Historical necessity'—'the logic of History . . .' Even before victory, prominent liberals who had fought Bismarck very hard over his domestic policies were hedging their bets. It began to be unthinkable that Prussian liberals should do anything that might by their actions allow Austria to

224

profit or injure the Prussian state. Thus Twesten, who had fought Man-teuffel in that famous duel, whom, later, Bismarck had done his best illegally to send to prison, could write in an open letter to the *National-zeitung*: 'We should prefer anything as an alternative to the defeat of the Prussian state. We are acting in the interests not only of Prussia but also of Germany, since we have been strengthened by recent events in the con-viction that no other power but Prussia can do anything for Germany. . . .'[3]

Historical necessity here was also cover for the yearning for a man of destiny. Liberal after liberal put his signature to the obituary notice of his own party by declaring that there was no liberal who could take Bis-marck's place. Bismarck himself, in those difficult weeks leading up to war, almost recklessly 'dared' the liberals in this sense. To Twesten and Unruh he pledged that when the war was won he would resign rather than con-tinue the fight against parliament. He would have resigned already, he de-clared, if only a suitable successor could have been found. And Unruh tamely agreed that no such person did in fact exist, if only because 'reac-tionary régimes have seen to it that in the higher ranks of the bureaucracy there is no liberal to be found who possesses the requisite energy and stamina, while at the same time enjoying general confidence.'[4] In effect Unruh was saying to Bismarck, You have made it impossible for us to learn to govern, so go on governing yourself and do what you like—so long as you recognize our budgetary authority.

And what Unruh was saying, amazingly, to Bismarck's face, others were saying among themselves. The south German historian Hermann Baum-garten, writing to Twesten, declared that since the Prussian liberals re-fused to join Bismarck's government they should be ready to form a ministry of their own. But . . . 'there is no liberal fit to take over the For-eign Ministry in present circumstances.' And he went on: 'Of course you may say: the difficulties created by Bismarck are Bismarck's fault; let him assume responsibility for them. But would this be any help to Prussia?. . . Would any liberal care to start by surrendering the duchies, by knuckling under to an Austrian-dominated Diet? I do not know of any liberals who would have a hope of mastering such a terribly difficult situation, *if only for the reason that hitherto they have had no opportunity of proving themselves in affairs of state, and because nobody, not even a genius, can solve political problems without practice and experience.*'[5] (my italics)

Who was going to learn to run the country, when, and how? *When and how, if it comes to that, had Bismarck learned?*

Very well, Bismarck had to run the country because he had prevented any liberal from learning how to do so. It was necessary, therefore, for liberals to revise their thinking. And so we find the distinguished Prussian historian Johann Droysen, another respected delegate to the Frankfurt Parliament of 1848, who once detested Bismarck, now swept up by the dazzle of his decisiveness in action—*any* decisive action until: "There is no getting away any longer from the fact that Count Bismarck has a rare capacity for statesmanship which it *would be unfair to judge according to so-called principles,* [my italics] that is to say, according to preconceived and hardened opinions and conclusions drawn from such and such precedents and ideas; whereas what is at stake is to take a step ahead, not merely to perceive new possibilities but also to realize them. . . . And this man, glowing coldly, passionately moderate, heedless of friend and foe, of parties and principles, entirely rooted in the facts, in the reality of this state, can act.'[6]

There were lonely voices against Bismarckism, but they were very few, and dwindling. Even the crown prince and Vicky, though at first they had contemplated with almost incredulous horror the idea of war with Austria, were carried away by war and victory—a war which Vicky was soon to justify to her mother at Windsor, and a victory which the crown prince did so much to secure. One of the few steadfast voices, and one of the most moving, was the voice of that old survivor of the Trieglaf circle and the Thadden friendships, Ludwig von Gerlach, who, paraphrasing in the light of Bismarck's victory, his own earlier arguments against Bismarckian policies, wrote after the peace had been ratified and Prussia's enemies punished for helping Austria, how he took 'as his point of departure the premise that God's law has its place not beside, still less below, but above the realms of diplomacy, politics and war. . . .' He chastised the erroneous notion that statesmen had no higher law than patriotic egotism.

' "National needs and demands"—"world-historical moments and world-historical missions"—"providential callings and providential goals" —these and all similar conceptions must find their place far below the holy majesty of God's commands, the same commands that the village child learns in school, but whose profundity and grandeur no human mind is capable of comprehending.'[7]

Within weeks Bismarck had captured the liberals and put himself at the head of the all-German nationalist movement. But it was not so simple as that: without anybody realizing what was happening, the entire political situation in Prussia was being transformed. By a remarkable coincidence the final results of the elections that had been in train since mid-June were announced on the very day of Königgrätz—though before the outcome of that battle was known—or that it had taken place. Even without that crowning victory the conservatives gained 114 seats, nearly all at the expense of the Left-Centrists and the Progressives, who lost 45 and 60 seats respectively. This gave the conservatives 142 seats, only nine less than the combined liberals. But in fact what was happening was the birth of a new alignment. Both conservatives and liberals were divided. The Ultra-Conservatives, including many of Bismarck's old supporters, such as Hans von Kleist-Retzow (to whom so many years before he had written his agonized confession about the temptations of the flesh), took it deliriously for granted that their champion would use his unassailable position to abolish the Constitution and crush the liberals for ever. Many of the liberals (though not the Unruhs and the Twestens) were also sure this would happen. But the great man had a trick worth two of that: he would make himself virtual dictator with the consent of parliament, and his old friends on the far right could think, and say, what they liked.

He knew from Unruh and Twesten how almost desperately eager the right-wing liberals were to cooperate with him and bridge the gap between them, and he intended to redeem his promise to recognize certain minimal parliamentary rights. On the very day after Königgrätz, in improvised quarters at Horwitz, where only the night before he had fallen into the farmyard midden, and where next day he was to start his extremely ticklish negotiations with the French and at the same time receive the Hungarian rebels as an insurance in case those negotiations failed, he had confirmed that promise by assuring the crown prince, as he had already assured his finance minister, Heydt (returned to serve under the once-detested Bismarck after Bodelschwingh's resignation), as well as Twesten and Unruh, that he would no longer rule in defiance of the Landtag. His solution was a bill of indemnity. He would go to parliament, admit that he had behaved unconstitutionally for the past four years, plead extenuating circumstances, and request the Landtag in the light of recent events to remedy matters by retrospectively legalizing the unauthorized expenditures.

It was a solution that takes the breath away with its bold simplicity. The Ultra-Conservatives moved heaven and earth to block it: they choked with indignation and disgust. The staunchest of the Progressives (e.g., Baron Leopold von Hoverbeck) were appalled at the ease with which so many liberals rushed to meet their fate (if Bismarck is allowed to get away with this, he will be able to get away with anything, they most correctly forecast), positively demanding to be conducted into the fold by the grey wolf with the amiably sardonic smile. But Bismarck won hands down. All the politicians were in Berlin; he was in Bohemia with his king, and he talked the king round, heaven knows how. So that in the end, when on 5 August William presented the bill to the House, it looked as though his chief minister was dispensing forgiveness instead of begging for it. It must have been a very tough struggle with the king, who nearly spoilt things at the very last moment by muttering: 'I have no regrets for having acted as I did, and I would do the same again in similar circumstances.'[8] These words were tactfully overlooked.

What Bismarck had achieved was mastery of a new middle party, a National Liberal party, from which the extreme right and the extreme left split off. It was to be his instrument for years to come. The liberal element, we have seen, broadly speaking consisted of those who put Prussia as the agent of German unification above ideals, or even principles, of government. The conservative element consisted largely of business men, entrepreneurs, manufacturers, merchants, bankers, financiers from the Catholic West, who were uninterested in dynastic glory or legitimacy but who knew success when they saw it and recognized in Bismarck the man who, above all others, could provide them with the base for an expanding economy. To these, very soon, would be added new voices from Hanover, Hesse, Frankfurt, and elsewhere.

Already, in a word, the old divisions conservative/radical, or army/ bureaucrat, were blurred and largely superseded by the needs and desires of a quickening bourgeois society. And soon new divisions would make for still greater change—as when the conservative Rhinelanders were themselves polarized into the Catholic right and the secular left—the latter joining what had been the Prussian right-wing liberals in a National Liberal party transcending all state frontiers.

The prerequisite for this operation was the web of treaties spun in the wake of the Austro-Prussian War. In the high summer of 1866 Bismarck found himself in the happy position of conqueror. With insignificant exceptions, all the German states had declared for Austria against Prussia and now they were made to pay. The fact that some had not fought very hard or effectively counted for nothing in their favour. Hanover, Hesse-Kassel, and Nassau had the misfortune to lie astride Berlin's communications with Prussia's western provinces; their liquidation as independent states and absorption into Prussia had long been one of Bismarck's primary aims. This involved, among other things, the deposition of the king of Hanover, the elector of Hesse, the duke of Nassau, and the end of their dynasties—a violation of the monarchical principle on the part of the Prussian king which made nonsense of William's own most solemn professions.

This was conduct held in aborrence by such devoted upholders of the divinity of kings as the Russian tsar, whose own father had refused to cast down even the Persian dynasty when it lay in the dust at his feet, knowing that once kings were seen to be expendable there would soon be no more of them. Indeed, one of the less thoroughly explored mysteries of the Bismarck era is how the upright and soldierly William allowed himself to be swept along into denying the very foundations of legitimacy by a minister whom he never really trusted. It can only be assumed that in the flush of victory the combination of anger and latent Hohenzollern acquisitiveness was too much for his proper judgement. He was, indeed, a very choleric man, as well as a tearfully emotional one; and just as he had allowed himself to be persuaded that Austria had treacherously assailed him, so he now felt that all who had sided with Austria—all Germany outside Prussia, in fact—had betrayed him. He laid himself wide open to Friedrich Engels' jibe in a letter to Karl Marx about 'the irreparable moral injury suffered by the Prussian crown by the Grace of God when it swallowed up three other crowns by the Grace of God.'

William wanted Saxony, too, and behaved like a spoilt child when it was denied him. But Francis Joseph in Vienna was determined, whatever else he gave away, not to leave his only loyal and active ally in the lurch, and Bismarck was content, so long as Prussia had effective command of the Saxon army. He knew that he was close to the limit of Napoleon's tolerance (Russia's too, perhaps). In addition to the annexation of Hanover, Hesse-Kassel, and Nassau he had seized for Prussia the free city of Frankfurt-am-Main. On top of this territorial aggrandizement he was in the process of establishing a North German Confederation to include the remaining states (some twenty of them) north of the Main, while entering into secret military alliances with the four southern states, Bavaria, Württemberg, Baden, and Hesse-Darmstadt. Saxony was punished with a heavy indemnity, while Frankfurt was submitted to the most frightful bullying, first at the hands of the commander of the occupying forces, our old friend General Manteuffel, then at Bismarck's own insistence. The Prus-

sians seem to have found the very existence of this great free city an affront, and the brilliant prosperity of Frankfurt especially brought to the
surface all the Junker distaste for merchants, bankers, financiers, and
Jews—added to which was the lingering taint of the 1848 revolutionary
Diet.

Bismarck was rough, too, with the Bavarians who had no wish to enter a
close alliance with Prussia, let alone one which would put their army at the
disposal of the North German Confederation—which meant in fact the
Prussian high command. They were given no choice. If you refuse an alliance, said Bismarck in effect, we shall treat you as a conquered foe, take
some of your territory, and demand a heavier indemnity.

These were tumultuous weeks. The pressures on Bismarck were acute;
the energy and attack with which he met them almost beyond understanding; and they were not ended at once by the signing of the various
treaties. For it was now that Napoleon, pushed intolerably by Drouyn and
Eugénie, came forward again with demands for 'compensations' on the
Rhine and was threatened by Bismarck with a war to seize Alsace.[9] Napoleon capitulated, blamed Drouyn, and dismissed him. But what about a
formal alliance in return for the 1814 frontier on the Rhine and the promise that at some future date France might annex Luxemburg and Belgium?
The alliance Bismarck would have nothing to do with, but he was prepared—though William clearly would not be—to talk about Luxemburg
and Belgium. Napoleon took him up on that so quickly that he had to
sidestep in order not to be pinned down to an agreement which the rest of
Europe would denounce, and, indeed, a threatening little crisis was later to
grow out of this imbroglio—but not until Bismarck had virtually the whole
of Germany safely in his hands.

Towards the end of September, after the formal victory parade in Berlin, Bismarck broke down. He had pushed himself too hard. But he had
the Indemnity Bill under his belt and was supreme in parliament; he had
driven Austria out of Germany and established Prussian mastery over all
Germany north of the River Main; he had fended off Napoleon and
achieved his revolution in map-making without effective interference from
the most interested powers—the powers who in 1815 had vowed to work
together to keep the Continent in balance. He had defeated his king, his
generals, and the liberals and brushed his old conservative supporters to
one side; he was worshipped throughout Prussia, feared throughout Germany, held in something like awe by the outside world. He was soon to be

presented with a vast sum of money to buy himself a country estate (ironically, it was parliament, not the king, who insisted on this), and promoted to major-general—the distinction he prized above all others: thereafter this surprising man was rarely to be seen out of uniform. And now, not surprisingly, he collapsed. Johanna got him out of Berlin into the remote countryside near Putbus, on the Baltic island of Ruegen. Before his illness, which was very real and caused him excruciating pain, he seems to have been living on two levels: to the outside world and to the defeated he was harsh, uncompromising, brutal, while to his old enemies in the Berlin Landtag he was gentleness itself. He had a troublesome time establishing with parliament the details of the annexations; Philip Eulenburg, his minister of the interior, was amazed at his patience: 'Nowadays,' he reported to Keudell, 'you would hardly know him. He replies to the silliest questions and objections with infinite patience and—I can find no other words for it—an almost childlike sweetness of temper and simplicity.'[10] This was the man who immediately after Königgrätz, and looking back over the struggles of past years, against parliament, generals, the king himself, could exclaim to one of his revolutionary Hungarian soldier friends, smiting the table with his fist: 'I have beaten them all! All!'[11]

Now, to Keudell himself he lamented that the best thing he could do was to depart: he had achieved as much as he could and was not sure whether he had it in him to do what still had to be done. 'In Pomerania,' he went on, 'when the women approach their time they have a saying, "I go to meet my peril." And that is how it is with me. For unless I quite give up and leave things to another—but I can think of nobody else to suggest—then I must face what comes even if it kills me.'[12]

And so, of course, he did. After a few weeks total prostration he started being himself again. For more than two months affairs of state had been ticking over while people settled down once more to the ordinary business of life, the rest of Germany had time to acclimatize itself to the new order, uncertain as this still was in detail. That order now had to be given shape and stamped with the authority of Prussia. For several weeks Bismarck, sequestered far away in his island fastness, had been reduced to lying all day in a chaise-longue, idly turning the pages of an illustrated volume, or simply staring into space. But soon the spell of the northern countryside, with the sea nearby and the breath of the infinite Arctic chilling the October sunshine, began to work once more and in no time at all he came alive. He had been carried off by Johanna barely able to move or speak, with stomach cramps and a return of agonizing pain in his damaged leg. But by the end of October he was hard at it, overwhelming his aides with memoranda (as a rule dictated to Keudell) on anything that came into his head—but above all about the shortcomings of his parliamentary colleagues and the projected shape of the North German Confederation.

His chief aide in all these matters—from how best to handle France to a whole range of questions affecting the proposed new constitution—was Dr. Lothar Bucher, a senior Foreign Ministry official whom for twenty years, from the war of the duchies onwards, Bismarck relied on more intimately than on anybody else. The interesting thing about Bucher was that he had been a revolutionary in 1848 and compelled to flee the country. After his return and conversion to Conservatism he kept some sort of contact with his old companions of the radical persuasion, of the extreme left, indeed. And in October 1865 he actually invited Karl Marx, long exiled from Prussia and established in London, to contribute a regular financial column to Bismarck's official newspaper, the *Staatsanzeiger*. Marx turned him down.

Bucher was good at extracting the essentials from every kind of state paper and also at drafting his own. When Bismarck arrived back in Berlin fit and well on the first day of December 1866 Bucher knew what he had to do. In the shortest possible time, to give objectors a minimal chance of organizing opposition, a constitution had to be drafted, and handed over for discussion and amendment to a special constituent council of ministers from each state in the new Confederation—in time for the first elections to the constituent parliament, or Reichstag, to be held on 12 February. The constitution was ready in draft, all sixty-four articles, by 9 December. It looked like a conjuring trick, and Bismarck was happy to give the impression that he had worked it out in his head and, as it were, jotted it down on the back of an old envelope in a couple of days of concentrated work with Bucher. In fact he had been putting his best experts to work for months. Starting with the abortive scheme produced at the Frankfurt Diet on the eve of the war, a variety of specialists had been producing drafts incorporating parts of various other federal constitutions—e.g., the American, the Swiss—together with features peculiar to German federalism, and provisions for the particular demands of Roon as minister of war and Heydt as minister of finance.

The fact remains that Bismarck and Bucher between them digested this mass of material and produced out of it a constitution that was to serve first the North German Confederation, then the new Reich born out of the Franco-Prussian War, for good or ill until 1918. All in a matter of days.

It has provided controversy for much longer. And perhaps nothing shows so clearly the remarkable and recurrent failure of so many German historians and politicians even to begin to understand the sort of animal Bismarck was than the immense, the immensely absurd and for-ever continuing argument (solemnity carried to infinity; irrelevance to the point of insanity) as to precisely what was in the great man's mind when he devised and promoted the 1867 Constitution—more particularly, was he seeking to create a German national government? Or was he simply concerned with establishing Prussian hegemony, elaborately camouflaged?

It seems to be the hardest thing in the world for Germans to understand that *Bismarck was not one of them* in any sense understood by them. He was Bismarck. He cared not at all for either the Prussian people or the German people. He was running Prussia in the name of the king of Prussia; he was now going to run North Germany in the name of the Confederation, and he was determined from the start to render his own power as chief minister more absolute than it was under the Prussian system. In this he succeeded.

Professor Pflanze has put this very well, but even he sees an ideal behind Bismarck's securing of his own power. 'The essence of the Bismarckian Constitution was its conservation, by the use of revolutionary means, of the Prussian aristocratic-monarchical order in a century of increasingly dynamic economic and social change....' Substitute 'Bismarckian' for 'Prussian' in that sentence and it makes perfect sense. But even better sense is made, once again, by Friedrich Engels. The remarkable thing is that the first of two letters to Karl Marx was written on 13 April 1866, stimulated by Bismarck's dramatic appeal to German nationalism at Frankfurt, two and a half months before Königgrätz. The jargon, alas, has to be accepted as the price to be paid for access to a fascinating mind: 'It is becoming ever clearer to me that the bourgeoisie has not the stuff in it for ruling directly itself, and that therefore where there is no oligarchy, as there is here in England, to take over, for good pay, the management of state and society in the interests of the bourgeoisie, Bonapartist semi-dictatorship is the normal form. It upholds the big material interests of the bourgeoisie even against the will of the bourgeoisie, but allows the bourgeoisie no share in the power of government. The dictatorship in its turn is forced against its will to adopt those material interests of the bourgeoisie as its own. So we now get Monsieur Bismarck adopting the programme of the Nationalverein. To carry it out is something quite different, of course, but Bismarck is hardly likely to come to grief through the German bourgeoisie.'[13]

And then, just after Königgrätz, on 25 July, Engels writes again: 'From the moment Bismarck by using the Prussian army carried out the Little Germany scheme of some of the bourgeoisie with such success, developments in Germany have taken this direction so resolutely that we, like others, must acknowledge the accomplished fact whether we like it or not.' And he goes on to speak of the inevitable absorption of the rest of Germany, including the Austrian German provinces, into a new Reich—and of Bismarck's inescapable future dependence on the bourgeoisie in his struggle with the particularist princes seeking to retain their privileges.[14] For 'bourgeois' here read 'National Liberal. . . .'

This, at any rate, is what happened, though not quite as soon as Engels expected: history is always slower than the men who try to make it. Little Germany was not achieved by the absorption of Germany south of the Main until five years later, when all the German states outside Austria were brought under Prussia's wing and called the German Empire. And it was not until 1938, twenty years after the Austrian Empire had been destroyed, that the next part of Engels' prophecy came true and Little Germany was succeeded by Great Germany, which did not endure.

This very peculiar symbiosis between Bismarck, as a 'semi-Bonapartist' dictator and Engels' bourgeoisie (first the Liberals, later the Conservatives) was the reality behind all the play-acting of the 'Prussian aristocratic-monarchical' order, which reached its apogee with Bismarck gone—dismissed by a monarch who confused with power and glory the silver eagle on his helmet, the decorations on his chest, the whiteness of his buckskin breeches, the shine on his jack-boots, and the jingle of his spurs.

The feature of the new North German Confederation which first met the eye was the inauguration of a parliament, the Reichstag, to be elected by adult male suffrage (unlike the Prussian Landtag, which was still elected on the absurd old three-class system). It was this Reichstag which would have as its first task the passing into law of a new constitution, and Bismarck's manipulation of it in its first days and the playing off of the Liberal deputies against the princely governments was as smoothly brilliant as anything he ever did. In achieving his network of peace treaties he had mixed persuasion with menace, hectoring with temptation, measuring one special interest against another. So now he used the liberal Reichstag as a threat to the princes, and then invoked the princes to curb the pretensions of the Liberals.

In fact, the first elections, with a very high poll, produced an overwhelmingly aristocratic assembly with a strong majority for the National Liberals—79 seats to compare with 27 Old Liberals, 19 Progressives (so had that once proud party dwindled in the heady atmosphere of war and conquest), 59 Conservatives, 39 Free Conservatives and a handful of splinter parties, mostly representing national minorities. No Socialists were returned, and Bismarck himself had the satisfaction of defeating Lassalle's successor as head of the German Working Man's Association, J. B. von Schweitzer. The complete failure of the Socialists and the obvious predilection of the common voter for the nobility (the 297 deputies included a royal prince, four nonroyal princes, two dukes, 27 counts, 21 barons and a number of high-ranking soldiers) did not prevent Bismarck from using the spectre of universal suffrage to frighten the bourgeoisie, just as he was using the bourgeoisie to frighten the aristocracy. And it was by playing on the special hopes and fears, the cupidity and the idealism of so many separate groups, almost it sometimes seemed of every individual, that he managed to push through a constitution which gave Prussia—i.e., Bismarck acting through the Prussian king—effective power over two-thirds of the people of Germany.

The old peaceful Germany was dying. The shortcomings of the princely courts had been blatant, in some cases vicious in their effects. Rule by royal or grand-ducal mistresses or professional intriguers was no way to develop the immense potentialities of the German people. Rule by enlightened patrons of the arts, as, for example, in Goethe's Weimar, did not help much either. But since 1849 there had been a number of states with genuinely liberal constitutions—indeed, all the states south of the Main, and some north of it. And so long as the spirit of nationalism was held in check many of the states were easygoing places which gave a better living to their subjects than might have been expected. There were some highly reactionary régimes, as in Hesse-Kassel, but others, most notably Baden and Württemberg, were advanced by any European standards. The multiplication of separate states had produced the multiplication of all kinds of cultural amenities, above all the splendid universities whose names in any truly civilized society would spell out a roll of honour—the battle honours of the mind: Göttingen, Jena, Heidelberg, Tübingen, Bonn—the Humboldt University in Berlin itself. Besides universities, great art collections, orchestras, and opera houses. Consider Saxony, the wonders of Dresden and Leipzig and its brilliant musical tradition from J. S. Bach through Schumann to Wagner. Consider the Baroque and Rococo inheritance of Bavaria and Württemberg, so closely akin to the German provinces of Austria. Think of Mannheim in Baden, the birthplace of the modern orchestra. Think of the superb efflorescence of extravagant yet perfectly controlled delight of the Residenz, the Archbishop's Palace at Würzburg, with Tiepolo's ceilings celebrating the glories of the old 'New World. . . .' And all this existing side by side with the grand Gothic of ancient cities—in a land riven and ravaged first by the Reformation, then by the Thirty Years War, at last humiliated by Napoleon Bonaparte—when Goethe in Weimar did not care who ruled, provided the arts of peace were allowed to flourish, and when the lands of the Rhineland, the Palatinate, looked to France rather than to Potsdam or even Vienna.

All this variety was coming to an end. The people of Germany were to be brought sharply into the nineteenth century by the philistine master of a parvenu kingdom which was culturally a wilderness compared with the older regions of the west and the south.

But a wilderness with a powerful ruling spirit: the idea of disciplined, sacrificial service—service to what? To whom?

To the Whole, to the Community, to the State, to the King who embodied the State.

What was it that attracted 'the tough, dour Junkers of the sandy, pine-infested plain of Brandenburg' to this doctrine, whose high-priest was Hegel, not a Prussian at all, but a native of Stuttgart in Württemberg, the Swabia from which the Hohenzollerns themselves had sprung? What was it that atracted Hegel, with all the universities of Germany to choose from, to Berlin? And not only Hegel?

The answer to both questions was power. The philosopher provided a rationale for the accumulation and the exercise of power; the manifest and visible power of the Hohenzollern state drew the philosopher.

The Great Elector, Frederick William of Brandenburg, had taken his country out of the Thirty Years War. With an inspired programme of recovery and rehabilitation, from the Peace of Westphalia in 1648 to his death in 1688, he had made the voice of Prussia count in the affairs of Europe. He played an important part in Dutch William's successful invasion of England; he built up a highly disciplined army, founded a navy, and started colonies in Africa. He was the first German ruler other than the 'universal' Habsburgs to look beyond his immediate neighbourhood.

When his great-grandson Frederick II came to the throne three generations later, in 1741, he found a tempered instrument ready to hand.

Frederick glorified power. He had no feeling for Germany. He despised all Germans. In the intervals of his almost incessant campaigning he did a great deal of writing, played the flute very well, and built Sans Souci at Potsdam. But although he ordered in the most arbitrary manner every detail of his subjects' lives it was to France he looked for intellect and taste. Voltaire was his hobby horse, but he did nothing for his own quiet genius, his humble subject Immanuel Kant, living out his life from cradle to grave at Königsberg in farthest East Prussia; he was equally unaware of the great Saxon who strove to bring Germany into the mainstream of Greco-Roman culture, Gotthold Ephraim Lessing. He had a concert every night in peacetime, but it was the gallant style of C. P. E. Bach and the elegant artificialities of Quantz, the blacksmith's son, that satisfied his musicianship and inspired his own compositions. He knew nothing of Gluck, his own exact contemporary, let alone Haydn and Mozart. He called J. S. Bach to Potsdam—not for his towering greatness, which was not recognized, but as a curiosity, a master of improvisation, above all: the marvels of 'The Musical Offering' were the result. For Frederick the arts were light entertainment. Power he wanted for itself, not for his people. He lacked the least sense of identity with his own people. Prussia was his inherited base, to be expanded by whatever means came to hand; the Prussian army his inherited instrument.

But the very rigour, also inherited, of his régime, lean and highly disciplined, attracted certain minds. Johann Gottlieb Fichte came to Berlin via Switzerland and Jena from a povery-stricken boyhood in Upper Lusatia; and there invented German patriotism, which was really Prussian patriotism, in which the will of the individual, the will of the German people became identified with the will of the universe, of God. And into Fichte's shoes in 1814 stepped Hegel after a long, long trail via Tübingen, Jena, Bamberg, Nürnberg, and Heidelberg—to preach in the end the glorification of the state. He spoke of the state not as a patriot or a politician but as a philosopher. Everything that a man was, he owed to the state. The state was the highest manifestation of human existence, all individual wills subordinated to the supreme good. It was God walking among men, the divine idea as its manifests itself on earth. Mankind advanced from the primitive community by a dialectical process, thesis and antithesis, until the grand culmination in one global community which must be attained, inevitably, by war and conquest.

How very odd that this one man, this abstract thinker from Stuttgart, should inspire the two supreme material phenomena of the twentieth century—Prussian militarism and Russian Communism. And how very far this harsh, bracing, almost hysterical self-righteousness of Potsdam from the cosy beer-drinking Michel with his tankard—or the lighter spirited wine drinkers of the Rhine and the Moselle.

Towards the middle of the century there was a strange cultural withering throughout nearly all Germany. It was as though a silence had fallen for a new voice to be heard. Nobody, of course, had come forward to fill the gap left by Goethe, Schiller, Hegel himself. Poor Schumann had died while Bismarck was still in Frankfurt. Music had become subsumed in Johannes Brahms from Hamburg (who had gone to live in Vienna) in the classical succession and the very self-conscious revolutionary Richard Wagner from Dresden—as cataclysmic in his way as his political contemporaries Bismarck himself and Karl Marx. But there was more involved than a drying up of creative genius. It was as though all the energies of a most various people were being collected and concentrated to one end. In the eighteen-forties and fifties, a silver age, the age that had succeeded the golden age of the eighteenth century, was drawing to a close. There were no successors to the Schlegel brothers, or to Tieck, with their superb translations of Dante, Shakespeare, Cervantes, Calderón. The sardonic voice of Heine was also stilled: admittedly he had spent the last twenty-five years of his life in Paris, but he could have returned from exile had he wanted to. He did not like the post-1848 Germany.

What was happening, of course, was that the inevitable period of reaction after the failure of 1848, which should have spent itself and then transformed itself into a state of freedom, either smoothly, imperceptibly, or with further violence, was in an important sense frozen by the advent of Bismarck, a naturally dictatorial figure, manipulating with extreme skill the spirit of nationalism, which in Germany was stronger than in any other land for the simple reason that it first had to create a nation. Bismarck created that nation—and in his own image. And the typical cultural figure of the Bismarckian era was the radical, or revolutionary.

Thus Heinrich von Treitschke, a liberal from Saxony, a man who at first abhorred Bismarck's domestic policies, was so spellbound by the glory of Germany uniting as an expression of power that he was drawn ever more closely to the presiding genius, until finally he prostrated himself at the feet of the man he had once denounced. He deserted Saxony, breaking his father's heart, and became the supreme apologist for blood and iron. Thus

Richard Wagner, another revolutionary, who had been out on the streets of Dresden with Bakunin in 1849, developed into another worshipper of German power. More than any man he owed a debt to German particularism, to the culture of the south, as when he was supported and sustained by poor young King Ludwig of Bavaria; but more than most men he came to idolize what Bismarck stood for.

We have run ahead. It is 1867. The North German Confederation has barely settled down. The war with France is still three years ahead, but the tone has been set. And the great material drive has already begun. The transformation of the German economy is under way. The peasant serfs of Prussia and the starving workers of Silesia and Baden are already being transformed. In the 1840s the English engineer responsible for building the railway from Berlin to Hamburg, Richard Lindley, imported as many British labourers as he could and paid them twice as much as their German fellows—because they were twice as strong and worked much harder, displaying an energy quite alien even to the Prussian labourers. Now the children of those labourers conscripted, formed the core of the most powerful and disciplined and successful army in Europe. A heady mixture was fermenting in Germany. Bismarck let it brew.

CHAPTER XV

THE SUPREME GAMBLE

The Bismarck who returned from his Baltic retreat to Berlin on the first day of December 1866 to launch the new North German Confederation was already the Bismarck of history, the mature and finished specimen, victorious, in command as to the manner born, apparently with all uncertainties behind him. Behind him too, as though they had never been, were the romantic dreams of his early years, his love of poetry, even it would seem the tenderness he had lavished on Johanna and then on Kathy Orlov. Apart from his regular Bible readings he seems to have read very little since his marriage. Johanna herself was still the stable centre of his world. His affection for his children was fierce, possessive, jealous. Marie was now twenty, Herbert nineteen, Bill seventeen. His family meant much to him, and outside his family life his sole interests were politics, estate management, food and drink, and the accumulation of a great fortune.

He was fifty-one, but he looked much older and very battered for his years. This was due in part to gross over-eating and drinking, in part to the immense strain to which he subjected himself. His activity was prodigious, his scheming incessant. From crisis to crisis the general high level of cerebration exploded into a positive fury as his mind became incandescent: he was then possessed as an artist is possessed in the act of creation; and, like many artists, he needed to sink back into himself to build up his strength after a major effort.

There was another aspect of his premature ageing: he was not one of those men who refresh their vigour by returning to the springs of their youth. He grew old, as it were, deliberately, as though distancing himself from all contacts and memories that might show up the terrible aridity of his almost exclusive preoccupation: power, how to keep it and extend it. Only his profound, his abiding attachment to the northern forests remained as an organic link with his early loves. He went into retreat on every possible, sometimes impossible, occasion, first to Schönhausen, then to Varzin with its 15,000 acres and seven villages, a richly forested estate in far Pomerania, near Köslin, which he bought with the 400,000 thalers (some $2 million) bestowed on him by a grateful Landtag after Königgrätz, in later years to Friedrichsruh, very close to Hamburg, his reward for beating the French and uniting Germany and making his king an emperor. But even here his very genuine passion for the cool, dispassionate splendour of the world of nature itself became corrupted. He was not content with the possession of enough land to lose himself in, to contain his daily rides, to give him good shooting and scope for good forestry, to shut the outer world away from sight and sound: he became possessed by a mania for acquisition. Power was not enough: he was determined to be rich as well. He was for ever adding to his properties, for ever demanding higher returns. He was greedy and not too scrupulous about money. We have seen how on the run-up to the war with Austria he had used his inside knowledge (the knowledge unique to him, of his own intentions and the timing of his proposed actions) to guide Bleichröder. He was to do this again and again in years to come: it clearly did not cross his mind that ministers in the latter half of the nineteenth century should not, must not, behave like private individuals in the money market. It was the same blind spot, and a large one, which had allowed him to use the appointment of judges known to be on his side unthinkingly, naturally, and greedily like a child.[1] He also kept up a continuous barrage of truculent complaint that he, the chancellor, should be required to pay taxes like any other mortal.

The most spectacular example of this aspect of his character was to be his handling of the personal fortune of the deposed King George V of Hanover, a very rich man indeed. On the whole, the northern states acquiesced in Prussian domination, but many Hanoverians, who were inclined to regard the Prussians as uncouth, were not at all reconciled to the deposition of their king. Considerable numbers attached themselves to the National Liberals, and one of these, Rudolf von Bennigsen (founder of the Nationalverein), became its leader. But others, like Ludwig Windthorst (later to become famous as the one man Bismarck loved to hate), were loyal to the old Guelph dynasty. It was Windthorst who conducted negotiations about the disposal of King George's fortune. It was formally agreed that a large part of it was his personal (as distinct from Hanoverian state) property, and as such would be held by the Prussian government, the interest being payable to the exiled king. There was strong opposition to this in the Prussian Landtag, but the treaty was signed in March 1868. *On the very same day*, however, the ex-king was charged with refusing to recognize the Prussian government and with building up a small army to fight again. Because of this William put his signature to an order confiscating his brother-monarch's entire fortune and handing it over to the government of Prussia to be used in countering Hanoverian subversion and separatism.

This meant in practice that it was handed over to Bismarck to use as he saw fit. It was soon known that he was using it as a private fund (aptly nick-named the Reptile Fund) largely to bribe editors and journalists of all kinds. But over the years the money was put to other uses not so widely known—as for instance an extremely secret payment in 1870 to King Ludwig of Bavaria, to win his support for the unification of Germany under a Hohenzollern emperor.[2]

This blind-spot had always existed. But it was enlarged with the years and by the beginning of 1867 the whole man had coarsened, so that it is painful to look back over the obliteration of so many splendid qualities: the extinction, perhaps, of the brilliant, impulsively generous, romantic, impetuous Bismarck of the early letters to Johanna by the precociously calculating Bismarck of the religious apologia addressed to his future father-in-law. One has to remember that this man so insensitive to corruption was an upright Pomeranian puritan who still read his Bible every day and who did not even enjoy corruption. As he approached and reached the summit of his glory he was a very unhappy man. And this was not just the old story of success turning to dust and ashes, as it must for anyone whose self-satisfaction stops short of imbecility. Even the most fleeting enjoyment of achievement seems to have been denied him. He could never be content with what he had and always was driven on, first by the raging ambition which lay beneath the detached, uncaring pose of cool indifference, later on by paranoia, which took the form of chronic suspicion of conspiracy. In his maturity he was no less a man possessed than he had been in the days of the young 'wild Bismarck': only the sharp focus of an immediate, realizable goal could discipline the demon in him, and the moment that goal was achieved the demon broke loose again. He found difficulty in knowing when to stop.

This is not what we have been taught about the man. Bismarck, we are told, was *par excellence* the statesman who knew where to stop. Nothing could be more wrong. We have already glanced at the equivocal nature of his celebrated moderation—the moderation which halted the Prussian advance after Königgrätz, which sent him back to the Landtag to acknowledge the illegality of his budgetary transactions and offer to turn over a new leaf. We shall soon come to the moderation displayed in the long twenty years after the defeat of France when the man of blood and iron settled down to become the powerful guardian of the peace of his country and all Europe, sleeplessly weaving his diplomatic spells to banish war. Is this a true picture?

In fact his calculated moderation was outweighed by his sometimes reckless violence. The young Bismarck who made a fool of himself in Berlin in 1848 is very clearly discernible in the mature Bismarck who, in the years of the *Kulturkampf*, drove quite deliberately into a head-on collision with the Roman Catholic Church and was lucky to escape without serious injury; who at this same period manufactured a completely groundless war-scare *vis-à-vis* France and was humiliated by the powers in consequence; who allowed his whole policy towards Russia to be ingeniously ordered by his obsessional hatred of his Russian opposite number, Gorchakov.

His genius is so familiar that it hardly needs stressing; but the flaws in that genius went very much deeper than is usually supposed. It is not enough, as is commonly done, to acknowledge that here Bismarck was mistaken, there he was short-sighted—treating as aberrations failures which in reality were an essential part of his character. Thus the man who fought his king and the generals so stubbornly after Königgrätz, throwing everything he had into the fight in the interests of moderation, was the man who four years earlier had defied parliament and made a ruin of constitutional government; he was the man who plunged Germany into civil war on his own responsibility and against the urgings of his sovereign; and he was the man who showed no moderation whatsoever after the defeat of France in 1871.

In later years there were to be innumerable witnesses to the profound internal *malaise* which ravaged the brilliancies of this extraordinary man. This was not simply the result of overstrain and over-eating. We remember the first impressions of both Schlözer and Holstein, his two assistants in St. Petersburg, and how, frustrated, he lay about all day in a dressing-gown, drinking, scheming, fulminating, drinking. Now, as he approaches the summit of his career, only a year after the triumphal setting up of the North German Confederation, we read of the demoralization and disarray induced in official Berlin by his peculiar temperament, when 'all established order is superseded by the morose arbitrariness of a single individual so that . . . gradually the whole machinery, thrown out of gear by misuse and coercion, begins to break down.'[3]

Behind this overbearing, insensitive bully, there is another Bismarck, without whom our picture is not complete. In 1869, three years after Königgrätz, he revealed his inner tension in writing to Roon, as often he must have revealed it behind closed doors, face to face with King William, during those stormy resignation scenes. An immense and overwhelming crisis suddenly loomed up out of the blue. It blotted out the light of the sun and the world stood still as he howled his agony. . . .

What had happened was that he had stubbed his toe on a bit of Prussian law he did not know about, or had forgotten. He had promised the chief postmaster's job at Frankfurt-am-Main to one of his Hanoverian supporters, and while he was away at Varzin the cabinet refused to authorize the appointment because the applicant had not completed the required three years in the Prussian service. One of the signatories to the refusal was Roon. To him Bismarck exploded: why had this been done to him? Was it because they had another candidate, was it wanton frivolity, was it petticoat influence? Whatever the cause, it was too much: 'Nobody has the right to ask me to sacrifice my health, my life, even my reputation for honesty and sound judgement, to satisfy a whim. For thirty-six hours I have not slept; the whole night long I vomited bile and in spite of cold compresses my head is still on fire. It is enough to drive me out of my mind. . . .' And he concludes in a colourful burst of mixed metaphor: 'If the cart we have been flogging along together is heading for a smash-up, at least people must know I have no share of the responsibility. . . . Perhaps we are both too hot-tempered to be able to row the boat together for much longer. . . .'[4]

If Bismarck could lash himself into such a frenzy against his oldest friend after nearly two months in the green and resinous solitudes of Varzin what can have been his state under the irritations of Berlin? This extreme irascibility, amounting to hysteria, was not by any means to be reduced by the fulfilment even of his furthest dreams. It increased as he grew older. In the 1870s it showed itself in some of his major actions.

It goes without saying that during the years when Bismarck at home was 'Prussianizing' the new Confederation and trying hard to bind the southern states more closely to it, the main external consideration was France. Domestic and foreign affairs were completely intertwined. It is impossible to tell whether in 1867 Bismarck was exaggerating the threat from Paris in order to bring the new Reichstag to heel and strengthen his hold over the southern states, or whether his first objective was to accelerate the movement towards German unity with an eye to a show-down with France. Perhaps he did not know himself. Feeling throughout Germany was uncertain to a degree. It was well-known that Bavaria and Württemberg were attracted more to France than to Prussia and would be unreliable allies in any Franco-Prussian confrontation. The reverse of that medal was the belief of the Bavarian Foreign Office after Königgrätz that Prussia was about to punish defeated Bavaria by breaking her up and awarding the Palatinate as compensation to Napoleon. Even such a shrewd and well-informed diplomat as the Bavarian foreign minister, Prince Chlodwig Hohenlohe-Schillingsfürst, convinced himself that Bismarck was thinking of dismembering Bavaria in favour of Napoleon at the very moment when Bismarck was telling Benedetti that Prussia would join with Austria, cross the Rhine, and take Alsace if Napoleon persisted in demanding the 1814 frontier.

That had been in August 1866, and it was nothing but bluff. Benedetti throughout almost the whole of his tour of duty in Berlin was sure that he enjoyed a special relationship with Bismarck—as indeed he did, but not quite as he saw it. He thought it was only the king who prevented Bismarck from ceding German territory in compensation first for France's neutrality in the Austrian War, then for her blessing to the North German Confederation—all with an eye to a future alliance. The relationship between the two men is brought vividly into focus in half a dozen words scribbled by Bismarck in the margin of a report from Benedetti to Drouyn, his chief in Paris, dispatched from Nikolsburg just three weeks after Königgrätz. Bismarck, Benedetti announced, 'is the only person in the entire kingdom who appreciates the advantage for Prussia in establishing, at the cost of some territorial sacrifice, an intimate and lasting alliance.'[5] Five years later this report was captured by Prussian troops; Bismarck found time to read it and scribble in the margin: 'He honestly believed it.'[6] How very characteristic that even when he put himself to the trouble of commenting on a fragment of history his words could be read in two senses, diametrically opposed. And it was characteristic of his whole *modus operandi* that Benedetti should be manoeuvred into being right in the letter of the word while quite wrong in the spirit. Had it suited his own purposes, Bismarck would not have minded transferring German soil to France; but he also knew that the question would not arise. He allowed Benedetti to suppose that King William might be persuaded to surrender part of his sa-

nce, knowing not only that this was out of the question—not,
to be suggested. Benedetti should have known that too, but
he most perceptive envoy of his day. So Bismarck might have
any shady dealer in 'antique' furniture, that if the unfortunate
f a fake was determined to believe he had found a bargain, who
was he to deny him satisfaction?

This, indeed, is a fair example of Bismarck's diplomatic practice,
stripped of the brilliance of his arguments, the resonance of his prose, the
aura of high office: he confused sleight of hand with bargaining. He was a
confidence trickster of genius, and his success was so great that he infected
his age.

It is a truism, of course, that long-dead statesmen would be judged by
the standards of their own age, not of our own. But such men, to qualify
for greatness, should at least reflect the best in their age, not the worst.
Bismarck's case is especially interesting because he was born at a time
when public and international morality were slowly and painfully improving, to reach a level far higher than our own, and he lived on to see the
start of an equally rapid decline—a decline for which, it may be strongly
argued, he himself was largely responsible. He did not reflect the best of
the second half of the nineteenth century, which aspired actively to peace
between nations and honesty at home. He made war and he glorified dishonesty. He threw the nineteenth century back (dragging the young twentieth century with it) to the level of Louis XIV or Frederick the Great. He
fell far, far back from Metternich. The fact that Louis Napoleon was also
an adventurer does not affect the issue: nobody has exalted that uneasy
monarch as Bismarck has been exalted. Bismarck was not simply one
gifted statesman among others: he was supremely gifted, a portent and a
national hero.

Poor Benedetti, infatuated with the belief that he enjoyed Bismarck's
confidence, doomed to be used by Bismarck as a cat's-paw, and then discarded. . . . As already remarked, he was not alone in his failure to see
where Bismarck was driving, which was to create a united Germany, less
Austria, while giving nothing away, even though this might be seen as a
direct affront to France and an upsetting of the European power balance.

Bismarck's conduct towards France underwent a sea-change in the early
spring of 1867. Until March of that year his position had been fluid and
indeterminate. He could lead Napoleon on to expect more than he would

ever be given; he could administer a snub (as at Nikolsburg, early in August 1866) when he decided that the French were getting a little above themselves. But his basic attitude remained friendly and all the signs were that he believed he could get what he wanted in Germany without giving anything away and without alienating Napoleon. Thus when, abandoning his demand for the 1814 frontier, Napoleon sent Benedetti in to try for Luxemburg and Belgium (neither of which was in Prussia's gift) and some sort of an alliance, Bismarck was benignly encouraging. England, he knew, would never stand for the annexation of Belgium, but there was no particular reason why the French should not have Luxemburg, and the idea of an alliance was still worth pondering.

He was so encouraging, indeed, that poor Benedetti abandoned all discretion and made the capital error of putting his confidences into writing: he incorporated the current French thinking in a draft agreement and actually entrusted it to Bismarck, who could hardly believe his luck. France was to have Belgium and Luxemburg in return for her consent to what Benedetti called a 'federal union' between the North German Confederation and the southern states, whose sovereignty would nevertheless be respected 'in just measure.'[7] This was most strangely an echo of Rechberg's attempt to jump Bismarck into signing an agreement with Austria only three years earlier. There was something about Bismarck that seemed to make seasoned diplomats lose all sense of reality and commit the most elementary *gaffes*. Benedetti was not alone in suffering from the illusion that he enjoyed a special relationship with him, but the price he was to pay was exceptionally high. Sometimes, indeed, there was no price: the appearance of confidentiality was one of Bismarck's most lethal weapons, but he also used this trick for purely exploratory reasons with no particular end in view, or simply to relieve his own tension, as we shall see when we come, for example, to his extraordinary outpourings a few years later to the British ambassador, Lord Odo Russell (later Lord Ampthill), who had to confess to his own government in London that his embarrassment at the great man's confidences was so great that he was hard put to it to know how to report them.[8]

But with Benedetti there was a definite end in view. It was to hold France off with hopes of benefits to come while Bismarck sorted out the German problem. And Benedetti played into his hands. His proposals showed that Napoleon was desperate for some sort of 'triumph' to prove to the French that he was still a dynamic leader and that France as well as Prussia was an expanding power. Taken in conjunction with his readiness to postpone his claim to the 1814 frontiers they showed that Napoleon had not been able to make up his mind to concentrate on a single objective, did not care where and what he received in 'compensation' so long as it was something. Above all they showed that he needed a settlement, understood that he was in no position to prevent the emergence of a new and powerful unified Germany, and had decided to make the best of a bad job and sue for Prussia's friendship.

It was an invitation to Bismarck to respond with a concession that would cost him nothing. Benedetti and Napoleon were turned firmly in the direction of Luxemburg. The position of that tiny country was complex. Rather as Holstein had been, it was a Grand Duchy which had been part of the old German Confederation, but the grand duke was the king of Holland. It contained a fortress area still garrisoned by Prussian troops on behalf of the Confederation. Now the Confederation was no more, but the Prussian troops remained. The best solution, Bismarck told Benedetti, would be for Prussia to keep out of what must be a passage of horse-trading between the emperor of the French and the king of Holland. He was sure (and he was correct in this) that the Dutch king would be only too pleased to sell the Luxemburgers and their land for an appropriate sum. He was also sure that the king of Prussia would not object, provided he was not asked to bless the transaction in advance.

It was at this stage that Bismarck had his break-down and crept away to Putbus, and from Putbus on 22 October he wrote to Goltz in Paris explaining the policy he was pursuing while he still lay low. The French, he said, 'must be induced to go on hoping and, above all, to retain their faith in our good will without being given any definite commitment.' Four months later he was writing that every day that passed was gain, winning time for 'the consolidation of our relationships in northern Germany and with southern Germany.'[9] But although he was keeping Napoleon at arm's length he was still amicably disposed. In December he could write to Goltz again insisting that 'since the start of his administration he had regarded this alliance as the natural expression of the lasting coincidence of the interests of both countries.'[10] Goltz was a fervent advocate of such a union, and it is impossible to tell whether Bismarck was here using him for his own tactical reasons, or whether he seriously contemplated an alliance. Be that as it may, in March there was a sharp and very public switch in his attitude. It was precipitated by Napoleon himself and complicated by the Dutch king.

On 14 February, two days after the elections for the first Reichstag, Napoleon felt constrained to assert himself in face of the new Germany. In his speech from the throne at the opening of the French parliament he ranged backward in time, boasted that France had halted the Prussians at the gates of Vienna without mobilizing a single regiment, and continued: 'Prussia seeks to avoid everything which might irritate our national sensitivity and is in agreement with us on the major European issues.' The recent enlargement of Prussia, he declared in effect, was no more than a natural step towards the realization of his dream of a Europe of nation-states in which the people of each separate state came together to work out their own destinies.[11]

The arrogance of Napoleon's boast gave offence to many Prussians, but the tacit admission of defeat was an open invitation to the bully in Bismarck. Why should he concede anything, even Luxemburg, to a France so feebly led?

The pressure of German public opinion was now real. Bismarck had contrived the Constitution to his satisfaction and was absolute master if he played his cards properly. But he had to play. He had, that is to say, for the first time since he came to power, to take into consideration parliamentary opinion as an expression of public opinion. Until now he had been fluid and free in all his activities, able and ready to improvise to suit the passing moment, able and ready to fight all opposition into the ground—provided he could only keep his king in order. Everything had been subordinated first to the assertion of monarchical control of the army, then to the defeat of Austria. The immediate goal had been the aggrandizement of Prussia, but now a much broader perspective opened. The North German Confederation had to be made to work and the southern states then had to be brought into at least some sort of union, if only economic, with it. This meant that Bismarck could no longer continue as one man against the rest: he would have to find allies; he would have to use all his skill in playing one party off against another. And it must have been very quickly clear to him first that king and people would never agree to the appeasement of Napoleon at the expense of Germany, and second the encouragement of a mood of hostility towards France would be a very good way of accelerating German unity.

The critical day was 19 March 1867. On that day two things happened. First, as an answer to Napoleon's boasting, and also to counter domestic criticism of his failure to unify Germany at one stroke (in deference to Napoleon it was supposed, in part correctly), Bismarck published to the world the texts of his treaties of alliance with the southern states, hitherto secret.

These made it clear that for all practical purposes the armies of all the German states stood together under Prussian control. To the Germans the revelation was a sensation, arousing in the anti-Prussian elements of the south the most bitter resentment, and in Bismarck's supporters a wry, almost shocked admiration of this latest manifestation of his unscrupulous genius. Was there nothing this man could not accomplish whether by fair means or foul? The answer, clearly, was no. In France the shock was damaging in the extreme. Only a few days earlier the redoubtable Thiers, seventy years old now, and recently back in politics after stormy years of exile and obscurity, had arraigned the emperor in a formidable indictment. Comparing Napoleon's feebleness of purpose with the courage, vision, and steadfast purpose of Bismarck, he declared: 'There is not another single mistake to commit.'[12] But already another error stood revealed. Once again Napoleon had been made to look absurd.

He felt humiliated and betrayed. The more so because on that very day his chase after Luxemburg was brought to an undignified end. The Dutch king agreed in principle to sell Luxemburg for 5 million gulden but not, he insisted, without the explicit approval of the king of Prussia. At the same time French agents in Luxemburg began to organize spectacular anti-Prussian demonstrations. The cat was now truly among the pigeons. Bismarck was presented with a fine excuse for washing his hands of the whole affair and posing as an injured innocent into the bargain. The ground had been cut from under his feet, he complained to the French: the whole point of the operation had been for Napoleon to leave Prussia out of any negotiations and face her with a *fait accompli*. He, Bismarck, could not and would not be asked to invite his sovereign to give away a foot of German soil. Furthermore, the street demonstrations looked like calculated provocation.

And so he let the situation boil, warning Goltz meanwhile that the extreme left in the Reichstag was planning to attack the government. But the attack when it came a fortnight later was not from the extreme left at all. It was led by no less a person than Bennigsen, the National Liberal leader, and Bennigsen, who was to allow himself too often to get too close to Bismarck and be used by him, had been encouraged and briefed by Bismarck himself. His initiative took the form of an interpellation: what steps did the government propose to take in defence of the union of that 'old German land,' Luxemburg, with the rest of Germany, and in particular of Prussia's right to garrison the fortress? Bennigsen was especially scathing about poor King William of Holland, 'a German prince,' for sinning against all that was most sacred by even contemplating selling to France land that had 'at all times been German.'[13] Napoleon was bewildered by this unexpected onslaught and not at all clear as to what had hit him; but he refused to be intimidated, and thus compelled Bismarck to take a harder and more obvious line. Prussia on her own, he told Dutch William, could not possibly sanction the deal: he must seek the views of all the signatory powers of the 1815 treaty—and, for good measure, those of the North German Confederation as well. He went further: Prussia must decline all responsibility for the treaty between France and Holland; she would reserve her action. He went further still: he invoked the spirit of nationalism. Neither the government nor he himself, he declared, could stand against the nationalist fury. '. . . we must, in my opinion, risk war rather than yield.'[14] But the decisive factor was nothing less than national honour. To his representatives at all the courts of Germany he dispatched a remarkable statement of principle: 'If a nation *feels* its honour has been violated, then this honour *has* in fact been violated, and appropriate action must ensue.' He stood, he announced to King William, powerless before the people's anger.[15]

Bismarck had made effective use of nationalist hysteria in the recent past; but this was the first occasion on which he had conjured it out of nothing and then pretended that it was a spontaneous outburst of emotion which he could do nothing to curb. It seems extraordinary that this man who had for so long stood alone, unmoved, immovable, in face of the most savage onslaught parliament and press could bring against him, was able to turn round and declare that he was the helpless slave of public opinion. Few queried this absurd presentation, and the reason for this was that almost the entire population of Germany was by now caught up in a passion of chauvinism. There was to be a repetition of this tactic on a much larger and more serious scale a very few years later, when Bismarck through his jackal press organized a popular clamour for the annexation of Alsace-Lorraine, and then pretended that he had been compelled by public opinion to seize more than he thought wise or politic, reluctantly and against his better judgement.[16]

What, in 1867, was he up to?

Not at that time to start a war with France; that was clear. He could have had one for the asking, and he knew very well that Napoleon was still in a poor condition to fight, with some of his best troops not returned from the sad Mexican fiasco and the re-equipment of the army far from complete. Moltke wanted war, and said so trenchantly. It was bound to come;

let it come while Prussia was strong and France in disarray. But apart from all other considerations Bismarck was far from sure that Prussia was as strong as Moltke assumed: the North German Confederation itself was only just learning to walk, while the military alliances into which he had pushed and pulled a reluctant and sometimes resentful South might, he believed, mean a good deal less in practice than they did on paper. As he had said to Goltz, 'every day is a day gained.'

It was now that he conducted the conversation, referred to earlier, with the Free Conservative leader, Bethusy-Huc: 'Unhappily I believe a war with France must come before long—her vanity, wounded by our victories, will drive her towards it. Yet, since I know of no French or German interest which calls for a resort to arms, I do not see it as certain. Only a country's vital interests justify the launching of a war—only its honour, which is not to be confused with so-called prestige. No statesman has a right to start a war simply because, in his opinion, it must inevitably come within a given period of time. . . .' And he went on with the moving phrases cited earlier in this narrative about war-cripples in the Wilhelm-strasse looking up at his window and thinking 'if that man up there had not made that wicked war I should be at home, healthy and strong.'[17]

All this was true, as far as it went. But did it go far enough? We have seen Bismarck actively provoke two wars, with Denmark and with Austria, and no doubt he could argue that in each case Prussia fought for a 'vital national interest.' Now, although he clearly did not want a war with France, he had already embarked on the course of provocation which was to end with Napoleon's declaration of war in August 1870. In the Luxemburg affair he saw a way of drawing North Germans together and using the threat of foreign attack to push through the first Reichstag's various desiderata which otherwise might have been long and bitterly resisted. He was not looking for a fight. He had a counter-proposal ready to appease Napoleon if it began to look like war: if Prussia backed France's claim to Luxemburg, would France allow her to keep the Danish part of Schleswig? (He was producing this possible solution to Goltz even while he was assuring the Dutch king that he was helpless in face of German nationalist feeling.) But was it necessary for Bismarck to push things as far as he did—first frightening William into withdrawing his consent to the sale of Luxemburg, then calling in the powers for a grand conference which ultimately neutralized Luxemburg, saved Prussia's honour, and not only deprived Napoleon of any gain whatsoever but, far worse, made him look a fool, and a greedy fool at that?

None of this was necessary to produce the tension required to weld the Germanies together. Bismarck himself knew very well, and had said so, that Napoleon might be forced to go to war to make up for his diplomatic humiliation—and yet he went out of his way to multiply that humiliation. It is impossible to escape the impression that he was not only magnifying the belligerence of France for his own internal reasons but also determined to destroy Napoleon, either provoking him to war and defeat or demoralizing him by making him punch-drunk. It is this sort of behaviour that makes the endless discussion as to whether or not he deliberately sought war in 1870 seem academic.

That he needed an exterior threat to weld Germany together was self-evident, and the most plausible threat was France, whose congenital belligerence was widely feared—and not only by the Germans, who stood closest to the threat implicit in it. France has suffered so much at the hands of Germany in three wars that nowadays it requires an effort of the imagination to think back to a time when she was the very image of predatory aggression: the Thirty Years War in the first half of the seventeenth century and the arrogant campaigns of Louis XIV in the second half; the unprovoked and greedy assault on the young Austrian queen, Maria Theresa, in the War of the Spanish Succession in 1741; the Napoleonic bid for the mastery of all Europe in the dawn of the nineteenth. For two hundred years France had made the pace, glorifying her warrior heroes: only the Prussian Frederick the Great, when he threw himself on Austria in 1741, had created an analogous disturbance, and even then the French had joined hands with him.

There was plenty of excuse for decent Germans, for Englishmen and Russians and Austrians too, to think of France as the supreme militarist power. And the behaviour of Louis Napoleon had done little to erase that impression. He himself may not have wanted war, but he was surrounded and upheld by people who did; and he needed glory and prestige of the kind most conveniently obtained on the battlefield. He made himself emperor in 1852. In 1854 he embarked on the Crimean War; in 1859 he beat Austria on the plains of Lombardy, in a war which could not have taken place had he not encouraged Cavour to goad the Austrians into making a false move (much as Bismarck was to goad them seven years later). In a word, it was very natural for any Prussian to regard the French in general and their new and flamboyant emperor in particular as a constant menace: others besides Germans felt this.

Ironically, Bismarck himself was one of the few who understood that Napoleon feared and hated war; but he also knew that there existed a strong war-party, which knew how to exploit that popular thirst for glory and drama which was the Achilles heel of the most intelligent nation on earth. He had to recognize that at any time Napoleon might be pushed into warlike action to avoid being driven from his throne in one of those wrathful outbursts of irritable violence which seemed to have become a feature of the French political scene.

Less sophisticated intelligences in Berlin were quite simply convinced that war was only a matter of time, Napoleon or no Napoleon. Moltke, for example, saw nothing in the emperor's climb-down and humiliation in the Luxemburg affair to make him change his mind. After it he was angrier than ever at the lost opportunity to put the French down while they were still half-way through their army reforms. He blamed Bismarck in person: 'This stand of his will cost us many lives later on,' he grumbled.[18] His views, and the views of a great many other Prussians of both high and low degree, were complicated by a congenital distrust, based on total incomprehension, of the French character—an attitude nicely expressed in his own words six years later when with France shattered (but not crushed), Alsace and Lorraine torn from her, her economy burdened by a savage indemnity, he could sadly and heavily express to the British ambassador, Lord Odo Russell (a friend of Germany if ever there was one), his regret that 'Britain showed, by her commercial policy, so decided a preference for an alliance with corrupt Catholic France to an alliance with kindred Protestant Germany.'[19]

There were plenty of North Germans who could not understand why victorious Prussia stopped at the Main and failed to coerce the southern states into immediate submission and some sort of union. This, of course, could have been done. But Bismarck had no desire to saddle himself with responsibility for a Catholic South which would regard the Prussians as alien oppressors from whom they might seek delivery at the hands of France. He had already pushed his luck. Immediately after the defeat of Austria the rulers of Hesse-Darmstadt and Württemberg had both sought to turn his anger at their siding with Austria by applying to join the new Confederation. Popular feeling in Bavaria, at odds with king and government, was also for union with the North. But when Prussia was suddenly transformed and augmented by Bismarck's ruthless annexations, enthusiasm dwindled.

With the boiling up of the Luxemburg crisis and the apparent imminence of war, the recoil was even stronger. Bitterness between the pro- and anti-Prussian factions was inflamed by Bismarck's publication of the treaties of alliance, which shocked the opposition and were seen by them as a betrayal of the peoples by their rulers: while the rulers themselves now shrank from the prospect of being dragged into a war with France, a consummation that promised nothing but woe to them. In a word, while Bismarck's Luxemburg policy helped him win the confidence of the German nationalists in Prussia, it also enlarged the gap between North and South, which was not at all what was intended.

Bismarck had many gifts, among the most valuable his ability to ignore defeat: if he could not turn manifest defeat into the appearance of victory, why then, he could pretend there had been no conflict at all. Faced with an unexpectedly formidable barrier on the banks of the Main, Bismarck publicly resigned himself to a placidly cheerful waiting game. This did not prevent him from seeking for ways and means of accelerating the movement towards unification. He was at it all the time. His brightest hope was centred on the establishment in 1868 of a so-called Customs Parliament, the Zollparlament. If the southern states would not enter into a political union, at least they might be prepared to institutionalize their existing economic union and through this work their way imperceptibly into political cooperation. For a man without illusions Bismarck set surprisingly great store by this conjuring trick, which was so obvious that not even the most simple-minded would be taken in by it. The southern states welcomed the Customs Parliament for what it was and made free use of it as a convenience; but they resisted all attempts to broaden its scope and increase the range of its authority. If Bismarck had reflected he would have realized that the Zollverein itself was so strong that it had developed an autonomous life of its own based purely on trade uncomplicated by politics—so much so that it had continued to function normally throughout the recent civil war; states in arms against each other had still profited from unrestricted mutual trade.

A very different scheme, and one which clearly showed which way his mind was moving, was his attempt, with the aid of the crown prince, to have William crowned as German emperor; nothing less than a revival of the Frankfurt scheme that he had rejected so scornfully twenty years before. This time the crown was to be offered not by the assembly of the people but by the princes. This scheme too came to nothing: in fact it was overtaken by quite unforeseen events which led to the final violent breakthrough.

All the time he was casting round and trying expedient after expedient to win over the southern states he was blandly counselling his subordinates not to worry: all would come right one day, but that day could not be rushed. Thus he could write to his envoy to Bavaria: 'I too think it probable that German unity would be advanced by violent events. But it is quite another matter to assume responsibility for bringing about a violent catastrophe and to choose the right moment to act. Arbitrary interference in the course of history on purely subjective grounds has always resulted in the shaking down of unripe fruit. In my opinion it is obvious that German unity is not a ripe fruit. . . . The gift of waiting while a situation develops is an essential requirement of practical politics.'[20]

With all Bismarck's utterances one has to bear in mind the nature of the audience. That particular observation was addressed to Baron Georg von Werthern, notoriously impatient and hot-headed, who had argued against Bismarck's policy of moderation after Königgrätz and was now, in Munich, passionate to bring the Bavarians to heel. It was he who a year later exclaimed in desperation, 'From the short period in 1867, when it was powerfully agitated and capable of exploitation, German national feeling has steadily declined, and I see no end to this process without a new crisis. . . . No one believes any more that Germany can move forward along the chosen path.'[21] In 1869 Bismarck still wanted to move quietly. He was disappointed, indeed taken aback, by the increasing reluctance of the South to join the North in any sort of union. He had gone as far as was possible in building North and South into a coherent military power through the intermingling of formations and commanders; but there was no military machine he could comfortably rely upon. The resistance of the South to Prussianization was steadily increasing and manifesting itself in a number of ways which would have caused a lesser man than Bismarck either to retire to sulk in his tent or else to break out with a show of violence. The failure of the Customs Parliament was a personal humiliation and would have been taken as such by most men, but not by Bismarck. Just as he had made that astonishing observation about national honour existing in the mind of the people, so he might now have said 'no man is humiliated who does not feel himself humiliated.'

He had taken too much for granted in his approach to the southern states. Perhaps because he had become accustomed to the ease with which he had been able to bully and bamboozle his own monarch and the parliamentarians of his native Prussia, he assumed that he could get his way throughout all Germany without too much effort. He quite simply did not know enough about the South, and he underestimated Catholic solidarity, the dynastic pride of the Wittelsbachs in Bavaria (a family older than both the Habsburgs and the Hohenzollerns), the reluctance of the princes to surrender their autonomy, and of the Liberal nationalists in the South to deliver the new Germany into the hands of Prussia, as well as of the particularists to surrender their independence to anyone. The better instructed among them also knew that in a unified Germany two out of every three Germans would be Prussians. This was not an alluring prospect, and the remarkable thing is that Bismarck ever thought it might be.

But although he was disappointed and taken aback, and although on occasion he could gamble recklessly, his gambling was invariably based on a calculated risk, and when not gambling he could be more cautious and circumspect than the next man. And so, while others grew desperate, he assumed the role of a wise, far-seeing statesman, tolerant, infinitely patient, prepared to wait for ever. As he said to Moritz Busch when inducting him as his special assistant: 'The question of German unity is making good progress; but it requires time—one year perhaps, or five, or possibly even ten years. I cannot make it go any faster, nor can these gentlemen either. But they have no patience to wait.'[22] ('These gentlemen' were the parliamentarians in Berlin.) The date was 20 February 1870, and Bismarck was already contemplating a new situation that might help him to force the pace.

The government of Spain had for some time been looking for a new monarch to succeed the Bourbon dynasty which had come to a disreputable end with the ejection of the notorious Queen Isabella in 1868. A year later, in September 1869, very secretly it offered the crown to a Hohenzollern, Prince Leopold, son and heir of Prince Charles Anthony of Hohenzollern-Sigmaringen, head of that branch of the family which had remained faithful to Swabia when early in the fifteenth century the first of the Prussian Hohenzollerns had set up his standard on, as it were, the north-east frontier, as margrave of Brandenburg. The two branches of the family had remained close, and Charles Anthony himself had for a brief period, in the fleeting days of King William's famous 'New Era' a decade before, served as minister-president of Prussia. Even now he was military governor of Prussia's Catholic provinces, Rhineland and Westphalia,

n Leopold was a serving officer in the Prussian army. In a word,
nches were seen by the outside world as one family, which in-
were: King William of Prussia had to give his explicit consent
member of that family could accept any crown that might be
he had recently done when Leopold's brother Charles had been
elevated to the throne of Rumania as Carol I.

When sounded out in September 1869, Leopold declined the Spanish
offer, chiefly because Spain itself seemed to be on the verge of civil war.
But it was not an unconditional refusal: all the Hohenzollerns were dynasts
by training and temperament, and Leopold made it clear that he might
accept later on, provided the proposal was formally approved not only by
the head of his own family, King William, but also by Napoleon (to whom
he was related through his grandmother, a daughter of Eugène de Beau-
harnais, Empress Josephine's son). In February of the following year the
Spaniards came forward again, this time with a formal invitation from
the Spanish regent, Marshal Juan Prim, presented by Don Miguel Salazar. The interesting thing was that while the Spaniards notified the Prussian king and his chancellor of their intention, as Leopold insisted, they
said nothing to Napoleon, even though Leopold had stipulated that this
also must be done. There was only one reason for this. All concerned knew
that the French would be up in arms at the prospect of a Hohenzollern on
the Spanish throne, and from the very beginning were at very great pains
to preserve total secrecy, Bismarck himself above all. Not even the government of Prussia knew for some time that an offer had been made.

What happened from 25 February 1870 on is part of the Bismarck
story, with Leopold and his father playing only subsidiary roles. Since the
seizure by the Western allies in 1945 of Prussian Foreign Office archives,
long-suppressed documents reflecting the progress and motivation of the
Hohenzollern candidature have come to light, providing much that was
until then only suspected concerning Bismarck's personal involvement—
enough to show that he lied extensively, consistently, and fluently, and
that in order to preserve his good name and to avoid making retrospective
and highly damaging admissions to the world in general and France in particular, the Wilhelmstrasse had determinedly suppressed (but not destroyed) certain key documents.[23]

We still do not know the whole story—for example, whether Bismarck
was actively engaged in exploiting the Spanish crisis even before February
1870. That he saw a situation that *could* be exploited was clear almost immediately after Isabella's flight, when he telegraphed from Varzin his ap-

preciation of the crisis as an embarrassment for France. 'A solution agreeable to Napoleon would hardly be of use to us.'[24] And very soon, in December, two of Bismarck's aides were in Madrid, followed in May by that ubiquitous contact man Theodor von Bernhardi. As far as is known they were sent as observers with a watching brief, but it seems improbable that there was no mention of Leopold as a possible candidate for the throne, even if only one among others. Certainly by mid-April 1869 there were indirect approaches to Charles Anthony and by May there were rumours convincing enough to worry Napoleon in the European press that Leopold had been offered the crown. On 8 May Benedetti was sent to ask Bismarck what, if anything, was going on. Bismarck agreed that Leopold had been sounded out but insisted that he had refused the offer.[25]

In other words, by May 1869 Bismarck knew all about the offer and also knew that Napoleon could not possibly take the prospect of a Hohenzollern on the throne of Spain lying down (but, of course, he knew that without being told). Yet in his memoirs he insisted that he played no part in the affair until July 1870: until then, he said, it had been nothing but a Hohenzollern family affair. This was a lie.[26]

On 25 February, in fact, he was formally brought into the picture by Charles Anthony himself, who was now eager for his son to accept the crown but wanted to manoeuvre William into taking the decision. In his letter, which presented the new offer as one of great urgency, Charles Anthony listed a number of practical reasons for acceptance, not least the probability that if Prussian Hohenzollern refused the Spanish crown, Bavarian Wittlesbach would pick it up. Was this desirable? To think of the glory it would bring to Hohenzollern made one almost dizzy: 'A dynasty which represents the centre of gravity of Central Europe and whose scions flourish by the Black Sea and beyond the Pyrenees—the one ruling over a nation of developing civilization, the other ruling over one whose civilization belongs to the past—a dynasty such as has not been known in history since Charles V—on such a dynasty, therefore, rests the responsibility of a high mission willed by Providence and of a reputation for knowing how to rule over elements of the most heterogenous kind.'[27]

Magnificent as the dream was, however, Charles Anthony was aware of the pitfalls: 'A Hohenzollern in Spain would give rise to a wild outcry in anti-Prussian Europe and either precipitate or defer the solution of many pending questions. This, however,' he modestly concluded, 'is a consideration which lies outside the sphere of my judgement.'

He thus turned the whole affair over to Bismarck, who, within days of

receiving Charles Anthony's letter, was pushing the Hohenzollern candidature as hard as he knew how in the face of the most stubborn resistance
from his sovereign.

Bismarck's first major onslaught came in a memorandum, dated 8
March, in which he argued with great élan but also in terms that were
oddly irresponsible. A Hohenzollern in Spain, he said in effect, would in
case of a Franco-German war tie down certainly one, probably two, French
army corps on the Spanish frontier; if a Wittelsbach took the crown rejected by a Hohenzollern there was a strong chance that both Madrid and
Munich would become the instruments of France, Austria, and Rome; or
Spain might turn republican and infect all Europe with the fever of revolution. On the other hand, acceptance by a Hohenzollern would redound to
the greater glory of the House and therefore to the strengthening of monarchical feeling at home and German prestige abroad. These points, and
others too, were flung down with no attempt to support them by close argument. And he was not above borrowing from Charles Anthony: 'It is
therefore to Germany's political interest that the House of Hohenzollern
should gain an esteem and an exalted position in the world such as does
not find its analogy . . . since the days of Charles V.'[28]

Bismarck knew better than anybody that William was not interested in
far-flung empires, but only in Prussia. He himself must have contemplated
Charles Anthony's invocation of Charles V with a sardonic twitch of the
lips. Now he was repeating that sententious invocation as his own idea to
William, who, by the time he reached the end of it, had torn the whole
memorandum to shreds in a dry, concise, penetrating marginal commentary, which showed that Bismarck's royal master possessed a far livelier and
shrewder mind than the servant liked to pretend. For example, puncturing
one of Bismarck's wilder flights of fancy, in which he insisted on the total
devotion to the monarchical principle of the Spanish army on which the
future monarch might safely base his rule, William observed: 'It seems to
me not so much the monarchical principle for which the troops fight well
as for the preservation of the rulers whom they support in a revolutionary
spirit in order to get into power. . . . Reliable support from an army which
has made all the revolutions for the last forty years is hardly to be expected!'[29]

The one thing William agreed with Bismarck about was the need to
keep the whole affair secret, which meant that discussion must be limited
to a minimum. And in fact on 15 March the king commanded Charles
Anthony to give a dinner in his own apartments which in everything but

name turned out to be a formal Crown Council. At 4:30 in the afternoon there asembled the crown prince, Prince Leopold, Bismarck as minister-president, Schleinitz as minister in attendance, Roon as minister for war, Moltke as chief of staff, Rudolf von Delbrück as minister of the interior, and Hermann von Thile, permanent under-secretary of state at the Foreign Ministry. With the king and Charles Anthony as hosts, these and these only were privy to the great secret of which Bismarck was later to disclaim all knowledge (to the end of his life he denied there had been a Crown Council at all, although the minutes were faithfully preserved).[30]

All except the crown prince and the king urged acceptance of the Spanish crown, though all by this time must have known that this act might drive Napoleon to war. For the first time even Leopold began to waver; but he still would not move without word from the king, and the king would not speak. It looked as though the dream were dissolving into nothingness. But neither Bismarck nor Prim were ready to give up. Bismarck sent his trusted Lothar Bucher with a staff officer, Major Maximilian von Versen, to report on the mood in Spain. They did so with extreme enthusiasm; but Leopold still refused to act without at least a declaration that acceptance was 'in the interests of the state.' The king had said his last word. Could Bismarck ignore his sovereign's will? He could and did. At the end of May, after a bout of jaundice, he tipped the balance, enraging poor William, who innocently imagined that the whole affair was over and done with. 'Today no less than before I feel no doubt that Germany has a vital interest here,' he wrote to Charles Anthony, 'I have once more begged HM the King to reconsider the question in this light and received the answer that as soon as any prince of the House of Hohenzollern showed any inclination to accept the crown he would raise no opposition whatsoever to this inclination.'[31]

It was this 'momentous letter' of 28 May, as Charles Anthony called it, which turned the tide.[32] Charles Anthony rejoiced; Leopold at last surrendered himself to his fate; Bismarck heaved a sigh of relief and took himself off to Varzin. There, demonstratively cut off from all official contacts, fortified by a great stock of Karlsbad water, he gave out that he had embarked on a 'drastic cure' and was not to be disturbed. What in effect he was doing was leaving the field clear for Charles Anthony, Leopold, and the Spaniards to make their own detailed arrangements in total secrecy while his own absence from Berlin would indicate to the world, particularly the French, that no mischief could be brewing. What the world did not realize was that he liked nothing better than to set a scheme in motion and then to wait at a distance while it worked itself out. In the matter of the Spanish candidature withdrawal gave point to his subsequent insistence that he had known nothing about the matter until July. . . .

It was now 3 June. With Bismarck far away in Varzin and the king at Bad Ems, Bismarck's men—Bucher, Versen, and his chief assistant, Thile—presided over feverish negotiations between Spaniards and Hohenzollerns, pressing the need for speed on the still reluctant Leopold. All this frantic activity took place in extreme secrecy in a land where the entire government had closed down for the summer. The Spaniards wanted the affair settled before the Cortes in Madrid shut down too. On 19 June Bucher managed to extract from Leopold a formal letter asking for William's blessing, and rushed off with it to Bad Ems. William gave his blessing, but with very bad grace. Through the crown prince he had discovered something of all this clandestine activity, which went directly against his own instructions and Bismarck's reassurances. Thile was rapped heavily over the knuckles and told unequivocally that no further action of any kind was to be taken until he, the king, had been informed. Thile passed on this instruction to his master, supposed to be incommunicado. Luckily, he wrote, the king had not asked for details 'which would have put me in an awkward position.' His Majesty had contented himself with a reproof, speaking 'not without a certain asperity, though at once adding that everything must be avoided that might put Your Excellency out of humour or "irritate your nerves." '[33]

This entire episode, and Bismarck's marginal commentary on the correspondence, illuminate with perfect clarity not only certain aspects of his relations with his sovereign but also the web of deceit which surrounded the whole Spanish question: 'That beats anything!' he commented. And' again: 'So H.M. wants the affair treated *with official Royal interference?*. . . The whole affair is only possible if it remains the limited concern of the Hohenzollern princes, it must not turn into a Prussian concern, the king must be able to say without lying: I know nothing about it.'[34]

It would be interesting to know where Bismarck drew his line between lying and not lying. That such a line existed somewhere in his mind is evident from that last remark; but to the outsider it remains invisible. It is interesting, too, to establish that from the moment of his withdrawal from the public scene he was kept fully informed by Thile of all the latest developments and that he himself intervened on a number of occasions.

At last, on 21 June, Salazar triumphantly dispatched his critical signal to the president of the Cortes: he would arrive in Madrid with Leopold's formal acceptance of the crown and the terms to be approved by the Cortes 'about the twenty-sixth.'

Critical because it went wrong. The signal was routed through the Prussian Foreign Ministry to the Prussian embassy in Madrid. There a cipher-clerk made a catastrophic error. Instead of 'about the twenty-sixth' (of June understood), the decode came out 'about the ninth' (of July understood). This made sense to the president of the Cortes, who decided that he could not keep the deputies hanging about in the sweltering heat of Madrid for another eighteen days. So he prorogued the Cortes, leaving this fearful secret hanging in the air. The amazing thing was that it had been kept so well for so long. But on 3 July the inevitable happened and it came out. The French press picked it up in a frenzy of outrage on the Monday morning (4 July), and instead of approaching Prussia quietly to urge the withdrawal of the candidature, Gramont struck a patriotic attitude: 'the interests and the honour of France are now in peril,' he proclaimed[35] (6 July). Keudell was breakfasting with Bismarck at Varzin when they received the newspapers containing Gramont's speech. He relates that Bismarck seemed taken aback by the violence of its tone. 'This looks like war,' he said. 'Gramont could not have spoken so recklessly if war was not decided.'[36] The proper thing, he went on, would be to order general mobilization and fall upon the French immediately. 'That would be victory for us. Unfortunately that will not do for a variety of reasons.' He made do the meanwhile with a paper war. 'The newspapers must be very rough . . . and as many of them as possible.'[37] The pot was to be kept on the boil. And so it was, but now it was the French who did most of the stirring.

Bismarck was lucky in the new French foreign minister, the duc de Gramont, whom he had known in Vienna at the time of the Schönbrunn Conference of 1864. Gramont had identified himself very much with the Austrian treaty in which he believed, since he himself could not imagine Austria ever relinquishing the idea of revenge for Königgrätz. He could be relied upon to act explosively and impetuously in any situation. He did so now, slamming out a dramatic declaration of affront and outrage. Bismarck must have smiled to himself very crookedly indeed when he read an echo of his own and Charles Anthony's invocation of the immemorial empire of Charlves V—but this time from the other side: the French people were not, Gramont declared, obliged to permit a foreign power to install one of its princes on the throne of Charles V and thus upset the European balance. . . .[38] It was from this moment, Bismarck himself admits, that he worked hard for war, and persisted until he got it. But he still stayed away at Varzin, allowing Gramont to make all the mistakes; and it was only when William started developing an independent policy in a determined effort to save the French from their own impetuosity that he finally entered the arena.

'It was a trap,' declared some of Bismarck's agents—Bucher and Versèn among them: the great man lured the French into a trap to destroy them at his leisure. Not so, say others, adducing all sorts of reasons—chief among them that Bismarck would never have removed himself to Varzin had he been planning war but would have stayed in Berlin to watch over the unfolding of his scheming. Further, the whole crisis arose from a hideous accident: if a cipher-clerk in Madrid had not made his improbable mistake Leopold would have been proclaimed king of Spain before Napoleon knew what was happening: there would have been no war.

And so the argument has swayed, sways, and will doubtless go on swaying. But is it really important one way or the other? We know very well that Bismarck did not go to war for fun. We know equally well that he was perfectly ready not merely to go to war but also to contrive a war if what he regarded as 'the vital interests' of Prussia were at stake. In 1870 his conduct in the Spanish affair indicated at the least a determination to elevate Prussia at the expense of France and in so doing to goad Paris into expressions of hostility which would induce all the German states to draw together. At the same time, if he was not seeking war he was quite relentlessly working for the public humiliation of Napoleon—which must have led either to war itself or to the end of the Second Empire. Certainly not even Bismarck could have foreseen the cipher-clerk's blunder. But what he must certainly have foreseen, and from very far back, was that even if Napoleon could hardly declare war when he woke up one morning to find Prince Leopold on the Spanish throne, the repercussions in France of this *fait accompli* would sooner or later have driven him to fight—or watch his empire fall to pieces, probably in violence, with consequences unpredictable for France and for Europe as a whole. This was the pattern Bismarck *must* have foreseen from the moment he started acting secretly in the Spanish affair. His whole activity, therefore, was directed against France in a way which no sovereign state could be expected to endure.

Too much stress can be laid on Gramont's speech, ill-judged as it was: for Gramont was heavily provoked before he made it. When he sent his unwise telegram demanding to be told to what extent the Prussian government was involved in the 'Hohenzollern intrigue,' Thile, in accordance with

his master's general instruction, blandly replied 'that the Prussian government knew absolutely nothing about this affair and that for it the affair did
not exist.'[39]

Nothing could have been better calculated to magnify the suspicions of
the French. And once Gramont had issued his challenge Bismarck in Varzin could sit back and let the crisis deepen without any open action on his
part—or so he thought. But 11 July was a particularly busy day, with telegrams flying about all over Europe—some of them emanating from Varzin—commanding an official policy of cool intransigence. At the same
time Prussia's controlled press let itself go in a manner far from cool. On
that day, too, Bismarck decided it was time to join his master at Ems, seizing the opportunity *en route* to talk to Gorchakov (who had just arrived in
Berlin from St. Petersburg) to make sure that Russia and Prussia understood each other. But he had no serious anxiety: all was going well. The
faithful Bleichröder, not at all in the picture this time, was worrying himself almost ill over the war talk in Berlin and Paris. Two days earlier he had
sent Bismarck news about the fitting out of six warships in Toulon harbour, 'certainly not bound for China,'[40] and also a report from a French
acquaintance, a highly placed official in Gramont's office, begging Berlin
not to take the Spanish affair lightly because French interests were too
deeply committed. He still hesitated to sell any of Bismarck's holdings, but
pleaded for an immediate word if only 'a single syllable,' if things looked
like getting any worse. And Johanna replied in person. Her husband was
too busy 'encoding and decoding' to reply himself, she announced, but she
could assure Herr Bleichröder that he did not believe in war, 'because despite the frivolity of certain people, he thinks it improbable that anyone
would suddenly fall upon *us* because *Spain* did not vote the way one
wanted her to.' 'Nevertheless,' she continued, obviously to Bismarck's dic-
tation, 'he thought there might still come moments when the belief in war
would be stronger than now, and since he needs the money here in any
case, it might be a good idea to sell the railway stock.'[41]

Meanwhile, without his knowing it (when was the last time anything
had happened in Prussia without Bismarck knowing?), King William in
Ems had been quietly and rather desperately undermining his chancellor's
whole position. It was not until Bismarck arrived in the Wilhelmstrasse on
his way to Ems on the afternoon of the twelfth that he discovered that
William had been, in effect, presiding over a feverish three-way traffic between Ems, Paris, and Sigmarigen which had just ended in the formal re-

nunciation of the Spanish crown by Prince Charles Anthony on behalf of his son, at that moment oblivious on holiday in the Alps (his last breath, he thought, of anonymous freedom). For two days king and prince had been bombarded with importunities and doubts—'The thought of an imminent *casus belli* because of a purely family matter,' wrote Charles Anthony, 'had become so unbearable that I had to hold myself in leash not to publish the decision already arrived at yesterday.'[42] The decision was to renounce the crown. Charles Anthony was waiting only for the king's emissary, who, to add to the element of farce that impinges on so many great occasions, had repeatedly missed his railway connections while all Europe held its breath.

All Europe except Bismarck, who was taken wholly by surprise. A bundle of telegrams, he later recounted, was handed to him even as he sat in his carriage in his own courtyard in the Wilhelmstrasse (why they could not wait until he had got indoors, he does not say), and he was shattered to discover that even 'after the French threats and the insults flung about in the Chamber and in the press, the king had continued to treat with Benedetti instead of coolly and aloofly rebuking his minister.'[43] Worse was to come. Bismarck had Moltke and Roon in for dinner that evening, and they were together when the news of Charles Anthony's decision came through. Bismarck's first thought was to resign then and there 'because, after all the insulting provocations of recent days, I saw in this surrender to blackmail a humiliation for Germany for which I was not willing to be officially responsible.' It was, he declared, 'a humiliation worse than Olmütz.'[44]

But soon he thought again about resigning. It was clear that the French were in a thoroughly belligerent mood, and Gramont might yet make a critical mistake which would put him unambiguously in the wrong. The first thing was to stop William informing Benedetti of Charles Anthony's surrender: France must get the news through normal official channels, and this was managed—the king was kept out of it. The second thing was to assure Gorchakov and others, but particularly Gorchakov, that he, Bismarck, had always desired peace and rejoiced that the crisis was over. All was well, and he would now go back to Varzin.[45]

He did nothing of the kind. On that same day, the thirteenth, he dispatched two telegrams which would have interested Gorchakov very much. The first was to the king in Ems warning him that German public opinion would demand satisfaction from France and urging him to recall Werthern, Goltz's successor, from Paris. While to Werthern himself he telegraphed that if 'a completely satisfying statement as to the intentions of France' was not very soon forthcoming he would urge the king to convene the Reichstag and solicit its view on the proper course to take.[46]

In fact he had done enough already. In Paris Gramont had not understood the extent of his own victory, or that it would only be a matter of days, if not hours, before it was made manifest to all the world. He was so blinded by resentment and wounded pride that he saw a deliberate insult in William's failure to acquaint him personally of Charles Anthony's decision, through Benedetti. The bit was fairly between his teeth, and he hardly needed to be urged on by the raucous expressions of chauvinistic public opinion which he himself had so effectively stimulated. As foreign minister he had direct access to Napoleon, and on the evening of the twelth without a word to his prime minister, Emile Ollivier, let alone the cabinet, sent off his last fatal instruction to Benedetti. That unfortunate envoy was to obtain from King William not only a formal endorsement of the renunciation but also 'an assurance that he will never authorize a renewal of the candidacy.'[47] Submission to the will of France had in this matter to be explicit, public, and everlasting.

Bismarck was still in Berlin. His sovereign, far away at Ems, believing that the crisis was well behind him, went for his morning stroll in the idyllic surroundings of the Kurpark on the banks of the River Lahn, flowing translucently by to join the Rhine at Coblenz. Suddenly he was aware of the all too familiar figure of the French ambassador, obviously seeking to waylay him. Politely he raised his hat and stopped. All the world and his wife gathered round, respectfully and properly distant (so much for the security of monarchs in those bad old days), as Benedetti delivered his message—he himself, it seems, hardly realizing its significance. William was very polite but coolly categorical. On no account could he consider entering such a binding undertaking. Benedetti ventured to argue, but the king would stand no more. He had nothing further to add, he said, raised his hat, and turned away. That afternoon he gave point to his refusal by cancelling a formal audience with poor Benedetti which had been arranged earlier. And in his irritation he took a critical step: he instructed his own Foreign Ministry's representative, Heinrich Abeken, who had accompanied him to Ems, to telegraph Bismarck in Berlin and tell him he might make the details of this last encounter public.

It was Abeken's telegram which arrived like a sudden shaft of sunlight to penetrate the depths of gloom in which the frustrated warriors had buried themselves—Bismarck, Moltke, and Roon. Bismarck saw at once that with the very slightest shift of emphasis Abeken's report, published to the world, would be such a slap in the face for Gramont and Napoleon that their reaction was bound to be furiously warlike. Too much has been made of the 'forgery.' There was no need for a forgery; the original wording needed only the slightest sharpening.[48] It is not necessary to believe Bismarck's own melodramatic account of the immediate effect of the telegram. All three men must have realized that the war which seemed to have receded from their grasp was now, suddenly and wonderfully, at hand.

On the evening of the next day, the Quatorze Juillet itself, the Paris newspapers came out with special editions and glaring headlines. By nightfall the Parisians had gone to war, the streets crammed with hysterical demonstrators yelling 'À Berlin!' On that day too the reservists were being called up in France, while the Landwehr in Germany were being secretly mobilized. Next day only Thiers and the left opposition voted against war credits in the Chamber of Deputies. Four days later, on the nineteenth, war was formally declared. But the southern German states, those that must take the brunt of the expected French attack, Bavaria, Württemberg, Baden, were already on a war footing. Nobody knew, nobody had the least premonition that the French were preparing to march to their own destruction, so universally was it taken for granted that the French army was still the finest and most powerful fighting machine in the world. It seemed highly likely that Austria in the south and Denmark in the north would, by joining hands with a triumphant France, seek to avenge their own past humiliations. At the very least, all the world expected a deep penetration into German territory, with the Germans hard put to it to contain the attack. Gorchakov was at pains to emphasize that Prussia had nothing to fear from Russia. English sympathies were almost entirely with the Prussians: here was the third Napoleon following in the footsteps of the first.

The third Napoleon could have disillusioned them. He was in acute pain, almost past enduring, from the stone. To mount his horse was torture. He could not think, and he had no heart for the war, but was driven on by Eugénie and the war party, sick with apprehension at the consequences if he failed to assert the honour and glory of France after so many rebuffs from Berlin. But even Napoleon in his most defeatist mood took it for granted that his armies would soon be in Germany. 'Whatever may be the road we take beyond our frontiers, we shall come across the glorious tracks of our fathers. We shall prove worthy of them. . . .'[49]

Moltke, too, fully expected a deep initial penetration, while the king, as commander-in-chief, thought it unnecessary yet to think of issuing maps of France.[50] Nobody, not Bismarck himself, understood the forces that had been at work in a double transformation-scene to strengthen Germany and weaken France, so that within a matter of weeks the whole balance of Europe was swung the other way. Indeed there was no balance left.

CHAPTER XVI

SEDAN, PARIS, AND THE NEW REICH

By the time the two great armies moved against each other on 28 July
1870, Bismarck had irretrievably set the German people on the path to the
mastery of Europe—or disaster. The moment was well timed. The French
army was ready 'to the last gaiter-button' the soldiers had assured Napoleon; but it was not ready at all. Even the great frontier fortresses, even
Metz itself, the key to the eastern defences, were unprovisioned and quite
unprepared to stand a siege; as for the army, which everyone expected to
march briskly into the Palatinate in order to separate the North Germans
from their southern allies (leading to the subversion or capitulation of the
latter) it simply was not there. The mobilization arrangements were so
faulty that formation commanders had no idea where their component
units were; battalions and squadrons wandered about looking for divisional
headquarters which did not seem to exist. Moltke, on the other hand, had
put his clockwork mobilization schemes into practice against the Austrians
four years earlier; they had worked well then; they worked still better now.
Using the new strategic railway lines to great effect, he brought three
armies to bear against the French line strung along the frontier between
Luxemburg and Switzerland: the First Army in the north, with 50,000
men under the veteran Karl von Steinmetz; the Second Army in the centre
under the king's nephew Prince Frederick Charles, with 134,000 men; and
in the south the crown prince's Third Army of 125,000. It was an imposing array, and Moltke's plan of campaign was all that could be expected of
a strategist of a clear-headedness amounting to genius, who valued simplic-

ity above all other qualities and was austerely free from the least impulse to show off.

But even though Prussian mobilization and logistics went like a dream, nobody behind divisional headquarters was altogether happy. The crown prince, with his southern army, felt abandoned and almost betrayed. He knew he could count on his two Prussian corps, but these were outnumbered by Bavarians, Württembergers, Badeners, whom he regarded as incompetent and did not trust an inch—until their fighting ability proved him wrong.[1] At the northern end of the line, Steinmetz, seventy-four, one of the heroes of the Austrian War but now regarded as burnt out by all except Moltke (who valued him in a tight corner and was expecting trouble in the north), had no intention of doing what he was told, and in fact was to ruin Moltke's plan and put the whole campaign at risk by fighting a private war of his own. Frederick Charles in the centre expected a furious assault to drive a wedge between his army and his cousin the crown prince's.

Everyone was braced for a vigorous and damaging French advance, and tension persisted and increased during the days of mobilization and deployment. It was not until 31 July that the king set out from Berlin to assume nominal command of his armies in the field, taking his chancellor with him. Four years earlier Bismarck had tagged along with the military high command as a Landwehr major, a politician who still had everything to prove, dressed up as a soldier. He was a major-general, already assuming the image of the iron conqueror, a gigantic figure in Prussian blue, complete with spiked helmet and heavy cavalry jack-boots reaching high up the thigh. But to the soldiers he was still a civilian in uniform.

His mood was complex. He had manoeuvred his own king and the emperor of the French into mortal combat. If the battle went against him, then everything was lost. But he did not really think the French could win. He had put himself into the hands of Moltke and Roon, but he trusted them as he trusted no other men in the world. He was far more concerned at this stage with the welfare of his own two sons, both officers in the dragoons, Herbert and Bill, who might well be killed in the war their father had made. . . . And with the future. Victory over France would clear the way for the unification of Germany, but there were still many obstacles to be overcome, not least his own king's reluctance to see Prussia, even an inviolate and dominant Prussia, merged with the rest of Germany. He had plenty to worry about during that first week, while the preliminary skirmishing took place and GHQ remained on German soil, at Mainz. But on 7 August they began at last to move forward, and then, the fate of Germany, his own future too, was for some time to come a matter for the soldiers. For once he had nothing to do.

The triumph, when it came at Sedan just three weeks later (Moltke's campaign against Austria and the rest of Germany had taken less than two weeks to reach its climax), was so overwhelming and apparently absolute that the victors forgot the tensions and alarms of the first days of the campaign, the shocking casualties suffered by the German armies, the sacrificial resistance of so many Frenchmen, the almost criminal blunders on the German as well as the French sides.

There were some bad moments for Bismarck and Moltke before the pattern began to clear. The maulings the Germans received at Wörth, near Weissenburg, on 5 August and Spicheren, just outside Saarbrücken, on 6 August were heavy blows to their pride and their confidence. But the fact remains that on each of these occasions they pushed forward in the end. At Wörth (the French named the battle Reichshafen after another village) the German Third Army under the crown prince lost 10,500 killed and wounded, the French under MacMahon 11,000, plus 200 officers and 9000 men made prisoner. At Spicheren the Germans lost 4500 and the French 2000 plus 2000 prisoners. Steinmetz distinguished himself by refusing to obey orders and sending his First Army southwards across the line of march of Prince Frederick Charles' Second Army.

There were worrying failures on the German side. For example, the Prussian infantry wavered badly under the impact of the French *chassepots* and the frightening *mitrailleuses* with their twenty-five revolving barrels, while the Prussian cavalry (like the French) at first beat itself to pieces against the new menace of rapid rifle-fire.

But what soon began to emerge was the superiority of the Prussian gunners and their armament. They were equipped with the percussion shells which, exploding on impact, had done so much damage as they burst among trees at Königgrätz, while the French were still using time-fuses, which meant that many of their shells buried themselves in the mud, exploding harmlessly. Nor was it simply a matter of weapons. The Prussian commanders showed themselves alert and adaptable; for example, they quickly learnt to let the gunners sweep a path for the infantry before advancing—the first artillery barrages. There was also the matter of morale. The French were to show that they would recklessly sacrifice their lives in battle. But they had no stomach for the war as such, were rightly critical of their senior commanders, and were all too liable to degenerate into a disorderly mob of looters and scroungers when not actually engaged in fighting for their lives.

Their commanders were far from negligible, but there was no one outstanding figure among them to set against Moltke. Napoleon was ill, in great pain, infirm of will and purpose, almost with the death-wish on him; but his position as commander-in-chief inhibited all decisive action on the part of his generals, and even when he handed over the supreme command to Marshal Achille Bazaine on 12 August, this brave but inadequate popular hero seemed unable to believe that he was really in command. Laboeuf at headquarters was the scapegoat for all the failures of his imperial master in the equipment and deployment of the army; MacMahon and Canrobert, both idolized and gallant veterans of the Crimea, were neither of them capable of handling great bodies of men, and knew it (Canrobert refused promotion beyond corps commander, while MacMahon allowed himself to be sentenced to disaster at Sedan by loyally obeying orders which he knew to be misguided).

Moltke's generals were not outstandingly brilliant. Steinmetz was the only one capable of losing the whole war in a single afternoon, and did his level best to do so at Gravelotte on 18 August. Frederick Charles was notoriously headstrong and impatient and, at St. Privat-la-Montagne, was to send IX Corps to its destruction through his recklessness: 8000 officers and men of the Prussian Guard, more than a quarter of the entire strength, were killed in barely twenty minutes as he sent them unsupported, exposed, and uphill into the French field of fire. But in spite of these failings, the superiority of the Germans (Germans from the south as well as from north of the Main and Prussia itself) was absolute. With better generalship the French might have avoided the débâcle of Sedan, but they would have been defeated all the same.

Moltke was in absolute command, his main problems the disobedience of a Steinmetz, the impatience of a Prince Frederick Charles, and the jealous circumspection of the crown prince's gifted chief-of-staff, General Leonhard von Blumenthal. There was nobody, however, to prevent him taking swift action to remedy blunders in the field, which he managed to dominate through the inspired creation and employment of senior staff officers, trained, as it were, to the minute by him—his demigods, as they came to be called: above all, three colonels—Paul Bronsart von Schellendorf, Karl von Brandenstein, and Julius von Verdy du Vernois—two of them to rise to be successive ministers for war. Among themselves these men dominated the commands, coordinating movement, lines of march, junctions, attacks, counter-attacks, reinforcements, rations, and munitions, deeply resented by many old-stagers, but invested with all the authority of the crown devolved through Moltke, and by their energy and efficiency making it impossible to ignore them.

This was the innovation above all others which made up for Moltke's chief defect. He was immensely gifted, but not infallible. His greatness lay in his coolness, his inspired common-sense, his brilliant swiftness of response to changing circumstances, to the upset of plans, themselves too rigid. He planned as though he had absolute control over everything that happened on the field of battle, but he knew that he had not. Even before he was made chief of general staff he had seen in the Danish War of 1864 what unimaginative generals could do to wreck an intelligent plan. In the Austrian War his master-plan had succeeded, but it had been threatened for a moment by Bismarck's intervention on the Hanoverian front and nearly ruined by the cautious slow motion of the crown prince and Blumenthal on the left wing. He had also seen that the comparatively new institution of chief of general staff cut little ice with many of the veteran commanders, who would not recognize their subordination to Moltke as the right hand of the nominal commander-in-chief, the king.[2] By 1870 that position had been clarified, but still too much depended on automatic obedience, on the exact dove-tailing of many obediences; and still Moltke was to indulge his two serious failings, which he passed on to subsequent generations of German commanders: the failure to recognize that it is asking for almost certain trouble to plan a grand encirclement depending on split-second timing and absolute obedience—when you know that not all your formation commanders are capable of obedience; and the failure to clarify beyond all doubt the chain of command. The existence of the demi-gods indubitably helped to confuse the chain of command, but they made up for this with the swiftness of their improvisations. Their presence, their flying visits to one HQ or another also injected very necessary flexibility into Moltke's sometimes too rigid planning.

At the other end of the scale, the part played by the junior officers—from the South as well as from Prussia—was something unimagined by the French. The senior German commanders on the whole neglected the bold and intelligent use of cavalry in reconnaissance, as did the French commanders too, as had the French, British, and Russian commanders in the Crimea, as had the French and Austrian commanders in Lombardy. (How odd that in the heyday of light cavalry, when the horse had the world at his feet, all the European armies without exception failed in re-connaissance, so that it was the commonest thing for large formations to bump into one another unexpectedly in the morning mist, as at Solferino in 1859, or to slip past each other in the night without making contact, as after Alma in 1854.[3]) But if the senior officers were negligent, many of their juniors on the German side showed a dash, a boldness, an *élan* of the kind more usually associated with Frenchmen than with Germans. Small unofficial patrols of lancers, the celebrated Uhlans, penetrated swiftly and deeply into enemy territory, upsetting lines of communication, putting the fear of swift encirclement into any troops they encountered, creating panic among the villagers.

After Spicheren and Wörth the German advance was slow and clumsy, the roads and railways overloaded, movement impeded by the preposter-ous entourage of princes and distinguished sightseers of every kind with their suites more in keeping with the age of Louis XIV than with the age of steel and railways. But it continued unrelentingly. Napoleon, under great stress, laid down the supreme command on 12 August, but his suc-cessor, Marshal Bazaine, was not up to the job. Risen from the ranks, he was brave and steady in the field as well as an accomplished tactician, but he lacked initiative and flexibility, and, at fifty-nine, was prematurely aged. Now he had the sense to take all the main army back under the guns of Metz in preparation for a critical retirement, via Verdun, to the River Marne. Before he was ready, however, German troops were blocking the Verdun road at Mars-la-Tour; the main French supply line was cut; Bis-marck was able to tell Johanna that the soldiers believed the French had shot their bolt and that the German armies would very soon stand before Paris.[4]

There were still serious worries to come, and heavy losses to endure. On the very next day at Vionville nearly 16,000 officers and men were killed or wounded on the German side, nearly 14,000 on the French. And when evening came Bismarck himself was given the shattering news that Herbert was dead: he had been seen to fall from his horse at the height of the cav-alry action at Mars-la-Tour. Bismarck, in his last letter to Johanna, had joked about his own reputation as the terror of the French ('The people here must take me for a bloodhound, the old women when they hear my name fall to their knees and plead with me to spare their lives. Attila was a lamb compared with me!'[5]); now he was beside himself with grief and rode off at once into the night from his billet at Pont-à-Mousson on the Moselle river, south-west of Metz—a ride of more than twenty miles over difficult country, until at last he found Herbert, safe if not quite sound: a bullet had gone clean through his thigh, missing the bone. To complete his relief, the younger son, Bill, also turned up: his horse had been shot under him; he had been given up for dead; but in fact he was only slightly concussed.

Bismarck, who had sent the two off to the wars with half a million others, wrote to Johanna next day with a full description: Bill had a marvellously hard head, and Herbert would be out of action for the rest of the war. 'Since God has so mercifully preserved our two I must not be bitter'; but he went on to criticize the poor leadership of the First and Second Armies—its 'squandering of the best soldiers in Europe,' its 'stupid misuse of the deathless bravery of our people. . . . We fight only with our fists, not with our heads, and yet we conquer. . . .'[6]

The next day was far worse. It saw the first pitched battle of the campaign, and for the Germans a very dangerous one, fought out between Gravelotte and St.-Privat-la-Montagne, still on the road from Metz to Verdun. To begin with, Bazaine behaved like a skilled commander. His deployment was brilliant and highly advantageous, even though the Germans could bring 188,000 men and 732 guns against the French 113,000 and 520 guns. It was now that Steinmetz at Gravelotte completely misjudged the French dispositions, and sent his First Army troops to be massacred in a ravine—infantry, artillery, cavalry, all hopelessly jumbled together; and it was at St.-Privat that Prince Frederick Charles did the same sort of thing, approving Prince August of Württemberg's decision to send IX Corps, unsupported, into the heart of the main French position.

A strong French counter-attack would have changed the day. The troops were there; but the directing brain was not. Bazaine had relapsed into passivity. The idea of a counter-attack did not cross his mind. He admitted as much when, a broken man, he was turned into the scapegoat for the French defeat, tried, and sentenced to death (a sentence commuted to twenty years' imprisonment: he escaped). He had given his corps commanders their orders, he said in his defence after the war; he had established them in commanding positions; it was up to them to look after themselves. Furthermore, he had been tired and in pain. So that in the end Gravelotte was a German victory, and a decisive one, at the cost of more than 20,000 killed and wounded to the French 12,000.

Moltke was an extraordinary man. Everyone in the German camp, from King William down, was shocked by the carnage that day. Poor William was almost on the verge of mutinying against himself when he learned of the loss of 8000 officers and men of his own guard in those fearful twenty

Otto von Bismarck in 1874

King William I of Prussia,
c. 1866

William I proclaimed Emperor
at Versailles, 19 January 1871.
Painting by Anton von Werner

Frederick III as Crown Prince, in 1875

The future William II as Crown Prince, with the Crown Princess Victoria
and their son, who was never to rule, in 1887

Alexander II,
Tsar of Russia, c. 1878

Alexander III,
Tsar of Russia, c. 1890

Family group. Left to right: Oskar von Arnim; Malwine von Arnim
(Bismarck's sister); Sybille (her daughter, Bismarck's niece); Johanna; Bismarck;
Bill (Bismarck's younger son)

The visit of Emperor William II at Friedrichsruh, 30 October 1888

Bismarck at his desk at Friedrichsruh

Bismarck in 1890. Portrait by Franz von Lenbach

minutes.[7] But Moltke never seems to have asked himself whether he himself must not share some of the blame. After all, Steinmetz and the others were his officers. But he rode across that terrible battlefield without seeming to turn a hair, leaving others to clear up the mess. He had something of the supreme detachment of the great naval commanders, with the difference that generals, unlike admirals, do not have to stand in the thick of the fight with their officers and men.

After the French disaster at Gravelotte Bazaine had to move very fast indeed or else find himself and his main army surrounded and effectively locked up in Metz. But he could not move in time. The last act of the main drama was beginning. As the Germans advanced upon Ste. Menehould and Vitry-le-François, leaving Metz far in their rear, they still had the great fortresses of Verdun and Toul in their way. But that way was never to be taken. The French now were in almost total disarray. Bazaine, after pretending that he had fallen back on Metz simply in order to collect his strength, had to admit that he could not get out. The commander-in-chief was out of play. Meanwhile Napoleon himself had gone off to Châlons-sur-Marne, where a new army was being laboriously assembled under MacMahon, that splendid veteran of Sevastopol and Magenta. Worn out, alternating between apathy and despair, in pain of such intensity now that it was almost lethal, the emperor had to agree that the only hope was to bring that army back under the guns of Paris. But he was defeated in this sensible decision by the furious resolution of Eugénie, who insisted that to fall back on Paris would be the end, the equivalent of abdication. The new army must go forward to the relief of Metz and the rescue of Bazaine. MacMahon knew that he was incapable of fighting through to Metz, and said so—until Bazaine himself came through with his fatal message saying that he could fight his way out if MacMahon would come to meet him.

And so the last act opened. Nothing more was heard from Bazaine, and MacMahon advanced, open-eyed, into disaster. When Moltke heard what was happening he could not believe his ears. It meant that with Bazaine cooped up in Metz and MacMahon moving away from Paris and into an exposed no-man's-land even closer to the frontier, he himself had only to swing north and get behind MacMahon's army. And so it was. MacMahon was totally surprised at Beaumont, and the army of Châlons was pushed ever farther north until it found itself being virtually herded into the frontier fortress of Sedan—with nowhere else to go except into neutral Belgium. On 30 August Bismarck took a hand, formally warning the Belgian government that unless all French troops crossing the frontier were immediately disarmed, the Prussians would pursue them into Belgium. 'Now we have them in a mouse-trap!' Moltke exclaimed next day.[8] The same thought in reverse was expressed by one of the true heroes of Sedan, General A. A. Ducrot, commanding the French I Corps: 'Nous sommes dans un pot de chambre, et nous y serons emmerdés.'[9]

Next day MacMahon himself was severely wounded and had to be evacuated. He had nominated Ducrot as his deputy, and Ducrot still believed it would be possible to pull out of Sedan, march west, and save the army to fight again. He was overruled when General Felix de Wimpffen, breathing fire and fury, arrived with authority from Paris to assume command. There was to be no retreat; in any case, the Prussians were nearer to blocking all possible exits than Ducrot realized. So Sedan was fought.

Poor MacMahon had never intended to stay in Sedan, which he had regarded as a staging post on the circular journey back towards Paris via Mézières. But when he saw that he had no choice but to stand and fight (so swiftly had the crown prince moved) the circle of hills above the Meuse seemed an ideal position—as ideal, indeed, as the position at Gravelotte chosen only a few days earlier by Bazaine. He still had no idea of the German strength, or that the crown prince was completing his superb forced march and had already with his cavalry reached the escape road at Donchéry—which meant that Moltke had achieved the extraordinary feat of wheeling an army of 150,000 men through an angle of 90 degrees and moving it nearly fifty miles in three days, with all its guns (but the troops had marched light, with three days' rations in knapsacks), through the steep, narrow, muddy lanes of the Argonne forest.

Now, on 1 September, they were all out in the morning mist, which was soon to melt into a radiant late-summer day. Moltke had chosen a hill-top commanding a spectacular view over the valley of the Meuse and into the very heart of Sedan, only two miles away. King William rode up there with his immense entourage and half the princes of Germany, together with war-correspondents and attachés from America, from Russia, from Britain—a fantastic array, and to add to the fantasy, a little apart from the dazzle of brilliant uniforms, there clustered the effective government of Prussia and the North German Confederation, a group of soberly clad civilian officials standing respectfully by an immense figure in major-general's uniform, Bismarck himself, with a skeleton chancellery staff. It was the last time in history that a soldier-king, a monarch, was to stand on a hill-top and look down on the battlefield; it was the first time as well as

the last that a civilian prime minister sat watching the progress of the battle he had brought about, while dictating telegrams dealing with its aftermath.

The day opened with an artillery bombardment, rather sooner than
Moltke had intended. And this was how it was to go on. There was, of
course, furious and bloody hand-to-hand fighting; heroic and forlorn last
hopes in the way of cavalry charges; infantry hurling themselves against a
ring of steel in vain attempts to break out. But in the end it was the shooting of the German gunners which counted most—consistently accurate,
fast, and deadly. It was by no means a cheap victory. The French lost
17,000 killed and wounded—and 104,000 taken prisoner. The Germans
lost over 9000. The chief of all the prisoners was Napoleon himself.
Deadly pale, in a torment of body, mind, and spirit, he had ridden about
the battlefield all day seeking the fiercest fighting, seeking death which
never came. When Wimpffen at last saw what he must do and caused the
white flag to be raised, Colonel Bronsart von Schellendorf was dispatched
by Moltke to find out what was happening. He returned with a member of
the emperor's suite bearing a letter from Napoleon himself:

'Monsieur mon frère,
N'ayant pas pu mourir au milieu de mes troupes, il ne me reste qu'à
remettre mon épée entre les mains de Votre Majesté. Je suis de Votre
Majesté le bon frère.

Napoléon.'

At last it was Bismarck's turn to move into action. Not for him the
dazed pause of almost unbelieving wonder at this miracle: the toppling by
German arms alone of the mightiest European power, France, the traditional great predator, paying the price for debasing the concept of glory by
confusing it for too long with military might (a consummation to be
echoed by Germany herself, and for the same reasons). The capitulation,
of course, had to be received by a soldier, and King William deputed
Moltke to represent him. But once the surrender was accomplished, then
the statesman must come to the front. Or so Bismarck supposed. It was
not to be as easy as that, however, and that same day was to show the first
signs of a profound conflict that was to overshadow the birth of the new
German Reich—and, in the end, to play a great part in its destruction: the
conflict between the soldiers and the civilians.

* * *

The first sign was very small indeed. When Moltke and Bismarck sat down to discuss the terms of surrender with Wimpffen and Castelnau in Donchéry they were to all appearances in perfect accord. It fell to Moltke to tell Wimpffen bluntly, and convince him by showing him the German positions on the map, that his cause was hopeless and he must accept the terms (ignominious surrender, no 'honourable capitulation' with weapons and bands intact) or be destroyed. It was then Bismarck's turn to outline his philosophy of victory. Wimpffen had put up an eloquent, spirited, and impressive argument for a generous peace. Harsh terms, he declared, would throw back the slow civilization of Europe and awaken all the dormant instincts of revenge. There would be wars without end. To this Bismarck retorted that the French should have thought of that before they started this war. It had been one thing for Prussia to make a moderate peace with Austria, a stable and gentlemanly state. But France had been a violent disturber of the peace of Europe as a whole for eighty years and for Germany for two centuries [sic]. If the French Empire had been solidly and properly established, if Napoleon had been respected as King William was respected, had he been master of his own house, if the succession were assured, then it might have been possible to talk of a generous peace and to count on the gratitude of the conquered. But, he went on, statesmen 'should not, in general, rely on gratitude, and especially not of a people.' French governments were in a state of constant flux. 'One can rely on nothing in your country.' France had declared war on Germany far too often. It must not be allowed to happen again. Germany must take whatever territory and forces were necessary to make further attack impossible.[10]

So far so good. It might have been Moltke himself speaking. But there was a sudden flurry in the dialogue which indicated to Moltke that Bismarck was already thinking in terms of a peace which, while securing Germany's frontiers, would allow the French to escape the total annihilation which he, as a soldier, was determined to inflict.

It was a question about the position of the emperor. When Napoleon had offered his sword in surrender, Bismarck asked: Was it his own sword or was it the sword of France? If the latter, it meant the surrender not merely of the French army but of the French state. And this could change things. Castelnau quickly replied that the emperor's surrender was purely personal, and a moment of conflict was passed. Moltke carried on as before, but he had taken note and was not to forget. The chancellor, the 'civilian in the cuirassier's jacket' as Bronsart von Schellendorf called him, was to be prevented at all costs from making any sort of a peace with the French until the army had finished with them.[11]

The conflict was soon open, Bismarck and Moltke angrily appealing against each other to the king, with Bismarck forced to use all his authority and power to prevent himself being edged out of the conduct of the war and the negotiations for peace. For Moltke, from the moment he saw at that critical midnight meeting in Donchéry that Bismarck was looking for a chance to end the war as quickly as was consonant with the imposition of crushing terms, started preaching the doctrine that while the politicians were responsible for foreign policy until the moment that war was declared, from that moment on the conduct of the affair must be left entirely to the soldiers, who must also be the ones to decide on such details as an armistice and the terms of peace. . . .

It does not seem to have occurred to Bismarck that he himself was largely to blame for the ascendancy of the military; it certainly did not occur to Moltke and his demigods (who did all they could to undermine and intrigue against their king's first minister) that they should be grateful to the man who had enabled the king to defend his army against parliamentary interference and establish it as the great power in the land, not by a *coup de main* of the kind dreamed of by Manteuffel, which would have left a bitterly divided Prussia, but by sheer force of character and suppleness of manoeuvre.

This was for the future. But for the time being all seemed well. At dawn on 2 September, Bismarck and Moltke were awakened in their Donchéry lodging with the news that Napoleon himself had slipped out of Sedan and was waiting in his carriage in a potato field close by. Bismarck dressed in a great hurry and went out to meet him and offered to bring him back to Donchéry, but Napoleon, now fearful for his life at the hands of his own people, was determined to avoid recognition by his subjects: they could discuss what to do next in a peasant's hut requisitioned for that purpose. The emperor wished to be conducted to the king so that he himself might sue for better terms than those laid down by Bismarck and Moltke to Wimpffen and Castelnau the night before. But Bismarck had no intention of allowing Napoleon to meet William until he had Wimpffen's formal surrender in his pocket (in this, the crown prince was at one with him), and while Moltke went off to report to the king the two sat on hard chairs talking about any subject other than politics while the minutes ticked by and turned into hours. At last all was settled. Napoleon was installed in a small château near Frenois. King William drove over to meet him there.

The crown prince was also in attendance, and was startled by the contrast between the ignominy of the emperor of the French and the brilliance and elaboration of his turn-out. 'All the imperial baggage wagons and carriages stood drawn up ready for the road; the French household appeared in their well-known rich liveries,' even the postilions were in gala dress, and powdered, 'as though for a trip to the races at Longjumeau.'[12]

After polite exchanges only one point of substance emerged: Napoleon insisted that as prisoner he could neither negotiate nor influence his government in any way. And where exactly was the government of France at that moment? At Paris, the emperor replied; and that was that. It was up to the empress and her advisers to continue the war if they cared to: he, Napoleon, no longer counted. And so he departed, accompanied by a special guard of honour, to internment among the splendours of the royal castle of Wilhelmshohe near Cassel. As the emperor waited for his carriage to start and carry him from the European stage for ever, he wept, affected not only by the emotions of the day, to which was added fear for his own life at the hands of his disaffected subjects, but also by the consideration and politeness of the king of Prussia.

He rode off, a flurry of wheels, a flashing of spokes and a clatter of hooves, a dazzle of imperial postilions and footmen, across Belgium to Wilhelmshohe, and thence to join Eugénie again at Chislehurst in Kent, and, three years after Sedan, to his grave at Farnborough.

The troubles of the Germans were only just beginning. With the whole of MacMahon's army, what was left of it, delivered into captivity, with the French main army under the supreme commander shut up in Metz (although another seven weeks were to pass before Bazaine, after a bloody attempt at a sortie, at last surrendered), the way to Paris was wide open, and Moltke set out upon it with every intention of occupying the capital and enforcing total surrender. The prospects were good. On 4 September, three days after Sedan, Eugénie, fearful of the Paris mob, had followed the example of a predecessor by fleeing the Tuileries. Next day saw the proclamation of the new republic. The gallant and puritanical General Louis Trochu, hero of the Crimean War, his bitter criticisms of the state of the French army on the eve of 1870 vindicated by the calamities of past weeks, was already in command of Paris and soon became president of the new Government of National Defence.

So Moltke set out via Rheims and Château-Thierry: the Army of the Meuse to follow the right bank of the Marne and the Seine, the crown prince's Third Army to follow the left bank. On 19 September the two armies joined hands at St.-Germain-en-Laye, a little to the north of Versailles. Paris was surrounded and must capitulate or starve to death. Moltke thought it might take six weeks.

Bismarck was not happy. His instinct had told him that it was a mistake to march on Paris. As early as 7 September he had written to Herbert, 'I myself would like to leave these people to stew in their own juice, while we settle ourselves comfortably in the conquered provinces before advancing farther. If we advance too soon we shall prevent them from falling out among themselves.'[13] This is a perfect example of the prescience that set him so far above his contemporaries. But in fact he did not press the matter. At Nikolsburg, after Königgrätz, he had fought to the point of resignation to stem the advance on Vienna. But in France, with everything in flux, with everything to gain from allowing the French to thrash about among themselves, could the Republican government possibly last? Napoleon had not yet abdicated; Eugénie was at large in London; nobody knew what forces might not arise in the vast hinterland of France under ruthless foreign pressure. Better to wait surely for all forces to fall apart, if only to decide whom to start negotiating with?

But, of course, Moltke did not want to negotiate. He was in a conqueror's mood, and so was the king. For Bismarck to quarrel with king and soldiers now could mean the ruin of his plans and of his own future. And in any case, he himself was not quite immune from the Francophobe fever: the French needed to be taught a lesson and made innocuous, either by the final acceptance of their own inferiority or by iron bars. It is very doubtful if Bismarck could have achieved anything at all but his own alienation from the king had he pressed his argument.

And so the conquering armies lumbered on, and the defeated began to pull themselves together. On 18 September, as the ring round Paris was closed, Jules Favre presented himself to Bismarck in quest of an honourable peace. The new republic had already lasted longer than Bismarck had expected, and he was ready to deal with it now. He wanted to finish off the war as quickly as possible, driven by the fear that the longer it went on the more likely was intervention from outside, above all from England. But the terms had to be his own: he did not intend to destroy France, as Moltke wanted to destroy her, but the gate must be firmly barred against her, and that barrier must be erected on French soil. Immediately after Sedan he had told his familiar, Moritz Busch, that all he required from France were the key points of Metz and Strasbourg: the possession of Alsace, he said, was 'an idea of the professors.'[14] But in fact his own newspapers urged on by him had been lashing the German people into a state of high hysteria about Alsace and Lorraine. It is impossible to know what Bismarck really thought about the demands he put to the French; we only know that he put them and pressed them—even though in the next breath he would be confiding that Metz was 'expendable.' Bismarck would be the last person to suggest that a man should be judged by his words rather than his actions. And his actions first drove Favre to continue the war, then ensured that for years to come the French would burn for revenge.

Favre's main request was not in the circumstances as preposterous as it seemed to Bismarck, who expected Paris to fall within a matter of days. The devoted French radical seemed to expect Bismarck to share his own bitter hatred of Napoleon and irritated him by asking too much and at the same time appealing to sentiment. He requested an armistice so that France could elect a new assembly and settle down to work out the terms of peace. Certainly France could have an armistice, Bismarck retorted through a cloud of cigar smoke, she was welcome to hold as many elections as she liked; but if she wanted an armistice she must first surrender into his hands the whole of Alsace, including Strasbourg and part of Lorraine, including Metz; further, if the blockade of Paris was to be lifted to allow supplies to be sent in from outside, then one of the protective forts must be surrendered. 'You want to destroy France!' exclaimed poor Favre, and wept; he returned to Paris in despair.[15] Bismarck would have been appalled had he known that Paris would hold out for more than four bitter months. He was still thinking in terms of diplomatic finessing—not at all sure, for instance, what government would in the end be strong enough to sign the peace; very much, as he said in a letter to Herbert two days later, concerned to treat Napoleon generously and keep him on ice, less because he might one day be restored, which seemed unlikely, than to keep the French guessing. 'The French must be kept wondering whether they may not get him back again,' to encourage them 'to quarrel among themselves.'[16]

In fact the Ferrières meeting was the start of a new and terrible phase in the war, perhaps in the history of Europe. Favre had innocently expected Bismarck to accept the fiction that the villain had been Napoleon, not the people of France. He was thrown off-balance when Bismarck failed to take his cue and instead responded with the sort of arguments he had used at Donchéry in the midnight conversation with Wimpffen and Castelnau after Sedan. He said now as he had said then: the French were and always had been natural aggressors; they must be stopped. And it was in that moment of rejection that the war was transformed from a war of professional armies into a national war of survival and revenge. The marvellous victory was tarnished, its splendour never to be recovered.

Already at Sedan there had been bloody incidents with civilians joining in the fighting. Now, while Gambetta and Trochu organized the great new people's armies, so-called *francs-tireurs* (resistance fighters, as they would be called today) sprang up on all sides, attacking and destroying the extended German lines of communication and bringing down fearful reprisals on the civilian population. The mood on both sides grew increasingly ugly: the French were no longer fighting for a dubious régime, or even for glory: they were fighting for their lives against a hated invader, and they fought with everything in their power and in accordance with no accepted rules of warfare. Bismarck, although he never put his thoughts down on paper, was himself now in the mood to brutalize and hurt. He did not hate the French as Moltke hated them: he was angered by their spoiling of his careful pattern; for getting in his way; for prolonging the war unnecessarily and vainly and all the time increasing the chance of outside intervention. He reacted as he was to react increasingly to opposition of any kind once he was back home in Berlin: he threatened. All villages harbouring *francs-tireurs* should be burned to the ground; all individuals, man, woman, child, thought to have fired on German troops or even plotted sabotage should be shot out of hand; the entire population in particularly defiant areas should be carted off *en masse* to prison camps in Germany.[17] This last expedient was never adopted, but there was a great deal of shooting and burning. And Bismarck, with his talk, his letters, his newspapers, did much to inflame and sustain the passion of hatred and contempt for all things French that swept through Germany. He himself did not really believe that Paris was Babylon. He could have effectively discouraged that belief in others. But it suited him to flatter it. He did not even reproach his own wife for her quite immoderate language. According to Holstein, she considered it 'disgusting' that wounded French soldiers should be nursed and cared for in German military hospitals: 'They ought to be left to die!' She also proclaimed that Paris, 'that mad Sodom,' should have been burned to the ground by incendiary bombs and reduced to rubble by high explosives.[18] If these words could be uttered by the great chancellor's nearest and dearest we need not be surprised when we find her aspirations echoed in the diary kept by Cosima Wagner, who recorded not only her own impressions but her husband's every spoken word: 'The *Illustrierte Zeitung*' she writes on 5 September (this was when everyone thought the

French were quite beaten) 'prints pictures of French soldiers (taken from the life), and from all these the wretchedness and the degeneracy of the people stare out at me—indeed, all the misery of mankind. In these sensual, bestial, besotted faces one sees complete idiocy.' A little later we find the great and unsensual composer echoing the hopes of the chancellor's wife as already quoted: 'Richard says he hopes Paris ("this kept woman of the world") will be burned to the ground; in his youth he did not understand Blücher, who had hoped for this, but now he understood him—the burning of Paris would be a symbol of the liberation of the world from the oppression of all that is bad.'[19]

Meanwhile Bismarck, who had no intention of burning Paris to the ground, became desperate—and so did the king. A few days after the Ferrières meeting Léon Gambetta, minister of the interior in the new Republican government, made his spectacular escape from the city in a balloon to join the government at Tours and become minister of war as well as minister of the interior. He showed himself to be a born war leader, and soon, even while the main imperial army under Bazaine was still holding out in Metz (there was a movement to raise the siege, so that Bazaine could march out and attack the Republican army), the great new peoples' armies of the North and of the Loire were being formed, with Garibaldi already operating enthusiastically in the Vosges. It was an extraordinary situation, and, once it was clear that the French had no intention of giving up, for the Germans sprawling across half France it was a very dangerous one, with their GHQ deep in enemy territory, their communications stretched. Desperate situations called for desperate measures. Towards the end of September Bismarck was thinking in terms of an imperial restoration to put an end to the revolutionary republicanism of the new régime. On 5 October the royal headquarters moved from the Rothschild mansion at Ferrières, near Montargis, to the royal palace of Versailles, where it was to remain until the end of January, instead of the week or two predicted. 'If only the king with all the princes and his staff would go away we could make short work of the business and soon bring peace within measurable distance.'[20] This *cri de coeur* from the crown prince's chief-of-staff was echoed by practically the whole army.

What on earth were the Prussian court, together with the entire government of Prussia and the North German Confederation, to say nothing of twenty princes and their followers, doing in the middle of the battle (for this was what the siege of Paris was), with vast armies being formed on every side, with Metz still invested, with most of the great fortresses—

Toul, Verdun—in French hands? Why did they not go home? Why did not even the war minister, Roon, go home to raise new armies, as the French were raising new armies? William was commander-in-chief, but at seventy-four a very nominal commander-in-chief. Bismarck might have gone home to run the government and organize foreign relations and peace negotiations from Berlin; but he dared not leave the field to Moltke; and his great quarrel with the military was now brewing.

The behaviour in the autumn of 1870 not only of Moltke but of practically the whole of the Prussian higher command—with the exception of the crown prince and Roon—was a promise of many tears in years to come. Bismarck resisted hard and furiously; in the end, as far as his own personal position was concerned, apparently successfully. But, in his extreme self-absorption, he was content to treat as a purely personal power-struggle what should have been a fight for principle: thus when, immediately after Sedan, he discovered that the soldiers were deliberately excluding him from their councils, even when matters affecting the future shape of France were under discussion, he did not present the matter as an attempt by the military to usurp the functions of the civil government but, rather, as an affront to him personally.

A major cause of friction between Bismarck and the soldiers rose from the tentative plan to raise the siege of Metz so that Bazaine could bring his imperial army into the field against the Republicans while there was still time. To this end Bismarck urged William to issue a safe-conduct for the recklessly brave Pyrenean, General Charles Bourbaki; he was to travel to London to consult Eugénie and, his mission accomplished, return to Metz. The plan came to nothing because the empress would not agree to Bismarck's terms, and very soon, on 27 October, Bazaine surrendered with his army intact. But he surrendered minus General Bourbaki, because Prince Frederick Charles, in command of the investing army, was at one with Moltke in determining to block Bismarck at every turn. He refused to allow the emissary back into the fortress, so that after a few days Bourbaki decided to offer his services to the Republican army being formed at Orléans. Frederick Charles's obstructionism achieved two things: it made nonsense of the word of honour of his uncle the king—and it released a particularly spirited general to become a dangerous threat to the German forces in Alsace.

Even when faced with this deliberate challenge to his authority as the chief servant of the king, Bismarck made no attempt to make it an issue of principle. Instead he wrote to the prince's chief-of-staff something very like a hard-luck letter: 'I appeal to Your Excellency's clear judgement and your own perception so that you will understand how discouraging it must be for me when, through this kind of failure to execute explicit royal orders, the danger arises that in the whole constellation of political calculations one single cog, which is necessary in its place, will refuse to work. *How can I have the courage to carry on with my work* if I cannot count on royal orders . . . being faithfully executed?. . .'[21] (my italics)

It was not until the middle of January that under extreme provocation from Moltke he demanded from William, and with surprising ease obtained, a categorical statement that he, the prime minister, was to be responsible for all dealings with the French authorities in the matter of the armistice and the ultimate peace-making; further, that he must be kept fully informed about the course of all future military operations and given the opportunity to express his views.

But this unequivocal statement came too late, and still not as a matter of principle. Moltke was shocked by it almost to the point of resigning; but he was able to convince himself that the king's declaration was really the aberration of an old, old man who had been duped by the infinitely cunning Bismarck; and in later years he laid it down formally, *as a principle*, that in time of war the soldier must be supreme. Had Bismarck concerned himself with principle as Moltke did this view might have been banished once for all, instead of surviving to bring Germany to ruin. But he preferred to make a personal issue of it. So that when, for example, he remonstrated with Moltke for communicating directly with General Trochu about the fall of Orléans, his intervention could be made to look like nothing more than pique on his part—stimulating Bronsart's observation, quoted earlier, to the effect that he was qualifying for the lunatic asylum.

Matters were exacerbated by the hot-house atmosphere in which court, government, and hangers-on were crowded together in Versailles. As it became apparent that the war was not to be ended at will tempers grew short, recriminations flew on every side, and exasperation with the French for continuing a struggle they were bound to lose turned in upon itself. In his table-talk, Bismarck was extremely free with his criticisms of the soldiers, and this got back to them, as his criticism of the Austrians twenty years earlier had got back to Vienna. As time went by, all differences began to crystallize round the furiously debated matter of the bombardment of Paris. The soldiers believed with absolute conviction that the decision whether to shell the city or not was exclusively one for themselves, to be determined on purely technical military grounds. Moltke, and almost all the higher command, including the crown prince, stood firmly against bombardment, insisting that it was an untidy, messy, expensive business which would only put up the backs of the inhabitants (they had discovered this already from the very damaging bombardment of Strasbourg): the proper, infallible procedure was to starve the Parisians into surrender, and the French being what they were, degenerate, soft, and greedy, would not hold out long! Bismarck, on the other hand (and he was supported by the very able crown prince of Saxony), wanted to bring about the surrender in the shortest possible time, and was convinced that a sharp bombardment would soon bring the French to their knees.

He was not at his best in this matter. Instead of arguing his case patiently and logically, he stimulated a press-campaign demanding the total annihilation, the razing to the ground, of Babylon. He convinced himself that there was a conspiracy against him. The whole affair, he wrote bitterly to Johanna, 'is enmeshed in an intrigue spun by women, archbishops, and professors.'[22] He convinced himself that Queen Augusta, the crown princess, and 'other English influences' were all involved, and his anger became black: he would, it sometimes seemed, tell anyone who cared to listen just what he thought of the crown prince and his women. Frederick, he informed his guests one evening, was completely under the thumb of his English wife: 'The assertion of the generals that they have not enough ammunition is untrue. They do not want to start [the bombardment] because the heir apparent does not wish it. He does not wish it because his wife and mother-in-law are against it.' And next evening, in different company: 'The principal reason why the bombardment is delayed is the sentimentality of the queen of England, and the interference of Augusta. . . . That seems to be characteristic of the Hohenzollerns—their women-folk always have a great influence upon them.'[23]

Not content with indiscretions of this kind, Bismarck was by now engaged in active warfare. Moritz Busch was instructed to make propaganda against the royal ladies, against certain churchmen, against the freemasons, and to stir up the popular demand for bombardment. He carried out this commission with quite startling nastiness. That Bismarck survived this disreputable episode was a direct contradiction of his own assertion. Augusta and Vicky, he insisted, could twist the king and crown prince round their fingers; in fact they were powerless in face of Bismarck. He could impugn the honour, too, of the higher command, by specifically declaring that the generals were only kept from bombarding Paris by those women; for the women influenced the crown prince, and very soon William would die and the crown prince would be king and master of those generals, whose futures would lie in his hands. It was because of this, he insisted, that Paris was not shelled. . . .

Is it to be wondered at that by the new year that most level-headed of generals, the quartermaster-general, Albrecht von Stosch, could record of the widespread feeling against Bismarck at Versailles: 'I have never yet known such bitterness against any man.'[24] This bitterness was not due simply to open differences, such as the bombardment, or access to information, or civilian authority in wartime, but above all to Bismarck's methods, his use of the smear, his mobilization of mob hatred against anyone who contradicted him, his refusal to acknowledge the good faith of anyone who opposed him. Not least his masquerading as a soldier. Bronsart's contemptuous reference to him as a civilian in a cuirassier's jacket is often quoted as an example of military arrogance. But in fact Bismarck's real offence was to insist on the supremacy of the civil arm while getting himself up as a soldier—not once but on every possible occasion.

His enmities were so complex, his schemings so elaborate. He was almost certainly wrong when he believed that the bombardment of Paris in October would have made a rapid end of the resistance; but he had a very good reason for wanting to shorten the war. Certainly Moltke, this man of transcendental common sense in purely military affairs, was politically illiterate. France was to be smashed, and if any other power objected or tried to interfere, then that power must also be smashed; this was the level of his statesmanship. He was incapable of understanding that other nations besides Prussia might, however misguidedly, have a point of view for which they were prepared to suffer, even die. He seemed incapable indeed of understanding the most elementary workings of cause and effect.

Thus, for example, only two years after the defeat of France and her subsequent spoliation, he was, in all innocence, to talk to Odo Russell like an idiot child: 'Germany,' he said, as reported by the British envoy, 'wished for peace, but France did not, nor could there be peace in Europe until the war of revenge had rendered the French harmless. . . . The late war had left sufficient fighting power in them to keep Europe still in constant alarm and a second war was necessary to obtain the guarantees they had unfortunately not been compelled to give before Paris that they would never again wantonly break the peace of Europe, so that other powers might disarm and place their armies on a peace footing. . . .'[25]

There was no need for Bismarck to attack Moltke personally; indeed, it is clear that the political intelligence of a man who could talk like that after 1871 was zero and not susceptible to persuasion. All that was needed was for Bismarck coolly and dispassionately to lay before William the issue of principle. William, who was no fool, would have understood, even though his personal sympathies were with the soldiers, even though he might disagree with Bismarck's demands for the bombardment of Paris and consider that particular matter to be none of his business; nevertheless he would almost without a doubt have conceded that his minister was in the right. And, months later, when at last Bismarck brought himself to make a reasoned statement of his case, he did. A great deal of the bitterness and muddle could have been avoided if Bismarck had acted immediately after Sedan, had insisted on the necessity for the prime minister to be kept fully in the military picture, and on his absolute supremacy when it came to making peace. There is nothing to suggest that he felt at all strongly about this principle—or that he was fully aware of it. All that he was concerned with was ensuring that he, Bismarck personally, should be in control. This made him weak.

He would also have made it far easier for himself had he sought to establish this principle in that first week of September, instead of nagging Moltke, who usually hardly listened to him. He had so much to think about that did not interest Moltke at all. Moltke was concerned with the humiliation of France, and that alone. For Bismarck victory was simply a critical stage on the way to the establishment of a unified imperial Germany with the Prussian king as emperor. His major worry was how to end the war quickly before other governments were moved to intervene; how to transform the military alliances of North and South Germany into a political union; how to bring about that union in such a way that he, Bismarck, was in the nearest thing possible to absolute control; how to make it appear that the unification owed nothing to the parliamentarians or to popular nationalism and everything to the princes (who were the very ones standing to lose most from it). In a situation reminiscent of his isolation in 1862 he was here manoeuvring in single combat against a variety of opponents who lacked a common cause: above all against King William, who regarded the imperial apotheosis with profound repugnance, seeing it as a fearful come-down for a king of Prussia; then the crown prince, who was keener on his father's acceptance of the crown than Bismarck thought he should be. ('The crown prince is as stupid and vain as anybody else. All this emperor-madness has gone to his head again.'[26]) What was happening was that the crown prince's enthusiasm for a free united Germany was a threat to Bismarck's way of doing things. Bismarck was intent on exploiting the delirium of popular nationalism which now engulfed all Germany without losing control of it, while the crown prince would have been only too happy to put himself at its head and be carried along by it. So that when Bismarck insisted on the need to move carefully in order not to injure the susceptibilities of the rulers of the southern states, the crown prince, liberal though he might be in some respects, replied in effect: We have the army; how can they resist us if we use force against them? Bismarck, who wanted the princes on his side, who also had no intention of sowing dragon's teeth for Prussia by enforcing a union of embittered foes, did not even trouble to argue. With bland effrontery he informed the crown prince that it was against his political principles to use coercion against an ally. . . .[27]

His plans fructified with surprising rapidity. The essence of his strategy was to isolate Bavaria and Württemberg, the two most awkward of the southern states, by bringing Baden and Hesse-Darmstadt quickly into the North German fold; after them, Württemberg—and then, he calculated, King Ludwig in Munich would not be able to face the prospect of exclusion from the new union.

The Reichstag was to meet on 24 November. On 14 November Baden and Hesse signed their treaties; on the twenty-third Bavaria. Most of the actual work had been done by officials in Berlin, Munich, Stuttgart, Karlsruhe, and Darmstadt; above all by the invaluable Delbrück, who was responsible for adapting the Constitution of the North German Confederation to the needs of the new Empire. It was Delbrück, too, who had to keep the Reichstag quiet (while Bismarck in Versailles wove his threads together) without alarming the southern states by reminding them too vividly that they were in effect submitting themselves to Prussia—and afterwards, when some deputies took exception to the concessions granted to Bavarian particularism (less important in reality than in appearance, it turned out, like most Bismarckian concessions). But very quickly it was all done. The whole of Germany, less Austria's German provinces, was by 23 November united in a new Confederation, and everyone took it for granted that the new Confederation would soon be the new Reich, the new Empire, with the Prussian king at its head.

Everyone, that is, except the future emperor himself, who resisted furiously, not only, as already stated, because Prussia meant everything to him, Germany very little, but also because he was becoming increasingly desperate at the slow progress of the war and thought it absurd to be discussing fripperies like the imperial title when Paris still held out and German troops were being slaughtered all over the falsely smiling land of France. He was also highly resistant to any suggestion that he was receiving the imperial crown from parliament and people. So much so, that as late as 19 December he refused even to receive a delegation from the Reichstag, offering a loyal address begging him to accept the crown. Nothing could be settled, he insisted, until the individual monarchs had ratified the separate treaties of union signed by their governments. In the end Bismarck forced his hand with a very characteristic manoeuvre. Ludwig II of Bavaria, still only twenty-five, had virtually bankrupted his country with his personal extravagances; at the outbreak of the war Bismarck had responded to an appeal by the Bavarian government for a secret advance of 3 million gulden towards mobilization costs;[28] now he discovered that Ludwig personally was in a serious financial pickle and hit on the idea of bribing him to write to William urging acceptance of the imperial crown and offering his homage. Such a missive coming from such a source, the head of the House of Wittelsbach, which was older than the Hohenzollern, and which regarded itself as the senior German dynasty, which had itself for a short time held the imperial title, even William would be unable to reject. And it was so.

Among the Bavarian contingent at Versailles—the doyen being Ludwig's uncle Leopold—was a handsome, extremely presentable courtier, Count Max von Holnstein, King Ludwig's master of horse. What nobody except Bismarck knew was that Holnstein was unprincipled, eager, and willing to jump on the Prussian band-wagon and prepared to do an equivocal job for him in return for cash—this was to return to Munich with a draft letter urging William to accept the imperial crown, which Ludwig was to copy out in his own hand and sign, in return for the promise of an annual pension of 100,000 thalers for King Ludwig and ten per cent of that for Holnstein. The arrangement was carried through to a swift conclusion. Holnstein galloped off to Munich with Bismarck's draft, which King Ludwig copied out in his own hand, then brought it back to Versailles and delivered it to Ludwig's uncle Leopold, who most reluctantly conveyed it to William. William was resentful—quite beside himself, indeed, the crown prince wrote in his diary.[29] He saw that his hand was being forced, that he would not be able to refuse.

For Bismarck the day was already won. William had not the faintest idea that the letter had been master-minded by his first minister, as the crown prince, in a rather surprised tone of voice, recorded in his diary. But not even the crown prince knew about the bribery. Very few did. Chief among these was Bismarck's banker, Gerson Bleichröder, who paid out the cash on Bismarck's behalf. And the crowning stroke was that the money came from the sequestered assets of the deposed king of Hanover, the notorious Reptile Fund, over which Bismarck had absolute control. Money looted from one German king thus went to bribe another—and all in the name of the king of Prussia, that proud and upright dynast: Hohenzollern robbed Guelph to pay Wittelsbach.

Even then the struggle was not over. Bismarck, who was almost worn out with his habitual one-man fight against the world, was himself in a state of near break-down. The bombardment of Paris still had not started. Opinion abroad was swinging behind France in her fight now against such overwhelming odds; William was sunk in the despair of frustration; the Russians had chosen this moment, with France leaderless and Germany deeply engaged, to denounce the Black Sea clauses of the Treaty of Paris on which the tsar has been brooding vengefully since 1855, an action calculated to make Britain spring to arms. Bismarck feared at first a war engulfing Europe, then a congress which would give Britain and Russia the chance to put pressure on Germany: in the end Britain mildly accepted the *fait accompli* and agreed that the congress should confine itself to Balkan affairs and refrain from discussing the Franco-German issue.

Bronsart was quite right when he observed that Bismarck was unhappy because he had played only a subordinate role in the war, the soldiers' war. But it went deeper than that. There was the genuine nightmare of the soldiers getting out of hand and ruining the future. The tension made him ill. So that in the very moment of his triumph he was prostrated. Even while the deputation from the Reichstag, after being put off for so long, arrived to present their address of loyalty to William, Bismarck was incommunicado. The crown prince very moderately recorded in his diary for that day that at this moment when Bismarck's views were urgently needed 'an attack of gout ... combined with the strained state of his nerves which necessitate the utmost quiet and care, is a cause of very serious inconvenience.'[30] Two days earlier Bismarck himself had written to Johanna: 'I keep tolerably well through rain and shine, weak with vexation over the usual matters, tortured with overwork beyond all reason—through the failure of others, not through real necessity, or I wouldn't complain. . . .'[31]

Christmas, not at all a happy Christmas, was approaching. Once upon a time Bismarck's idea had been to announce the foundation of the Reich on New Year's Day; but when Christmas came there was still no settlement and William still resisted, even though he knew he would have to give way in the end—or abdicate. And the crown prince, for all his liberal reputation, was now almost indecently eager to get the new Reich established (he had dreams, indeed, of reviving the old title of the Holy Roman Empire for the benefit of Hohenzollern). But at last all was decided. William yielded, and the situation was a sad commentary on his entire reign: the reign of an upright ruler who was weak and gave his blessing to some procedures which revolted him and to others which he did not understand.

Of course William had no idea that his chief minister had bribed in his venerable name a half-mad young ruler in Munich who might have been his grandson. But without his master's weakness Bismarck could never have functioned as he did; he needed an upright king to cover his deviousness and a weak king to bend to his will. William filled the bill almost to perfection. His appearance was splendid, his uprightness was well-known, and his weakness he had displayed from the moment in 1848 when, as Prince of Prussia, he had fled to England leaving his wife and his elder brother, the king, to face the revolutionaries. Almost never in his entire career did he carry through a firmly expressed intention in face of Bismarck's threats or blandishments. As he gave way in the abdication crisis of 1862, so he gave way over the Congress of the Princes in 1863, over the war against Austria in 1866 (and the subsequent peace settlement). Now he was giving way over the new imperium, and he was to continue thereafter. And so we shall find him nine years later, in 1880, in his eighty-third year, with Bismarck now working on him grimly and relentlessly to make him cut loose from his oldest friend, Russia, to ally himself with Austria, once more bursting into tears—and giving way ('My whole moral strength is broken'[32]).

So in Versailles, protesting loudly and angrily to the last in a charade that made an unpromising start for the birth of a new state, he allowed himself to be elevated above his fellow-princes without looking too deeply into how it had been managed. Charade was his own angry word. 'I have just come back from the emperor-charade,' he wrote to Augusta in Potsdam. 'I cannot tell you how utterly depressed I have been feeling in these last days, partly because of the high responsibility, partly because of the pain at seeing the Prussian title superseded.'[33] It was this title that worried him most. If he was to be emperor he wished to be known as emperor of Germany, or emperor of the Germans. The crown prince wanted that too. But Bismarck, who did not care one way or the other, knew that the southern states would not agree. Rather than let the whole thing fall to pieces, the crown prince accepted that the title German emperor would do. But William himself went angrily to bed with the matter undecided. It was not until on the great day itself, when his son-in-law the grand duke of Baden stood forward to call for three cheers for Emperor William, that the crisis was surmounted. And even then the newly minted emperor was so angry with his prime minister that when he moved along the ranks of princes and generals, he passed him by without stopping to shake him by the hand.

Bismarck did not care. He had got what he wanted. The whole affair was a charade for him too. . . . 'This imperial birth was a difficult one,' he wrote to Johanna a few days later, 'and kings at such moments have wonderful cravings, like women before delivering to the world what they can no longer withhold. As midwife, I several times most urgently wished I was a bomb to go off and blow the whole edifice to pieces.'[34]

But did either of these men, on this great day, which was also the bicentenary of the founding of the kingdom of Prussia, realize quite how very much out of drawing the whole performance was? Posterity has come to regard the scene in Louis XIV's preposterous hall of mirrors as the grand celebration of victory over France. Had this been so, as a symbolic act if a Napoleonically vulgar one, there would have been some excuse for it. But it was not so. Paris had not yet fallen, was still being bombarded, and more days were to pass before the French sued for an armistice, more weeks before the signing of the peace. So that this showy gathering of princes and their courtiers, of generals and humbler representatives from all the fighting regiments, a blaze of uniforms and medals, all doing homage to the ruler of a new empire, was taking place on the soil of a nation still at war. Bismarck hated it. He read out his proclamation in expressionless tones and with the grimmest of countenances, and that was that.

He was never one to enjoy his triumphs, always hurrying on to the next one. But it was he who was responsible for this whole rushed and tasteless performance. The empire could not wait. The iron had to be struck while it was hot. Give the princes and their armies a chance to disperse and they might never come together again in the pattern he needed. For although some sort of union was inevitable, Bismarck was not interested in some sort of a union: he would rather have none at all than a union brought about, as it were, from below. So it had to be Versailles. It had to be done quickly. How could the whole circus be transported to Germany? And where in Germany? Would the southern states agree to do homage in Berlin? There was still no Germany. So there was something symbolic in another way in this proclamation of the new Reich on foreign soil, in the presence of princes and soldiers. It was to go on like that, moulded for another twenty years by a man who fought the soldiers all along the line— and yet wore their uniform ('What's the use of it to me?' he growled when congratulated on his promotion to lieutenant-general on the eve of the ceremony; but he accepted the promotion all the same), by a man who had perfected his style of management in the 1860s and, oblivious of social change (how could anything change when he had not sanctioned it?), thought he could go on like that for ever. But things did not stand still.

France was dealt with very soon, but there were still to be some alarms. On the very day of the foundation of the Reich, Moltke, William himself, and all the senior officers present had half their minds on a very dangerous situation that was developing at St.-Quentin to the north. Here only the brilliance of one of the younger Prussian generals, August von Goeben, saved the First Army from being overwhelmed by a superior French force in a formal battle on 19 January. While only four days before, far away in the Vosges, the steady and competent General Werder had been so shocked by the sudden discovery of the weakness of his position *vis-à-vis* General Bourbaki (the man who would have been captured in Metz but for Prince Frederick Charles's bad faith) that he signalled Moltke for permission to retire from Belfort so that he could make sure of holding Alsace. Moltke told him to stand and accept battle where he was, and there followed a three-day struggle of extreme and punishing severity in appalling winter weather. It was not until 24 January that poor Bourbaki, his spirit broken, decided that the only way to escape a massacre was for his troops to fight their way out through the bleak Jura mountains along the Swiss frontier. When Paris refused to countenance this move he fought on for two more days, then tried to shoot himself; but his successor three days later took 80,000 men across the border at Les Verrières into ignominious internment.

That was on 1 February. Bismarck had been very sharp indeed when five days earlier he had met Favre's first tentative and private proposals for an armistice. With the king's commission, so to speak, in his pocket, empowering him to negotiate an armistice without interference from the military, it was as though he was determined to prove that a civilian minister could be as harsh and relentless as any soldier. In fact, while repelling Favre's overtures, he was still hoping with half his mind for a message from Eugénie offering peace with a Restoration France. But on the twenty-eighth poor Favre had appeared at German GHQ once more, this time as the bearer of a formal offer of an armistice on specific terms: no triumphal entry of German troops into Paris; no attempt to disarm the Garde Nationale; the Paris garrison to march out with full military honours, not to be treated as prisoners of war; everything to be held in suspense for three weeks pending the election of a National Assembly which could authorize formal peace negotiations. If Germany would not agree to these terms, then the French would go on fighting until they dropped; then France would collapse; then Prussia would have the task of feeding and administering Paris. And so on.

It was a brave effort; but it was nothing but bluff, and Favre should have known by now that Bismarck was not a man to tolerate bluff. He was in effect sent packing with nothing but a three weeks' respite in which to hold a general election and set up a new government. But before he went back to Bordeaux he made one fateful decision. The extreme south-east of France, where Bourbaki had been fighting so well and was now actually threatening Belfort, was to be exempted from the armistice: Favre allowed himself to hope that Bourbaki might achieve a victory which would be advantageous when it came to negotiating the peace; but Moltke knew that our old friend General Manteuffel, now commanding Steinmetz's army (he was to finish up as governor of Alsace-Lorraine), was at that moment moving fast to relieve General August von Werder's army in front of Belfort. And thus it was that Favre was responsible for that last terrible act, so devouring of men on both sides, so humiliating for the French, who had to watch with incredulity as their last army marched into captivity in Switzerland.

When the newly elected National Assembly met at Bordeaux three weeks later, the veteran Adolphe Thiers was chosen as head of the executive, in effect as president of a Republican France. And France now was reduced to a single asset: the character of her new leader, then in his mid-seventies, whom Bismarck respected and liked (it was sad for the new Germany that her so exacting creator would never have tolerated a Thiers in his government at home). And on 21 February, a Tuesday, Thiers duly appeared at Versailles. By the end of that week it was all over. There was next to nothing to discuss. Everyone knew Bismarck's terms in outline, and largely in detail. He might himself still like to say that he could have done without Metz but was pushed by the military into demanding it. It made no difference. Too much fuss has been made about Metz. Bismarck certainly wanted at one time to keep the historic fortress-city and encouraged popular agitation for its retention, even though he might also have had qualms about taking such an indigestibly French region into the Reich. But, Metz or no Metz, he was determined to hold Strasbourg, all of Alsace, and part of Lorraine. Straightforward strategic considerations apart, he needed this slice of the Rhineland as the cement to hold North and South Germany together.

Thiers managed to save Belfort, which meant so much to the French: the German high command attached less importance to the famous Belfort 'gap' and did not care about it so long as they held Strasbourg and Metz; and in exchange for Belfort Bismarck obtained agreement to a victory parade through Paris. As for the indemnity: Thiers himself had been expecting a demand for 5 billion francs; when Bismarck asked for six he gasped aloud. But Bismarck was only playing with him: 5 billion, he considered, was as much as France could pay (many thought it far too much) and the funding of it was to be managed by his faithful Bleichröder, who was now approaching the summit of his glory. The money was to be paid in just under four years, and German troops were to be withdrawn stage by stage with each instalment. Even without the loss of Metz it would have been a harsh and punishing settlement and one calculated to rankle until redressed. It is sometimes said that Bismarck's terms were not so bad as those imposed on Prussia by Bonaparte. Should Bonaparte himself be praised for being less barbaric than Tilly or Genghis Khan?

The new conqueror was neither a Genghis Khan nor a Napoleon. He was a statesman of the second half of the nineteenth century whom the Germans saw fit to turn into a national hero and who managed so to impose himself on the outside world that he came to be extolled for wisdom and moderation. At Versailles he made a deliberate calculation, as he had made a deliberate calculation at Nikolsburg four years earlier. This time it was an erroneous calculation, for which others had to pay. It opened the way to Armageddon a generation later.

At least one man in high position knew that Germany had taken the wrong turning. On the last day of December 1870 the crown prince confided to his diary his sense of despair: 'The longer the struggle lasts the better for the enemy and the worse for us. . . . We are no longer looked upon as the innocent victims of wrong, but rather as arrogant victors, no longer content with the conquest of the foe, but determined to bring about his utter ruin. . . .' In its sympathy for France in her death throes, he went on, the world was coming to hate Germany, 'this nation of thinkers and philosophers, poets and artists, idealists and enthusiasts; and see her only a nation of conquerors and destroyers, to which no pledged word, no treaty, is sacred, and which speaks with rude insolence of those who have done it no injury. . . . At the moment it must seem as though we are neither loved nor respected, but only feared. . . .'[35]

Frederick saw, but he lacked the strength to act on what he saw; and in any case, like almost all his fellow-Prussians, he was himself soon carried away by the intoxication of power.

PART THREE

TO WHAT END?

Bismarck has made us great and powerful, but
he has robbed us of our friends, the sympathies of
the world, and—our conscience.
—CROWN PRINCE FREDERICK OF PRUSSIA,
31 December 1870

Oh how the German nation errs if it thinks it will be
able to put the rifle in one corner and turn to the arts and
the happiness of peace! They will be told above all you must
continue your military training! And after a time no one will
really be able to say what is the purpose of living. For soon
the German-Russian war will loom on the horizon.
—JACOB BURCKHARDT, 1871

CHAPTER XVII

BARREN YEARS

We move now from fact into legend. In a matter of eight years Bismarck had welded the old, fragmented Germany into the most formidable military power in the world and in so doing had himself risen to a position of almost mesmeric authority, which, with the might of the Prussian-led army behind him, made him, inevitably, the arbiter of Europe. Exit the militant conqueror; enter the elder statesman, a paragon of peace and wisdom. That is the legend. It is true that he made no more wars: he did not need them. But peace? Does it make sense to call the later Bismarck a man of peace simply because he was satisfied with the Germany he had made and found the best way to buttress and sustain it was to keep all Europe desperately guessing, and fearing, so that when he had gone there was nobody capable of keeping within bounds the tensions he had created?

The new Bismarckian era may conveniently be dated from 1 April 1871. Bismarck was fifty-six and there were no further aspects of his character to reveal themselves. Only the emphases changed. This means that in a study of his life-work, his achievements and failures, we can very soon escape from detailed chronological unfolding: for the next twenty years in everything he did he was simply ringing the changes on the many aspects of a highly complex character. His contemporaries did not know this. To them he now emerged as Jupiter. They had started by underrating him; they were now to make up for this by overrating him. They knew nothing of the real man behind the face of bronze, and even those few like, for example, the British ambassador, Lord Odo Russell, to whom from time to time he revealed himself, had no conceivable means of conveying to their masters the strangeness of this man of iron who preferred to foster instability when he might have stood on rock.

It is easy enough to see how the legend took root. Statesmen and diplomats in all countries were so overwhelmed by the new German presence and the consummate skills of its creator that it was the most natural thing in the world to assume that he must always know precisely what he was doing, and why, and that whatever he did must make sense. Or, in the words of a distinguished British historian, 'Bismarck is judged to be right because he is the master diplomatist; he is the master diplomatist because he is right.'[1]

There was also the matter of relief when the worst fears aroused by the great new military state in the heart of Europe proved unfounded. Even before the peace was signed, Disraeli in London could offer the House of Commons one of his brilliantly prophetic insights: 'This war represents the German Revolution, a greater political event than the French Revolution of the last century—I do not say a greater, or even as great, a social event. . . . You have a new world, new influences are at work; new and unknown objects and dangers with which to cope, at present involved in that obscurity incident to novelty in such affairs. . . . But what has come to pass in Europe? The balance of power has been entirely destroyed.'[2]

The same thought was put more brutally in the hearing of the Austrian ambassador to Berlin, Count Felix von Wimpffen, by a Prussian acquaintance in response to an expression of concern for the future of the balance of power: 'We ourselves with a million soldiers are the equilibrium of the future.'[3] Bismarck himself, with all his calm authority, was for the rest of his career to be haloed, as it were, by 'the iron radiance of a million bayonets.'[4]

Calm authority?

His fifty-sixth birthday he celebrated with a scornful and hectoring attack in the Lower House on all those minority groups and parties which were committing the unforgivable sin of opposing him, chancellor of the new Reich, minister-president, and foreign minister of Prussia. For over a year, during the hidden run-up to the war with France, its successful prosecution and conclusion, and the crowning of King William as German emperor, he had been able to spare little time for domestic politics. Now that he had his great work behind him he might have been expected to return to Berlin with magnanimity in his heart and a determination to use his unique position to heal past divisions, make his peace with past opponents, and set about turning the new united Germany into a model power, protected from attack from outside by her unrivalled strength, while at home quietly developing the immense potential, human and material, spiritual and practical, of her various parts.

He was the cleverest man in Europe and the most skilled in diplomacy and statesmanship; his vision, though blinkered, was almost blindingly intense; he was supported by the most powerful army in the world; his achievement was more than enough for his lifetime and his glory knew no limits. He had been made a prince and presented with the Grand Cross of the Hohenzollern Order in diamonds and a vast new estate of seventeen thousand acres, nearly all of it valuable timber in good order: Friedrichsruh, in Lauenburg-Holstein, near Hamburg, bigger and richer than Varzin. The honours, he said, he despised; the land he gloried in, adding to it, as to Varzin and Schönhausen, as much as he could. He had nothing to do at home but work out a satisfactory political system designed to engage and bring on the best available talent and provide a solid and enduring matrix for his successors: it was already obvious by 1871 that Germany had embarked, without any further help from the central government, upon a new and tremendous wave of industrial expansion which would bring her economic power into step with her military might. So Bismarck had nothing to do abroad but make Germany trusted. . . .

It could have been done, but already by his treatment of defeated France he had made it impossible. He had sought to ensure, by taking Alsace-Lorraine, by taking Strasbourg and Metz, that France could never attack again. But this very action made it certain that she would burn for revenge, and that the other powers would sympathize with her. Had Bismarck been a truly great statesman he would have concentrated all his forces on securing pepetual amity with France, with Austria, with Russia—and with England. He did not even consider this obvious and humane course.

The tragic error over Alsace-Lorraine might have been put down to an aberration in the heat of war, but it proved to have been an earnest of the way Bismarck intended to go on, at home as well as abroad. Starting with his birthday speech on 1 April 1871, he now entered on a course of fairly wild plunging that lasted five years and poisoned the atmosphere of the new Germany and of Europe as a whole. It ended in a first-class European crisis and what was for all practical purposes a nervous breakdown on the part of the man who could have presided as a tranquillizing influence but instead, by the kindest interpretation, preferred to practise violence at home while in foreign affairs seeking security for Germany by setting the other powers against each other. Less kindly regarded, his conduct for years to come was directed above all at making himself the dominant figure in Europe as he was already the dominant figure in Germany.

The birthday speech was the opening shot in what came to be known rather bombastically as the *Kulturkampf*. In July 1870, while Bismarck's thoughts were elsewhere, Pope Pius IX, recently deprived of the remnants of the Papal States, proclaimed the doctrine of papal infallibility and proceeded to impose rigid papal authority over Catholics everywhere. This led to divisions among the faithful in all lands, not least in Germany. Bismarck at first refused to pay any attention to the warnings of German Catholics who resented this assumption of authority, which entailed the wholesale dismissal and excommunication of Catholic priests, schoolmasters, etc., who refused to toe the line. But with France satisfactorily disposed of, he suddenly realized that while his back was turned and his attention concentrated on the destruction of French power, life at home in Prussia had not stood still waiting for his permission to proceed. Pius IX's new activism was deplored by many German Catholics, but others it had stimulated. And at the Prussian Landtag elections in November 1870 these had put forward their own candidates with a strong clerico-social programme. They gained fifty-seven seats and formed themselves into an independent conservative opposition called the Centre Party, with its own newspaper. This new party made so much ground that when the first elections for the new imperial Reichstag were held in March, they won fifty-three seats and, under Ludwig Windthorst, the strongest character among German politicians after Bismarck himself, shocked the chancellor into sudden action. Windthorst was a hunch-backed Hanoverian with a vitriolic tongue and a first-class mind who had never reconciled himself to the subjugation of his historic kingdom by the Hohenzollerns. Bismarck knew very well that he was bound to attract as allies Polish nationalists, Hanoverian loyalists, and, very soon, deputies from Alsace and Lorraine as well.

Bismarck was congenitally suspicious of papal pretensions. All other considerations apart, he could not forget that Pius had been restored to the Vatican and maintained there by French bayonets after the troubles in 1848. But he played down the fears of others because there were more important matters to be settled first. Even so, in 1869, he could write to Prince Hohenlohe in Bavaria: 'There is a party in Rome which is consciously trying to disturb the spiritual and political peace of Europe.' He genuinely believed that the Ultramontanes, of all lands, were united in a conspiracy to gain command of all the world. In 1870 he set his press jackal, Moritz Busch, to denounce a Silesian journal for charging him with anti-Catholicism, when really all he objected to (he declared) was 'a small, subversive coterie' which had nothing in common with honest German Catholics. 'In complaining of the Ultramontanes we were thinking . . . of the party of the *Münchener Volksboten* and similar organs, whose slanderous jibes stir up the Germans against each other, and who encouraged the French to attack Germany and are partly responsible for the present war, inasmuch as they represented the French victory to be easy and certain and the German people to be disunited! . . .'[5]

But although he was at pains for a long time to speak of the Ultramontanes as a vicious little coterie, not to be confused with the Church, he soon argued himself, as Odo Russell put it, into the conviction that 'the pretensions of the Vatican were fundamentally inconsistent with the supremacy of the state. . . . He could not conceive that a faithful child of the Church could also be a loyal son of the fatherland. The Syllabus, the Vatican Decrees, constituted a challenge to German unity.'[6]

It was characteristic that with all his distrust of the Ultramontanes, when sounded out in September 1870 by the archbishop of Posen as to whether Prussia would offer the pope asylum should it be needed after the defeat of his mainstay, Napoleon III, he easily accepted the idea. The presence of the pope, he felt, would add to Prussia's prestige; at the same time he would expect the pope to show his gratitude by instructing all the faithful to support his, Bismarck's, government. He really believed that this was the way the papacy still worked. As things turned out the occasion did not arise. Instead of welcoming the Holy Father to the new Reich, Archbishop Count Mieczylaw von Ledóchowski was to find himself in prison, as the *Kulturkampf*, now being called by some 'the struggle for civilization,' gathered bitterness and intensity.

The great conflict had opened with a rather misleading emphasis on the national minority parties, the Poles and the Hanoverians above all. Even when in July Bismarck took his first step against the pope by demonstratively abolishing the Catholic department of the Prussian Ministry of Public Worship and Education, he was still far more concerned with the dangerous linkage between Rome and politically dissident groups and parties than with the papal challenge to secular authority as such. But by the autumn of 1871 he had taken soundings and discovered that even in the Catholic South—in Bavaria, in Württemberg, in Austria as well—there was a great deal of alienation and unease in face of Pius's new course. In

November he issued his first serious challenge. He decided to set up a special schools' inspectorate, which would give the Prussian authorities mandatory powers to inspect all schools and report on their teaching.

The man he found to draft and push through the statute giving body to this decision, Adalbert Falk, was an upright and experienced civil servant, who was also an ardent anticlerical, a rationalist of the deepest dye. His general outlook was shared to a greater or lesser degree by most German Liberals, and his appointment thus brought the Liberals closer to Bismarck than ever before. From the Hanoverian Benningsen downwards they seemed quite unaware that in fashioning a rod to beat the pope they were making a scourge for their own backs. Falk had been personally recommended by the extremely open-minded and unfanatical Delbrück, hard-working and self-effacing, the man who for many years effectively ran the expanding German economy on Bismarck's behalf. As his campaign grew ever harsher and more bitterly divisive, even highly intelligent men, like Virchow, were carried away by the feeling that they were engaged on an honourable crusade against reactionary obscurantism. Few paused to wonder what Bismarck was doing at the head of such a crusade.

What in fact he was doing now, what he was doing by the middle of 1873 when Virchow had enthusiastically christened the crusade the *Kulturkampf*, was losing his temper and by his bullying tactics not only reuniting the divided Catholics in opposition to his policies, but turning many of the Protestant conservatives into active opponents, including his old estranged friend and mentor, Ludwig von Gerlach, infinitely far from Rome in reason and instinct, but adamant in his refusal to concede that any secular government had the right to interfere in matters of religious education.

Germany, so recently unified, so young, was thus torn and riven quite wantonly in a manner which would have severely strained the most long-established and settled society. And the violence continued for years. By 1873 two archbishops were in prison and 1300 parishes had no priest. The affair had gone far beyond Bismarck's own personal feelings about the papacy as such. He was, quite simply, out of his depth. He did not understand the strength of Catholicism. To him it was alien, exotic, dangerously conspiratorial, but artificial. He did not understand the strength of ideas. Odo Russell came close to the truth when he reported to Whitehall: 'I fancy that Bismarck utterly misunderstands and underrates the power of the Church. Thinking himself more infallible than the Pope, he cannot tolerate two Infallibles in Europe and fancies he can select and appoint the next Pontiff as he would a Prussian General, who will carry out his orders to the Catholic clergy in Germany and elsewhere. . . . '

And he continued: 'The German Bishops who were politically powerless in Germany and theologically in opposition to the Pope in Rome—have now become powerful political leaders in Germany and enthusiastic defenders of the now infallible Faith of Rome, united, disciplined, and thirsting for martyrdom, thanks to Bismarck's uncalled for and illiberal declaration of War on the freedom they had hitherto peacefully enjoyed.'[7]

In the end he had to abandon the fight. In May 1872 he had loudly proclaimed in the Reichstag that there would be no Canossa for him, 'either in body or in spirit.' Just a year later he proclaimed the notorious May Laws, worked out by the conscientious Falk, secularizing many aspects of German life, including marriage. At the 1874 elections the Catholics responded by rallying round the Centre Party, which increased its strength in the Reichstag from sixty-three to ninety-one seats.

Later that year, when Bismarck was taking the waters at Bad Kissingen in Bavaria, he was shot at in his carriage by a young Catholic journeyman, Heinz Kullmann. The bullet grazed his right hand as it was raised to acknowledge the cheers of worthy citizens standing to watch him pass. The wound was not serious, but Bismarck made the most of it. It was easy to suggest that the attempt had been part of a Catholic conspiracy. He chose the moment for attacking the Centre Party as the inspiration of the would-be assassin: 'You may try to disown this assassin,' he thundered, 'but he is clinging to your coat-tails all the same!'[8] But it availed him very little.

Four years later it was all over. Pius died in 1878 and was succeeded by the conciliatory Leo X. Bismarck did not go to Canossa 'in body,' but he certainly did so 'in spirit.' Falk was quietly thrown over, most of the anti-Catholic laws were dismantled, and in no time at all the National Liberals discovered that they were being abandoned to clear the way for a grand *rapprochement* between Bismarck and the Conservatives.

To this day there has been no completely satisfying explanation of the *Kulturkampf*. But the answer seems to lie in a mixture of three main elements. Perhaps most importantly of all, Bismarck as chancellor of the new Reich could not hope to control the Reichstag as he had contrived to control the Prussian Landtag with the king of Prussia at his back. He needed a strong, nationally minded party behind him, and the National Liberals fell naturally into place: only through them could he hope to keep in being and develop the national fervour required for the consolidation of the new

Reich. And, indeed, the chance to get back at the priests was a temptation irresistible. Only Eduard Lasker among the prominent Liberals had the percipience to see that the great struggle was essentially no more than a Bismarckian manoeuvre in the grand manner.

But, of course, it was not a purely cynical manoeuvre. Cynicism there was in plenty, but, as always with Bismarck, cynicism was mixed up with primitive emotions. Later on, in the years of retirement, he was to throw poor Falk to the wolves. He himself had been far too busy, he declared in his reminiscences, even to read the May Laws, which had been drafted by Falk: 'The error in the conception of the Prussian laws was made obvious to me by the picture of dextrous, light-footed priests pursued through back doors and bedrooms by honest but awkward Prussian gendarmes, with spurs and trailing sabres.'[9] Poor Falk, who was carrying out to the letter what his master had prescribed, who as education minister also had done more than any man to build up the very fine German educational system, as the servant of this terrible master had to be sacrificed.

The pope he could deal with as he could deal with the head of any other foreign power, but he distrusted the Curia extremely. The picture of slippery, wily priests making rings round honest Protestant policemen came naturally to him and fitted in with his idea of a sinister international conspiracy, typified by those 'French priests who incited the country people to murderous attacks upon our troops, attacks in which they themselves took part . . . those priests who sullied the cloth, sneaking into our camp as spies under the pretence of bringing the last rites to the dying.'[10] And this instinctive revulsion against an alien and largely incomprehensible presence was reinforced by his obsession with Poland—which he was to represent as the main cause of the *Kulturkampf:* 'The *Kulturkampf* was decided for me predominately by its Polish side. . . . In Posen and West Prussia, according to official reports, whole villages, thousands of individuals, had been brought up as Poles under Catholic influence and re-educated according to Polish ideas and formally described as Poles, although in the previous generation they were officially German.'[11]

It is misleading, however, to consider the *Kulturkampf* in isolation, as a self-contained issue. In its conception it was simply one manifestation of the obsessive urgency with which the creator of the new Reich sought at home to make his position no less commanding and unassailable throughout Germany than it had been for some years in Prussia, and abroad to thwart the organization of any possible anti-German coalition by a vengeful France. In both cases this supremely flexible opportunist was losing his touch and starting to box himself in, a development which before 1870 he would never have tolerated. At home he was making himself too dependent on the backing of one or other of the great parties; abroad he was forcing himself into too close an accord with Russia and Austria. For by turning France into the implacable foe of the new Germany he had offended against the very canon he had so passionately upheld to Leopold von Gerlach in earlier days: he had reduced his freedom of manoeuvre by, in his own words, putting part of the chessboard out of bounds. Certainly he was not yet committed to a fixed pattern: he could quarrel with Russia and make it up again. Certainly he had not bound himself for ever to the National Liberals: he could throw them over quite ruthlessly, including the trusted, the indispensable Delbrück, and turn to the Conservatives, including the Centre Party itself. But what in effect was happening was that instead of exploiting his unassailable position inside and outside Germany to show himself above partisan struggles, against predation, against vindictiveness, his need to dominate had become absolute.

He offended against his own canon in another way too: the chessboard was further reduced by the effective exclusion of England from his calculations: there were one or two tentative efforts to bring England into play and achieve some sort of an alliance with her; but these efforts drained into the sand the moment Bismarck was certain that he had organized his relations with Vienna and St. Petersburg to his liking. England he never understood. Above all in the Gladstone era he was convinced, and rightly, that there was a critical incompatability between his own aim, to secure by whatever means a Europe that was safe for Germany, and the Gladstonian aim, to secure a Europe that was safe not only for England but also, or by virtue of this, a harmonious concert in which all might prosper. Bismarck did not care whether others prospered or not.

This absolute concentration on his own personal hegemony went far beyond the domineering impatience towards the less gifted and the tiresomely obstructive which is exhibited to a greater or lesser degree by almost all commanding personalities. Over the years, the temperament which had made it unthinkable for Bismarck in youth to play second fiddle to anyone had so hardened as to make it impossible for him in maturity to cooperate on terms of give and take with any other living soul. It hurt him now to defer even to the monarch he had turned into an emperor; while the demands of the generals in the recent war and their attempts to exclude him from participation in the conduct of that war had bitten very deeply indeed.

With all his measureless self-regard he was full of superstitious fears and in a mood to suspect conspiracy on every side. He evidently never realized that by making it impossible for parties and factions to function constructively in opposition, he was manufacturing the climate for intrigue. There was plenty of this. And one of the driving spirits of the opposition was Augusta, not at all grateful for being made an empress, and ready to support any individual, faction, party, institution, prepared to stand in Bismarck's way—up to and including the papacy itself. But Bismarck's inflamed and jealous imagination all too easily transformed personal intrigue into an international conspiracy: he really believed in a world-wide Popish plot.

During this period, the worst years of his life so far, he continued the habit, formed at Versailles, of unburdening himself to Odo Russell, holding forth in terms of such startling disloyalty to his own people, from his imperial master downwards, that the English diplomatist, fascinated as he was, sometimes hardly knew where to look. Wearily the great statesman rambled on. He wanted only to get out and have done with office; his colleagues were impossible to work with: but would the emperor dismiss him or allow him to resign? He would not, partly because His Majesty could never make up his mind about anything, partly because it amused him to play one minister off against another.

About his hatred for the empress he made no bones at all: 'Her Majesty' (Russell is paraphrasing) 'had the advantage over him of breakfasting with the emperor every morning and of looking over the papers with His Majesty, when she found daily opportunities of fighting the battles of her spiritual and political directors and of undermining the emperor's confidence in him, whose services His Majesty had unhappily never appreciated. . . .'

All this, he went on, meant that he had to squander his energy combating her influence, 'which often called for the old emperor's tears. . . . The Prussian government was like a cart with eight horses harnessed to its wheels [sic]. He could no longer consent to be one of them and wear out his strength in administrative detail. . . .'[12]

This was in the autumn of 1872, when in fact he had persuaded William to let him resign his position as Prussian minister-president in favour of Roon. It did not last long. Roon was supposed to cast his conservative mantle over the chancellor's liberal expedients—and also to save the great man wear and tear. Bismarck had evidently imagined that his old patron would do the hard work and rubber-stamp his decisions. When this did not happen he was furious. Roon, he complained to Odo Russell, 'was in his dotage':[13] the experiment lasted just ten months.

One of the points at issue between Bismarck and his emperor was the future government of France. Although there could be no question of France's hitting back in the near future, she was recovering with unexpected rapidity. Hag-ridden as he was by the fear of an ultimate war of revenge, Bismarck's first task was to keep France isolated, above all to prevent her making an alliance with either Russia or Austria. And to this end he had decided to back Thiers, in the belief that a Republican France would not easily find allies among the dynasts. At the same time he set considerable store by an understanding between Russia and Austria which would restrain the two powers from encroaching upon each other's interests in the Balkans and keep them both friendly towards the new Germany.

The one preoccupation led him directly into one of the most disreputable episodes of his career, the other to a minor triumph of diplomatic public relations.

The triumph was the creation of the Three Emperors' League, a fantasy which was, for a short time, stronger than many a more formal alliance. It was a very pretty and elegant piece of diplomatic tapestry, with various incompatibles all smoothly woven together: if Bismarck had been content with this sort of operation, of which he was the consummate master, he would have been a greater man than he was, and Europe and the world would have benefited.

The first step, in 1871, was the reconciliation of William and Francis Joseph: they met at Ischl, the Austrian emperor's favourite hunting-box— while Bismarck and the mordantly anti-Prussian Beust conferred at Salzburg and Gastein. Beust obviously could not long survive this *rapprochement*: his sustaining interest had been preparation for the day when Austria and his own native Saxony would be revenged for Königgrätz. He was succeeded as Austrian foreign minister in the autumn of 1871 by the somewhat flamboyant Hungarian Count Julius Andrássy, once condemned to death *in absentia* for his part in the Hungarian revolt against the Habsburgs, now, as a result of the great Compromise of 1867 (the transformation of the Habsburg Empire into the Dual Monarchy, with

Hungary autonomous in all but military and foreign affairs) firmly in the saddle, pro-German, almost violently anti-Russian, and above all interested in working to subordinate Vienna to the interests of Budapest.

With Beust gone, the way was clear for the acceptance by Francis Joseph of an invitation to Berlin. That was in August 1872. Suddenly Alexander II of Russia announced that he would like to visit Berlin at the same time. All three emperors thus met in September of that year, and Bismarck saw his chance to use the occasion to create at least a shadow of the old Holy Alliance which had brought together Alexander's uncle, Francis Joseph's grandfather, and William's father. In the following year William proceeded in state to St. Petersburg, accompanied by Bismarck and Moltke, and there a military convention was concluded: each side, if attacked by another power, would come to the other's aid with 200,000 men. Since there was no immediate prospect of any other power attacking either Prussia or Russia, it was clearly the spirit of the agreement that counted. And this, indeed, was to be true of the entire construction. In June Alexander proceeded to Vienna, there to sign a harmless convention about mutual consultation. In October William followed him to Vienna, and there the formal protocol of the *Dreikaiserbund*, the Three Emperors' League, was signed.

Rather than anything else, it was a declaration of common interest: there was no firm alliance. In Bismarck's mind it was above all an insurance against France. But it is permissible to wonder whether this martial-sounding demonstration on the part of the absolutist powers, the so-called Northern Courts, was as clever as its creator assumed it to be. Certainly it proclaimed a formal reconciliation between Austria and Prussia on the one hand and Austria and Russia on the other. But as a demonstration of overwhelming power it so obviously lacked real foundation that those outside it were not intimidated but, rather, irritated, perhaps quite disproportionately. England above all, for Disraeli was in no mood to contemplate with resignation a Europe dominated by a league of abolutist powers, the greatest of them, Russia, then regarded, rightly or wrongly, as a standing threat to the British position in the Mediterranean and the East. Further, with the Balkans an abiding theatre of dispute between them, there could be no real and lasting *rapprochement* between St. Petersburg and Vienna.

In fact the *Dreikaiserbund* was not to last long, but the making of it, for what it was worth, was an elegant example of Bismarck's diplomatic virtuosity, though it was here virtuosity performing in a void. His strongest emotions were deeply engaged much nearer home, finally exploding in the great war scare of 1875 ending in a débâcle, a humiliation, which would have put an end to the career of any lesser man.

Bismarck was in a strange, almost desperate mood during the early and mid-1870s: certainly half exhausted by his exertions of the past decade, but also driven by the need to command and assert himself and display purposeful activity in a period which most imperatively demanded relaxation and consolidation. The comings and goings of emperors, the state trips between Berlin, Vienna, and St. Petersburg, he could more or less benignly grace with his incomparable authority, gently steering the principals in the required direction with a nudge here, a slight check there. He could set up and maintain an imperial system so designed that it was built round himself as the controlling element. But when it came to directing the day-to-day conduct of affairs he was at odds with almost everyone, and with himself into the bargain.

Imperial Germany, booted and spurred, had clattered on to the world stage with all the insecure brashness of a parvenu, determined to cut a great figure, and quite failing to understand the inevitable effect on her neighbours of the sudden appearance of a strong, dynamic, restless, and highly belligerent power, apparently free of all inhibitions, in the heart of Europe where no power had been before. Bismarck, who had engineered this power, who despised the sabre-rattling nationalism which he had encouraged and exploited, who insisted now that he was a man of peace, nevertheless made no consistent effort to moderate that impact. Indeed, by his own actions he appeared to give his blessing to the Francophobia which most Germans with their idiotic talk of the hereditary enemy seemed now to be taking for granted as an immutable law of nature. On another level, he did nothing to restrain the anti-Catholic, anti-clerical excesses of the *Kulturkampf,* which he had unloosed and over which he still presided. And he seems to have asked no questions at all about the speculation mania now arising out of the dangerously booming economy.

For these first years of the new Reich came to be known as the *Gründungszeit,* the foundation time. Real industry, of course, expanded mightily, and there was plenty of it. But there was a still more feverish stampede to get rich quickly. Established banks, hitherto decently sober in their conduct, launched themselves into speculative ventures of the most dubious kind. There was no limit to the credulity and greed of the speculators, who included some of the highest in the land, all determined to cash in on the great expansion, already under way before 1870, and now fantastically accelerated by the overbearing optimism which arose from the intoxication of victory, the glorying in newly discovered strength, above all the immediate availability of the 5 billion francs' indemnity which the French contrived to pay off much sooner than expected. If ever there was a call for a statesman to stand up and preach a little sobriety and restraint it was now. But Bismarck seemed unaware of the danger until it was too late.

All Europe, indeed, was booming at that time. Western man, inspirited by technological progress, industrial expansion, and the tremendous increase in the supply of mined gold, was smitten by one of his recurrent bouts of immoderate greed. Unrestricted economic growth (the term was not yet invented) was seen as a law of nature: everyone could get rich all the time and for ever—everyone, that is, belonging to the middle and the upper classes. And it looked as though this might be true. While Marx and Engels poured out their prophesies of woe, immense and stimulating profits were being made; as though at a touch of a magic wand, by anyone who cared to apply himself seriously to the business of accumulation. The mysterious but unshakeable belief in inevitable 'growth,' the strength of faith required to justify unbridled greed, were not to be approached again for close on a hundred years, when, after the second world war, the 'working-classes' were corrupted by that same mania for acquisition that had distinguished their 'betters' in earlier days. The speculative fever in Germany, centred on the very new stock exchange, was never again to be equalled until the madness which ended in the great crash of 1931. And as in 1931, the collapse when it came started in Vienna when on 9 May 1873, Black Friday, the bottom fell out of the stock market at the very moment when the shining city was packed with visitors, from the Russian tsar downwards, for the Great Exhibition, the biggest ever seen, which was to mark Austria's recovery from the catastrophe of her defeat by Prussia. Francis Joseph was deeply shocked to discover that one in four of those paladins of democracy, the deputies to the parliament in Vienna, had been exploiting their inside knowledge and influence to enrich themselves: some of the most prominent were waist-deep in corruption, while the rot had spread to the exclusive aristocracy of the so-called First Society, which was supposed to be above such things. The scandal was great, but it was also prophylactic.[14]

Prussia was in the same case, but here Bismarck, who was not shocked, managed to conceal the extent of corruption from his sovereign, who would have been deeply sunk in shame had he known about it. Bismarck could hardly take a high moral line himself, since his own financial transactions through the faithful Bleichröder were by no means lily-white. But the scandals gave him some bad moments. When all was said, it was *his* Germany and *his* system which had encouraged the swindlers, the speculators, the fraudulent entrepreneurs, who now fell apart, dragging down with them into the pit tens of thousands of the innocently acquisitive. It had been he who had rejected the advice of Ludwig Bamberger, a leading Liberal politician and banker, that Germany should spread out the instalments of the French indemnity, to prevent too many millions flooding into circulation all at once. It was he who with his sequestration of the Hanover millions and the private employment of them (as bribes) through Bleichröder was setting an example in corruption. He was lucky to get away with so few national scandals. Lasker, perhaps the most independently minded of all Bismarck's Liberal allies, was as usual, the most fearless in exposure, and it was he who forced the public investigation into a major railway scandal which cost Bismarck's minister of commerce, Count Heinrich Itzenplatz, his career and was the ruin of his old and tried supporter Hermann Wagener, the first editor of the *Kreuzzeitung*. Many years before it had been Wagener who had caught Bismarck's imagination with his schemes to an enlightened social order to save Prussia from the worst excesses of capitalism. It had been to Wagener, too, that Bismarck had expounded his faith in the special Prussian virtues of loyalty, sobriety, honour, etc. These qualities were at a discount. Now his old comrade-in-arms was doomed to die in poverty and he would not raise a finger to help him: it was not safe for him to declare himself. There were too many skeletons in too many cupboards: least said soonest mended. And it was all the easier to sweep unpleasant facts under the carpet because, as in Austria, plenty of the Liberal deputies were also involved in financial scandals of one kind and other, a detail which severely inhibited the Liberal Lasker in his moral crusade.

The fact remained that less than three years after the fall of Paris France had paid off her indemnity in full and was already rebuilding her army, while the German economy had suffered a heavy set-back—and this at a moment when Bismarck was conducting his stately sarabande with the three emperors. The financial scandals he could not talk about, but they told on his nerves and were thus at least in part responsible for the madness—there is no other word for it—which was increasingly manifest as the *Kulturkampf* developed, and which reached a climax in the disastrous year 1875.

*   *   *

His very odd state of mind was best reflected in the notorious Arnim affair, which ran in parallel with the *Kulturkampf* and the leisurely approach to the Three Emperors' League.

Count Harry von Arnim, a senior career diplomatist, was a leading light of that far-ramified Pomeranian clan already encountered in the persons of Bismarck's first chief at Aachen and of his brother-in-law, the husband of Malwine. There were Arnims everywhere: an Arnim had married the writer Bettina Brentano, Goethe's unrequited lover; an Arnim, Count Harry's own son, had married Elizabeth Russell, the author of *Elizabeth and her German Garden*. Count Harry himself was vain, unstable, faulty in judgement, but clever—one of those doubly unhappy men whose ambitions far exceed their powers. He was nearly ten years younger than Bismarck, his chief, and dreamed of supplanting him. His chief assets were on the one hand his friendship with the chancellor's old enemy, the empress, on the other his connections with the conservative Junkers who had once patronized and supported Bismarck but were now uniting against him.

Bismarck, of course, knew Arnim well, had taken him to London with him on his unfortunate visit in 1862, sent him to represent the North German Confederation at the Vatican, used him as a special representative with the French for the winding up of the war, and finally appointed him as ambassador to Paris once the peace was signed. He disliked and distrusted him profoundly as an intriguer and a potential rival, but Arnim was too well seen in the highest circles of the land to be got rid of easily. At first all went quietly enough, but by the autumn of 1872 Arnim began to show something like the same independence of judgement and antagonism to official foreign policy that Bismarck himself had displayed in Frankfurt twenty years earlier. Bismarck was determined to go on backing Thiers as the natural head of a Republican France: a republic was still what he wanted, as a deterrent to *rapprochement* between France and Austria or Russia. Arnim, who lacked imagination and sensibility, did not trust Thiers an inch, saw him as an astute, devious, self-seeking politician leading the poor simple German Michel by the nose. Sooner or later, he insisted, the Thiers system, built on nothing, would fail, and then a revolutionary régime under Gambetta would sweep into power to threaten Germany with an army already surprisingly recovered. And so on. The solution was for Germany to get rid of Thiers and restore a royalist government while there was still time.

Leaving aside the rights and wrongs of this judgement, nothing could be more calculated to infuriate a dictatorial chancellor and foreign minister, who had planned and organized the downfall of the great antagonist and was now engaged in the delicate business of restoring neighbourly relations while hanging on to the spoils of war and ensuring her continued isolation. Bismarck's first reaction was surprisingly mild, though comical to anyone who remembered his own ambassadorial dispatches: it was the task of an ambassador to carry out his government's policy, not prescribe it, he argued patiently, and even though he then came out with his celebrated declaration that he expected his ambassadors 'to wheel into line, like soldiers, on command,' he let the man down very lightly.[15]

But Arnim would not, or could not, take a hint. He was merely reporting on the situation as he saw it, he retorted, not trying to play politics. This was not true. He was making a bid for power. He was trying to secure a seat in the Upper House, and he saw himself as the natural successor to his overbearing chief. He began to play his own game hard, informing his master in the Wilhelmstrasse that he was the emperor's envoy, not the chancellor's and, as such, had the right to report to his sovereign directly. When in October 1873 he turned up in Berlin to exploit his influence at court it was in effect a declaration of war.

Such stubborn insubordination was not to be borne. Bismarck, collecting his forces, was already fighting back by accusing Arnim of actively plotting the overthrow of Thiers and his replacement by a Royalist. In a long and almost hysterical memorandum to the emperor he declared that Arnim with his intrigues had succeeded in destroying the balance of power in Europe and was conspiring with the Jesuits and Germany's enemies in the Vatican. This outpouring, dated 19 June 1873, was almost certainly never sent to William, but the very fact that it was written at all, ending with yet another offer of resignation, showed a temporary loss of grip. As it was, he contented himself with seeking an audience with William at Babelsberg, from which he returned home on the edge of nervous collapse. A few days later Johanna carried him off to Varzin and there he remained, almost without interruption, for the rest of the year, the first of the long retreats which were such an eccentric feature of his active life and especially of his years of glory. In September he broke his seclusion to travel to Berlin to discuss aspects of the *Kulturkampf* with Falk, and it was then that he had his last meeting with Arnim and opened a window into his own soul. Seated at his great desk in the Wilhelmstrasse, twice the size of any ordinary desk, he looked across with that baleful gaze at his overweening subordinate, whom he was about to destroy. 'For eight months,' he said, 'you have damaged my health and disturbed my peace of mind! You are conspiring with the empress! You will not stop intriguing until you sit at this desk here—and then you will see what it is all worth. Nothing!'[16]

But he went on fighting for what was worth nothing, and now with no holds barred. Not for the first time, he seemed unable to realize his own strength, putting himself out far too much and too publicly, to the detriment of his own reputation. For the emperor could not conceivably have got rid of him at this stage, no matter how wistfully he may have longed to do so. William was in his seventies and had become so used to his sombrely demanding taskmaster that he could not have managed without him: perhaps he even needed the pain? To complicate matters, it was an especially difficult time for him. He was suddenly, bewilderingly, horribly, back in 1862, and Bismarck now, as then, was the only man who could save him. The parliamentarians, no longer the Prussian Landtag, but the imperial Reichstag now, were once more interfering with the army. While Bismarck sought to lose himself among his beloved trees at Varzin, the emperor's military advisers had drafted a new bill designed to settle the size of the army for all eternity. The Reichstag rebelled: its members were determined to keep at least some parliamentary control over the army and its budget; the budget, they insisted, must be debated every three years as hitherto (the lifetime of a parliament between elections under the new Constitution), or, as an utmost concession, every four. William, regardless of the lessons learnt so hardly ten years earlier, was no less determined to show once for all that the military establishment was his affair alone, wholly free from civilian interference.

This time Bismarck was at least in part on parliament's side: he was still wooing the Liberals; furthermore, his difficulties with Moltke in the recent war had shown him that the soldiers were quite strong enough already. From his sick-bed in Varzin he proposed and effected a compromise: the army should be debated every seven years. This solution pleased nobody, but it cut the knot and prevented a new constitutional crisis. Parliament had demonstrated its ultimate control of the army, while the emperor and his soldiers at least had room to plan ahead and work towards a revision of the compromise when the first seven years was up—if not sooner.

It was this suppressed crisis that gave Bismarck his chance to push William into action against Arnim, to recall him from Paris and pack him off to Constantinople. That might have been the end of the affair, with Arnim accepting a temporary set-back and planning for the day when his hated master would retire, or fall, or die. Instead he lost all sense of the possible and started fighting back, a performance which demonstrated his fatal lack of judgement for all to see: anyone who could imagine that he might beat Bismarck in a contest of underhand intrigue, blackmail, and vilification must have lost touch with reality. Arnim began by publishing secret papers about the origins of the *Kulturkampf*, offending so sharply against public-service protocol that Bismarck had every reason to insist on his suspension by the emperor pending a formal enquiry. It was soon discovered that he had abstracted large numbers of secret documents from the files of the Paris embassy, and these he refused to give up when called upon to do so. But Bismarck was now in a very black mood indeed. He was not satisfied simply with the dismissal of an erring subordinate: he wanted him arraigned and prosecuted in the criminal courts, a course which William refused to countenance.

We are now in June 1874. The Arnim affair itself has been sputtering on since the autumn of 1872. Simultaneously Bismarck has been exhibiting ever increasing exasperation in the *Kulturkampf*, more convinced than ever of a conspiracy between the Centre Party in Germany and the Vatican and the Jesuits of France. In January of that year the old Conservatives had been shattered; the Catholic Centre Party had made important gains, but the Liberals, on whom Bismarck now counted, also did well. It was in July that Kullmann made the attempt on Bismarck's life which gave the chancellor his great chance to savage the Centre Party and to browbeat the emperor. Kullmann had belonged to a Catholic youth movement; and his outrage aroused such a white heat of anti-Catholic feeling and at the same time so elevated Bismarck's personal popularity that the emperor could no longer hold out in the Arnim affair. It had begun to seem to poor William that his turbulent minister was specially protected by a guardian angel who preserved him from all perils and with unfailing punctuality smote his enemies to the ground. Surely this could only mean that he had a divine purpose to fulfil! The first fruit of this conviction was the emperor's agreement to Arnim's arrest. The pretext was that Arnim was about to fly the country and bombard the world's press with further secret revelations.

It was a difficult moment for Bismarck. All the popularity he had gained in the past months seeped away as the world saw only a powerful dictator vindictively destroying an able and honest, if wrong-headed, subordinate for daring to stand up to him. And the trial when it came was indeed a fairly disreputable affair. Bismarck kept himself out of it, and so did Manteuffel, whom Arnim had approached for support when he made his first bid for membership of the Upper House. Bismarck himself managed to create a useful diversion by stirring up excitement in the Reichstag in the days preceding the trial, assailing the Centre Party with venom, even to the point of suggesting its complicity with Kullmann's murderous attempt. In a word, by the time the trial opened in December Germany was full of revived emotion about Popish plots, and some of that indignation rubbed off on Arnim.

The trial lasted three weeks, Arnim was convicted and given three months, pending appeal, but slipped out of the country to Switzerland for medical treatment (he was, in fact, mortally ill). From Switzerland he issued an anonymous pamphlet, *Pro Nihilo*, so indiscreet, so unbalanced, so damaging, that he laid himself open to a charge of treason and was sentenced to five years *in absentia*. Within two years he was dead. Nobody else was to challenge Bismarck seriously, though many sought to undermine him, for the rest of his career.

The year 1874 had been a bad one. The Three Emperors' League apart, nothing had gone right for Bismarck since the grand triumph of 1871. His life was suddenly and disconcertingly full of uncertainties and ambiguities. No longer the strenuous but simple days when he had fixed on his goal and then stretched all his powers of manoeuvre, deception, and attack to attain that goal. He no longer had a goal, except the rather dreary and unsatisfactory business of consolidating his personal power and keeping it. The Germany which he had created, and to which he now was required to give a good deal more personal attention than he was accustomed to giving to internal domestic affairs, was in a very far from healthy state. The economy had by no means recovered from the spectacular disasters of 1873. The railways were losing money at an alarming rate. The enterprises of Herr Krupp, the very steel upon which Prussian invincibility was founded, were doing badly: between 1874 and 1876 four thousand workers had to be laid off. Alfred Krupp, with his brand-new villa, or palace, of two hundred rooms at Essen, was forced to mortgage his vast conglomerate to obtain a 30-million-thaler loan put up by a powerful banking condominium—a development which sent the military high command into a flutter of agonized apprehension.[17] In 1874, too, the transactions of the brilliantly able railway king, industrialist, entrepreneur, speculator, and Conservative deputy, Bethel Henry Strousberg, who had bankrupted himself in half a dozen countries, carrying tens of thousands down to ruin, were sensationally exposed in a popular magazine with a mass circulation at the very moment when Bismarck had imagined that the financial scandals of 1873 were at last dying a natural death. On the military front Moltke let scarcely a day pass without uttering dire warnings about the consequences, more or less immediate, of French rearmament. The *Kulturkampf* had further gained in bitterness, and Bismarck had reacted with renewed acrimony to the new challenge of the augmented Centre Party after its electoral successes at the beginning of the year. He himself, as often as not, was ill. He was grossly overweight, bloated, ravaged; his teeth were in a terrible state, but he would not see a dentist; he could not sleep; his bad leg tortured him, and to old pains were added new. He had no real friends. He was still not quite sixty, at the summit of his glory, and submerged in self-pity. 'Before I was a minister,' he wrote to his old and distant friend, Kathy Orlov's husband, early in the new year, 'I had a large number of friends and very few enemies, even among my opponents; now it is the other way round and I ask myself whether this is due to my own character or whether it is the natural outcome of a ministerial career of a more than usually protracted kind.' He went on to talk of the loneliness of kings: all the kings of Prussia, he asserted, had died unmourned; 'How then, can an unfortunate minister hope to escape this coldness, this hatred, which is visited by power upon all who exercise it?'[18]

How, indeed?

The year then beginning, 1875, was worse. Up to the end of 1874 Bismarck had been concerned less with French rearmament as such than with a new terror: the Royalist régime seen as a rallying point and a centre of intrigue for all those opposed to his anti-papal line. He had shown something of his very black mood in the spring of that year in an extraordinary circular addressed to the courts of Europe in which he went so far as to proclaim that any close identification of the French government with the Catholic clergy could lead to war. Now, more jaundiced still, he allowed his judgement to run wild in the absurd matter of a Belgian, a Catholic artisan, who had written to the archbishop of Paris offering to kill the German chancellor, for 60,000 francs. When the archbishop very properly passed the letter to Berlin, instead of enjoying the joke Bismarck furiously required the Belgian government to punish the offender. When it was pointed out to him that no known legal code allowed for the punishment of a crime that had not even been attempted, Bismarck mounted a very high horse indeed, and in a formal note of remarkable frigidity, requested the Belgians to amend their penal code to cover this deficiency.[19] The fact that he circulated this note to the major European courts and had it published in the German press was as clear an indication as it is possible to imagine that his nerves were not under control.

This is important since it must bear directly on the fiasco of the great war-scare of a few weeks later.

Bismarck had known very well from the beginning that France would never lie down under the terms of peace he had forced on her. Rudolph Stadelman, comparing the great man's attitude towards the defeated French with his attitude towards the defeated Austrians five years earlier, has remarked on the strange fatalism which seized hold of him at Versailles, leading him into paths from which he knew there could be no issue except through violence.[20] How was it that the man who at Nikolsburg showed himself so acutely aware of the desirability of moderation in victory could at Versailles be so excessive? The simple answer has already been suggested: it is that Bismarck had never practised moderation in the interests of international concord but only in the immediate interests of the Prussian state as understood by him.

Here is the great divide between Bismarck and Metternich, who, with all his manifest faults, was possessed of a vision of a united Europe dwelling in harmony and concord. Bismarck was not interested in Europe, but only in Prussia, *his* Prussia: later in Germany, *his* Germany. He did not want a strong and healthy France as a neighbour. He was obsessed with 'the nightmare of coalitions,' with the perils of war on two fronts (the phrase had not been invented; but Bismarck invented the fear), specifically with the horror of a Germany caught between France and Russia. He had needed a strong Austria after 1866, or so he thought. He was sure that he could manage Vienna in the interests of Prussian security: his error was in believing that Austria meant what he cared to make her mean.

But France? It was clearly impossible for Germany to overrun the whole of France and stay there: the best thing to do was to cripple her, keep her isolated, and frighten her with menaces if she should show signs of reasserting herself—and, if necessary, cripple her again. It was not a very constructive programme for the most intelligent statesman of his age. One day in May 1875 Moltke was regaling the Belgian ambassador to Berlin with his by now habitual tale of woe. The French volcano, he declared, was by no means burned out: another war was unavoidable. The Belgian took it upon himself to enquire what another war might be expected to settle that the first had failed to settle: '*Mais quand vous aurez vaincu de nouveau la France, qu'en ferez-vous?*' And Moltke had no answer. He sighed, like one oppressed: '*Je ne sais pas, ça sera assurément fort embarrassant.*' And he then worked himself into a tirade against war even more passionate than his words to Odo Russell: 'Ah, war! War! When one has seen it at close quarters as I have done one can only hold it in profoundest detestation! It is the worst of all the scourges of mankind and assuredly one must do everything possible to avoid it!'[21] There is no reason at all to doubt the great soldier's sincerity—only his capacity for connected thought. For at this very moment he was thinking and quite freely talking of preventive war.

Bismarck's thinking at this time was little, if at all, superior to Moltke's. What had happened was that both men in their different ways had allowed themselves to embark upon a major war without asking themselves what would happen next. They were now in their different ways very painfully finding out. Bismarck had achieved some sort of unity for Germany and tamed its various parts—but at what a price! It seems likely that the fatalistic mood referred to earlier had in great part been induced by the belated understanding that there was nothing he could do within the realm of practical politics vis-à-vis a defeated France except reap the bitter harvest. He was not by nature a fatalist, however, and so, first at home, then abroad, he felt driven to assert himself at every point in order to conceal from the world—perhaps from himself as well—the bankruptcy of the policy which had won a united Germany at the cost of ensuring the lasting enmity of a resurrected France and the nightmare of a war on two fronts.

Against this background the events of the spring of 1875 make sense. For it is only when our inherited awe of Bismarck is moderated that we can begin to understand some of his more mysterious initiatives. The actions which seem totally inexplicable only because it is assumed that, leaving political morality aside, everything Bismarck did was wise, considered, far-seeing, and infinitely clever, may be seen for what they are: mistakes—sometimes quite silly ones.

'Ist Krieg in Sicht?' 'Is War in Sight?' This was the notorious and excruciating headline, blazoned across the front page of the Berlin Post, on 8 April. It brought crashing out for all to hear the alarm bells which had been ringing in the ears of the diplomats for some time past. These knew all about Moltke's warnings. They knew also that two months earlier Bismarck had imposed a ban on the export of saddle-horses when he learned that the French were seeking to buy ten thousand remounts in Germany. They knew that the Wilhelmstrasse, backed by Moltke, was making much of a French army reorganization which gave every regiment an extra battalion—increasing the strength of the army, that is to say, by one-quarter.

They had read and pondered only three days before the sensational *Post* article, a less sensational but even more ominous outburst in the *Kölnische Zeitung*, in which France was charged with preparing for war and with joining Italy and Austria in a Catholic coalition directed against Protestant Germany (this on the strength of a meeting in Venice between Francis Joseph of Austria and Victor Emmanuel of Italy). They knew that Bismarck himself had planted this article, and when they read 'Is War in Sight?' they knew that he had planted that too—the appalling style notwithstanding.

It is true that after blaming all the evils of the world on French rearmament, the author reflected with calculated sobriety: 'Yes, war *is* in sight, but the threatening clouds may yet blow over'; trained observers, however, were not greatly reassured by this. All that was needed to make the sinister picture finally clear was an article in Bismarck's own personal mouthpiece, the *Norddeutsche Allgemeine Zeitung*, cheerfully assuring the world that in fact there was nothing to fear from Italy or Austria, but a great deal to fear from France. All over Europe the stock exchanges panicked. Poor Emperor William, staying in Baden as so often with his daughter and son-in-law, wrote in extreme agitation to his chancellor demanding an explanation. There was nothing to worry about, Bismarck airily replied: the article in the Cologne paper, which had started all the trouble was, to the best of his understanding simply part of a stock-exchange ramp, possibly instigated by the Rothschilds.[22] That article had in fact been written by his own chief press agent, K. L. Aegidi, who had emphasized to the editor of the *Kölnische Zeitung* that every word must be printed as written: 'every word has been carefully weighed as in an official document.'[23]

Not in the least suspecting that his own chancellor was telling a deliberate lie, William took it upon himself to inform the French military attaché that, although someone unknown had been trying to set France and Germany against each other, it was all over now: he, the emperor, would never countenance a war. Even as he spoke Bismarck continued weaving his spells behind the old man's back. He began on that very day by nudging the British Foreign Office, sending his ambassador to convey one of Moltke's alarmist reports. Ten days later, on 21 April, one of his most trusted subordinates, Joseph von Radowitz (son of Frederick William IV's old general and minister), seized the occasion of a dinner party given by Odo Russell to inform the French ambassador, the vicomte de Gontaut-Biron, that since France was clearly meditating revenge Germany had everything to gain by attacking her before she was ready with allies and a reformed army: 'Why should we wait?' He went so far as to invite the somewhat bemused Frenchman to admit that Germany would be justified in such a course 'on political, philosophical, even on Christian grounds.'[24]

Had this 'indiscretion' been committed in Bismarck's despite, as he afterwards said had been the case, it would have been the immediate end of Radowitz. Instead, on 1 May, Bismarck himself informed Count Károlyi, the Austrian ambassador, that Germany might find that her duty lay in taking action against France. Károlyi promptly passed on the news to Odo Russell, who, on 2 May, himself received a visit from Moltke, who talked some more about preventive war and this time sought to justify it on the lines that the aggressor was not necessarily the government that launched an attack but rather the government which provoked another to take active measures in self-defence. When Russell politely rejected this argument, Moltke replied in effect, Well then, let all the powers openly declare their support for Germany, then France will see that her dreams of vengeance are in vain. Had he not been a professional diplomat, Russell might have replied, Let Germany restore Alsace-Lorraine and ask the powers for a guarantee against French aggression and peace may be secured.[25]

On 3 May Bismarck renewed the pressure, this time in a dispatch to his ambassador in Paris who was informed of the chancellor's profound conviction that France was preparing for war and instructed to take steps to dispel any impression of a relaxed atmosphere in Berlin which might have been given by his subordinate Ernst von Bülow in a recent conversation with Gontaut.[26] The pot was to be stirred and stirred again.

But this time the unthinkable had happened. Bismarck was for once not in command of the kitchen. He was so accustomed by now to outmanoeuvring anyone who opposed him that it simply did not cross his mind that the French foreign minister, Louis Decazes, might play his own game and beat him at it. This, however, is what happened.

When Gontaut reported to Paris on his remarkable conversation with Radowitz, Decazes kept his head: not for him the clumsy blundering of his predecessor, Gramont. Quietly and with malicious satisfaction he circulated Gontaut's dispatch to all the major powers, with the warning that Germany needed watching. A little later he called in that creature of high fantasy, the celebrated correspondent of *The Times*, A. O. de Blowitz, and laid all the telegrams before him. On 6 May that newspaper published de Blowitz's dispatch and shocked the world. Bismarck had been very neatly hoist with his own petard: France preparing to attack Germany had been turned into Germany preparing to attack France!

Such was the cumulative effect of these events that even Lord Derby, that most inert and indecisive of British foreign secretaries (Lord Salisbury, his successor, was to write of him that 'making a feather-bed walk was as nothing' compared with the difficulty of making him look into the future[27]), was stirred to action. He dispatched a polite warning to Berlin and at the same time exchanged views with the Russians, who were even more worried than the British. The highly gifted Russian ambassador to St. James's, Count Peter Shuvalov, who had recently talked to Bismarck in Berlin, reported to Derby that in his opinion the state of our hero's nerves was a danger to Europe.[28] ('How much he could do if he were less irritable!' one of his ministers, Lucius von Ballhausen, was to write in later years. 'But it is his temperament, and he as well as others have to suffer.'[29])

By chance Alexander II of Russia and his chancellor, Gorchakov, now in his seventy-ninth year, were about to pay a state visit to Berlin. Gorchakov, still as vain as a peacock, and with Britain now behind him, ecstatically seized the opportunity to round off his career by presenting himself as the supreme arbiter of war and peace—and at the same time to take Bismarck down a peg or two: the two had had an up-and-down relationship ever since they had been colleagues at Frankfurt and Gorchakov had for some time been feeling that Bismarck had grown too big for his boots. So Tsar Alexander talked to Emperor William, his nephew, very seriously and privately about the danger of a general conflict should Germany attack France, and the nephew (seventy-eight) in all sincerity assured his uncle (fifty-seven) that nothing was further from his mind; Gorchakov tackled Bismarck about Radowitz's indiscretion. Nothing whatever to do with me, Bismarck replied in effect, and why, anyway, was St. Petersburg making so much of it? But Gorchakov would not be put off lightly. He pressed Bismarck for an assurance that he had no intention of attacking France then or ever. And Bismarck in the face of the most humiliating diplomatic defeat of his career, displayed once again that amazing self-command which in a crisis he could, as it were, suddenly switch on even when his nerves were in shreds. Gorchakov patronized him insufferably. 'I do not want anything written,' he was kind enough to say. 'Your word is good enough for me.'[30] And instead of exploding, the great man meekly gave his word, knowing that Gorchakov would now take all the credit for saving the peace of Europe. And this in fact happened. Russia alone, he assured all and sundry, had stayed Bismarck's hand. The version put about by Bismarck himself years later in his memoirs is untrue. The crisis was not the irresponsible invention of Gorchakov and Gontaut in unholy collaboration. It was deliberately fabricated by Bismarck himself to rally German opinion and to assert his own authority and the authority of the new Reich in Europe. He had been trying to bully France as he had successfully bullied first the Prussian liberals, then all Germany, and as a result had been publicly humiliated in a manner to him quite insupportable: 'Bismarck has put European opinion to the test and now he has got his answer,' exclaimed Lord Derby.[31] And so he had. Only a profound lapse of judgement could have made him think that any good could come of this operation. There is no need to look for any hidden and subtle or venal motive. His mood and behaviour in all things over the past four years clearly point to the fact that he had been, and still was, in what may perhaps be kindly described as a state of mental and emotional dislocation.

It was still only May, and although he had contained himself in face of Gorchakov he was at the end of his tether. While Andrássy in Vienna rejoiced at his defeat, while Gorchakov went about declaring that nothing more could be expected of a man who drank and ate and overworked so much, he went to the emperor and asked yet again to be relieved of his office—this time perhaps more seriously than ever before. William said no, but told him to take indefinite leave. On 5 June he withdrew to Varzin and did not return to Berlin until November. When he returned to Berlin his actions were more coherent, but although he was soon to enter on the period of almost unexampled supremacy, the great statesman whose touch was so infallible that when he took an incomprehensible step it was immediately assumed that it was a move of exceptional cleverness or wisdom, he was never again to be so absolute a master of his actions and intentions as he had been before the unification. And the war-scare left a fatal legacy: his devouring hatred of Gorchakov rankled ever after, affecting his relations with Russia in years to come.

'Behind our backs, Bismarck raves like a maniac,' confided Odo Russell to a colleague on the eve of Bismarck's departure to Varzin.[32] And even when he returned to Berlin half a year later he was far from restored to any sort of contentment with his lot. Even apart from his diplomatic humiliation, it had been a bad year. There had been little comfort in his own home: his daughter's fiancé, a gifted young Eulenburg, had quite suddenly died, plunging the Bismarck household into gloom and anguish. He had news of his beloved Kathy Orlov's death (she was only thirty-five). His own health had deteriorated still further. How low he had sunk in the past twelve months may be seen by comparing his New Year letter of 1876 to

Kathy's sorrowing widower with the gloomy enough letter of the year before.

His pain, he conceded, could be as nothing compared with the anguish of his old friend over the death of Kathy or with the misery of his own daughter, Marie, of Johanna, also, over the death of young Eulenburg.

All the same, he had suffered too, and he quickly moved from sympathy to self-pity: 'I myself have been ill all twelve months of the year, especially in Varzin, where I could neither shoot nor ride nor work—could hardly walk. Most of the summer I spent in bed. I could not summon up the courage to deny my old master the last powers remaining to me, so long as he would not release me of his own free will; but straightforward physical collapse will soon put a term to it. My doctors threaten me with death within the year if I don't completely pull out of all business, and I myself thirst after peace and am filled with an irresistible longing for an existence which will allow me to live out the days remaining to me in total seclusion. . . . Forgive me for this outpouring, my dear Nikolai. . . . But I feel the need to tell you of my unhappiness, while at the same time beseeching God not to punish me for it. . . .'[33]

The irresistible longing was successfully resisted for another fifteen years, and retirement, when it came, was involuntary and bitter.

CHAPTER XVIII

APOGEE

As we watch the great man wearily and painfully making the long journey back from Varzin to the Wilhelmstrasse in November 1875 (two hours on the road followed by seven and a quarter in the train), still flaring with bitterness and hatred after his diplomatic humiliation five months earlier—as, in the new year, we overhear this nerve-racked titan pouring out his misery to the bereft husband of his beloved Kathy, we ask ourselves how he ever managed to transform himself into the bringer of peace, the arbiter of Europe, all-wise, all-seeing, stern, harsh even, but benign, terrible only to his enemies. And the simple answer is that he did nothing of the kind. The image of the hero above good and evil was a figment of the German national imagination. Perhaps his countrymen had to idolize him because unless he was a truly great man there was no excuse for their submission to him and for their acceptance of his manners: '. . . a ruler of the great Germanic type, lionlike in temperament as in the glance of his powerful eyes; dangerous to enemies and allies, demoniacally defiant in his strength, crushing, pitiless. . . .'[1] It is an alarming thought that the most able of Bismarck's early biographers, Erich Marcks, should have offered this model of a primitive Nordic god as a suitable prime minister for a great industrial power preparing to enter the twentieth century.

In fact this image of Bismarck, even though it ignores the tears, the self-pity, the hypochondria, is much closer to the truth than the commonly accepted story that after 1871 there was a great change. Peace-making is a creative act, springing from a genuine desire for harmony and concord on which to base the prosperity of nations. For Bismarck peace-making was no more than an expedient. At no time was he interested in anything but

331

the security and prosperity of Germany. From 1871 this meant keeping the new Reich out of a war which could bring no benefit to Germany and might destroy her. It was to him inconceivable that this irreproachably civilized object might be attained by the fostering of conciliation, compromise, understanding, trust between the powers: this 'ruler of the great Germanic type' trusted nobody inside or outside Germany. Peace in his view, which he made crystal clear, could be maintained only by mutual fear, by setting one potential enemy against another, by sowing discord and suspicion between allies, actual or potential, by keeping all the threads in the puppet-master's hand to make sure that the governments of the powers danced to his tune. The tune was by no means always discordant; sometimes it was seductive. But the motives were unchanging and they were not civilized at all.

This way of carrying on brought short-term advantages only because Bismarck was a titan; a titan, moreover, who, at least in foreign affairs, could pull back swiftly and with perfect composure if he saw that he was pushing too fast and too far. But it spread swiftly through the German governmental system and was inherited by inferiors incapable of understanding when they had gone too far—or of withdrawing gracefully if they belatedly understood. The most important point to bear in mind when considering Bismarck's career is not that for a number of years he made war and then stopped, but that he cheated and made mischief all his life.

In a word, the Bismarck of the new Reich was identical with the Bismarck who had unified Germany under Prussian leadership after three wars. There were to be no more wars; but the means he now employed to keep the peace were the selfsame means he had used to win power and to bring about the wars which gave it to him.

We are by now familiar with those means. We have also seen how Bismarck went to pieces after 1871, partly from physical and mental exhaustion, but more because he did not know what to do next. He had achieved his ambition by developing to a fine art a technique which enabled him, in Professor Medlicott's phrase, 'to consummate short phases of provocative policy with a swift and crushing use of force.' This, indeed, was the only technique he knew, and he floundered badly when, in the *Kulturkampf*, he applied it for the first time to an object, the Roman Catholic Church herself, against which force of a truly crushing kind could not, in the nature of things, be brought, and when to the war scare of 1875 he brought to bear all the devious and deceitful apparatus of his preliminary sapping operations against Denmark, Austria, and France without the prospect of war as the liberating climax. We have seen how he behaved when successfully crossed or baffled.

In the years to come, from 1875 onwards, he learned how to adapt that technique for the consolidation of his own position at home and for securing the avoidance of war in a Europe over which he had gained ascendancy for Germany by the simple (simple in the dazzling, Bismarckian sense) device of keeping all the powers at arm's length from each other, suspecting each other of subtly villainous designs, and, above all, wondering what Germany would do next. This went on for exactly fifteen years. The old Emperor William would die at ninety-one in 1888, and the unfortunate crown prince, already fifty-seven, whose succession Bismarck had for so long viewed with gloomy apprehension, would himself already be dying. He reigned for only ninety-nine days, most of the time in an extremity of pain. Bismarck, unrelenting, made things as hard for him as he could.

His son succeeded him as William II when he was only twenty-nine. Bismarck had known him all his life, had encouraged him in his brash opposition to his parents, and took it quite for granted that he would be able to manage him without the least effort or consideration. This was his last major error: within two years he was gone, driven out by his new master. The world is so properly aware of William II's failings, of his responsibility for the disaster which swept away his dynasty in 1918 and, consequentially, led to the dismemberment of the Reich itself in 1945 and the removal of Prussia from the map of Europe, that in the popular imagination the truth of the matter is still found in the famous *Punch* cartoon, 'Dropping the Pilot,' in which a fatuously complacent young Kaiser negligently contemplates the giant figure of his stricken mentor, sombre in sea-boots and donkey-jacket, as he leaves the great ship for the pilot-cutter. In fact the dismissal of Bismarck was the most sensible act of William's career. The trouble was that it was much too late. When the time came, so powerful and all pervading was the army he had sought to use but which had successfully used him, that there was no escaping its domination.

The diplomatic history of those years, years in which the Bismarckian system reached its apogee, is intricate, complex, and fascinating. It has been deeply explored by able historians and reconstructed in great detail. It is the history of Europe's advance towards the precipice: what happened between 1894 and 1914 was no more than acceleration of a process already in train. The whole Western world, including Russia, was seized by a spirit of vulgar and parvenu acquisitiveness going hand in hand with an obsession with prestige which amounted to a disease. All the powers were afflicted by this disease, but in Germany alone was it, as it were, built into the system.

There is no place in a study of this kind for a month-by-month recension of that history, which tells us little new about Bismarck—though an understanding of Bismarck is essential to an understanding of that history. For fifteen years he rang the changes on the several aspects of a highly complex character by now sufficiently familiar. The diplomatic juggling and sleight-of-hand, the threats, the cajolings, which punctuated the years of his European supremacy, differ in no particular from earlier performances which we have looked at in some detail. The hide-and-seek game with the powers during the Balkan crisis of 1875–77; the celebrated performance of the 'Honest Broker' in the chair at the Congress of Berlin in 1878; the sealing of the Austrian alliance in 1879, with poor Emperor William once again in tears at what he saw as his chancellor's betrayal of Russia; the renewal of the Three Emperors' League in 1880–81 as an important move in the deliberate and successful attempt to wreck Gladstone's dream of a renewed Concert of Europe; the conclusion of the Triple Alliance, bringing Italy in with Austria, in 1882; the sudden enthusiasm for colonies in 1884 (part of a scheme which had little to do with any desire on his part to found a colonial empire); the Bulgarian crisis of 1885–86, which showed our hero at his nastiest; the crowning inspiration (we are told) in 1887 of the Reinsurance Treaty with Russia, concluded with apparently no regard for the existence of the Austrian Treaty of eight years earlier—all these and more besides were excercises in the so familiar style, at best quite sterile, at worst harmful to Germany and the world.

Bismarck's days in this crowning phase of his career were busy enough, but nothing of even relative permanence was achieved in them; it was one thing after another, the last very frequently contradicting the first. But at least, his advocates exclaim, he steered Europe away from war for the rest of his life! More particularly, he preserved Germany from a war on two fronts. Did he? Nobody beside France had the least desire to go to war with Germany, and it did not require a genius so to organize things that France would not dare go to war, so long as Germany behaved herself. Some Austrians wanted to go to war with Russia, but there was no immediate danger of this happening. Russia certainly went to war with Turkey in 1877, under extreme pressure, but although when the Russians got to the gates of Constantinople a year later the danger of a European conflagration became immediate, it was not Bismarck who averted that danger. Austria restrained herself in spite of Russia's breach of a secret agreement about the Balkans; Britain and Russia (in the person of her most accomplished diplomat, Count Peter Shuvalov) worked out the necessary amendments to the Treaty of San Stefano long before they met in Berlin under Bismarck's aegis. During these years Bismarck's main contribution to keeping the peace was to lie low and say as little as possible. It was a little later that his restless shuffling of alliances produced an unhealthy and enduring tension all over Europe. The quickness of the hand deceived the eye; the eye knew it was being deceived, but could not see how. It was only a matter of time before something, somewhere, exploded. The apostle of peace and moderation was in fact regarded by the governments of the other powers as a disturbing, dangerous, unpredictable element, whose ceaseless activity made it impossible for the Continent to settle down.

The German people, of course, knew nothing of this. It was all too easy for this new, uncertain, insecure nation to believe what its great leader told them: namely, that the new Reich was surrounded by jealous neighbours pressing in on her, who at any time might combine to destroy her. Bismarck himself came to believe in the reality of his own fantasy, which became in fact a self-fulfilling prophecy. On the other hand, when he spoke of 'the nightmare of coalitions' it almost certainly never occurred to him that he himself had created the 'two fronts' which troubled his dreams.

At this point perhaps it would be proper to make clear that in contemplating Bismarck with something less than total admiration I am not suggesting that his foreign contemporaries were paragons of virtue. Disraeli, for example, played at *Realpolitik* almost as unfeelingly as Bismarck himself, if a good deal less effectively. Gorchakov was full of uncharitableness, and a fluent if ineffective liar in the theatrical yet boring Russian manner. Decazes could hold his own with anyone in the matter of deviousness. The English, however, never as a nation prostrated themselves before Disraeli; it would never have occurred to any Russian to make a national hero out of Gorchakov; while Decazes was simply one more gifted politician in the sober (as opposed to the furious) French tradition. The Germans, on the other hand, did prostrate themselves before Bismarck and make a national hero of him. Although some protested, these were few and they went unheeded: many were imprisoned, or intimidated by a very unpleasant police force, Bismarck's police; many more slipped away to start new lives in the freer air of Britain or America. The rest submitted. What they were sub-

mitting to was the authority of a man who by now was profoundly corrupted by power in the classical manner, all his splendid qualities choked
by the rank growth of the destructive forces within him.

It was a poor society over which this man presided. Once Germany had
been rich in growing-points: her kings and princes, unprepossessing as
most of these were, had at least actively encouraged the talents available to
them, had taken a pride in their cities and sought to vie with one another.
Now all lay under the iron hand of the supreme Philistine in Berlin—or,
rather, his ministers, who almost without exception were no more than
glorified bureaucrats, closer to the civil servants staffing their departments
than to their master who ruled them now from far away for the greater part
of the year, from Varzin, from Friedrichsruh, from Bad Gastein, from Bad
Kissingen—but above all from Varzin—seven and a quarter hours by train
(day travel, starting at breakfast time: no sleepers), then two hours by
road—with a trumpeting postilion. . . .

Not only was he possessed by a demon (as he himself admitted, and as
his admirers so misguidedly boast); not only was he corrupted (as neither
he nor his admirers, nor even many of his opponents will admit); he also
suffered from a vulgar failing impossible to reconcile with the sort of
greatness claimed for him: the inability to understand that by trusting nobody, he made it inevitable that nobody could trust him. This failing was
always with him. It was relatively unimportant when he was advancing
purposefully and single-mindedly through blood and fire and every kind of
chicanery towards the physical destruction of those who stood in his way.
But now, embarked on the path which was to lead to the Congress of Berlin and the network of defensive treaties, it began to matter a good deal. So
much so that in the end his main purpose was defeated. That purpose was
to mould Europe into a safe haven in which the new Reich could flourish
and extend her influence. Instead he made Germany the most distrusted
power in Europe. Having alienated France, he proceeded to alienate first
Britain, then Russia—until he brought his country face to face with the
very situation he was most anxious to avoid, the threat of war on two
fronts.

No sooner was Bismarck back in Berlin at the start of 1876 before he
was causing raised eyebrows in London and St. Petersburg as he twisted
about in a very unsettling manner in an effort to insure Germany in face of
any war that might break out.

His supreme fear at this time was for Germany to be embroiled in a war for which she was not ready. A related fear was, as he confided to Odo Russell, that Austria and Russia might become too intimate behind Germany's back. He needed time.

The immediate international problem was a new eruption of the perennial Eastern Question, which had been quiescent for some years. The occasion was a violent revolt of the Christian Serbs of Bosnia-Herzegovina against Turkish misrule. Alexander II in St. Petersburg, unlike his father, Nicholas I, had no obsessive interest in the protection of the Christian subjects of the Porte and was not, at least for the time being, proposing to do anything about Constantinople. But there was a strong war party in Russia, made articulate by Pan-Slav propagandists and fortified by angry generals who were determined not only to march to the rescue of their fellow-Slavs but also to drive Turkey out of Europe and seize Constantinople into the bargain. Austria, in the person of her new foreign minister, the Hungarian patriot Julius Andrássy, shared the traditional English view that Turkish overlordship of the Balkans was a necessary check to Russian expansionism; but the emperor Francis Joseph himself, still deeply humiliated by the loss of his Italian possessions and his defeat by Germany, saw in the acquisition of Bosnia-Herzegovina balm for his shaken dignity. France stood outside the whole affair, interested only in any development which might help her to avenge Sedan. Germany had no direct interest in the Balkans, and Bismarck said so. Ideally he would have liked to see Russia embroiled in a debilitating war with Turkey while the rest of Europe looked on. This, in fact, was precisely what was to happen, but in the new year of 1876 it seemed an improbable issue: his great fear was the development of a war the direction of which he would be unable to control and which could be the ruin of the young Reich.

This Balkan crisis marks the beginning of Bismarck's reputation as a moderator and a peace-maker. But how could he have acted otherwise? For the first time since 1863 he found himself standing on the periphery of events. The newly created German Reich, still only shakily established, was in no condition to risk a war with a resurgent France allied with Russia or Austria. There was an alternative development, equally unfavourable to its position in the longer run, improbable as it seems to us looking back. Austria and Russia might sink their differences and unite in a brotherly embrace from which Germany was excluded.

So Bismarck was a good deal less tranquil than he appeared to be at this time. His domestic problems were accumulating and he was floundering a little in his relations with the powers. His advantage was that all the world saw him through a distorting haze. He had emerged from nowhere to dominate a continent, the man above all others who knew what he wanted and was ruthless in getting it. It was psychologically impossible for his fellow-statesmen in other lands to understand that now that he had put himself at the head of a powerful new empire, his own creation (fighting three wars, proving himself a master of chicanery as well as of the bludgeon, acting always with what seemed absolute singleness of purpose), he did not know where to go. Everyone expected him to lead Europe. But where to? He had no plan. His very lack of a plan was taken as a sign of great depth. Deep meanings were read into every action, into every abstention from action, so that the paradox arose that in a few years he recovered by passivity the reputation for statesmanship which he had jeopardized so sorely with his war-scare of 1875. Nobody understood that the passivity was enforced.

Thus, in December 1875, when Andrássy presented the Turkish government with a strong note demanding immediate and radical reforms, Bismarck joined with the powers in welcoming the Austrian initiative. When this came to nothing (as Bismarck himself had expected) because the Porte either could not or would not make its provincial governors mend their ways, he surprised the British with a very private approach through Odo Russell, suggesting intimate cooperation between Germany, who needed peace, and Britain, the power most concerned with maintaining the *status quo* in Turkey and thus in preserving the peace of Europe: Germany, he blandly explained, would like to be Britain's partner in this worthwhile mission. Russell himself believed Bismarck to be sincere, but the British government suspected that what he really wanted was to embroil Britain with France in the Middle East.[2]

Obtaining no satisfaction from London, Bismarck promptly turned to St. Petersburg, suggesting that Russia and Austria should divide the Balkans between them while Germany benevolently looked on—Britain being bribed into acquiescence by allowing her to take Egypt (Disraeli had very recently concluded his celebrated purchase of the Suez Canal with £4.5 millions of Rothschild money, borrowed at two and a half per cent). Gorchakov, no less sceptical than Lord Derby and Disraeli, suspected a plot to embroil Russia certainly with Austria, probably with Britain and France as well.

In fact at this stage Bismarck was genuinely seeking an insurance policy, and he proved this by moving closer to Austria after being cold-shouldered by Britain and Russia. The path of a man seeking to avoid war while keeping all the powers at odds with one another was thorny indeed. That he had only himself to blame for the mistrust he engendered seems not to have occurred to him. And, indeed, both London and St. Petersburg were in some measure right: for example, France was sensitive to a degree about British activity in Egypt, and Bismarck knew it. When we recall the brilliant way in which he kept open all possible lines in his war-making days, it is evident that he was perfectly capable of seeking the peace for Germany's protection, of working to reduce the heat in a dangerous situation, while at the same time laying snares for the very statesmen for whose cooperation he was suing.

While Bismarck had stayed hidden in Varzin for the greater part of 1875 the world had not stood still, and from time to time even he was forced to take cognizance of its movement. In the summer of 1875 the *Kreuzzeitung*, the old Conservative paper with which he had quarrelled many years before, carried a surprisingly forthright attack on his government which was also a nasty piece of anti-Semitism. Germany had been living, it declared, under the unsavoury rule of Jews: The Bleichröder-Delbrück-Camphausen era, it called it: 'Jews actually govern us now.'[3] Leaving aside the anti-Semitism, there was just enough truth in the article to touch Bismarck on the raw: a rather more selective and discriminating attack on corruption in high places would have been very hard to answer. There was, in fact, nothing corrupt about Bismarck's minister of the interior, Rudolf von Delbrück, the man who kept the country on an even keel while Bismarck himself schemed and made war or peace or secluded himself in his northern forests. Otto von Camphausen was an honest minister of finance, who fitted in well with Delbrück. But there was plenty of corruption elsewhere, and Bismarck knew it.

At first he ignored this attack, but when he returned to Berlin in November his guns were cleared for action, and in February 1876 he moved into the attack in a speech to the Reichstag so virulent that it drove many decent and moderate Conservatives to make a gesture of solidarity with the anti-Semitic extremists of the *Kreuzzeitung*: a number of Bismarck's old Pomeranian neighbours, fellow-Junkers, were provoked into publishing an uncompromising and formal declaration defending the newspaper against their old leader.[4] It was a very bitter moment indeed, all the more bitter because precisely at that moment Bismarck was immersed in the initial phase of one of those sustained bouts of brooding from the bottom of which he would dredge up new ideas. And the new idea in question, far from clearly formulated in his mind, which was to take another four years to crystallize, was by one means or another to escape from his dependence on the Liberals, and build a new alliance with a Conservative flavour.

Thus in a sense the *Kreuzzeitung* had pre-empted his thinking. Delbrück and Camphausen were to go.

The German economy was still in a bad way and Bismarck had to find ways and means of raising taxes. This would have been easy enough if, like any other prime minister, he could have gone to parliament, put his case, and asked for a vote of funds. But the last thing he wished to do was strengthen the Reichstag's power by going to it with a begging bowl. He was determined to raise the necessary revenue by indirect taxation of a blanket kind—specifically he was thinking of a state tobacco monopoly: indirect taxes did not have to be renewed each year by parliament. The *Kulturkampf*, of course, was still in full swing, the country still divided. And his own particular nostrum, universal suffrage, was turning sour: although he knew very well that Germany was becoming a great industrial nation, certain implications of this transformation had not entered his consciousness. He still thought of the masses in terms of peasants. And the fact that his own country, Prussia east of the Elbe, was still overwhelmingly agrarian helped to conceal from him the fact that in other parts of the Reich a strong urban working class was building up, the members of which were inclined to use their votes to return Socialists to the Reichstag.

There was a new power abroad. Wilhelm Liebknecht and August Bebel were the heroes of an increasing number of honest Germans. Liebknecht, expelled from Prussia by Bismarck's police in 1865, and Bebel, a Saxon wood-turner, had founded the Peoples Party of Saxony in 1866 under the shock of Bismarck's war with Austria. Three years later, at Eisenach, they had founded the first wholly Socialist party—the Social Democratic Labour Party. They alone among politicians had opposed the war with France and the annexation of Alsace-Lorraine. Both had been imprisoned in 1872 as Enemies of the State (for libelling Bismarck). Both, after two years in gaol, were more active than ever. Bismarck was appalled. He was to spend the rest of his career trying by one means or another to crush Socialism out of existence. But since very soon he was to turn against the Liberals too, he made it very difficult for any radical or any reformer of any kind to pursue a moderate course, with the result that the Socialists grew ever stronger and more rigidly Marxist and the polarization of Germany between the propertied classes and the rejected proletariat became fatally established.

In 1876 all this lay in the future. It was to be some time before Bismarck finally decided on the definite course at home which enabled him once more to play a greater role abroad.

Until now he had paid very little attention to economic and fiscal policy, just as he had paid no detailed attention to the rapid industrialization of his country and the growing importance of the urban classes, lower and middle (it is doubtful whether he even realized the extent to which the great Junker estates were being bought up by rich commoners). It must have been at Varzin in 1875 that for the first time he seriously began to realize that phenomena of this kind were interlocking parts of a general situation. His skilful exploitation of the Zollverein in his early days gives a misleading impression: then, as already remarked, he had been interested less in the Prussian economy than in using the Zollverein as a weapon in his struggle with Austria. Now once again he was being forced to think in terms of economics. 'I am no real expert in these fields,' he confided informally to a group of parliamentarians in 1875 in that easy manner which always made his hearers feel especially favoured, and continued with one of his characteristic exercises in disloyalty, 'but my present advisers, however well-qualified they may be when it comes to routine business, have no creative ideas. I have to count upon myself to think up plans for reform and to pick up the instruments for their implementation wherever I can find them.'[5]

To anyone with his wits about him those words would have indicated that Bismarck was thinking about turning against the National Liberals, whose free-trade policies were becoming ever more unpopular with the large industrial and agrarian interests, and who were also rather too readily inclined to presume on Bismarck's need of their support. It is true he had nowhere to go at the moment; for unless he could get the Centre Party on his side, together with the Old Conservatives, he could not outvote the Liberals. But that this was the way his mind was working soon became obvious. For the advisers he dismissed so casually were none other than Delbrück and Camphausen, the men who kept the economy running for him, and held the government together during those long retreats to Varzin and Friedrichsruh (to say nothing of the almost obligatory summer 'cures' at Gastein and Kissingen), both convinced free-traders in the nineteenth-century Liberal manner. And, sure enough, within a year of Bismarck's complaint—the first step in the process of coldly undermining his most faithful subordinates—Delbrück had gone, offering his resignation officially for health reasons but in fact because he saw which way the wind was blowing.

After Delbrück's departure in April 1876, others saw it too. Camphausen was to battle on for two years: Bismarck still needed him. Just as in the sixties, for example, he had worked for a confrontation with Austria but did not know how and when it would be, and found it desirable to remain on reasonable terms with her until he decided that the time had come to strike her down, so, on a lesser scale, he remained on terms with the Liberal free-traders, and with Camphausen in particular—until he had decided that the time had come to cast them aside. That could not be until he was in a position to capture the Conservatives and the Centre Party; that could not be until he could liquidate his conflict with Rome; and that could not be while Pius IX remained pope. Pius was eighty-four and showed no signs of dying.

The emperor William was only seventy-nine, and he looked like dying first; and Bismarck, among his other worries, became obsessed with the conviction that with William dead the crown prince would be able to weld Liberals and Conservatives into a coalition in which Bennigsen and Windthorst might be induced to co-operate, thus once and for all dispensing with his, Prince Bismarck's, services. He was determined to pre-empt this happening, pending the day (Pius IX dead) when he would be able to patch things up with Rome, call off the *Kulturkampf* and win over the Centre Party.

In the spring of 1877, an early, indeed a premature, move in this direction was an unexpected and outrageous attack in the Reichstag on one of his own ministers, the head of the new Admiralty, General von Stosch—an intimate of the crown prince, whose chief-of-staff he had been at Königgrätz and at Sedan. This very honest soldier, hard-working and efficient, a member of Bismarck's own class, had taken over the job of planning the small new navy because there were no sailors available. Bismarck had for long been convinced that, like Arnim, Stosch was plotting to supplant him. He now saw him as the most likely successor when the crown prince became emperor, and he resolved to render his position untenable in advance. The attempt backfired. For two weeks after his public humiliation by his chief, the admiral hung on, knowing that he had the favour not only of the crown prince but also of the emperor and the empress; but Bismarck proceeded to lay down such a barrage of libellous press criticism that on 24 March the poor man had no choice but to offer his resignation.[6]

William for once was firm: on no account would he allow his old friend to go. Three days later Bismarck, almost beside himself with rage, slammed in his own resignation: either Stosch or I! And for more than a week he was left to wonder whether his bluff was not at last being called: for instead of bursting into tears and pleading with his chancellor in his customary manner, William allowed Bismarck to stew in his own juice. Even at this critical time, however (and it speaks volumes for his reckless courage, as well as his capacity for hatred), Bismarck kept up his offensive—this time against the imperial family itself. He instructed the wretched Moritz Busch to launch a sustained and personal press attack on the empress Augusta and her circle. The old familiar story of petticoat influence was served up once again, but this time with a malevolence passing all bounds. Bismarck, the great chancellor and creator of the Reich, was being forced out of office by a gaggle of malicious and irresponsible women, the libel ran; and Busch's onslaught was illustrated with examples of alleged misbehavior on the part of Augusta provided by Bismarck himself.

Even under this display of insolence, presumption, and open disloyalty, poor William lay down. He was eighty now, and (with Russia on the verge of war with Turkey) fearful of attack by France, simply could not bring himself to dismiss the servant who had become his scourge. He refused to accept Bismarck's resignation, but sent him out of Berlin on a long spell of leave. This was April 1877. Bismarck did not return from Varzin until February of the following year. But for many weeks after his departure Busch continued to pour out attacks on Augusta, the crown prince, and Vicky. William let it happen.

Many Germans were shocked and saddened by the emperor's failure to stand up to Bismarck and dismiss him after he had assailed the empress and her family so outrageously. The crown princess herself was in despair, and said so to Queen Victoria. Her feelings were shared by many. But how could William, in extreme old age, support himself without this man, who had made him what he was and guided him for better or for worse every inch of the way for fifteen historic years? Perhaps more than anyone this strange monarch, so bluff and open on the surface, so timid and emotional below, understood the nervous crises which could shake the very foundation of his iron chancellor, causing him to conjure fears from the air and nourish hatred and resentment as other men nourish hope or resignation.

343

* * *

For the greater part of 1877 Bismarck was in almost as distressed and distressing a condition as he had been in that terrible year 1875. Sometimes the self-pity would come welling up unashamedly in front of anyone who was there to see. Thus on a Sunday in October 1877 he treated Busch, Bucher, Holstein, and other visitors to Varzin to an especially heart-felt lament. He had, he said, obtained little pleasure or satisfaction from his political life. He had made no one happy thereby, neither himself nor his family nor others: 'There is no doubt, however, that I have been the cause of unhappiness in great numbers. But for me three great wars would not have taken place, eighty thousand men would not have been killed and would not now be mourned by parents, brothers, sisters, and widows. . . .' And he went on, as one war-lord speaking of another: 'I have settled that with God, however,' and then, descending into bathos almost unimaginable: 'But I have had little if any pleasure from all that I have done, rather a great deal of vexation, care, and trouble. . . .'[7]

And yet he was still scheming. If he could not dispense with the Liberals altogether because the pope would not die, at least he could split the party and drive its left wing into the wilderness. If he could push Lasker and his colleagues into limbo, then he would find it easier to destroy the Socialists at will and generally tighten up police rule. So in December 1877 he invited Bennigsen down to Varzin and offered him all the kingdoms of the earth—i.e., the vice-chancellorship of the Reich. But Bennigsen would not be caught. He might have faced a split in his own party in exchange for a genuine opportunity to influence national policy directly; but he knew that on his own he would be Bismarck's prisoner. He refused to join forces with the chancellor unless he promised ministerial posts to two or three other right-wing liberals. This was not Bismarck's plan at all, and the matter fell to the ground. But not without further uproar. Bismarck, it will be remembered, was supposed to be on indefinite leave—sick-leave, in effect; and William was shocked when he heard that his chancellor, instead of resting, was actively conspiring with the accursed Liberals. For a time the atmosphere between them was very tense indeed. Under the impact of a very sharp letter from his sovereign, dated 30 December 1877, Bismarck once more took to his bed.[8]

He was up again very soon. In February 1878 Pius IX at last died, and Bismarck had to be ready to profit by the change. On his very first day as pope, Leo XIII sent a message to William expressing his hopes for a reconciliation. Although it was to take some time before the *Kulturkampf* could be formally ended, Bismarck could already see the pattern of the future, knew that he need not trouble himself with Bennigsen any more, and could look forward to capturing Windthorst and the Centre Party.

Perhaps because of this he was more ready than he had been to apply himself to the international scene, which was becoming very heated indeed, a movement that culminated in the Congress of Berlin five months later, convened to sort out the dangerous consequences of Russia's victory over the Turks.

Even before this could take place, however, domestic affairs once more took precedence. On 11 May William was fired upon by an out-of-work plumber called Max Hödel, who missed. Three weeks later a second and much more serious attempt on his life was made by a middle-class intellectual, a doctor of economics, Karl Nobiling, who committed suicide at once. The Hödel attempt gave Bismarck the pretext to introduce a second anti-Socialist bill (Hödel was supposed to have once belonged to the Social Democratic Party), which was thrown out as the first had been. The Nobiling attempt came when he was feeling frustrated almost to the point of violence. William was wounded so badly that nobody thought he could recover, yet Bismarck's immediate reaction on hearing the news at Friedrichsruh was not to express concern for his sovereign but to rub his hands together and exclaim: 'Now we shall dissolve the Reichstag!'[9] And this was done. The way was clear for the anti-Socialist bill which was now his most passionate desire. Nobiling made his attempt on 2 June. The Congress of Berlin was agreed to on 3 June and was scheduled to open on the thirteenth. The Reichstag was dissolved two days before. And as the plenipotentiaries arrived in Berlin the emperor lay gravely ill, leaving all his ceremonial functions to the crown prince to fulfil. This was the domestic background for one of the most celebrated international occasions of modern times.

Few of those present in the Radziwill Palace at Berlin had the least conception of the stresses under which their host had been working up to the very eve of their arrival in his capital—or, indeed, that even while the congress was in full session under his very assertive chairmanship, at least half his mind was engaged with domestic affairs.

This was one of the penalties of playing Pooh-Bah, of insisting on holding all the strings, of not trusting anyone but himself to speak for Germany. Bismarck's foreign guests at the great assembly, the last full-dress diplomatic gathering of all the powers, friends and foes together, in the history of the Old Europe, had for the past three years all been very much concentrated upon foreign affairs, and especially on the never-ending problem of the day, the Eastern Question: how to prevent the approaching disintegration of the Ottoman Empire from dragging the powers into a general war. All could take their domestic backgrounds more or less for granted, leaving the day-to-day running of their countries quietly ticking over under the more or less competent guidance of departmental ministers (this applied even to M. William Waddington, the representative of the new French Republic, and the only French foreign minister to have been educated at Rugby and Trinity and to have rowed for Cambridge in the Boat Race). All had been surprised in the past three years by the way in which Bismarck, usually so restless and so peremptorily demanding, had been hanging back, instead of taking the leading role as intermediary in the Balkan crisis, which, with proper reservations, they were inclined to attribute to him as the due of an imposing and victorious statesman with no obvious axe to grind in the vexed matter of the Eastern Question.

In fact, Bismarck had been—still was—so wrapped up in the task of organizing his empire and setting it on a new course as yet only mistily apprehended that, for him, the manner in which the great dispute was settled was of little consequence, so long as it was settled one way or another without Britain and/or Austria declaring war on Russia and perhaps setting off an avalanche to bring disaster to the new Reich.

What happened between 1875 and 1878 was that the Andrássy memorandum had, as Bismarck expected, failed in its purpose: the Turkish government either would not or could not compel its satraps to carry through the proposed and promised reforms. The situation in the Balkans was becoming desperate. One revolt against Turkish misrule followed another. Disorder spread from Bosnia to Macedonia and Bulgaria. (The French and German consuls were both killed in the rioting at Salonika.) And the Turks finally threw away all sympathy, even in England, and united all Europe against them, when in May 1876 the news reached the West of what became known as the Bulgarian atrocities: the massacre of some fifteen thousand men, women, and children and the burning of their villages. Insignificant when compared with twentieth-century European holocausts, this enjoyable act of terror shocked our more civilized forebears, still in the first flush of hope in the triumph of human decency—and in England Gladstone's mellifluous thunder so excited public opinion that for Disraeli it was no longer possible to continue the familiar English game of propping up corrupt and horrible old Turkey, regardless of the fate of her

Christian subjects, for the sake of holding Russia in check. The Bulgarian affair was all that was needed to force King Milan of Serbia to give way a month later to the public clamour for war. But in no time at all the Serbs were getting the worst of it; and now the Russian tsar began to find it impossible to hold out any longer against popular demand, fanned by the Pan-Slav militants, for a war to drive Turkey out of Europe for ever.

Tsar and chancellor (still Gorchakov) resisted manfully, holding crude nationalism and racial hysteria equally in contempt. When Count Valuyev, the Russian minister for home affairs, scathingly referred to these manifestations as 'Slavophile onanism'[10] he was reflecting the thoughts of the inner government of the Russian Empire, but not of increasingly powerful and articulate elements in the army and the bureaucracy. In April of the following year the call for a war of liberation was too strong to be resisted; and, of course, once Russia was committed to a war, that war became a holy crusade. So overwhelming then was the Russian effort, so courageous the Turkish resistance after fearful initial disasters, that public opinion in Europe, above all in England, began to swing the other way. And when nine months later, in January 1878, the Russians stood at the very gates of Constantinople, their centuries-old dream and England's traditional nightmare, and Britain sent her fleet through the Straits as a precautionary measure, it began to look like another sort of war. The day of hurrah-patriotism had dawned. All over Europe the dynasts and the cosmopolitan and aristocratic statesmen were surrendering to the mob, or seeking to exploit its emotions, or both; Pan-Slavs in Russia, nationalists in Germany, revanchists in France, jingos in Britain—a phrase taken from the musical hall song: 'We don't want to fight, but by jingo if we do/ We've got the men, we've got the ships, we've got the money too/ The Russians shall not have Constantinople.'

With Russia on the point of doing just that, even Bismarck had to agree to a European congress: and when, with remarkable dispatch, Russia imposed on the defeated the Treaty of San Stefano, which took no account of the interests of other powers, above all defying Britain and outraging Austria by reneging on the private agreement about spheres of influence in the Balkans reached on the eve of the war, a conference became a matter of great urgency.

One would have said that the tireless diplomatic activity aimed in the first place at forcing reforms on Turkey, then on keeping war away from Europe, would have been very much to Bismarck's taste. But he did not wish to play politics with Russia and Austria at this moment, and he was not interested in the Balkans. All his life he referred to the Serbs and their neighbors as a gang of sheep stealers. It was in December 1876, with the Serbs clearly beaten and the Pan-Slav clamour for war rising to a storm in Russia, that he uttered in the Reichstag his celebrated remark to the effect that for Germany there was no interest in all the Balkans 'worth the healthy bones of a single Pomeranian grenadier.'[11] His immediate aim was to keep friendly with Austria and Russia without obviously favouring either, and to this end he worked for a restoration of the Three Emperors' League. But he was driven by events to declare himself, and in a rather ignominious manner.

When, in the summer of 1876, Gorchakov, in a supreme effort to keep his country out of war, called for a European conference of all the powers, and in particular suggested that Bismarck, whose country was not directly involved, should take the chair, Bismarck declined the invitation. To his own office he argued that the net result of such a conference would be disagreement between 'our three friends,' while he, Bismarck, would be blamed impartially by all.[12] But he was soon driven into a corner. At the end of September Russia, encouraged by William himself, categorically asked whether she could count on German support in case of a war with Austria; almost simultaneously Andrássy put the same question in reverse. Austria was easy to fob off, but Bismarck understood that Russia was now presenting the bill for her conduct in the 1870 war when she had mobilized 200,000 men on the Austrian frontier as a deterrent to Austrian intervention. He could not meet it. He could not conceivably stand by while Russia defeated Austria and then in all her pride turned her appalling strength to face Germany alone. Germany, he told Gorchakov, would only intervene in a war between Austria and Russia if one or other of them seriously threatened the existence of the other as a power.[13]

This was the end of Germany's special relationship with Russia and the beginning of the entanglement with Austria which was so to limit her freedom of action in years to come. Bismarck did not see this then. He disliked very much being forced to declare himself in certain circumstances against Russia. But he was so accustomed to his total, anarchistic freedom of action that he could not believe he was losing it now. He still believed he could make anyone do anything. Thus a year later, in February 1877, we find him playing with the idea of an alliance with England directed against France to preclude any chance of the French invading Germany under cover of a war between Austria and Russia. The British were inclined to believe that he himself was planning to march on Paris if Russia went to war with Turkey.

That same month Russia concluded the secret pact with Austria, which enabled her to go to war knowing that Austria would not intervene, that Germany had no thought of doing so, that England could not. Bismarck was still on the outside and was not brought in again until the late spring of 1878, after the Russian victory, when the powers insisted on his taking the chair at the Congress of Berlin. By the time the congress opened on 13 June the immediate danger of war had been averted and the revision of the Treaty of San Stefano largely effected in secrecy between Russia, Britain, and Austria. Bismarck, presenting himself now as the 'honest broker,' had little influence on this. At Berlin he received no thanks from the Russians for working to soften some of the Western demands. Russia, he insisted, should be grateful to him for standing between her and the full weight of the Anglo-Austrian demands. But Russia was not grateful: she felt betrayed by Bismarck in a moment of profound national humiliation. In consequence, he was driven still closer to Austria, so that before long Germany would find herself inexorably involved in any ill-conceived adventure that deeply harassed power might enter into. And Austria was deeply harassed not only because of the disaster of the 1866 war, Bismarck's work, but, more particularly, because the spirit of revolutionary nationalism, despised by Bismarck but encouraged by him for his own ends, had spread from Germany to the component nations of the Habsburg Empire.

The Congress of Berlin was in more than one sense Bismarck's apogee. By a stroke of good luck, the would-be assassin's bullet, he was more absolutely master of the German scene, both in appearance and in fact, than he had ever been or was ever to be again. The emperor lay on his sick-bed, too ill to govern but not ill enough to be formally excluded from government in favour of a regent. The crown prince thus had no powers. The Reichstag had already been dissolved. Bismarck, presiding over the great gathering in the Radziwill Palace could do what he liked. And for once he also put himself out to vie with the court when it came to official entertaining. The Russians and the Austrians, of course, knew him of old, but Disraeli, now Lord Beaconsfield, had encountered him only once, and then very briefly, in London sixteen years before. He was fascinated by what he found: '. . . I sat on the right hand of P. Bismarck and, never caring much to eat in public, I could listen to his Rabelaisian monologues: endless revelations of things he ought not to mention,' he wrote to Queen Victoria. And again: 'The contrast between his voice, which is sweet and gentle, with his ogre-like form is striking.' And again: 'His views on all subjects are original, but there is no strain, no effort at paradox. He talks as Montaigne writes.' It was on this occasion that Bismarck warmly congratulated Disraeli for se-curing Cyprus for Britain.[14] But perhaps the best of all Disraeli's *aperçus* was contained in a letter to Lord Tenterden: 'P. Bismarck with one hand full of cherries and the other of shrimps, eaten alternately, complains he cannot sleep and must go to Kissingen.'[15]

That was towards the end (the congress lasted almost exactly a month) when Bismarck was increasingly impatient to get away from the midsum-mer heat in Berlin. He had kept the proceedings moving briskly, ruthlessly harrying the Turks when they tried to presume on the fact of an anti-Russian front among the powers, keeping the negotiations from breaking down even for a moment, making it clear to all concerned that he had no interest in the Balkans, whether strategic, ideological, or humane, and that he was determined to quarrel with nobody. His completely self-centred and unsentimental view of the Balkan situation was what appealed to Disraeli, who liked to think of himself as a *Realpolitiker*—which in some degree (in a very high degree when compared with Gladstone) he was. But he was not in Bismarck's class. None of the others was in Bismarck's class when it came to freedom from scruple and inhibition, not even Gorcha-kov, not even Gorchakov's brilliant and burningly ambitious junior and rival, the Russian ambassador to St. James's, Shuvalov, who was playing a devious and complex game to do with his own advancement.

For in considering the effect produced by Bismarck on his contem-poraries, it becomes apparent that it was this *total* lack of any pretence of public decency (his private outbursts of remorse were another matter) which hypnotized them. Only the year before Disraeli had been very angry with the great man. Europe was on the boil and Bismarck had gone off to Varzin and made himself so inaccessible that Odo Russell, with nothing to do, had gone home to England: 'And how about Germany?' Disraeli ex-claimed in exasperation to Lord Derby: 'When I am told its prime min-ister is in solitude and cannot be disturbed, and that the Queen's ambas-sador is here because it is no use being at his post, I listen to eccentricities which must not be permitted to regulate events affecting the destiny of generations and emperors.'[16]

But permitted they had to be, and were; and within the year Disraeli was under Bismarck's spell. Looking back from a great distance it seems that he managed to project a magic aura which dulled or blurred the sensibilities of almost all who came within his orbit. For just as the upright Hohenzollern king and emperor allowed himself to be corrupted and persuaded into courses which he knew to be wrong, just as the German liberals allowed themselves to be seduced into regarding as a national saviour this nihilist who piled trophies at the feet of a sovereign and of a people he despised, so now diplomats and politicians who knew a good deal about his bullying and his deviousness began to elevate him above themselves on no other grounds, when it came down to essentials, than that he lied and bullied with greater skill, conviction, and persistence than any of them.

It was as though, as far as foreign statesmen and diplomats were concerned, this remarkable man with his absolute effrontery, his absolute lack of scruple, offered a refreshing model of what life might be for them if only they could liberate themselves from the usual half-lies, evasions, conventional equivocations, imposed upon them by respect for, or fear of, public opinion, loyalty to their royal masters or mistresses, deference to parliamentary masters, the desire to shine in history—and so on. Disraeli, for example, could never forget that he was a Jew in the service of a Christian monarch, an adventurer representing a deeply traditional society; Waddington could never forget the University Boat Race and his Rugby and Repton upbringing (he also felt responsible to the new Third Republic); Andrássy had no fewer than three masters—the emperor Francis Joseph (whose extreme rectitude crumbled when it came to the thought of seizing Bosnia-Herzegovina), the parliament in Vienna, and, above all, his fellow-Hungarian magnates who wanted no part in any Balkan adventure because the Dual Monarchy in their Magyar eyes contained far too many Slavs already. Gorchakov, sly and cunning in the immoderate Russian manner (and now half senile, as all Russian statesmen ideally seem to be, for reasons unfathomed this side of Smolensk), was bound by loyalty to his own class and very much the creature of a tsar who took honour very seriously indeed, even if he sometimes got it wrong.

Only Bismarck stood alone, the putative servant of a monarch whom he despised; the betrayer of his own class; the effective master of a Reich that was not really a Reich because he refused to breathe life into it—the master of Europe, who cared not a rap for the welfare of Europe, elevating first Prussia, then Germany, as exercises in the use of impersonal power, humiliating the Liberals, then raising them up to smash the Conservatives and fight Rome, now in the process of casting them down in favour of a new and carefully limited alliance with the Conservatives in the construction of a Bonapartist state with himself, not the monarch, as the centre of power. How right he was (though not as usually understood) when he remarked in old age that he did not hold with absolute monarchies (though not for the reasons he gave).

What one sees in Bismarck's fellow-Germans was a love-affair with success and military glory, the first in compensation for the past impotence of fragmentation, the second as the reward (at least for the Prussians) for years of patient regimentation in the name of the state; what one sees in his fellow-statesmen was, perhaps, obeisance to a false idea of realism in politics. They were saluting a man who was the living embodiment of the absolute of immediate self-interest, untrammelled by principles of any kind, by any sense of responsibility towards anything or anyone except a God created in his own image.

Nobody would hold up Gorchakov or Disraeli as particularly principled men, but they both had their inhibitions. Like most of humanity they lived in that misty half light which is only transcended by the saints—and by the Bismarcks. Of course, Gorchakov sought a Russian advantage detrimental to the European community; so, for his own country, did Disraeli; so did Andrássy and Waddington. But they all believed in Europe. Bismarck did not. Since Europe manifestly existed, who was the realist? 'The problem is neither German nor Russian, but European,' Gorchakov had written, sententiously enough, in a note from St. Petersburg. In the margin Bismarck wrote: '*Qui parle Europe a tort, notion géographique.*'[17] On another occasion he wrote: 'I have always found the word "Europe" on the lips of those statesmen who want something from a foreign power which they would never venture to ask for in their own name.'[18]

What Bismarck failed to see, with all his perspicuity, was that the holding of a name in vain does not render that name meaningless: his own Bible reading should have told him that.

Paradoxically, the idea of Europe should have meant more to Germany than to any other power; for it was only to a harmonious Europe that she could accommodate herself without fear. Bismarck, as already observed, preferred discord to harmony, tension to relaxation. A few months after the congress, in November 1878, he declared as much in so many words to the crown prince: 'It would be a triumph for our statesmanship if we succeeded *in keeping the Eastern ulcer open*, thus jarring the harmony of the other powers in order to secure our own peace.'[19]

Of course at the Berlin Congress it was Bismarck's immediate task to do what he could to reduce the international temperature. There were certain fixed demands which he could do nothing to change. A secret agreement between Russia and Austria on the eve of the Russian declaration of war had stipulated, for example, that in the event of a Russian victory St. Petersburg would refrain from creating 'a large compact Slav state' in the Balkans; further, that Austria should, among other things, lay claim to Bosnia-Herzegovina. This agreement was completely ignored by the man chosen by the tsar to conclude the peace with Turkey—the overbearing and ambitious Count N.P. Ignatiev, a rabid Pan-Slav whose contempt for the West was exceeded only by his ignorance of it. For him the agreement with Austria might not have been, and he saw no reason to take into consideration British interest in the Straits: Constantinople was Russia's legitimate goal. But Ignatiev's gains now had to be surrendered to save another war. At the same time Russia made it absolutely clear that she would on no account give up Bessarabia on the one hand or Kars and the Black Sea port of Batum on the other. Agreement on these matters was reached between the principals without very much help from Bismarck, and the man who did the work, who, in effect, presided over the Russian surrender, was Peter Shuvalov, one of the most brilliant diplomats of the day, who nevertheless was afflicted with that disability common to almost all temperamentally cold fish—of underrating the strength of the passions of ordinary mortals.

It is worth dwelling on this for a moment, because Bismarck himself set far too much store on Shuvalov. Nobody would call Bismarck cold, but, passionate as he was, he shared Shuvalov's inability to see that lesser mortals had their feelings too. This did not immediately matter within Germany: he could trample on anyone with feelings. But he could not trample on the tsar, and he should have known more than he did about the relations between the tsar and Shuvalov, who was working to get himself back into the high favour he had once held as one of Alexander's oldest friends. He was a man of quite remarkable adroitness and address, a profound reactionary who for most of his life had been doing his best to undermine his sovereign's reforming operations while retaining the confidence he had won as Alexander's boyhood friend; he impressed not only Bismarck but also Disraeli. He was one of those dangerous men who are able to conceal a burning ambition and an ice-cold nature behind a blandly expansive and extrovert exterior. He displayed, wrote Disraeli to Lady Bradford from Berlin, 'marvellous talent and temper. He is a first-rate parliamentary debater, never takes a note, and yet in his reply never misses a point.'[20]

Yet with all his cleverness he lacked human understanding. Russia in 1878 was threatened with war. Alexander, opposed by an active war party of considerable weight which saw Constantinople open for the taking, shrank from war. Shuvalov, with his brilliant diplomacy, averted war. Bismarck backed him. Both these supremely intelligent operators failed to see that Alexander, far from being grateful to Shuvalov, would be bound to see in him the chief agent of Russia's abasement—with Bismarck as his active seconder. Bismarck made things worse by making it perfectly clear to all the world that he expected Alexander to dismiss Gorchakov and replace him with Shuvalov. He went on pressing Shuvalov's claims for a long time to come, and the conflict between Bismarck and Gorchakov grew into an undeclared war, 'the Two Chancellors' War.' Once again the strange insensitivity to predictable human reaction seriously upset the scheming of this man in some respects so supremely sensitive. His cool judgement about Russia was fatally impaired by this personal antipathy.

It is too much, however, to attribute the entire swing of Bismarck's policy away from Russia, the faithful if sometimes rather overbearing old ally, and towards Austria, the old antagonist, as many have done (including rather interestingly Karl Marx: 'The most characteristic thing in Bismarck is the way in which his antagonism to Russia originated. He wanted to depose Gorchakov and install Shuvalov. Since he failed to get his way, the rest followed as a matter of course'[21]). It was much more, surely, the old familiar reflex, which made him show fight at the least challenge to his primal supremacy in whatever field he might be occupying.

Thus one of the reasons for his repeated failures to follow through his own initiatives for a formal understanding, or alliance, with England was that he knew very well that he could never hope to have any control over British governmental policies, even if such could be said to exist. France he was happy with only when he had beaten her and isolated her—and then not for long. Russia he could not hope to command directly. He had a much better hope of commanding Austria, or at least determining the broad lines of her policy. And with Austria shackled to him he could offer Russia a partnership based on reinforced German strength which any tsar would find it hard to refuse. This, at any rate, was what happened when in that critical year after the Berlin Congress he nearly overturned poor William's reason by deserting Russia in order to conclude a close alliance with Austria—and then turned back to Russia to bring her into a new Three Emperors' League.

*   *   *

We remember how, long before he was chancellor, at the time of the Crimean War, Bismarck had exclaimed in the course of one of his brilliant harangues addressed to his then master Otto von Manteuffel: 'Let us never tie our trim Prussian frigate to the worm-eaten Austrian galleon!' Now he was saying: 'Perhaps of all the powers, Austria is the one whose internal condition is the healthiest, and the rule of the Imperial House is firmly established among the component nationalities. But in the case of Russia nobody knows what eruption of revolutionary elements may not suddenly occur in the interior of the great empire.'[22]

To what extent this was a serious consideration it is impossible to say (Russia had been freshly caught up in the revolutionary ferment which was soon to culminate in the assassination of the tsar in 1881). More immediately to the point was another observation made in that year of great decision, 1879: 'If I must choose I will choose Austria, a constitutionally governed, pacific state, which lies under Germany's guns; whereas we cannot get at Russia.'[23]

The year of 1879 was a time of critical change not only for Bismarck's foreign policy but for his domestic policy as well, and the two reacted upon each other very closely. It was the year in which he turned against the National Liberals, abandoned the *Kulturkampf*, and made his peace with the Conservatives. It was the year in which Germany went over from free trade to protection.

Even before the Berlin Congress, as we have seen, Bismarck's new thinking was becoming clear—with the resignation of Delbrück, the humiliation of Camphausen, and the first onslaught on the Socialists. The attempted assassination of the emperor had played into his hands, and we have seen how his first thoughts on hearing the news of the second and more serious attempt was that here was the perfect opportunity to dissolve the Reichstag—and also to outlaw the Social Democrats. The general election of the late summer of 1878 was therefore a critical campaign, and it was fought with such venom that it filled many decent Germans with an enduring revulsion from party politics. Bismarck was out to destroy the Liberals and stifle at birth any possibility of a strong and coherent party for the crown prince to command when he succeeded to the throne (as, it was thought, must very soon happen: nobody expected William to make a complete recovery). Professor Eyck has gone so far as to suggest that Bismarck was not really interested in fighting the Socialists as such, but rather assailed them above all in order to split the Liberals between those who would defend the Socialists on the ground of liberal free speech and those who would rally to Bismarck's side. This may indeed have entered his calculations—and this view is supported by the fact that he introduced two anti-Socialist bills one after another, carelessly flung together and, as everyone knew, bound to fail. But it is only part of the story. Bismarck was determined to destroy Socialism as he was determined to destroy Liberalism.

It is clear that at this time he was slowly but steadily assuming the attitudes that were to characterize him until the end of his career. He was in the process of boxing himself in domestically, as well as in his foreign relations. Looking back, it is impossible to fit him with any party label over the twenty-eight years from 1850 to 1878. He used the Liberals as he used the Conservatives (but more purposefully and dynamically), as he used the monarchy and the army, as he would have been perfectly happy to use the Socialist Lassalle, had there been any advantage in it. But although he rode to his greatest triumphs in a chariot harnessed to the National Liberals, he remained always completely detached. He himself did not realize it at the time, but with the achievement of unification the National Liberals had given him all he needed of them, all, indeed, they had to offer. It took him some years to work through the disorientation which followed the dizzy triumph of 1871: where next to go? It should have been obvious that unless he proposed to continue his career of military conquest this revolutionary (this 'white revolutionary,' if it pleases) was bound to finish up as a Conservative. Not because he had started as one, or had seemed to do so, in the 1847 Prussian Diet, but because he needed to hold what he had—a very simple fact overlooked by so many who have speculated rather helplessly about Bismarck's behaviour during the eleven years from 1879 until his fall.

As already remarked, he did not understand this himself. He still believed he was keeping many lines open. But life itself was closing in and limiting his movements. Not only his, but also the movement of German politics in general. Bennigsen, for example, has been reproached for failing to seize the opportunity to infiltrate Bismarck's government: had he done so, the argument runs, he would have been able to establish a bridgehead for his followers.

This is high fantasy. Bismarck had tried to seduce Bennigsen in order to emasculate the National Liberals. Since he failed in this he had to destroy them. As Liberals they had thrown away their chances many years before.

There was only one way of countering Bismarck now, and that was by an *ad hoc* coalition of Liberals and Conservatives combining to turn him out. If such a miracle combination had emerged, successful action on its part would almost certainly have entailed the emperor's abdication, so utterly dependent had William come to be on the man who now used him as a convenience. Bismarck owed everything to William, and yet he could speak of him as a stranger, as when he urged Disraeli never to trust princes or courtiers and continued with a dubious confidence to the effect that his illness had not been brought on by the French war, as people imagined, but by the 'horrible conduct of his Sovereign. . . . In the archives of his [Bismarck's] family remain the documents, the royal letters, which accuse him after all his services of being a traitor. . . .'[24]

How could a Bennigsen alone hope to hold a bridgehead in face of a man who could speak in such terms of his master to the prime minister of a power to which Germany was not even allied and at what was virtually a first meeting? Bennigsen knew, of course, that it was impossible; but for a short time he still believed that Bismarck would be compelled to give way to his demands. He was reckoning without the death of a pope.

He was reckoning, too, without the malevolence of Bismarck, though by now he should have known enough about the man. The chancellor's attack on Lasker in the post-congress election campaign of July was a model of electioneering at its demagogic worst. Lasker, his fellow-Jew, Ludwig Bamberger, and others who opposed Bismarck were to be destroyed—a fitting reward for all they had done for him and for unification in the past. And it is now that Herbert von Bismarck, the elder son, last seen as a serving officer in the 1870 war, for the first time begins to edge into the picture as both a passive and an active principal of nastiness. 'In the archives of his family . . .' Disraeli's words to Queen Victoria suggest for the first time the concept of the Bismarck family as a dynasty which was to emerge so strongly in the years to come. Herbert was now in his thirtieth year and beginning to fight his father's battles, his own personal ones as well, with much of his father's toughness and no part at all of his charm.

In the 1878 elections he put himself up for a number of separate constituencies; but although his father pulled every wire, issued peremptory voting instructions to local authorities, exploited to the limit the newspapers under his control (he was now using his younger son, Bill, and his son-in-law Kuno von Rantzau as 'press bandits,' to use William von Bismarck's own phrase), compelled the faithful and sycophantic Bleichröder to throw his own weight into the campaign, and especially into the vilification of Lasker (Bleichröder's friend of long standing), it did not avail. Herbert was defeated on all fronts.

These repeated rebuffs must have had a great deal to do with the subsequent exaggeration of the unpleasant side of Herbert's character. At the time Herbert took the line that he was glad to be out of the running for parliament, which he despised. By standing for election he had done his duty by his father and his country; rejected, it was a blessing to have escaped from 'the filth that necessarily clings to parliamentarianism.' Nothing was more clearly sour grapes. For Herbert was to import his own 'filth' into all his official relationships and intrigues. Even during the 1878 elections he began by priming his brother-in-law on the line to take in the press. Lasker was to be the chief target of the malice of Bismarck father and son. He was to be misrepresented in every possible way—above all, he was to be shown as an agent of red revolution. 'It is especially important that Lasker and [Eugen] Richter [the Progressive Party leader] should always be put on the same footing as "preaching insurrection," and carefully prepared excerpts from their inflammatory speeches must be dished up over and over again.' With this sort of thing in mind, it is fascinating to see Bismarck *père* lashing himself into one of his rages after Herbert's defeat as a result of what he virtuously called 'the mendacious electoral campaigns of the Liberals.'[25]

Herbert may have felt all the more bitter because he had failed repeatedly where others had succeeded. There were many victories over the Liberals in those midsummer elections. Bismarck himself was not yet in command of the Centre Party, but he could count on its support on certain issues, and when that happened, the combined Conservative vote gave him an absolute majority of sixty. Thus it was that in September his third and most serious attempt at an anti-Socialist bill passed easily.

Ever since the almost successful attempt on the emperor's life on 2 June the country had suffered from a condition of anti-Socialist hysteria. It was everywhere taken for granted that Nobiling's attempt had been a calculated act of Socialist terrorism. The strange mental odyssey of Heinrich von Treitschke, the celebrated publicist and philosopher, from a violently anti-Bismarck position in 1866 to an extremity of militarist reaction had been virtually completed by 1871 and very soon was translating itself into virulent anti-Socialism: 'an invitation to bestiality,' was his considered verdict on any show of sympathy for the aims of the Social Democrats. Even while the great congress had deliberated in Berlin the law courts in that city had been sentencing quite harmless individuals to crippling fines and punitive prison sentences for offering the mildest criticism of the emperor. The election itself, as we have seen, was fought in an atmosphere poisoned with suspicion; the Socialists were atheistical conspirators, and the Laskers and Richters were said to be of their number. It was at this time too that the anti-Semitism already proclaimed in the *Kreuzzeitung* attack began to figure largely in German politics. Bismarck himself, although he frequently spoke slightingly of Jews, never tried to persecute them; his son Herbert, on the contrary, became one of the leaders of the pack, and from now on Gerson Bleichröder, his father's 'special Jew,' was the chief object of his venom.

So the third anti-Socialist bill when it came to be passed had an easy birth. Its only effect on the growth of Socialism was to accelerate it, to turn mild idealists into doctrinaire Marxists, to polarize left and right, to divide the new nation into two mutually hating, mutually uncomprehending camps.

The depth of Bismarck's hatred of Socialism is rarely stressed as it should be. There was a strain of insanity running through it. Sometimes it has been presented as an artificial mood especially engendered to rally the Conservatives. But in fact it was elemental. The new law was almost bottomless in its silliness. People might still call themselves Social Democrats and they could still put themselves up for parliament. Germany was a free country, wasn't it? Or, to quote Bismarck himself speaking many years before in a rather different context: 'The demand is undoubtedly justified that every Prussian should enjoy that degree of freedom which is consonant with the public welfare and with the course which Prussia has to follow in the politics of Europe; but no more.'[26] Now, in maturity, he detailed in his anti-Socialist law some of the freedoms he considered Germany should be without. These included the right to form clubs, associations, organizations of any kind in support of 'Social Democratic, Socialist, or Communist activities designed to subvert the existing political and social order in ways that threaten the public order and *particularly the harmony of the social classes.*' (my italics) The same applied to publications, public meetings, and the raising of funds. And for all practical purposes the sole judges of whether or not a given political activity broke the new law were the police. Punishments ranged from prison sentences and very heavy fines to enforced removal or expulsion to remote districts. Licences essential for the pursuit of a hundred and one professions or trades could be, and were, withheld or cancelled. The whole nexus of book production was particularly vulnerable in this respect: booksellers, publishers, binders, printers, could all be closed down, and were. Most oppressive of all, the individual state governments making up the new Reich were empowered to declare 'a minor state of siege' for periods of up to a year in districts or cities where Social Democratic agitation appeared to imperil the public order.

The police in such circumstances were entrusted with virtually absolute power, and the new law was hardly on the statute book before they had moved in to suppress forty-five out of a total of forty-seven major party newspapers. And when they had made a fairly clean sweep of all collective or communal manifestations of any activity that might be construed as Socialism, they turned their attention to individuals, throwing many leading Socialists out of their homes, expelling them from their districts, and driving them to take refuge in other parts of Germany—or abroad.[27]

On the face of it Bismarck's triumph was complete. The entire network of Social Democratic activity was torn to pieces and destroyed. The infant trade union movement was strangled. But in fact the very thing that Bismarck most feared, a conspiratorial and fighting opposition, was being born. And the party itself in the Reichstag could not be destroyed. Even under the most intense persecution, with leaders fled abroad or in prison, its voting strength increased. At the January election of 1877 the new party polled 493,000 votes and won 12 seats in the Reichstag. After the body blows of the law of 1878 and the police drive of the next two or three years, which led to a heavy diminution, numbers began to pick up again, and by 1884 had reached nearly half a million. In 1890, the year of Bismarck's fall, this number had been increased to nearly a million and a half—1,427,000.

The anti-Socialist law of September 1878 was only the beginning of a campaign, which Bismarck had no doubt he would win, to eradicate Socialism from the German consciousness. It was not until five months later that he announced in the Reichstag his intention not merely of suppressing Socialism but of removing the very causes of it by paternalist legislation. For the moment he had even more important matters on his personal agenda.

His mind was at last made up about the necessity to abandon free trade and turn over to a policy of tariffs. Certainly the great new industries, which had outgrown their strength, needed protection; and now it appeared that his landowning neighbours needed it too; traditionally committed to free trade in grain, they were finding themselves hard hit by a mounting flood of exports from the prairies of America, the Black Earth of the Russian Ukraine, the Hungarian *puszta*. In favour of protection were both wings of the Conservatives, and some National Liberals; against it were the Progressives, more National Liberals—and the Socialists (outraged by what they saw as a proposed tax on the workingman's bread).

The dovetailing was neat. Bringing himself rather belatedly to contemplate the effects of the continuing economic depression, Bismarck soon decided that protection was a necessary medicine. For quite other reasons he was determined to break the National Liberals and destroy the Progressives. Under the banner of protection he could now summon the Conservatives to do his work for him. In October he was petitioned by two hundred deputies to sanction the abandonment of free trade. In December he announced that he would be putting before the Reichstag a programme of tariff reform.

The real crux, however, was the introduction of indirect taxation, already heralded, which the Centre Party promised to support in exchange for certain concessions. Bennigsen, who was still hoping and striving to keep the National Liberals in the saddle, was happy to accept certain tariffs and ready for a degree of indirect taxation, but only in return for some sort of a constitutional guarantee which would give the Reichstag a measure of parliamentary control over the imposition of such taxes—e.g., through an annual budget debate and vote—even if this meant that Lasker, Bamberger, and others would break away. Bismarck had not the least intention of surrendering what in his eyes was the main advantage of indirect taxation—to which he had so bleakly sacrificed poor Camphausen. And in no time at all the German people learned that their chancellor had buried his quarrel with Windthorst and the Centre Party, so long the target of his most outrageous invective.

Here was another example of the luck which attended so many of Bismarck's critical manoeuvres. For some time it had been evident to Windthorst that the chancellor was on the way to liquidating the *Kulturkampf* and making his peace with Rome: in fact, Bismarck had hoped to perform this somersault quite soon after Pope Leo's accession; but the new pope, while indicating his eagerness for reconciliation, had demanded in return a little more than the perfunctory obeisance that Bismarck was then prepared to make; nothing less, indeed, than the repeal of the May Laws. In the summer of 1878 it was too soon for this, but even then it was clear that some sort of a *rapprochement* between Bismarck and the Centre Party was very much in the wind. The debate over protection and indirect taxation gave Windthorst a most favourable opportunity to offer himself and his party in place of the Liberals. As a staunch Hanoverian, as the man entrusted by King George V of Hanover to look after his interests, it had been impossible for him to have anything to do with the man who had seized the king's fortune and, in the shape of the Reptile Fund, converted it to his own use. In June 1878, however, while the congress was in full session at Berlin, King George conveniently died, and it became politic and respectable for Windthorst to seek a meeting with his old enemy to secure what he could for the widowed queen. His crossing of the threshold of the chancellor's residence in the Wilhelmstrasse to attend a formal reception created a major sensation. Next came the resignation of poor Adalbert Falk, cast as the scapegoat for the excesses of the *Kulturkampf* and, two days later, on 15 July, the passing of the Tariff Bill.[28]

It was in the course of the debate over this bill that Bismarck turned upon the Liberals the sort of abuse he had hitherto reserved for Windthorst and the Centre Party. Towards Lasker and his associates, but particularly Lasker on whom in the past he had so much relied, who even now was highly selective in his opposition, and who was known to all the world as a man of outstanding honesty and dedication, he showed his most unpleasant face. Lasker, he declared, was a perfect example of those useless ineffectuals who are parasites upon the body politic: 'they sow not, neither do they reap, they toil not, neither do they spin, and yet they are clothed. I shall not say how, but at least they are clothed. Those gentlemen whom our sun does not warm, whom our rain does not wet.'[29]

Windthorst was triumphant. The Liberal Party, he gleefully declared, was bankrupt. And so it was. How could any party, right or left, ever hope to mature if its elected deputies were banned from ministerial office? But the Conservatives were not much better off. Like the Liberals before them, they imagined they were using Bismarck, who in fact was using them. Altogether symptomatic of the new régime was the appointment in place of Adalbert Falk of Robert von Puttkamer, a distant cousin of Johanna's. For Puttkamer was a reactionary Junker of the most rigid and unimaginative kind. The *Kulturkampf* itself had long ceased to have any serious meaning, and Bismarck was now only too pleased to undo almost the entire complex of the May Laws in return for a papal blessing. He was, he believed, free of all past obligations, independent of all parties, able to move swiftly and at will in any direction he chose.

This was an illusion: certainly he was no longer tied to the Liberals, but from now on he depended so much on balancing between the parties that he spent more time and energy in the Chamber than ever before, week in week out, wearing himself into a fury of exasperation and frustration. Certainly he was tied to no one particular party, but so long as the Constitution existed he was tied to them all. And since his original stipulation in 1871 that the chancellor was to be the sole 'responsible minister,' since his subordinate ministers were more like glorified civil servants than politicians, since no parliamentarian could become a minister unless he resigned his seat, it was clear that the first parliamentarian in Germany had manoeuvred himself into a position that was barely tenable. There were times when he grumbled his envy of England: given a different history, he would say, Germany too might enjoy the benefits of parliamentary government in the English manner; there were times when he would announce with a sigh that he would have liked nothing better than to step down and give a Windthorst, or even a Bebel or a Liebknecht, the chance to form a government—but the emperor, alas, could never be persuaded (the second part of this statement at least was true). His real feelings, however, were reflected far more accurately in the frequency with which he reverted to his old dream of a *coup*, a *Staatsstreich*, which would abolish the Constitution and do away with all clogging opposition, all ambiguities for ever.

CHAPTER XIX

THE OLD ENTERTAINER

Nobody would deny that the abandonment of free trade in favour of protection accelerated the transformation of Germany into the strongest industrial power on the European Continent and an active challenger to Britain. Even if his motives were not purely economic, Bismarck deserves more credit for this than he is normally given. As Friedrich List, the instigator of the Zollverein, had urged earlier in the century (and as certain Russian economic thinkers had argued at the same time and for the same reasons), Britain, the standard-bearer of free trade, had laid the foundations of her own industrial might under the shelter of a tariff barrier, which was only dismantled when it suited her.

When the new Reich took to protection it already had a good deal to build on. Without benefit of prohibitive tariffs, the German states (above all Prussia with her great extent and rich mineral deposits) had developed a powerful steel industry and by the time of the unification were well on the way to building up a chemical industry which would soon be supreme. By the end of the century the new Reich was to capture for herself sixteen per cent of the global market for manufactured goods, while Britain's share was to fall from thirty-two per cent in 1870 to eighteen per cent in 1900. For sheer hard work, enterprise, attack, and *imagination*, the best of the German industrialists were showing the way.

A particularly clear illustration of this enterprise is the story of the chemical industry.

Towards the middle of the century, when the young Bismarck was settling down to marriage and beginning to look for a job, a number of German universities were producing first-class chemists: after all, they had

364

Justus Liebig to inspire them, one of the key influences of our age. But they were starved of research facilities, and some of them moved to England to seize the better chances offered there. One of these, August Wilhelm Hoffmann, rose to become director of the Royal College of Chemistry in London: among other achievements he discovered how to distill coal-tar to make benzene. One of Hoffmann's pupils was a young Englishman called Perkin, later Sir William Perkin, and it was he who produced the first of all the aniline dyes, 'Perkin's mauve.' For some years fabrics coloured with British artificial dyes held the field. In 1865, however, Hoffmann decided to return to Germany, and there a new generation of young scientists trained by him swiftly laid the foundations for the vast German chemical industry—dyestuffs, fertilizers, drugs, etc. German enterprise was proving itself, and Britain was already showing the beginnings of what was to become a chronic disease—the slowness of the so-called 'practical' men on whom she prided herself, from manufacturers to naval and military planners, to seize upon, exploit, and develop the discoveries and the inventive genius of the so-called dreamers, whom she despised.

The German electrical industry, which was also to lead the world, was another story. Here it was more of a straight race, which the Germans won with ease, so that the pioneers, above all Werner Siemens and Georg Halske, built up a native industry from scratch—and after unification the great firm founded by them, now one of many, was soon establishing subsidiaries in Britain and other lands which they had overtaken.

Coal, iron, steel, textiles, chemicals, electricity—here was the composite base for that almost delirious expansion of the shipbuilding industry which, at the turn of the century, was to complete Germany's remarkable feat of building herself up for a time into the strongest power in the world.

The drive of the new industrialists and engineers was formidable. But the idiosyncrasies of the Constitution were such that although there was universal suffrage for the Reichstag, Prussia, which embraced by far the greater part of German industry, was still governed under the post-1848 Constitution with an electorate divided into three estates according to income. There had been a time when the young Bismarck had reprehended this system. He wanted a division based on group interests and occupations rather than on wealth; but he failed to make a change when he came to power, and in Prussia the system survived the unification and lasted until 1918, effectively disenfranchising the workers and depriving the middle classes of their proper weight.

Bismarck could never make up his mind about the place of parliament. Absolutism he certainly rejected and for the reasons he often gave: it could lead to no good (also, it was inconceivable for him personally to contemplate serving under a master whose word was law, as the word of the Russian tsar was law). There had to be some sort of a parliament, and Bismarck's remarkably vague idea of an ideal parliament seems to have demanded an institution where men could stand up and criticize the government with impunity without being able to coerce it. Hence the stubbornness with which he resisted demands for a ministry responsible to parliament, its members chosen from parliament itself. And yet he abhorred (it is not too strong a word) the bureaucracy. 'The bureaucracy is cancerous from head to foot; only its stomach is healthy,' he had written with unexpected coarseness to his old friend Wagener in the summer of 1850, 'and the laws it passes as excrement are the most natural filth in the world.'[1] He retained his contempt for bureaucracy to the end—even as he turned his own ministers into bureaucrats. A little later he tried another tack. 'Parliament,' he had argued in his 1853 memorandum to the then Prince of Prussia, later his sovereign William I, 'must be equipped with the means to obstruct new laws and taxes and to exercise a controlling criticism over the governmental system, namely over the financial housekeeping and the inner administration.'[2] This sounds comical enough when we recall how as prime minister he treated the Landtag in the budget crisis of 1862—and on subsequent occasions. Until we read on: 'Parliament must never have the power to force the crown to act against the will of the king, or to coerce the king's ministers; otherwise it will unfailingly misuse that power.' 'Parliament,' he states again, even more categorically, 'must be allowed no formal control over the budget or any part of it. Pending approval of a new budget, the previous one must remain in effect. The crown must have the authority to continue levying taxes, once granted, without the approval of parliament.'[3]

This kind of self-contradiction ceases to be comical; it becomes pathological. Here, ready-made, is the theory of 'the Gap' which enabled Bismarck as chancellor to levy taxes to pay for his monarch's army against the will of parliament in 1862. Here, also, is a fair reflection of his political thinking, as distinct from his political genius.

For what emerges from Bismarck's words and actions over the decades is the surprising incoherence of his political thinking. His genius was almost exclusively concerned with the concrete and the immediate. The explanation of the frequency with which he contradicted himself in relaxed conversation as well as in formal memoranda was not, as might naturally be assumed, the outcome of perversity, or a sense of mischief (though both these qualities abounded in him), but, far more, of the absence of any settled point of view, of an inability to think in abstract terms.

Indeed, his brain seemed to function at its proper superb level only when confronted with an immediate and concrete challenge. For the first twenty years of his public life—the first eleven of these as a diplomat without power—the challenge was clear-cut: Prussia must be great; then Prussia must be Germany, and Germany must dominate Europe. All under his direction. It was a fighting programme, and for it he mobilized all his marvellous talent for discerning not only the immediate concrete advantage but also alternative paths to the immediate goal. He was really only happy when he was fighting. We recall the observations of his second secretary at the St. Petersburg embassy, Kurd von Schlözer, in those far-away days before Germany was Germany: 'His whole being is a ferment of impulses and desires, to be expressed, manipulated, shaped. He is determined to command the political arena, to master the chaos in Berlin, but he does not yet know how.'[4] And again: 'The big question is "Will he suit Prussia? Will Prussia suit him?"—This violent spirit suddenly bursting out on to such a narrow and limited stage.'[5]

Well, he had burst out of the limited stage of Prussia. He had given himself all Germany to play with. He wanted to play with all Europe, but now there was nowhere to go without a war of conquest which would have brought all Europe down on Germany—or, if successful, extended German dominion over alien races, the last thing he desired. Bismarck, with all his manifest failings, was too sensible for that. He was not a Louis XIV or a Bonaparte; he was not a Hitler to convince himself of Germany's right to rule over inferior peoples; he was not a Lenin, driven by the insane conviction that he and he alone knew what was good for humanity. He was simply Otto von Bismarck, a man goaded by a restless and overweening ambition, sustained by contempt for his fellow-men, but saved from the nethermost circle of Hell because, sinner that he was, he rarely—at least until his later years—lost sight of the fact that he was a fallible human being.

And so this enthralling bundle of contradictions enters upon his last decade of power, 'all dressed up,' as they say, 'and nowhere to go.' The schemer had no concrete goal to scheme for; the fighter had nobody to conquer. But he had to scheme and he had to fight. As a compulsive actor he also had to go on performing. We recall that letter to his sister, written in those far-off days when he had been consigned to cold storage in St. Petersburg, when he compared himself to a worn-out trick rider forced to go through his paces yet again. Then, of course, he had in fact hardly started; now, eighteen years later, there is nothing more for him to learn. He is the old entertainer—but it is he himself he is entertaining: he cares little for his effect on other people, but he has to keep himself amused. Just once, in a way, we catch a glimpse of his old enjoyment at surprising people—as when at a very solemn moment in the negotiations for a revival of close relations with Russia after the post-congress rupture, he plays on the Russian ambassador, Peter Saburov, a trick he had learned from that fatal interview with Benedetti (fatal for Benedetti, that is) in 1866, when the unfortunate little Corsican had written out in his own hand Napoleon's proposed deal involving Luxemburg and Belgium—and had allowed Bismarck to pocket the note, to be produced with devastating effect three years later. This time Bismarck himself offered Saburov pencil and paper, asking him to be good enough to note down the terms of a suggested three-point agreement. But Saburov remembered Benedetti and, 'assuming an embarassed air,' explained that he was not authorized to enter into any *written* agreements: 'I saw by the chancellor's smile that he had understood that we were both thinking of Benedetti, without mentioning his name. Taking back his pencil, "Well", he said, with affability, "dictate the three points to me: I will act as your secretary." '⁶

But he did not often enjoy himself like that: as a rule his jokes could not be shared. He alone could enjoy the full flavour of his more elaborate diplomatic flights. It was in 1881 when, bewailing his lot, as so often, to Odo Russell he exclaimed: 'The only recreation in my overworked existence is to talk about foreign affairs.'⁷ He might better have said 'to play with foreign affairs'; or better still, 'to make up foreign affairs.' For he was by then embarked upon the complex series of manoeuvres which were supposed to make Germany safe, but which in fact created a trap into which she later fell. To some extent these manoeuvres were governed by genuine fears— those intermittent gusts of panic which drove him from time to time off course—but pride also played a decisive part; so did his need to be up and fighting—when he was not prostrate at Varzin or Friedrichsruh; so also did the need to entertain himself. Nothing but the satisfaction of private enjoyment as an actor and deceiver can account for the labyrinthine windings of his path for the next few years.

The defensive treaty with Austria of October 1879 was the first act in a period of compulsive diplomatic activity which brought into being the Dual Alliance—later, with the accession of Italy, to be the Triple Alliance. The climax was the so-called Reinsurance Treaty with Russia, triumphantly signed in June 1887. Through the years between Bismarck is supposed to have demonstrated a consistent skill and perspicuity unsurpassed in diplomatic history. And certainly, as exercises in ingenuity and finesse, his various initiatives could hardly be bettered. But a point that is frequently overlooked is that this sort of secret diplomacy, which was all very well for a Kaunitz in the climate of his time, was already becoming inappropriate before Metternich's day was over; and by the middle of the nineteenth century, when cabinets and rulers were increasingly dependent on and prisoners of the nationalist enthusiasm, or hysteria of the masses, it was anachronistic. The fact that others beside Bismarck could still indulge in diplomacy of this kind by no means sanctified his practice.

What we are concerned with here is the true secret diplomacy, involved in the making of secret treaties, not the perfectly legitimate and proper art of negotiation behind closed doors, which is nowadays confused with secret diplomacy. Bismarckian diplomacy might be defined as secret agreements exacerbated by leaks. Nothing could have been better calculated to keep everyone guessing and uneasy. That is to say, he allowed others to see that something was going on, but gave them no idea what it was. The consequences were inevitable: rumour multiplied. Sometimes the secrecy was absolute. The Reinsurance Treaty with Russia of 1887 was a case in point. This baroque masterpiece, quite incompatible with the Austrian Treaty of 1879, was due for renewal in 1890 at the very moment when Bismarck was forced out of office by William II, who refused to renew it (to the tsar's distress). But nobody knew of its existence until 1896, when Bismarck himself, from his enforced retirement, referred to it in one of his malevolent, cat-out-of-the-bag excursions into journalism. Today this sort of diplomacy, which bound whole peoples to honour with the sacrifice of their lives secret agreements of which they knew nothing, is confused with agreements secretly negotiated which, once arrived at, must be approved or ratified (or not) by parliament. Secret treaties are blank cheques in the hands of irresponsible politicians; but open negotiations are non-diplomacy.

The Austrian Treaty was very secret indeed—although poor William desperately worked to publish it. In brief, it stipulated that each contracting party, Austria and Prussia, would go to the help of the other if attacked by Russia and would stand benevolently neutral if attacked by any other power—unless that power was supported by Russia. This was the arrangement which for all practical purposes brought Germany into the war against Russia in 1914. Of course, Bismarck was far from wholly and exclusively to blame for that: he would never have allowed Germany to slip into the position in which she would have had to fight if Russia declared war on Austria, regardless of the strength of Russia's allies. But he made straight the way to it.

Why did he devise that treaty with Austria? Did he himself know? His own words contradict themselves so fluently, almost inconsequently, that one could be forgiven for wondering; but in fact the reason was clear enough. He started by working up a rage about the military threat from Russia. Late in 1878 the War Office in St. Petersburg had moved fully equipped cavalry in greater numbers and closer to the German border than ever before. This was partly due to the natural transfer of forces from south Russia and the Principalities to the western borderlands after the conclusion of the Turkish War and the Congress of Berlin, partly a demonstration of Alexander's indignation and pique at the spectacle, as he saw it, of Germany conspiring with the other powers to humiliate him at the Berlin Congress. On top of this, early in 1879 the Russian press began to lash itself into an anti-German fury on a variety of grounds: Bismarck's attempt to unseat Gorchakov in favour of Shuvalov was becoming an international joke, deeply resented inside Russia; the new protective tariffs on grain threatened to hit Russian landowners very hard indeed; Germany was conspiring with Austria to cheat Russia of her rightful dues by rigging the boundary commissions set up by the Treaty of Berlin. And so on.

Bismarck responded to this campaign with public anger and a private mixture of irritation and satisfaction: irritation because he found it hard to endure criticism of any kind from any source whatsoever, satisfaction because it gave him the excuse he needed to urge his emperor (and his own Foreign Ministry) to look to Austria as a natural ally in face of the imaginary Russian threat.

He needed Russia. The revival of the Three Emperors' League was his supreme object—on the face of it a reasonable object, since no combination of powers on earth would dare attack Germany, Austria, and Russia in close alliance. But he was not going begging to Russia and there was no hope at all that Austria might be induced to extend a hand of friendship towards her except in exchange for concessions in the Balkans which Russia could not be expected to make. Austria and Russia, therefore, both had to be tricked.

Russia also had to be taught a lesson. Her assumption that the new Germany depended on her, as the old Prussia had done for so long, must be shown to be false. St. Petersburg must be made to realize that now it depended on Berlin. It would have been easy enough to create a situation in which Germany could ally herself to Russia at, as it were, Russia's request. But the constant danger of a violent clash between Austria and Russia— the inevitability of such a clash, indeed, if things continued as they were—made any exclusive attachment out of the question. Austria was already making sheep's eyes at the West, at England above all. In no time at all Russia might find herself faced with a revival of the Crimean coalition—with Germany doomed either to being dragged into war in her wake or to ignoble neutrality unbecoming to a great European power.

The solution was to go first for a defensive alliance with Austria, the very prospect of which should frighten Russia into seeking a *rapprochement* with Germany and the consummation of which would give him, Bismarck, the whip-hand over Austria and a large measure of control over her foreign policy.

He was beginning to think in terms of an Austrian alliance as early as April 1879, as he revealed in conversation with General Lothar von Schweinitz, the extremely pro-Russian ambassador to St. Petersburg. Throughout the early summer, while Bismarck matured his own plans, the ambassador reported mounting anti-German feeling in St. Petersburg. On 7 August the tsar himself complained to his old friend Schweinitz. If matters did not quickly mend, he said, 'Cela finira d'une manière sérieuse.'[8] Bismarck, who had already gone off to Gastein to meet Andrássy, seized upon these words as a threat. At long range he put all his weight into the task of stampeding William into thinking the worst of his nephew Alexander. But William would not be stampeded, and when a week later the tsar followed up his warning to Schweinitz with a personal letter to William himself, one of those imperial Russian communications, hierarchical in tone, solemnly reproachful, full of self-pity and hurt dignity, the poor man was shocked and bewildered into dispatching his faithful General Manteuffel posthaste to seek an explanation—and then he himself went to meet his nephew at the frontier town of Alexandrovo to assure him that it was all a terrible misunderstanding, that Russia had done no wrong, that he, William, would answer for Germany's eternal devotion to the great Russian friend.

But on his return from Alexandrovo to Berlin William had a further shock: he was faced with a telegraphed demand from Bismarck in Gastein for his assent to a treaty with Austria unambiguously directed against Russia. At first he was incredulous, then beside himself with indignation—all the more so because his own chancellor and nominal servant was far away in Austria, talking directly to Andrássy, while he, William, German emperor, had to make do with telegrams from Gastein or Vienna and briefings from subordinate officials in Berlin. Andrássy was about to retire. Bismarck was determined to catch Austria in his net while her pro-German foreign minister was still in place. He made another vain attempt to persuade Andrássy into a new triple accord with Russia and an equally vain and still more perfunctory effort to get Austria to guarantee Germany against attack from France. But he did not pursue these stipulations: what he wanted now, and quickly, was to tie Vienna to Berlin.

To this end he extended his play-acting far beyond court circles. Even his own most responsible subordinates must be made to believe he feared attack from Russia. Alexander in his letter to William had used another phrase in the minatory style favoured by Russian autocrats when addressing foreign monarchs, at least since the days of Ivan the Terrible: *'les craintes qui me préoccupent et dont les conséquences pourraient devenir désastreuses pour nos deux pays.'*[9] If this was not a threat, said Bismarck in effect, then he was a Dutchman. He knew very well it was nothing of the kind. He knew that Russia was in no fit state to fight Germany, let alone attack her. But with Russia forever the vast, mysterious, unsettling power looming out of the infinite East, it was always easy to pretend, perhaps even half to believe in his own pretence. A little later, referring in conversation with Saburov to Alexander's letter, he was to say: 'I know very well that it was a letter from a nephew. But it is a nephew whose every gesture represents a force of two million bayonets.'[10]

On 31 August he stoked the fires in a letter to Bülow from Gastein. Referring to Manteuffel's mission and the subsequent Alexandrovo meeting as evidences of their sovereign's deplorable weakness, he remarked: 'Any new agreement with Russia would be built on sand. No further reliance can be placed on the tsar. His nerve has gone.' It made no difference, he continued, whether this was due to congenital indecisiveness or to dishonesty: all that mattered was that 'we cannot base the future of Germany on one too easily excited individual, and in all the length and breadth of Russia we have no other friend.'[11]

What nobody knew was that six weeks earlier Bismarck had held private conversations at Bad Kissingen with Saburov (then Russian ambassador-designate to Constantinople), who was determined to bring his own country together with Germany again, even if he had to do so single-handed. Bismarck had been just sufficiently forthcoming to give Saburov hope and send him off in a hurry to his tsar, then summering at Livadia on the Black Sea coast. By mid-September he was back again with Bismarck, now in Berlin, and well on the way to re-establishing the old relationship. But the Austrian Treaty was almost ready, and Bismarck was determined to give not an inch to William. He knew by now that his opening to Austria (though the Russians knew nothing of the terms of the agreement) was having its expected effect. Alexander was softening, but William must not know this until the treaty was signed. William still balked. He would never sign, he declared, and meant it: 'Prince Bismarck,' he wrote on 28 September, 'himself states in his communication that I shall find it difficult to ratify this treaty. Not simply difficult, but impossible: it would go against my conscience, my character and my honour to conclude behind the back of my friend—my personal, my family, my political friend—a hostile alliance directed against him.'[12]

But conclude it he did, initialling the draft only five days later, and writing in the margin: 'Let those who made me take this step answer for it on high in the hereafter!'[13]

Bismarck, of course, had threatened resignation once again, and once again, as so often before, poor William gave way to that implacable intensity of purpose.

Nor was it a simple point of honour on which he gave way. In his eighty-third year William in some directions could see a great deal more clearly than his chancellor—at least when that chancellor was blinded by prejudice and bad temper, as he was in this early autumn of 1879. For what particularly upset William was what seemed to him an unbelievably one-sided arrangement: Germany was required to guarantee Austria against attack from Russia, which was the thing most feared in Vienna, while Austria was not required to guarantee Germany against attack by France, the thing most feared in Berlin. It seemed to William obvious that the proposed treaty would drive Russia into the arms of a vengeful France and calamity must ensue.

He was right, although the scenario took longer to work itself out than William had foreseen—largely because Bismarck still had a trick up his sleeve. But why at this stage of his career and of Germany's development did he need to deal in hidden tricks?

Partly it was a matter of over-insurance. Professor Taffs has an extremely vivid passage, *à propos* of the 'Is War in Sight?' crisis of 1875, suggesting the nightmare fears conjured up by an over-imaginative and congenitally distrustful autocrat in a state of nervous exhaustion and fed by idiotic reports from his own secret agents, venal and absurd, a Bismarck 'whose strange threats and inexplicable demands were inspired by terrors which were as real to his mind as they were exaggerated in fact.'[14] I think she goes a little too far (although when contemplating a man of Bismarck's complexity it is very hard to go too far in any direction, so out of drawing by any human scale was he); but there is enough truth in her picture to make it necessary to take account of it.

Partly it was enjoyment in lying for its own sake, one of the few pleasures left to him in his middle sixties. Although, unlike some others (V. I. Lenin, perhaps, most notably), he did not prefer lies to the truth even when the truth would serve better, he certainly enjoyed lying when a good opportunity presented itself, and he brought high accomplishment to the practice of it.

Partly it was delight in play-acting—the sort of acting commented upon by Schlözer all those years ago when the newly appointed minister-president of Prussia, his tongue loosened by champagne, exhibited such huge delight in his capacity for pulling the wool over the eyes of all parties and all men impartially.

Bismarck *always* had a trick up his sleeve, usually more than one. And he sometimes forgot its existence, or was impatient, and if it was no longer needed simply shook it out without bothering to stoop and pick it up. His relations with England, for example, could always be relied upon to provide him with a spare trick, which in fact he never had to use. Thus even while in 1879 he was teasing and bullying Alexander, torturing William, and bending Francis Joseph to his will, he found time for a game on the side with Disraeli. On 16 September he instructed his ambassador in London, Count Münster, to enquire of Disraeli what the British attitude would be if Germany found herself compelled to resist Russian pressure. The implication was that Bismarck would welcome an alliance with Britain in face of what the British had for so long, rightly or wrongly, understood to be the Russian threat to her imperial lifelines. Münster joyfully reported that Disraeli had responded, as well he might have done, with considerable interest and warmth. On 8 October, however, the unfortunate envoy was abruptly told, without explanation, to drop the whole matter and say no more about it.[15]

What had happened was that on 7 October the Austro-German Treaty had been signed, while, shortly before that, Saburov had returned to Berlin from Livadia bearing Alexander's authorization to enter into negotiations for a Russo-German treaty. It is fairly obvious that Bismarck had here been using Britain as a forcing card, believing that the news of his advances would get back quickly to St. Petersburg and fill the tsar and Gorchakov with salutary apprehension. That card was no longer necessary, so he discarded it without a backward look once Austria was on the bank and Russia to all appearances firmly hooked. It does not seem to have occurred to him, for all his sensitivity, that inexplicable and unpredictable initiatives and reversals of this kind were bound to add to the unease of Europe as a whole. British perfidy was one thing; it was traditional; it was expected; the Continental powers would have felt lost and insecure had they been deprived of their belief in the unexampled duplicity of the British Foreign Office. Britain had been at it a long time. But Germany was not an old, established power; she was the newest member of the club, newer even than Italy, if taking up a great deal more room; and a less egocentric statesman than Bismarck might, with profit in the long run, have endowed German imperial diplomacy with at least the look of a sense of responsibility—which itself might then (who knows?) have encouraged the development of such a sense in his successors.

After the signing of the Austrian Treaty it took Bismarck rather longer than he expected to achieve a formal restoration of the Three Emperors' League: over a year and a half, in fact, until the midsummer of 1881. The Austrians were very reluctant indeed to enter into any binding agreement with a Russia which did not recognize their extended Balkan interests. Alexander in St. Petersburg was much easier. Even before the Austrian Treaty was signed Bismarck had Saburov charmed into a state of dazzlement. He was stern with the Russian at first, then warmly and jocosely expansive. It was a pity there had been this trouble between St. Petersburg and Berlin, he said in effect. He had never intended it. In 1876 he had offered in all solemnity, he said, to go all the way with Russia, 'through thick and thin,' in exchange for nothing more than her backing in the matter of Alsace-Lorraine. Unfortunately Russia had refused. Things were a little different now, but never mind. There was no need whatsoever for the tsar to be upset about his dealings with Austria.[16]

He showed Saburov the draft of an agreement with Vienna which was clearly no more than a generalized mutual expression of good-will. Saburov guessed (perhaps Bismarck intended him to?) that a more formal and specific agreement must exist, but he had no idea that that agreement was in fact directed exclusively against Russia. Bismarck made light of the whole affair. Austria, he explained benignly, needed to have her hand held. Also she was moving too close to Britain. He had acted swiftly, above all, 'to raise a barrier between Austria and the Western powers'.[17] That being accomplished, Germany and Russia could proceed with the task of reconstituting, with Austria, the Three Emperors' League.

Russia still needed a little wooing, but Bismarck started playing hard to get in consummate style. He would admit reluctantly that yes, the unexpected return of the sick and aged Gorchakov to his desk had indeed caused him to entertain second thoughts about the league; and yes, 'It is true that you have much cavalry on the frontier and that our staff are passing sleepless nights because of this.'

In the past he had told his soldiers not to worry, he explained, but lately Moltke had insisted to the emperor that if that sort of thing had occurred on the French or Austrian frontiers Germany would have had to order 'at least a partial mobilization.'[18] Bismarck said no more to Saburov. He left the thought hanging, making no demands. It was a judicious tightening of the line while he was wrestling in Vienna with the new foreign minister, Andrássy's successor, the colourless, quite unmemorable, but stubborn Haymerle, who was proving very difficult. Since Austria was now guaranteed against Russian attack by Germany, why should she allow herself to be locked into a system which accepted the *status quo* in the Balkans? In return for allying herself with Russia she would demand a green light for her annexation of Bosnia-Herzegovina, and the Sanjak of Novi Bazar, occupied by agreement with the powers in 1878; she would also require to be recognized as the natural protecting power over the kingdom of Serbia.

Bismarck was hard put to it to keep these demands from Saburov: the tsar would have been indignant had he known of them. But he managed it, and the new alliance was sealed. Not before he had been compelled to tell a deliberate lie, however. The lie was preceded by a devastating truth. Saburov asked him point blank whether Haymerle was holding off because 'he believed Austria to be sufficiently protected by the Treaty of Alliance with Germany.' No, Bismarck energetically replied, 'Austria would be much mistaken, if she thought herself completely protected by us. I can assure you that this is not the case. Our interest orders us not to let Austria be *destroyed*, but she is not *guaranteed against attack*. A war between

Russia and Austria would place us, it is true, in a most embarrassing position, but *our attitude in such circumstances will be dictated by our own interest and not by engagements which do not exist.*'[19] (my italics)

By now Bismarck's pursuit of his triple alliance of emperors had been made very much more urgent by the reappearance in the spring of 1880 of Gladstone at the head of a new administration in London—a Gladstone preaching with great fervour the concept of the European concert. Bismarck was determined at all costs that his alliance of the Northern Courts must not be swamped by attempts to achieve a genuine European harmony which would reduce Germany to the position of one power among others and, worse, elevate to pre-eminence in Europe a spokesman who induced in him a hatred which verged on the pathological. For good reasons and for bad, Gladstone stood for everything he loathed and feared. Already Saburov was gently teasing him by pointing out that although Gladstone might be Austria's enemy, he was not Russia's enemy:[20] it was, as Saburov well knew, supremely important to Bismarck for England and Russia to be permanently at loggerheads in the Middle East. As late as 1884 he is writing off in something like a panic to Schweinitz in St. Petersburg at the first signs of a better understanding between the two traditionally antagonistic powers. Was Giers, the new chancellor, Gorchakov's belated successor, deluding himself that England could be Russia's friend? Or did he imagine that the inevitable decline of English power under a weak and incompetent ministry would favour Russia? He should be asked 'whether the common interest of monarchical Europe, thus also of the Russian crown, can conceivably gain if England becomes inwardly subverted and republicanized by an indefinitely extended Gladstonian régime. The republic's progress in England is not merely confirmed by expert observers but is a natural consequence of radical governmental principles directed towards the destruction of the ruling oligarchy.' The English crown, he went on, being rooted in that oligarchy, the consequences of its destruction were obvious. 'On top of republicanism is the inept handling of British interests: questions of life and death such as the Irish question, the Anglo-Scottish agrarian question, the Egyptian affair and the socio-political situation in India could lead to a major catastrophe for the British Empire which would also bring great danger to the rest of Europe. . . .'

After this little lesson in the interdependence of the powers, the kind of kindergarten talk which so often in Bismarck's homilies stood out with bizarre effect against the brilliance of his insights, he finishes up by begging

Schweinitz to let him know at once his considered opinion as to whether the current Russian view of Gladstone 'springs from the conviction that any injury to England, even its final downfall, is a goal to be striven for, or whether they are building some sort of hopes on the friendship of that man of whom Lord Palmerston expressed the conviction that he would end his days in a lunatic asylum.'[21]

At that moment Bismarck himself had ahead of him another six years in office. The three imperial dynasties were all to be swept away within twenty-four years of his departure; the British crown survived Gladstone and two world wars.

Bismarck was in deadly earnest about Socialism. He was responsible above all others for turning what might have developed into a broadly based reformist movement uniting honest workingmen with middle-class idealists into an angry, conspiratorial party with a strong revolutionary flavour. By allowing him to do this the German Liberals, in Professor Stern's phrase, succeeded only in alienating the working-class electorate without repressing it. It was all the sadder because, more than most, Bismarck saw the need to improve the lot of the workers, above all the new industrial workers. At first sight it might seem that he was following in the footsteps of Stein: Stein who had stared the French Revolution in the face and had refused to be frightened by the revolutionary troops when they overran Westphalia, had believed that enlightened social policies could avert revolution. But Bismarck was a very long way from that enlightened reformer: 'If the nation is to be uplifted,' Stein had insisted, 'the submerged part must be given liberty, independence, property, and the protection of the law.'[22]

Bismarck gave it social security, but without liberty and independence and, at least where politics were concerned, without the security of the law. In the matter of social insurance, it is true, he was as far ahead of the rest of the world as he was ahead of his own country. A long, hard fight had to be fought before he triumphed with his Sickness Insurance Law of 1883, his Accident Insurance Law of 1884 and his Old Age and Disability Insurance Law of 1889. Historians and economists have argued without end about Bismarck's motives. To what extent were they humanitarian in inspiration? To what extent were they simply concerned with cutting the ground from under the feet of the Socialists? The one thing we can be sure about is that once Bismarck had seen the political desirability for raising up the poor and the oppressed, it would have been wholly and absolutely out of character for him to permit any other individual, group, party, or class to take the necessary action and acquire the credit for it. The state in its care for the common people must be shown to be superior in all ways to any political party. He, Bismarck, was the state.

Of freedom, of course, he had no true conception. Like almost all others of his class, and of the middle classes too, he was terrified of the mob and was determined to crush all who might be accused of inflaming its passions. He was not one of those Junkers of whom the great soldier Scharnhorst had once so scathingly remarked that they were too stupid to make concessions; but he was closer to these than to those of his contemporaries who saw which way the world was moving. After all, in 1879 he had wanted to introduce a bill providing for the dismissal without a pension of all civil servants. And in Prussia, where he had no parliament elected by universal suffrage to deal with, and where the highly developed bureaucracy provided, as it were, the armature of law and order for the whole Reich, he showed what he meant without any statute to uphold him. Falk's successor as minister of the interior, the reactionary Puttkamer, did not need a law to exclude Socialists from the civil service: he simply saw to it that there was no promotion for any civil servant who might be considered to hold liberal (let alone Socialist) views. He also, by purely administrative action, got rid of a great many senior judges and magistrates of a liberal cast of mind, holding their places in suspense, as it were, until they could be filled by officials who thought as he did.

It was a strangely turbulent period. While on the one side Bismarck was weaving his net round Austria and Russia with marvellous coolness and delicacy of touch, inside Germany, at a time when the need for quiet and steady growth in material wealth as well as national confidence was plain for all to see, he reverted to bullying and hectoring as at the height of the *Kulturkampf*. The switch from Liberal to Conservative support had not gone as smoothly as he had expected. He could not rely on the Centre Party—indeed, sometimes he had to treat it as an enemy—while the Liberals who, he thought, were shattered as a moral force had resurrected themselves by the simple process of splitting into two. In the summer of 1880 the best of them—including Max von Forckenbeck, the veteran Progressive and mayor of Berlin, and Ludwig Bamberger, the Liberal economist—formed a secession party, which did brilliantly well at the 1881 elections and at once moved towards the man who had recently taken over Windthorst's place as Bismarck's *bête noire*, Eugen Richter, now leader of the Progressives (who had made a reputation by his courageous outspokenness against the militaristic excesses of a state which exalted the army above all other institutions). By the time the next elections came round three years later they had united to form the Freethinking Party, which returned over a hundred deputies to the 1884 parliament.

Thus instead of standing aloof above the state, Bismarck was being forced to pick up allies where he could find them. He even had to flatter the Socialists to obtain their support for his first social insurance bill by assuring them of the instruction and enjoyment he had derived from his long and stimulating conversations with Lassalle nearly twenty years earlier. He also found it helpful to back one of those uneasy twilight figures of the late nineteenth century who foreshadowed the sinister and all-powerful demagogues of our own time.

The Prussian specimen of this genre was Pastor Adolf Stöcker, a covetously ambitious Evangelical who had been taken up by the court and who now decided that his supreme mission was to save Germany from Socialism. (Naturally, he was as interested in saving the mob from itself as in saving his aristocratic patrons from the mob.) It was through the rhetoric of Adolf Stöcker that endemic German anti-Semitism was elevated to the dignity of a political principle. There was very little racial bias at that time: provided a Jew became a good Christian in Berlin then (a good atheist in Moscow today) all would be well: he ceased to be a foreign body rejected by the natural juices. It was just bad luck that Stöcker's brilliant oratory, like Treitschke's mordant prose, so confused the common man that he thought he was being encouraged to unleash his 'instinctive' feeling, which was that there were too many Jews in Berlin and that they stank. Since the son and heir of the chancellor himself also felt like this, and said so loudly, the common man had cause to feel himself in good company.

Bismarck let it happen. Stöcker's oratory was most helpful in the 1881 election, and Bismarck gave him a free rein even when he attacked his faithful and indispensable Bleichröder. Nemesis took a hand less than ten years later when the revered pastor, now firmly hitched to the star of the emperor William II, played a critical and disreputable part in the downfall of the man who had once disreputably encouraged him.

The 1881 elections in which Stöcker carried so much weight, at least where Berlin was concerned, took place at a time when various major centres, including most of Hamburg, found themselves under a 'minor state of siege,' when at least six hundred Socialists were in gaol simply for being Socialists, when thousands more were being ejected from their homes, and when the distaste for Bismarck's method in general and the activities of his police in particular were sending thousands of the liberally inclined (over and above involuntarily exiled Socialists) to uproot themselves and start new lives in Britain and America, greatly to the lasting advantage of these countries, irretrievably to Germany's loss. And Bismarck himself was so sick of wrestling with parliament that he went as far as he could, short of a physical coup, to deliver the country for which he had made himself reponsible into the hands of the emperor and the military cabinet—and, in doing so, sealed his own doom.

On 4 January 1882 he caused a royal edict to be issued proclaiming that the king-emperor in person was responsible for all governmental policy; further, civil servants were bound by their oath of office to support that policy. Three weeks later, on 24 January, Bismarck himself informed the Landtag that the first minister was the servant of the king-emperor, who was thus the real minister-president of Prussia.[23] Eight years later, William's grandson was to take him at his word.

Why did this man of violent and autocratic temper allow himself to be harassed and tortured by the parliamentarians he despised? Why did he put up with parliament at all? In 1862 he had talked of a coup to abolish the Constitution and he was talking in the same way more passionately than ever twenty years later. He did not believe in parliament: his record was enough to show that the reasons he gave from time to time for rejecting an absolute monarchy amounted to no more than idle rationalizations. He clung to parliament because he needed parliament, and he turned himself into an accomplished parliamentarian because that parliament had to be managed—not for the unpredictable duration of a Western style ministry but for a lifetime—his, Bismarck's lifetime. He needed parliament because in the management of parliament, and in that alone, he was indispensable. Abolish the Constitution, suspend the Landtag in Prussia and the Reichstag in Germany and substitute rule by royal and imperial decree, then William would no longer have to put up with the only man who knew how to work the Constitution, control parliament, and keep democracy at bay. With a profound sigh of relief the ageing monarch would be free to sink back into the sustaining arms of his trusted military advisers and appoint a strong man from among them to rule in his name—a Manteuffel, or one of the newer generals with political ambitions, a Waldersee or an Albedyll. Bismarck would no longer be indispensable or even necessary. So, much as he detested parliament he had to work with it—and master it.

This situation goes a long way to explain the especially bitter taste of German politics. Nobody who respected parliament as an institution (and, in spite of flattering words, Bismarck no more understood British parliamentarians than he understood his own) could conceivably have behaved as Bismarck behaved towards the National Liberal leader Eduard Lasker, his opponent in many things but his invaluable support in others, and a man universally respected.

Lasker died, at fifty-five, when he was visiting America. The United States House of Representatives passed a formal resolution offering its sympathy to the Reichstag for the loss of an outstanding and patriotic member. Bismarck flatly refused to pass the resolution on and returned it to Washington on a technical pretext. When Lasker's body was brought back to Germany Bismarck forbade any government representative to attend the funeral. When some days later this extraordinary behaviour was criticized by one of Lasker's colleagues, Bismarck stood up and launched into a virulent diatribe, virtually accusing the dead man of being an enemy of the state.[24]

The time was January 1884. It has been argued in Bismarck's defence that the elections then taking place were exceptionally bitter, with the new Freethinking Party making its début and the Socialists staging a comeback. But this was not the first time he had behaved disgracefully in face of this very distinguished politician and jurist, whose real offence was to exhibit more independence of mind than most of his fellow-Liberals. The first time had been during the 1878 elections referred to earlier, when Herbert Bismarck had been standing for the Reichstag in a number of constituencies and his father's bought press was instructed by Herbert that Lasker was to be smeared and misrepresented in every possible way.[25]

It is a matter of record that these three election campaigns—1878, 1881, and 1884 filled so many decent Germans with such disgust that, to their own terrible cost, they left politics to the gutter. The man responsible for this disaster was the great hero-statesman who could not bring himself to pay tribute, or allow others to pay tribute, to a devoted colleague and patriot, now dead—for no other reason than that on occasion that colleague had dared oppose him.

*   *   *

At the time of the 1878 elections, Herbert was twenty-nine. Soon after his electioneering failure he began to move upwards, and before long it was clear that the chancellor saw in his son his ultimate successor.

Certainly he brought Herbert along very fast. The young man served for over a year as first secretary at the London embassy, was then promoted minister at The Hague, and in 1885 at thirty-six, became deputy secretary of state under the able but extremely idle Count Paul von Hatzfeldt. It was only a matter of time before Hatzfeldt, squeezed between two Bismarcks, threw in his hand and Herbert took over from him. This was in 1886, when Herbert was still only thirty-seven. His father exaggerated his successes, ignored his rudeness and his heavy drinking, seemed oblivious of his lack of subtlety and his vile temper. At home he kept his son down and snubbed him outrageously; in the Wilhelmstrasse he could do no wrong. This may have been in part because the father knew in his heart that he had wrecked his son's private life, when, in 1881 he categorically forbade him to marry the Princess Elisabeth Carolath—with whom he had fallen heavily in love. It was an astonishing situation. Elisabeth Carolath, born Hatzfeldt (a distant cousin of the state secretary) was unhappily married and now put her divorce in train to marry Herbert. Herbert was a grown man of thirty-two, and by temperament violent and demanding. But his terrible father wore him down, raging and weeping, pleading, threatening, promising. He would kill himself, he declared, if Herbert married the princess. He would cut him off without a penny. Instead of simply walking away from this insane performance and telling his father what he thought of him, Herbert, worn to rags, gave in. The unfortunate princess was left naked, as it was, to face a scandalized and scandalizing world. William I was not the only man who could not stand up to Bismarck.

And what was it all about? Nobody was ever told. We remember the furious outburst to Roon years earlier about the postmaster at Frankfurt. . . . It seems most likely that Elisabeth was considered to be consorting with the enemy. She was closely related to Schleinitz, one time foreign minister, Bismarck's chief in his St. Petersburg days, and the confidant of the empress Augusta his old enemy, who for many years had been the minister for the royal household. Bismarck, who still in his eighties spent sleepless nights burning with hatred for the schoolmasters of his youth, would have rejected with all his being any family connection with this abhorred creature.

* * *

And yet this man who was so often a monster could still appear as a charmer, worth a hundred, a thousand, ten thousand ordinary men.

To most people he turned a stony and rejecting countenance, when he was not actively bullying them. 'It was a psychological necessity for Bismarck to make his power felt by tormenting, harrying, ill-treating people. His pessimistic view of life which had long since blighted every human pleasure left him with only one source of amusement, and future historians will be forced to recognize that the Bismarck régime was a constant orgy of scorn and abuse of mankind collectively and individually.'[26]

This was Holstein in his memoirs. Admittedly in his later years Holstein had come to hate his old master of the Petersburg years; but he had a shrewd eye, and in fact he is saying little more in that depressing indictment than Schlözer had said in his letters from St. Petersburg twenty years earlier.

And yet he could still suddenly come alight. Thus in those bleak, lost days in 1875, when the man who had looked as though he would develop into a great statesman now that Germany was firmly established and could dispense with diplomatic trickery and iron and blood, began to reveal himself as something a good deal less than that, his old friend Motley could visit him at Varzin and, translated into paradise, be warmed and stimulated by the affectionate welcome and the brilliant conversation of the old friend who could behave towards him with that self-deprecatory modesty which he could still on occasion produce with such humbling effect. His charm on those rare occasions must have dazzled: this vast, gross monument of a battered hero with all the cares of the universe on his shoulders, suddenly bursting into radiance. . . .

Since the days of Kathy Orlov there had been precious little radiance in his life. He loved his family with a jealous love, and cherished Johanna as the centre of an existence that lacked any centre of its own. But many years had passed since he had been deeply involved in her life. 'Despite all love,' wrote one of his most faithful admirers, who had a critical eye nevertheless, Baroness Hildegard von Spitzemberg, he was 'not very interested in the personal lives of his family. Even in the midst of wife and children there is a peculiar aloofness about him.'[27] This aloofness was ever present, unaffected by the stream of almost compulsive comment and reminiscence, usually highly indiscreet, with which he favoured anyone who might be there to listen. Many years earlier, in 1851, when he had been trying to prepare Johanna for the great world at Frankfurt, apologizing for dragging her from contented obscurity into the world of fashion, explaining how he is paving the way for her by making friends with the wives of some of the great aristocrats of Europe, begging her to learn French, revealing himself as eaten up by ambition even while he made fun of ambition's appurtenances, he had added in effect: never mind, my beloved, if you don't want to learn French the others can learn German; 'I married you to love you in God for your own sake and for my own heart's needs and to have a place for my heart in an alien world, to escape from the chill of all the barren winds that blow and to find the warm fire burning in the hearth to draw near to when outside is frost and storm; not to possess a fashionable wife for the society of others. . . .'[28]

Well, Johanna gave him a fireside. But as the years went by he sank deeper into himself. 'He was very sensitive to bodily pain and discomfort,' wrote an anonymous observer, 'from which he suffered severely, even to the point of tears. He complained a lot at times in an exaggerated way. At such times he had a need to be sympathized with by those nearest him and to be treated lovingly, and he was bitter if this did not happen in sufficient measure.'[29]

Johanna cared for him in illness, stood by him in his long periods of depression or fulminating rage, fed him far too much and too richly; but she provided no intellectual stimulus whatsoever. Bismarck of course did not want it; but once he had opened to her the storehouse of his experience and taught her the elements required of a diplomat's wife there can have been very little left for them to talk about. Except gossip. Johanna was a glutton for gossip, and her tongue became more malicious with time, so that in later years the Bismarck drawing-room became less and less frequented: people feared her and found the malice too much. Apart from the delights of gossip and scandal-mongering, she found her pleasure now in her grandchildren, whom she adored. The rest of the world counted for very little. Her husband himself must have felt on occasion somewhat of a *tertium quid*. With his paranoid fixation on petticoat intrigue, with his suspicion of a court dominated by his great enemy the empress and her daughter-in-law, the crown princess, he needed a refuge. He needed a home. The beloved woods were his, but the houses were for all practical purposes Johanna's. And Johanna ran them very much for the children and the grandchildren.

He could no longer ride. He could enjoy his trees and make money from his timber, but otherwise he could only eat and drink and scheme. He was eating himself to death, and Johanna seemed to be abetting him. At sixty-eight he weighed just on twenty stone. The head of his chancellery, Christoph von Tiedemann, a favoured guest at Varzin, was particularly fascinated by his master's eating habits. 'They eat here always until the walls burst,' he reported to his wife in 1880. Luncheon was a massive meal, with a roast and game. Dinner had 'six heavy courses followed by dessert. At midnight tea was brought round. Next morning, as always, Bismarck complained of sleeplessness.' To another visitor he complained that it was often seven in the morning before he fell asleep, but then spoiled the effect by adding that he slept on until two in the afternoon.

On another occasion Tiedemann recounted how Bismarck, having complained that he had no appetite, immediately fell to and made short work of a 'three-man portion of every course.' Apparently when the great man had a stomach upset Johanna was in the habit of comforting him with the best *foie gras*. On one occasion, when her husband was thus suffering, she telegraphed to Berlin for a fresh supply. When the handsome terrine was presented at table next day Tiedemann was fascinated by his master's behaviour. He, of course, had the first go at it, taking out a very large segment; and then, as it made the round of the table, followed it with a jealous eye so obvious that nobody else dared help himself to more than a token portion. When it came back to him, scarcely diminished, he finished it off.[30]

In 1883, when Bismarck was sixty-eight, Johanna belatedly took fright at her husband's condition. His illnesses over the past decade had read like a medical dictionary: neuralgia, rheumatism, gout, migraine, gall-stones, varicose veins, influenza, jaundice, shingles, piles, gastric upsets, constipation, stomach-aches and cramps. As early as 1872 he had written to William complaining of 'this pressure on my brain that makes everything that lies behind my eyes seem like a glutinous mass. I am not able to hold my thoughts continuously. In addition there is this unbearable pressure on my stomach, with unspeakable pains.'[31]

Now the doctors decided that he had cancer too. Johanna went into action and got hold of Ernst Schweninger, a faintly raffish and disreputable character who had been struck off the register for a sexual offence against the medical proprieties, and had built himself up a fashionable and rather dashing unofficial practice in Berlin. Schweninger had more character than either the emperor or Herbert. You will do as I tell you, he announced in effect to his formidable new patient, or I shall abandon you. For a start you will give up food and drink.

The very brash young man had nothing to lose by being thrown out and everything to gain by staying. He stayed. Bismarck must have been frightened. He obeyed his new doctor. It was discovered that the cancer was a false alarm. Schweninger took up residence in the Bismarck household, proceeded to order his august patient about as though he were a delinquent schoolboy, put him on a strict diet (mainly fish, which meant mainly pickled herring), drastically curtailed his drinking, persuaded him that it was possible to relax sufficiently to enjoy a good night's sleep, and taught him how to do so. There was nothing magical about his treatment, only force of a will that must have had a hypnotic quality. Schweninger started his régime in November. At Christmas Bismarck wrote to William in a letter of unrelieved flattery and apparently deeply felt obligation (compare his remarks about poor William to Odo Russell and others) that his health had so much improved that for the first time in many years he had been able to ride for several hours in his woods with Herbert and Bill. He was careful, however, to add that, although physically much better, he was not yet quite up to the stresses of mental work. . . .[32]

CHAPTER XX

UNHAPPY ENDING

Very soon he was back in the Wilhelmstrasse physically transformed and with his celebrated 'nerves' under better control than for many years past. Only three years earlier, in 1881, he had been worrying himself almost into a state of nervous collapse at the news of the assassination of Alexander II before the final ratification of the treaty which set up the Three Emperors' League. Two fears had then seized him: would the new tsar, Alexander III, noted for his dislike of Germans, back out of his father's agreement? Worse, was Russia on the edge of revolution? It seemed most frighteningly likely. What would the Poles do if the Russian Empire fell apart? How long would it take for red chaos to spread to Germany? Bismarck had made no attempt to hide his extreme agitation. Schweinitz, long suffering in St. Petersburg, was urgently enjoined to dispatch without fail a morning and an evening telegram every day until further notice reporting all well; if no telegram arrived, then the chancellor would know that revolution had broken out. . . .

He was never again to display this sort of open panic: henceforth his nervous tension, still frequently close to breaking point, found sufficient release in bad temper, bullying, and passages of almost perversely complex diplomacy. On the whole he seemed, thanks to Dr. Schweninger, to be enjoying these last years.

But to what end? We are now well into the final period of his career, which too many historians (by no means all of them idolators of Bismarck) have held up as his crowning glory. We are asked to kneel in admiration of the stupendous virtuosity of this man, now nearing his seventies, but positively exploding with youthful vitality, ripe with the wisdom of the ages, wily as the serpent, holding all Europe in the palm of his great hand, commanding peace. Virtuosity there was; but more often than not it was brilliance in a void. Bismarck's restless, endless sequence of devices and expedients, bewildering in its wanton complication, when contemplated with a less than loving eye appears not so much as a series of solutions, even temporary solutions (which in fairness to him is all that he, as distinct from his adorers, would have claimed) to real problems as instant responses to factitious problems manufactured for the occasion by the solver.

He had by all means created a power in the centre of Europe which had to be taken into active consideration by any other power contemplating any action anywhere in the world. That power, drilled and heavily armed, was in a position, simply by virtue of its formidable presence, to keep the peace of Europe at least as effectively as Britain was keeping the peace of the seas. But this was not enough for Bismarck. Certainly, and all credit to him, he wished to keep Germany out of war. Equally certainly he was not content to sit still. He wished not only to maintain the peace but also to command it and to be seen to be commanding it.

The trouble was that although he was indeed the most commanding figure in Europe he could no longer control events as he had controlled them in that blissful dawn when all problems could be solved by Prussia's bright sword. What had made him what he was, what had distinguished him from all other statesmen of his time, was his capacity for positive and purposeful action. From his early days in Frankfurt he had cut his own way, bending others to his will or breaking them. It is easy to be purposeful when planning for war, less easy when planning for a peace which will nevertheless secure your position at the top of the heap. The conclusion of the Three Emperors' League may be seen as the last of his actions forming a part of a calculated pattern. Henceforth he ceased to act positively and was limited to *reacting* to changing circumstances or the actions of others. And even though his reactions were often bold and brilliantly ingenious, so that to the world they appeared as aspects of a complex but unfathomable design, he himself must have realized, had he sat back and considered his position, that he was now almost permanently on the defensive: even the celebrated Reinsurance Treaty was no more than an expedient, an attempt to escape from a dangerous situation, not, as he later boasted, a diplomatic master-stroke.

So many of his fears were as baseless as his fears of a Russian revolution in 1881. That revolution was not even attempted for another twenty-four years. It did not succeed until 1917, and then only as a direct consequence of the 1914 war, which itself was very largely a no less direct consequence of Bismarck's Austro-German Alliance of 1879. The killing of Alexander II, in a word, was the last effective revolutionary action for years to come. The terrorists, pathetically few, were crushed. The new unbending tsar certainly despised all foreigners in the grandest and stiffest Russian manner, Germans above all; but he was a dynast first, and he took for granted the need for solidarity with his fellow-monarchs—provided this did not conflict with what Bismarck would have called the vital interests of his realm. Sooner or later these vital interests, real or imagined, were bound to collide in the Balkans with those of Austria, but until that happened the Three Emperors' League was safe. It had no teeth, however, and only those intoxicated with the beauty of diplomatic finesse for its own sake could admire it as a masterpiece. What was it intended to achieve? Instead of exercising his genius to steer the jealous and uneasy rivals, Austria and Russia, away from the danger area, Bismarck, reposing a profound faith with no discernible foundation on this highly artificial imperial alliance, positively threw them at each other.

The most that can be said is that it gave him a breathing-space, and perhaps this is all he asked. Contrary to legend, he was never a man to look, except in the narrowest sense, far ahead. The capacity to set a course for a limited objective, a particular and distant goal, is not the same as looking ahead: it calls for the one-track concentration, the patience and swift opportunism of the hunter rather than the questing, exploring vision of the statesman. Bismarck had the swiftest, subtlest, most exact perceptions of everything in the immediate field of vision which might conceivably bear on the fulfilment of a simple and clearly formulated purpose; but there was never any question of building for the future. This may have been due in part to that paradoxical streak of humility which showed up so strangely against the self-assurance of this most overbearing of men—a humility expressed from time to time in his observations on the limitations of statecraft and the need to go with the tide—or attend to the sound of the Almighty's footfall. But it was also in very large part due to an absence of human understanding. When all his powers were directed towards the execution of the task in hand, whether the contriving of a major war, the destruction of an individual who had crossed his path, the winning of an election, the negotiation of a treaty, or the brain-washing of his sovereign, he too frequently lost sight of not very distant consequences—as, for example, of the war with France in 1870 and still more the peace terms of 1871.

He could indeed be blind. For example, it is impossible to believe that the creator of the Three Emperors' League had appreciated the inevitability of Austro-Russian conflict in the Balkans unless a sharp and sustained congress of all the powers could meet, excogitate, arrive at an agreed solution (which must also include an agreed solution to the Anglo-Russian quarrel over the Straits), and set up the machinery to impose it. There was an astonishing blindness here. And there was an astonishing blindness about his approaches to France after the departure of MacMahon from the presidency in 1879. Jules Ferry, who became premier in 1880, was known to be more interested in imperial expansion than in Europe, and Bismarck decided to exploit this preoccupation in the interest of a Franco-German reconciliation. He seems to have believed that all he had to do to persuade the French to fall into his arms with tears of gratitude and submission was to support them in their colonial adventures, especially when such support could appear to be directed against England.

Ferry may have been more interested in Indo-China than in the Rhine, but even if he himself (although born at St.-Dié in the heart of the Vosges) was ready to forget Alsace-Lorraine in exchange for Bismarck's good offices in the larger world, he would never have been allowed to do so. At the height of his wooing, in November 1888, Bismarck confided to the French ambassador in Berlin, the baron de Courcel, that his constant anxiety since 1871 had been to conduct himself in such a manner that France might come to 'forgive Sedan as she had earlier forgiven Waterloo. . . .'[1]

Something was going very badly wrong with the quality of our hero's judgement if he believed this could happen. At the same time he was, to all appearances, trying to tempt Ferry with the dream of a grand Continental system directed against Britain's maritime supremacy and calling for determined French activity against the British in Egypt.

In the following year the French suffered a defeat in Tonkin and Ferry went down, sunk by the big guns of a comparative newcomer, a new portent for Germany, the vengeful radical Georges Clemenceau, who had Sedan written on his heart, to say nothing of Strasbourg and Metz, and was now developing the powers that for the next thirty-five years were to be largely devoted to the undoing of Bismarck's Germany. In that year, too, the Three Emperors' League fell to pieces when a grand crisis blew up in Bulgaria, bringing Austria and Russia once more angrily face-to-face.

In so far as Bismarck at this time was making any sense at all it seems likely that he was governed by two false assumptions: the assumption that both France and Russia were so exclusively obsessed with their differences with England that each would be ready to pay heavily for German backing; and the assumption that Austria could be relied on to bow to his will. In fact he had no proper conception of the Austria, the Austria-Hungary, rather, of the 1880s—when Budapest, as opposed to Vienna, was making the pace, when the old Emperor Francis Joseph was being driven to distraction in his vain effort to control and subdue the fervid nationalism which he, Bismarck, had for his own purposes done so much to encourage: Austria was gathering the momentum of desperation which was to sweep her into the abyss—and with her Germany, shackled to her by Bismarck.

There is no doubt that Schweninger gave Bismarck a new life. What did he do with it? Certainly nothing to prepare his country and his government for the day when he would be gone. On occasion he murmured that he feared all would be lost, undone, when he was no longer there to put things right. But he took no action to prevent the fulfilment of that prophecy. He seemed, moreover, content to concentrate his hopes for the future, such as they were, on his son Herbert, who was, to say the least, an inadequate repository for even such minimal treasure. Herbert was growing nastier as he grew older: arrogant, coarse, drunken (in fairness, it should be recorded that he managed in England to make friends with Lord Rosebery—a strange choice for this violent anti-Semite, since Rosebery had recently married a Rothschild), and the nastier he became the more his father seemed to admire him. Holstein, who saw a great deal of both of them in these years, observed that the old man thought his son must be a good judge of men because he was 'even more mistrustful and pessimistic' than himself.[2] Of course, Herbert was by no means a nonentity, but he was a light-weight, and to cast him as the successor to an autocrat of genius was ludicrous: even when he was promoted to be foreign minister in 1886 he had to function as his father's voice.

The family mood at this time, at Varzin, at Friedrichsruh, bears very directly on the public face of Bismarck. It was philistine and intellectually squalid. At his best, Bismarck himself talked only of the past, often entertainingly, often with scabrous bluntness invariably with himself as hero, the rest of mankind villains or fools. Johanna had neither mellowed nor matured. Count Eulenburg recorded a steady falling off in the number of visitors: few were prepared to face the malicious gossip of Johanna and her daughter, Marie—who, with her unpleasant husband, Count Kuno von Rantzau, was almost always where her mother was because Johanna's only amusement now was to play with her grandchildren. In the winter of 1887–88 Holstein recorded a chilling exchange between husband and wife which plunges to the heart of the mood which governed Bismarck at the summit of his fame. At dinner one evening the princess, Johanna, was holding forth to the company at large on the inadequacy of her mother-in-law, the long dead Wilhelmine Mencken (whom she had never met): 'I hope the worthless creature is now being tortured for it!' she exclaimed. Bismarck took no exception to this outburst: 'Yes,' he commented, 'my pessimism can be traced back to my mother and the training she gave me in childhood.'[3]

Enough has been said to make it clear that the repellent aspects of Bismarck's character, as well as his errors of judgement, were not (as they are commonly presented) aberrations scattered through a lifetime of noble endeavour but, rather, the symptoms of a deep-lying sickness. Also, of course, these unheroic aspects did not present themselves to all the world in a broad and ordered perspective: very few had occasion to experience in their lives, or even to observe, the whole range and force of his destructive qualities. Further, while he was fighting for the mastery of Germany he staked his own political life on each throw, and might well have lost it.

The deterioration in his character went back a long way. It seems to have set in irrevocably about half-way through his Frankfurt period, when he began to fret impatiently for power. We turn back to the earlier days, to his letters to Johanna before and after marriage with a sense of shock. What has happened to the exultant sensibility displayed by the young Bismarck (*not* an adolescent but already in his late thirties) as he describes his moonlight swimming in the Rhine, the alien vastness of the Hungarian *puszta*, Kathy Orlov by the sea at Biarritz, the blazing Pyrennean sunsets? Something must have remained: he could not otherwise have borne the solitudes of Friedrichsruh and Varzin. And even in old age he can recall with a smile the activities of that pair of 'tom-tits' which distracted his attention from the needs of his king and the most urgent affairs of state at Bad Gastein in 1862. But nothing of this appeared in his life away from his beloved woods. And if indeed there in solitude he had time to remember the man he had once been, this would help to explain that curious quality of bitterness in his attitude towards a world which he dominated so absolutely that he had no grounds for bitterness at all, unless a sense of his own inner failure.

The most marked deterioration of all came in that final decade, when he appeared to forget everything but the need to cling to power and the determination to keep that power in the family. Holstein was convinced that this deterioration, which struck many others too (and is amost painfully evident in his public actions the moment one looks at those actions with a sceptical eye) was due to Schweninger's treatment. 'But for Schweninger he might be dead,' he wrote; 'but he would have died great. Schweninger marks the dividing line between hyper-tension and ossification. . . .'[4]

In fact, in so far as Holstein is here referring to his master's social behaviour, both he and Kurd Schlözer nearly thirty years earlier had characterized the Bismarck of St. Petersburg in much the same terms. In so far as he is referring to public actions Holstein is not a reliable guide: on more than one occasion he showed himself incapable of grasping Bismarck's perfectly evident purpose. In particular, he never understood his master's acute awareness of the imperative necessity for Germany to keep on friendly terms with Russia—*unless* France, Britain, and Austria could be brought together into a firm and formal alliance with the Reich. Holstein has been unfairly maligned as the conspiratorial and sinister *éminence grise* of the Wilhelmstrasse, the man who, when Bismarck had gone, was more responsible than any other in Germany for the 1914 war. He was not like this at all. He was a shy, dedicated, deeply knowledgeable official who preferred to work behind the scenes, but he was not perceptive when it came to penetrating motives and reactions, whether of his own people or of the rulers of other powers. The real weakness of Bismarck's policies from 1871 until the end was their incoherence and inconsequence: sometimes he seemed interested in nothing at all but keeping Europe on edge. He knew so well how to do this, and he also knew better than anyone in the world how to go into reverse and extricate himself from a difficult situation. The trick was quite simple: it was to stop what he was doing and do the opposite without asking whether he could afford to lose face. He was one of the very few public men to understand that if you do not care about face you have nothing to lose.

There were four main considerations in the forefront of his mind once the Three Emperors' League was attained: how to keep as close to Russia as possible and minimize Germany's commitment to Austria; how to secure the friendship of France; how to destroy Socialism once for all; above all, how to weaken the crown prince so that he, Bismarck, would be able to survive the emperor's death. He was convinced that Frederick, if given the opportunity, would set up a new Liberal ministry as soon as he came to the throne. When Bismarck was given his new life by Schweninger in the winter of 1883–84, he was sixty-eight; William was eighty-six; the crown prince already fifty-two. From now on Bismarck referred to the new German Liberal Party as 'the crown prince's party,' and the ministry he feared as 'the Gladstone ministry.' To undermine both in advance of the emperor's death became an obsession with him, and that obsession assumed some very odd shapes and lay behind some curious distortions of both his foreign and his domestic policies—if, indeed, 'policy' is the word for the expedients he put forward on his last six years of power.

The most striking example of a policy not worthy of the name was the grand colonial adventure, the breaking out of Germany into Africa and the south seas. A considerable mystery has been made of how and why Bismarck was converted to colonialism; but of course he was never converted. He simply exploited the colonial idea, very briefly, for his own purposes, as in earlier days he had exploited the nationalist idea. Even when in 1884 and 1885 he presented his proud supporters now with a corner of Africa, now with a handful of islands in the south seas, he himself remained as contemptuous of all colonial dreams as ever. Let the Maritime Powers play with Africa and Asia to their hearts' content, had been his line; it will keep them out of mischief nearer home and also, with a stroke of luck here and a cunning nudge there, put them at each other's throats. Italy could be set against France in Tunis; Britain and France against each other in Egypt; Russia and Britain could be kept for ever glowering at each other through the Straits. But with the rise of popular interest in empire-building he began to see how a colonial adventure could be turned to his own account.

The pretext was economic. Bankers, entrepreneurs of various kind, above all the merchants of the old free Baltic ports had been urging the need for overseas bases and trading posts since the unification—in a small way even earlier. The real future of Germany as a power, they insisted, depended upon her gaining access to the foodstuffs and raw materials of distant and barbaric lands. The scramble for Africa, with Britain and France in the lead, had made their demands more urgent. After the Congress of Berlin the switch from free trade to protection offered the colonial lobby a new opportunity, and in 1882 the foundation of the Colonial Union (Ko-lonialverein) injected into the German political scene a pressure group too powerful to be ignored.

Not that Bismarck was any longer interested in ignoring it. The colonial dream was now beginning to appeal to patriotism of the flag-waving kind which was all too soon to bring catastrophe to Europe but which, for the time being, came in very useful to Bismarck. By presenting Germany with colonies he could win votes; not only that, he could strengthen the National Liberals against the new Liberals who were opposed to colonial adventures, thus weakening the position of the crown prince. At the same time, and on another front altogether, he could so arrange his empire-building as to cause the maximum irritation to Britain. This would please France, whom he was now most actively wooing. Adverse British reaction would inflame anti-British feeling in Germany, which would also tell against the crown prince, with his closeness to England.

There has been a natural tendency among historians to look for deeper reasons for Bismarck's sudden interest in colonialism. But this sort of wanton, almost inconsequent, deviousness was perfectly in character. The man who would glory in keeping 'the Eastern ulcer' open in order to assure the continuance of bad blood between Russia and Britain was still in the business of destruction rather than construction. He himself told Alexander III at the grand meeting of the emperors at Skierniwice in Russian Poland in the early autumn of 1884, at the very height of the colonial excitement, that 'the sole object of German colonial policy was to drive a wedge between the crown prince and England.'[5] Delete the word 'sole,' because no action of Bismarck's, with the exception of his preparations for war, was ever governed by a single object, and we may believe him. Years later Herbert gave the same explanation to Schweinitz: 'When we launched our colonial policy we had to assume that the crown prince's reign would be a long one, with English influence predominant. It was to be ready for this that we embarked on a colonial policy which was popular and also conveniently adapted to bring us into conflict with England at any given moment.'[6]

In fact the colonial cry did not prove as popular as Bismarck had hoped. The masses were not interested and voted Socialist. Moreover, England would not quarrel. Bismarck did his best to provoke her into angry reaction. He quite deliberately picked on two sensitive spots to open his drive—south-west Africa, adjacent to Cape Colony, and some islands to be known as the Bismarck Archipelago, provocatively close to Australia.

While this was going on, and while he also laid claim to Togoland and the Cameroons (deliberately confusing not only Britain but also, and characteristically, his own unfortunate ambassador to London, Count Münster, as to his wishes and intentions), the British, apart from a few newspaper editors, kept their heads. And although Bismarck managed to work up two artificial crises, the second by a really outrageous personal attack in the Reichstag on Lord Granville, Gladstone's foreign secretary, the creation of Germany's colonial empire proceeded with the minimum of friction. The way in which Bismarck dispatched Herbert to London in the summer of 1884 to mediate where no mediation would have been required if only the unfortunate Count Münster had been properly informed and instructed, suggested that at least a subsidiary aim of this play-acting was to impress William with Herbert's abilities so that he would be the more ready to accept him in succession to Hatzfeldt as foreign secretary.

In fact, the last thing Britain wanted was to be embroiled in a useless quarrel with Germany: she had quite enough on her hands in Egypt and the Sudan. Gladstone was determined that Bismarck should have what he wanted; he was not, however, prepared to be blackmailed. One passage in Herbert's report to his father not only illumines as nothing else his unlovely character but is also a foreshadowing of that particular strain of overbearing arrogance which certainly had its roots in the Prussian military caste, but which was spread by Bismarck himself like an infection throughout Germany: 'To discuss with Mr. Gladstone the essence of the foreign policy of a great state,' Herbert wrote, 'is useless, because he is quite unable to understand it.'[7] No British statesman has ever received a greater compliment—whether fully deserved or not is a matter for discussion. Certainly Gladstone knew how to take the wind out of Bismarck's sails (he and Granville both saw through the electioneering tactics and declined to be made use of in this way), and it must have been humiliating as well as irritating for Bismarck to listen to this most-hated man blandly assuring the world that Britain welcomed with joy and sympathy 'the extension of Germany to these desert places.'[8] Henceforth, the implication was, the two great peoples would advance hand in hand, spreading instruction and enlightenment to the heathen.

Anything less likely to appeal to Bismarck, with his very specialized religious faith, it would be impossible to imagine. He abandoned his colonial drive as suddenly and casually as he had started it. Ferry had resigned in March 1885, and it took Bismarck only a few months to discover what he should have known before: namely that the difference between Sedan and

Waterloo was basic; the first stood for the loss of Alsace-Lorraine, the second only for the abandonment of a stupid dream. This meant that he need no longer provoke England to please France. Very soon, indeed, he would be wooing England—and working up another war-scare against France.

Before that happened he had to watch the de-materialization of his own dream, the Three Emperors' League, the concert of the Northern Courts. As anyone could have predicted, the whole apparatus came to grief in the Balkans. The occasion was the assertion of independence by Bulgaria. And the joke was the reversal of roles.

Russia, it will be remembered, had promised Austria not to set up 'a large compact Slav state' out of the leavings of the Ottoman Empire— and, after her successful war against the Turks, had gone back on her word and established a very large Bulgaria looking to St. Petersburg for protection. One of the main tasks of the Congress of Berlin had been the dismantling of this construction. The new Bulgaria was broken up: a part of it, with Sofia as its capital, was taken from Turkey and set up as an independent principality under the young Prince Alexander of Battenberg, whom the Russians expected to keep in leading strings. Another part, known as Eastern Rumelia, reverted to Turkish suzerainty, but with a measure of autonomy. The Russians at once proceeded to give the Bulgarians, and anybody else who cared to watch, an exhibition of that clumsy and heavy-handed way with subject peoples which their successors have brought to such a high pitch of unproductive ineptitude (Russian relations with Poland were another matter: here, as to this day, deep feelings of inferiority led to fear and hatred). Prince Alexander soon began to show signs of modest resistance to Russian commands. In 1885 the Bulgarians in Eastern Rumelia revolted against their Turkish overlords and demanded union with their brothers under Prince Alexander. Immediate uproar. For the committed student of Russian affairs the working out of the consequences makes a fascinating study: all others would be better employed reading *Alice in Wonderland*. To cut a long story short, Alexander finally abdicated after being kidnapped by a group of Russian officers; Austria, in a turmoil of recrimination, was finally and irrevocably alienated from Russia, and the Three Emperors' League was dead.

This was the background to the celebrated Reinsurance Treaty with Russia, which thus had its origin in a time of great stress, a time, particularly, in which Bismarck was very far from being in control: so many things were now happening which he neither initiated nor desired, nor could effectively influence one way or the other. This perfectly normal condition of humanity was in perfect opposition to his temperament and his habit. 'I will make my own music, or none at all,' he had written to his cousin fifty years earlier to explain why he could not make a career in government service. He still felt the same. He had made his own music on a Continental scale for those nine marvellous years, from 1862 to 1871. He could never accustom himself to the fact that those days were past. The Bulgarian affair, which involved Germany only indirectly, brought it home to him and he responded with anger. He was particularly angry because he was already nourishing a quarrel with Prince Alexander and with the Battenbergs as a clan.

Nearly a year before the Bulgarian crisis he had learned with grim disapproval that for the past year Alexander had been secretly engaged to Princess Victoria of Prussia—secretly from him, but with the enthusiastic backing of her mother, the crown princess, and the rather grudging consent of her father. Bismarck had never been happy about the choice of a German prince to rule over a new country which he regarded as inherently unstable and which might at any moment land him in complications with either or both of his two imperial allies; but he had contented himself in 1879 with rather distantly warning the young prince (he was only twenty-two) that he was on his own and would be wise to play the game strictly according to the rules laid down by the Treaty of Berlin. Enough at that time had been more than sufficient, and he was prepared to put up with no more. Now, five years later, the Prussian royal family was proposing to marry into this hornet's nest. It was too much. Alexander was told in terms both chilly and offensive of the German government's firm opposition to formal announcement of his engagement. There the matter rested—until within a matter of months, the Battenberg family popped up yet again. This time it was the turn of Alexander's younger brother, Henry: he was to marry Queen Victoria's youngest daughter, Princess Beatrice. Bismarck exploded at the news: he was, he felt, bullied, plotted against, most ill-used. Nothing more was needed to convince him that the English queen and the Prussian crown princess were conspiring actively together to extend British influence in Germany. About Prince Henry and Beatrice, he could do nothing, but he brought into play all his old force to persuade William to forbid the marriage between a Hohenzollern and a Battenberg. That was in March 1884, and William, as so often, gave in.[9]

Thus, when Alexander finally abdicated and was expelled from Bulgaria two years later, he received no sympathy from Bismarck, who might have been expected to withdraw his objection to the marriage now that the Bulgarian connection was no longer an obstacle. Not at all. He was so angry with the whole family and anything to do with it, so enraged against the crown prince and the crown princess, so alarmed by the sudden immense popularity of the handsome young prince, who had defied one after another Serbia, Russia, Austria, that he was resolved to finish him for good. He was seized with quite a new nightmare: if Alexander were to be allowed to settle down in Germany married to a Hohenzollern princess he would be the natural choice of the crown prince as head of a new Liberal government which would put an end to Bismarck. And so he launched what was to be his last assault on his old and failing master's nerves, and one of the most disreputable. He built the unfortunate young prince into a monster of irresponsibility and intrigue: with his English connections, his dangerous liberal leanings, he would appeal to the worst elements in the land were he allowed to make his home in Germany—to that unholy coalition of new Liberals, Catholics, and Socialists who now formed an anti-government majority in the Reichstag. The old emperor responded. To save the empire from disruption he forbade the marriage. Alexander of Battenberg was effectively banished from the scene, and Bismarck was able to turn to other things.[10]

His domestic policy had been a failure for years past: its only success had been his own retention of power. The Socialists, far from being defeated, were stronger than ever; the dream of a steady and reliable parliamentary majority (whether Liberal or Conservative was a matter of perfect indifference to him), was as far away as ever. But he was still a fighter, and in September 1886 he inaugurated yet another grand manoeuvre designed to undermine the crown prince and the Liberals while there was still time. Once more the army was trundled into the front line—Bismarck's front line. But this time Bismarck had to pay for it.

He had already been compelled to give more ground than he liked to the army when, in 1883, he had allied himself with soldiers in order to defeat a sudden and unexpected attack on army expenditure, the pampering of expensive and useless cavalry regiments, and the deification of what Eugen Richter derisively called 'parade' troops. William had nearly had an apopletic fit at the thought of any civilian daring even to criticize his beloved Guards. These men, in his eyes, Richter on the left, Windthorst on the right, were not politicians; they were traitors. But the 'traitors' were in a strong position. There was no longer a Roon at the Ministry of War. The present incumbent, General A. von Kameke, was no fighter and in any case was suspect, regarded by Bismarck with weary suspicion as being too liberal and too close to the crown prince. To get rid of him and to meet the parliamentary challenge Bismarck had no choice but to appeal to the military establishment. This meant for all practical purposes putting himself into the hands of Moltke's putative successor, the able but extravagantly ambitious and restlessly intriguing quartermaster-general, Count Alfred von Waldersee, or the less colourful, less ambitious, but very hard-headed chief of the emperor's military cabinet (the position for so long held by Edwin von Manteuffel), General Emil von Albedyll.

Albedyll was chosen because he was less personally dangerous to Bismarck than Waldersee, who more or less openly aspired to the chancellorship. But Albedyll had his own ambition. For long he had been striving to realize Manteuffel's ideal: the right of direct access to the sovereign by the chief of the military cabinet, instead of through the minister for war. Further, he insisted that the new minister for war should be none other than General Bronsart von Schellendorf, who, as the most politically minded of Moltke's demigod colonels, had been so outspokenly contemptuous of Bismarck during the Franco-Prussian War. ('This civilian in a cuirassier's jacket!') From 1883 the army had been much stronger relative to the politicians. The one real success of this manoeuvre from Bismarck's point of view was that at last he was able to push his old hate, General von Stosch, from the Admiralty, a victory over the crown prince which warmed his heart. The unseen irony of this transaction was that Stosch was succeeded by another general, Count Leo von Caprivi; and it was Caprivi who was brought forward to the chancellorship when Bismarck fell.

This reorganization of the high command had been forced on him by events and was therefore untidy. But now, in 1887, he embarked upon a full-scale calculated action in the mature Bismarckian manner, his true aims hidden in a cloud of deception: the cool and perfectly timed conjuring up of yet another war scare to achieve a limited domestic objective. It was his last great exercise in this style. It ran so true to type that it was no more than a variation on a pattern established as a theoretical ideal in the Frankfurt days, when he had no power, and for the first time realized in the Schleswig-Holstein affair in 1864.

It was one more action in his unresting campaign to break the Liberal opposition before William died and the crown prince became the first liberal monarch. It involved staging the debate on the army estimates a year before it was called for under the seven-year rule. The *Septennat* did not expire until 1887, but he believed that by going to the Reichstag a year early, challenging the Opposition to deny a further term of seven years (he knew they would stick at three years), and by invoking the threat of war he could dissolve the Reichstag, call a fresh general election, and annihilate the Opposition on a wave of patriotic fervour. And this is what happened. The elections of 1887 brought in a firm majority of National Liberals (now indistinguishable from the stuffiest Conservatives) and Centre Party, who promptly combined to form a coalition known as the *Kartel*. The new *Septennat* was then passed.

The opportunity for this performance was provided by the French in the person of that mock-heroic figure, General Georges Boulanger, who had been made minister of war by the peace-loving Charles de Freycinet, Ferry's successor. Ministers of war on white horses notwithstanding, there was not the slightest possibility of France attacking Germany, but for a short time Boulanger's posturing presented Bismarck with the opportunity he desired. The new army bill must be passed or there would be war, he insisted. You can have all the money you want, declared the opposition, but only for three years; then we can think again. This was not what Bismarck wanted. The Reichstag had at all costs to be kept from reaching a compromise. The great and venerable Moltke was brought down to the Chamber in his eighty-eighth year to utter a solemn warning that all would be lost unless the bill was passed. Moltke may have believed in the danger, but certainly Waldersee and the active higher command did not. Bismarck used every possible means to provoke the Opposition into resisting—and succeeded. The bill was thrown out and the Reichstag was dissolved. The new elections of February 1887 brought him his heart's desire. The crown prince's party was halved, and although the Socialists were still very strong the success of the National Liberals was beyond their wildest dreams (220 seats out of 397). Instead of showing their disapproval of the man who, only eight years earlier, had done his best to destroy them, they flocked to serve under his banner, shoulder to shoulder with the Conservatives who had profited by that act of mayhem. Within two months the Army Bill was passed. Strengthened by Bismarck's handling of the Liberal attack on the army estimates in 1883, the soldiers had been gaining in confidence. They were never to look back. But if Bismarck had known that there was no danger of immediate French attack, now that the Three Emperors' League was mortally stricken by the Austro-Rumanian quarrel in the Bulgarian crisis of 1885–86, he was again apprehensive about the possibility of a Franco-Russian alliance. Indeed, he no longer wanted to repair the league, which remained technically in being until June 1887. Haymerle had gone from the Ballhausplatz, but his successor, Count Gustav von Kálnoky, would have liked to salvage it; so would Giers in St. Petersburg; but Tsar Alexander would have nothing more to do with it. He had reverted to his natural mood of dismissive aloofness, and seemed determined on splendid isolation.

Bismarck registered this situation. He made no immediate attempt to argue Alexander out of his mood of total withdrawal. Instead he began to think of constructing a Russo-German alliance, excluding Austria. His first step was to give Shuvalov the text of the Austrian Treaty of 1879 in order to demonstrate that although he was inhibited from allying himself with Russia in an aggressive war against Austria there were no other limitations to his unsleeping devotion to the Russian cause. Russia in return, he hoped, would promise her neutrality if Germany felt constrained to enter upon a preventive war against France. But this was too much for Alexander, and the main feature of the new treaty as signed was that each contracting power would stay benevolently neutral if the other were involved in war with a third party, but with two specific exceptions: Russia would not guarantee her neutrality if Germany attacked France and Germany would not guarantee hers if Russia attacked Austria.

In further articles Germany agreed to recognize Bulgaria as a predominately Russian sphere of influence and promised all support short of war should Russia be forced to close the Straits to hostile warships. The treaty was signed on 18 June, the sixth anniversary of the Three Emperors' League. The Austrians, of course, knew nothing about it. Nor did anybody else. It remained one of the best kept diplomatic secrets of the age—until, nine years later, from his retirement, Bismarck publicly attacked the new young Emperor William II for fatally damaging Russo-German relations by failing to renew it.

Would the Reinsurance Treaty have prevented the First World War had it been renewed in 1890 and thereafter? Far from it. That war was started by Austria's overbearing and reckless ultimatum to Serbia. Russia, no less recklessly, then declared war on Austria. A war of aggression? . . . The Austro-German Treaty called for Germany then to go to the support of Austria, which happened. Had the Reinsurance Treaty still been in force it could have made no difference. . . . Russia's distress when the new German emperor refused to renew that treaty in 1890 arose not because she felt suddenly open to attack but because the young Kaiser's rebuff confirmed her worst fears about the general mood in Berlin. In a word, the Reinsurance Treaty, of which so much was later made by Bismarck, was no more than one element in a pattern of obsessional treaty-making which had no more enduring object than to keep five balls in the air all at once. In the last resort everything depended on Bismarck himself, as the only man who could command war or peace at will. It is inconceivable that had he been chancellor in 1914 he would have allowed Germany to be dragged into Armageddon by an Austria visited by the death-wish. But it was he who set the scene for a consummation of this kind.

Even in the summer of 1887 Alexander in St. Petersburg had every reason to be bewildered by Germany's real intentions.

For some time the Russians had been tightening official restrictions on foreign trade and on the activities of foreigners inside Russia, specifically a ban on the foreign ownership of Russian land. This was the outcome partly of one of those so familiar Russian withdrawals—for fear of contamination, dilution, corruption, heaven knows what—and partly a response to Bismarck's monstrous expulsion from Germany in 1885 of 30,000 Poles who, through no fault of their own, were technically citizens of the Russian or the Austro-Hungarian Empire. All this was going on even before the Reinsurance Treaty was signed, and now Bismarck hit back with interest added.

The German press (which knew nothing of the Reinsurance Treaty) launched itself into a violent anti-Russian campaign in protest at the hardship caused to German property-owners in Russia and to German exporters in general. Far from checking the excesses of this campaign, Bismarck actively encouraged it. And in November 1887, at the very moment when Alexander (very reluctantly persuaded) was paying an official visit to Berlin, he brought things to a climax by instructing the Reichsbank, in face of the agonized and uncomprehending pleas of Bleichröder, to refuse any further loans against Russian bonds. This was the notorious *Lombardverbot*, intended as a characteristically Bismarckian flourish to frighten the Russians and bring them to heel.[11] It worked the other way. France saw a heaven-sent opportunity and seized it with verve. Within two or three years Russian industry was so dependent on the accumulated savings of the French that Alexander had no choice but to recognize the despised Republic as a friend, a stay, a potential ally. Four years later, with Bismarck in retirement and the Reinsurance Treaty lapsed, the unthinkable happened. A French naval squadron paid a visit to Russian waters and in July 1891 the Autocrat of all Russia stood bareheaded to the strains of the revolutionary 'Marseillaise' on the deck of a French man-of-war in Kronstadt harbour: the Franco-Russian alliance was in the making.

There was one other aspect of Bismarck's activity which contributed to the general confusion that crucial year, 1887. To Lord Salisbury in London he addressed a long and mysterious missive which could mean only that, with the Reinsurance Treaty in his pocket, he was seeking to combine Britain and Austria in an anti-Russian front which would frighten off the French. Britain, Germany, and Austria were 'saturated states,' he carefully explained to this remarkable statesman whose scepticism matched his own in depth and greatly exceeded it in discrimination. The peace of Europe was threatened by none of these countries; but France and Russia were another matter, and Germany had only one course open to her: to secure alliances for herself which would ensure her against the possibility of being called upon to fight two powerful neighbours at once.[12] Whether this was an invitation to Lord Salisbury to respond with the offer of an alliance or not, just over a year later, in January 1889, Bismarck himself came forward with a formal offer of an Anglo-German treaty directed against French aggression: he was by now more fearful than ever of a Franco-Russian accord. But nothing that Salisbury, first as foreign secretary, then as prime minister, had seen of the great chancellor's behaviour since the last abortive offer of 1879 (when Bismarck had himself broken off his own overtures to Britain as soon as he was sure that he had captured Russia for his Three Emperors' League) had in any way invested him with the appearance of a trustworthy ally. Salisbury refused the invitation. He was hardly to be blamed. He was not alone in his scepticism. Only two years before, Shuvalov, the most persuasive Russian advocate of a German alliance, had observed to a French diplomat: 'You need not worry. We shall not allow Germany to dominate us. The age of illusions is past.'

The German general staff knew no more than anyone else about the Reinsurance Treaty. It was convinced that there would soon be war with Russia and argued in the Moltke tradition that the sensible thing to do would be to bring it on as soon as possible. Waldersee, still quartermaster-general but already effectively chief-of-staff, had been elevating his military attachés all over the world into a virtually independent diplomatic service. Just as Albedyll at the hand of the military cabinet could cut out the War Ministry and report directly to the emperor, so now Waldersee was using his attachés to cut out the Foreign Ministry. For many years this system had obtained as a special case in St. Petersburg, where the tsar as supreme commander insisted on a personal military link with his fellow commander-in-chief in Potsdam, so that the so-called Flügeladjutant often knew things that were hidden from the ambassador. Bismarck had grumbled about it on occasion but had failed to insist on its abolition—just as in the Franco-Prussian War he had failed to insist as a *matter of principle* on the subordination of military to civil rule. Now his chickens were coming home to roost.

Towards the end of 1887 he found that the military attaché in Vienna had so far forgotten protocol as to initiate discussions with the Austrian high command about the disposition of Austro-German troops in the event of a likely war with Russia. Bismarck roared. He hauled Waldersee in person over the coals, told Moltke, Albedyll, and Bronsart what he thought of them, and very pointedly invited the Ballhausplatz to cooperate with the Wilhelmstrasse in protecting foreign policy from the interventions of the soldiers.[13] His roar could still inspire terror in all but the strongest and awe even in these. But who, when he was gone, could hope to keep down the very men he had lifted up? And even as he roared, he was finding himself increasingly dependent on those men. Later that winter, on 6 February 1888, he introduced into the Reichstag a measure which could only have been directed against Russia, the new secret ally. By reorganizing the reserves he added nearly three-quarters of a million men to the army's war establishment.

It was in introducing this measure that he delivered the last of that long series of great speeches, extending over a quarter of a century, which raised German oratory to a level never attained before or since. It was an emotional *tour de force*. 'We no longer ask for love, either from France or from Russia. We run after nobody,' he declared. And: 'We Germans fear God and nothing else on earth; and it is the fear of God which causes us to love peace and cherish it.'[14] Moltke wept. Bismarck was mobbed, and a great crowd followed his carriage, escorting him—like a prima donna or a monarch—to the chancellery. There was a feeling in the air that united Germany had come of age. Indeed, in a sense she had. . . .

For even in this moment of triumph the stage is almost imperceptibly being peopled by a new cast. They tiptoe about at first because the old emperor is still alive and nobody quite knows what sort of an epoch the crown prince will usher in. But they are there in strength, mostly soldiers, and Bismarck brought them there, all except one, the most important of them all. Waldersee, Albedyll, Bronsart, Bronsart's successor as war minister, his old companion of the demigod days, Verdy du Vernois—and a little younger, but already in 1888 forty years old and beginning to reveal his ambition, the dire figure of the future Prussian minister of state and Grand Admiral of the Fleet, Alfred von Tirpitz.

Above them all, the man who was to lead his country to ruin by glorifying military above civilian advice: the crown prince's son and heir, Frederick William Victor Albert, the future Kaiser William II, now twenty-nine years old and married—another of history's little jokes—to Augusta Victoria, the daughter of Bismarck's early victim, the unhappy Augustenburg.

Bismarck had spoken on 6 February 1888. On 9 March William, in his ninety-first year, at last died. Already now our hero, this loyal servant of Hohenzollern, knew that his obsessional striving to nullify the new emperor in advance had been unnecessary and vain. Frederick had cancer of the throat. He had only ninety-nine days to live. Already there had been a court battle, a vicious struggle between German and British doctors and their partisans, over the correct treatment. Now, with his new master almost in the grave, the old servant spared him nothing. For some time he had been looking to the new William, whose flamboyance, brashness, and general unpredictability had long been a matter of deep distress to his parents, particularly his English mother, who had indeed been worried by these faults since his early childhood. Bismarck had exploited this situation by encouraging the son to work against them. But there was no longer anything to work against. Poor Frederick on the throne was in no condition to initiate anything at all. One of his very few actions was to invite Prince Alexander of Battenberg to return to Berlin and accept a new appointment in the army. Bismarck, unable to forego his feud with the new empress, perhaps also fearing Alexander once again as a threat to his own position, insisted that the invitation should be cancelled: Russia, he declared, the tsar himself, would take it as an insult, and untold harm would be done to Russo-German relations.

Frederick gave way, as his father had so often done before him. But his difficult servant was not satisfied. Instead of quietly accepting the dying emperor's submission, Bismarck seized the occasion to punish the empress, who had nowhere to turn for advice and support. He whipped up another press campaign against 'the English woman' even more virulent than his campaign against Augusta and her daughter-in-law over the bombardment of Paris.

And to make things worse, the whole operation from start to finish was based on a deliberate lie. The Russian tsar did not care in the least what Germany did with Alexander, provided he kept out of Bulgaria. Bismarck was heavily snubbed when he tried to embroil Russia by instructing Schweinitz in St. Petersburg to ask Giers for a formal declaration that a visit by Prince Battenberg to Berlin would be regarded as an unfriendly act. Giers did not pretend that Russia regarded Alexander with affection and trust, but stated categorically that it would not occur to him to imagine that such an action would mean any change in Germany's policy of friendship.[15]

Even in face of this rebuff Bismarck persisted in his lie: the presence of Alexander Battenberg in Berlin would mean war with Russia, he insisted. And the greater part of the German press, the National Liberal press most notably, still fulminated.

Matters came to a head when Queen Victoria, who wished to visit her dying son-in-law, was warned off by Bismarck, who officially informed Whitehall that Russia would be enraged. The response was a classic snub from Salisbury: 'I am sorry not to be able to comply with Prince Bismarck's wishes,' the prime minister replied, 'but he is asking me to assist him in thwarting the wishes of his Emperor and my Queen to gratify the malignant feelings of the Russian Emperor. This would certainly be inconsistent with my duty and, if German cooperation can only be held at this price, we must do without it.'[16]

The queen herself, contemptuous of Bismarck's behaviour, was in fact tumultuously received when she arrived in Germany, as though the press campaign did not exist; but she advised her daughter to forget about the Battenberg marriage (which in any case Alexander no longer wanted). She met Bismarck, politely, but so kept him on his toes that he emerged wiping the sweat from his forehead, exclaiming: 'What a woman!' This unwilling respect did not prevent him from persecuting her daughter after Frederick's death, when he had, or thought he had, nothing to fear from anybody any more.

Bismarck's last offence against Frederick was to stay away from his funeral. One of his first acts in the new reign was to assail his widow with more violence than ever before. The dowager empress was quite alone, exposed to a hostile chancellor, a hostile emperor (her son), and a hostile court. Frederick on his deathbed, unable to speak, had laid her hand in Bismarck's as a silent pledge. But within three months Bismarck had seized on the publication of parts of Frederick's diary as a means of humiliating the widow. Nothing could have been milder than the criticisms of the chancellor confided to these papers, but Bismarck was beside himself. He knew the diary was genuine and said so to his jackal, Moritz Busch (who had been lately master-minding the campaign against 'the English woman'), but he deliberately perjured himself by declaring it to be a forgery and instituting criminal proceedings against the unfortunate professor who had published extracts from it. Before the new emperor he laid a formal complaint, which William agreed should be published—without realizing, apparently, the monstrous implications of, for example, the following almost unbelievable passage designed to show that the late emperor was not to be trusted: 'I was not permitted by King William to discuss the more confidential aspects of our policy with the crown prince, because he feared indiscretions leaking out to the English court, which was full of French sympathizers.'[17]

We do not know what went on in the young Kaiser's mind when he allowed himself to be tempted by the old chancellor to publish to the world this slander on his own father, which was also the gratuitous self-exposure of a disloyal servant. We do know that within two years the Kaiser rid himself of a chancellor who, now on his own direct showing, could himself not be trusted. Pretexts abounded. In the end the break came over matters of social policy. For a long time Bismarck who knew all about the emperor's character deficiencies but had quite failed to appreciate his acute intelligence (to say nothing of his unforgiving stubbornness) quite casually left him out of account, behaving as though he imagined he could run the country without paying even lip-service to his new master. His last diplomatic exercises were concerned with trying to persuade Lord Salisbury into an Anglo-German alliance, sponsoring and encouraging the Mediterranean agreements between Britain and Italy and Austria (designed by him to associate British sea-power with the Triple Alliance), and with a ludicrous affront to Switzerland about revolutionary conspiracies on her soil. William II meanwhile was paying his chancellor back in his own coin, behaving rather as though the Bismarck family did not exist, demonstratively visiting Constantinople, making vainglorious speeches to anyone who would listen, and, in particular, discovering a new role for himself as champion of the working class.

It was now only a matter of time before the fatal clash, as William clearly saw. But Bismarck still underrated his new master, and instead of summoning all his powers to win control of parliament, government, and army, continued to remove himself from the scene of action whenever he felt he had had enough of Berlin—which was most of the time. This did not prevent him seeking to block with total rejection the Kaiser's attempts to put through protective labour legislation. He, Bismarck, had given the German working class the most advanced social services in the world, he said in effect (and truthfully); but the emperor's notions of shorter working days, protection of women and children from exploitation, and all the rest, amounted to an open invitation to further excessive demands. The government alone knew what was good for the masses and could provide it: hence the three social insurance acts. If the Reichstag rejected his anti-Socialist law he would bring force to bear instead. If the emperor was not prepared to fight the Socialists to the bitter end, then he, Prince Bismarck, must go.

William was already looking around for a successor, and he had at least the wit to pass Waldersee by and choose Caprivi, the man who had succeeded poor Stosch at the Admiralty, and who was remarkable among the German high command for his good sense and sobriety of language. There were several last straws. The first was Bismarck's crude and deliberately provocative attempt to wreck his sovereign's pet scheme, an international labour conference to be held in Berlin: he went so far as to urge foreign ambassadors to advise their governments to have no part in it. Another was his pointed reminder to all Prussian ministers that nobody was entitled to discuss business with the sovereign except through the head of government (Prussian Law of 1852). Another was his attempt to draw Windthorst into a Conservative Centre coalition without consulting, or even informing, the emperor. Another was his deliberate and open defiance of his master and the Reichstag on the eve of the labour conference by ordering the arrest of all Socialist agitators and their confinement in army barracks.

That was on 13 March 1890, and the young emperor had had enough. On the next day, the day before he was due to open the conference, William warned Bismarck that he proposed to call on him next morning in the chancellery. He arrived very early indeed. But his note of the previous evening, it was said, had arrived after the chancellor had retired for the night and thus had only just reached him. So now the emperor was kept waiting while Bismarck dressed. When the great man appeared his master bitterly reproved him. How, for example, could he, the Kaiser, possibly avoid consulting with departmental ministers if Bismarck hid himself away in the country for half the year? Bismarck appeared inattentive. Rather demonstratively he tried to slip some papers under others on his desk and when William asked to see them he refused to hand them over. William grabbed at one of them, as was expected. It was a confidential dispatch from St.

Petersburg which included a reported comment by the tsar on the character of his fellow-monarch, the newcomer at Potsdam: '*C'est un garçon mal élevé et de mauvaise foi*. . . .' The Kaiser's feelings as he read can be imagined. There was nothing he could say—except, as he turned away from that baleful and implacable gaze, rap out a formal instruction for the immediate rescinding of the order forbidding ministerial access to the king-emperor.[18]

Bismarck, so free with threats of resignation in the past, did not resign immediately. William had to send him a virtual ultimatum, not once but twice: Either . . . Or . . . It took three days, and when the letter of resignation at last arrived it contained a lecture on, of all things, the imperative need to preserve constitutional forms (as, for instance, the cabinet order of 1852) and the danger of being pushed into ill-considered action by a sabre-rattling general staff. . . .[19]

It was, of course, a most honourable retirement. Lieutenant-General Prince Otto von Bismarck-Schönhausen was created duke of Lauenburg and gazetted field-marshal. He had not lost his mordant humour. The new title, he said, would do when he was travelling incognito; and to Herbert he remarked, how very odd it was that the emperor should appoint his best general to the chancellorship and his best chancellor to be field-marshal.[20]

But there was nothing further to come. He had eight more years to live. For some time he played with the idea of making a triumphant return, and he actually got himself elected to the Reichstag; but the weeks and months and the years went by without his entering the Chamber. Instead he put forward his point of view and exercised his malice in a series of widely read newspaper articles, often highly indiscreet, sometimes treacherous, like the one in 1896 in which he attacked the emperor for his wanton sacrifice of Russian friendship, supporting his case by revealing the highly secret Reinsurance Treaty to all the world. William in the first flash of incredulous dismay spluttered dire threats. But there was nothing he could do. The German people had made a national hero of Bismarck: more than most peoples they needed a figure of that kind, and they had no other.

The national hero in retirement had almost at once embarked on his memoirs, driving poor Bucher (conscripted to do the devilling) to distraction with his contradictions and falsifications (whether intentional or not) and his general refusal to admit that he had played any part in any plan or action that had failed. He even disclaimed to Bucher all responsibility for the *Kulturkampf* and insisted that he had had nothing to do with the dismissal and arraignment of Arnim. There is no doubt that the strains and stresses entailed in reaching some sort of a compromise between the truth and Bismarck's view of it hastened Bucher's death in 1892. Thereafter there was no systematic attempt to produce a definitive autobiography. Bismarck pottered at the text when he felt in the mood, illuminating almost everything he touched upon and producing some memorable prose, still outstanding for its quality in a language so splendid but so rarely respected as it should be by its inheritors. As an historical record in the strict, objective sense *Thoughts and Memories* does not hold water; but as an essay in unconscious self-revelation it is pure gold.

Towards the end of 1895 Johanna quietly died at Varzin, and for the three years remaining to him Bismarck settled at Friedrichsruh. For some years all the world had been beating a path to his door, and the Kaiser himself turned up in style to congratulate the vanquished enemy on his eightieth birthday. Bismarck was not only a legend still, he was a legend which grew from year to year, and William II, that most insecure of monarchs, felt the need to have a share in it. So the great man, immense, very stiff in the joints, leaning on a stick while one of those crop-eared mastiffs at his side contemplated the All Highest with something of the malevolence that its master felt but was too polite to show, received as his due the salute of a squadron of cavalry and the studied tribute of the showman-monarch, who was only now beginning to mature into the joke figure of Europe, the sick-joke figure, who was, for example, to greet Nicholas of Russia as the Admiral of the Atlantic wishing well to the Admiral of the Pacific while still, almost hysterically, hoping to be loved by England.

It was all very well for Bismarck to look down from his great height at the posturing figure of the dynast whose excessive power he himself had done so much to secure and guarantee. It almost certainly never occurred to him that one of his great disservices to Germany had been to accustom her people to accepting boastfulness and bullying as proper means of self-expression. But what is one to make of the second thoughts about the powers of parliament with which he favoured enthusiastic audiences at Kissingen and Jena on his way back from Herbert's wedding in Vienna (he had married a Hungarian, Countess Hoyos)? Now he modestly confessed that in drawing up the Reichs Constitution in 1871 he had given too much power to the crown, thereby reducing the influence of the Reichstag. Parliaments should have freedom to criticize, to warn, 'sometimes to direct the government': and again: 'People must not assume they are obeying God when really they are obeying a senior civil servant. . . .'[21]

He died on the night of 30 July 1898. His emperor had paid a final visit, to no useful purpose, seven months earlier. Since then, the old man's breathing had troubled him extremely; a ravaged hulk, he was rarely out of a wheelchair. His family was with him when he died, but he had no real friends. As soon as he was dead the egregious Moritz Busch for the first time in his career showed courage and initiative by publishing the letter of resignation, written eight years earlier, which placed so much responsibility on such irresponsible shoulders. He had insisted on being buried at Friedrichsruh, and so he was. Here Herbert von Bismarck, almost at the end of his own tether, firmly stood up to William, who was determined on a grand state funeral in Berlin with himself as the centrepiece.

Franz Schnabel, the South-German historian, who has seen deeper into Bismarck's failings than the majority of his colleagues, could nevertheless succumb to the temptation of compartmentalizing, as it were, those failings, thus sealing off the virtues and keeping them artificially pure. For example, what marvellous breadth of vision, he declares, was displayed by Bismarck in his celebrated conversation with the exiled Liberal, Carl Schurz (and in his own memoirs later) when he showed his profound understanding of the European need for the Habsburg Empire and went on to say that if it were allowed to vanish from the scene, 'new creations in this area could only be of a revolutionary character.'[22]

This apocalyptic view was certainly prophetic, but surely every statesman of the period worthy of the name would have taken it for granted—as it was certainly taken for granted even by that dedicated Czech nationalist, František Palacký who, in 1848, sought Bohemian autonomy—but under the Habsburg crown. Far more significant than Bismarck's understanding of Austria as a European necessity was his readiness to unleash revolution and chaos over half Europe if this was necessary to bring Austria to her knees.

What kind of a statesman was it, one asks again, who could even contemplate such a course as a remote contingency?

The tragedy of Bismarck, apart from the profound personal tragedy of a man of wonderful gifts corrupted, was not that he subordinated morality to the supposed needs of the state: most other statesmen of his time did that, including Gladstone. The tragedy was that he exalted the amoral con-

cept of politics into a principle; and that, as a corollary, because he succeeded with such dazzling skill through the nine miraculous years which
culminated in the foundation of the Reich, his countrymen surrendered to
that principle. In engineering his wars and in the end giving too much
power to the soldiers in order to fight parliament the better, he encouraged
his successors to give the soldiers their heads and allow them to draw up
their wholly apolitical plans—plans which involved, for example, the violation of pledged neutrality, as well as mobilization schemes which, once
sanctioned, no civilian government could put into reverse. Bismarck had
fought the soldiers when it suited him, but only for himself; not for Prussia
or for Germany.

The German people saw it happening and lacked the will to stop it.
Bismarck and the people each corrupted the other. To say that Bismarck
was a direct precursor of Hitler is evidently untrue; but it is not untrue, I
think, to say that those aspects of the German character which made it
possible for Bismarck to rule for just on thirty years were those same aspects which made it too easy for a Hitler to take power and keep it. As for
the soldiers, he had the power to put them firmly in their place, but he
needed them too much.

He was right to distrust them. Their successors did not shine as politicians. First, in 1917 they very cleverly sent Lenin into Russia to spread
chaos and disruption; then, in the 1930s, they very cleverly supported
Hitler. In the vast and terrible processes set in motion by the German high
command, which came into its own under Bismarck, Prussia was destroyed, quite simply removed from the map, and united Germany divided. Königsberg, the ancient coronation city of the Hohenzollern (and
the home of Immanuel Kant), is now Russian Kaliningrad. Schönhausen
was burned down by Russian troops: what is left of it, with Kniephofen
and Varzin, is now swallowed up in Poland. Malwine's daughter Sybille,
Bismarck's beloved niece, the nicest of all that clan, was living at
Schönhausen when the Russians broke through; she was eighty years old
and shot herself before they came. What remains of the glory? Friedrichsruh; a grave; an equivocal memory.

NOTES ON SOURCES

I have used the following abbreviations for certain key sources. The titles of all other works referred to are given in the notes that follow.

GW   *Bismarck: Die gesammelten Werke,* edited by H. von Petersdorff, F. Thimme, W. Frauendienst, W. Schüssler, W. Andreas, W. Windelband, G. Ritter, R. Stadelman, et al. (Berlin, 1923–33). 15 vols; vol. VI has four parts, the pages of each separately numbered, and vol. XIV (the letters) two parts, page numbers running through; vol. XV contains the Memoirs, *Gedanken und Errinerungen.*

Kohl   *Die politischen Reden des Fürsten Bismarck,* edited by Horst Kohl (Berlin, 1892–95). 10 vols.

APP   *Die Auswärtige Politik Preussens, 1858–1871,* Historische Reichskommission (Berlin, 1932–39). 10 vols.

GP   *Die grosse Politik der europäischen Kabinette, 1871–1914*

OD   *Les origines diplomatiques de la guerre de 1870–71* (Paris, 1910–32). 29 vols.

Busch   *Tagebuchblätter von Moritz Busch* (Leipzig, 1899). 2 vols.

PART ONE: PREPARATION

CHAPTER I: THE PRUSSIAN INHERITANCE

1. Kohl I, pp. 8–10; and see Ch. III below.
2. Busch I, p. 250.
3. Erich Eyck, *Bismarck and the German Empire,* 3d ed. (London, 1968), p. 11.

4. To Johanna von Puttkamer, 23 Feb. 1847, GW XIV, p. 67.

CHAPTER II: MISLEADING DIRECTIONS

1. To Heinrich von Puttkamer, 21 Dec. 1846, GW XIV, pp. 46–48.
2. R. S. Lucius von Ballhausen, *Bismarck-Erinnerungen* (Stuttgart and Berlin, 1921), pp. 137–38.
3. Erich Marcks, *Bismarck, eine Biographie 1815–1851* (Stuttgart, 1940), p. 40.
4. GW XV, p. 5.
5. Busch I, pp. 247–48.
6. 10 Aug. 1836, GW XIV, p. 8.
7. See GW XIV, pp. 8–11, and Marcks, op. cit., pp. 120–24.
8. Marcks, op. cit., p. 141.
9. To Johanna von Puttkamer, 13 Feb. 1847, GW XIV, pp. 57–58.
10. GW XIV, pp. 13–17.
11. To Johanna, 13 Feb. 1847, GW XIV, pp. 57–58.
12. Marcks, op. cit., pp. 147–59.
13. Bismarck to his father, 28 July 1842, GW XIV, pp. 18–19.
14. Marcks, op. cit., p. 166.
15. See ibid., pp. 217–224.
16. To Heinrich von Puttkamer, 21 Dec. 1846, GW XIV, pp. 18–19.
17. Ibid.
18. Ibid.
19. To Heinrich von Puttkamer, 4 Jan. 1847, GW XIV, pp. 48–49.
20. Fürst Philipp zu Eulenberg-Hertefeld, *Aus 50 Jahren* (Berlin, 1923), p.28.
21. Robert von Keudell, *Fürst und Fürstin Bismarck* (Berlin, 1901), p. 47.
22. To Bernard von Bismarck, 31 Jan. 1847, GW XIV, p 50.
23. To Johanna, 1 Feb. 1847, GW XIV, p. 53.
24. To Johanna, 17 Feb. 1847, GW XIV, p. 59.
25. To Johanna, 25 Feb. 1847, GW XIV, p. 68.
26. To Johanna, 24 Feb. 1847, GW XIV, p. 68.
27. To Johanna, 7 Feb. 1847, GW XIV, p. 55.
28. To Johanna, 4 Mar. 1847, GW XIV, p. 74.
29. Ibid.
30. To Johanna, 17 Feb. 1847, GW XIV, pp. 59–60.
31. To Johanna, 7 Feb. 1847, GW XIV, p. 55.

CHAPTER III: A SMALL BEGINNING

1. Constantine de Grunwald, *Tsar Nicholas I*, trans. Brigit Patmore (London, 1954), p. 74.
2. To Johanna, 8 May 1847, GW XIV, p. 86.

3. To Johanna, 18 May 1847, GW XIV, p. 89.
4. To Johanna, 7 Feb. 1847, GW XIV, p. 54.
5. To Johanna, 23 Feb. 1847, GW XIV, pp. 65–66.
6. To Johanna, 1 Feb. 1847, GW XIV, p. 51.
7. GW XV, p. 17; and Kohl I, pp. 8–10, 17 May 1849.
8. To Johanna, 21 May 1847, GW XIV, p. 89.
9. To Malwine von Bismarck, 24 Oct. 1847, GW XIV, p. 100.

CHAPTER IV: CHAMPION OF REACTION

1. E. Ashley, *Life and Correspondence of the Hon. John Temple, Viscount Palmerston*, rev. ed. (London, 1876), vol. I, p. 103.
2. Ibid, pp. 104–105.
3. GW XV, p. 19.
4. Ibid.
5. GW XV, p. 20.
6. GW XV, p. 22.
7. Kohl I, p. 46, 4 Apr. 1848.
8. To Johanna, 3 Apr. 1848, GW XIV, p. 109.
9. To Hermann Wagener, 9 June 1848, GW VII, p. 13.
10. Marcks, *Bismarck, Eine Biographie*, p. 487.
11. GW XV, p. 39.
12. GW XV, p. 34.
13. GW I, p. 1.
14. Kohl I, p. 94, 21 April 1849.
15. To Frau von Puttkamer, 4 Nov. 1849, GW XIV, p. 150.
16. Kohl I, pp. 111–12.
17. Ibid., pp. 264–65, 3 Dec. 1850.
18. Graf Carl Friedrich Vitzthum von Eckstädt, *Berlin und Wien in den Jahren 1845–1852* (Stuttgart, 1886), p. 304.

CHAPTER V: 'I AM PRUSSIAN . . .'

1. To Johanna, 20 Jan. 1851, GW XIV, p. 190.
2. To Johanna, 28 Mar. 1851, GW XIV, pp. 206–207.
3. To Johanna, 5 May 1859, GW XIV, p. 517.
4. To Johanna, 28 Apr. 1841, GW XIV, pp. 206–207.
5. To Johanna, 7 May 1851, GW XIV, p. 209.
6. To Johanna, 9 Aug. 1857, GW XIV, pp. 475–76.
7. To Johanna, 8 July 1851, GW XIV, p. 231.
8. To Johanna, 27 June 1852, GW XIV, p. 271.
9. To Johanna, 26 June 1851, GW XIV, p. 228.
10. To Johanna, 1 May 1851, GW XIV, p. 207.

11. To Johanna, 3 May 1851, GW XIV, pp. 207–208.
12. Ibid.
13. Heinrich Ritter von Srbik, *Deutsche Einheit* (Munich, 1935–42), vol. II, p. 175.
14. To Leopold von Gerlach, 22 June 1851, GW XIV, pp. 219–24.
15. To Hermann Wagener, 5 June 1851, GW XIV, p. 217.
16. To Johanna, 3 July 1851, GW XIV, pp. 229–30.
17. To Hans Hugo von Kleist-Retzow, 4 July 1851, GW XIV, p. 230. The suppressed passage is in Leonhard von Muralt, *Bismarck's Verantwortlichkeit* (Göttingen, 1935), pp. 89–90.
18. Motley to his wife, 30 July 1855, in *The Correspondence of John Lothrop Motley* (London, 1889), vol. I, p. 177.
19. Ibid., p. 173, 27 July 1855.
20. To Kleist-Retzow, 4 July 1851, GW XIV, p. 231.
21. GW XIII, pp. 177 and 468.
22. GW I, pp. 375–76.
23. GW III, pp. 37–39.
24. Ralph Flenley, *Modern German History*, 4th rev. ed. (London and New York, 1968), p. 152.
25. To Leopold von Gerlach, 27 Jan. 1855, GW XIV, p. 290.
26. To Otto von Manteuffel, 27 Jan. 1855, GW XIV, p. 290.
27. To Otto von Manteuffel, 15 Feb. 1854, GW I, p. 427.
28. To Leopold von Gerlach, 13 Oct. 1854, GW XIV, p. 368.
29. To Otto von Manteuffel, 15 Feb. 1854, GW I, pp. 427–30.
30. GW XV, p. 73.
31. To Johanna, 27 Aug. 1855, GW XIV, p. 413.
32. To Otto von Manteuffel, 14 Sept. 1855, GW II, pp. 71–73.
33. To Otto von Manteuffel, 13 Apr. 1855, GW II, p. 40.
34. Ibid., p. 41.
35. To Leopold von Gerlach, 11 May 1857, GW XIV, p. 469.
36. Ibid., p. 465, 2 May 1857.
37. Ibid., p. 486.
38. Ibid., p. 470, 30 May 1857.
39. Ibid., p. 471.
40. Ibid., p. 466, 25 May 1857.

CHAPTER VI: COLD STORAGE ON THE NEVA

1. To Leopold von Gerlach, 2 May 1857, GW XIV, p. 464.
2. Christoph von Tiedemann, *Persönliche Erinnerungen an den Fürsten Bismarck* (Leipzig, 1898), p. 5.
3. Lucius von Ballhausen, *Bismarck-Erinnerungen*, p. 85.
4. F. de Martens, *Recueil des traités et conventions conclus par la Russie avec*

les puissances étrangères (St. Petersburg, 1874–1909), vol. VIII, pp. 453–54.

5. Eyck, *Bismarck and the German Empire*, p. 211.
6. Mar. 1858, GW II, pp. 302–22.
7. GW II, p.142; GW XIV, p. 441.
8. GW II, pp. 232ff.; and A. O. Meyer, *Bismarcks Kampf mit Oesterreich am Bundestag zu Frankfurt* (Leipzig and Berlin, 1927), pp. 549–53.
9. To Johanna, 15 Jan. 1859, GW XIV, pp. 496–97.
10. Count Josef Alexander von Hübner, *Neun Jahren der Erinnerungen eines oesterreichischen Botschafters in Paris* (Berlin, 1902), vol. II, p. 150.
11. To General Gustav von Alvensleben, 5 May 1859, GW XIV, p. 517.
12. To Baron Alexander von Schleinitz, 12 May 1859, GW III, p. 37.
13. Ibid., p. 38.
14. Otto Pflanze, *Bismarck and the Development of Germany* (Princeton, 1963), p. 127.
15. Christoph von Tiedemann, *Aus sieben Jahrzehnten* (Berlin, 1905), vol. II, p. 484.
16. To Malwine, 29 June 1859, GW XIV, p. 544.
17. Friedrich von Bernhardi, ed., *Aus dem Leben Theodore von Bernhardis*, (Leipzig, 1893–1906), vol. III, p. 305.
18. Pflanze, op. cit., p. 133, quoting Rudolf Haym, *Das Leben Max Dunckers* (Berlin, 1891), p. 213.
19. Kurd von Schlözer, *Briefe eines Diplomaten*, ed. Heinz Flügel (Stuttgart, Deutsche Verlag-Anstalt, n.d.), p 97, 18/6 April 1859. The double dates in letters from Russia arise from the difference between the Julian and Gregorian calendars.
20. Ibid., p. 100, 28/16 Apr. 1859.
21. Ibid., p. 103, 21/9 May 1859.
22. Ibid., p. 113, 31/10 Aug. 1860.
23. Ibid., p. 113, Oct. 1860.
24. Ibid., pp. 116–17, 26/14 Nov. 1860.
25. Ibid., p. 117.
26. To Leopold von Gerlach, 2/4 May 1860, GW XIV, p. 547.
27. To Schleinitz, 10 Sept. 1860, GW III, P. 148.
28. Ibid.
29. To Alexander von Below-Hohendorf, 22 Aug. 1860, GW XIV, pp. 561–62.
30. Norman Rich and M. H. Fisher, *The Holstein Papers* (Cambridge, England, 1955–63), vol. I, p. 5.
31. To Malwine, 26 Mar. 1861, GW XIV, p. 568.
32. GW III, p. 100.
33. Keudell, *Fürst und Fürstin Bismarck*, p. 84, 21 Apr. 1861.

CHAPTER VII: THE CALL TO ACTION

1. Ludwig Bamberger, *Count Bismarck, a Political Biography*, trans. Charles Lees Lewis (London, 1869), p. 113.
2. General Albrecht von Roon, *Denkwürdigkeiten* (Berlin, 1905), vol. I, pp. 339–40, and vol. II, pp. 521ff.
3. Gordon A. Craig, *The Politics of the Prussian Army 1640–1945*, rev. paperback ed. (London, Oxford, New York, 1964), p. 67.
4. Ibid., p. 141, quoting Erich Marcks, *Kaiser Wilhelm I*, 4th ed. (Leipzig, 1900), pp. 178–79.
5. H. L. von Schweinitz, *Denkwürdigkeiten des Botschafters H. L. von Schweinitz*, ed. H. von Schweinitz (Berlin, 1927), pp. 242–43.
6. Gordon A. Craig, 'Portrait of a Political General: Edwin von Manteuffel and the Constitutional Conflict in Prussia,' in *Political Science Quarterly*, Vol. 66 no. 1 (1951), pp. 1–36.
7. Prince Kraft zu Hohenlohe-Ingelfingen, *Aus meinem Leben* (Berlin, 1887–1888), vol. II, pp. 244–46.
8. Pflanze, *Bismarck and the Development of Germany*, p. 163, quoting Karl Twesten, *Was uns noch retten kann* (Berlin, 1861), pp. 81–82.
9. Roon, op. cit., vol. II, p. 21.
10. Craig, *Politics of the Prussian Army*, pp. 153–54, quoting from *Roon Nachlass*, Manteuffel to Roon, 6 July 1861.
11. Bernhardi, *Aus dem Leben*, vol. IV, p. 256.
12. Johanna to Keudell, 7 Jan. 1862, in Keudell, *Fürst und Fürstin Bismarck*, p. 88.
13. To Malwine, 17 Jan. 1862, GW XIV, p. 581.
14. To Johanna, 21 May 1862, GW XIV, p. 586.
15. To Johanna, 2 July 1862, GW XIV, p. 590.
16. To Count Albrecht von Bernstorff, July 1862, GW III, pp. 381–82; also GW XV, pp. 173–74.
17. Kurt Promnitz, *Bismarcks Eintritt in das Ministerium* (Berlin, 1908), pp. 44–49.
18. Graf C. F. Vitzthum von Eckstädt, *St. Petersburg und London in den Jahren 1852–1864* (Stuttgart, 1887), vol. II, pp. 158–59.
19. Brunnow to St. Petersburg, 5/17 July 1862, quoted in J. Y. Simpson, *The Saburov Memoirs, or Bismarck and Russia* (Cambridge, England, 1929), pp. 4–5.
20. To Johanna, 19 Aug. 1862, GW XIV, p. 612.
21. To Malwine, 20 Aug. 1862, GW XIV, p. 613.
22. Johanna to Keudell, 7 Sept. 1862, in Keudell, op. cit., p. 96.
23. To Roon, 14 Sept. 1862, GW XIV, p. 619.
24. Johanna to Keudell, 24 Sept. 1862, in Keudell, op. cit., p. 97.
25. GW XV, pp. 177–80.

PART TWO: ACHIEVEMENT

CHAPTER VIII: ONE MAN AGAINST THE REST

1. Emperor Frederick III, *Tagebücher 1848–66*, ed. H. O. Weisner, (Leipzig, 1929), pp. 160–61.
2. To Schleinitz, 12 May 1859, GW III, p. 38.
3. Kohl II, p. 30, 30 Sept. 1862.
4. GW XV, pp. 194–95.
5. Ibid.
6. Kurd Schlözer, *Briefe eines Diplomaten*, pp. 135–36.
7. Kohl II, pp. 78–79, 27 Jan. 1863.
8. Ibid., pp. 79–80.
9. Ibid., p. 87.
10. Erich Eyck, *Bismarck, Leben und Werk*, 3 vols. (Zurich, 1941–44), vol. I, p. 460. This is the original version of Eyck's splendid work. *Bismarck and the German Empire*, referred to earlier, is a single-volume English-language abridgement by the author himself, which contains certain passages not in the main work.
11. Fürst Nikolai Orloff, *Bismarck und Katharina Orloff* (Munich, 1944), p.103.
12. To J. L. Motley, 17 Apr. 1863, GW XIV, p. 639; and Motley, *The Correspondence of John Lothrop Motley*, vol. II, pp. 126–27.

CHAPTER IX: NEW MANNERS; NEW WAYS

1. W. O. Henderson, *The Rise of German Industrial Power 1834–1914* (London, 1975), p. 113.
2. Ibid., pp. 115 and 117.
3. To Johanna, 5 July 1862, GW XIV, p. 612.
4. Heinrich Ritter von Srbik, *Quellen zur deutschen Politik Oesterreichs* (Oldenburg, 1934–38), vol. II, pp. 719–21ff.
5. GW XIV, p. 628.
6. GW VII, pp. 69–72.
7. GW VII, p. 72.
8. APP III, pp. 131–32.
9. See Note 4 above.
10. See Ch. XII below.
11. Heinrich Friedjung, *The Struggle for Supremacy in Germany* (London, 1935), p. 29. This is an admirable translation and abridgement, by A. J. P. Taylor and W. L. McElwee, of Friedjung's two-volume classic, *Der Kampf um die Vorherrschaft in Deutschland* (Stuttgart, 1897).
12. To Malwine, 26/14 Mar. 1861, GW XIV, p. 568.
13. To Bernstorff, 25/13 Nov. 1861, GW III, pp. 289–90.
14. 8 July 1866, GW VII, p. 140.

15. E. N. Anderson, *The Social and Political Conflict in Prussia* (Lincoln, Nebraska, 1954), p. 343.
16. See Sir Frederick Ponsonby, *Letters of the Empress Frederick* (London, 1928), and the three volumes of correspondence between Queen Victoria and her eldest daughter, all edited by Roger Fulford, *Dearest Child* (London, 1964), *Dearest Mama* (London, 1965) and *Your Dearest Letter* (London, 1971).
17. Crown Princess to Queen Victoria, 27 Sept. 1887, in Ponsonby, op. cit, pp. 246–47.
18. 21 May 1863, in Fulford, ed., *Dearest Mama*, p. 211.
19. Frederick III, *Tagebücher 1848–1866*, p. 198.

CHAPTER X: SERVANT INTO MASTER

1. GW XV, p. 233.
2. Ibid., p. 234.
3. Count Friedrich von Beust, *Aus drei Viertel-Jahrhunderten* (Stuttgart, 1887), vol. I, pp. 332ff.
4. Hohenlohe-Ingelfingen, *Aus Meinem Leben*, vol. II, pp. 334–35.
5. *Queen Victoria's Letters 1862–78* (London, 1926), vol. I, p. 108.
6. Franz Schnürer, *Briefe Franz Josephs an seine Mutter 1838–1872* (Munich, 1930), p. 320.
7. Keudel, *Fürst und Fürstin Bismarck*, p. 126.
8. Ibid.
9. GW II, p. 240.
10. Kohl I, pp. 264–65, 3 Dec. 1850.
11. APP VIII, p. 133.
12. APP IV, p. 435.
13. Ernst Vogt, *Die hessische Politik in der Zeit der Reichsgründung* (Munich and Berlin, 1914), p. 212.
14. Eyck, *Bismarck, Leben and Werk*, vol. I, p. 586.
15. OD IV, p. 62.
16. To Johanna, 17 July 1864, GW XIV, p. 672.
17. Vogt, op. cit., p. 212; and L. D. Steefel, *The Schleswig-Holstein Question* (Cambridge, Mass., 1932), p. 256.
18. Srbik, *Quellen zur deutschen Politik Oesterreichs*, vol. III, p. 621.
19. APP IV, pp. 300–303; Eyck, op. cit., vol. I, p. 587.
20. Eyck, op. cit., vol. I, pp. 587–88.
21. Lord Robert Cecil, (later Marquess of Salisbury), *The Quarterly Review* (London), April 1864; also in *Essays by Robert, Marquess of Salisbury, 1861–1864* (London, 1905), pp. 230–31.
22. Friedjung, *The Struggle for Supremacy*, p. 54.
23. Francis Joseph to Albert of Saxony, 16 Feb. 1864, *Staats-Haus und Hof Archiv*, Vienna.

24. Bismarck to Count Robert von der Goltz, 24 Dec. 1864, GW XV, p. 262.
25. Keudell, op. cit., p. 153.
26. Steefel, op. cit., p. 256.

CHAPTER XI: OPPORTUNISM AS A FINE ART

1. Busch I, pp. 247–48.
2. W. F. Monypenny, and G. E. Buckle, *The Life of Benjamin Disraeli, Earl of Beaconsfield* (London, 1910–20), vol. VI, p. 332.
3. Friedjung, *The Struggle for Supremacy*, p. 102.
4. Ibid., pp. 120–21.
5. Conversation with General Stefan Türr, 11 June 1866, GW VII, p. 126.
6. Kohl II, pp. 166–67, Apr. 17, 1863.
7. Ibid.; Pflanze, *Bismarck and the Development of Germany*, p. 197.
8. Friedjung, op. cit., p. 55.
9. A. J. P. Taylor, *Bismarck: The Man and the Statesman* (London, 1955), p. 79.
10. Kohl II, p. 253, 21 Jan. 1864.
11. Bernhardi, *Aus dem Leben*, vol. V, pp. 224–25.
12. Ibid., vol. VI, p. 102.
13. Pflanze, op. cit., p. 278, quoting L. Parisius, *Leopold Freiherr von Hover-beck* (Berlin, 1897–1900), vol. II, pp. 15–16.
14. To Johanna, 30 Oct. 1864, GW XIV, p. 687.

CHAPTER XII: TO THE BRINK—AND OVER

1. Pflanze, *Bismarck and the Development of Germany*, p. 251, quoting Walter Lipgens, 'Bismarcks Österreich-Politik vor 1866,' in *Die Welt als Geschichte* X (1950), pp. 244–77.
2. To Johanna, 7 Oct. 1864, GW XIV, p. 681.
3. Beust, *Aus drei Viertel-Jahrhunderten*, vol. I, pp. 403–404; Eyck, *Bismarck, Leben und Werk*, vol. II, pp. 32–34.
4. Fritz Stern, *Gold and Iron* (New York and London, 1977); see especially pp. 37–47.
5. C. W. Clark, *Franz Joseph and Bismarck*, Harvard Historical Studies, vol. 36 (Cambridge, Mass., 1934), p. 198.
6. Ibid., pp. 542–47.
7. Roon, *Denkwürdigkeiten*, vol. II, pp. 354–55; Stern, op. cit., p. 63.
8. Stern, op. cit.
9. Clark, op. cit., p. 290.
10. Stern, op. cit., p. 64.
11. OD II, pp. 453–54.
12. Ibid.
13. Orloff, *Bismarck und Katharina Orloff*, pp. 88–89, 3 Oct. 1865.

14. Ibid., p. 113, 21 Oct. 1865.
15. Ibid., p. 115, 30 Oct. 1865.
16. Ibid.
17. To Hermann von Thile, 23 Oct. 1865, GW XIV, p. 707.
18. GW V, pp. 396–99; OD VII, p. 214.
19. Hermann Oncken, ed., *Die Rheinpolitik Kaiser Napoleons III von 1863 bis 1870* (Berlin, 1926), vol. 1, pp. 147 and 165.
20. Ibid.
21. Raymond Mortimer, ed., *Queen Victoria: Leaves from a Journal* (London, 1961), p. 34.
22. Károlyi to Mensdorff, 14 Apr. 1866, in Srbik, *Quellen*, vol. V (i), pp. 486–87; Roon, op. cit., vol. II, p. 400; and GW V, p. 461.

CHAPTER XIII: GERMAN AGAINST GERMAN

1. Stern, *Gold and Iron*, p. 48.
2. GW VII, p. 117.
3. GW VII, p. 127; and Lord Augustus Loftus, *Diplomatic Reminiscences*, 2d series (London, 1894), vol. I, p. 60.
4. Oskar Regele, *Feldzugmeister Benedek* (Vienna, 1960), p. 436.
5. To Johanna, 16 June 1866, GW XIV, pp. 717–18.
6. GW VII, pp. 186–87.
7. Keudell, *Fürst und Fürstin Bismarck*, p. 297.
8. To Johanna, 9 July 1866, GW XIV, p. 717.
9. GW XV, p. 279.
10. GW VI, pp. 78–81; GW XV, p. 279; and Frederick III, *Tagebücher*, pp. 470–73.
11. Keudell, op. cit., p. 398.
12. GW VI, pp. 45–55.
13. GW VII, pp. 148–49.
14. GW VI, pp. 83, 120; GW VII, p. 156; and W. E. Mosse, *The European Powers and the German Question* (Cambridge, England, 1958), pp. 243–47.
15. GW VII, p. 156, 10 Aug. 1866.
16. GW VII, pp. 234–35; GW XV, p. 278.

CHAPTER XIV: 'I HAVE BEATEN THEM ALL!'

1. *Rudolf von Ihering in Briefen an seine Freunde* (Leipzig, 1913), pp. 196–98, quoted by W. H. Simon in *Germany in the Age of Bismarck* (London, 1960), p. 111.
2. Ibid., pp. 205–207, quoted in Simon, op. cit., p. 108.
3. Julius Heyderhoff, and Paul Wentzcke, eds., *Deutscher Liberalismus im Zeitalter Bismarcks: Eine politische Briefsammlung* (Osnabrück, 1967), pp. 255–56.

4. Stern, *Gold and Iron*, p. 87, quoting Heinrich von Poschinger, ed., *Erinnerungen aus dem Leben von Hans Viktor von Unruh* (Stuttgart, 1895), pp. 243–50.

5. Heyderhoff and Wentzcke, op. cit., p. 296, quoting Hermann Baumgarten to Karl Twesten, 17 May 1866.

6. Rudolf Hubner, ed., *Briefwechsel von Johann Gustav Droysen* (Berlin and Leipzig, 1929), vol. II, pp. 871–72, quoted in Simon, op. cit., p. 105.

7. Ernst Ludwig von Gerlach, *Die Annexionen und der Norddeutscher Bund*, 6th ed. (Berlin, 1866), pp. 3–5, quoted in Simon, op. cit., p. 125.

8. Eyck, *Bismarck, Leben und Werk*, vol. II, p. 305.

9. See Notes 12 and 13 to Ch. XIII above.

10. Keudell, *Fürst und Fürstin Bismarck*, p. 309.

11. To Count Artur Seher-Toss, GW VII, p. 140.

12. Keudell, op. cit., pp. 309–10.

13. 13 Apr. 1866. *Karl Marx und Friedrich Engels: Briefwechsel* (Berlin, 1930), vol. III, pp. 326–27.

14. *Ibid.*, pp. 349–50, 25 July 1866.

CHAPTER XV: THE SUPREME GAMBLE

1. Stern, *Gold and Iron*; especially Ch. 12.

2. Ibid., pp. 133–34.

3. Lucius, *Bismarck-Erinnerungen*, p. 28.

4. To Roon, 29 Aug. 1866, GW XIV, pp. 756–57.

5. Eyck, *Bismarck, Leben und Werk*, vol. II, p. 284; OD XI, pp. 164 and 241.

6. Eyck, loc. cit.; APP VIII, p. 120.

7. OD XII, pp. 116–17, 170–75; and Oncken, *Die Rheinpolitik*, vol. II, pp. 82–83ff.

8. Winifred Taffs, *Ambassador to Bismarck: Lord Odo Russell, First Baron Ampthill* (London, 1938), pp. 17–18.

9. OD XIII, pp. 200 and 226; Oncken, op. cit., p. 201.

10. OD XIII, pp. 273, 322, 367; Oncken, op. cit., pp. 146–50; APP VIII, p. 212.

11. Pflanze, *Bismarck and the Development of Germany*, p. 378; Emile Ollivier, *L'Empire libéral*, 17 vols. (Paris, 1895–1912), vol. IX, p. 233–37; APP VIII, p. 397.

12. Ollivier, op. cit.

13. Hermann Oncken, *Rudolf von Bennigsen* (Stuttgart, 1910), vol. II, p. 33.

14. GW VI, pp. 323–31; APP VIII, p. 615.

15. APP VIII, p. 641; GW VI, pp. 322–23.

16. For an examination of the annexation policy see Walter Lipgens, 'Bismarck, die offentliche Meinung und die Annexion von Elsass und Lothringen,' in *Historische Zeitschrift* 199 (1964), 31–112.

17. GW VII, pp. 186–87.

18. E. Kessel, *Moltke* (Stuttgart, 1957), p. 533.

19. Lord Odo Russell to Lord Granville, 2 Mar. 1873, in Paul Knaplund, *Letters from the Berlin Embassy 1871–74 and 1880–85*, American Historical Association Reports (Washington, 1944), p. 92.

20. To Baron Georg von Werthern, 11 Jan. 1869, GW VI(b), pp. 1–2.

21. APP X, p. 553; Pflanze, op. cit., p. 414.

22. Busch I, p. 4.

23. This whole affair is described and analyzed in the editor's introduction to *Bismarck and the Hohenzollern Candidature for the Spanish Throne*, ed. Georges Bonnin, (London, 1957). See also R. H. Lord, *The Origins of the War of 1870* (Cambridge, Mass., 1924) and Ludwig Dehio, *Bismarck, Frankreich und die spanische Thronkandidatur* (Munich and Oldenburg, 1962). The best modern analyses are S. William Halperin, 'The Origins of the Franco-Prussian War Revisited: Bismarck and the Hohenzollern Candidature for the Spanish Throne,' in *Journal of Modern History* 45 (1973); Josef Becker 'Zum Problem des Bismarckischen Politik in die spanische Thronfolge 1870,' in *Historische Zeitschrift* 212 (1971); and Jochum Dittrich, 'Ursachen und Ausbruch des Krieges 1870–71,' in Ernst Deuerlein and Theodor Schieder, eds., *Reichsgründung 1870–71* (Stuttgart, 1970).

24. 3 Oct. 1868, GW VI(a), p. 412.

25. 11 May 1869, GW VI(b), p. 82.

26. Bismarck's own account of the events leading up to the Franco-Prussian War is in GW XV, pp. 301–11.

27. 25 Feb. 1870. The complete letter is in Bonnin, op. cit., pp. 63–65. It was previously published (with omissions indicated by Bonnin) in K. T. Zingeler, *Karl Anton, Fürst von Hohenzollern* (Stuttgart and Leipzig, 1911), pp. 237–39.

28. To William I, 9 Mar. 1870, GW VI(b), pp. 271–74; and Bonnin, op. cit., pp. 68–72.

29. Bonnin, op. cit., pp. 69–72.

30. Ibid., pp. 291–94.

31. 28 May 1870, GW VI(b), p. 557; and Bonnin, op. cit., p. 158.

32. Prince Charles Anthony to Bismarck, 31 May 1870, in Bonnin, op. cit., p. 162.

33. Thile to Bismarck, 19 June 1870, ibid., p. 191.

34. Bismarck marginal commentary on above, ibid.

35. Lord, op. cit., p. 42; Ollivier, op. cit., vol. XIV, pp. 109–10.

36. Keudell, *Fürst und Fürstin Bismarck*, p. 429

37. Lord, op. cit., pp. 46, 155. See Busch I, pp. 28ff for Bismarck's manipulation of the press.

38. Lord, op. cit., p. 42; Ollivier, op. cit., vol. XIV, p. 110.

39. Lord, op. cit., pp. 30–31, 121–22.
40. Bonnin, op. cit., pp. 237–38.
41. Stern, op. cit., p. 128.
42. Prince Charles Anthony to William I, 12 July 1871, in Bonnin, op. cit., pp. 250–51 (complete) and Zingeler, op. cit., pp. 236–37 (incomplete).
43. GW XV, pp. 305–307, and Lord, op. cit., pp. 68ff.
44. Ibid., GW XV, loc. cit.
45. Lord, op. cit., pp. 201–204, 224–25.
46. Ibid., pp. 219–20.
47. OD XXVIII, p. 255, 12 July 1870.
48. For an analytical discussion of the Ems telegram affair see especially William L. Langer, 'Bismarck as a Dramatist' in A. O. Sarkissian, ed., *Studies in Diplomatic History and Historiography in Honour of G. P. Gooch* (London, 1961), pp. 201ff.; Lord, op. cit., pp. 220 and 231–32, gives Abeken's original telegram and Bismarck's revised version.
49. Napoleon's Order of the Day, 28 July 1870. Michael Howard, *The Franco-Prussian War: The German Invasion of France 1870–71* (London, 1968), p. 78.
50. Ibid., p. 77. Howard's book is incomparably the best account in any language of the war and its military background.

CHAPTER XVI: SEDAN, PARIS, AND THE NEW REICH

1. Frederick III, *Das Kriegstagebuch von 1870–81*, ed. H. O. Meisner (Berlin, 1926), p. 9; and Ponsonby, *Letters of the Empress Frederick* (London, 1928), p. 79.
2. For a discussion of the development of the institution of chief of staff see Craig, *The Politics of the Prussian Army*, esp. Ch. II, pp. 45, 63, 78 and Ch. V, pp. 193ff.
3. Edward Crankshaw, *The Fall of the House of Habsburg* (London, 1963), pp. 62–63; and *The Shadow of the Winter Palace* (New York and London, 1976), p. 142.
4. To Johanna, 16 Aug. 1870, GW XIV, p. 785.
5. Ibid.
6. To Johanna, 17 Aug. 1870, GW XIV, pp. 785–86.
7. See Howard, *The Franco-Prussian War*, pp. 167–82, for the full horror of Gravelotte.
8. Leonhard, Graf von Blumenthal, *Tagebücher aus den Jahren 1866 und 1870–71*, ed. Albrecht Graf von Blumenthal (Stuttgart and Berlin, 1902), p. 110.
9. Howard, op. cit., p. 208.
10. See especially Busch I, pp. 151–53.

11. Howard, op. cit., pp. 219–22, has a vivid account of the negotiations based on a variety of sources.
12. Frederick III, op. cit., p. 99.
13. To Herbert von Bismarck, 7 Sept. 1870, GW XIV, p. 791.
14. Busch I, p. 172.
15. Howard, op. cit., p. 232.
16. To Herbert von Bismarck, 23 Sept. 1870, GW XIV, p. 793.
17. Busch I, pp. 256, 294–96. For unfavourable reactions see Frederick III, op. cit., p. 292, and Ludwig Bamberger, *Bismarcks Grosses Spiel,* ed. Ernst Feder (Frankfurt, 1932), pp. 152–53.
18. Rich and Fisher, *The Holstein Papers,* vol. II, p. 64.
19. Cosima Wagner, *Die Tagebücher* (Munich and Zurich, 1976), vol. I, pp. 272 and 281.
20. Blumenthal, op. cit., p. 193.
21. GW VI(b) pp. 552–53.
22. To Johanna, 28–29 Oct. 1870, GW XIV, pp. 797–98.
23. Busch I, pp. 40–41.
24. Ulrich von Stosch, ed., *Denkwürdigkeiten des Generals und Admirals Albrecht von Stosch* (Stuttgart, 1904), p. 227.
25. Odo Russell to Lord Granville, 2 Mar. 1873, in Taffs, *Ambassador to Bismarck,* pp. 92–93.
26. Eyck, *Bismarck, Leben und Werk,* vol. II, p. 550.
27. Ibid.; see also O. Becker, *Bismarcks Ringen um Deutschlands Gestaltung* (Heidelberg, 1958), pp. 747–49; Friedrich III, op. cit., pp. 220 and 223.
28. Stern, *Gold and Iron,* p. 133.
29. Friedrich III, *Kriegstagebuch,* p. 212.
30. Ibid., p. 224.
31. To Johanna, 14 Dec. 1870, GW XIV, p. 802.
32. Eyck, op. cit., vol. III, p. 333.
33. Ibid., pp. 563–64.
34. To Johanna, 21 Jan. 1871, GW XIV, p. 810.
35. Frederick III, op. cit., pp. 202–203, 31 Dec. 1870.

PART THREE: TO WHAT END?

CHAPTER XVII: BARREN YEARS

1. W. N. Medlicott, *Bismarck, Gladstone and the Concert of Europe* (London, 1958), p. 12.
2. Disraeli in the House of Commons, 9 Feb. 1871, *Hansard,* 3d series, vol. CCIV, pp. 81–82.
3. Wimpffen to Beust, 13 Aug. 1870, quoted in Helmut Böhme, ed., *The*

Foundation of the German Empire, trans. Agatha Ramm (Oxford, 1971), p. 16.

4. Helmut Böhme, *Deutschlands weg zur Grossmacht*, p. 25, quoting a contemporary newspaper article.

5. Busch I, pp. 288–89.

6. Taffs, *Ambassador to Bismarck*, pp. 11–12.

7. Lord Odo Russell to Lord Granville, 18 Oct. 1872, in Knaplund, *Letters from the Berlin Embassy*, p. 71.

8. 4 Dec. 1874, Kohl VI, pp. 214–26.

9. GW XV, p. 335.

10. Busch II, p. 289.

11. GW XV, p. 333.

12. Lord Odo Russell to Lord Granville, in Taffs, op. cit., p. 18.

13. Ibid.

14. Edward Crankshaw, *The Fall of the House of Habsburg*, pp. 256–60.

15. Eyck, *Bismarck, Leben und Werk*, vol. III, p. 140. For the Arnim affair see especially G. O. Kent, *Arnim and Bismarck* (Oxford, 1965); also, for Bismarck's own story, GW XV, pp. 556–60.

16. Eyck, op. cit., vol. III, p. 142.

17. Henderson, *The Rise of German Industrial Power*, p. 170.

18. Orloff, *Bismarck und Katharina Orloff*, pp. 162–63, 10 Feb. 1875.

19. Eyck, op. cit., vol. III, pp. 157–58.

20. Rudolf Stadelmann, *Das Jahr 1865 und das Problem von Bismarcks deutsche Politik* (Munich, 1933), p. 41.

21. Rudolf Stadelmann, *Moltke und der Staat* (Krefeld, 1950), p. 281.

22. Eyck, op. cit., vol. III, p. 162.

23. Ibid., p. 160.

24. Ibid., pp. 164–65.

25. Lord Odo Russell to Lord Derby, 2 May 1875, in Taffs, op. cit., pp. 89–91.

26. Eyck, op. cit., vol. III, p. 168.

27. To Lady Salisbury, 4 Oct. 1879. Lady Gwendoline Cecil, *Life of Robert, Marquess of Salisbury* (London, 1921), vol. II, p. 89.

28. Eyck, op. cit., vol. III, p. 172.

29. Lucius, *Bismarck-Erinnerungen*, p. 66.

30. Eyck, op. cit., vol. III, p. 174.

31. Ibid.

32. W. N. Medlicott, *Bismarck and Modern Germany* (London, 1965), p. 117.

33. 4 Jan. 1876, Orloff, op. cit., pp. 163–64.

CHAPTER XVIII: APOGEE

1. Medlicott, *Bismarck and Modern Germany*, p. 119, quoting from a lecture by Erich Marcks to an English audience in 1902.

2. See for example Taffs, *Ambassador to Bismarck*, pp. 118–122.
3. Stern, *Gold and Iron*, p. 187, quoting *Kreuzzeitung* for 29 June 1875.
4. Ibid., p. 191.
5. Hans Rothfels, *Bismarck und der Staat: Ausgewählte Dokumente* (Stuttgart, 1954), p. 62.
6. F. M. Hollyday, *Bismarck's Rival: A Political Biography of Albrecht von Stosch* (Cambridge, Eng., and Durham, N. Carolina, 1960), pp. 164–70.
7. Busch II, p. 468.
8. William to Bismarck, 30 Dec. 1877. *Kaiser Wilhelm I und Bismarck*, Horst Kohl, ed. (Stuttgart and Berlin, 1901) pp. 277–78.
9. Eyck, *Bismarck, Leben und Werk*, vol. III, pp. 226–27.
10. Quoted in Sydney Harcave, *Years of the Golden Cockerel* (London and New York, 1970), p. 221.
11. Kohl VI, pp. 446ff.
12. To Ernst von Bülow, 14 Aug. 1876, GP II, pp. 31–34.
13. Lothar von Schweinitz, *Denkwürdigkeiten*, vol. I, pp. 355–56 and 359–64; *Briefwechsel* (Berlin, 1928), p. 120; GP II pp. 80–84.
14. Lord Beaconsfield to Queen Victoria, 17 June 1878, in Monypenny and Buckle, *Life of Benjamin Disraeli*, vol. VI, p. 332.
15. Lord Beaconsfield to Lord Tenterden, 2 July 1878, quoted in B. H. Sumner, *Russia and the Balkans, 1870–78* (Oxford, 1937), p. 505.
16. Lord Beaconsfield to Lord Derby, 4 Sept. 1876, in Monypenny and Buckle, op. cit., vol. VI, pp. 52–53.
17. GP II, p. 87.
18. Eyck, op. cit., vol. III, p. 244.
19. Ibid., p. 267.
20. The Marquess of Zetland, ed., *The Letters of Disraeli to Lady Bradford and Lady Chesterfield* (London, 1929), p. 179.
21. 10 Sept. 1879. Marx-Engels, *Briefwechsel*, vol. IV, p. 497.
22. Emil Ludwig, *Bismarck, The Story of a Fighter*, trans. Eden and Cedar Paul (London, 1927), p. 528.
23. Ibid., p. 533.
24. Lord Beaconsfield to Queen Victoria, 17 June 1878, in Monypenny and Buckle, op. cit., vol. VI, p. 332.
25. Stern, op. cit., pp. 198–99.
26. Memorandum of 1853 to Prince William, GW I, p. 375.
27. Gordon Craig, *Germany 1866–1945* (Oxford, 1978), pp. 145–47.
28. See Stern, op. cit., pp. 203–205 especially, for Bleichröder's part as go-between.
29. Ibid., p. 206, quoting from Horst Kohl, *Fürst Bismarck: Regesten zu einer wissenschaftlichen Biographie des ersten deutschen Reichskanzlers* (Leipzig, 1891–92), vol. I, pp. 222–24.

CHAPTER XIX: THE OLD ENTERTAINER

1. To Hermann Wagener, 30 June 1850, GW XIV, p. 159.
2. GW I, pp. 375ff.
3. Ibid.
4. Schlözer, *Briefe eines Diplomaten*, p. 113.
5. Ibid., pp. 116–17.
6. J. Y. Simpson, ed., *The Saburov Memoirs, Bismarck and Russia* (London, 1929), pp. 83–85.
7. Lord Odo Russell to Lord Granville, 17 Jan. 1881, in Knaplund, *Letters from the Berlin Embassy*, pp. 188–89.
8. Wolfgang Windelband, *Bismarck und die europäischen Grossmächte, 1879–1885* (Essen, 1940), p. 66.
9. Ibid., p. 67.
10. Simpson, op. cit., p. 73.
11. Windelband, op. cit., p. 73.
12. Ibid., p. 79.
13. Ibid., p. 80.
14. Taffs, *Ambassador to Bismarck*, p. 105.
15. Eyck, *Bismarck, Leben und Werk*, vol. III, pp. 333ff.
16. Simpson, op. cit., p. 55.
17. Ibid., pp. 86–87.
18. Ibid., p. 100.
19. Ibid., pp. 173–74.
20. Ibid., p. 130.
21. Medlicott, *Bismarck, Gladstone and the Concert of Europe*, pp. 341–43. The full text of Bismarck's dispatch to Schweinitz of 26 February 1884, previously suppressed by the German Foreign Office, is given by Medlicott in the original German.
22. From Baron Karl vom und zum Stein's 'Nassau Manifesto,' quoted in C. P. Gooch, *Studies in German History* (London, 1946), p. 196.
23. Eyck, op. cit., vol. III, pp. 378–79.
24. Ibid., p. 378.
25. Stern, *Gold and Iron*, p. 198.
26. Rich and Fisher, *The Holstein Papers*, vol. I, p. 118.
27. R. Vierhaus, ed., *Das Tagebuch der Baronin Spitzemberg* (Göttingen, 1960), p. 218.
28. To Johanna, 14 May 1851, GW XIV, pp. 211–12.
29. Otto Pflanze, 'Towards a Psycho-analytical Interpretation of Bismarck,' in *American Historical Review* 77, p. 434, quoting from 'Bismarcks Persönlichkeit, ungedrückte persönliche Erinnerungen,' in *Süddeutsches Monatsheft* 19 (1921), pp. 114–115.
30. Christoph von Tiedemann, *Aus sieben Jahrzehnten* vol. II, p. 484.

31. Bismarck to William I, May 1872, GW VI(c), p. 19.
32. Bismarck to William I, 25 Dec. 1883, GW XIV, pp. 945–46.

CHAPTER XX: UNHAPPY ENDING

1. Courcel to Ferry; *Documents Diplomatiques Français 1871–1914*, 1st series, vol. V, p. 495.
2. Rich and Fisher, *The Holstein Papers*, vol. II, p. 200.
3. Ibid., p. 64.
4. Ibid., p. 133.
5. Ibid., p. 161, 19 Sept. 1884.
6. Schweinitz, *Briefwechsel*, p. 193.
7. Eyck, *Bismarck, Leben und Werk*, vol. III, p. 147.
8. Agatha Ramm, *Political Correspondence of Mr. Gladstone and Lord Granville 1876–1886* (Oxford, 1960), vol. II, pp. 242–43 and 251.
9. The best account of the Battenberg story is in Count Egon Corti, *Alexander of Battenberg* (London, 1954).
10. Corti, op. cit., pp. 287–94.
11. See especially Stern, *Gold and Iron*, pp. 442ff.; Hugh Seton-Watson, *The Russian Empire, 1801–1917* (Oxford, 1967), pp. 571–72.
12. Eyck, op. cit., vol. III, pp. 496–97.
13. Craig, *Politics of the Prussian Army*, pp. 267–70.
14. GW XIII, p. 347.
15. Eyck, op. cit., vol. III, p. 520.
16. Ibid., vol. III, pp. 515–16.
17. Lord Salisbury to Sir Edward Malet; Eyck, *Bismarck and the German Empire*, p. 302. See Ch. VIII, note 10 above.
18. GW XV, pp. 512–15; Karl Nowak, *Kaiser and Chancellor* (London, 1930), pp. 204–208; Lucius, *Bismarck-Erinnerungen*, pp. 521–22.
19. See especially the posthumous volume of Bismarck memoirs, published as *Gedanken und Erinnerungen* (Stuttgart and Berlin, 1919), vol. III, pp. 81–110.
20. W. Bussmann, *Staatssekretar Graf Herbert von Bismarck* (Göttingen, 1954), p. 567.
21. Bismarck's speeches delivered in his 'retirement' to audiences in many towns and cities occupy two hundred large quarto pages in GW XIII.
22. Franz Schnabel, 'The Bismarck Problem,' in Hans Kohn, ed., *German History, Some New German Views* (London, 1954), p. 73; the original German appeared in *Hochland* (Munich) for October 1949. See also Ch. XIII, note 18 above.

SELECT BIBLIOGRAPHY

Anderson, E. N. *The Social and Political Conflict in Prussia.* Lincoln, Nebraska, 1954.

Bamberger, Ludwig. *Count Bismarck: A Political Biography.* London, 1869.

———. *Bismarcks grosses Spiel.* See Feyder, ed., below.

Becker, Oskar. *Bismarcks Ringen um Deutschlands Gestaltung.* Heidelberg, 1958.

Beust, Graf Friedrich von. *Drei Vierteljahrhunderten.* Stuttgart, 1887. 2 vols.

Blumenthal, Graf Leonhard von. *Tagebücher des Generalfeldmarschalls Grafen von Blumenthal aus den Jahren 1866 und 1870/71,* ed. Albrecht Graf von Blumenthal. Stuttgart and Berlin, 1902.

Böhme, Helmut. *Deutschlands Weg zur Grossmacht.* Cologne, 1966.

———, ed. *Probleme der Reichsgründungszeit, 1848–79.* Cologne and Berlin, 1968.

Bonnin, Georges, ed., *Bismarck and the Hohenzollern Candidature for the Throne of Spain.* London, 1952; New York, 1960.

Bronsart von Schellendorf, Paul. *Geheimes Kriegstagebuch.* Bonn, 1954.

Buchheim, Karl. 'The Via Dolorosa of the Civilian Spirit in Germany.' See Kohn, Hans, below.

Busch, Moritz. *Tagebuchblätter.* Leipzig, 1899. 2 vols.

Bussmann, W. *Staatssekretär Graf Herbert von Bismarck.* Göttingen, 1964.

Clark, C. W. *Franz Joseph and Bismarck,* Harvard Historical Studies, vol. 36. Cambridge, Mass., 1934.

Corti, Count E. C. *Alexander von Battenberg,* tr. E. M. Hodgson. London, 1954; New York, 1955.

———. *The English Empress.* London, 1957.

Craig, Gordon A. *The Politics of the Prussian Army, 1640–1945.* Oxford and New York, 1955.

———. *The Battle of Königgrätz.* Philadelphia, 1964; London, 1965.

———. *Germany, 1866–1945*. Oxford and New York, 1978.

Crankshaw, Edward. *The Fall of the House of Habsburg*. London and New York, 1963.

———. *The Shadow of the Winter Palace*. London and New York, 1976.

Curtius, Friedrich, ed. *Denkwürdigkeiten des Fürsten Chlodwig zu Hohenlohe-Schillingsfürst*. Stuttgart, 1907. 2 vols.

Dehio, Ludwig. *Gleichgewicht oder Hegemonie*. Krefeld, 1948.

———. *Bismarck, Frankreich und die spanische Thronkandidatur*. Munich and Oldenburg, 1962.

———. 'Bismarck und die Heeresvorlagen der Konfliktzeit,' in *Historische Zeitschrift*, 144 (1931).

Demeter, Karl. *Das deutsche Heer und seine Offiziere*. Berlin, 1970.

Dittrich, Jochen. 'Ursachen und Ausbruch des Krieges, 1870/71,' in Ernst Deuerlein and Theodor Schieder, eds., *Reichsgründung 1870/71: Tatsachen, Kontroversen, Interpretaten*. Stuttgart, 1970.

Eulenberg, Fürst Phillip zu. *Aus 50 Jahren*. Berlin, 1925.

Eyck, Erich. *Bismarck, Leben und Werk*. Zurich, 1941/44. 3 vols.

———. *Bismarck and the German Empire* (single-volume condensation of the above). New York, 1951; translated as *Bismarck und das Deutsche Reich* (Munich, 1976).

———. *Auf Deutschlands politischen Forum*. Zurich and Stuttgart, 1963.

———. 'Holstein as Bismarck's Critic,' in Sarkissian, ed., below.

Feyder, E., ed. *Bismarcks grosses Spiel: die geheimen Tagebücher Bambergers*. Frankfurt-am-Main, 1932.

Flenley, Ralph. *Modern German History*, 4th rev. ed. London and New York, 1968.

Friedjung, Heinrich. *Der Kampf um die Vorherrschaft in Deutschland*, 10th ed. Stuttgart and Berlin, 1897. 2 vols. Abridged and translated as *The Struggle for Supremacy in Germany* by A. J. P. Taylor and W. L. McElwee (London, 1935).

Frederick III. *Das Kriegstagebuch von 1870–71*, ed. H. O. Meisner. Berlin, 1926.

———. *Tagebücher 1848–66*, ed. H. O. Meisner. Leipzig, 1929.

Fulford, Roger, ed. *Dearest Child; Dearest Mama; Your Dearest Letter*. London and New York, 1964, 1968, 1971 (1972). Three volumes of correspondence between Queen Victoria and the Princess Royal, Crown Princess of Prussia, later German Empress.

Gall, Lothar. *Das Bismarck Problem in der Geschichtsbeschreibung nach 1845*. Cologne, 1971.

———. 'Das Problem Elsass-Lorthringen,' in Deuerlein and Schieder, eds., above.

Gerlach, Leopold von. *Denkwürdigkeiten*. Berlin, 1891. 2 vols.

Gerlach, Ludwig von. *Aufzeichnungen aus seinem Leben und Wirken*. Schwerin, 1903. 2 vols.

Gooch, G. P. *Studies in German History.* London and New York, 1948.

Grant, Robertson C. *Bismarck.* London, 1918.

Hamerow, T. W. *Restoration, Evolution, Reaction.* Princeton, 1958.

——. *The Social Foundations of German Unification, 1858–1871.* Princeton, 1969 and 1972. 2 vols.

——, ed. *Otto von Bismarck: An Historical Assessment.* Princeton, 1969.

Henderson, W. O. *The Rise of German Industrial Power 1834–1914.* London, 1975; Berkeley, Cal., 1976.

Hohenzollern-Ingelfingen, Prinz Kraft zu. *Aus meinem Leben 1848–71.* Berlin, 1897–1907. 4 vols.

Holbein, Hajo. *A History of Modern Germany, 1840–1945.* New York, 1969.

Hollyday, F. B. M. *Bismarck's Rival: Albrecht von Stosch.* Durham, N.C., 1960.

Howard, Michael. *The Franco-Prussian War.* London, 1960; New York, 1961.

——. 'William I and the Reform of the Prussian Army,' in Gilbert Martin, ed, *A Century of Conflict: Essays for A. J. P. Taylor.* London and New York, 1966.

Kent, George O. *Arnim and Bismarck.* Oxford and New York, 1968.

Keudell, Robert. *Fürst und Fürstin Bismarck.* Berlin, 1901.

Kissinger, Henry. 'Bismarck, the White Revolutionary,' in *Daedalus* (Summer 1968).

Knaplund, Paul. *Letters from the Berlin Embassy, 1871–74 and 1880–85,* American Historical Association Report, vol. 1. Washington, D.C., 1944.

Kohn, Hans, ed. *German History, Some New German Views.* London and Boston, 1954. See also Alfred van Martin and Karl Budiheim.

Langer, W. L. *European Alliances and Alignments,* rev. ed. New York, 1950.

——. 'Bismarck as Dramatist.' See Sarkissian, ed., below.

Lipgens, Walter. 'Bismarck, die öffentliche Meinung und die Annexion von Elsass und Lothringen,' in *Historische Zeitschrift* 199 (1964), pp. 31–112.

Loftus, Lord Augustus. *Diplomatic Reminiscences,* series 2, vol. 1. London, 1894.

Lord, R. H. *The Origins of the War of 1870.* Cambridge, Mass., 1924.

Lucius von Ballhausen, R. S. *Bismarck-Erinnerungen.* Stuttgart and Berlin, 1921.

Ludwig, Emil. *Bismarck: Geschichte eines Kämpfers.* Berlin, 1926.

Macartney, C. A. *The Habsburg Empire, 1790–1918.* London, 1968; New York, 1969.

Mann, Golo. *Deutsche Geschichte.* Frankfurt-am-Main, 1956.

——. 'The Second German Empire: The Reich That Never Was,' in E. J. Feuchtwanger, ed., *Upheaval and Continuity: A Century of German History.* London, 1973; Pittsburgh, 1974.

Marcks, Erich. *Bismarck, eine Biographie 1815–51,* rev. ed. Stuttgart, 1939.

Martin, Alfred von. 'Bismarck and Ourselves, A Contribution to the Destruction of an Historical Legend.' See Kohn, ed., above.

Marx, Karl, and Engels, Friedrich. *Briefwechsel,* vol. 3. Berlin, 1930.

Matter, Paul. *Bismarck et ses temps.* Paris, 1907–1909. 3 vols.

Medlicott, W. N. *The Congress of Berlin and After*. London, 1938.
———. *Bismarck, Gladstone and the Concert of Europe*. London and New York, 1956.
———. *Bismarck and Modern Germany*. London and Mystic, Ct., 1965.
———, and Coveney, Dorothy, eds. *Bismarck and Europe*. London, 1971; New York, 1972.
Meinecke, F. *The German Catastrophe*. Cambridge, Mass., 1950.
Meyer, A. O. *Bismarcks Glaube*. Munich, 1933.
———. *Bismarcks Kampf mit Oesterreich am Bundestag zu Frankfurt*. Leipzig and Berlin, 1927.
———. *Bismarck und Moltke vor dem Fall von Paris und beim Friedenschluss*. Berlin, 1943.
———. *Bismarck, der Mensch und der Staatsmann*. Stuttgart, 1949.
Moltke, H. K. B., Graf von. *Geschichte des deutsch-französischen Krieges von 1870–1871*. Berlin, 1891.
Monypenney, W. F., and Buckle, G. E. *The Life of Benjamin Disraeli, Earl of Beaconsfield*. London, 1910–1920. 6 vols.
Mosse, W. E. *The European Powers and the German Question, 1848–71*. Cambridge, England, and New York, 1958.
Muralt, Joachim von. *Bismarcks Verantwortlichkeit*. Göttingen, 1935.
Newton, Lord. *The Life of Lord Lyons*. London, 1913. 2 vols.
Noll von der Nahmer, Robert. *Bismarcks Reptilienfonds*. Mainz, 1968.
Ollivier, Emile (bibl 780). *L'Empire libéral: Etudes, récits, souvenirs*. Paris, 1895–1912. 16 vols.
Oncken, Hermann. *Rudolf von Bennigsen*. Stuttgart, 1910. 2 vols.
———. *Die Rheinpolitik Kaiser Napoleon III von 1863 bis 1870 und der Ursprung des Krieges von 1870–71*. Stuttgart, 1926. 3 vols.
Orloff, N. *Bismarck und Katharina Orloff*. Munich, 1936.
Palmer, Alan. *Bismarck*. London and New York, 1976.
Pflanze, Otto. *Bismarck and the Development of Germany: The Period of Unification*. Princeton, 1963.
Ponsonby, Sir Frederick, ed. *Letters of the Empress Frederick*. London, 1928.
Poschinger, H. von. *Fürst Bismarck und die Parlamentarier*. Breslau, 1894–96. 3 vols.
Ramm, Agatha. *Germany 1789–1919: A Political History*. London and New York, 1967.
Reiners, Ludwig. *Bismarck*. Munich, 1957. 2 vols.
Rich, Norman. *Friedrich von Holstein, Politics and Diplomacy in the Era of Bismarck and Wilhelm II*, vol 1. Cambridge, England, and New York, 1965.
———, and Fisher, M. H. *The Holstein Papers*. Cambridge, England, and New York, 1955–63. 4 vols.

Richter, Adolf. *Bismarck und die Arbeiterfrage in preussischen Verfassungskonflikt.* Stuttgart, 1933.

Richter, Werner. *Bismarck, eine Biographie.* Frankfurt-am-Main, 1962.

Ridley, Jasper. *Lord Palmerston.* London, 1970; New York, 1971.

Ritter, Gerhard. *Staatskunst und Kriegshandwerk: Das Problem des 'Militarismus' in Deutschland.* Munich, 1954–64. 4 vols.

Roon, A. T. E. von, Graf. *Denkwürdigkeiten aus dem Leben des Generalfeldmarschalls Kriegsministers Grafen von Roon.* Breslau, 1897. 3 vols.

Rothfels, Hans. *Bismarck und der Staat, Ausgewählte Dokumente,* 2d ed. Stuttgart, 1954.

———. *Bismarck, der Osten und das Reich.* Stuttgart, 1960.

———. 'Problems of a Bismarck Biography,' *Review of Politics* IX (1947).

Sarkissian, A. O., ed. *Studies in Diplomatic History and Historiography in Honour of G. P. Gooch.* London and New York, 1961. See also Eyck and Langer, above.

Schlözer, Kurd von. *Briefe eines Diplomaten,* ed. Heinz Flügel. Stuttgart, n.d.

———. *Petersburger Briefe.* Berlin, 1921.

Schmidt-Volkma, Erich. *Der Kulturkampf in Deutschland 1871–1890.* Göttingen, 1962.

Seton-Watson, Hugh. *The Russian Empire, 1801–1917.* Oxford and New York, 1967.

Seton-Watson, R. W. *Disraeli, Gladstone and the Eastern Question.* London, 1935.

Simon, W. M. *Germany in the Age of Bismarck.* London, 1968.

Simpson, J. Y. *The Saburov Memoirs.* Cambridge, England, 1929.

Schweinitz, H. L. von. *Denkwürdigkeiten.* Berlin, 1927. 2 vols.

———. *Briefwechsel.* Berlin, 1928.

Srbik, H., Ritter von. *Deutsche Einheit.* Munich, 1935–42. 4 vols.

———, ed. *Quellen zur deutschen Politik Oesterreichs 1859–66.* Oldenburg, 1934–38. 5 vols.

Steefel, L. D. *The Schleswig-Holstein Question.* Cambridge, Mass., 1932.

———. *Bismarck, the Hohenzollern Candidacy and the Origins of the Franco-Prussian War of 1870.* Cambridge, Mass., 1962.

Stern, Fritz. *The Politics of Despair: A Study in the Rise of the Germanic Ideology.* Berkeley, 1961.

———. *The Failure of Illiberalism: Essays on the Political Culture of Modern Germany.* New York, 1972.

———. *Gold and Iron: Bismarck, Bleichröder, and the Building of the German Empire,* London and New York, 1977.

Stosch, Ulrich von, ed. *Denkwürdigkeiten des Generals und Admirals Albrecht von Stosch.* Stuttgart, 1904.

Sumner, B. H. *Russia and the Balkans 1870–80.* Oxford and New York, 1937.

Taffs, Winifred. *Ambassador to Bismarck: Lord Odo Russell, First Baron Ampthill.* London, 1938.

Taylor, A. J. P. *Germany's First Bid for Colonies.* London and New York, 1938.

———. *The Struggle for Mastery in Europe.* Oxford and New York, 1954.

———. *Bismarck, the Man and the Statesman.* London and New York, 1955.

Tiedemann, Christoph von. *Persönliche Erinnerungen an den Fürsten Bismarck.* Leipzig, 1898.

———. *Aus sieben Jahrzehnten,* vol 2. Leipzig, 1905.

Tirpitz, Alfred Friedrich von. *Lebenserinnerungen.* Leipzig, 1920.

Treitschke, Heinrich von. *Aufsätzen, Reden, Briefe.* Berlin, 1929. 4 vols.

Verdy du Vernois, Julius von. *Im Grossenhauptquartier, 1870–71: Persönliche Erinnerungen.* Berlin, 1896.

Victoria, Queen. *Letters,* 1st series, ed. A. C. Benson and Viscount Esher, 3 vols.; 2d and 3d series, ed. G. E. Buckle, 6 vols. London, 1907, 1926, 1930.

Vierhaus, R., ed. *Das Tagebuch der Baronin Spitzemberg.* Göttingen, 1960.

Vitzthum von Eckstädt, Carl Friedrich, Graf. *Berlin und Wien in den Jahren 1845–52.* Stuttgart, 1886.

———. *St. Petersburg und London in den Jahren 1852–1864.* Stuttgart, 1887.

Wagner, Cosima. *Die Tagebücher.* Munich and Zurich, 1976. 2 vols.

Waldersee, Alfred Graf von. *Denkwürdigkeiten des Generalfeldmarschalls Alfred Grafen von Waldersee,* ed. H. O. Meisner. Stuttgart, 1922–25. 3 vols.

Waller, Bruce. *Bismarck at the Crossroads, 1878–80.* London and Atlantic Highlands, N.J., 1974.

Wehler, Hans-Ulrich. *Bismarck und der Imperialismus.* Cologne and Berlin, 1969.

———. *Krisenherde des Kaiserreiches 1871–1918.* Göttingen, 1970.

Windelband, Wolfgang. *Bismarck und die europäische Grossmächte, 1879–85,* 2d ed. Essen, 1942.

INDEX

ACKNOWLEDGEMENTS

The author and publishers wish to thank the following who have kindly given permission for the use of copyrighted material:

George Allen & Unwin Ltd., for extracts from *Germany in the Age of Bismarck* by W. H. Simon (1968).

George Allen & Unwin Ltd. and Alfred A. Knopf, Inc., for extracts from *Gold and Iron: Bismarck, Bleichröder and the Building of the German Empire* by Fritz Stern (1977).

George Allen & Unwin Ltd. and Macmillan Publishing Co., Inc., for extracts from *Bismarck and the German Empire* by Erich Eyck (1958).

The American Historical Association and Professor Otto Pflanze, for an extract from "Towards a Psycho-Analytical Interpretation of Bismarck," published in *American Historical Review* No. 77 (1972), pp. 433–34.

Verlag C. H. Beck, for extracts from *Bismarck und Katharina Orloff* by Nikolai Orloff (1944).

Georges Bonnin, for extracts from *Bismarck and the Hohenzollern Candidature for the Spanish Throne*, published by Chatto and Windus (1957).

Cambridge University Press, for extracts from *The Holstein Papers* by Norman Rich and M. H. Fisher (1955–63).

David Higham Associates Ltd., on behalf of Michael Howard, for an extract from *The Franco-Prussian War*, published by Rupert Hart-Davis (1968).

David Higham Associates Ltd., on behalf of A. J. P. Taylor, and Hamish Hamilton Ltd., for an extract from *Bismarck: The Man and the Statesman* (1955).

K. F. Koehler Verlag, for extracts from H. O. Meissner's *Kaiser Friedrich III: Tagebücher 1848–66* (1929) and *Friedrich III: Das Kriegstagebuch von 1870–71* (1926).

Frederick Muller Ltd., London, for an extract from *Ambassador to Bismarck* by Winifred Taffs.

Oxford University Press, for extracts from *The Politics of the Prussian Army 1640–1945*, translated by Gordon A. Craig (1955).

R. Piper & Co. Verlag, for extracts from *Tagebücher* by Cosima Wagner, edited by Martin Gregor-Dellin and Dietrich Mack (1976).

A. J. P. Taylor, for an extract from the English translation of *The Struggle for Supremacy in Germany* by H. Friedjung.

Maurice Temple Smith Ltd. and the University of California Press, for an extract from *The Rise of German Industrial Power* by W. H. Henderson (1975).

Every effort as been made to trace all the copyright holders but if any have been inadvertently overlooked, the publishers will be pleased to make the necessary arrangements at the first opportunity.

Picture Credits:
With the following exceptions, all illustrations are from the Archiv für Kunst and Geschichte, Berlin: "Princess Katharina Orlova" and "Family Group," BBC Hulton Picture Library; "The Morning after Königgrätz," Heeresgeschichtlichen Museum, Vienna.